ROUTLEDGE LIBRARY OF BRITISH POLITICAL HISTORY: LABOUR AND RADICAL POLITICS 1762–1937

VOLUME XI

ROUTLEDGE LIBRARY OF BRITISH POLITICAL HISTORY:
LABOUR AND RADICAL POLITICS 1762–1937

ENGLISH RADICALISM
The End?

Edited by
S. Maccoby

London and New York

First published 1961 by George Allen & Unwin Ltd.

Reprinted 2002 by Routledge
11 New Fetter Lane, London EC4P 4EE

Simultaneously published in the USA and Canada
by Routledge
29 West 35th Street, New York, NY 10001

Routledge is an imprint of the Taylor & Francis Group

Typeset in Times by
Keystroke, Jacaranda Lodge, Wolverhampton
Printed and bound in Great Britain by
Antony Rowe Ltd, Chippenham, Wiltshire

British Library Cataloguing in Publication Data
A catalogue record for this book is available from the British Library.

Library of Congress Cataloging in Publication Data
A catalog record for this book has been requested.

English Radicalism: The End?
ISBN 0–415–26576–2

English Radicalism: 6 Volumes
ISBN 0–415–26570–3

Routledge Library of British Political History: Labour and Radical
Politics 1762–1937: 11 Volumes: ISBN 0–415–26562–2

Publisher's Note
The publisher has gone to great lengths to ensure the quality of this reprint
but points out that some imperfections in the original book may be apparent.

ENGLISH RADICALISM
THE END?

BY

S. MACCOBY
M.A., Ph.D.

LONDON
George Allen & Unwin Ltd
MUSEUM STREET

TO THE MEMORY OF
SAM AND ESTHER MOLIVER
AND OF
BESSIE WEINBOUM

PREFACE

SOME years ago a sixth volume was promised to complete
English Radicalism's eventful history. It was foreseen
then that a small Radical remnant would survive for a long
time, a remnant almost equally adverse to traditional Toryism and
to a Labour Party tied to Trade Unionism and the defence and
justification of some of the most disquieting features of the national
life. Yet what was not foreseen was the possibility that the call for
a Radical Liberalism, made by Joseph Grimond, the Liberal
Leader, would produce so massive a vote as that of the General
Election of October 8, 1959. But this volume tells the story of
previous notable "revivals" which took the political commentators
by surprise and which, like that of 1959, were followed by
suggestions for a "progressive" alliance of Radicals and "moderate
Labour" men which might give the country a more desirable
alternative to Toryism than alleged combinations of Trade Union
"bosses" and "Red" politicians.

Three successive defeats at General Elections have at last
induced some Labour Parliamentarians to think regretfully of what
they had over-confidently turned their backs on when abandoning
such evocative nomenclature as "Radical Reform" so that the
suggestion has been seriously advanced of trying Labour and
Radical or Labour and Reform as a new party-name. Indeed, the
candid admission has been made that Labour, as a polling-style,
is an electoral liability with the "new middle-class" of highly-paid
craftsmen and process-workers who tend to associate it with slums
and poverty and to view it with some of the distaste accorded to
the Nationalization panacea. There is a seeming measure of
justification, at any rate, for the question-mark left in the title of
this volume, *English Radicalism: The End?*

This book could not have been written in its present form,
without long reading and re-reading of the file of the great
Radical weekly, *The Nation*. The Bradford City Library, which
generously made its file available, and the Durham County
Library, which provided much other material, hard for the private
citizen to come by, must be gratefully thanked for never deserting
a would-be writer trying to complete his self-imposed task.

English Radicalism: The End?

It remains to acknowledge the liberality with which the present owners of *The Nation* copyright, the proprietors of *The New Statesman*, have allowed long illustrative extracts to be used over a large part of this work and the similar liberality shown by the proprietors of *Whitaker's Almanack* who have kindly given permission for many successive annual volumes to be quoted in confirmation of dates, names, and events mentioned in the text. Messrs. Hutchinson, too, have allowed important extracts to be made from the late Sir Almeric Fitzroy's *Memoirs*, and from the late Viscount Addison's *Four and a Half Years*; quotations from the *Observer* are by permission; and the Controller of H.M. Stationery Office has authorized some use of *Hansard* and the *Parliamentary Papers*. Finally, Caroline Playne's revealing studies of "public opinion" in Britain during the war-years, 1914–1918, have been freely drawn upon as has the daily newspaper press.

CONTENTS

English Radicalism: The End?

BOOK FOUR

The Last Radical Programmes of Lloyd George

BOOK ONE

Before the First World War

CHAPTER I
BEFORE AND AFTER 1906

"General Election. To the Parliamentary Electors of the Borough of Middlesbrough.

"Gentlemen,

"The resignation of Mr. Balfour and his Ministry give you another opportunity of electing a member. . . .

"You did me the honour to elect me as your representative in 1892, and later in 1895 . . . whilst in 1900 I was unsuccessful by the small minority of 55. Since then the Liberal and Labour Electors have paid me the high compliment of asking me again to champion their cause. . . .

"I have been and am opposed to the policy of Mr. Balfour and the late Government, who, in my opinion, have proved themselves the most incompetent and extravagant administration this country has experienced for many years.

"Their management of the Transvaal War was a scandal, their introduction of Chinese Labour into South Africa was an insult . . . their endowment of the Liquor Trade without a mandate from the electorate was a shameful piece of jobbery, their Education Act has inflicted hardship on many of our best citizens whilst their neglect of legislation for the better protection and improvement of the working classes has been criminal.

"To crown all this the Right Hon. Joseph Chamberlain, the self-elected leader of the Conservative Party, has endeavoured to rush the country into a policy of Protection, and destruction of Free Trade, which has done so much to cheapen the food of the people and to better the condition of the working classes. . . .

"Should you honour me by electing me as your Parliamentary Representative, I shall support any Government which pursues a safe and rational Foreign Policy, the object of which, I believe, should be the maintenance of peace with all our neighbours. I shall support an amendment of the Education Act which will ensure Religious Equality and Public Control and the Abolition of all Sectarian Tests. I shall support any measure which will give the people full and absolute control of the Liquor Traffic.

"I shall support Home Rule for Ireland, the extension of the Workmen's Compensation Act to all workers, the amendment of the Conspiracy Laws with a view to protecting the funds and legalising the position of Trade Unions, and any sound scheme of Old Age Pensions.

English Radicalism: The End?

"I am in favour of the following Reforms—Improvement of the Land Laws, Taxation of Land Values, One Man One Vote, Registration Reform, State Payment of M.P.s and Election Expenses, Extension of the Franchise to the Jury Boxes so as to give the ordinary working-man offender the right to be tried by his peers, the Abolition of all Special and Class Juries, Amending the Shipping Laws so as to secure greater safety and better treatment in our Mercantile Marine, and any measure calculated to raise the social status and uplift the great mass of our ever-increasing population.

"I am also in favour of dealing with the Veto of the House of Lords. . . . With regard to Imperial Defence I am opposed to any form of Conscription, and believe every encouragement should be given to our Auxiliary Forces.

"For 26 years I have fought on the side of my fellow-workers . . . I ask to be sent to the House of Commons free and un-trammelled and clear of the dictation of any small I.L.P. clique such as is endeavouring to intimidate the voters of this town. . . ."

> J. Havelock Wilson's Liberal-Labour Election Address of January 1906 when he successfully displaced a Tory and left "Independent Labour" at the bottom of the poll. The voting was Wilson, 9251; Sadler, 6870; George Lansbury 1380.

"Labour candidates and their supporters have made ample use of current electioneering cries for their own ends. 'Dear Food' and 'Chinese Labour' have been worked for all they are worth. In view of the lead given them by Liberal and Radical candidates, some of them Ministers of the Crown, they would have been more than human had they not done so . . . these two cries alone, apart from the merits of the Labour programme, and apart from the wave of Socialism now going through the industrial classes, have gained many seats both for Radicalism and Labour.

"It is not my intention here to touch upon the merits of 'Dear Food' and 'Chinese Labour', beyond remarking that the whole political history of England may be ransacked without finding greater electioneering frauds. . . .

"We have seen, then, . . . that some adventitious circumstances have helped the entrance of that Labour party into the House of Commons. But what is its real programme? Mr. Keir Hardie has classified the policy of the Labour party as laid down by its annual congresses into reforms that are fundamental and reforms that are merely expedient, including among the latter Registration Reform and Payment of Members . . . fundamental matters include meals for school-children; amendment of the Unemployed Workmen Act . . . and public subsidies for land afforestation and reclamation, and in aid of Trades Union sick funds. Then come old age pensions; acquisition of the whole of the schools of the country; and the conferring of full powers upon the municipalities for the acquisition of land. To balance these proposals, which obviously involve an extravagant national and local expenditure —regardless of economics . . . a graduated income tax and the reduction of military expenditure are advocated . . . the Trades Disputes Bill . . . is mentioned as a matter in which the Labour party will brook no delay. . . . All, or nearly all the above proposals, and with the addition of proposals for a minimum wage and an universal eight hours working day, are again set out in a further article. . . .

"Opposition to the class of 'wealth and privilege' have been openly declared . . . Mr. Keir Hardie is very outspoken. . . , he said, '. . . that the advent of a Labour party, strongly imbued and leavened with Socialism, is a menace to the privileges and monopolies which enable the denizens of Mayfair to live in riotous excess, whilst their victims, both in England, India and South Africa, reek in poverty.' "

An article entitled "The Labour Party—A Unionist View" in the March 1906 number of the *Nineteenth Century*.

A T the Bradford Conference of January 1893, where the
Independent Labour Party was founded, Mr. Keir Hardie,
it is related, "claimed that the balance of power in the
country was even then" in its hands.[1] This was, of course, one of
the typical exaggerations of those seeking to build up mass-
followings quickly and, in point of fact, the day-to-day grind of
persuading the average working-class voter that his temporal
salvation depended largely on his putting his cross against the
name of a candidate who claimed to stand exclusively for "Labour"
was only just beginning. Those who expected that millions of the
"workers" would fall over one another in their rush to enlist under
the new banner were proved, in the event, to have been much too
optimistic. After all, Mr. Keir Hardie lost his own seat before
long, and the best-known M.P. surviving the 1895 General
Election who could advance as good a claim to the label of "Independent Labour", Mr. John Burns, had strong views on some of
the follies he thought Keir Hardie to have perpetrated during his
three years in Parliament.[2] But Burns too, behaved, on occasion,
like an egotistic political adventurer, trading on the name of
"Labour", in the eyes of some of the ten to twelve "Liberal
Labour" M.P.s, half of them Miners' representatives, who since
1885, had found Gladstonian politicians ready, it seemed, to
accord them reasonably generous treatment as candidates and
brother-members.[3] Had not Broadhurst, the ex-stone-mason,
been given office by Gladstone in 1886 and Burt, the ex-pitman,
in 1892?

It should not be thought that scepticism as to the motives and
ultimate wisdom of Keir Hardie and Burns—not to mention

[1] This is the summary of the *Annual Register*, 1893. The full boast, according
to the *Workman's Times*, was this: "At the next General Election, whether it
came in six months or six years, they could decide absolutely who should occupy
the Government benches . . . if the General Election did not come for two years,
they would be able to command 25 per cent of the electorate."

[2] Cf. *South Western World*, August 10, 1895 for Burns on Hardie's "Parliamentary anarchism", "unscrupulous demagogy", and the way he had "outbid
everything in the way of political seduction and bribery to get votes".

[3] Cf. *Workman's Times*, June 20, 1890 for Schnadhorst's announcement that
the Liberal Party would support Labour candidates "where possible". By 1891
the famous Liberal organizer was going further. The *Workman's Times* of
March 27, 1891 quotes him writing thus to the Secretary of the Metropolitan
Radical Feberation: "The difficulties attending the question of Labour representation are very grave: but they do not arise from the leaders of the party.
Wherever a demand for a Labour candidate exists, and a suitable man is within
reach, the Liberal headquarters earnestly bespeak for him the generous
support of the [local] Liberal Association."

Hyndman, Tillett, Tom Mann, and the rest—was confined to the Liberal-Labour Parliamentary Benches.[1] After all, the best type of Victorian working-man was a shrewd and laborious craftsman, far from ready to be made an instrument for the self-aggrandizement of "agitators" who, some suspected, had gladly laid down their tools for ever in order to practise more profitable arts.[2] Moreover, though "Socialism" had been prudently left out of the name of the Independent Labour Party, Socialist propaganda dominated its platforms.[3] And if the hard-headed craftsman suspected that "Socialism" made far too many easy assumptions of the inherent virtues of the "working classes",[4] what did the Socialist propagandists even greater harm for a whole generation was the suspicion of Atheism and Free Love which rumour had attached to Socialism and Socialists since the days of Robert Owen.[5] But more of this will be said later.

The "bad times" towards the end of the Boer War and afterwards, when the Liberal and Radical Opposition were working up a storm of denunciation of the Tory Ministries of Salisbury and Balfour, improved "Independent Labour" chances considerably. In point of fact, at numbers of by-elections in pit or industrial areas, the Liberal Leadership saw to it that strongly-backed "Labour" candidates, whose personality and views did not arouse too much opposition, were also adopted as Liberal candidates or, at least, promised the Liberal vote. Thus did the ex-weaver,

---

[1] Cf. A. W. Humphrey, *A History of Labour Representation*, pp. 87–8, for George Howell, the Gladstonian Liberal-Labour M.P. for Bethnal Green North East, from 1885 to 1895, venturing to criticize even Owen and Ruskin.

[2] Distrust of the "agitator" still exists, of course, and not, as once, mainly in employing circles, seeing the troubles worked up, even in "socialized" industries, by "unofficial strike" leaders whose public and private ambitions are sometimes suspect. But there is nothing now akin to the strength of feeling produced by whole generations of denunciation of the "agitator" as instanced, for example, in some of the savage anti-Union cartoons of the strike-fever period of the spring of 1834 or, to go forward to 1871, the furious attacks on those working-class leaders who ventured to defend the Paris Commune. (Cf. *Penny Illustrated Paper*, June 24, 1871 under "The Apostles of Crime".)

[3] Cf. A. W. Humphrey, *A History of Labour Representation*, p. 134, for the defeat of the proposal to name the party, the Socialist Labour Party.

[4] Hannah More's *Will Chip* and, indeed, a number of other anti-Jacobin tracts of the previous century, had based themselves on the thriftier and more laborious artisan's sense of superiority to the wasteful and the idle.

[5] Cf. W. L. Sargant, *Robert Owen and his Philosophy*, pp. 438–9: "But there is one subject on . . . which he was supposed to hold opinions, more universally offensive perhaps, than even his ravings against religion. It was said that he was an enemy to marriage and a favourer of promiscuous intercourse between the sexes. No charge could be more false . . . he would have granted divorce for incompatibility. . . ."

D. J. Shackleton, become M.P. for Clitheroe on August 1, 1902; the ex-workhouse boy, Will Crooks, M.P. for Woolwich on March 11, 1903; the ex-pitman, John Johnson, M.P. for Gateshead on January 19, 1904, and another ex-pitman, Thomas Richards, M.P. for West Monmouth on November 3, 1904.[1] Of course, this Liberal self-denial was destined to pay handsome dividends at the next General Election and, meanwhile, even where men like Shackleton and Crooks held themselves as completely uncommitted to the Liberal Front Bench as Keir Hardie himself,[2] some shadow of a moral claim over their Parliamentary allegiance had been established.

Sometimes, of course, a direct Liberal-Labour clash could not be avoided despite all the efforts and diplomacy of the Opposition leadership. Thus, there was fury among South-West Durham Liberals when it transpired, on the death of their Barnard Castle member, Sir Joseph Pease, that his well-paid and generously-treated election agent, Arthur Henderson, ex-ironfounder and Methodist, had consented to undertake an "Independent Labour" candidature which excluded even the notion of his running on a Liberal as well as a Labour basis. By the standards of that day, Henderson's action was not very straight-forward[3] for he had been paid for over seven years to nurse the constituency's Liberalism and Radicalism. Naturally, the local Liberal organization selected another candidate, and Henderson, just snatching victory, with the aid of pitmen, quarrymen, steelworkers, and railwaymen, in a three-cornered contest, became an "Independent Labour" M.P., on July 24, 1903, in the full sense of the term. Of course, he had polled less than $35\frac{1}{2}$ per cent of the votes cast against 35 per cent for the Tory and under 30 per cent for the Liberal.[4] His platform denunciations, too, of the Tories' Boer policy, of Chamberlain's "Dear Food" agitation, of Balfour's Education Act of 1902, and

---

[1] Cf. *Whitaker's Almanack, 1905*, pp. 139–44, for the way this very widely-used reference source classed these men as *L.* for Liberal with (*Lab.*) in brackets alongside. Burns, also now figured as *L.* for Liberal though, in his case, that was followed by (*Lab. late S.*), the *S.* standing for Socialist.

[2] Cf. *The Reformers' Year Book, 1906*, p. 33, for his return to Parliament in 1900 after five years' absence, as junior member for the then two-member borough of Merthyr Tydfil.

[3] Mary Agnes Hamilton's *Arthur Henderson*, pp. 42–3, has a not very convincing piece of special pleading.

[4] *Northern Echo*, July 26, 1903, for the polling figures: Henderson, 3370; Vane, 3323; Beaumont, 2809. Both Henderson's opponents belonged to wealthy landed families, familiar to the constituency for generations.

of the stream of rate-reductions allowed, of late years, to landlords and parsons, "allegedly" hard-hit by the fall of corn prices, were little more than echoes of those of the Opposition Press and Front Bench.[1] But if the Labour Representation Committee, founded in 1900, on the initiative of the Trades Union Congress, claimed to see special reason for optimism in the Barnard Castle result, it was not entirely because Henderson had made the need for a reversal of the Taff Vale Judgement, imperilling the Unions' funds, a main plank in his platform. It was partly because Henderson, the fifth M.P. accorded the Committee's recognition and support, was, from one point of view at least, the first of the five who had won a seat when strongly challenged by both the historic parties.

By 1904 it was becoming steadily clearer that the sitting Tory Ministry would be heavily defeated whenever a General Election should come. That was why the Liberal leadership was so intent on keeping up maximum electoral pressure and why its efforts to prevent by-election rivalry between Liberal and Labour, from which only the harassed and divided Tories could gain, sometimes enlisted even "Independent Labour" support. Thus, in January 1904, after an "Independent Labour" candidature had imperilled but not, ultimately, defeated an Opposition bid to win a Tory seat, the Labour Representation Committee's own Chairman of 1902-3 telegraphed to the victorious Liberal: "Great triumph for progress. Hearty congratulations, R. Bell, M.P."[2] And if "Independent Labour" zealots were scandalized into formal reproof,[3] that did not prevent two more "Independent Labour" M.P.s, Shackleton and Henderson, in the mounting by-election excitements of 1904, from personal intervention in securing two further by-election gains for Opposition though, in those two

---

[1] Cf. *Ibid.*, file for July 1903. This halfpenny Radical daily, published in near-by Darlington, dominated the constituency's political reading.

[2] A. W. Humphrey, *A History of Labour Representation*, p. 163. Bell had already helped Opposition by-election candidates at Cleveland, Newmarket, and Liverpool. He was General Secretary of the Amalgamated Society of Railway Servants and had, in 1900, become junior M.P. for Derby, in a very close contest, by running in double harness with a Liberal against two Tory candidates. He and Shackleton were eventually invited, under Asquith, to very acceptable posts in the Civil Service.

[3] *Ibid.*, for the Labour Representation's Executive criticizing what had been done as a "serious departure from the principles on which this movement was founded, and a breach of the provision of the constitution safeguarding the independence of the Labour Party".

cases of Harborough and Devonport, it could be urged there was no competing Labour candidature to harm.[1]

If 1904 had not brought the half-expected collapse of the Tory Government, distracted not merely by the now-forgotten Irish Devolution disputes but by the crippling contentions between full-scale Chamberlainite Tariff Reformers, more moderate Balfourians, the Conservative "Free Fooders", the Conservative Free Traders and, finally, those, like Winston Churchill, preparing to desert altogether and "rat" to Opposition, that only made it the more likely that the collapse would take place in 1905.[2] A General Election was certain to follow quickly, under the auspices of the Opposition, and, in view of by-election results, that General Election might well prove catastrophic for Conservatism and an immense opportunity for "all the forces of progress". One of the factors, however, capable of robbing a "progressive" victory of much of its decisiveness, was a long series of angry contests in which competing Radical and "Labour" candidates should strive to claim a Tory seat for themselves, thoroughly "split the progressive vote" and ultimately allow the Tory back on a minority poll. During the course of 1905, accordingly, the outline of many tacit electoral bargains between Opposition and "Independent Labour" became clearer, and such bargains, indeed, might be considered merely an extension to other undivided two-member boroughs of what had already happened in Merthyr Tydfil and

---

[1] The files of Keir Hardie's *Labour Leader* and Hyndman's *Justice* will be found, over a course of years, almost competing in denouncing the allurements of Whiggery and urging the necessity of so rigidly aloof an attitude on the part of "Labour" that many considered it impracticable. On occasion, of course, especially where money for election purposes was in question, this rigid attitude could be abandoned with startling suddenness. Hyndman's Social Democratic Federation was charged with having accepted Tory money in 1885, and the *Labour Leader* numbers of the Woolwich by-election period of 1903 hardly showed any strong objections to taking the *Daily News*'s £1000 Fund for election expenses on behalf of Will Crooks. All the same Will Crooks found it advisable not to have Liberal politicians on his platform, Lloyd George, for example, when intervening on his behalf, doing so in the form of an address to the local Free Church Council. Similarly, Shackleton and Henderson did not speak from a Liberal Party platform, in their by-election interventions, but claimed to be defending "Free Trade".

[2] Cf. Sir Almeric Fitzroy's *Memoirs* under 1904 and 1905 for an "inside" view of Government troubles by the Clerk of the Privy Council. On January 31, 1905, for example, he was noting: "my information goes to show that those with the best means of judging look upon the position as most critical. The ranks of the party are steeped in lukewarmness and discontent . . . many of the Unionist Free Traders would welcome the early defeat of the Government. . . . The chief danger arises from the dissatisfaction of Unionists with the Irish Administration".

Derby at the 1900 General Election. At Merthyr, in 1900, the anti-war, "pro-Boer" Radicals had given their second vote sufficiently to Keir Hardie[1] to allow him to return to Parliament instead of an Imperialist pro-war Liberal, and, at Derby, Richard Bell had been similarly assisted to Westminster by the Liberals' second vote.[2] In contrast, too, to Keir Hardie, Bell seems to have been grateful enough to voice the Opposition Leadership's case for reasonable co-operation among all "the forces of progress", in the inner circles both of the Labour Representation Committee and the T.U.C.'s Parliamentary Committee.[3] By some such method it presumably was that Ramsay MacDonald joined Broadhurst as one of the two "progressive" nominees for Leicester men's two votes, and that Philip Snowden, G. H. Roberts, G. J. Wardle, James Parker, J. T. Macpherson, T. Summerbell, and Walter Hudson were similarly provided for at Stockport, Halifax, Preston, Sunderland, and Blackburn, Norwich, Newcastle.[4]

The old undivided two-member boroughs lent themselves particularly to this type of electoral bargain, but the movement spread to other electoral areas, too. Thus, since 1885, Manchester had been divided into six separate one-member constituencies and Salford into three, and Opposition held only one of the nine seats.[5] At the pollings of January 1906, however, all the eight Tory seats were won from them, partly, at least, because only one "Progressive" candidate had been nominated for each.[6] Two of the eight captors of Tory seats were the Labour men, Clynes and Kelley, and though tangible proof was sometimes hard to come by, it would have been political innocence, indeed, to assume that it was by pure coincidence alone that "straight fights against the Tory" had taken place throughout Manchester and Salford and

---

[1] Though he would doubtless have denied this, it was the opinion of many competent election judges.

[2] Cf. *Whitaker's Almanack, 1901*, for the figures. At Merthyr, they were: D. A. Thomas, 8598; Keir Hardie, 5745; W. P. Morgan, 4004. At Derby, where the situation more exactly forecast those of 1906 because only one Liberal and one Liberal-Labour were nominated against two sitting Tories, the voting was: Roe, 7917; Bell, 7640; Bemrose, 7389; Drage, 6776.

[3] Cf. *The Reformers' Year Book, 1907*, for Bell preferring to stay Liberal-Labour after the formation of a Labour Party under Keir Hardie's Chairmanship.

[4] *Whitaker's Almanack, 1907*, for all these men reaching Westminster.

[5] *Ibid., 1906*.

[6] *Ibid., 1907*, shows Winston Churchill and Hilaire Belloc as two of the victors and Balfour himself as one of the victims.

that no element of hard bargaining, unrevealed to the "public", entered into the story.

Of course, "arrangements" of the kind depicted above were not too difficult to make when it was a matter of partitioning Tory seats, not yet won, between two sets of claimants, needing one another's support or, at least, neutrality. But, on the Labour side, a mixture of private ambition, of a sense of mission on behalf of the "workers" and, sometimes, even of good electoral opportunity made it certain that there would be claims, and even "outrageous" claims, on which compromise would be difficult or impossible. Thus the Amalgamated Society of Engineers and its General Secretary, G. N. Barnes, had marked out the Blackfriars Division of Glasgow for themselves though the Gladstonian, A. D. Provand, who had represented it from 1886 to 1900 and had been ejected by Bonar Law at the "Khaki Election", was anxious to fight the seat again. Provand had the special merit of being the originator of Shop Hours legislation in protection of shop-assistants[1] but, in the event, he was left at the bottom of the poll and Barnes was sent to Westminster instead of Bonar Law.[2] At Chester-le-Street, again, represented for twenty years by the Liberal mining magnate, Sir James Joicey, Joicey's decision to accept a peerage found W. J. Taylor of the Durham Colliery Mechanics' Association expeditious enough in enlisting support to get himself a Labour nomination before the Liberal Association had completed its inquiries for a new candidate. Even so, it gave Taylor a hearing and might have been prepared to accept him if it had not found that he had had his hands tied so tight by his Labour backers that he would not be able to come out as a Liberal as well as a Miners' candidate.[3] Thereupon, an eloquent Congregational minister accepted the Liberal and Labour candidature but was too

[1] Cf. *Hansard*, February 24, 1892, for the Second Reading on Provand's Shop Hours Bill when he defeated the Government by 175 votes against 152. The Government subsequently undertook legislation of its own which Provand found insufficient because only protecting shop-assistants under eighteen.

[2] *The Reformers' Year Book, 1907*, p. 24, for the figures: Barnes, 3284; Bonar Law, 2974; Provand, 2058. Barnes went on to become Labour's representative in Lloyd George's War Cabinet during 1917.

[3] Cf. *Northern Echo*, January 5, 1906, for the angry "Old Liberal" correspondent who claimed that Taylor had, in the near past, consented to have his name go on to a list of possible Liberal-Labour candidates and had "played fast and loose with the Liberal Party". On January 9th, the *Northern Echo* gave a long leading editorial to the theme that "progressives' disunity is the reactionaries' opportunity" and begged that a three-cornered fight should be avoided. Taylor had apparently not improved matters by declaring himself a member of the I.L.P.

late to stop Taylor's triumphant progress to Westminster in a three-cornered contest.[1]

Of course, Labour swoops of this kind were far from universally successful, as Keir Hardie was himself to find despite his persistent and almost fanatical ambition to create a political situation in which a Labour group in the Commons would hold the balance of power. He had hoped and worked for such a situation since the 1892 Election and had, at times, even dreamed of breaking away from Opposition an Independent Radical Wing, perhaps under Lloyd George, to co-operate with Independent Labour and the Irish to seize control of the House of Commons.[2] Now he had determined that J. Havelock Wilson, who had been M.P. for Middlesbrough from 1892 to 1900 and had only been ejected by the narrowest margin during the "Khaki Election", should not return as a Liberal-Labour member but that George Lansbury should become "Independent Labour" M.P. instead. Wilson, founder of the National Union of Seamen and Firemen, was not, perhaps, an exemplary character[3] and there may well have been something in Keir Hardie's suspicions that he had not been above "selling" the seamen on occasion for a private consideration from

[1] Cf. *Ibid.*, January 9, 1906: "The miners' candidate, Mr. J. W. Taylor, has gained the distinctive advantage of an early start. . . . His friends have now secured committee rooms in every quarter of the constituency. . . ."

[2] Cf. *Labour Leader*, March 7, 1903, for an Open Letter addressed to Lloyd George. "For over a hundred years," Hardie declared, "the Whigs have played the game of gagging their dangerous rivals. No one can read the records of the last 130 years without being struck by the skill shown by the Liberals in inveigling the leaders of the people into their net and always with the same result. The earnest reformer, once he has tasted the cloying sweets of office, loses the taste for strenuousness; finds a thousand good reasons why he should cling to office, even after he knows he has been befooled and the people betrayed. . . . But remain aloof, you would in time become the recognised leader of that force in politics which desires genuine reform. . . . There would be a cleavage between Whiggism and Radicalism. . . ." All the same, when coming to estimated figures, Keir Hardie saw to it that independent Labour was written down for 50, the independent Radicals for 25, and the Irish for 85, so that he was still dishing not merely the Whigs but the Radicals too if it should ever come to rival claims for leadership. And writing for the *Nineteenth Century* number of January 1906 on "Labour at the forthcoming Election" Keir Hardie was busy trying to make the infant Liberal Government's flesh creep. "Unless," he claimed, "the Liberal majority is very large, the existence of the Government will be to some extent at the mercy of this combination of the Irish and Labour parties." Such single-minded concentration on the mechanics of winning power—albeit for the representatives of the "labouring masses"—does not now seem the wholly admirable thing it may have appeared before the days of Lenin, Mussolini, Stalin, and Hitler.

[3] Cf. *J. "Havelock" Wilson, M.P. Daylight on his Career. Exposure and Challenge. Astounding Revelations*, for some disclosures of his book-keeping and expense accounts. This pamphlet must have been indirectly financed by the Shipping Federation before Wilson came to terms.

their employers.[1] But that Keir Hardie could, even for a moment, cherish the belief that his vigorous personal support and the Labour Representation Committee's endorsement could make the cause of a newly-introduced Londoner[2] prevail against the strongly-established position of Wilson, himself a North-Easterner and powerfully backed by the new Government in the shape of Lloyd George, shows that he was still over-sanguine.[3]

Two other constituencies shall be examined before a summing-up. At Darlington it must have taken prodigies of tact and rare Liberal and Radical self-abnegation to accept from London an Amalgamated Society engineer, endorsed by the Labour Representation Committee, as the one "progressive" candidate against the Liberal-Unionist of local origin, Pike Pease. Alderman

[1] Cf. *Northern Echo*, January 12, 1906, reporting Hardie at Middlesbrough: "So long as Mr. Hardie . . . contented himself with explaining the aims and objects of the Labour movement he was listened to with respect but the moment he declared that Mr. J. Havelock Wilson had applied to have his candidature endorsed by the Parliamentary Committee of the Trades Union Congress and had been refused, the storm burst, and after declaring that he would never allow a man to be returned to Parliament without protest who would do as he had done before, fight Labour and support capitalists at every opportunity, he sat down."

[2] Cf. *Ibid.*, January 11, 1906, for a biting examination of Lansbury's election record to date, showing him "to have been consciously or unconsciously an instrument for returning Tory members" by splitting the "progressive" vote. "At a bye-election in 1895," reported the *Northern Echo*, "he stood as a Socialist candidate for Walworth. He only secured 347 votes, but his intervention had the effect of handing over the seat to a Tory. Again, at the General Election in 1895, he stood for the same constituency, and though his vote dropped from 347 to 203, it had the effect of securing the return of a Tory. . . . At the general election of 1900 Mr. Geo. Lansbury was put forward as a Socialist [for Bow and Bromley], and although it was a Liberal seat the Liberals decided not to oppose him, allowing Mr. Lansbury to have a straight fight with a Tory. The result, however, was again the same, for Mr. Lansbury was defeated by a majority of 1845 and a Liberal seat was handed over to a Tory. After such a record it takes a fair amount of effrontery to come to a constituency like Middlesbrough and pose as a friend of the working man. . . ."

[3] Cf. *Ibid.*, January 10, 1906, for full reporting of the Lloyd George visit under the headlines: "LLOYD GEORGE AND LABOUR"; "A STIRRING APPEAL TO PROGRESSIVES"; "MR. WILSON COMMENDED"; "IMPOSING DEMONSTRATION AT MIDDLESBROUGH". Of Wilson Lloyd George said : "No truer, trustier or pluckier comrade than Mr. J. Havelock Wilson do I ever want to go into action with. He is the sort of man I can tiger hunt with . . . there are some people I would not go ratcatching with." The *Northern Echo*'s report continued: "Referring to the contest in Middlesbrough, he wanted to say one word about the attempt to split the Progressive vote. The previous night he spoke in support of the Labour candidate at Darlington and appealed to the Liberals of Darlington to give him their support, and he believed they were going to do it. In Wales they gave a refuge to Keir Hardie when he was rejected by his own people. But here was a Labour man, who knew the needs of Labour, and Keir Hardie and his friends were trying to turn him out purely because he was willing to co-operate with the friends of the Labour cause. 'That,' exclaimed Mr. Lloyd George, 'seems exalting personal cantankerousness to the level of a political faith.' "

Mitchell could certainly not complain of the help he got—the daily strenuous campaigning of the Radical *Northern Echo* on his behalf, a visit and speeches from Lloyd George, messages from John Burns and Dr. Clifford, and much else. Yet it must have been obvious early that constituency feeling had been misread for Mitchell hardly ventured, before long, to stress the "Labour" character of his candidature, urging more and more that it was "progressive".[1] In the end, Pike Pease went back by 4575 votes against Mitchell's 4087. But Mitchell was probably less calculated to antagonize a good deal of the still vitally important "respectable" element on the "progressive" side than was the agent of the Gas Stokers and General Workers' Union, Pete Curran, who had arrived, with the endorsement of the Labour Representation Committee, to take over Jarrow in the name of Labour. As the sitting Liberal baronet was the aged Sir C. M. Palmer, who had founded and still controlled the great ship-building and other enterprises of the area, and as Curran had been prosecuted in the past for intimidation in the course of a strike, the first reaction, at least, of "respectable" ship-yard artisans to Curran's candidature was very far from enthusiastic. Of course, Curran's Election Address employed the usual electoral patter to convince the innocent that his candidature was the fervent and oft-expressed wish of a great bulk of the constituency's workers.[2] Curran was

[1] Based on the *Northern Echo* file and a small collection of posters, handbills, and other election material in the writer's possession. It is significant that there was no Labour candidate at the next three elections for Darlington, and that, in January 1910, though the Conservative recovery elsewhere was very marked, at Darlington such a complete outsider as the foreign-born adventurer, the afterwards notorious Tribich Lincoln, running as a Liberal and Radical, captured the seat from Pike Pease. Of course, the unmasking of Tribich Lincoln ruined Liberal chances in Darlington, for ever as it proved, but no Labour candidature was revived till 1922 and no victory won till 1926.

[2] Cf. *Ibid.*, January 10, 1906, for the Election Address which opened thus: "Fellow Citizens, It is now close upon four years since I received an invitation from a conference of Organized Workers of the Division to come forward and contest the seat in the direct interests of Labour. Since that period, however, in conjunction with supporters well known in the National Labour Movement, and supporters representing the local Organized Workers, I have addressed over two hundred meetings in the Division, and have received every encouragement. I have also received resolutions of endorsement from a majority of the Trade Union branches in the Constituency and, in addition to that, they are likewise represented by direct delegation on my Election Com mittee." Thus smoothly was it hoped to disguise the fact that Curran was not, of course, a native or resident of Jarrow and was widely suspected of being merely another loud-mouthed marshaller of unskilled immigrant labourers. When Palmer died, however, and Curran, louder-mouthed than before, contrived, with a smaller vote, to win the seat in an extraordinary four-cornered contest, his victory, in conjunction with another won at the same time by

rejected at the polls by 8047 votes against 5093 but that was a result which was to induce him to try again a year and a half later when the aged Sir C. M. Palmer had died.

The outcome of all this polling throughout the country has often been described, and especially the Conservative catastrophe of numbers in the Commons reduced from 369 to 157 while the Liberals totalled 381, with 19 Liberal-Labour men as supplement to raise the figure to 400. Of course, such massive voting strength behind the Government's Front Bench reduced many of the hopes that Keir Hardie had been cherishing of a Labour-Irish combination, holding a balance of power and partly able, at least, to dictate the Government's course. Yet there were ample compensations even if the dating of "real progress", with a Labour majority and Government, of course, in charge, had once again to be delayed till the Election after the next or, perhaps, even the Election after that. As one Labour calculator had it: "Labour (in the general sense) increased its numbers from 14 to 49, and in the place of but four Independents a solid section of 30 men pledged to support neither of the historic parties obtained places in the new House of Commons."[1] Indeed, Keir Hardie, soon Chairman of a Parliamentary Labour Party of thirty, not only with its own Whips and Committee Room in the House of Commons but with the Labour Representation Committee outside converted into a national Labour Party, was cheerfully and confidently busy, before long, on further extensive plans on behalf of the "workers". Especially was the Government Front Bench to be displayed, if it hesitated about conceding every Labour demand, as a very indifferent friend to the masses, and there were, besides, the normal administrative decisions on Indian, Colonial, Foreign, and Armament policy to rely on for further "proof" that there was

Grayson for "extreme Socialism", caused those fearful of what were considered revolutionary incitements, some temporary disquiet. But one dose of Curranism, apparently, was sufficient for the constituency, which returned to Palmer control at the next General Election of January 1910 and stayed Liberal till October 1922.

[1] This was F. W. Pethick|Lawrence, educated at Eton and Trinity College, Cambridge, who after buying but failing to save the *Echo* newspaper, was now issuing both *The Reformers' Year Book*, from which this extract is taken, as an annual and the *Labour Record and Review* as a monthly. The *Labour Record and Review* advertised itself as giving "a complete story of the doings in Parliament with short extracts from all the speeches delivered by the Labour Members". After 1907, Lawrence's energies were mainly concentrated on the struggle for Women's Suffrage and he did not enter Parliament till 1923. He was Labour Secretary of State for India and Burma, 1945–7.

little difference between Liberal and Tory Governments save, perhaps, greater hypocrisy on the Liberal part. Here is a prompt summary of the 1906 Session on these lines issued in *The Reformers' Year Book*, *1907*:[1]

The history of the Session of Parliament . . . has been the history of the failure and political cowardice of the Liberal Party, and has indisputably demonstrated that though there are within its ranks some able and conscientious men, the vast majority are indifferent, and not a few actively opposed, to any real reform.

The Liberal Government has failed entirely to justify the confidence reposed in it by the electorate, not only upon the newer questions as they have arisen, such as the war in Natal, but on the very matters upon which it was returned to power, of which the chief was the continuance of Chinese Labour in the Transvaal.

Nor has the record of individual members of the party, in general, been more satisfactory. A few, on occasion, have been found to be willing to vote against the Government in defence of their principles; but for the most part, they have been content to take the official view . . . as in the case of their cowardly abandonment at the twelfth hour of the deputation to the Duma. . . .

The sands of the Liberal Party, with its great traditions, are running out. Reformers call upon it in vain for enthusiasm or for action. Its inspiration is gone. One by one its compeers on the Continent are dying. It cannot long survive.

To the Socialist Party we look to take its place. Already in many of the municipal elections the line of cleavage is between Socialist and anti-Socialist candidates. Already in the General Election a vote of 275,000 was given in favour of declared Socialists, being over half the total vote given for Labour candidates of all kinds. Already in the House of Commons, the Independent Labour Party, with its strong Socialist leanings, has achieved remarkable success. Already it has compelled the attention and the strenuous opposition of the Forces of Reaction. . . .

This was hot gospelling with a vengeance, unmarked, too, by the slightest acknowledgement of the way Liberal legal consciences had had to be stretched "to put Trade Unions above the law" and undo, for the future, the effects of the Taff Vale Judgement.[2] But the Socialist path did not prove so easy to tread as

---

[1] From F. W. Pethick Lawrence's Preface.

[2] Cf. *Hansard*, February 22 and March 28, 1906, for the introduction of two competing Trade Disputes Bills, the first by Hudson for "Labour" and the second by the Attorney-General for the Government. At first, the Government resisted the suggestion that Union funds should be completely immune whatever the damage or illegalities Union policy might have led to in the course of a trade dispute. But, before long, the Government's "partial immunity" was

27

some, at least, of the hot gospellers had imagined. For one thing, organized Conservatism began an electoral recovery of increasing proportions, as by-elections soon showed, and hot gospelling of the kind instanced above seemed normally to send more antagonized Conservatives to the polls than converted Socialists. Then there were the literary Socialists, like Shaw and Wells, who would not remember what harm to "Socialism" Blatchford had done a couple of years before in blurting out provocatively his disbelief in Christianity[1] and who now went on to outline the "new" views of Love, Marriage, and the Family in a fashion that many of the old school must have found even more abhorrent than Blatchford's Unbelief.[2] To remember the anger excited by the Socialist

being converted virtually into the "complete immunity" desired by "Labour. (Cf. *Hansard*, April 25 and August 3, 1906, for vital stages.) Some opponents early called upon the House of Lords to be ready to stop what was being done (*Nineteenth Century*, May 1906, pp. 881–4) but it was not thought expedient.

[1] No anti-Socialist pamphlet was complete before long without quotations from the *Clarion* article of September 23, 1904: "I do not believe that Christianity, or Buddhism, or Judaism, or Mohammedanism is true . . . I deny the existence of the Heavenly Father. I deny the efficacy of prayer. I deny the providence of God. I deny the truth of the Old Testament or the New Testament. I deny the truth of the Gospels. I do not believe that any miracle was ever performed. I do not believe that Christ was Divine. I do not believe that He died for man. I do not believe that He ever rose from the dead. I am strongly inclined to believe that He never existed at all." Possibly Blatchford was proud of this as an improvement on a "notorious" passage in Paine's *Age of Reason* but his circulation manager and the Independent Labour Party must quickly have uttered the cries of distress that brought a change of course. Here is one anti-Socialist sneer on the change, from Cayley Calvert's *Socialism?*: "Finding their avowals of atheism and sneers at religion were not universally popular, the Socialists have recently been shifting their ground. *But they cannot.* The spirit of unbelief in revealed religion breathes through almost all their publications, so it's no use Mr. Glasier going back to Charles II's reign . . . or *Justice* stating a man may "square his accounts with heaven how he likes" or Mr. Blatchford belatedly quoting the Sermon on the Mount."

[2] Cf. J. H. Bottomley, *Socialism, Atheism, and Free Love, Explained and Exposed* (1907, Second Edition), for this Conservative Agent picking the following extract from the *Manchester Dispatch* of October 22, 1906, reporting Shaw thus: "'Thou shalt not commit adultery.' Why not? The marriage contract 'for better or for worse' is the very last word in human wickedness. A contract ought only to be a contract for the better. If a marriage is a bad job, it ought to be instantly dissolved. . . . Adultery is the quickest and most effective way out of a bad marriage contract." Of H. G. Wells the following was written: "During the last few weeks a prominent Socialist, Mr. H. G. Wells, has published a book entitled 'In the days of the Comet' showing that the natural goal of Socialism is 'Free Love'." *The Times* in its review (September 15, 1906) said: "He— Mr. Wells—foresees the objection that, even if men could be persuaded not to quarrel about property, they would still be liable to quarrel about women, and he is prepared with his solution of that problem also. Socialistic men's wives, we gather, are, no less than their goods, to be held in common. Free love, according to Mr. Wells, is to be of the essence of the new social contract. One wonders how far he will insist in the tracts which he is understood to desire to write for the Fabian Society, and what the other Fabians will say." And even

Sunday Schools, now started in a few places, and the *Red Cate-chism* taught the children there—an anger which played its part in breaking for ever the hold on the capital of the Radical-Socialist Progressives of the London County Council—is to keep another relevant factor in mind.[1] Finally, of course, there were the obvious passages from "Socialist" propagandists, past and present, to show that Socialists meant to abolish the Crown and the Peerage,[2] disband the Army and Navy,[3] abandon the Colonies and the Empire,[4] and concentrate on the confiscation of all private property so that the lazy and shiftless might reap where the diligent and contriving had sown.[5] All told, it was a story that awoke stronger emotions than had, perhaps, been bargained for by Keir Hardie and the *Labour Leader*.

Despite Socialist handicaps of the kind just described, handi-caps doubtless underrated by Keir Hardie and the I.L.P.,

Mrs. Philip Snowden's fancy picture of Socialism as economical because "instead of a hundred kitchen fires and cooks we shall have one" caused rage in the heart of another anti-Socialist pamphleteer. "Having exiled the King," inveighed Cayley Calvert, "and banished Religion, Socialism proposes next to *lay its unhallowed hands on the home*, and give in place co-operative barracks, where various families will sit down to tea together in happy harmony, and share tea-spoons. . . . How this idea will commend itself to the ordinary English-man, who has been wont to pride himself upon his house being 'his castle' remains . . . to be seen."

[1] A. P. Hazell's Preface to the *Red Catechism for Socialist Children* has this: "On the occasion of the London County Council Election, in March 1907, an attack was made on the Socialist Sunday Schools by the Tory or 'Moderate' Party. . . . The Tory Press, including in particular the *Daily Mail*, the *Daily Express* and the *Daily Telegraph* exhibited much bitterness. . . . A discussion was also raised in Parliament on the matter, in the hope of bringing Cabinet pressure to bear on the L.C.C. . . . it was at last decided, on June 11th, to perpe-trate the gross injustice of refusing the schools to Socialists."

[2] Cf. Cayley Calvert's *Socialism?* quoting Comrade Jackson of Battersea: "The Socialists are working for revolution . . . the King is useless, and I hope he will be the last one."

[3] *Ibid.*, pp. 6–7: "The Declaration of Principles of the Socialist Party of Great Britain informs us that the armed forces of the nation exist only to conserve the property of the capitalist. . . . Kindred Socialist Manifestors advocate abolition of the naval and military forces altogether."

[4] *Ibid.*, p. 7, quoting Comrade Rossiter speaking at Newington Butts: "What is the Empire to us? Nothing! We must crush the Imperial spirit in the British people, and England must be satisfied with the home market alone."

[5] Cf. *The Anti-Socialist* periodical whose launching to head the stream of anti-Socialist pamphleteering in the manner of the *Anti-Jacobin* was being hope-fully arranged by the Anti-Socialist Union in 1907. In its basic declaration of principles, the *Anti-Socialist* defined Socialism thus: "It is a ruinous scheme to take all the factories, workshops, businesses, railways, land, buildings, machinery, shops, houses, capital and savings from their present owners, with or without compensation, and hand them over to the Government. THIS IS ROBBERY. It is a scheme to compel every able-bodied person, willing or un-willing, to work as a Government servant under the orders of an army of officials. THIS IS TYRANNY."

"Labour's" ceaseless claims to be converting the masses at a rate which would soon put it into power, in place of the "shuffling professors of Liberalism", were not long in arousing anxiety among "moderate" Liberals and even among some who called themselves Radicals. Of course, a good deal of the anxiety came from the never-ending Socialist street-corner propaganda[1] with which the masses were being "beguiled", it was asserted, into such beliefs as that the first Socialist Chancellor of the Exchequer would be able, as a mere preliminary to more far-reaching measures, to remove the entire weight of taxation, then resting on working-class shoulders, on to the backs of the rich.[2] But apart from objections to the "confiscatory taxation" such offers involved, there were objections, too, to the ruinous shortsightedness many professed to see in the Socialist approach whether to the economic complexities of wealth-production at home, or to the dangerously swaying Balance of Power abroad, or, finally, to the problems of an Empire which contained many populations unsuitable for speedy pushing-forward to the Socialists' universal panacea of Adult Suffrage and the Ballot Box.[3]

It is interesting to examine how Lloyd George, the very Radical President of the Board of Trade in the Liberal Government, sought to reassure himself and the Government's vast majority as to the real prospects before them. Despite the boasts of Labour propagandists[4] and the occasional nightmares of the

---

[1] Cf. *Labour Leader*, August 16, 1907, for the leading article, entitled "Unsurpassed Propaganda", which claimed that the 1907 summer "has been the most successful in the history of the movement. . . . Nothing like this season's I.L.P. propaganda has ever been attempted by any political organisation in the country. It is estimated that our branches have been holding at least 2000 meetings a week. Thirteen new branches . . . were formed last week."

[2] Cf. Philip Snowden's *The Socialists' Budget*, p. 31, for "Indirect taxation for revenue would find no place in the Socialist Budget" which was speedily interpreted by an opponent in *Some Socialistic Proposals, A Brief Analysis* as meaning "the total exemption from taxation of the industrial working classes".

[3] In the *Labour Ideal Series*, projected in 1906, it was Ramsay MacDonald who had been asked to write on *Labour and the Empire*, and one anti-Socialist critic, if still finding much to object to, was almost pleased to find little of the rabid anti-Imperialism of Hyndman, Bax, or Quelch.

[4] Cf. *Political Caricatures, 1906*, p. 92, for the great Liberal cartoonist, Carruthers Gould, on *The Ox and the Frog*, a pictorial-political version of Aesop. A small Keir Hardie, marked I.L.P., is represented as a somewhat inflated frog, calling out to a huge ox, marked Liberal Party, "I shall soon be bigger than you!" And the patient ox, in the large meadow, is made to reply: "All right, I don't mind. There's plenty of room for both of us—but take care you don't burst." This first appeared in the *Westminster Gazette* of October 10, 1906.

more "moderate" Liberals, the supersession of the powerful
reigning majority by Labour was, he claimed, almost impossible
for a generation. It was folly to believe that the entire working-
class vote would automatically go to Labour after a few more years
of propaganda, and, indeed, if some of the more spiteful forms of
Labour agitation even against Liberals were continued and
"moderate" Liberals, in consequence, driven to combine with
Tories in anti-Socialism, the results for Labour would be most
unpleasant. But, perhaps, Lloyd George should be allowed to
speak for himself in the form of a Cardiff speech of October 11,
1906. It was addressed, of course, in the first case, to a Welsh
audience, and in it Lloyd George had the peculiar advantage of
being able to claim that the leader of Welsh Labour, the Liberal-
Labour "Mabon", was on his platform, leaving others to go on to
the thought that if there was one Welsh seat in the hands of
"Independent Labour" and, indeed, that of Keir Hardie himself,
that was the ill-requited result of Welsh Liberals quixotically
helping a non-Welshman in 1900. Here is one salient passage
of an address which, it was claimed, "did much to smooth over
some jealousies which had arisen between Liberalism and
Labour":[1]

The working man is no fool. He knows that a great party like ours
can, with his help, do things for him which he could not hope to
accomplish for himself without its aid. It brings to his assistance the
potent influences drawn from the great middle classes of the country,
which would be frightened into positive hostility by a purely class
organization to which they did not belong. No party could ever hope
for success in this country which does not win the confidence of a large
portion of this powerful middle class. That is an asset brought by
Liberalism to the work of progress which would never be transferred to
a Progressive party constructed on purely Labour lines, and I would
strongly urge the importance of this consideration upon those who wish
to drive Liberalism out in order to substitute another organization. You
are not going to make Socialists in a hurry out of the farmers and
traders and professional men in this country, but you may scare them
into reaction. They are helping us now to secure advanced Labour
legislation; they will help us later on to secure land reform and other
measures for all classes of wealth producers, and we need all the help
they give us. But if they are threatened with a class war, then they will
surely sulk and harden into downright Toryism. What gain will that

[1] Cf. H. Du Parcq, *Life of David Lloyd George*, iv, 627, for the claim. The
speech was very widely reported in the newspapers of October 12, 1906.

be for Labour? Of course, if the Labour leaders could ever hope to
detach every working man from both political parties and recruit them
into a Labour combination, then I agree such a party might be all-
powerful. But those who know anything about political history can tell
you this is an impossible feat. There are hundreds of thousands of
working men who never under any pressure or provocation quit the
parties that they join. . . . There are many more who will always
remain true to the members, upon the election of whom time after time
they have often spent much enthusiasm. . . . There are numbers who
are treated well by employers to whom they are attached. There are
many who doubt, and will continue to doubt, the wisdom and feasibility
of the Socialist ideal.

You must recollect that up to the present there has been no real
effort to counteract the Socialist mission amongst the workmen. When
that effort is made you may depend upon it it will find adherents even
amongst working men. You have to reckon with an enormous power
of wealth, the influence of highly trained intelligence or organisation;
you have also the incalculable influence of conflict of Labour interests,
personal and sectional rivalries. There will be alternative remedies,
amongst which working men will be divided. For instance, take, if you
like, Tariff Reform, and . . . the blighting but potent seduction of
drink. . . . Does anyone believe that within a generation, to put it a
the very lowest, we are likely to see in power a party pledged forcibly
to nationalise land, railways, mines, quarries, factories, workshops,
warehouses, shops, and all and every agency for the production or
distribution of wealth? He who entertains such hopes must indeed be
a sanguine and simple-minded Socialist.

Able speaking of this kind may explain why Lloyd George had
become a Cabinet Minister before serving in any junior office[1] and
why he was to rise so rapidly in national importance. It is certainly
remarkable to find him laying his finger so unerringly on the
principal obstacles to a rapid advance of "Independent Labour"
to the Treasury Bench, obstacles, in fact, that Keir Hardie had
already been planning, on occasion somewhat shamefacedly, to
evade or surmount. The wisdom of omitting "Socialist" from the
name of the party had been accepted by Keir Hardie from the
first;[2] he had later accepted the wisdom of preventing the Labour

---

[1] There were some parallels to Joseph Chamberlain's career in this and
some later developments, and Chamberlain, too, had begun at the Board of
Trade.

[2] Cf. A. W. Humphrey, *A History of Labour Representation*, for the Labour
Representation Committee's Newcastle Conference of 1903. The result is
summed up thus (p. 157): "The Socialist resolution was rejected at Newcastle,
and the 'class war' as a declared policy, by 86 to 35. Conference also refused
allow candidates to run as 'Labour and Socialist', and would only allow to
'Labour'."

Representation cause from being confined to working-men and Trade Union secretaries so rigidly, by definition, that he himself, Burns, MacDonald, and Snowden would all have been excluded;[1] and, finally, he did not jib at the unofficial bargains for sharing two-member seats with the Government, begun in preparation for the 1906 Election and, in some cases, at least, continued long afterwards. When, in fact, a Socialist Party of Great Britain had announced its appearance in 1905 and tried to enlarge its appeal in 1907,[2] its attacks on the Independent Labour Party and the Labour Representation Committee for ignoring or repudiating Socialism and the class-struggle whenever a petty personal,[3]

[1] *Ibid.*, p. 159, for the Trades Union Congress of 1903 debating the Labour Representation Committee and facing a proposal "to set up the same test for membership of the Committee as existed for membership of the Congress—working at a trade or being paid secretary of a union; under which conditions Mr. J. R. MacDonald—whose work for the Committee had been invaluable and whose energy and skill were second to none—and Messrs. Burns, Pease, and Hardie would have been among the excluded." The suggested test was defeated by 209 to 53.

[2] *The Manifesto of the Socialist Party of Great Britain*, dated at London on June 12, 1905, announced that the party had been launched exactly a year before as a "revolutionary Socialist party" on the basis of the class-struggle and "the abolition of all class distinctions and class privileges". It must have spent the intervening year collecting the material, hurled in the *Manifesto* against Hardie, Burns, the I.L.P., etc. etc., and repeated, with additions, in the *Manifesto*'s second edition of 1907, the edition which added, also, to previous attacks on Hyndman and his Social Democratic Federation, the charge that he was pressing for compulsory military training.

[3] Cf. *Ibid.*, Second Edition, p. 12: "The so-called 'Independent' Labour Party is independent only so far as it is free to sell to the highest bidder. The I.L.P. is in reality run by a set of job-hunters, whose only apparent political principle is to catch votes on varying pretexts and by still more varying means. . . . The Labour Representation Committee came into existence . . . as far as the trade union officials were concerned because they saw a chance of Parliamentary jobs. At the first meeting of the L.R.C. Mr. John Burns opposed putting the movement on a working-class basis. Mr. James Sexton, of the Liverpool Dockers, said that the Socialist resolution was magnificent but not war—not conducive to Parliamentary jobs he meant. . . . Mr. Steadman said they should elect those who had borne the heat and burden of the day—*i.e.*, men of the Steadman stamp. At Newcastle Mr. John Ward stated that they wanted to get their feet on the floor of the House of Commons, and would not be particular how they did it. Mr. J. Keir Hardie said they did not want Toryism, Liberalism, or Socialism, only Labourism. Wonderful to narrate, this is the same Keir Hardie who sits as a delegate on the International Socialist Bureau. . . . Messrs. W. Crooks, D. Shackleton and A. Henderson supported Mr. Benn, Liberal candidate for Devonport, and Mr. Bell, ex-Chairman of the L.R.C. got his seat . . . by an arrangement with the Liberal Party. Mr. D. Shackleton is a defender of child-labour, and Mr. A. Henderson is an opponent of the legal reduction of the hours of labour. After all their cry of independence and after all their falling out with Mr. Burns . . . they selected as Chairman of their Parliamentary group the same Mr. John Burns, the defender of Asquith the murderer of the miners at Featherstone, thus choosing as their leader one of the most bitter enemies of the working class."

financial,[1] or electoral[2] advantage seemed to be obtainable were savage enough to warrant everything Lloyd George had said on "the incalculable influence of conflict of Labour interests, personal and sectional rivalries". Choice morsels from the Socialist Party's *Manifesto* were, before long, figuring in anti-Socialist attacks upon Keir Hardie, the I.L.P., and the Labour Party.

In view of the obvious importance of the personal story of Keir Hardie in the forcing of a definite cleavage between "Labour" and Liberalism, even of the Radical kind, this chapter might well terminate with the shortest of biographical notes upon him. His early life was thus summarized for *Who's Who*:[3] "*b.* Scotland, 15 Aug. 1856, working-class parents, both Scotch. At work in the mines from 7th until 24th year; elected Secretary to Lanarkshire Miners' Union; *m.* Lillie, *d.* of Duncan Wilson, collier, 1880; appointed editor *Cumnock News*, 1882; resigned 1886; Labour candidate for Mid-Lanark, 1888; elected for S.W. Ham, 1892." It is hardly necessary to stress the strenuousness of effort and self-education behind a bald recital of this kind even if it omits his early oratorical practice and success as a Temperance speaker.[4] Nor is it, perhaps, wise to try and separate fact from fiction in the stories that grew up about the safe seat and great advantages elsewhere that were promised Hardie if he abandoned a Labour candidature of 1888 that threatened to split the Gladstonian vote at a critical period in the struggle to eject the Tory Government of Lord Salisbury on the Irish Coercion issue. Though the actual Mid-Lanarkshire poll when it came on April 27, 1888 was Philipps, Gladstonian, 3847; Bousfield, Unionist, 2917, and Hardie, 617,[5] Hardie had already begun making a sufficient mark

---

[1] Cf. *Manifesto of the Socialist Party of Great Britain*, Second Edition, p. 11: "Soon after it came into existence the I.L.P. spent about £5000 in election expenses, and it is significant that to this day no explanation has been given as to where this money came from." *Ibid.*, p. 2: "The source of a large portion of the funds of the I.L.P. is still wrapt in mystery. Recently two mysterious individuals, no doubt 'independent labourers' (or were they 'suffragettes'?) gave the party, through Mr. Hardie, a donation of £1000 and another person, similarly anonymous, gave £100."

[2] *Ibid.*, p. 2: "The I.L.P. has continued its policy of bargain-making with capitalist politicians. At the General Election Mr. Ramsay MacDonald at Leicester and Mr. James Parker at Halifax were amongst the candidates who entered into compacts with the Liberals. When this is remembered it is easily understood why the by-elections at Leicester and Halifax were not contested."

[3] *Who's Who, 1914*, p. 919. Hardie had the additional disadvantage of illegitimate birth.

[4] *Men and Women of the Time*, Fifteenth Edition, Autumn 1899, p. 476.

[5] *Whitaker's Almanack, 1889.*

at meetings of the Trades Union Congress[1] to induce the Gladstonian leadership to give him the unopposed run against the Tory that made him the member for South West Ham from 1892 to 1895. This three years' membership, despite the opening ridicule cast upon the cloth cap and wagonette cornet-blasts of his first arrival at Westminster, was undoubtedly to help him to make his *Labour Leader* and I.L.P. an increasing problem for the Gladstonian leadership. Yet he was again allowed an unopposed run against the Tory in 1895, and if ejected this time in the "reaction" of that year, pro-Boer Welsh Radicals always claimed that they had helped him back to Parliament for Merthyr in 1900.[2] And, in 1906, the opening chances, at least, seem to have been that he would be allowed an unopposed return together with the Radical senior member, D. A. Thomas. But some of his Government- and "capitalist-" baiting proved too much for a section, at least, of the Merthyr Liberals, and a late candidature against him was attempted, doomed to failure from the beginning. Yet annoying though Hardie found it to have to fight a contest when he would have preferred to be completely free to go to the aid of "Independent Labour" candidates of his choice, there was gain in it for him as well as loss. He could claim to have shown once again how all the entangling wiles of Liberal capitalists could be defeated and disgraced by steadfast adherence to the cause of "Independent Labour".[3]

[1] A. W. Humphrey, *A History of Labour Representation*, p. 109, gives considerable prominence to Keir Hardie's attack, at the 1887 T.U.C., on the Liberal-Labour ex-Minister, Broadhurst, for voting against a Miners' Eight Hours Bill and "stumping the country" to catch votes for Liberals. His attack on Broadhurst in 1889 as "not a fit and proper person" to hold the office of Secretary of the Parliamentary Committee of the T.U.C. was backed by accusations of Broadhurst's "supporting employers of labour and holding shares in sweating companies". Broadhurst countered by asking where the money was coming from to print and circulate charges against the Parliamentary Committee, the first reference to the occasionally mysterious provenance of Keir Hardie's funds.

[2] He was, of course, a pro-Boer of special vehemence, as was Lloyd George who was to claim that no non-Welshman could have won Merthyr in 1900 save as a "persecuted" pro-Boer.

[3] Cf. *Whitaker's Almanack*, 1907, p. 145, for the Merthyr polling figures: Thomas, 13,891; Hardie, 10,187; Radcliffe, 7776.

CHAPTER II

LLOYD GEORGE AND THE "PEOPLE'S BUDGET"

"They say: 'You are taxing the landlord because the value of his property is going up through the growth of population, through the increased prosperity of the community. Does not the value of a doctor's business go up in the same way?'

"Ah, fancy their comparing themselves for a moment! What is the landlord's increment? Who is the landlord? The landlord is a gentleman ... who does not earn his wealth. He does not even take the trouble to receive his wealth. He has a host of agents and clerks to receive it for him. He does not even take the trouble to spend his wealth. He has a host of people around him to do the actual spending. ... His sole function, his chief pride is a stately consumption of the wealth produced by others. What about the doctor's income? The doctor is a man who visits our homes when they are darkened with the shadow of death; who, by his skill, his trained courage, his genius ... wins life out of the fangs of the Great Destroyer. All blessings upon him ... to compare the reward which he gets for that labour with the wealth which pours into the pockets of the landlord purely owing to the possession of his monopoly is a piece ... of insolence which no intelligent man would tolerate."

> Lloyd George evades an issue by rhetoric at Limehouse, July 30, 1909.

"The seed which Mr. Lloyd George is at present scattering may for the moment produce Liberal blossoms, but there can be no doubt that ultimately Socialist fruit will ripen. ... When a German Junker reads these speeches he will, with his insufficient knowledge of Socialism, swear that they have been delivered by a red-hot Socialist Democrat. ... The tone of these speeches is so seditious ... they deal with ... the House of Lords with such lack of respect that they could have been delivered by a Social Democrat. These Liberal speeches appeal to the passions of the masses. ... The speech which the Chancellor of the Exchequer delivered at Newcastle leaves nothing to be desired in the way of inciting the people. ..."

> Vorwärts, October 13, 1909, comments, from the German Socialist angle, on Lloyd George's Limehouse and Newcastle speeches.

Lloyd George and the "People's Budget"

"Tariff Reform alone will not make a new heaven and a new earth; but there is no hope without it. There will be no agricultural revival without it. Without it there can be no firm basis for unemployment insurance. Free imports, leaving the home markets at the mercy of every external influence, necessarily keep industrial insecurity at the maximum; and a single season of dumping might upset the whole financial basis of any system of Unemployment Insurance in any trade. . . . Mr. Lloyd George's method is impotent even to attempt a remedy for unemployment. He can only aggravate the disease and make it mortal. The people's Budget would be the people's curse.

"Tariff or Budget? These, then, are the rival policies. The Tariff would be a powerful instrument for every constructive purpose. The Limehouse style is saturated with the spirit of political destructiveness. The Budget means pulling down. The Tariff means levelling up. Socialistic finance and Single-Chamber domination—the strange creed of class hatred at home and sentimental fraternity abroad—would sink the masses in a slough of despond as surely as it would bring the greatness of England and the existence of her Empire to an end. The statesman who asks the nation for authority to resist 'futile expenditure' on naval armaments invites the masses to dwell in a fool's paradise which would be shattered by the guns of some stronger Power."

The *Observer*, December 12, 1909, offers Conservatives an Election programme.

I T was seen, in the last chapter, how in the course of an important speech of October 1906, Lloyd George, the very Radical President of the Board of Trade, told a Welsh audience that the tendency to panic, already observable in some who faced ever louder "Labour" claims to be on the very verge of power, had little or no existing justification. But he gave a warning, too, directed, doubtless, principally to the "moderate" Liberals, that his argument was based on the assumption of real activity by the Government in effecting political and social reform for, otherwise, the "Labour" claims might prove more justifiable than "moderates" would, in the least, care for. As Lloyd George put it:[1]

But I have one word for Liberals. I can tell them what will make this I.L.P. movement a great and sweeping force in this country—a force that will sweep away Liberalism amongst other things. If at the end of an average term of office it were found that a Liberal Parliament had done nothing to cope seriously with the social condition of the people, to remove the national degradation of slums and widespread poverty and destitution in a land glittering with wealth; that they had shrunk from attacking boldly the main causes of this wretchedness, notably the drink and this vicious land system; that they had not arrested the waste of our national resources in armaments, nor provided an honourable sustenance for deserving old age; that they had tamely allowed the House of Lords to extract all the virtue out of their Bills, so that the Liberal statute book remained simply a bundle of sapless legislative faggots fit only for the fire; then would a real cry arise in this land for a new party, and many of us here in this room would join in that cry. But if a Liberal Government tackle the landlords, and the brewers, and the peers, as they have faced the parsons, and try to deliver the nation from the pernicious control of this confederacy of monopolists, then the Independent Labour Party will call in vain upon the working men of Britain to desert Liberalism that is so gallantly fighting to rid the land of the wrongs that have oppressed those who labour in it.

This is already an outline of the programme which advanced Lloyd George to the position of the people's hero before very long and left Keir Hardie and the Labour Party very far behind. In fact, if Hardie had been told, say in 1907, that the next Election would only yield a Labour Party of 40, including the Liberal-Labour miners absorbed in 1909, and that the Election after that would barely raise the figure to 42, with many fewer votes polled

---

[1] H. Du Parcq, *Life of David Lloyd George*, iv, 630-1. The speech was delivered at Cardiff on October 11, 1906.

nationally, he would have been incredulous.[1] He would have been still more incredulous if told that, by 1914, the entire Labour Movement of his brand was being written off as a mistake, merely serving to divert the masses from the strongest possible industrial action.[2] Yet so it was, despite hopes that had sometimes risen very high, especially during the oncome of sharp depression in 1907. For, in 1907, the anticipatory shivers that had already been passing down "moderate" Liberal backs worsened for a time as the result of two notorious but not, as it proved, very representative by-elections, held in July 1907.[3] At Jarrow the eloquent if not very "respectable" Labour candidate, Pete Curran, established himself in a Liberal seat on a most "Socialistic" programme, and the same thing happened at Colne Valley where Victor Grayson's "Independent Socialism" seemed almost of the "revolutionary" continental pattern. Obviously, two Parliamentary Sessions, largely wasted on finally abortive Education Bills promised to the Dissenters, and a third Session of the same pattern almost inevitable in 1908 owing to commitments to Temperance "fanatics", were allowing both Conservative "reaction" to rise high on the Right Wing of "public opinion" and "Socialist" extremism on the Left. Serious unemployment, for example, might almost have ended in 1906, but the American slump of 1907 had promptly threatened its revival. And, in any case, there were sufficient memories of the "bad winters" of 1902–5 among craftsmen, and sufficient pockets of surviving "distress" among unskilled and "general labourers" to make Tariff Reform offered

[1] Cf. *Whitaker's Almanack, 1911*, for big Conservative gains at the expense of Liberal and Labour in January 1910. At Sunderland and Preston, for example, the Liberal and Labour members were both defeated, Will Crooks lost at Woolwich, and there were other Labour losses at Chatham, Jarrow, and Colne Valley, the last two to Liberals. And in the December 1910 elections, there was a fall of 134,888 in the aggregate national poll from the figures of the previous January though it is only fair to add that some candidatures had been abandoned. (Based on *Whitaker's Almanack, 1912*.)

[2] Cf. A. R. Orage, *Guild Socialism*, p. 5: "Labour's adventure into politics during the last decade has been an exhausting deviation and an appalling waste of time and nervous energy . . . an economic struggle must necessarily be waged in the industrial sphere. . . . The daily and weekly Socialist bulletins should tell, not of some trivial success at a municipal election, or of some unusually flowery flow of poppycock in Parliament, but of wages so raised that rent-mongers and profiteers find their income *pro tanto* reduced." See also G. D. H. Cole, *The World of Labour*, p. 395: "To attack the Parliamentary Labour Party nowadays may look rather like flogging a dead horse. If a General Election came to-morrow there is not the least doubt that 'Labour' would lose many seats, and that those it retained would be by Liberal favour and sufferance."

[3] The results were both reversed in January 1910.

39

from the Conservative side,[1] or Right to Work and Maximum
Eight Hour Bills from the "Socialist",[2] much more interesting to
great numbers in the industrial areas than Government's rather
stale quarrels with parsons and publicans.

Of course, a majority as large as that returned in January 1906
was not without its counter-resources. The Liberal Publication
Department experimented with quite a variety of leaflets aimed at
setting out Government's record to the best advantage and
emphasizing how much better still it would have been but for the
constant mischiefs wrought by the House of Lords. *20 Things
already Done by the Liberal Government,*[3] *What the Liberal*

[1] Apart from the Tariff Reform Union's own propaganda, handbills of the
National Union of Conservative and Constitutional Associations came, towards
the end of 1907, to concentrate more and more on Haldane's admissions as War
Secretary that money had been saved on meat-contracts and Army horseshoes
by accepting the possibility of foreign supply. *The Horse Shoe Scandal* and
American Horseshoes for the British Army are two leaflet-titles of note; under
yet another, *Horseshoes. How the Radical Government serves the Working Man*,
five Labour M.P.s were quoted as opposed to such disregard of unemployment,
actual or potential in Britain; and a fourth asked: "British Iron and Steel
workers, Farriers, and Shoeing Smiths, HOW DO YOU LIKE IT? Farmers and
Labourers, what do you think of this ONE-SIDED FREE TRADE? The money taken
from you by Taxation is spent by the Radical Government in encouraging
Yankee Trusts to dump down their goods in Britain, to your detriment . . .
British Workmen go unemployed while the Americans refuse to accept British
products save on payment of an enormous toll to American workers. . . ."
[2] Cf. *Reformers' Year Book, 1907*, p. 122, for a special note on the Right to
Work "movement". It was to be the State's duty to provide work or pay for
the unemployed but the Socialists had ambitions of building up "armies of
workers" permanently maintained for development work and representing the beginning of the national organization of labour and the end of the capitalist system.
[3] To give the atmosphere of the day, it might be well to recount these twenty
points as follows: Full Self-Government granted to the Transvaal; The issue of
licences for the importation of Chinese coolies into the Transvaal stopped. All
the Chinese now there are to go back. . . ; The Army put on a business footing,
its efficiency increased and its costs lessened; The Navy kept strong and
supreme; The right of effective combination restored and secured to the
Workers, and Trade Union Funds safeguarded; The right of compensation for
accidents given to 6,000,000 workers, and for injuries to health in certain
dangerous trades; Merchant shipping laws amended. Position of seamen in
regard to food, living room, and illness improved; Greater safety of workers
secured by the Notice of Accidents Act; Laundry workers brought under the
Factory Acts; Trade Unionism more fully recognized by the State as employer;
Farmers given (a) Compensation for damage done by game; (b) Freedom of
cropping; (c) Compensation against unreasonable disturbance. . . ; Access to the
land for small-holdings and allotments made more easy by the Land Act of
1907; Education authorities enabled to provide meals for school-children;
Property qualifications for magistrates abolished; A Court of Criminal Appeal
set up. . . ; The Law as to Patents amended so as to safeguard home industries
and the home consumer; 1d. taken off the tax on tea; The shilling duty on
exported coal abolished; 3d. taken off income tax on earned incomes of less than
£2000; The National Debt reduced and the National Credit raised; Free Trade
adhered to. The door barred and bolted on all attempts to increase the price of
food by taxation.

Government has done for the Nation, What the Liberal Government has done for the Miners, The Budget of 1907; A Nest-Egg for Old Age Pensions, What the Liberal Government has done for the Farmer and *The Government and the Workers* are some typical leaflet-titles under which Ministers' achievements were listed and praised—and, by contrast, there were leaflet-titles like *The Wrecked Education Bill* and *The Lords as Wreckers* under which the political iniquities of Tory Peers were recounted. And as the election to Parliament of two such "Socialist extremists" as Curran and Grayson in July 1907 was followed in the autumn by a strong anti-Socialist leaflet campaign by the Conservatives,[1] it must be presumed, especially as the lost seats had been Liberal, that the Liberal Publication Department was also called upon for decisions in regard to Socialism. Yet the decisions could hardly have been different from what they were—no pamphlet-wars against "Socialism" of a nature calculated to arouse animosity on the Labour Benches and, perhaps, prevent relatively harmonious co-operation when the time to "settle accounts with the House of Lords" should appear to have come.

It seems to have been finally resolved to take part of an Asquith speech of October 19, 1907, head it boldly as *Liberalism and Socialism*, and make that serve as Government's response to the situation.[2] The Tories' efforts to make use of anti-Socialism for their own party ends were derided; Liberalism was treated as having accepted the view "that in preparing the road for a better future there is a large place for the collective effort and organised energies of the community"; but Socialism, as the Socialist doctrinaires defined it, was described as threatening "the most sterilising despotism that the world has ever seen" because personal initiative would, in effect, be destroyed. Here is one passage showing a good deal of sympathy with Socialists' discontent followed by another, claiming that Socialism's theories were not the right answer but Liberalism's "path of social reform":

In this, as in other controversies . . . it will clear the ground and the air if we can only persuade our rhetoricians, who are numerous and

[1] Three of the leaflets issued were under titles as extreme as *Socialism Means Atheism, What Socialism Means; Your Child Everybody's Child,* and *Socialism and the Family; The End of Home Life.*

[2] *Liberalism and Socialism. From a Speech by the Rt. Hon. H. H. Asquith, M.P., Chancellor of the Exchequer, at Ladybank, on October 19th, 1907.* It was, of course, widely and rightly assumed that Asquith would, before long, succeed Campbell-Bannerman as Liberal Leader and Prime Minister.

noisy, to define their terms. What do they mean by Socialism? There is a very real sense, as a great Liberal statesman said a few years ago, in which we are all Socialists nowadays. Anyone who looks around with unprejudiced eyes at the structure of society as it actually is, and realises, not only the enormous disparities in the distribution of material comfort and happiness, but the still more striking discrepancies between opportunity on the one side and talent and character on the other, will not only find it difficult to reconcile what he sees with even the rudest standard of ideal justice, but will be tempted to be amazed at the patience, even the inertness, with which the mass of mankind acquiesce in what they deem to be their lot. No wonder that constant contemplation of and reflection upon such a spectacle has driven and continues to drive some of the best and finest spirits of our race into moral and intellectual revolt.

And here is the promised passage, suitably headed "Where Liberalism and Socialism part Company", in which Asquith attempted to make his criticism of doctrinaire Socialism:

If you ask me at what point it is that Liberalism and what is called Socialism in the true and strict sense of the term part company, I answer, when liberty in its positive, and not merely its negative sense is threatened. Liberty means more than the mere absence of coercion or restraint; it means the power of initiative, the free play of intelligences and wills, the right, so long as a man does not become a danger or a nuisance to the community, to use as he thinks best the faculties of his nature, the earnings of his hands or his brain, the opportunities of his life. The great loss counterbalancing all the apparent gains of a reconstruction of society upon what are called Socialistic lines will be that liberty will be slowly but surely starved to death.... To Socialism, so understood, Liberals are prepared to offer a convinced and un-compromising opposition. But I am not so much afraid of its advent in this country as many excellent people seem to be ... our most advanced Labour members ... before the foundations of the new Jerusalem on Socialistic lines are well and truly laid, ... have to get rid, not only of a great deal of solemn parade and ceremonial ... but also to get rid of some of the elementary sentiments and passions of human nature that are incarnated in the average Briton. When, therefore, Lord Balfour of Burleigh appealed to his countrymen to form a new organization to deal with Socialism, this appeal left me very cold. I do not under-rate the activity or the progress of the Socialist propaganda, or the importance of meeting it with a constant and persistent exposure of many of its cloudy though alluring fallacies; but the real danger lies in leaving evils unredressed and problems unsolved on the ground that, except by revolutionary expedients, it is beyond the competence of statesmen to deal with them.

Passages like these afford an explanation of why, some six months later, Asquith succeeded the dying Campbell-Bannerman in the Prime Ministership.[1] And if by that time, too, there was a growing acceptance of Asquith's view that the prospects of the Socialist propaganda could be exaggerated, much new justification was becoming available. Thus the creator of the Labour Party, Keir Hardie, and its Chairman for its first two Sessions of 1906 and 1907 proved far from suitable for the difficult day-to-day work of leadership on the floor of the House of Commons. He was a missionary by nature rather than an organizer and came near to wrecking his infant party by trying to commit it "unnecessarily", as most of his Parliamentary colleagues considered, to "extreme" views of Women's Suffrage.[2] But when Henderson succeeded to Hardie's place in 1908, the aura of quasi-sainthood certainly left it and something much more matter-of-fact and pedestrian took its room. Then, despite adverse influences from the American depression of 1907, there had already been indications in 1906 that the seriousness of the whole problem of Unemployment might be passing as the tremendous resources of a British Empire, enlarged even during the last decade by the Sudan, the Transvaal, and the Orange River Colony, were set in quicker motion by a period of trade "advance" in commodities, like tin and rubber, in which all the economic advantages were with Britain. From November 1, 1907 to October 31, 1908, in fact, while seven Conservative by-election gains from Government took place, Labour and "Socialism" gained nothing and sometimes polled disgracefully.[3] In one famous election for North-West Manchester, the poll of April 24, 1908 was as follows: W. Joynson-Hicks, Conservative, 5417; Winston S. Churchill, Liberal, 4988; Dan Irving, Socialist, 276.[4]

Of course, other factors, too, entered into the account. Thus there was the "patriotic" anger and alarm excited by what was coming to be regarded as the growing German challenge to

---

[1] In April, 1908.

[2] Cf. Hamilton Fyfe's *Keir Hardie*, p. 133: "Intrigue against him had started long before. An attempt was made to prevent his being elected chairman. In the year after his election he threatened to withdraw from the Party because it declined to share his enthusiasm for the Pankhursts' Suffragette movement. . . . He was for straightforward support of the demand . . . MacDonald and Henderson did not take that view. They looked at the matter tactically. . . . Would Hardie's policy win elections or estrange possible Labour voters? . . . Had nobility and fearlessness been qualities common among his following, he would not have laid down the chairmanship 'with the feeling of one liberated from bonds' as his friend, Bruce Glasier, put it."

[3] Cf. *Whitaker's Almanack, 1909*, p. 155.

[4] *Ibid.*, p. 164, for the by-election necessitated by Churchill's promotion.

Britain's naval and Imperial position, a challenge, too, thought to be backed by German invasion-plans. When the Government Front Bench found itself forced by what it considered ignorant clamour to concede a great Dreadnought-building programme,[1] and when the *Daily Mail* sent so accredited a Socialist as Blatchford of the *Clarion* to report, alarmedly, on what he found in Germany, Socialist reliance on a Socialist International's call to the "German workers" to stop the Kaiser, was not likely to make many converts at the polls. And then there was the fact that 1908 was the year when the Aged Poor were granted their Old Age Pensions Act and the pitmen their Eight Hour Bill, to persuade voters, who did not vote Conservative in order to end "dumping", the "German menace", and the "oppressive" Licensing Bill of 1908,[2] to vote Liberal instead, rather than Labour. Indeed, Asquith, on becoming Prime Minister in April 1908, was thought by some to have agreed, if not very enthusiastically, to[3] Lloyd George's succeeding him at the Exchequer mainly because Lloyd George's very Radical record and reputation might make his promotion a Government asset with the masses. Since 1906 Lloyd George had been the Cabinet's most Radical voice, calling for a popular programme likely to win over the "millions" to resolute and even enthusiastic support for Government's Front Bench, and he had been joined, in the Cabinet, by a close collaborator when Winston Churchill succeeded him as President of the Board of Trade. Already by the end of 1908, the Lloyd George-Churchill combination, which dated back to Churchill's crossing the floor in 1904, was beginning to show signs of dominating the Cabinet.[4] By April 1909, when Lloyd George's provocative

[1] Cf. *Edwardian England, 1901–1910*, for G. P. Gooch (p. 17), on the final surrender, in 1909, to the full demands of the "We want eight and we won't wait" panic-mongers: "the false rumour of secret acceleration of the German navy programme led to a panic which was reflected in the laying down of eight Dreadnoughts in a single year". Lord Fisher, at the Admiralty, seems to have been largely responsible.

[2] Cf. *To the British Working Man. The Licensing Bill 1908. What It Means To You* for one Conservative handbill, decorated with a disgruntled artisan, pictured walking past a closed public-house, watched by one policeman while a second officer controls the approach to a Workmen's Social Club.

[3] Cf. *Edwardian England, 1901–1910*, for Professor Hearnshaw's: "Mr. Lloyd George, who had forced himself upon Mr. Asquith as his Chancellor of the Exchequer. . . ."

[4] Cf. Sir Almeric Fitzroy, *Memoirs*, i, 320 (by permission of Messrs. Hutchinson), for the Clerk to the Privy Council noting, on December 21, 1908, the acute Cabinet controversy raging on the Navy Estimates which were under hot attack from Lloyd George and Churchill because of the considerably increased demands they made on the Exchequer. Later in the *Memoirs* Fitzroy was to

"People's Budget" made its appearance, there might be some private criticism among his colleagues of what he was doing and why, but there was apparently little attempt to enforce serious modification.[1]

Of course, both Lloyd George and Churchill were eager for material which should not only stop the growing success of "Conservative reaction", now irritatingly able to ascribe some recent rises in living-costs to Ministers,[2] but which should also bring back "Labour" from fantasies of being on the very threshold of Downing Street to the day-to-day necessity and advantage of working amicably with Government. In point of fact, Labour had already had more than one rude lesson in the truth that, in existing circumstances, many attempts to snatch at "Liberal" seats would merely let the Tory in and leave Liberals resentful enough to threaten the safety, at the next Election, of the large proportion of Labour members who sat by virtue of pacts, avowed or unavowed, with local Liberal Associations. Moreover, the whole financial basis on which the Labour Party had been erected and financed was under legal attack by anti-Socialist Trade Unionists who were, before long, to obtain the tremendous triumph of the Osborne Judgement.[3] The Law's final ruling, feared already, which

surmise that the Lloyd George-Churchill combination had set themselves to thwart McKenna, the First Lord of the Admiralty, partly because they recognized in him the sharpest financial critic, in the Cabinet, of the kind of Budget plans being prepared for 1909.

[1] Cf. *Ibid.*, pp. 376–7, for Fitzroy's Budget note of May 1, 1909 and his impression that Lloyd George and Churchill had succeeded in wearing down the opposition of "more important" Cabinet colleagues who had certainly had no original intention of endorsing some of the Budget's principles.

[2] Cf. *The Working Man's Expenses*, the Conservative handbill, N.U. No. 707, with the conclusion: "There you have it shown that it costs 2/4½d. a week more now than it did three years ago for coals, butter, sugar, bread, oil and potatoes. Other things are dearer also. Out with that Fraud of Frauds, a Radical Government."

[3] Cf. *Morning Leader*, January 2, 1909 for W. V. Osborne, Secretary of the Walthamstow Branch of the Amalgamated Society of Railway Servants, in whose name the action, against his Society's management, was to go through the Chancery Division, the Court of Appeal to final triumph in the House of Lords on December 21, 1909. He claimed that he had joined the Society as a non-political body but that he and his would now lose sick pay, death grants, orphan payments and, perhaps, even the right to work in the trade, if he withdrew from the Society. "The object of all this," he continued, "is to send to Parliament a number of members—tied, paid, and controlled by an outside body—whose very conditions of servitude are the renouncing of country, constituency, conscience, and manhood, and who are to act in accordance with the dictation of their paymasters, securing in return salaries which are extracted by coercion from the pockets of their political opponents." *The Times* of December 5, 1908 had already contained a letter from a Trade Unionist M.P., who sat for Burnley, Mr. F. Maddison, protesting that, "I, who detest State

decided that, on the basis of existing Statutes, the Unions had no right to spend their members' contributions on politics, meant that the Government would once again have to be approached, in worse circumstances than in 1906, for new legislation, and that, meantime, Payment of Members from the Treasury had become urgent. Negotiations behind the scenes, indeed, which ultimately decided that Labour and other members would be entitled to draw, if they so desired, £400 a year from the State must have had a bigger part than is often admitted in conditioning the attitude of some on the Labour Benches, hitherto merely receiving £200 a year from funds originating in the Unions.

The Labour members, then, when offered, in 1909, the benefits of Churchill's Anti-Sweating and Labour Exchanges Acts and the even more stimulating gifts of the "People's Budget" were, perhaps, no longer in the over-confident mood of 1906 and 1907, when Downing Street sometimes seemed only two Elections away at most. Indeed, the tactful Government decision in July 1909, on the occasion of a mid-Derbyshire vacancy, to allow the local Liberal Association to adopt the Labour candidate as its own and so permit Independent Labour to raise its count in the Commons to 33 against Government's 386,[1] once more aroused the type of "Labour" rejoicing prepared to see something profoundly significant in a single accession to the Labour Benches. Of course, there was still some Labour niggling even about the Labour Exchanges Act though the measure must have represented much consultation of the Fabians, Toynbee Hall, and the Trade Unions in regard to methods of helping the Unemployed.[2] But with

Socialism, am made to pay my share to the salaries of seven Socialist members of Parliament who were run as official candidates of the Independent Labour Party and who receive £1400 per year. . . . Liberals and Tories, an overwhelming majority in the Unions, are taxed to keep going a political machine worked by Socialist leaders."

[1] Cf. *The Case against Radicalism, 1909*, p. 109, for the official Conservative Handbook's sour comments on "Liberal Wheedlings and Socialist Contempt." The local Liberal Association actually went as far as inviting the I.L.P. to join it in celebrating the "progressive" victory, only to be rather gruffly rebuffed (cf. *Sheffield Daily Telegraph*, August 23, 1909).

[2] Though it was being proposed ultimately to employ a staff of some 800 in Labour Exchanges, distributed throughout the country, the *Labour Leader* of June 18, 1909 found G. N. Barnes asserting that "the number of unemployed will probably not be lessened by a single person." And the *Manchester Guardian* of May 21, 1909 had already quoted Keir Hardie to the effect that "there was nothing new in Labour Exchanges. . . . There should have been such exchanges under the Unemployed Workmen's Act of the last Government, but owing to the reactionary policy . . . pursued by the Local Government Board, that provision had never been put into operation."

regard to the "People's Budget" of Lloyd George, the Labour Party was half-prepared to admit that the Radical Chancellor had annexed a good deal of its *raison d'être*.

Two perfect examples of the type of Labour comment called out by the "People's Budget" show how Lloyd George's hopes of re-establishing harmonious co-operation between Government and "Labour" had some basis. Here, for example, is Keir Hardie himself as reported in a speech at Woolwich, delivered on August 26, 1909:[1]

> He began to feel almost, nowadays, that his occupation as a Socialist agitator had disappeared . . . Mr. Lloyd George went to Limehouse and denounced the dukes and other mighty and respectable persons of that kind in a way which, up to quite recently, they had only heard on Socialist platforms. . . . There were those who said that the Socialists were not making much progress, and yet when they looked at the present Budget that would in itself give them more idea of the progress that is being made than any example he could possibly quote.

Keir Hardie obviously felt that his audience had been attracted as much by the Limehouse oratory as by the Budget. But here is a Socialist editor, well before Limehouse, enrolling himself behind Lloyd George for, perhaps, the next decade.[2]

> "We shall be quite frank about Mr. Lloyd George's Budget," said the *New Age* of May 6, 1909, "it is splendid. Two minor defects apart, the Budget is not only more than we had dared to hope even after Mr. Lloyd George's Swansea speech, but almost as much as we should have expected from a Socialist Chancellor in his first year of office. . . . We cannot deny, and we have no intention of denying, that the author of the present Budget is good enough statesman for a Socialist to support during the next five or ten years at any rate. . . . It is certain that a vista of Socialist reconstructive statesmanship is opened up on all sides by Mr. Lloyd George's Budget."

[1] *Woolwich Pioneer*, August 27, 1909. The Limehouse speech had been delivered on July 30th but its echoes were obviously reverberating still in London's working-class quarters for it would be hard to find another passage of this type in Keir Hardie's addresses.

[2] Cf. *New Age*, May 13, and June 17, 1909, for other views on the Budget. It would almost appear that Orage, the editor, had been warned behind the scenes against over-enthusiasm for Lloyd George which might militate against the success of the pure Socialist gospel. On May 13th, certainly, he wrote: "We cannot for the life of us see why the Budget should not be claimed as a victory for Socialist ideals", and, on June 17th, still in a posture of self-defence, he was urging: "We contend that if Mr. Snowden were Chancellor at this moment the Budget would be very little different; and is not Mr. Snowden a Socialist? You cannot legislate in advance of your majority."

The Budget speech of April 29, 1909 with which Lloyd George
had attempted—and, as has been seen, with some success—to
inaugurate a new political era, was not an immediate and convincing Parliamentary triumph.[1] It was, of course, his first
Budget speech; the months of preparation, when he was dealing
with unfamiliar material, needing, in view of his ambition to be
the first "social reform" Chancellor, more than ordinary readjust-
ments as Budget Day approached, had apparently wearied him;
and, all told, his four hours' speaking was not impressive. Some
members, indeed, may not have realized, till they read the printed
reports, what bold fiscal and party strategy was implicit in the
Budget plan and how likely it was that it would dominate the rest
of the Session, and, perhaps, even the rest of the life of the 1906
Parliament. It gave the Chancellor a strategic advantage to begin
with, to be able to claim that the combined effect of Old Age
Pension and Dreadnought expenditure gave him a bigger prospective deficit to contend with, £15,762,000, than had possibly ever
been the case in peace-time before. Moreover, some new Navy
and Social Reform expenditure would contribute to bring the
extra new revenue he would have to find to sixteen and a half
millions. He proposed, therefore, to reduce National Debt
repayment by three millions; to introduce both a petrol duty and a
graduated tax on motor-cars; to raise the Income Tax on all
unearned income and all earned income over £3000 to 1s. 2d. in
the pound; to collect a further super-tax of 6d. in the pound from
incomes of over £5000 while increasing the child-abatement
allowances for incomes under £500; and to increase both Stamp
Duties and Death Duties. Nor was this yet all. While Liquor
licensing charges were to be raised to yield an extra £2,600,000 a
year, and spirits and tobacco taxation to be increased to yield even
more, a wholly unprecented tax of twenty per cent was to be raised
on the "unearned increment" of land-values and a tax of a halfpenny in the pound on "undeveloped" land and minerals.

If those familiar with the political climate of the time will see
abundant reasons for "progressive" joy in much already recited,
joy, perhaps, all the greater from the knowledge that there would
be a great deal of gnashing of teeth among Brewers, Landlords,

[1] Cf. *Hansard*, under April 29, 1909, for a corrected version of the speech.
The *Daily News* and the *Daily Chronicle* of April 30th show next day's com-
ments of the popular pro-Government sheets, and the *Daily Mail* and *Daily
Express* of Government's opponents.

and Peers, the list of the Budget's attractions for the "progressive" is not yet exhausted. One hundred thousand pounds a year was going to be found for the expenditure of the Labour Exchanges, intended specially to help the unemployed; £200,000 a year more would be made available for Afforestation and other development plans, also capable of easing the Unemployment problem;[1] and, finally, a National Insurance plan and further Pension possibilities were foreshadowed for the future.

Though Treasury experts and, in private, some of his own colleagues were despondent about the Chancellor's deficiencies as a financier;[2] though his tendency to encourage spending, of which he approved, instead of paying heed to the tradition that a Chancellor's main task was retrenchment, awoke doubts, even abroad, as to the future of British Public Finance,[3] Lloyd George, it must be admitted, did better during the long Budget struggle in the Commons than many had thought possible. The whole problem

[1] Cf. *The Reformers' Year Book, 1907*, p. 122, for the possibility of regarding this as a concession to the "extreme" Socialism of the Right to Work Council which had aimed at using Unemployment emergencies to get corps of workmen enrolled which, even when the emergency passed, were to be prevented from disbanding because their continued existence and, it was hoped, their increase would prove the beginning of the end of "private capitalism". As *The Reformers' Year Book* had it: "There are slums to clear, houses to build, land to redeem, and waste places to afforest. To get this work done there is need of armies of workers, engaged not temporarily to tide over a depression, but permanently to complete an undertaking, the amount undertaken swelling or diminishing each year according to the state of trade. These armies must consist, not of society's failures, paid less than a fair wage, but of men capable of earning a high one. Other workers would then naturally be drawn into municipal manufacturing departments to provide their fellows with all the needs of a decent life, and thus not only should we provide employment for numbers to whom the ordinary relief works can bring no relief, but we should strike a deadly blow at the sweater. To guard, by these methods, against unemployment is the beginning of the national organization of labour and of the end of the capitalist system." It can safely be said that it was not only Tories who shuddered at the implications of writing and thinking of this kind.

[2] Cf. Sir Almeric Fitzroy, *Memoirs*, i, 379, under May 13, 1909: "the difficulties into which the Chancellor of the Exchequer is falling point to some catastrophe to his reputation before the long-drawn controversy on the Budget comes to an end. Those whose business is to watch him are in despair at his indifference to large financial issues, and now confine their efforts to keep him out of the most obvious pitfalls."

[3] Cf. *Morning Post*, September 1, 1909, for the views of the French economist, Jules Roche, on why Budget Deficits were threatened: "Radicalism which has governed since the last elections, has put into practice the method adopted by us of so-called social laws voted unexpectedly without investigation . . . the law on Old Age Pensions has immensely exceeded the credits anticipated, and a deficit has been the result. It has even shown itself particularly menacing for the Budget of 1910. . . . As in every country, the period of social policy promises blessings but produces ruin. England is beginning to enter upon this path. Let her persist in it a few years, and one will see where it will land the country which liberty made the richest in the world."

of land-valuation bristled with technical difficulties of a kind, lending themselves to constant "exposure" of the "ignorance", "presumption", and "vindictiveness" of the Chancellor. And, of course, by the time forty days, prolonged sometimes through the night to the following morning,[1] had been spent in Committee on the grievances of injuriously affected interests, many amendments had been offered or found necessary. Meanwhile, too, there had been the Tariff Reform cry, inside Parliament and out, that much more than the sixteen and a half millions the Chancellor claimed as necessary to avoid a deficit could have been raised from taxing foreign imports and, yet, the Unemployed benefited much more substantially from the resulting discouragement or even total prohibition of "dumping" than they ever would be by Labour Exchange and so-called "Development" expenditure, offered as a sop to the "Socialist" enemies of Society. Nay, by the time the Budget was being debated in the Lords, there were bankers' estimates available, from Lords Rothschild and Revelstoke, of a Budget-induced flight of capital from London which could thus be summarized by Conservatives:[2]

By driving away capital this year to the extent of at least £100,000,000 sterling over and above the ordinary outflow of money for investment abroad, the Budget has already deprived the working classes of an immense sum which would otherwise have been absorbed in enterprise and mainly distributed in wages. In this way alone Mr. Lloyd George has directly caused to the people more direct loss in one year than his "people's Budget" could make good in ten, even if his contentions regarding it were sound.

Yet, if the case finally made out against the Chancellor had its strength, the Government Benches had quickly discovered that, aided by their powerful popular Press, a growing mass-sentiment in favour of the Budget as a "People's Budget", adverse to "plundering land monopolizers", could be readily stoked up. In fact, a Budget League was created to stir the masses further, and it was hoped, not altogether vainly, that, behind such a League, a combined Liberal and Labour "movement" could be organized capable, not merely of reversing the long tide of Conservative by-election successes, but, perhaps, even, of reproducing the

[1] Cf. *Hansard*, June 22nd, for the beginning of the vital Committee stage on the Finance Bill.
[2] Cf. *Tariff or Budget*, p. 7. This pamphlet, consisting largely of J. L. Garvin's anti-Budget writing in the *Observer* during the second half of 1909, had a wide sale.

triumphant polling-results of the "movement" against "Chinese Slavery". The long tide of Opposition by-election successes was, indeed, halted, during the summer, and an exultant Winston Churchill was able, at Norwich on July 26th, to deal thus with those who said the Budget was "hung up":[1]

So it is. It is hung up in triumph over the High Peak; it is hung up as a banner of victory over Dumfries, over Cleveland, and over Mid-Derby. The miniature General Election just concluded has shown that the policy embodied in the Budget, and which inspires the Budget, has vivified and invigorated the Liberal Party; has brought union where there was falling away; has revived enthusiasm where apathy was creeping in.

In point of fact, the Budget League[2] produced stir enough to cause some Conservative doubt as to whether it might not be wiser to let a much-amended Budget go through, under protest, than to risk what might happen, at a General Election, if the "People's Budget" were rejected by the Peers. To stop this hesitancy in high Conservative quarters certainly took strong agitation from those who feared that if the "Radical Plunderbund" got a "Revolution by Budget" through in 1909, it would merely be encouraged to repeat and expand the process year by year.[3]

To the Budget campaign in the country, the Chancellor contributed two of the most important speeches of his career, speeches whose mass-appeal proved such as to convert him, till 1914, into by far the greatest platform attraction in the country. No other speaker seemed to combine so entertaining a line of almost music-hall patter, in derision of his opponents and the "people's", with "progressive" and "democratic" sentiments, favourable to the poor and the needy. The effect of the Limehouse speech, delivered on July 30th in the heart of London's East End, appeared so temporarily overwhelming as almost to decide the issue of the

[1] *The Times*, July 27th.

[2] *The Budget, the Land and the People, the New Land Value Taxes explained and illustrated*, represents the kind of literature it was preparing for cheap issue and in large quantities. This booklet of a hundred pages was first issued on August 17th, and there was a second edition in September. More significant, perhaps, was the issue of what was intended to be a regular annual by the founder of *The Reformers' Year Book*, Joseph Edwards, under the title of *Land and real Tariff Reform being the Land Reformers' Handbook for 1909*.

[3] Cf. *Observer*, August 8, and August 15, 1909, for two editorials from J. L. Garvin. "There would be no end to the process set up by this Budget" affirmed Mr. Garvin. "The new method would be used as the master-key for every Radical problem. There would be another and another Budget, as vicious and injurious as the present one, but even more plausible."

51

Budget struggle.[1] But the echoes even of the most frenzied mass-applause ultimately died away, and the Conservatives resumed the contest, still apparently undecided what action, if any, to take in their stronghold of the Lords.

It was when the Budget had passed through its difficult and prolonged Committee stage in the Commons and was almost ready for presentation to the Lords that the Chancellor made his Newcastle speech of October 9th. He apparently felt the need of explaining away the many amendments he had found it advisable to accept before passing on to jeer at dukes and landlords. Here is a characteristic passage:[2]

The Budget is through all its most troublesome stages, and it has emerged out of its forty days and forty nights in the wilderness rather strengthened and improved. We have made alterations and modifications. You cannot apply any great principle or set of principles without necessary hardships. We have done our best to meet every hard case . . . and done it amidst the taunts of the very people who pressed them upon us whenever we listened to them, as I have had to do for five months. I have done five months' hard labour.

Although we have made alterations and modifications, the Bill in its main structure remains. All the taxes are there. The land taxes are there. The super-tax is there. The poor fellows who are receiving only five thousand a year and £10,000 and £20,000 a year will have to contribute just a little more to the expenses of the country. And then there is the man to whom somebody has left a fortune. He will have to contribute a little more. . . .

What is the chief charge against the Budget by its opponents? That it is an attack on industry and an attack on property! . . . It is very remarkable that since this attack on industry . . . trade has improved. It is beginning to recover from the great crash which first of all came from America, the country of high tariffs, and it has improved steadily. It has not quite recovered; it will take some time . . . but it is better. Industries which were making losses last year are beginning to make profits this year. The imports and exports have gone up during the last few months by millions. . . . Only one stock has gone down badly— there has been a great slump in dukes. . . . They have been scolding like omnibus drivers because the Budget cart has knocked a little of the gilt off their old stage-coach. . . .

[1] Cf. *Observer*, August 8th: "Some Unionist journals were responsible for suggestions of a surrender. . . . There was in some Opposition quarters a movement of panic . . . the members of the Plunderbund persuaded themselves that there was going to be a Unionist surrender. They danced in each other's arms in this ecstatic delusion. They told each other that all was over but the shouting. They cried that victory was theirs. They wrote of *The Flight of the Opposition.* They plunged into orgies of premature rejoicing."

[2] Cf. *Northern Echo*, October 11, 1909.

Of course, this was hardly a frank admission that an apprentice-Chancellor, in a far more ambitious Budget than most, had made far more than the usual number of miscalculations and mistakes, but it proved effective enough politically with biased or uncritical audiences. So did the great portion of the speech, devoted to the alleged iniquities of landlordism which can be aptly summed-up in one of Lloyd George's sentences on the gross over-charging for land, needed for industrial, housing, or even school development: "I can give you cases where landlords have charged thirty, forty, even a hundred times the value of the land."[1] The Chancellor had obviously begun collecting from businessmen associates in the Liberal Party facts and figures, not always reliable or fairly stated, which might make the basis of future political campaigns after the Budget was enacted. But the temptation to quote the Chancellor on mining royalties and ground-rents in the Rhondda or on the Yorkshire landlord who had showed comparative moderation when charging for land, for miners' cottages, only eighteen times its alleged agricultural price[2] shall be avoided in order to concentrate on a soon notorious peroration offering "rare and refreshing fruit" to the masses and threatening the Peers with "a revolution" if they unconstitutionally prevented the enactment of the Budget.

"Who talks about altering and meddling with the Constitution?" declaimed the Chancellor. "The Constitutional party, the great Constitutional party. As long as the Constitution gave rank and possession and power to the Lords it was not to be interfered with . . . as long as the Constitution enforced royalties and ground rents and fees and premiums and fines, and all the black retinue of exaction; as long as it showered writs and summonses and injunctions and distresses and warrants to enforce them, then the Constitution was inviolate. It was sacred. . . . But the moment the Constitution looks round; the moment the Constitution begins to discover that there are millions of people outside park gates who need attention, then the Constitution is to be torn to pieces.

"Let them realise what they are doing. They are forcing a revolution, and they will get it. The Lords may decree a revolution, but the people will direct it. If they begin, issues will be raised that they little dream

[1] H. Du Parcq, *Life of David Lloyd George*, iv, 693. The speech will be found to contain detailed treatment of the burdens said to have been imposed on mining developments in South Wales and Yorkshire by landlords, who shared none of the commercial risks.

[2] There seems something ominously inexact about the landlord's quoted terms "£6 or £10 an acre". "£6 or £7 an acre" or '£9 or £10 an acre" would have carried greater conviction.

of . . . the question will be asked whether five hundred men, ordinary men chosen accidentally from among the unemployed, should override the judgement—the deliberate judgement—of millions of people who are engaged in the industry which makes the wealth of the country.

"That is one question. Another will be, Who ordained that a few should have the land of Britain as a perquisite? Who made ten thousand people owners of the soil, and the rest of us trespassers in the land of our birth? Who is it who is responsible for the scheme of things whereby one man is engaged through life in grinding labour to win a bare and precarious subsistence for himself, and when, at the end of his days, he claims at the hands of the community he served a poor pension of eightpence a day, he can only get it through a revolution, and another man who does not toil receives every hour of the day, every hour of the night, whilst he slumbers, more than his poor neighbour receives in a whole year of toil? Where did the table of that law come from? Whose finger inscribed it? These are the questions that will be asked. The answers are charged with peril for the order of things the Peers represent; but they are fraught with rare and refreshing fruit for the parched lips of the multitude. . . ."

This kind of oratory, with a far greater appeal to the masses than anything the Labour Party could yet produce, must certainly have contributed to rule out the possibility of a party compromise such as certain Court circles went on suggesting. The mere notion of offering further Budget concessions would have broken up Asquith's Government and Majority[1] while, on the other side, a Conservative by-election victory won, late in October, in such a working-class area as Bermondsey encouraged the Tory Press and Peers to demand an end of the hesitations of their leaders.[2] On November 22nd, finally, when the Second Reading of the Finance Bill was moved in the Lords, the Tory leader, Lansdowne, rose to proffer his fateful amendment by which the Lords declared, after six days of debate and in a division of 350 against 75, that they were not justified in consenting to the Bill until it had been submitted to the judgement of the country. The Government reply, on December 2nd, was to carry, by a great majority in the Lower House, a resolution claiming that the Peers had invaded

[1] It was obvious that Asquith could no longer risk the resignation of Lloyd George and Churchill as he might well have done previously. And by December 3rd, Lloyd George already felt confident enough to threaten resignation, in public, unless something like the later Parliament Bill was insisted upon.

[2] Cf. *Observer*, October 31st: "The death sentence upon the 'poor man's Budget' has been pronounced by one of the poorest constituencies in the land. If the Limehouse method failed in a dismal warren of social wretchedness, where can it hope to succeed?" The voting had been Dumphreys, Conservative, 4278; Hughes, Liberal, 3291; Salter, Socialist, 1435, and, of course, Government organs consoled themselves by claiming "Majority for the Budget, 448."

the financial privileges of the Commons and, far more important, to announce that a Dissolution had been advised.

It would seem that Government's more Radical supporters were elated enough by their having secured a General Election on their own chosen grounds of "Peers against the People" and "Peers against the Constitution" for some very optimistic polling forecasts to be made. There were even those who hoped that the existing Government majority over Conservatives of 386 against 167 would not fall significantly enough for either Irish Home Rulers or "Independent Labour" to be able to dictate Government's future course though, of course, combined "log-rolling" by over one hundred and twenty Irish and Labour members was also an ugly possibility.[1] There were Conservatives, too, who were inclined to think that, after the shattering defeat of January 1906, it was too much to expect them to draw level with Government at a single General Election, expecially in the circumstances engineered by the tricky Chancellor. But events showed that, aided somewhat by electoral survivals like University Representation and Plural Suffrage and aided, too, by a distinct middle-class distaste for the mob-tactics Lloyd George was employing, Conservatives did a good deal better than many had expected. They reduced Government members proper to 275 against their own 273 and succeeded, too, in inflicting on "Independent Labour" a number of the rudest electoral shocks which served, temporarily at least, to abate the flood of prophecy foretelling the speedy and inevitable triumph of a party reduced from 45 to 40.[2]

[1] Cf. Sir Almeric Fitzroy, *Memoirs*, i, 391, under January 6, 1910: "some Liberals talk of the Government retaining a majority of 200."

[2] Two of the lost Labour seats were at Preston and Sunderland in both of which places the 1906 partitioning of the representation between Liberal and Labour was overthrown by Conservatives. Chatham saw another Labour loss to Conservatism, and Jarrow and Colne Valley two losses to Liberals.

CHAPTER III

THE YEARS 1910 AND 1911

"They said: 'Who has hate in his soul? Who has envied his
  neighbour?
Let him arise and control both that man and his labour.'
They said: 'Who is eaten by sloth? Whose unthrift has
  destroyed him?
He shall levy a tribute from all because none have employed
  him.'
They said: 'Who hath toiled, who hath striven, and gathered
  possession?
Let him be spoiled. He hath given full proof of transgression.'
They said: 'Who is irked by the Law? *Though we may not*
  remove it,
If he lend us his aid in this raid, we will set him above it.' "

    Kipling denounces the Radical-Labour *entente* in the City
of Brass (1909).

    "Of all the London newspapers, *The Daily News,* has the
most obvious claim to represent the political Nonconformity
which came into power at the general election of 1906 . . . its
statement of the Government's case for Home Rule . . . called
Fifty Points for Home Rule which is having a wide sale . . . says
at the start that 'Unionism is only a scarecrow creed dressed up
in the rags and tatters of superstition and prejudice. . . . There
are some people . . . who are content that they have solved the
Irish question when they have talked vaguely about the Pope
and Irish poverty. . . .' All through these *Fifty Points* . . . one
meets this *suppressio veri*. . . . The twenty-fourth point, Ireland
and a German Invasion, is that it is 'nonsense scarcely requiring
an answer' to assert that 'a Home Rule Ireland would receive
the invader and give him a base from which to attack
England. . . .' The idea . . . is only a 'sensational picture
painted by Unionist agitators.' . . . If a German force landed
in Ireland now . . . it would have to face a loyal executive
Government and a British army corps in occupation of every
strategic point. . . . If a German force landed in a Home Rule
Ireland, it would find an executive Government . . . at the
invader's disposal, in return for a guarantee of complete
independence. . . . The twenty-fifth point, headed Threatened
Ulster Rebellion, is that Ulster's protest against Home Rule
is only the 'bluster' of the 'old ascendency party' on being asked
to 'surrender their class privileges. . . .' 'The Unionist bullies,'

as *The Daily News* calls the Ulster Members, are not 'the masters of a political caucus' which would govern Ireland 'with the remorseless hostility and violence with which Russia governs Poland.' . . . The Nonconformists are therefore being misled when they are told that the talk about rebellion is merely the 'brag and bluster' of Ulster Members . . . and that 'the ordinary intelligent Irish Protestant' has no part in it. . . ."

Home Rule polemics from M. J. F. McCarthy, *The Nonconformist Treason* (1912).

"We therefore most certainly favour strikes: we shall always do our best to help strikes to be successful, and shall prepare the way as rapidly as possible for the General Strike of national proportions. This will be the actual Social and Industrial Revolution. The workers will refuse any longer to manipulate the machinery of production in the interest of the capitalist class, and there will be no power on earth able to compel them to work when they thus refuse."

Tom Mann's *The Industrial Syndicalist* (March 1911) offers Labour a change.

I T may well be that, if the Conservatives had obtained, at the General Election of January-February 1910, the 300 seats which some had hoped for instead of the 273 actually won,[1] the whole future course of British politics would have been different. Even as it was, there was much anxiety among Ministers, whose Press supporters might loudly be claiming a Government majority of 124 by the simple device of adding 40 Labour men and over 80 Irish Nationalists to the 275 Liberals and Radicals, but who knew that their position on the Front Bench would henceforward be a most uneasy one. Some Ministers, in their franker moments, admitted to a majority of 2 only over the regular Opposition which, in certain circumstances of Labour and Irish irritation, could become a minority of 120.[2] In fact, if the Irishmen who had thought fit to oppose the Budget because of the "excessive" taxation of Irish whisky,[3] had renewed their opposition to the revived Budget of the 1910 Session, the Government would have broken up. The Irish leader, Redmond, who now had power of life and death over the Cabinet, did not, of course, throw Ministers out over such a bagatelle as somewhat dearer whisky

[1] Cf. *Observer*, August 29, 1909, for even higher hopes: "The calculation at the present moment—a calculation checked by experienced politicians . . . is that the Unionist Party, in the worst event, would not come back from a General Election less than 320 strong. Even in that case the Radicals and Socialists together would be far inferior in numbers and ruinously dependent on the Irish vote; and the real power of the demagogues would be destroyed." It almost looks as though Garvin had been accepting calculations, based on by-election results, which notoriously, in the British system, allow Opposition to whip up any and every Government critic and enemy (especially after a Ministry has been in office for years) in a fashion that cannot often be reproduced over the country as a whole at a General Election.

[2] Cf. Sir Almeric Fitzroy, *Memoirs*, i, 394, under February 11, 1910: "One of them told me yesterday that he considered that the Government had only a majority of *two*." A few days later he reported that members of the Government were openly discussing the possibility of a defeat on the Address.

[3] Cf. *Hansard*, May 24, 1909, for Irish ingenuity in making any and every possible charge against the addition of 3s. 9d. to the existing duty of 11s. per gallon. According to T. P. O'Connor, who claimed that the publicans had already added 1d. per glass to the price of whisky, it was all "an unfair, unjust, exaggerated case of indirect taxation of the poorest of the poor in Ireland" besides doing great harm to the important distillery trade (two-thirds of whose product was supposedly exported) and to the Irish barley-farmer. And Timothy Healy alleged "universal dissatisfaction and discontent" with perilous possible consequences, the probable closing of all the smaller distilleries with dangerous resulting unemployment and the monstrous fiscal injustice represented by his claim that: "if an Irishman spent 4½d. for a glass of whisky 4d. went to the Government, whilst of 4½d. spent in England on beer only a halfpenny" so went. There were further grievances on publicans' licence duties on which concessions were finally made for the small Irish publican.

even if that gave certain rhetorical advantages on Irish platforms to the small minority group of "Independent Nationalists". Instead, he quickly demanded, in view of Home Rule's past treatment by the Peers, speedy Ministerial action to secure far-reaching reductions in the power of the House of Lords not merely in regard to Budgets but in regard to all legislation demanded by a majority in the elected and representative House.[1]

For weeks British Government had to work in circumstances of critical uncertainty while one section of the Cabinet, headed, it would seem, by Lord Chancellor Loreburn, opposed any idea of bargaining with Redmond while another, including Lloyd George and Churchill, favoured a compact which would end all ideas of a compromise with the Lords.[2] Ultimately the Prime Minister seems to have had to convince the Nationalists of Government's good faith by postponing the rapid re-passage of the "People's Budget" through the Commons and making the new House's first major work the passing, amid long and angry debates, of the three Resolutions on which the later Parliament Bill was based.[3] In certain economic circumstances, the further delay of two months imposed on the enactment of a Finance Bill, already long overdue, could have resulted not merely in Exchequer and Money Market inconvenience,[4] but in a "loss of confidence" capable of doing serious hurt to trade and employment. If industry, however, had now taken a sufficiently marked upward turn from the harmful effects of the American slump of 1907 not to be afflicted by "loss of confidence", the extra risks that were being run, under the

[1] Sir Almeric Fitzroy, *Memoirs*, i, 394: "Redmond's declaration, which is reported this morning [February 11th] that he could not support the Government unless he had the guarantees necessary for an effective campaign against the Lords, has produced a great sensation. . . . There is a section of the Cabinet, of which the Lord Chancellor is a prominent figure opposed to any transaction with Redmond. . . . They are willing to leave him to do his worst."

[2] Cf. *Ibid.*, p. 398, under February 22nd: "The Lord Chancellor said this morning that they might be out in a few days, and the general feeling is that, while Redmond is personally anxious to do his best for them, he is not master in his own house and may give them a fall at any minute"; and under February 26th: "The section of the Cabinet which has been throughout opposed to any transaction with the Irish Party is becoming more restive . . . the hope of the more violent lies in the inertia of the Prime Minister."

[3] *Ibid.*, p. 400, under April 2nd: "Redmond's bluster has been carefully designed to conceal the real intention to keep the Government in power as long as they are willing to reap the reward of their subservience."

[4] *Ibid.*, under March 18th: "The financial deadlock is causing a sense of deep resentment in the City, where it is ascribed to sullen indifference on the part of Ministers to everything but their own *amour-propre*."

combined pressure of "British and Irish demagogues", failed not to be gloomily stressed by the City and the Opposition.

Budget matters were eventually reached on April 18th, and there was virtual agreement between the Front Benches that further "unnecessary" delays would be intolerable. According to Lloyd George, expenditure for the year 1909–10 had been £157,945,000 and revenue, £131,697,000, but the apparent deficit of £26,248,000 would be more than made up out of the arrears of revenue left uncollected because of the non-passage of the Budget. When these were gathered in, there would be a surplus of £2,962,000, and £1,300,000 only would have been lost. One of the few interesting problems that arose during several days of abbreviated debate turned on the number of "Independent Nationalists" who would follow William O'Brien into the Opposition Lobby because of the Budget's alleged "cruel injury to more than one Irish industry". The figures by which O'Brien's attempt to defeat the Second Reading were rejected—328 against 242— give an indication of the balance of forces in the Commons. And, on April 28th, the Lords passed the belated Finance Bill without a single Division, despite the varied arguments that might still have been brought to deny the mandate of a Government with a majority of 2.[1] It was, of course, intended to show the nation that directly any sort of a tenable case was established for arguing that the majority of the electorate desired a Government Bill, the Peers would conscientiously abstain from Opposition. Certainly, the Ministerial case for a Parliament Bill and a new General Election, after the Peers should have rejected it, might be held to have been considerably weakened in many eyes and especially in those of the King, the ultimate use of whose prerogatives was already in question.[2]

But on May 6th occurred the death of King Edward VII, and, out of consideration for a new monarch, likely to be faced almost at once by party-disputes on the possible use of his prerogatives, a head-on collision between Government and Opposition was avoided for some time. Instead, a prolonged series of confidential

---

[1] Cf. *Hansard* between April 18th and 28th.

[2] Cf. *Edwardian England, 1901–1910*, p. 59, for Edward VII's anxieties and forebodings. When he died on May 6th, one diarist reported: "Some Tories of the baser sort are disposed to attribute the King's death to the unscrupulous tactics of Ministers, and you are gravely told that the King's visit to Sandringham was due to the want of some vent for his anxieties after his interview with the Prime Minister" (Sir Almeric Fitzroy, *Memoirs*, ii, 409 under May 23rd).

conferences between Government and Opposition leaders was arranged which, before being finally abandoned in November, seems sometimes to have come within measurable distance of success. The possible party compromises under discussion at these conferences will be mentioned later but, first, should be treated some of the more significant Parliamentary occasions before the Adjournment, on August 3rd, for a Recess timed to end on November 15th. The Budget statement for the 1910–11 year was made on June 30th and could hardly, in the circumstances, be a very contentious one. But the Chancellor gave notice of a National Insurance scheme preparing for 1911 and contrived, too, to allot part of his expected surplus to finding Old Age Pensions, as from January 1, 1911, for some unfortunates hitherto disqualified as paupers. And to pass over "extremist" displays, mainly from Irish and Labour members, on the subjects of Indian "coercion"[1] and "excessive" Naval expenditure,[2] is to be given a little more space for dealing with the most discussed Sessional activity of the Labour Party which, as it happened, was concerned not with Payment of Members, Reversal of the Osborne Judgement, or Women's Suffrage,[3] but with the provision for the Royal Family under the new Civil List.

It was George Barnes, to whom the rotating Chairmanship of the Labour Party had now come, who took the lead in the Civil List debates of July 22nd, 26th, and 27th.[4] There was a very long history of "popular" opposition to "excessive" provision for the Royal Family, and among the demands put forward by the Labour

---

[1] Cf. *Hansard*, July 26th, for Edwin Montagu's introduction of the "Indian Budget" and the debate that ensued on some of the measures being taken in India against "terrorists" and the "seditious" portion of the Press. An anti-Government amendment secured 48 votes against 277.

[2] *Ibid.*, July 14th, for Dillon's amendment raising 70 votes against 298.

[3] The Labour member, D. J. Shackleton, had charge of the Sessional Bill to extend the Parliamentary vote to women occupiers, and at Second Reading, which was as far as it got, the Bill won 299 votes against 190. See *Hansard*, July 11th and 12th.

[4] Cf. *Hansard* for these days. It was on July 22nd that Lloyd George had moved the business, basing himself on the Report of a Civil List Committee of twenty-one. The income proposed for a future Princess of Wales was £10,000 to be increased to £30,000 in the event of widowhood; the younger sons of the King were to have incomes of £10,000 after attaining the age of twenty-one and £15,000 more per annum was to be added if they married; the daughters were to have incomes of £10,000 when attaining the age of twenty-one or marrying; and finally, the new Queen if left a widow was assured of an income of £70,000. On these resolutions of July 22nd, carried, after the defeat of amendments from Barnes and Keir Hardie, by 197 to 19, the Civil List Bill was based which obtained its First Reading on July 25th. Second Reading was on July 26th, and the Committee stage on July 27th.

group were the reduction of the Civil List from £470,000 per annum to £385,000, the abandonment of the proposed financial provision for a future Princess of Wales, the similar abandonment of the provision for the King's younger children when they should have come of age and marry, and, finally, the transfer of the revenues of the Duchies of Lancaster and Cornwall to the public Exchequer. Barnes's first two divisions of 26 against 206 and 21 against 218 were hardly inspiring, but Keir Hardie in the House, and Labour stalwarts in the country, would not have forgiven a tame abandonment of opposition and so the effort continued. It was on July 26th, and on the proposal to transfer the Duchy revenues of Cornwall and Lancaster to the Exchequer, that Barnes raised his figures to 52 against 221. Labour, at any rate, could now claim that it had been a Radical in Office, Lloyd George himself, who had proposed "excessive" Court expenditure and that the old Radical task, once willingly undertaken by men like Burdett, Dilke, and Bradlaugh, of attempting to curb such expenditure in the name of the poverty-stricken multitude, had now devolved, like so much else, upon the Labour members.

It was on July 29th, when the long Summer Recess was almost upon Parliament, that the Prime Minister made an important announcement on the conferences that had been proceeding since June 17th between a team of four Government representatives, composed of Asquith himself, Lloyd George, Birrell, and Lord Crewe, and one of four Opposition representatives, made up of Balfour, Austen Chamberlain, and the Lords Lansdowne, and Cawdor. The Prime Minister's carefully-balanced phrases, studied and commented upon all over the world, are worth repeating at some little length.[1]

"The representatives of the Government and the Opposition," reported Mr. Asquith, "have held twelve meetings, and have carefully surveyed a large part of the field of controversy. The result is that our discussions have made such progress, although we have not, so far, reached an agreement, as to render it, in the opinion of all of us, not only desirable, but necessary, that they should continue. In fact, I may go further and say that we should think it wrong at this stage to break them off. There is no question of their indefinite continuance, but if we find, as a result of our further deliberations during the recess, that there is no prospect of an agreement that can be announced to Parliament in the course of the present Session, we should bring the conference to a close."

[1] Cf. *The Times*, July 30th.

It hardly needs great acumen to detect that this communication had its special message for two anxious sets of non-participants, the Irish Nationalists, who, though they held Government pledges,[1] must have been rendered uneasy by the prolongation of Ministers' conferences with Home Rule's leading opponents, and the Irish Unionists who feared that the Conservative Leaders might be tricked or cajoled into a specious "compromise" which would, in effect, be a "betrayal". Both Irish Nationalists and Unionists now had the assurance that their doubts should be ended, one way or the other, before the end of the year. And it was, in fact, during October that the great effort seems to have been made to reach what might have been compromise-decisions over a large area of acute political controversy.[2]

No exact account has ever been given of what went on at these prolonged conferences of party leaders, and it may well be that no exact account will ever become available. But, even at the time, there were broad hints that much more was being discussed than the Lords' Veto and Home Rule. And long afterwards, during Lloyd George's Premiership, there were repeated allusions which seemed to indicate not only that a remodelled House of Lords and a safeguarded Home Rule had been under discussion, with a Coalition Government to carry them through,[3] but that Conservatives had been agreeably surprised to find the Chancellor far from blind to the case for more Military Training or against "dumping" and the running-down of British Agriculture. It seems, however, that the rank-and-file Tory Commoner and, even more, the rank-and-file Tory Peer were growing increasingly suspicious of the conferences and increasingly disinclined to authorize the distasteful compromises that might soon be called for. The claim to keep for a "reformed" House of Lords, still decisively weighted towards the stiffest Conservatism by a strong

[1] There had been a March meeting between Mr. Redmond and members of the Government at which the pledges seem to have been given.

[2] Cf. Sir Almeric Fitzroy, *Memoirs*, ii, 418, under October 15th: "Political life has this week resumed its course. The first Cabinet Council took place on Wednesday (12th), the King held a Council on Thursday (13th), and the Conference continued its sittings with a frequency that greatly agitated those who prophesy without knowing. Notwithstanding, however, the gloomy vaticinations of some and the scarcely veiled hostility of the extreme sections of both parties, I believe much of the lumber in the way of mutual understanding has been cleared out, and a path prepared along which statesmen with a soul above mere politics may find salvation. I had an opportunity of talking to Cawdor at some length on the subject and was much struck by the moderation of his tone."

[3] Cf. Frank Owen, *Tempestuous Journey*.

hereditary contingent, either the full Veto powers of the old or, at least, the modified power to "hang up" Commons Bills till the "people" had been consulted, was certain to break up the conferences, and broken up they were, as was officially announced on November 11th.[1]

It will be instructive to give the comment regretfully written into his diary by a well-placed observer, the Clerk to the Privy Council, who had confidants in both camps. On November 15th he wrote this.[2]

The Tory Party and their associates seem bent on political suicide. The lessons of the last twelve months have been lost, and they are engaged in precipitating a crisis which prudent statesmanship could have avoided not only with honour, but advantage.

I hold no brief for the Government, which contains reckless and menacing elements, but Asquith, on going into the Conference, held these elements in check, and I have the best reason for knowing that the Government representatives went a long way towards making every possible concession to the views and feelings of their opponents, in order to reach an accommodation that should stand the test of time; and I further know that an arrangement which finally brought both parties into substantial accord was within an ace of being concluded. Other counsels unfortunately prevailed, influences which had been held in suspense and kept at a distance infiltrated into the area of negotiation, external advices asserted themselves, and the foolish cry, "Better perish at the hands of the constituencies than of the Conference," was raised with fatal effect.

Meanwhile the "extreme Radical" Press had been taking a speedy Dissolution for granted, even before the King had been consulted, and the King, for his part, had apparently decided against the constitutionality of permitting the Prime Minister to announce a Dissolution directly Parliament reassembled on November 15th and before the House of Lords had had any chance of examining Ministers' proposed Parliament Act.[3] It would have been most

---

[1] Cf. *The Times*, November 12th. There had been twenty-one meetings of the party leaders.

[2] Sir Almeric Fitzroy, *Memoirs*, ii, 422.

[3] Cf. *Ibid.*, p. 422, under November 16th: "The situation undergoes remarkable changes: no sooner has one party taken the false step of bringing the conference to a close, in order that the judgement of the constituencies should be invoked, than the other caps the indiscretion by attempting to force a dissolution at the bidding of its extreme supporters without having a technical case to claim from the Crown the exercise of its prerogative in that regard. Lord Morley, in discussing the matter this morning, was perfectly frank in agreeing that the King's position in refusing Mr. Asquith's request was a very strong one. . . ." What Lord Morley did not tell the Clerk to the Privy Council was that a Cabinet Minute was then in the King's hands

improper, as well as highly dangerous, for Ministers, at this stage, to take the "extreme Radical" stand of threatening to resign, and so the principal business in Parliament, on November 15th, proved to be Lord Lansdowne's demand that Government's Bill should be placed before the Peers, who were prepared, he claimed, for reform and the admission of representative elements. The Government's Bill was given a First Reading on November 16th, and on November 17th Resolutions for Reform of the Lords, on lines suggested by the Liberal ex-Premier, Rosebery, were accepted according to which half the future Upper House might have been chosen by the hereditary Peers amongst themselves and the other half have been made up of representative and nominated elements.

It is now known that King George's hand had meanwhile been forced in a way that he always resented, and that "pledges" the Prime Minister was presumed to have given, in a speech of April 14th, to keep the Irish, Labour, and "extreme Radical" elements in the Commons united behind him,[1] were used to constrain the King to agree not only to a Dissolution but to a creation of Peers afterwards if necessary. It was even sought to make a great concession of the fact that the Cabinet was willing to agree that the King's promise to create Peers should be kept secret unless and until a constitutional crisis threatened.[2] The most trusted member of the King's entourage, Sir A. Bigge, the later Lord Stamfordham, drew up a trenchant document[3] for the King to use in the decisive interview with the Prime Minister and Lord Crewe

reiterating the request for a speedy Dissolution and presuming that, if that Dissolution resulted in the return of "an adequate majority in the new House of Commons" in favour of Ministers' policy, the Royal prerogative of creating Peers would be available, "if needed, to secure that effect should be given to the decision of the country". The Cabinet Minute is to be found in Harold Nicolson's *King George V*, p. 136.

[1] Cf. *Hansard*, April 14th, for the Prime Minister's "pledges" on introducing the Parliament Bill on April 14th: "In no case shall we recommend Dissolution, except under such conditions as will secure that in the new Parliament the judgement of the People, as expressed in the Election, will be carried into law."

[2] Cf. Harold Nicolson, *King George V*, p. 137, for an extract from the Royal Archives in which Lord Knollys, Joint Private Secretary to the Monarch, after an interview with Asquith and Crewe on the Cabinet Minute of November 15th, advised compliance with the Cabinet's wishes because "What is now recommended is altogether different in every way from any request to be allowed publicly to announce that you have consented to give guarantees. It is a great compromise on the part of the Cabinet."

[3] The document is quoted, in part, below and was copied by Harold Nicolson, from the Royal Archives at Windsor for his *King George V*, pp. 137–8. Further trenchant writing from Bigge will be found in the book.

in which the issue was settled, against the Monarch, by a Cabinet resignation being made the alternative:[1]

"The King's position is: he cannot give contingent guarantees," wrote Bigge. "For by so doing he becomes a Partisan & is placing a powerful weapon in the hands of the Irish and Socialists who, assured of the abolition of the veto of the House of Lords would hold before their electors the certainty of ultimate Home Rule & the carrying out of their Socialist programme. The Unionists would declare His Majesty was favouring the Government and placing them [the Unionists] at a disadvantage before their constituencies. Indeed, it is questionable whether His Majesty would be acting constitutionally. It is not His Majesty's duty to save the Prime Minister from the mistake of his incautious words on the 14th of April. . . . What is the object of the King giving the Cabinet to understand that, in the event of the Government being returned with an adequate majority in the new House of Commons, he will be ready to exercise his constitutional powers, *if his intentions are not to be made public until the occasion arises.* Why should not the King wait till the occasion arises? . . . Is this straight? Is it English?"

The impending Dissolution was announced on November 18th and considerable outstanding Sessional business, including the Finance Bill, was pushed through before November 28th. Government's opponents, of course, guessed that Dissolution was hardly the wish of the Crown and had, too, the further argument that Ministers had no constitutional case for a Dissolution while their Bill on the Upper House was still before the Peers, who had not rejected it even though they were discussing possible alternatives. There were other indictments possible of Government's course, and especially the charge that, just as the whole "Constitution" was being destroyed as the price of eighty grossly over-valued Irish votes,[2] so the price of forty Labour votes, hitherto un-

---

[1] Cf. *King George V*, p. 138 for an extract from the King's diary: "I agreed most reluctantly to give the Cabinet a secret understanding . . . I disliked having to do this very much, but agreed that this was the only alternative to the Cabinet resigning, which at this moment would be very disastrous." There is a less guarded account as given, in August 1911, by the King to Lord Derby in Randolph Churchill, *Lord Derby*, pp. 126–7.

[2] Cf. *Whitaker's Almanack, 1912*, pp. 186 and 190, for the way in which the shrinkage of the Irish Catholic population since the 1840s and the great growth of population in Britain sometimes made a British Conservative M.P. represent up to twenty times the electorate of the smaller Irish boroughs. The five smallest boroughs represented by Nationalists were Kilkenny with 1742 electors, Newry with 2021, Galway with 2306, Waterford with 3104, and Limerick with 4470. By contrast, five of the "Greater London" constituencies in Middlesex, represented by Conservatives, were Harrow with 35,379 electors, Enfield with 28,571, Ealing with 25,073, Hornsey with 23,450, and Brentford with 20,071.

disclosed, was now revealed, by a pre-Dissolution pledge, to be the conferment on the Trade Unions of the right to raise and expend political funds. Organizations founded for the industrial protection of their members and endowed by Parliament, for that very reason, with great privileges and immunities, would now be increasingly turned into political machines for financing municipal and Parliamentary candidatures on the part of their loudest or most ambitious officials. The Courts had sought, in the Osborne Judgement, to protect the ordinary Trade Union member from being converted into the tool of a tiny minority of would-be Socialist politicians.[1] But now the protection of the Law was to be removed by Statute and millions of working-men left without defence against the machinations of those still intent on climbing to Downing Street, with the aid of Political Funds extorted from often unwilling Trade Unionists with better uses for their money. It was a Conservative case, which sometimes went well when there was a sincere Conservative Trade Unionist to back it or a notorious Labour climber, with a besmirched record known to the constituency, to point to as evidence of what must be avoided.

In view of the recriminations on the Osborne Judgement that were to continue for years, and in view, too, of a great new wave of strike-unrest whose beginnings were already faintly to be heard towards the end of 1910,[2] it may not be thought untimely to set down a shortened Labour survey of the great political disputes which had been raging on the "People's Budget" and the Lords' Veto. No Labour writing of 1910 has been found so terse and pertinent as that issued in 1921 when William Stewart, Keir Hardie's biographer and friend, thus summarized much of the *Labour Leader*'s files for 1909 and 1910:[3]

[1] Cf. *The Case against Radicalism, A Fighting Brief for Unionist Candidates, Agents, and Speakers*, p. 317. This was the big Conservative manual for the first 1910 Election, and even before Ministers' pledge to set aside the effects of the Osborne Judgement, it had denounced the notion as "tyranny of the worst kind" coming particularly badly from a Parliamentary Labour Party "who never cease fulminating against the alleged tyranny of capital".

[2] Cf. H. Du Parcq, *Life of David Lloyd George*, iv, 766–7, for a clear indication from the Chancellor in an address delivered in the City Temple on October 17th. "The great unrest amongst the people in all the civilized countries of the world," he said, "is beginning to attract special attention. . . . Everything points to the fact that the storm cone has been hoisted and that we are in for a period of tempests. . . . You have got it in Portugal, in Germany, in France, in Austria. . . . You have also got it in the North of England, in South Wales, and in Scotland. . . ."

[3] William Stewart, *J. Keir Hardie, A Biography*, pp. 291–4. Stewart, it may be mentioned, found employment on the *Labour Leader* under Keir Hardie for

English Radicalism: The End?

In the two general elections of 1910 the man in the limelight was Mr. Lloyd George. . . .

All through the year the great constitutional controversy continued, and the people became so engrossed shouting for or against Lloyd George that they forgot all about Sir Edward Grey, a much more fateful statesman. . . .

The rival partisans debated hotly as to whether the House of Lords should be ended or mended, as to how many new Peers it would be necessary to create to render that House impotent, or as to how many times a reformed Second Chamber should be allowed to throw out a Bill. . . ; and while this political comedy . . . was proceeding, the diplomats and Imperialists were not idle.

Lord Roberts continued his propaganda for compulsory military service . . . Mr. Haldane's "nation in arms" was materialising in spite of protests from Hardie. . . . The Admiralty was getting its Dreadnoughts built. Germany was adding to its fleet. France was raising the peace-time strength of its army, and more fateful than all, British and French financiers were investing their millions in Russia. . . . In the midst of the evolution of a policy in which he took a special interest . . . King Edward died. . . .

It would be unfair to Keir Hardie and the large section of the Labour Party, which felt like him on Foreign Affairs, to fail to point out that the last few lines, quoted from his biographer, do not represent merely wisdom after the event. The possibility of a great European War was in their minds even in 1910, and they had objected strongly to the exchange of visits between King Edward and the Tsar not merely because The Triple Entente, which it cemented, threatened to prolong the reign of "tyranny" in Russia but also because it threatened to drag Britain into the next great continental War as an ally of the Tsar.[1] It was, in fact, at the International Socialist Congress of September 1910 at

many years and was a contributor, besides, to the *Clarion* and *Forward*. Like Hardie himself, he had worked with his hands after leaving the elementary school and began his journalism by conducting, at Dunfermline, his native place a local Socialist monthly, *The Worker*, which ceased in 1899 whereupon he moved to Glasgow and work for the *Labour Leader*.

[1] Cf. William Stewart, *J. Keir Hardie, A Biography*, pp. 263-4, for some of the anger excited by the King's State visit to the Tsar at Reval in June 1908 which did not, however, prevent the carrying-through of a species of return visit from the Tsar to Cowes in August 1909. The indignant *Labour Leader* characteristically surmised that Stock Exchange and Russian Loan considerations provided much of the motivation and countered, indignantly, with statistics of the "crimes" of Tsarism—the 169 members of the First Duma arrested on its forcible dissolution, the 74 members of the Second Duma who suffered similarly, the 19,000 persons allegedly "butchered" by the Black Hundred in the course of two years, and the 3205 political executions which allegedly occurred during the same period.

Copenhagen that Keir Hardie, in the course of discussions as to how working-men themselves might try to halt war-preparations and declared war, too, boldly advised consideration of "the general strike, especially in industries that supply war material". But perhaps Keir Hardie's biographer should be allowed to continue his summarization of the *Labour Leader* in explanation of his hero's attitude towards political developments and party manœuvres after King Edward's death:[1]

Liberals and Tories called a temporary truce. They mingled their tears for the dead monarch, combined their cheers for the living one, and then went on with the farce, "The Peers *versus* the People. . . ."

It is strange to reflect that during the whole of this General Election the subject of war was never mentioned. Foreign policy was never mentioned. Armaments were never mentioned. . . . As a decoy-duck Lloyd George was a success. He attracted the fire that should have been directed against Grey and Haldane and the British war-lords. Only the Socialists were alive to the impending danger . . . the Socialists of France, Germany, Belgium, Britain, the nations that were, even then, being drawn into the whirlpool of blood. . . . But the people never heard them. . . . The people were singing the "Land Song". They were listening to Lloyd George and "waiting and seeing" . . . what Mr. Asquith was going to give them. . . .

Writing like this dominated though it is by over-tones from the trench-massacres of 1914–18 has some obvious merits. Yet, unconsciously perhaps, it disguises the fact that the I.L.P. theorists of 1910 and even of 1921 vastly over-simplified the facts of international life, and never more so, perhaps, than when, like

---

[1] William Stewart, *J. Keir Hardie, A Biography*, pp. 294–307. It is probably worth mentioning that the General Election referred to is, of course, that of December 1910 and that in his anxiety not to spoil a purple passage Stewart exaggerated the absence of Foreign policy and Armament discussions from the Election meetings and literature of the end of 1910. And quite apart from the considerable Radical block of M.P.s and writers who worked hard for an Anglo-German accommodation and the foundation, before long, of an Anglo-German Association, one of Stewart's warlords, Haldane himself, undertook, early in 1912, an exploratory mission to Germany which had important results in initiating a real Anglo-German *détente* that lasted to the very outbreak of war. The *Labour Leader*, of course, and Stewart, after it, were inclined to find altogether greater significance in the I.L.P.'s anti-militarist campaign of November 1910 in many of the country's larger urban centres, the climax of which was planned to be an Albert Hall meeting in December with Hardie himself presiding and representatives of France, Germany, Belgium, Britain, and America addressing the assembly. Though General Election campaigning overtook the Albert Hall demonstration against militarism and Imperialism referred to above, it was held, all the same, Jaurès speaking for French working-men, Vandervelde for Belgian, Molkenbuhr for German, Mills for American, and MacDonald and Anderson for those of Britain.

Keir Hardie, they ascribed to Stock Exchanges, Foreign Offices, and Armament Contractors the sole responsibility for the dangerous tension that existed.[1] Competing Nationalisms, each with its own sense of unique and privileged mission, were Europe's greatest peril, and share-brokers, diplomats, and even battleship constructors had had little or nothing to do with making them so. Moreover, though Europe's armed and brigaded Nationalisms were being faced in 1910 by the awkward new questions put by Norman Angell's *Great Illusion*,[2] both the new questions and the old, as they had heretofore been raised by Radicals and Socialists, campaigning for International Arbitration and Disarmament, proved to have but little power to stay the course of events.

To turn to the "practical politics" of 1911 is to be reminded that the General Election of December 1910 had certainly not settled the problem of the Lords' Veto beyond a peradventure. Even though Conservatives had not improved their numbers in the Commons, their improved polling had been such that some considered that they had demonstrated their possession of greater popular support than Liberalism and Labour combined.[3] There were members of the Government, indeed, who considered that there were still possibilities of dispute between Ministers on one side and Labour and Irish members on the other which could break up the Administration, and, in point of fact, such dispute possibilities were on the increase, for many months to come, owing to Labour, and ultimately Irish, complaints of Ministers' sanctioning the use of police and military in the mounting "industrial unrest" of the time.[4] The reappearance of Balfour as

[1] Cf. H. N. Brailsford, *The War of Steel and Gold*, for a statement of Hardie's position more eloquent than Hardie himself could ever have contrived. He praised it very warmly in the *Labour Leader* of November 5, 1914 when it reached him for review. E. D. Morel's *Morocco in Diplomacy*, issued in 1912, if severe on the diplomats, was not written from a Socialist or even a Labour angle, for Morel was, at the time, among many other things, a Liberal candidate.

[2] *Who's Who, 1914*, p. 42, claims that the book (by August 1913) had appeared in Britain, America, France, Germany, Holland, Denmark, Sweden, Spain, Italy, Russia, Japan, and China, while in India, there had been translations into Hindi, Bengali, Urdu, Marathi, and Tamil. The *Great Illusion*'s main thesis was that it was illusory to imagine that the victorious side in any likely war would gain anything save higher taxes and increased National Debt.

[3] Cf. Sir Almeric Fitzroy, *Memoirs*, ii, 426: "The popular vote in Great Britain is almost evenly divided, and, but for the abnormally large number of uncontested seats, would be against the Government."

[4] Cf. *Whitaker's Almanack, 1912*, p. 463, for the first violent outbreak noted under November 7, 1910: "The most serious rioting known for many years broke out among the miners of the Rhondda and Aberdare valleys. For some hours Tonypandy was in the hands of a mob who plundered the shops. A

Prime Minister was, in short, not beyond the bounds of possibility nor his chances of winning an Election[1] if he substituted a genuine Reform of the Lords for the Veto Bill and guaranteed that a Conservative policy of safeguarding the Nation's Industries would not be allowed to raise the cost of living. Balfour, too, might well have been helped by the great Imperial pageantry preparing for George V's Coronation on June 22nd so that, all in all, the three parties that made up the Majority were very well-advised not to quarrel too violently and too publicly. It was, in fact, Conservative divisions between "Die-Hards" and the rest that appeared most conspicuously by the time the Parliament Act, introduced on February 21st, received the Royal Assent on August 18th, and, meantime, Ministers had pushed National Insurance, Payment of Members, and a £1,500,000 plan for Sanatoria a fair way towards realization. But these shall be treated later, and attention shall be concentrated first on novel international and industrial phenomena, whose importance had been growing while the constitutional crisis had been in question.

In international affairs, July 1911 was marked by the sharp German *riposte* to the French occupation of Fez in circumstances that Berlin suspected to the point of sending German naval forces to Agadir in South-West Morocco "to protect German interests". There may have been those in the German Government willing to test whether Britain under "Radical" rule and threatened with a constitutional crisis in which King, Lords, and Commons were all deeply involved, would be able or willing to act strongly enough to prevent Germany from extracting some strategic advantages from the Moroccan situation. For some weeks, certainly, British diplomacy failed to get from Berlin adequate explanations and assurances so that some suspected that a German quasi-protectorate of South-West Morocco might be in question as Germany's price for an agreed extension of French and Spanish "rights" over

strong force of Metropolitan Police was drafted into the district, and severe fighting took place." The arrival of troops was reported under November 21st, and the attack on the Cambrian Colliery, Clydach Vale, by 3000 strikers on March 22, 1911.

[1] Cf. Sir Almeric Fitzroy, *Memoirs*, ii, 427, reporting Lord Morley as believing that if Balfour took office after a difference between Ministers and the King, and a Dissolution followed, "he thought it likely that the country in despair of any other expedient would give the Unionists a majority . . . they could ask the country for a homogeneous support, whereas Ministers could only rely on a composite majority, a section of which was able to turn them out at a moment's notice".

the rest of the country. It was finally the Radical Chancellor himself who, on July 21st, consented in a speech he was due to deliver in the City of London, to act as the Cabinet's mouthpiece in a warning to Berlin that Britain did not intend to allow Germany to dictate a settlement.[1] As this was the first occasion when Lloyd George enjoyed some of those pleasures of "patriotic leadership", which came to him in such large measure after 1914, the section of his speech directed at Germany is worth requoting. Here are the Radical Chancellor's words:[2]

I believe it is essential in the highest interests, not merely of this country, but of the world, that Britain should at all hazards maintain her place and her prestige amongst the Great Powers of the world. Her potent influence has many a time in the past, and may yet be in the future, invaluable to the cause of human liberty. . . . I would make great sacrifices to preserve peace . . . but if a situation were to be forced upon us in which peace could only be preserved by the surrender of the great and beneficent position Britain has won by centuries of heroism and achievement, by allowing Britain to be treated, where her interests were vitally affected, as if she were of no account in the Cabinet of Nations, then I say emphatically that peace at that price would be intolerable for a great country like ours to endure.

This speech, though it caused great resentment in Germany, may well have played some part in reducing Berlin's estimate of what profit the situation could be made to yield.[3] The need for moderation in Berlin became even more obvious, during August, when the Conservative Leaders, bitterly critical though they were of the means which had been used to extract advance promises from the King of a mass-creation of Peers if that should prove necessary to carry the Parliament Act, just prevented their extremer followers from raising sufficient votes to provoke a crisis.[4] And as the Houses adjourned for over two months after

[1] Cf. Lord Riddell, *More Pages from my Diary, 1908–1914*, p. 21, on why the Chancellor was half an hour late at the Mansion House banquet. The delay was due to a conference with Asquith and Grey as to the precise terms of the speech.

[2] *The Times*, July 22, 1911.

[3] Cf. Lord Riddell, *More Pages from my Diary, 1908–1914*, p. 21, for the German Government's attempt to get the Chancellor reprimanded or dismissed, and the German Ambassador's astonishment on learning that he had been "the voice of the Cabinet".

[4] Cf. *The Times*, August 11, 1911, for the final vote, when the motion not to insist on the Lords' amendments was carried by 131 against the "Die-Hards' " 114. Of course, the Conservative Leaders may well have hoped to undo the Parliament Act, in whole or in part, when they won an Election and were able to put their suggested Reforms of the Upper House into operation. To have allowed the King's prerogative and the House of Lords to be cheapened together by the mass-creation of up to 400 Peers would certainly not have helped.

the Parliament Act was placed on the Statute Book, it might well have appeared dangerous, at Berlin, to over-rate the possible strategic effects of the industrial unrest which had also prevailed in Britain for some time, and was, in fact, showing signs of mounting to a climax.

Basically, the cause of the industrial unrest of 1910–12 was the fact that, for some time, wages had been rising rather more slowly than the cost of living.[1] But there was also some importation from the Continent of the strange amalgam of Anarchism and Marxism which, under the name of Syndicalism, took on a temporary importance because of its tendency to turn away with increasing distaste from "Labour" politics and politicians and to put its faith in "direct action" in the industrial sphere.[2] The prolonged ten-months pit-strike in South Wales that had begun in the autumn of 1910 must count as Syndicalism's first contribution to the British industrial scene, but it was far out-done in importance, during the summer of 1911, by a series of strikes among seamen, dockers, carters, railwaymen, and others, resulting, on occasion, in incendiarism, violence, and even bloodshed. The attempted "general strike" on the railways, during August, was not only unprecedented in itself but led to some unprecedented consequences as even the shortest summary of the events of that summer and autumn makes plain.[3] The Government, deeply

[1] Cf. *Britannica Year Book, 1913*, pp. 69–70, where the qualification was, however, made that the food-producing countries had suffered badly from abnormally low prices in the immediate past and that manufacturing countries had gained heavily at their expense. The partial readjustment that was proceeding was, it was felt, a beneficent one "for the world in general".

[2] Cf. Arnold White, *English Democracy, Its Promises and Perils*, pp. 80–4, for an Anarchist appeal to the striking pitmen of 1893 which anticipated much of the Syndicalist thinking of 1910 and afterwards. Here is one brief extract: "It matters not which party is in power; all are alike, thieves in the pay of thieves. Politicians of all shades, Conservative, Liberal, or so-called Labour, are simply humbugs who would draw you from the more effective method—your own action. They talk on trivialities and side-issues while you are starving. . . . No! If you would be free you must take the matter in your own hands. You must put an end to the system that enslaves you. You must sweep away masters altogether, and take back all the wealth you have made. . . . Miners, be determined! Insist on your rights. If you dare to set the example, the workers of the world will follow. . . ."

[3] Cf. *Whitaker's Almanack, 1912*, p. 464: "Disaffection broke out on the Lancashire and Yorkshire Railway and extended to the London and North-Western Railway, the advice of their leaders and of the Conciliation Board being disregarded by the men. Aug. 15th. The representatives of the various railway organizations decided upon a general railway strike in 24 hours if the men's demands were not met . . . on the following day it was announced that the Government had given assurances of ample protection to the railways which would enable an efficient though restricted service to be given. The whole of

concerned by Morocco developments that might bring disaster if Britain were paralysed by a railway stoppage, certainly intervened with some speed, urgency, and temporary success.

Before Parliament reassembled on October 24th to complete the Session, there were numerous new indications that the country was moving towards still more contentious politics. On September 1st, members of Parliament became, in the angry phrase of some Conservatives, "professional politicians" in receipt of £400 per annum; on September 22nd Lloyd George, though deep in difficult bargaining with the Friendly Societies and the doctors on the financial details of his yet unpassed Insurance Bill, committed the Cabinet to carrying, during the 1912 Session, a Bill for the Disestablishment and Disendowment of the Church in Wales; and on October 22nd, the Irish Leader, Redmond, told his followers that they would find the Government Home Rule Bill, also preparing for 1912, very much to their liking. It was plainer than ever, according to indignant Conservatives, that, without allowing the intermission of a single Session, the corrupt Government Coalition was preparing to take advantage of the Parliament Act, just fraudulently forced upon the King, to impose Home Rule and Welsh Disestablishment upon an unconsulted nation. The Lords, of course, would reject such things in 1912 and 1913 but when passed in a Third Session, during 1914, they would be taken, over the Lords' Veto, straight to the Statute Book. By that time, moreover, the Radical Chancellor would almost certainly have prepared another "plundering" Budget over which the Peers would have lost virtually all their rights. It is, perhaps, plain in what an agitated Opposition atmosphere it was that the first great Ulster

the Aldershot command was held in readiness to guard the railways, and contingents dispatched to various parts of the country, and warships were ordered to the Mersey. Further prolonged conferences were held on Aug. 17th, in which the Prime Minister and Mr. Buxton took part, but no agreement was arrived at, and the railway strike began. . . . Manchester, Bristol, and other centres became involved . . . and a large force of military was distributed throughout the affected area. On Aug. 19th, at Llanelly, 2 men were shot dead and 3 injured by volleys fired by troops during an attack on a train, and at the same place, while looting and firing a goods train, an explosion of gunpowder took place killing 5 people. The railway strike came to an end on Aug. 19th. . . . The Government agreed to the immediate appointment of a Special Commission to enquire into the whole question. . . . Oct. 3rd. The Railway Commission held its last sitting for the hearing of evidence. . . . Oct. 20. The Report of the Railway Commission . . . was received with great dissatisfaction in labour circles. . . . Oct. 31st. The unrest in the railway world again reached a crisis. . . . The London and North Western and Great Western companies announced a scheme of increased wages and shorter hours. . . ."

protest demonstration was staged on September 23rd,[1] and the "Balfour must go" campaign pressed to success by November 8th[2] against a Leader deemed deficient in toughness.

[1] Cf. G. Dangerfield, *The Strange Death of Liberal England*, pp. 78–82, for the Craigavon meeting addressed by Sir Edward Carson and resulting, before long, in plans for an Ulster Provisional Government and Ulster Volunteers to resist attempts to enforce a Home Rule Bill.

[2] *Ibid.*, p. 76, for the succession of Andrew Bonar Law whose "father had once occupied an Ulster manse" and about whom "the really dangerous thing was that he was too close in spirit to Ulster's bigotry". A more resolute fighting lead was, of course, hoped for than had been given by Balfour.

CHAPTER IV

POLITICAL CONTROVERSY, 1912-13

"1912. *January 17th.*—Lord Morley . . . spoke with some gravity of the political outlook which, in his judgement, had been aggravated by the laxity and miscalculation of the Prime Minister in dealing with . . . Women's Suffrage. . . . Lord Morley confirmed . . . Asquith's indolence in shirking a difficulty, confident in his ability to furnish at least some provisional solution when the situation . . . threatens to get out of hand. . . .

"*January 24th.*—Lord Morley . . . deplored Winston Churchill's recklessness [in creating Belfast trouble by accepting a Home Rule invitation] as well as the manner in which it had been met. [by the Orangemen.] The last chance for the introduction of the Home Rule Bill in a calm atmosphere had, he said, been destroyed. . . .

"*February 12th.*—There is a section of the Cabinet headed by the Lord Chancellor and Lord Morley, who are angry with Winston Churchill's indiscreet declaration that her fleet is a luxury to Germany. . . . The comments of the German Press are enough to show the mischief that has been caused. . . .

"*March 1st.*—The coal strike has come upon us in spite of the efforts of the Government . . . but for the Prime Minister's invincible objection to bestir himself except at the last moment, active intervention should and might have been entered upon a month ago. . . . Whatever was the strength of the miners' position—and I believe much of it might fairly and safely be conceded—they should have been told that a general strike would not be allowed. It should, in short, have been treated as a conspiracy against the safety of the State. . . . It might no doubt have meant a breach with the Labour Party and the early collapse of the Government; but other causes are bringing about its doom . . . the unpopularity of the Insurance Bill. . . .

"*December 6th.*—Morant saw me to-day upon the administration of Maternity Benefit. . . . According to him, Lloyd George and Masterman care nothing for the economic soundness of the Act or the hygienic efficiency of its administration; they are only concerned with the political effect of presenting the benefit. . . . Placards and posters . . . have been poured forth from the Liberal publishing agency. . . .

"1913. *January 27th.*—The threats of the women of what they will do in the event of their hopes being disappointed have reached such a pitch that . . . valuable lives are in danger. . . .

"*June 9th.*—The King's luncheon to the [Balkan] Peace delegates was . . . happily arranged, but quite fruitless of conciliation. . . . Lord Morley encouraged me to talk about the position of the Government which disagreeable as it was . . . did not appear to him to threaten its existence. He put the Marconi muddle in the first place of its embarrassments.

"*July 15th.*—The Home Rule debate presented no novel feature: the same dreary reiteration of irreconcilable points of view. . . . Signs of growing acrimony are not wanting, and the King is gravely concerned by the problem he will have to face next year. The Tory Party have committed themselves so deeply in Ulster, without awaking the expected response in the British constituencies, that they have no way of retreat open."

From Sir Almeric Fitzroy's *Memoirs*.

I T will hardly be denied that the politicians of 1912–14, even those whose names were "household words", misjudged some of their principal problems. Yet the Women's Suffrage agitation was already proving by violence, destined to grow very serious during 1912,[1] that the reigning *status quo* at Westminster would no longer be accepted as sufficient reason why the refusal of "just" claims should be patiently and indefinitely endured, and the weary work recommenced of trying anew to build up a Westminster Majority. The Syndicalist agitation in the Trade Unions, which had already provided some rude shocks for the politicians in 1911, was destined, during 1912, to provide further shocks in the mines and at the docks, despite the obvious return of growing prosperity.[2] Nor will the searcher of political memoirs find much awareness of the possibility that Italy's descent of 1911 upon the Tripoli coast, followed by severe maritime pressure upon the resisting Turks, would furnish sufficient temptation to the rival Christian States of the Balkans to get them to close their ranks as the Balkan League and precipitate the Balkan Wars of 1912–13 which led on so fatally to World War in 1914. Even when

[1] Cf. *Daily Mail*, March 2, 1912, for the reopening of militancy on an hitherto unparalleled scale: ". . . at 6 o'clock yesterday evening a brigade of militant Suffragettes scattered along the Strand, Haymarket, Piccadilly, Bond Street, Oxford Street, Regent Street, made simultaneous attacks on the shop-windows. . . . Some drew hammers from their muffs, many had handbags filled with heavy weights. . . . The few moments that followed saw an extraordinary scene. From every part of the crowded and brilliantly lighted streets came the crash of splintered glass. . . . Scared shop-assistants came rushing out . . . policemen sprang this way and that. Five minutes later the streets were a procession of excited groups, each surrounding a woman wrecker being led in custody to the nearest police station. The arrests numbered 148." The immediate cause of this major outburst, soon to be followed by the conspiracy charges against Mrs. Pankhurst and the Pethick Lawrences and the counter-resort to hunger-striking was the conviction, on the part of the Pankhursts' Women's Social and Political Union, that the Prime Minister, an admitted anti-Suffragist, was tricking them when representing that a Government Franchise Bill, intended greatly to enlarge the male electorate, would be drafted in such a way as to permit Parliament, on a free vote, to add Women's Suffrage amendments. Certainly, on January 27, 1913, the Speaker was to decide, in a fashion Asquith was suspected to have foreseen, that the introduction, in Committee, of a Woman's Suffrage amendment, would alter the Bill too profoundly in character and measure of enfranchisement, to be permissible.

[2] Cf. *Britannica Year Book, 1913*, pp. 568–9, for such information as: "The demand for workers exceeded the supply in the cotton, woollen, and worsted trades, as well as, during certain seasons of the year, in the coach-building and engineering trades and the Clyde ship-building industry, while female workers were also found scarce in the clothing and laundry industries. . . . British trade has had three 'record' years in 1910, 1911, and 1912, each surpassing all others before it in the figure for imports and exports. . . ."

the implementation of the National Insurance Act, finally put on the Statute Book at the very end of 1911, was in question, the serious strains that would result on the Civil Service and on the public temper before the finish, were hardly foreseen by Lloyd George, the Minister responsible. In the short run, at any rate, the Insurance Act's prolonged "teething" troubles with Benefit Societies, the British Medical Association, workmen, and employers lost the Radical cause, to Lloyd George's consternation, many more votes than it gained.[1]

Possibly the Cabinet's most blameworthy piece of optimistic shortsightedness concerned the Irish situation. At the beginning of 1912, though there had already been some loud warnings from Ulster, Ministers still preferred to regard the Ulster preparations against Home Rule as "bluff".[2] That Ulster Protestants would refuse to accept the dictates of the species of "democratic majority" that "unprincipled log-rolling", in Ulster's view, had built up at Westminster was not fully accepted until civil war was almost at hand. But that the new Conservative Leadership, under Bonar Law, should unswervingly refuse to recognize the slightest moral claim in Westminster's "democratic majority" to force or coerce Ulster out of the United Kingdom—this was probably the

[1] Cf. Beatrice Webb, *Our Partnership*, pp. 473–7, for the very different atmosphere that had reigned in 1911. Mrs. Webb, who had quickly detected a number of dangerous weaknesses in Lloyd George's proposals—the "costly and extravagant" collection of Insurance revenues, for example, "the slovenly administration" that seemed inevitable, and the "growth of malingering" by workmen—yet admitted "the splendid reception by all parties" of the plan in its opening stages. Mrs. Webb, who had just begun her famous and ultimately vain crusade for the "national minimum of civilized life" was, of course, a rival promoter of a scheme she had failed to get Ministers to accept but there was a good deal of justification for some of her views. Of Lloyd George's "demagogy", she observed, "He has taken every item that could be popular with anyone, mixed them together and produced a Bill which takes some twenty millions from the propertied class to be handed over to the wage-earners, *sans phrase*." And of the original whole-hearted Conservative support, because Lloyd George had made Insurance not free but part-contributory, she had had this to say: "Everywhere among the governing class one meets the naïve delight at making the men pay—a delight which makes them overlook the heavy state contributions, the cost of collection, the absence of prevention, the exclusion of the weakest, and even the danger of malingering—all these real evils are to be cancelled by the extracting of pennies from the workman's disposable income, extracting them so that he shall feel extraction."

[2] Cf. George Dangerfield, *The Strange Death of Liberal England*, pp. 88–90, for Winston Churchill's attempt to call the bluff, if bluff it was, by agreeing to address a Belfast meeting on February 8, 1912. Five extra battalions of infantry and two extra squadrons of cavalry had finally to be imported to allow the meeting to be held in a marquee on the Celtic Football Ground. Even so there had been a potentially dangerous situation for weeks, and anti-Catholic demonstrations in the ship-yards.

supreme shock to the normal Radical politician or journalist. Blinded by electoral statistics and Division figures, he hardly saw the Opposition's strong case for the essential immorality of all Radicalism had done to "win" the last three Elections—the building-up of the "Chinese Slavery lie" for 1906, the "rare and refreshing fruit" offered the masses as "bribe" in 1909, and the "Peers versus the People sham" of 1910 which had permitted the King to be "coerced" in 1911 and the Upper House, not reformed, but rendered powerless to prevent "log-rolling" majorities from getting their way even when it conflicted with the nation's will.

The whole situation, as between Government and Opposition, could hardly have been better epitomized than when the Prime Minister attempted, during his introduction of the long-expected Home Rule Bill on April 11, 1912, to reprimand Bonar Law for the violence of the language he had been using. The passage, quoted from Bonar Law by the Prime Minister, was: "The present Government turns the House of Commons into a market-place where everything is bought and sold. In order to remain a few months longer in office, His Majesty's Government have sold the Constitution." And the Prime Minister then began the query, "Am I to understand that the Right Honourable Gentleman repeats here, or is prepared to repeat on the floor of the House of Commons", only to be interrupted with a defiant "Yes" from Bonar Law before he had completed his sentence. Asquith may well have thought that he had established an advantage over a too-hasty opponent for he invited Bonar Law to continue by observing: "Let us see exactly what it is: It is that I and my colleagues are selling our convictions." To which Mr. Bonar Law's rude reply was, "You have not got any." There were others, beside Conservatives, who considered that Asquith's final comment, withering though it was intended to be, did not succeed: "We are getting on with the new style."[1] Yet Asquith's prestige had certainly risen, of late, after the major part he had taken in handling and, to some extent, settling the great Coal disputes of the previous weeks.[2]

[1] Cf. George Dangerfield, *The Strange Death of Liberal England*, p. 95.
[2] The *Daily Mail* on February 29th had reported: "A series of eleven conferences concerning the coal strike yesterday ended in a deadlock." On March 1st, it was reporting, "Strike Begun, A Million Men Out", and also the Government's resolve to take a firm line against "the dwindling minority" of coal-owners who declined to accept the principle of the minimum wage. Before *Daily Mail* headlines, on March 28th, were able to report, "Strike Breaking Up",

There were other things besides Asquith's settlement of the Coal Strike that encouraged the Radical belief, during 1912, that the "cause of sane and ordered progress" would continue to overcome the formidable obstacles in its path. Thus Lloyd George's Budget statement of April 2nd announced, despite the Coal Strike, the largest surplus on record, and, wisely enough, in view of current controversies on Ministers' programme of Home Rule, Welsh Disestablishment, and Insurance Act enforcement, no controversial use of the surplus was proposed. In fact, when, on June 24th, the suggested division of over six and a half millions of surplus was announced, a million more for the Navy was allotted because of a new German Navy Law, Uganda and East Africa were allowed half a million of Loan to help their transport systems to cope with increasing exports of cotton and wheat, and no less than five millions was assigned for reduction of the National Debt, making a total Debt Reduction, Lloyd George claimed, of seventy-eight millions since Ministers had taken Office.[1] When the current Trade Boom permitted even the Limehouse Chancellor to be written up in the *Star*, the *Daily News*, and the *Daily Chronicle* almost as another Gladstone for Debt Reduction, while yet entitled to gratitude from the Big Navy Men and the Imperialists, too, it is obvious that not all the factors in the political situation were adverse to Ministers. Here, in fact, is Lloyd George recording, on July 13th, two days before the entry into force of the Insurance Act, that some of his worst fears were over:[2]

There are in this country 13,000,000 of working men and working women who under this Act are compulsorily insurable. It is a nasty word, I know, but you will thank me for it exactly as we are thanking Mr. Forster for making education compulsory. There were 14,000,000 when the Act was brought in. Those under the age of 16 were cut out, and there were other exceptions of that kind. We estimated that 1,000,000 would join the Post Office, and that 12,000,000 would join Societies. That was an estimate before the Act had come into

Asquith had had to take a very firm line against the other party to the dispute, the Miners' Federation, which had, at first, tried to dictate its own national minima of "five and two" (five shillings per day for men and two for boys) instead of accepting the district arrangements of Ministers' compromise Coal Mines (Minimum Wage) Bill. It is plain that "public opinion" turned decisively against "Syndicalist" extremists among the pitmen when they seemed to be disregarding the "unparalleled scenes of privation and distress" reported by the *Daily Mail*, March 25th, from "the great industrial centres of the North", where very serious unemployment (from lack of coal) was spreading.

[1] Cf. *Hansard*, April 2, and June 24, 1912.
[2] Quoted from H. C. Dent, *Milestones to the Silver Jubilee*, p. 66.

operation. Now I can announce that before the Act comes into operation there are 9,500,000 members of Approved Societies. Nine-and-a-half millions! By Monday there will be 10,000,000, and in three weeks or a month—I have got the information from those working on these Societies—you will find that not merely the whole of the 12,000,000 will be in, but at least half of the Post Office contributors will also join Societies.

Other factors, too, could be held to be working in Ministers' favour besides the noteworthy improvement in their prospects of being able to implement the Insurance Act at the Statutory dates. Thus the very considerable fraction of Ministers' supporters, who liked to describe themselves as Radicals, and even as "advanced Radicals", rather than as Liberals,[1] were delighted that, in addition to Home Rule and Welsh Disestablishment, Ministers had been persuaded to undertake two further commitments to the "most democratic progress" in their Sessional programme. The Trade Unions Bill, to help the Unions to overcome the adverse effects of the Osborne Judgement on their political activities, was naturally relied on to win some Labour gratitude and to improve some electoral prospects if only in the shape of the abandonment of threatened Labour candidatures whose first effect might well be to "let in the Tory" owing to the rivalry among the friends of "progress". But it was the Franchise and Registration Bill, introduced on June 17th, that provided the more "advanced" of Government supporters with the chance of striking the almost perfect blow for "greater political equality and justice" and yet making sure, at the same time, that its probable effects should be their almost indefinite retention of power. It was the plural voter —the man hitherto registered in several different constituencies because of business or personal occupation of premises in each— whose electoral rights were to be reduced to the same level as the ordinary man's, the ability to throw one Parliamentary vote only.

[1] *Who's Who, 1914,* shows Sir W. P. Byles, M.P. for North Salford and Tom Wing, M.P. for Houghton-le-Spring in this category. William Abraham, President of the South Wales Miners' Federation and M.P. for the Rhondda since 1885 also described himself as Radical and not as Labour, while his Parliamentary allies, Thomas Burt and Charles Fenwick, identified themselves sufficiently with the Liberal Front Bench's policy to allow themselves to be classed as Liberals. Barnet Kenyon, elected for Chesterfield in 1913 to represent the Derbyshire Miners, acknowledged Government support by writing himself "Liberal and Labour". It should be added, in this connection, that many of the constituency organizations supporting the Government called themselves Liberal and Radical Associations in order to attract and retain the support of the "advanced".

It was calculated that 525,000 plural votes altogether would thus be cancelled, and an almost unparalleled blow struck at Conservative voting strength. Nor was this all. The plural vote of the University graduate, and the University seats themselves, were to be abolished in the name of political equality.[1] And, finally, the poorer working-man who had hitherto, it was claimed, found his way to the Voters' Register barred by over-exigent Registration conditions would now find it made so much easier that, perhaps, two and a half million new voters might be enfranchised.[2] If, indeed, the same measure of enfranchisement were allowed to women, ten and a half million further voters would be created. This Radical electoral Paradise, was it was promised, to be supplemented later by a Redistribution Bill which, according to Conservatives, would probably be found to be motivated by the same Radical party-spites and ambitions.[3]

By the time the Franchise and Registration Bill had been given its Second Reading on July 12th, the Government's Sessional record had begun, for "reformers", to take on imposing proportions. Home Rule's Second Reading had been carried on May 9th by 372 votes against 271 and the Committee stage begun on June 11th; Welsh Disestablishment had been taken to Second Reading by 348 votes against 267 on May 16th; and the involved London Port disputes, bringing a lightermen's strike on May 21st and ultimately an attempt to stop every port in the country,[4] always seemed to show Ministers, as in the case of the pit disputes of March, more moderate and more responsible than the extremists on both sides of Industry. A mixture of firmness and humanity, it could be claimed, was also being shown to those fomenting the Suffrage disorders,[5] which had now completely antagonized the

[1] Cf. *Hansard*, June 17th, for J. A. Pease, President of the Board of Education, introducing the Bill. His figure for University votes to be cancelled was 49,000.

[2] *Ibid.* The period of continuous residence required for registration was reduced to six months and lists showing additions to the Register would be issued every month. This eagerness to register the "tramp vote" had, in the past, been caustically denounced by Lord Salisbury.

[3] Cf. *Ibid*, July 8th, for the beginning of the Second Reading proceedings which ended on July 12th, after speeches by Mr. Balfour, Mr. Asquith, and Mr. Bonar Law, in a Government majority of 290 against 218.

[4] Cf. *Daily Chronicle*, June 11th: "A national strike of transport workers was declared last night." But on June 12th, the headline news was: "NO NATIONAL STRIKE. PORTS RESPOND ONLY PARTIALLY." (Re-quoted from H. C. Dent, *op. cit.*)

[5] Cf. *Britannica Year Book, 1913*. Diary of Events, under June 24th: "Mrs. Pankhurst and Mrs. Pethick Lawrence, Suffragist leaders, released from prison." They had only been sentenced to nine months on May 22nd, had gone on hunger-strike and had been forcibly fed to the point of danger.

public, and even to those Syndicalists who had tried to turn the troops from their duty during strikes.[1] It was an added merit with some that, despite Ministers' extensive commitments to all manner of "progress" from Home Rule, Welsh Disestablishment, and Franchise Reform to a new Trade Union Bill and full Insurance Act implementation, they had not hesitated to launch a new campaign for "progress" in yet another field. The Lloyd George speech, preparing the way for a new Land campaign was made at Woodford on June 29th.

Normally a two months' Summer Adjournment of Parliament, beginning with some of the worst August weather on record,[2] could have been trusted to damp down politics, for the time, almost completely. But quite apart from the growing accusations of a "Marconi scandal" capable, if true, of bringing down the Cabinet,[3] the tough struggle proceeding between the British Medical Association and Lloyd George on panel conditions and pay,[4] and the ever more threatening news from the Balkans,[5] the Ulster Unionists, backed almost unreservedly by Bonar Law, had arranged, for September, a series of anti-Home Rule displays intended to arrest the attention of the country and the world. By the time the Press of Britain and many nations overseas had

[1] Cf. *Britannica Year Book, 1913*. Diary of Events, under June 22nd: "Mr. Tom Mann, Syndicalist leader, released from prison after serving six weeks of his sentence." Three men sentenced, on March 22nd, for an article in the *Syndicalist* inciting soldiers to mutiny, were also shown some mercy.

[2] Cf. *Daily Telegraph*, August 27th: "August 1912 has surpassed itself, and incidentally has beaten all British records." Next day, the *Daily Telegraph* had this: "Every additional day of rain makes the situation more serious. . . . The loss which has already been incurred beyond repair on account of damaged or wholly ruined crops—cereals, hay, and potatoes—cannot be calculated. . . ."

[3] *The New Witness* campaign of Cecil Chesterton was, apparently, animated partly by the desire to ruin the two Jewish members of the Cabinet, Herbert Samuel, Postmaster-General, and Rufus Isaacs, Attorney-General, but the Liberal Chief Whip and Lloyd George were also involved.

[4] Cf. Dr. Addison, *Politics from Within, 1911-1918*, pp. 20-2, for Dr. Addison, a medical M.P. for a very Radical London constituency, giving the Chancellor the helpful advice, on the medical profession's anger at the idea of merely extending the cheese-paring "sick-club" system, which allowed the Chancellor to offer the improvements that gave him the final victory over the British Medical Association. "In those days," wrote Addison of the Chancellor, "he was a left-wing Radical, as I was, and grasped at any practical proposal likely to be useful to humble folk."

[5] Cf. *The Times*, October 14th, after a summer of constantly worsening Balkan news: "War between Turkey and the whole of the Balkan League is now only a matter of a few hours. . . . We have to face the one grim fact that the conflict which all Europe has been dreading for thirty years is at last to be precipitated. . . . Grave though the present position may be, it will be graver when battles have been lost and won. The real danger is not to-day, but hereafter."

reported, with obviously growing respect, the Ulster demonstrations, opened at Enniskillen on September 18th and brought to a climax at Belfast on September 28th with the unprecedented rites, marking Sir Edward Carson's beginning the signing of the Solemn Covenant, the Ulster leaders could certainly congratulate themselves. They had succeeded reasonably well in assuming the appearance of standing on a righteous defensive and in disguising the fact, very largely, that combative Orangeism tended to be based on a credulous and violent intolerance at least as repulsive as anything in the opposite camp.[1] The Solemn Covenant, signed before long by 218,206 men and 228,991 women within Ulster and 19,162 Ulstermen and 5,055 Ulsterwomen living outside, was in these terms:[2]

'Being convinced in our consciences that Home Rule would be disastrous to the material well-being of Ulster as well as of the whole of Ireland, subversive of our civil and religious freedom, destructive of our citizenship, and perilous to the unity of the Empire, we, whose names are underwritten, men of Ulster, loyal subjects of His Gracious Majesty King George V, humbly relying on the God Whom our fathers in days of stress and trial confidently trusted, hereby pledge ourselves in Solemn Covenant throughout this our time of threatened calamity to stand by one another in defending, for ourselves and our children, our cherished position of equal citizenship in the United Kingdom, and in using all means which may be found necessary to defeat the present conspiracy to set up a Home Rule Parliament in Ireland; and, in the event of such a Parliament being forced upon us, we further solemnly and mutually pledge ourselves to refuse to recognise its authority.

[1] *Rome and Germany, The Plot for the Downfall of Britain,* a 376-page work by Watchman, issued apparently in 1908, represents very well the favourite reading-matter, about this time, of extreme Protestants, British and Irish. A characteristic opening passage is this: "Great Britain has been, and still is, the one great Protestant nation in the world, the chief upholder and example of civil and religious liberty, the principal guardian of and witness to the Bible, and the foremost agency in distributing it throughout the world. She is therefore the one great enemy of Rome, and the chief, and practically the only formidable opponent to the pretensions and superstitions of the Romish priesthood. . . ." And how "the Vatican and the Jesuits" had been hoping, since the Boer War, to make use of the pro-Boer fanaticism of much of British Nonconformity to weaken Britain sufficiently to allow Germany to deliver a mortal blow made a story just as fascinating. Then there was *The Unknown Power behind the Irish Nationalist Party, Its Present Work and Criminal History* (Second Edition, 1908 edited by Lord Ashtown), and Michael McCarthy's *The Nonconformist Treason or the Sale of the Emerald Isle* of 1912. F. Frankfort Moore's *The Truth about Ulster* of 1914 would not have been found so admirable by Orangemen but still shows the author credulous enough to believe that Protestant properties in Belfast were being "raffled for" at the Nationalist clubs after Gladstone had introduced his first Home Rule Bill in 1886 (pp. 56–7).

[2] Cf. *Britannica Year Book, 1913,* p. 512.

In sure confidence that God will defend the right, we hereto subscribe our names, and, further, we individually declare that we have not already signed this Covenant.

It was, doubtless, correct party tactics for the Prime Minister, speaking in his constituency on October 5th, just before the resumption of the Parliamentary Session on October 7th, to take a somewhat scornful line towards Sir Edward Carson's Movement and the Opposition's attitude of approval. To judge, in fact, from his speech of October 5th and his Closure resolutions of October 10th in the Commons, he was still either unable or unwilling to face the possibility that Ulster, or at least its major part, would have to be excluded from the Bill. The promises given to Redmond envisaged no such possibility, and the more Radical part of Government's supporters in the Commons, not to mention the Labour members, might have combined with over eighty Irish Nationalists to make his continued Prime Ministership impossible if, at this stage, Asquith had shown signs of giving way to Ulster and Opposition "intimidation".[1] It seems, indeed, that right up to the outbreak of the 1914 War there were continuous demands from the Radical elements in Government's ranks for a stronger policy in regard to Ulster "lawlessness" and a somewhat over-ready belief that the commencement of Government prosecutions against Carson, "Galloper" Smith, and a handful of others would end the increasing disregard to Parliament and the Law being prepared and enacted in Ulster. And, it may well be, that the Radical calls for prosecutions and even arrests did spur on Ulster drilling and arming to the pace reached by 1914. In October 1912, at any rate, in view of his own Radicals' dangerous misreading of the situation, Asquith had no other course open than to push Home Rule, Welsh Disestablishment, Franchise Reform, and Trade Union (anti-Osborne Judgement) Bills through the Commons, by Closure when necessary, and to trust that, sooner or later, Opposition might be driven to offer to parley on Ulster's

---

[1] Cf. Dr. Addison, *Politics from Within, 1911–1918*, p. 35, for one of the Radical group, who ultimately helped Lloyd George to overthrow Asquith, saying this of the Prime Minister of 1914: "The feeling in the Liberal Party, and, I believe, in the Labour Party was directed as much against the Prime Minister as against Lord Carson and the organizers of the Ulster movement. . . . Few of us could understand, and it is impossible to understand now, how the Government could look on at the organized and open preparations for civil war." But it was just these preparations that forced Redmond ultimately to agree to consider a modification of the Home Rule to which he had committed Asquith in 1910.

behalf. It was not unreasonable to hope, for example, that Opposition might be influenced towards what Asquith regarded as a more "responsible" attitude by the Balkan thunderclouds that had already become one of Ministers' main preoccupations and were fated to remain so until August 1914.

Unfortunately the road to an Ulster compromise was not facilitated by the bitter party recriminations on the Land Enquiry Committee of Government supporters which Lloyd George had now set to work.[1] The Land Enquiry Committee was, of course, a party venture, but, as Conservatives saw it, it was the culmination of a Radical campaign dating back to 1906 by which, when other electoral conditions became unfavourable, voters in town and country were, on specious pretexts, to be offered the plunder of the landlords as an inducement to vote Radical at a General Election, say, in 1915.[2] Nor were Conservative tendencies to find union and stimulation by turning fiercely against their opponents reduced by the temporarily unsuccessful effort of Bonar Law, in his "Ashton Speech" of December 16, 1912, to establish a Tariff Reform policy-basis acceptable to every section of the Conservative Party. The revival of Radical confidence reported after the "Ashton Speech" had had a "mixed" reception in the Conservative Press seemed, for example, to make it all the more important for Ulster Unionists to convince the electorate, before Home Rule was pushed a second time through the forms of the Parliament Act, that their talk of resistance was not an empty threat. There had doubtless been some discussion already of arming the Ulster Volunteers but matters were to go much farther, during 1913, when arms-smuggling on the largest scale was not only being discussed but planned and prepared. And, meanwhile, despite such Ministerial satisfactions as had been obtainable from

[1] Cf. *Britannica Year Book, 1913,* p. 513: "Meanwhile, with Mr. Lloyd George's active encouragement, yet another political issue had been made prominent . . . in the shape of an organized agitation for land-tenure reform and increased taxation of land-owners, promoted more particularly by a section of the Radical party who had long been advocates of the single-tax theory on Henry George's lines. . . . The unpopularity of the Insurance Act made it opportune . . . to divert electioneering attention on the Radical side to something more attractive. . . . Intense exasperation was created on the Conservative side."

[2] *To Colonise England, A Plea for a Policy,* a 211-page volume published at a shilling and with contributions from a considerable number of Government M.P.s, was an early effort issued in 1907. And even before the two bulky Reports of the Land Enquiry Committee were ready in 1914, defensive Conservative writing had been required under such titles as *The Land Question: Exposure of Socialist and Radical-Socialist Fallacies.* A non-party survey of the rural position, issued in 1913, was Robertson Scott's *The Land Problem.*

organizing a Balkans Peace Conference in London and setting each part of the Insurance Act to work at the statutory date, Marconi trouble in plenty was fated to overtake the Government during the first half of 1913.[1] And if no corruption, but only indiscretion, was finally revealed in Government's Chancellor of the Exchequer, Attorney-General, and ex-Chief Whip, even that was certain to make it considerably harder to drive a fiercely-contested Parliamentary programme through. A new airship-panic, too, a trifle more warrantable, perhaps, than the "German waiter" panic soon to follow it, could hardly be counted as a pro-Government influence since nothing could be said for the Ministerial programme to compete, for thrills, with such compelling headlines as:[2]

WANTED AN AIR MINISTER

ENGLAND AT GERMANY'S MERCY

NORTH-EAST COAST SURVEYED NIGHTLY BY DIRIGIBLES

FURTHER APPEARANCES OF AIRSHIP AT WHITBY

The 1913 Session had begun on March 10th after only two days Recess. And to spare the Government Coalition some of the fatigues which had helped to drag out the 1912 Session to March 7, 1913, it was resolved virtually to cut out the Committee stage from the Home Rule and Welsh Disestablishment discussions, to reduce Committee discussion of the Bill to end Plural Voting, to make a merely nominal beginning with an Education Bill and to leave "Land Reform" out of the Sessional programme altogether.

---

[1] Cf. *Everyman*, April 4, 1913: "It does not take a very large pebble to ruffle the pools of public opinion, and the Marconi Inquiry is producing some very formidable ripples. Viewing the mass of things said on the question by organs of every shade of political conviction, two things at least emerge. One is a general attitude of respectful sympathy towards a Cabinet which has been plunged into a situation of extreme delicacy and complexity. The other is a justly high and scrupulous regard for the best traditions of British honour. . . . It is rumoured that the Marconi [Select] Committee intend to close the enquiry after hearing the evidence of Mr. Samuel, and without summoning the journalists who, in the earlier stages of the proceedings were to have been heard." There were, of course, reprobatory resolutions in the Marconi Select Committee, first, and in the House of Commons afterwards which, if carried, would have compelled the resignation of both Lloyd George and Sir Rufus Isaacs and possibly broken up the Government.

[2] *Whitby Gazette*, February 28, 1913 as quoted in *The Strange Death of Liberal England*, p. 115. The *Daily Mail* had already called for "a large provision of dirigibles" and continued to agitate until, by May 5th, it had obtained, according to *Whitaker's Almanack, 1914*, "an influential meeting at the Mansion House to draw attention to the vital necessity of Great Britain being fully equipped with aircraft".

By the standards of the day, Ministers were showing some temporary conciliatoriness on Land and Education, if not on Home Rule, Welsh Disestablishment, and Plural Voting, by taking the course they did, and the Lords, when rejecting the three vital Bills, that were being pressed through to the Statute Book, as Radicals hoped, under the Parliament Act, thought it wise to use conciliatory language too. Plural Voting, as such, was not defended though Ministers' attempt to snatch a party advantage by dealing with only one of the several parts of the electoral machinery, needing amendment, could not be accepted. Even Home Rule and Welsh Disestablishment, it was declared, if proved to be the popular will at a General Election, would not again be rejected but provided with better safeguards.

It was obviously not a situation beyond a "realist" compromise of the kind ultimately imposed by events. But for the time, and until the Great War forced its own logic upon the politicians, there were too many obstacles. One mighty obstacle, of course, was Asquith's commitments to Redmond and the Irish Nationalist Party whereby Home Rule was to be carried under the Parliament Act and without a new General Election. Indeed, if Asquith had attempted to evade or reinterpret his obligations to Redmond, he would have had a Radical revolt to deal with on the "democratic" ground that, apart from other things, the Parliament Act was virtually being set aside to ease a faint-hearted Front Bench's difficulties with an Ulster lawlessness that should have been nipped in the bud early. Another major obstacle to compromise was the strong hope of Bonar Law and many Conservatives that Ulster defiance would yet break up the uneasy Asquith-Redmond coalition before there had been more than the threat of bloodshed. And they may already have guessed that even if the long-hesitant Prime Minister steeled himself to order military action with possibly irretrievable consequences, the Government's difficulties would grow worse. A shooting-down of a dozen Ulster Volunteers, followed by angry Conservative demonstrations in Britain and wide-spread officers' resignations in Ireland, could, it appeared, hardly fail to destroy the Government.[1] The one thing apparently overlooked by all the political tacticians calculating how, and by

---

[1] Cf. *Britannica Year Book, 1913*, p. 511, for Bonar Law having ventured to forecast Ministers' being "lynched in London" if they ordered bloodshed in Ulster. The forecast was made after the Home Rule debating of June 1912 in Parliament.

whom, Redmond might ultimately be cajoled into greeting to the "provisional exclusion" of four,[1] five, six, or seven Ulster counties from the Home Rule Bill and whether such an agreement could be reached in time to prevent bloodshed and save Asquith's Government, was the growing readiness in Nationalist Ireland to organize, drill, and arm like the Ulstermen but for ends that, in some cases, alarmed Redmond himself.[2]

One man, at least, there was who showed himself determined to allow neither the Home Rule imbroglio nor Marconi-scandal-mongering to arrest the further course of "progress". Acknowledging party congratulations on having been cleared by the Marconi Majority Report, the Chancellor both turned savagely on his critics and nailed the "Land Question" defiantly to the Ministerial mast-head. Extracts from his speaking are worth giving since the retention of the "progressive" initiative in the hands of the Radical Chancellor meant continuous by-election frustration and failure for "Independent Labour" and "Socialist" candidates who tried to force their way to Westminster regardless of Ministers and the local Liberal and Radical Associations mobilized behind them. Without turning here to discuss the considerable importance for their own day of the Chesterfield by-election of August 1913 or the North-East Derbyshire result of May 1914,[3] it might be well to quote from a Lloyd George speech of June 30, 1913:[4]

---

[1] Cf. *Hansard*, June 19, 1912, for a Back-Bench Liberal, Agar-Robartes, moving in Committee the exclusion of Antrim, Armagh, Down, and Londonderry. There were indications that this was taken by some as the beginning of long-range bargaining.

[2] Redmond, of course, did not approve the organization of the Dublin slums into "Larkinism" first and a "Citizens' Army" afterwards. And not till June 1914 was he brought to "countenance" the National Volunteers, aware as he was of possible Gaelic, Sinn Fein, and Republican "follies" that might completely antagonize British opinion before Home Rule became the law of the land under the Parliament Act.

[3] Cf. G. D. H. Cole, *The World of Labour*, pp. 396-7, for the heavy defeat inflicted on "extremists" when a "Liberal-Labour" miner was successfully chosen to succeed one who had been merely "Labour". The figures were Kenyon, Liberal-Labour, 7725; Christie, Unionist, 5539; Scurr, Socialist, 583. The North-East Derbyshire result of May 1914 presented what had counted as a "Labour" seat to the Conservatives in the following poll: Bowden, Unionist, 6469; Houfton, Liberal, 6155; Martin, Labour, 3699. Meanwhile the Labour leader himself, J. R. MacDonald, had come under "extremist" criticism for allegedly discouraging a Labour attempt to win Leicester's second seat on June 27, 1913 in case it imperilled the *entente* with Leicester Liberals by which he held his own. On that occasion voting had been Hewart, Liberal, 10,863; Wilshere, Unionist, 9279; Hartley, Labour, 2580.

[4] Cf. *Daily News and Leader*, July 1, 1913.

At the back of the Tory mind you find this: Tories firmly believe that Providence has singled them out to govern this land. . . . In 1906 they were turned out of power. They thought it was just a temporary visitation. . . . But when a second election came with the same result and a third election came and Radicals were still in power, the Tories became troubled. They saw Radical Bills go through Parliament, and, what was still worse, they found that Tories were expected to obey them as if they were common people. They found Radicals on the Benches as Magistrates and Radicals becoming Judges. They found Radicals as Ministers receiving Kings and Presidents. They saw Radicalism governing the Empire. . . . And they said, "There is no knowing that it might not even happen again. There is the Plural Voting Bill." They found trade prospering, and the country going on, and at last their balance is completely upset. . . .

Supposing I had devoted as much time and energy to defending privilege and monopoly in land, in the Church Establishment, in the liquor traffic, in the House of Lords, as I have devoted to assailing them, do you think a word would have been said in the Tory Press . . . with regard to this [Marconi] matter? No, what has happened to us has happened because in office we have stood by the people who put us there. . . .

Great principles have been preached by the Tory Party. We mean to hold them to them. . . . I hail this new altruism of the Tory Party. Just think of the noble declaration of Lord Robert Cecil: "No man has the right to put himself into a position where his public duty shall conflict with his private interests." I welcome that. We will enforce it. . . .

Here is a campaign on the land question. All parties want it. They feel that something has got to be done to improve conditions in rural life, and the country demands it. A committee was engaged in investigating the subject, and while they were ploughing laboriously through the facts the Tories rushed in in advance and said: "Let us have our programme in before these fellows begin"; and then came the programme. What is it? The labourer is suffering from an inadequate wage. The tenant farmer is suffering from inadequate security. The tenant in the towns has been oppressed by tyrannical conditions. What is the answer of Lord Lansdowne? I will tell you what it is. More money for the landlords. Houses are bad, atrociously bad. But the obligation to build and repair is an obligation of those who own the land. . . . So Lord Lansdowne said: "Yes, houses are bad. Houses are deficient. It is an obligation of those who own the land to build and repair. Let us transfer that obligation to the taxpayer." Then you come to the other proposition, land purchase. Advance money at a low rate of interest to enable the farmer to buy where the landlord is willing to sell . . . a low rate of interest means a high purchase money. . . . What happened in Ireland under the Wyndham Act? . . . The value of the land went up by between five and six years' purchase for the landlord. In addition to that they had another two or three years' purchase by bonus. That is their idea of solving the land question. . . . The poor miserable labourer who cannot feed and clothe and house his children adequately . . . what has Lord Lansdowne got for him? An open mind. For the landlord, all the burdens, the heaviest burdens of his estate, shouldered by the State, the value of his land put up by hundreds of millions at the expense of the State. An open mind for the labourer. . . .

There was, of course, some rhetorical confusion of the issue in the angry Lloyd George's speaking. There is the best of reason for believing that the average purely agricultural estate was in a bad way and quite unable to give labourers town-housing standards at rural rents. Estates that were doing so were really being subsidized from a more flourishing part of the landlord's income, if he had one, than farm-rents. It was doubtful, too, if Rent Courts, judging on purely economic standards, would have been able to lighten the farmer's burden sufficiently to make a Labourers' Minimum Wage Act a practical proposition though here Lloyd George was doubtless reckoning, also, on putting part of the farmer's rates on the landlord in the fashion that Radicals had agitated for half a century. It was the income of town property-owners, of course, that promised the most glittering agitating field for the popular politician[1] with leaseholders offered, perhaps, enfranchisement on "reasonable" terms, occupying ratepayers cheaper rates by making ground-rents rateable, and the whole town-population better and cheaper housing and amenities thanks to an increase of the local authorities' powers of compulsory acquisition on "fair terms". Filled out with more tasty matter on the harm done to farmers and to food-production by the landlords' game and the harm done to Industry and its workers by mineral-royalties and way-leaves, the Chancellor felt confident that he had the stuff for winning the next Election.

There was, nevertheless, some reluctance on the part of a Cabinet section to being committed to everything Lloyd George might have in mind,[2] and the existing compromise was continued

[1] Cf. *Everyman*, November 15, 1912, for a "progressive" new weekly unable to refrain from a sensational article and street-plan under the title of the "LONDON OCTOPUS". It dealt with the London properties of Lord Northampton, the Duke of Bedford, Lord Howard de Walden, Lord Portman, the Ecclesiastical Commissioners, Earl Cadogan, the Duke of Westminster, and the Duke of Norfolk.

[2] Cf. Lord Riddell, *More Pages from My Diary, 1908–1914*, under July 19, 1913, for indications that Lord Crewe was leading the questioners and that though Lloyd George reported, "all parties are sympathetic with the labourer", and that Grey had been brought to admit "that you cannot leave the farmer in the cold" either, plenty of trouble was likely to develop about the notion of charging benefits for both mainly "on the land".

by which the "Land Campaign" received only a somewhat reserved party blessing and a quantum of party funds.[1] The material gathered by the Land Enquiry Committee was to be published;[2] Lloyd George, with what allies he could find, was to be free to push it vigorously; but Government, as such, would, for the time at any rate, remain uncommitted to immediate and detailed action. Were not Ministers' energies, for the 1914 Session, largely pledged already to the three Parliament Act Bills for Home Rule, Welsh Disestablishment, and "Equal Franchise"? And were not controversial Naval Estimates expected, in addition, from Winston Churchill, controversial Budget clauses from Lloyd George and, above all, a controversial Home Rule Amendment Bill from the Prime Minister himself if intermediaries were fortunate in difficult private negotiations with Redmond on the one hand, and Bonar Law on the other?[3] Even the Dissenters' reported anger at their Education grievances being taken ever more lightly by Ministers, who owed their power to the Dissenting chapels' crusade against the Conservatives' Education Act of 1902, was not to be disregarded.[4]

The long-discussed opening of the "Land Campaign" came

[1] *Ibid.*, under July 9, 1913. By that time £15,000 had been spent on the Land Enquiry, and the problem of publishing the results in a cheap and possibly subsidized form had arisen as well as the shape, direction, and cost of the "Campaign" to drive home the results.

[2] *Ibid.*, under the same date, which shows Lloyd George being "strongly urged that the facts must be absolutely accurate" even by his own group of confidants. "L.G. agreed that this was vital", reported Riddell of the *News of the World*, "a few mistakes might spoil the whole campaign", and, in fact, the Chancellor had been making a close study of Joseph Chamberlain's possible mistakes in launching his "Tariff Reform" camapign of 1903. As a result the two big volumes called, *The Land*, the *Rural* of October 1913 and the *Urban* of 1914 were not the purely partisan documents they might easily have been. Indeed, Lloyd George himself must have been taken aback by such admissions as that the famous "People's Budget" had had a noticeably harmful effect on cottage-building for letting to working-men. (*The Land, Urban.* Vol. 2, pp. 82–3.)

[3] Cf. Lord Riddell, *More Pages from My Diary, 1908–1914*, under November 1913, for "a large section of the Radicals" having declared war on Churchill's enlarged Naval Estimates with the *Daily Chronicle* as their principal mouthpiece.

[4] Cf. Lord Riddell, *More Pages from My Diary, 1908–1914*, under November 12th, 13th, 15th and 16th, for some informed reporting from behind the scenes. One of the great Dissenting grievances was the single-school area, normally a country village provided only with a National School run on Church of England principles, and now Ministers, after having professed the brave truths of their 1906 Bill, were charged with running away from them completely in proposals of "conveying the dissenting children to the nearest County Council Schools in omnibuses. Nicoll waxed very wrath about this plan, which he compared to conveying little lepers in tumbrils. He added that the Committee which had been appointed proposed to issue a manifesto damaging to the Government."

with two meetings addressed by Lloyd George in October 1913, the first at Bedford on October 11th and the second at Swindon on October 22nd.[1] It was apparently to have continued, partly with the help of paid propagandists, until the next General Election in 1915 when it might have been made to furnish some of the principal planks in Ministers' platform. And if the Campaign's results were not uniformly happy,[2] it certainly did promise electoral victory in numbers of what would today be called "marginal constituencies" besides depriving a somewhat shaken Labour Party, scoffed at unendingly by the Syndicalists and Guild Socialists, of still more of its political *raison d'être*. The Great War, of course, ended the "Land Campaign" before it had run its predestined course but it did not die entirely fruitless. The era of Rent Restriction Acts, that began in 1915, was easier to initiate because of the "Land Campaign" and so were the post-war Housing Schemes on the grand scale. Indeed, the "Land Campaign" itself was revived and modernized when, between 1924 and 1929, Lloyd George made the famous attempt to offer the post-war working-class voter a "progressive" alternative to Labour.

The "Land Campaign", however, was only in its opening phases and the Parliamentary Session, fixed to begin on February 10th, was still a comfortable distance away when, partly by accident, a major disaster nearly overtook the Cabinet. The *Daily Chronicle* had been voicing opposition to exaggerated Naval demands for some time, and a Cabinet group had also been forming, critical of Lloyd George's complaisance for Churchill and critical also of Churchill's supposedly thrusting himself

[1] Lord Riddell, *More Pages from My Diary, 1908–1914*, under October 1913. Churchill's aid had also been secured in announcing "the minimum wage for agricultural labourers in his speech at Manchester" though, as appeared later, Churchill expected, in return, the Chancellor's continued acceptance of Admiralty Estimates that were already causing dismay in the Radical camp.

[2] Cf. Dr. Addison's, *Four and a Half Years* for this London Radical M.P.'s diary notes on the "Land Campaign" in London as it was functioning by the midsummer of 1914. On June 30th he wrote: "Walter Isaac and myself went over speakers' reports on the Land and Housing Campaign and then reviewed the results of their efforts so far with Wallace Carter, Secretary of the National Liberal Federation. Regretfully decided that four of the speakers must be found employment, if any, outside London. They know more about cabbages than slums. Some others are to be admonished. . . ." And under July 14th is reported the admonishment: "Interviewed the open-air speakers of the Land Campaign in London with Wallace Carter and Isaac, and gave them a heart-to-heart talk, telling them they had better realise that the poor Londoner was not interested in cabbages and Wat Tyler's rebellion but did want his tenement made decent and habitable . . . we shall have to issue them with much fuller instructions and a better handbook of local illustrations. . . ."

forward into the field of a possible "Ulster Settlement". How acute Cabinet antagonisms had become even before the *Daily Chronicle*'s notorious Lloyd George interview was given to the world on New Year's Day, 1914, may be surmised from diary entries made by a well-placed observer in frequent and friendly contact with a number of Ministers. On December 13, 1913, Riddell, controller, among other things, of the *News of the World*, entered into his *Diary*[1] a report of serious Cabinet differences both on Churchill's Navy Estimates and on his supposedly having organized an "Ulster Settlement" dinner at which he and Morley, conferring with Austen Chamberlain and F. E. Smith, had discussed some exclusion of Ulster from the Home Rule Bill.[2] Prompt reaction from Irish Nationalists and their special Radical associates was certain, and the same diary entry, in fact, recorded the gloom of another Minister, Masterman, when reporting Ulster's leading Nationalist, Devlin, as totally opposed to the notion of any Ulster exclusion because, for one thing, the Irish Leaders could not, even if they would, carry their following with them for the proposal. And next day's entries by Riddell reported McKenna as repeatedly blaming Lloyd George for failing to control expenditure and bitter, too, about the "Ulster Dinner"; Masterman as naming Samuel, Pease, Hobhouse, and Runciman as the Ministers combining against the size of the Navy Estimates; and, finally, Lloyd George as refusing to join in any move to drive Churchill from office though admitting that Churchill had been extravagant and that he himself, as Chancellor, had, for two years, been "too easy" with Churchill's figures. But now that the First Lord recognized the strength of party antagonism he had aroused, Lloyd George professed to feel sure that the Estimates would be amended.

Obviously there was a strong section of Ministers,[3] whose

[1] Lord Riddell, *More Pages from My Diary, 1908–1914*, pp. 189–90.

[2] Cf. Sir Almeric Fitzroy, *Memoirs* under December 4, 1913, for another diarist behind the scenes reporting that Morley had pressed at the last Cabinet, with Churchill's assistance, for a conciliatory approach to the Opposition but that Lloyd George had led the critics. Redmond, too, had done his utmost to deter the Cabinet from consultations with the Opposition Leaders and the result had been that a late speech made by Asquith at Leeds had been disappointingly stiff. There are indications, however, in the Fitzroy *Memoirs* that Morley, with the immense prestige of having been Irish Secretary for Gladstone both in the 1886 and 1892 Home Rule Cabinets, was not deterred by the "Ulster Dinner" critics from continuing his speech for a possible way out of the Irish impasse and that Asquith was not unaware of it.

[3] The Sessional history of 1914 makes it plain that Pease's Board of Education and Samuel's Local Government Board were two of the Departments asking for money, in considerable amounts, to undertake "social advances" of some scope.

Departments had been waiting for years for the wherewithal to undertake the important social and administrative "advances" expected by working-men Radicals from a "progressive" Government, and who were in revolt against the Admiralty's constant "working of the German naval scare" (with the help, too, of the Opposition Press) in order to make ever larger and more questionable demands on the Treasury. Before long, in fact, Churchill's resignation was being canvassed with equanimity and successors, including Samuel, were being considered, prepared to stand up to the Admirals, the "Scare Press", and the worst Churchill might seek to do, after being forced out, whether on "abandoned sea-power" or on Ulster. Lloyd George, meanwhile, with professions of the greatest personal and political regard for Churchill, was preparing to take, at last, a stronger line with the Admiralty Estimates and one which it was plain would restore his credit with the Radical party zealots, still regretting the great days of "Peace, Retrenchment and Reform".

It was with Lloyd George in this mood, that a *Daily Chronicle* reporter secured the first big newspaper "scoop" of 1914. From what later transpired on the circumstances of the notorious interview reported in the *Daily Chronicle* of New Year's Day, 1914, the Chancellor showed marked indiscretion in allowing sympathy for a newspaperman, who had had a hard job in tracking him down.[1] to win from him an unrehearsed commentary on events. It was a commentary meant, doubtless, to forward Anglo-German relations, but, unfortunately, it was regarded both by the Foreign Office and the Admiralty as much weakening the British case then being made in regard to German policy. Here is one extract which explains why the Chancellor seemed, for a time, to have increased the strains in an already seriously divided Cabinet almost to breaking-point:[2]

The German army is vital, not merely to the existence of the German Empire, but to the very life and independence of the nation itself, surrounded as Germany is by other nations, each of which possesses armies almost as powerful as her own. We forget that, while we insist upon a sixty per cent superiority (so far as our naval strength is concerned) over Germany being essential to guarantee the integrity of

---

[1] Cf. Lord Riddell, *More Pages from My Diary, 1908–1914*, under January 17, 1914, for the newspaperman's three calls before persuading Lloyd George to speak.

[2] *Daily Chronicle*, January 1, 1914.

our own shores—Germany has nothing like that superiority over France alone, and she has, of course, to reckon with Russia on her Eastern frontier. Germany has nothing which approximates to the two-Power standard. She has therefore become alarmed by recent events, and is expending huge sums of money on the expansion of her military resources.

It took weeks to restore some harmony to a badly-shaken Cabinet, and at one time there was talk of Lloyd George going and of Asquith resolving to dissolve Parliament in that event. In the end Lloyd George's indiscretion probably helped Churchill to keep some of the Estimates he might otherwise have had to surrender, and there was no Cabinet resignation to increase the Government's already formidable list of problems for the 1914 Session.

CHAPTER V

"PROGRESS" IN 1914

"April 8th.—John Burns assured me that the Board of Trade experts gave the present boom another four or five years, and he believed the Chancellor of the Exchequer would be able to budget for a large normal increase of revenue, if not as large as last year. The peace in the Balkans had resulted in an immense expansion of English trade in that quarter, and what was more curious, the political predominance of France and Spain in Morocco had given the trade advantage to us, presumably owing to the distaste of the Moors for the methods of the other Powers. . . .

"April 29th.—The dramatic *coup* by which the Ulster malcontents introduced in a single night an unknown quantity of arms . . . following upon the collapse of the military plans a month ago, has given an immense momentum to the pacifists in the Cabinet . . . no conspiracy to precipitate bloodshed was entertained by the Cabinet. The most that was in the minds of the Government as a whole was some kind of demonstration which would test the confidence to be reposed in the troops, and for that there was some reason. . . . Not only at the Curragh, but at other stations, leaflets have been distributed urging them to disobey orders . . . the language of the Tory newspapers and the clamour . . . render a section of the Unionist Party in the highest degree suspect. . . . The Government are open to the charge of slackness and want of forethought in dealing with the elements of Ulster discontent, of not having measured its force. . . .

"July 28th.—The menace of European war has come with startling abruptness. . . . Lord Morley . . . sympathetic as he is towards France . . . cannot brook this country becoming a party to what he regards as a Slavonic movement against Teuton influence. Russia and all she stands for is still for him identified with barbarism, and he looks upon any tendency hostile to Germany that has its roots in Slav aspirations as prejudicial to the interests of civilisation. I understood there were other members of the Cabinet who thought with him, but at this stage it is not certain where the preponderance will ultimately lie."

From Sir Almeric Fitzroy's *Memoirs*.

"In and around towns there is a large amount of land of considerable value for building purposes which is either vacant

98

or used as accommodation land or agricultural land. Such land, if vacant pays no rates at all, and if used for accommodation or agricultural purposes is rated only upon its value for such purposes—a sum far below its market value as building land. This is objectionable for two reasons:

"(a) The value of the land is in large measure due to and is continually enhanced by the industry of the community and the expenditure of the local authorites. It therefore seems unfair that the owner should not contribute to local expenditure . . . in proportion to the full market value of the property.

"(b) In many cases where a town is rapidly expanding, land, which would be built upon if offered at a reasonable price, is kept out of the market, either because the owners take a more sanguine view of its probable increase in value . . . or because they prefer to keep it in its present condition for personal or sentimental reasons. The present rating system encourages this proceeding."

> From *The Land, The Report of the [Liberal] Land Enquiry Committee* (1914) to show why Conservatives condemned even "moderate" passages as Radical landlord-baiting for electioneering ends.

"Farm servants have declined from approximately 136,000 in 1881 to 87,000 in 1911, while gamekeepers have increased in the same period from 42,500 to 59,900 . . .

> UNSATISFIED DEMAND FOR FARMS . . .
> UNDER-DEVELOPED LAND . . .
> SCANDAL OF THE DEER FORESTS . . .
> USE FOR THE HILLS . . .
> SCOTLAND'S TOWN PROBLEM: OVERCROWDING . . .

Over a fifth of the population is living more than three persons per room; nearly one half of the population more than two persons per room . . ."

> *Public Opinion*, July 17, 1914, extracts some plums from *The Report of the [Liberal] Scottish Land Enquiry Committee* and follow up with summaries of the quite drastic recommendations on behalf of Tenant-Farmers, would-be Smallholders, urban House Tenants, etc., etc.

PERHAPS before the weightier politics of the fateful 1914 Session are discussed—the three Parliament Act Bills, the series of Irish crises, the Austro-Serb conflict, and the on-come of the Great War—an attempt should be made to deal with less dramatic and now practically forgotten activities of the Session which the "advanced" of the time considered important steps in the "march of progress". It was being resolved, for example, to find an extra £2,750,000 per annum for Education, and that not inconsiderable sum for those days, was to be confined, for the first year, to the necessitous school areas. Half the cost of feeding necessitous school-children was to be taken over by the Exchequer; and grants were also to be obtainable by local authorities for physical training, open-air classes, maternity centres, and technical secondary, and higher education. More millions were to be spent to supplement the Insurance system, with Exchequer grants made available in aid of sick married women and deposit contributors and, much more ambitiously, made available also for establishing a system of medical referees and providing centres for the co-operation of panel doctors and the organization of health lectures.[1]

The money for these Education and Public Health advances was to come, in a somewhat unorthodox fashion which caused its own disputes, from the Budget, and it is obvious from the medical or, at least, the Public Health bent of most of the "advances" that Lloyd George had been taking medical counsel. In point of fact, he had for years been making use of Dr. Christopher Addison, Radical M.P. for Hoxton, in circumstances that soon brought the latter political promotion. Dr. Addison's account of his pre-war co-operation with the Chancellor is worth quoting:[2]

Ever since the Insurance Act days we have been close friends, and breakfasts . . . have been the times of our confabulations. Health

[1] Cf. *Hansard*, May 4, 1914, for Lloyd George's three-hour Budget speech. But see also *Beatrice Webb's Diaries, 1912–1924* (ed. Margaret Cole), under February 20th and April 22nd, for the revelation that Insurance deficits had been accumulating under the head of "excessive sickness of married women" which turned out to be due to the risk of pregnancy having been omitted, according to Mrs. Webb, by ignorant Government actuaries. Her help had been invited by Lloyd George; Margaret Bondfield and Mary Macarthur had been brought in; and the final result, with the help of Dr. Addison and Herbert Samuel, had been a Public Health scheme for Mothers and Infants.

[2] From *Four and a Half Years*, under Friday, July 3, 1914. (By permission of Messrs. Hutchinson.)

services, children, housing, land always, and Radical social reform projects generally are the topics—except for political gossip. We encourage each other to dream dreams but to base them on existing realities.

Generally my job is, when we get so far on a subject, to go away and draft a memo. on it and hammer it into as practical a shape as I can, getting what help I need from suitable men. This job really is easy, when it might be difficult, because the chiefs, whom I tell frankly what I am after, are so decent about it. They are, particularly, Pease at the Board of Education and Samuel at the Local Government Board, Masterman at the Insurance Commission and Montagu at the Treasury. The man, of all others, who helps is Morant. . . .

At these breakfasts a useful preliminary is to ask L.G. if he has read the memo. we have presumably come to talk about. With rare exceptions he has. . . . The time for talk is when the family is scattering. . . .

After breakfast my task is to get another stage on with the subject. . . . Sometimes this is easy, sometimes difficult, sometimes impossible. On those days when something else has become more urgent I have learnt to mark time. . . .

The social services proposals announced for Budget grants this year have been developed at these breakfast talks—schools for mothers, improved maternity services, health services. . . .

To-day [July 3, 1914] I had presumably come to report progress on the settlements of the departmental turmoils about nursing grants, medical consultants, etc., but what L.G. really wanted to talk about was the position that had been reached over land valuation and the Budget—including the inquisitorial Form IV.

I suggested that if he wanted to lose the General Election, should it come before next year, he would be well advised to send out a million Form Fours. . . .

We then had a few minutes on Nursing and other grants. . . .

The 1914 Budget, it is obvious, had been framed ambitiously and not without an eye to a General Election before a year was out. Moreover, the £9,800,000 per annum extra the Chancellor was proposing to find from taxation was also to be raised in a fashion calculated mightily to please the masses and even the "lower middle classes". Whereas Children's Allowances, in the case of incomes of under £500, were to be doubled, income tax and super-tax on the incomes of the wealthy were to be made to yield so much more that the net increase of income-tax revenue was to be £5,250,000 and of super-tax revenue £2,500,000, with a further £250,000 to be made available from foreign investments. Nor was this all. Death Duties were to be made to yield £650,000 per annum more, Settled Estate Duty £150,000 more and, to the completer dismay of some even on the Government side of the House,[1] a million was to be taken from the Sinking Fund. And there was a still more controversial section of the Budget, ostensibly to "save some municipalities from bankruptcy", but, in truth, largely to satisfy the Radical ambition to get into the position for putting much heavier burdens on ground landlords. A national system of valuation for local taxation, it was explained, needed to be set up, separating the site from the improvements, and site-value rating would follow which would permit rate-reductions on houses, shops, and other "improvements" especially in the hardest-pressed areas. This part of the year's financial plan came, perhaps, nearest to the dreaded "legislation by Budget" which Conservatives had been forecasting since 1909 and, in point of fact, there were sufficient Government critics and drafting complexities for some, at least, of Lloyd George's plans to go awry. A Speaker's decision of June 22nd, for example, that the Finance Bill must be confined to taxation compelled the excision from the Finance Bill, as such, of the local authority clauses. And by the time the taxation sections, helped through by the guillotine, had become law on July 31st, much more was in the melting-pot than the remaining sections of the Chancellor's original Budget scheme.

It does not seem, from the course of later events, that Lloyd George's reputation with the masses suffered appreciably from some of his Budget frustrations of 1914. Indeed, it might be well, at this stage, to give a very sharp-sighted observer's picture of the masses' own reputed party in 1914. According to Mrs. Webb's famous *Diaries*,[2] the Labour Party Conference of late January 1914 had been a personal triumph for Ramsay MacDonald, the discontented I.L.P. critics of the first day having been "steam-rollered", with the help of the Miners' and Textile Unions, who did not desire, as MacDonald knew, the links with the Liberal Party to be broken. Helped by a commanding figure, a fine voice, and "clever dialectics", MacDonald had proved more than a

[1] Cf. *Hansard*, July 7, 1914, for the Government majority falling to 23. Dr. Addison in his diary entry for the day blamed rich men on the Government side for abstaining.

[2] *Beatrice Webb's Diaries, 1912–1924*, pp. 17–18, under February 6, 1914. It was the special Party Conference at Glasgow she was commenting upon at which MacDonald had denied having made any secret bargains with the Government. And only six days later, Mrs. Webb was again ruefully commenting on MacDonald's attachment to every "old Radical shibboleth".

match for his opponents, whether on the platform or in the audience, and would be Labour's Leader for as long as he desired. In his "old-fashioned Radicalism" and his liking for Lloyd George, he was really representative of the bulk of Trade Unionists who might have been persuaded by the I.L.P. that a Labour Party could help them and that some working-men should enjoy the prestige of the M.P.'s name and the £400 salary, but who wanted such M.P.'s, all the same, to stick as close as possible to the Liberal Party. The British workman, Mrs. Webb considered, still believed in the right of the middle and professional classes to run the government and did not credit (and rightly for the most part) his own work-mates with the ability to do so. And a little later in the famous *Diaries*,[1] Mrs. Webb, while making reservations for Snowden, Hardie, and Arthur Henderson, dismissed all the rest of the Labour Party (except its Leader) as merely a comfort-loving "lot of ordinary workmen" who stuck to MacDonald to save themselves from confusion. MacDonald himself was reported to be critical of almost the whole of the "ostensible" programme of his party, opposed to striking out in a "constructive Socialist direction", bored with his own Labour colleagues and attracted by the Front Bench Liberals, to whom he had given steady support. If he had been able, he would have stopped the three-cornered contests in which Labour and Liberal rivalry often presented Conservatives with a seat on a minority vote. But years of Labour Representation propaganda and the "ambition of every local Labour leader" to get into Parliament put this beyond MacDonald's effective power.

Nor did Beatrice Webb become less mordant after she had been enlisted by the Chancellor to help with Budget problems.[2] She felt Keir Hardie was "used up", the rank-and-file "puzzled and disheartened", and the Labour members, conscious of having "utterly failed to impress the House of Commons and the constituencies" as a live force.[3]

[1] Under February 12, 1914. What makes all this criticism more authentic is, of course, the fact that Mrs. Webb would have liked, if she could have done so truthfully, to report very differently on the ability and willingness of Mac-Donald and his party to strike out "in the constructive Socialist direction".

[2] Under April 22, 1914 the *Diaries* report the Webbs' resumption of relations with two Liberal Cabinet Ministers, Lloyd George and Herbert Samuel, with a view to using the Insurance deficit, perplexing Lloyd George, to persuade him to find some extra resources for a Public Health expansion under the aegis of Samuel's Local Government Board.

[3] *Beatrice Webb's Diaries, 1912–1924*, p. 23, under April 22, 1914.

The Sessional events of 1914 were, indeed, particularly apt for those on whatever side of politics, who desired to belabour or bewail the Parliamentary Labour Party's alleged uselessness or helplessness.[1] The rural poor, for example, seemed to have everything to gain, not from the Labour Party, but from the Village Rehousing and Agricultural Wage Board plans boldly suggested by Lloyd George's Land Enquiry Committee.[2] And that Committee's clearly-drafted schemes of attack upon urban overcrowding and urban slums[3] certainly appeared to promise a more realistic and effective solution of some of the principal problems of the urban worker's life than the Land Nationalization projects of the Socialist propaganda societies or the watered-down versions of such "extremism" that had had, perforce, to be allowed, on occasion, to emerge as Labour Party or T.U.C. resolutions. Moreover, whether on the Budget of 1914 or on the "three vital Parliament Act Bills" for "Equal Franchise", Welsh Disestablishment, and Home Rule, "Labour" seemed to have nothing effective to contribute except the niggling and mostly petty amendments, designed, not for use, but to sound well at "working-class meetings" or to read well in the rival columns of the *Daily Citizen* or the *Daily Herald*.[4] "Labour", for example, was, at least, as

---

[1] The Syndicalists and Guild Socialists were, of course, very prominent in this form of activity, and the British Socialist Party, not to mention the Anarchists, were specialists in "revelations" both of the uselessness and of the "financial corruption" of the Labour members. Beatrice Webb, hopeful especially of the rank-and-file ("The Labour Movement rolls on—the Trade Unions are swelling in membership and funds, more candidates are being put forward"), was more charitable but even she girded occasionally that the Fabians "are by their adhesion to the present Parliamentary Party bolstering up a fraud—pretending, to the outside world, that these respectable but reactionary Trade Union officials are the leaders of the Social Revolution".

[2] Cf. *The Land, The Report of the Land Enquiry Committee*, Vol. 2, pp. 160–1: "The Government has definitely decided to deal with the rural problem, not by letting cottages below an economic rent, but by *raising the economic status of the workers*, and thus enabling them to pay for a sanitary dwelling *out of their wages*. No doubt, even after this has been done, there will be a residuum of people who for various reasons are unable to pay an economic rent for a healthy cottage without help from the local authority. But these cases will be exceptional. . . ."

[3] *Ibid.*, p. 28, for the justification: "The fact that a large proportion of the population are grossly overcrowded, or have to live in houses unfit for habitation or both, has a disastrous effect, not only on their health but their morality."

[4] In October 1912 the Trades Union Congress had sponsored the *Daily Citizen* which it tried to keep in safer and more "moderate" paths than the "rebel" *Daily Herald*, whose appearance, in April 1912, had been made possible by the financial backing of the wealthy H. D. Harben. Beatrice Webb found the *Daily Citizen* "smug, common, and ultra-official" and the *Daily Herald* "iconoclastic and inconsistent in the policies it takes up and drops with fiery levity". But she noted also the "team of clever and intellectually unscrupulous young

ready as the "extreme Radicals" to criticize the long "tolerance" of "Ulster treason" which had been displayed by a Cabinet with suspect aristocratic affiliations extending right into the "enemy camp". And it was partly, at least, to win the cheers of "Labour" as well as those of the Radicals and Irish, that Winston Churchill and Lloyd George made the soon notorious Bradford and Huddersfield speeches of March 14th and 21st in the character of Ministers, determined, now that every "reasonable" concession to Ulster had been offered, that further defiance of Parliament and the Law would not be tolerated. As these speeches led straight on to the worst Ulster crisis yet, followed, in turn, by a Downing Street crisis, some detailed attention should be given to their background. It was, after all, not usual for a Minister who, like Churchill at Bradford on Saturday, March 14th had threatened the use of force against his opponents, in a phrase as grim as "there are worse things than bloodshed", to be cheered enthusiastically not only in a provincial hall but at his first appearance in the Commons afterwards.[1]

It had been on March 5th that the "three Parliament Act Bills" for Home Rule, Welsh Disestablishment, and "Equal Suffrage" had been reintroduced for the 1914 Session but, as was already widely guessed in political circles, difficult negotiations between Ministers and the Irish Party had been proceeding beforehand, in order to allow the Prime Minister, when moving Home Rule's Second Reading for the third and decisive time, to announce important concessions to Ulster.[2] Under heavy pressure from Ministers, who could truly say that a Government break-up was probable if force was uncompromisingly employed against Ulster and bloodshed occasioned, Redmond, Dillon, T. P. O'Connor, and Devlin were finally brought to agree to the offer made to Ulster when the Prime Minister spoke on March 9th.[3] Of course,

journalists with Will Dyson, the cartoonist at their head, and Lansbury exercising an emotional paternal influence." When war came, the *Daily Citizen* which had lost heavily was abandoned but the *Daily Herald* managed to survive by converting itself into a weekly till the war was over.

[1] Cf. Sir Almeric Fitzroy, *Memoirs*, ii, 541, for the impression made on Asquith.

[2] Cf. *Ibid.*, under March 4th, for Morley reporting the Irish acceptance of concessions which would have been deemed impossible a fortnight before. Morley believed "public opinion" would be impressed but was pessimistic as to the Opposition's being satisfied.

[3] Cf. Lord Riddell, *More Pages from My Diary, 1908–1914*, under March 6th, for Lloyd George, who had consented to do Asquith's bargaining for him, with the Irish, telling Riddell of the toughness of the job and of Asquith's tendency to shirk a row and unpleasantness generally.

Redmond had his bargaining advantages, too, for fifty Radicals,[1] besides most of the Labour men, were regarded as ready to back Redmond against their own Front Bench rather than have "Ulster treason" allowed to dictate terms to Parliament for which Redmond was unprepared. It could be argued, moreover, that every weakening of Ireland's national case not only played into the hands of W. O'Brien's intransigent minority group[2] but strengthened also the appeal of the infant Republican Guild Socialism of James Connolly[3] and the anarchic "Larkinism" of the Dublin slums.[4]

Still another of Redmond's bargaining advantages came from the rigidity of the Parliament Act itself. Asquith could not offer Ulster any modification of the Home Rule Bill proper for that measure had to be carried, in 1914, in the precise form in which it had already passed the Commons, during the previous two Sessions, if the Veto of the Lords on any Home Rule at all were to be circumvented under the Parliament Act. Asquith's offer, in short, could only be that an Amending Bill would be contrived to follow the Home Rule Bill through Parliament and to become law before any part of Home Rule became operative. Under the suggested Amending Bill, moreover, though all Ulster's counties, and the cities of Belfast and Londonderry, were given the right, if they desired it, to hold a species of Referendum to exclude themselves, even by bare majority, from the operation of the Home Rule Bill, that self-exclusion was limited to a six years' period. Some of the toughest bargaining between Ministers and the Irish must, indeed, have been on the self-exclusion procedure and what was to follow after the six years were over. To meet Redmond's needs and yet to leave a door open for further manœuvre, the provision was to be that self-excluded counties would, at the end

[1] Sir Almeric Fitzroy, *Memoirs*, under December 4, 1913: 'There are no less than fifty Liberals who would vote with Redmond if he declined to accept any compact . . . made with the Opposition."

[2] *Ibid.*, "Redmond has to show that he can get more for Ireland than O'Brien and at the same time avert being over-trumped by Devlin" who sat for West Belfast and represented "sacrificed" Ulster Catholics.

[3] *The Workers' Republic* of 1898–1903 represented Connolly's less mature agitation but after American experience, between 1903 and 1910, he returned a more formidable figure.

[4] Cf. W. P. Ryan, *The Irish Labour Movement*, for the inability even of an account highly biased in "Jim Larkin's favour (and without a good word for the Irish employers, the Dublin police, the Royal Irish Constabulary or, for that matter, the "obedient official element" of the British T.U.C. which refused to allow itself to be committed to "Larkinism") to disguise the strong hostility of the Irish Catholic Church to Larkin's methods and personality.

of the six-year period, come under the Irish system unless the Imperial Parliament otherwise determined. Even if the possibility of further exclusion was thus left open, the right to indefinite self-exclusion was not accorded which Ulster and the Opposition could not have rejected without greatly weakening their case. As it was, Sir Edward Carson was able to take his stand on the strong position of: "We do not want a sentence of death with a stay of execution for six years", and the Opposition to move a formidable Vote of Censure on March 19th which permitted Carson to demand a fair offer and to leave for Belfast shortly afterwards amid tremendous Opposition cheering. He had made his position much stronger, on March 9th, by agreeing to put the Government's proposals before an Ulster Convention if the six-years time-limit were withdrawn, and Bonar Law had come to his aid, on March 19th, by offering Lord Lansdowne's assurance that the House of Lords would not stand in the way if a Referendum on Home Rule, as modified by the Government's new proposals, were put to the country and carried.[1]

There was, doubtless, some awareness in all parts of the House that the position in Ulster was approaching a crisis and Ministers, in fact, had had reports, early in March, that there were Ulster Volunteer plans for undertaking the worst "outrage" yet, the seizure of arms from Government depots in North-Eastern Ireland.[2] In fact, after Government's "new offer" to Ulster had been made, on March 9th, Lloyd George and Winston Churchill, carrying a somewhat hesitant Prime Minister with them, had resolved on Churchill's platform "menaces" of March 14th at Bradford and Lloyd George's "lurid oratory" at Huddersfield a week later, on March 21st.[3] It looks, indeed, as though more than platform menaces were in question for, undoubtedly, the precautionary military and naval measures ordered to protect Government supplies in Ulster could have become the first steps in Ulster's "coercion",

[1] Cf. *Hansard,* March 9th and March 19th.

[2] Cf. J. E. B. Seely's account in his book *Adventure* of what information came to him as War Secretary.

[3] Cf. Lord Riddell, *More Pages from My Diary, 1908–1914,* under March 14th, for the circumstances in which Lloyd George had encouraged Winston Churchill to make a speech "that will ring down the corridors of history," the speech whose most important and eloquent passage affirmed that "there are worse things than bloodshed" when Parliamentary government itself was at stake owing to the defiant illegalities being encouraged in Ulster. The speech was almost a preparation of "public opinion" for the measures of force which might have been asked of the Army and Navy and was momentarily welcomed as restoring "fine fighting form" to the Liberals.

and just as undoubtedly there would have been the warmest applause for such "coercion" from strong Radical and Labour elements as well as the Irish.[1] It was because many of the Army officers at the Curragh who, in any case, from their class origins, had little love for a "Radical Government" under Irish Nationalist "dictation", strongly suspected what they were about to be asked to do, in aid "of the civil authorities in Ulster", that the next sensational developments, on March 23rd and 25th, took place. On March 23rd Parliament had to be told that there had been some tendering of resignations by Army officers but that there had been a return to duty when explanations had been given. On March 25th, however, it had become plain that Seely, the War Secretary, alarmed by the prospect of mass-resignations spreading to Britain and even, it was said, to Egypt and India,[2] had allowed General Gough, from the Curragh, to commit him to what in angry Radical eyes looked like "a private bargain with a few rebellious officers". To make matters worse, Sir John French, Chief of the Imperial General Staff, and the Adjutant-General had also become involved.

It was not difficult for the Prime Minister, despite his painful sense of the shattered prestige of his Government, to win enthusiastic applause from the Radical, Labour, and Irish Benches when, on March 25th, he made what some considered a bold counter-offensive against the peccant officers of the Curragh.[3] Whatever the consequences might be, Mr. Asquith declared, the Government would never yield to the claim of any body of men in the service of the Crown to demand from the Government in advance what they would or would not be required to do under circumstances that had not arisen. Five days later, on March 30th, even greater applause came from the Radical Benches when he

---

[1] Cf. Sir Almeric Fitzroy, *Memoirs*, under March 25th, which, after mentioning the naval side for which Churchill had assumed the responsibility, treats the military side thus: "The plea of the Government that nothing considerable was intended is belied by the fact that an officer of standing was a few days ago sent over to Ireland, with two juniors, to organize an Intelligence Department, and has been working, as I saw by a letter under his own hand, fourteen hours a day. . . . The White Paper issued this morning is a miserable document of shifts and gaps. . . ."

[2] Cf. Lord Riddell, *More Pages from My Diary, 1908–1914*, p. 206. It was apparently Sir John French who did the alarming: "I had messages", he told Riddell, "from all over the country which told me that Gough's resignation would be followed by hosts of others, and that the disaffection would speedily spread to Egypt and India."

[3] J. A. Hobson's *The Traffic in Treason* is the best-known pamphleteering attack on Ulster from the Radical and Labour point of view.

announced that in view of the resignation of the War Secretary, of
Sir John French, and of the Adjutant-General, he had felt it to be
his duty, for a time, at any rate, to take over the office of Secretary
of State for War. In 1914, this involved the Prime Minister's
leaving the House and submitting to re-election, and again there
was a great demonstration of enthusiasm for him, as he left, by
Radicals who claimed that he was going "to trounce the Army".[1]
In point of fact, in view of what had gone before, this was now
well beyond his power, and on April 26th there was announced,
perforce, the greatest piece of Ulster defiance yet, the monster
gun-running which had landed and distributed 35,000 rifles and
a million rounds of ammunition to complete the arming of an
Ulster Volunteer Force now returned as 111,000 strong.[2] Next
day, when General Macready took over military and police control
in Belfast, Ministers obtained a reliable military representative in
Ulster but one who received only the most cautious and unheroic
directives.[3] Ministers were no longer relying on force to extricate
them from their difficulties. They were beginning to have more
hopes from the mediating action of the Crown and to trust that
the widespread organization of Irish National Volunteers being
planned against "King Carson" would sober the Opposition
Leadership if not the Ulster Volunteers.[4] It was presumably no
secret that while Home Rule,[5] Welsh Disestablishment, and

[1] Cf. Lord Riddell, *More Pages from My Diary, 1908–1914*, under March
30th: "The P.M. has made the dramatic announcement that Seely, French, and
Ewart have resigned, and that he will become Minister for War. The Radicals
are delighted, and regard this as an intimation that the P.M. intends to trounce
the Army. I am confident that he proposes to do nothing of the kind. . . . He
does not believe in a democratic Army, I am quite sure, and will not go further
in that direction than is absolutely necessary." The last sentence quoted shows
how, for a few days infuriated Radicals and Labour men went as far as discussing a democratization of the Army.
[2] Cf. H. W. Nevinson, *More Changes, More Chances*, p. 405.
[3] The story is told in his own *Annals of an Active Life*.
[4] On July 13th (July 12th, the normal "Boyne Day", being a Sunday) "King
Carson" was reported thus: "I will give the Government the alternatives: Give
us a clear cut for Ulster, or come and fight us. In a very short time unless they
are prepared to leave us alone, we will recognize the Provisional Government,
and no other Government.
   "The Provisional Government have given me authority to act at any moment,
and in any way I like, to assert your authority, so as to prevent Home Rule being
put on the Statute Book." *Whitaker's Almanack, 1915*, p. 474, reported under
July 4, 1914: "An open display of armed force was made in Belfast, 2000 Ulster
Volunteers marching through the streets with rifles with fixed bayonets."
[5] Cf. *Daily News and Leader*, May 26th, reporting the great Parliamentary
event of the previous day, under the headline "HOME RULE THROUGH THE
COMMONS". Redmond's dictum on the occasion is worth repeating: "The
Union, as we have known it, is dead."

"Equal Suffrage" were being advanced nearer the Statute Book during May, June, and July at Westminster, the first large-scale gun-running for the Nationalist Volunteers[1] was arranged which, on July 26th, succeeded, despite troop precautions that only brought ultimate disgrace, in landing 3000 muskets.[2]

Though there were Radicals who objected violently to the exertion of Royal influence[3] and Asquith persisted, for some time, with behind-the-scene negotiations with Bonar Law and Carson, the King's authority had to be invoked, after all, during the second half of July. By that time Ministers were in trouble in a variety of different directions—the Home Rule Amending Bill was being vitally altered in the Lords while the Home Rule Bill itself was denied discussion;[4] the over-ambitious Budget was threatening to dislocate the Sessional time-table besides producing other mishaps;[5] and the international situation was growing steadily more disquieting after the Sarajevo assassinations of June 28th. A Buckingham Palace Conference, under the Chairmanship of the Speaker, was finally arranged to begin on July 21st[6] with a short

[1] *Whitaker's Almanack, 1915*, gave under the date of June 9, 1914: "Mr. Redmond announced that the Irish Party had given its countenance to the Nationalist Volunteer movement." In view of what the Ulster Volunteers were busy with, Redmond was apparently unable any longer to resist pressure in his own ranks for a stronger course.

[2] Cf. *The Times*, July 27th: "Some 3,000 rifles were landed from a yawl at the Hill of Howth, and received by a body of several hundreds of Volunteers. A battalion of the King's Own Scottish Borderers and a small force of [Irish] Metropolitan Police intercepted them on their march to Dublin. An attempt to disarm the Volunteers was resisted. The troops charged with fixed bayonets, and shots were exchanged. Ultimately the Volunteers escaped with their arms. When the troops returned to Dublin, they were furiously stoned by a mob and they were obliged to fire three volleys. Three men and a woman were killed."

[3] Cf. Dr. Addison, *Politics from Within, 1911–1918*, i, 34–5, for Liberal and Labour members suspecting "almost to a man", after the circulation of all manner of rumours, that Palace influence would ultimately be used to force the Government out and compel an Election in circumstances that would, of course, be weighted against them and against Home Rule.

[4] Cf. *Hansard*, July 8th, for the Amendment moved by Lord Lansdowne and carried by 138 against 39 under which the whole of Ulster was to be excluded indefinitely. There were others.

[5] Cf. Lord Riddell, *More Pages from My Diary, 1908–1914*, under June 23rd, for McKenna's criticisms of Lloyd George after the Speaker's decision of the night before had necessitated the jettisoning of a considerable part of the year's Finance Bill. He talked of a shocking muddle and of the absurdity of the Chancellor's hoping to pass in a week a very complicated measure with some of its main provisions in the schedules. Three months would have been needed, and the House was in no mood for such heavy, tiresome legislation. There are other reports of the Prime Minister "writhing" under the indignity of his Government's position.

[6] *Ibid.*, p. 216, for an account which seems to show that the first confidential contacts between Northcliffe and Lloyd George, which were to become so

Royal appeal, and Asquith and Lloyd George were to represent
Ministers, Bonar Law and Lansdowne the Opposition Leader-
ship, Redmond and Dillon the Irish Nationalists, and Carson and
Craig the Ulstermen. The kernel of the short appeal from the
King was this:[1]

> My intervention at this moment may be regarded as a new departure.
> But the exceptional circumstances under which you are brought
> together justify my action.
> For months we have watched with deep misgivings the course of
> events in Ireland. The trend has been surely and steadily towards an
> appeal to force, and to-day the cry of Civil War is on the lips of the most
> responsible and sober-minded of my people.
> We have in the past endeavoured to act as a civilising example to the
> world, and to me it is unthinkable, as it must be to you, that we should
> be brought to the brink of fratricidal strife upon issues apparently so
> capable of adjustment as those you are now asked to consider. . . .

There can be little doubt but that the Royal appeal had sufficient
effect on the Opposition Leadership and the Ulstermen to induce
them to forgo their hopes of wrecking Home Rule entirely or, at
least, forcing the exclusion of the whole of Ulster from its effects.
On the other hand, they refused to contemplate leaving more than
half Ulster under a Dublin Parliament whatever might be the
statistical justification for claiming that Tyrone and Fermanagh
could not like Counties Antrim, Armagh, Derry, and Down be
counted as Protestant but must be accepted as containing a
population more than half Catholic. The obvious Ulstermen's
answer was to point out that many more Protestants in the
remaining twenty-six Irish Counties were being left to Dublin
than the total number of Catholics in the Six Counties whose
exclusion from Dublin control was being demanded. It would
appear that three years of preparation to take over, as a Provisional
Government, a viable Ulster sub-State had convinced Carson and
Craig that suggestions of partitioning Tyrone and Fermanagh on
a confessional basis could not be accepted. Had not the Ulstermen
offered to surrender their claims to the three Ulster counties of
Donegal, Monaghan, and Cavan?

With the break-up, after four sittings, of the Buckingham Palace
important after war came, developed from co-operation on this matter.
Apparently, Lloyd George was instrumental in getting Northcliffe the information which, to the fury of the Liberal Press that mistakenly laid the blame on
Asquith, allowed *The Times* and the *Daily Mail* the major "scoop" of exclusive
announcement.

[1] *The Times*, July 22nd.

Conference on July 24th, the situation both at Westminster and in Ireland would normally have become much more critical. There was certainly some anxious Radical and Labour discussion of the possibility that the King might now consider himself to have sufficient ground for declining to sign the Home Rule Bill until there had been a General Election.[1] In fact, a Royal breach with the Ministers and their resignation or dismissal were also among the subjects mooted. But the newspapers of the next few days contained such alarming intelligence from the Continent[2] that the relative importance of even the most exciting or vindictive Lobby gossip sank rapidly. It is worth examining the well-kept diary of one fast-rising Radical M.P. to see what "progressive opinion" had been busy with from the time the Buckingham Palace Conference had been announced. Dr. Addison's diary entry for July 20th ran thus:[3]

At the House in time to hear the Prime Minister's statement on the Irish Amending Bill. He announced the Conference at Buckingham Palace, which was received with a puzzled silence and profound distrust on our side. The only man who evoked any enthusiasm was Redmond, whom the rank and file of our party will back up, notwithstanding Cabinet wobblers . . . reported as being Harcourt, Crewe, Morley, and Winston . . . Morley, they say, is living in a state of continual funk and offers his resignation every other day. There never was a time when it was more important for Asquith to sit tight and maintain the rights of Parliament than the present. If he does not he will smash up the Liberal Party and lead to the opening up of other big questions beside Ireland, amongst them the rights of the Monarchy.

And his entry for July 21st is almost as revealing, running thus:[4]

Attended at the House a meeting of Liberal members to consider the present position of Irish affairs. Sir Thomas Whitaker[5] supplied the wanted lead. . . . We are determined, so far as members can, to apply ginger to the Government; to stick to the Nationalists throughout and to refuse absolutely to dissolve Parliament until Plural Voting and the

[1] Cf. Dr. Addison, *Politics From Within, 1911–1918*, pp. 33-4.
[2] Cf. *Daily Express*, July 25th, for the headlines, "NEW EUROPEAN PERIL, AUSTRIA THREATENS SERVIA WITH WAR", and *The Times*, July 25th: "The outstanding feature of the situation is the proposal made by Sir Edward Grey that the four Great Powers not immediately interested in the Austro-Servian conflict should confer together with the object of inducing Russia and Austria-Hungary to suspend military operations while the four Powers endeavour to arrange a settlement." (Re-quoted from H. C. Dent, *op. cit.*)
[3] Dr. Addison, *Four and A Half Years*, i, 27.   [4] *Ibid.*, pp. 27-8.
[5] Cf. *Who's Who, 1914*, p. 2231, for this leading member on the Government side who had been M.P. for Spen Valley since 1892. He had been made a Privy Councillor in 1908, his special subject was "Temperance Reform", and his name should have been spelt Whittaker.

other Parliament Act Bills are through. The Tories are counting on the failure of the Palace conference, followed by a dissolution. This being so, they have of course no inducement to agree. . . . I hear that the King's speech to the conference will make a bad impression on our people. . . . Lord Stamfordham also is reported to be against us and disposed to persuade the King to insist on a dissolution, as a condition of signing the Bill.

By July 27th, however, the urgency of the European situation was breaking through into the diary even of a member concentrating above all on forcing the "Parliament Act Bills" through, on the one hand, and, on the other, doing his utmost for the "social reforms" that were about to take him to Ministerial rank. Here is Dr. Addison's diary entry for July 27th, followed by those for July 28th and July 31st:[1]

All the excitement is about the gun-running episode in Ireland. There is no getting away from the difference in treatment meted out to the Nationalist gun-runners by police and soldiers when compared with that given to Ulster gun-runners. . . . Everything, however, even Ireland, is now overshadowed by this Austro-Servian affair and the horrible fear of European complications.

Tuesday, July 28, 1914.

Things even blacker than yesterday as to the European situation. We got the Feeding of Children Bill, with substantial alteration, through Committee in the morning. The latest phase of the Irish business seems to be making towards a settlement. We were kept late at the House on Milk and Dairies Report[2] . . . but made good progress.

On Friday July 31. . . . Two meetings of Ponsonby's[3] Foreign Affairs Group—the second largely attended. Only one motion was put to a division, the effect of which was that we should be neutral whatever happened in Belgium or elsewhere. If I remember rightly, nineteen voted for it, four against it (of whom I was one), but most did not vote at all. Everybody felt, I think, in abject misery at the prospect of what war would entail. What haunted me was the thought of the poor folks in Hoxton. The City was already in a panic and people rushing to lay in stores of food and hoarding up gold. I found myself with a few shillings and drew £7 which would be enough to tide us over a few days.

[1] Cf. Dr. Addison's *Four and A Half Years*, i, 27–31.

[2] Addison, as a medical man, was taking a special interest in what the public sometimes called the "Pure Milk Bill", and those who can remember the retailing of milk almost direct from cowsheds in the heart of the cities will understand why.

[3] Cf. *Who's Who, 1914*, p. 1684, for Arthur Ponsonby, M.P. for Stirling Burghs since 1908 when he had succeeded Campbell-Bannerman, the Prime Minister, to whom he had been Principal Private Secretary. Born in 1871 of distinguished Whig stock (he was a great-grandson of "Earl Grey of the Reform Bill") he had been Page of Honour to Queen Victoria, 1882–7, and had later served in the Diplomatic Service and the Foreign Office. Government Back-Benchers obviously respected his opinions on Foreign Affairs.

By this stage, indeed, the furious exchanges expected on the Peers' major alterations in the Home Rule Amending Bill had been prevented by the resolve, on July 30th, to defer the Second Reading in the House of Commons so that the nation might face the war-peril with a united front. Moreover, the financial situation was already causing the gravest anxiety because of the huge and possibly irrecoverable credits from London which, in those days, financed a large part of the world's trade[1] and which, if lost or even threatened, seemed likely to cause major business havoc in Britain and serious unemployment. Then the normal movements of much of the world's shipping and food were being so strongly affected by the precautions taken by owners and Governments, fearing a major war, that food-shortages seemed possible in London. Here are headlines from the *Morning Post* of July 31st and August 1st, and the *Morning Post* was not a sensational journal:

ON THE BRINK OF WAR

HOME RULE POSTPONED

BLACK DAY IN THE CITY

FOUR MORE FAILURES ON THE STOCK EXCHANGE (July 31st).

BANK RATE 8 PER CENT.

STOCK EXCHANGE CLOSED

RUSSIAN ARMY MOBILISES

FLOUR, BEEF, SUGAR AND EGGS ALL DEARER (August 1st).

On Saturday August 1st, Sunday August 2nd, and Bank Holiday Monday August 3rd, while millions of still care-free Britishers were pleasure-making or reading the first exciting war-news from the Continent, there took place the final diplomatic exchanges that, at 11 p.m. on August 4th, brought the British Government into a war in which Austria, Serbia, Russia, Germany, France, and Belgium were already involved. Originally, there had been almost universal distaste for the mere idea that the suspect Balkan cliques of Belgrade, who probably had a good deal of responsibility for the Sarajevo assassinations, could involve the

---

[1] *Beatrice Webb's Diaries, 1912–1924*, p. 28, give under the date August 28, 1914: "Lloyd George was convinced that the Germans had methodically prepared for war in the financial as well as in the military sphere and had succeeded in getting comfortably into debt for some 200 millions. Consequently her merchants were flush of money."

major part of Europe in war.[1] And when Tsarist Russia resolved to mobilize in Serbia's defence, the long tradition of anti-Tsarism in British popular politics seemed to make it all the more unlikely that Britain would eye the Slav allies against Austria with any favour. Even when Germany, coming to Austria's support, mobilized against Russia and demanded immediate clarification of France's attitude, in view of the Franco-Russian alliance, there was little visible change in the prevailing anti-Serb and anti-Russian temper of the man-in-the-street who saw of course, not the slightest reason, at this stage, why Britain should intervene. Yet British intervention of a kind had already taken place on August 2nd under "secret" Franco-British arrangements not yet revealed to Parliament, and this was but a prelude to complete British intervention unless the German intention of using Belgian territory, with or without Belgian permission, in the fighting against France was abandoned.

Perhaps this part of the story should be told in the very words employed in the House of Commons, on August 3rd, by the Foreign Secretary, Sir Edward Grey. This is what a tense and crowded House heard from the Minister:[2]

On Sunday I gave the French Ambassador the assurance that, if the German Fleet comes into the Channel or through the North Sea to undertake hostile operations against the French coasts or shipping, the British Fleet will give all the protection in its power.

I understand that the German Government would be prepared, if we would pledge ourselves to neutrality, to agree that its fleet would not attack the northern coast of France. That is far too narrow an engagement for us.

If, in a crisis like this, we ran away from our obligations of honour and interest with regard to the Belgian treaty, I doubt, whatever material force we might have at the end, whether it would be of very much value in face of the respect we should have lost.

We have not yet made an engagement to send the Expeditionary Force out of the country. The mobilisation of the Fleet has taken place; that of the Army is taking place.

[1] Cf. Julian Symons, *Horatio Bottomley*, p. 162, for the attitude taken by the ultra-popular weekly, *John Bull*, and not immediately abandoned even after Britain's declaration of war on Germany: "*John Bull* . . . asserted that the [Archduke's] murder had been planned and carried out by the Servian Secret Service. . . . A facsimile of the document planning the assassination was reproduced. . . . An article referred to Servia as 'a hot-bed of cold-blooded conspiracy and subterfuge' and ended 'Servia must be wiped out! On August 8th, four days after the outbreak of the war . . . a powerful article appeared headed 'To Hell with Servia'."

[2] Cf. *Hansard*, August 3, 1914.

We cannot issue a proclamation of unconditional neutrality.

We must be, and are, prepared for the consequences of having to use all the strength we have at any moment—we know not how soon—to defend ourselves and take our part.

It was the Opposition and Redmond[1] who accepted Grey's case unreservedly, but there were known to be critics among his own Government colleagues and Back-Benchers, while the Labour men seemed committed against it both by a Manifesto of August 1st[2] and Trafalgar Square resolutions of August 2nd.[3] The best-remembered speech of August 3rd, apart from Grey's own, was, in fact, that of the Chairman of the Labour Party, Mr. Ramsay MacDonald, and as he seemed, at first, to be voicing criticism on behalf of the whole Labour group, it is from his speech that an extract shall be taken rather than from that of Ponsonby, the Foreign Affairs guide of Government's own Back-Benchers. Of Grey and the policy he had been pursuing MacDonald had this to say:[4]

I think he is wrong. I think the Government which he represents and for which he speaks is wrong. I think the verdict of history will be that they are wrong. We shall see . . . if the right hon. gentleman had come here to-day and told us that our country is in danger, . . . we would be with him and behind him. If this is so, we will vote him what money he wants. Yes, and we will go further. We will offer him ourselves if the country is in danger. But he has not persuaded me that it is. He has not persuaded my hon. friends who co-operate with me. . . . If the right hon. gentleman could come to us and tell us that a small European nationality like Belgium is in danger, and could assure us that he is going to confine the conflict to that question, then we would support him. What is the use of talking of coming to the aid of Belgium, when, as a matter of fact, you are engaging in a whole European War. . . ? The right hon. gentleman said nothing about Russia. We want to know about that. We want to try to find out what is going to happen, when it is all over, to the power of Russia in Europe. . . . Finally, so far as France is concerned, we say solemnly and definitely

[1] *Hansard*, August 3, 1914, for Redmond feeling able to give Ministers the assurance that their troops could safely be removed from Ireland and the defence of the country against the enemy entrusted to Irishmen themselves. One strong Government supporter, Dr. Addison, put very high praise for Redmond's speech into his diary entry for the day (*Four and A Half Years*, i, 34) but was obviously over-optimistic in considering that "his speech snuffed out Ulsterism and the Anti-Home Rule movement as one snuffs out a candle. Everybody felt this."

[2] Quoted above.

[3] Cf. *The Labour Year Book, 1916*, p. 17, for such language as: "we protest against any step being taken by the Government of this country to support Russia, either directly or in consequence of any understanding with France".

[4] Cf. *Hansard*, August 3rd.

that no such friendship as the right hon. gentleman describes . . . could ever justify . . . entering into war. . . .

In the light of History, MacDonald and other critics of the way Britain had become enmeshed in the wiles and ambitions of the Franco-Russian alliance are seen to have had much to justify them even if they did not make sufficient allowance for the Foreign Office's constant troubles with Germany's growing expectations and armed might. In the short run, after all, the overrunning of East Prussia by the Tsarist forces, during August 1914, probably produced, in proportion, a worse crop of invasion-horrors[1] than the "Prussian atrocities in Belgium" which were so widely and successfully used in increasing anti-German feeling in Britain and the world. And, in the long run, the whole appalling consequences of a war that led from the trench-massacres of the Western Front to the Versailles *Diktat* and from that, in turn, to the Hitler revenge-animus that brought a second World War, more terrible than the first, were so catastrophic that, could their possibility have been foreseen in August 1914, the whole course of events would have run very differently. It seems doubtful, for example, whether MacDonald would have been allowed to resign the Labour Party Chairmanship[2] after it became certain, during the next few days, that the Germans were actually overrunning Belgium and pushing on to deal with their French enemies in

[1] Cf. *Labour Leader*, July 8, 1915, for a Manifesto from the National Executive of the German Social Democratic Party which claimed that: "Four hundred thousand people in East Prussia have been forced to flee as refugees; 1620 civilians have been murdered and 433 wounded; 5410 male civilians (amongst them helpless old men), 2587 women, and 2719 children have been removed to Russia; 24 towns, 572 villages, and 236 farms, totalling 36,553 buildings have been entirely or partly destroyed, and about 200,000 homes have been entirely or partly plundered and devastated."

[2] Cf. *The Labour Year Book, 1916*, pp. 16–17, for a declaration from the National Executive of the Labour Party, issued on August 7th, still blaming Sir Edward Grey for his policy of "understandings with France and Russia only" as "bound to increase the power of Russia both in Europe and Asia, and to endanger good relations with Germany". But it was on that very day that MacDonald, finding the majority of the Parliamentary Labour group unwilling to allow him to continue critical on the Vote of Credit, resigned and Henderson took his place. No doubt the almost complete failure of the Neutrality League to stay the rapidly-mounting war-excitement may have had something to do with the situation inside the Parliamentary Labour Party. The Neutrality League's Advertisement No. 2, beginning "ENGLISHMEN, DO YOUR DUTY and keep your country out of a WICKED AND STUPID WAR. Small but powerful cliques are trying to rush you into it," appeared on August 5th in the *Daily News* and nine other papers. Protest meetings, letters to the newspapers, and distribution of the Neutrality League's leaflets had been among the forms of anti-war activity vainly appealed for.

despite both of Belgian resistance and the British declaration of war. And it seems just as doubtful whether Morley and Burns of the Cabinet and Charles Trevelyan of the junior Ministers would not have been joined in their resignations by the considerable group of colleagues who, on August 3rd, were nearly as dismayed by the prospect of being dragged into a great war against Germany in the wake of the Franco-Russian alliance.

Perhaps, before war-events begin to dominate the account, the Back-Bench Radical, Dr. Addison, who was about to be appointed Parliamentary Under-Secretary to the Board of Education in Trevelyan's place, should be allowed to tell in his own words the story of how the rapid onrush of war, on August 3rd and 4th, affected the "advanced" of Government's rank-and-file and the "Labour" members with whom they associated. Part of Dr. Addison's diary entry for August 3rd reads:[1]

There were two meetings of the Foreign Affairs Group. One bright feature was that Ramsay MacDonald and Henderson attended, and hoped to get the Labour Party to join the Liberals in a campaign to favour strong measures to relieve war distress and to work for an issue which would be the crushing of Kaiserism and all that it meant. They were reported, however, to be at sixes and sevens, and I learned afterwards that MacDonald had only a few followers in the Labour Party in support of his attitude of opposition to the war. . . . The panic in food prices continued.

And for August 4th, his entry was this:[2]

All the Motions on Ways and Means, which usually take hours in the Division Lobby, were passed in a few minutes. Amongst them, I am glad to say there was the Education (Provision of Meals) Bill, under which we could pay 50% of the cost of feeding children. The Chancellor explained the scheme for State Insurance against all shipping risks—probably the most Socialistic measure after Insurance to which this Government has ever been committed. . . .

All sorts of rumours of Cabinet resignations are going about. Buckmaster told me that, before the receipt of the German Chancellor's proposal . . . Simon, Harcourt, Pease, Burns, Morley, as well as himself, had intended to resign if we became involved.

I had a talk with Simon. He said that an important consideration with him was that, as we were in it, we must put our whole strength in seeing it through and do our best to combat the distress at home without party division. If a block of them were to leave the Government at this juncture, their action would necessitate a Coalition Government which

[1] Dr. Addison, *Four and a Half Years*, i, 32–3.
[2] *Ibid.*, pp. 33–5.

would assuredly be the grave of Liberalism. Most of us felt that Liberalism was already in its grave—at any rate that is what I feel like. When one thinks of all our schemes of social reform just set agoing and of those for which plans had been made in this year's Budget, one could weep. . . . Insurance must go on: the feeding of children is safe: and we must snatch what we can of others. . . . The State has become committed to a few great enterprises in connection with the relief proposals [war-distress relief]. The Housing Bill . . . to allow the Government to spend three millions in housing at Rosyth and other places where there are Government employees and to provide four millions for rural housing . . . had had to be split in two before the war crisis and we had reluctantly agreed to abandon the rural part in consequence of opposition. The Bill for Rosyth housing received a Third Reading to-day and, to our joy, the rural portion, which had been given up as lost, was resurrected in a separate Bill and went through all its stages in a few minutes.

BOOK TWO
The War Years, 1914–18

CHAPTER VI
DIFFICULT WAR YEARS BEGIN

"1. The national organization that has been set up for the purpose of dealing with any distress which may arise in consequence of the war is not intended to deal with cases of ordinary poverty. . . .

"4. Obviously the best way to provide for persons thrown out of their usual employment as a result of the war, is to provide them with some other work for wages. Wherever possible, such work should be work which is normally required to be taken in hand either by public authorities or private employers. It is only when these fail that recourse should be had to relief works. . . .

"7. Where the demands of the normal labour market are inadequate the Committee should consult the Local Authorities as to the possibility of expediting schemes of public utility. . . .

"10. Where relief works are provided, each man should only be employed a certain number of days per week. . . .

"12. Single men who are physically fit and within the prescribed ages—for enlistment in the Army, Navy, or territorial forces should not ordinarily receive assistance from the Local Committee until other applicants have been provided for.

"13. Relief without work should only be given when no other means of assistance are available. . . .

"17. So far as practicable, allowances should be made not in money, but by way of food tickets on local shops or stores. These tickets should be given to the women rather than to the men."

> From the *Memorandum for the Guidance of the Local Committees for the Prevention and Relief of Distress* (*August 20th, 1914*), issued while the initial war-dislocation made an urgent official problem.

"THE MOBILIZATION OF WOMEN. . . . If it were to degenerate into the supplying of cheap labor, it would bring a great train of misery . . . it is only as women's labor ceases to be either cheap or docile that any successful advance can be made. The White Paper just issued on the State of Employment reports that 80,000 additional laborers will be required for agriculture this summer, and 91,000 casual laborers in addition for the harvest. This deficiency will, in part, be supplied by women, and it ought to be arranged that every woman who enlists for this service becomes a trade unionist. Either we believe in

democracy . . . or we are only posing . . . if the dockers are
slow to recognise their obligations to society in a great crisis,
the reason is that society has treated the dockers, not as
citizens, but as a body of labor existing for the service of its
employers and for no other purpose in life."

> *The Nation*, March 27, 1915, continues a strong pro-
> Trade Union line, disturbing even to some of its Radical
> backers, aware of growing labour-shortages and rising
> wage-pressures.

"When the war broke out and progressively as it continued,
there was mobilisation of all national resources except constructive political thought. . . . To stifle political thought was
the fixed purpose of the men and the Parties that had brought
us into the war. . . . We urged the civilians to think, if only in
justice to the soldiers . . . we were it seems discouraging the
Army and encouraging the enemy. . . . Similarly you were the
friend of every country but your own, and probably in the pay
of the enemy, when you urged that there was no dishonour
and many obvious advantages, not to mention the saving of
precious human lives, in an endeavour to bring the Great War
to a close, like most wars before it, by negotiation, provided
that you surrendered none of the specific obligations of honour
for which you had ostensibly drawn the sword. But if you
shouted on the housetops that your Generals were incompetent
fools . . . your depots empty of ammunition, your enemy's
resources illimitable, you were doing your utmost to steady the
nation's nerves."

> E. D. Morel describes, in 1924, and with obvious reference
> to the Northcliffe Press's "Shells" campaign against
> Kitchener of May 1915, the obstacles met by the Radical
> and Socialist anti-war minorities.

AFTER war was declared on Germany on August 4th, Ministers were doubtless relieved to find, in view of the wide-spread neutralism which had existed in Radical circles,[1] that no effective "popular" anti-war movement developed. Indeed, even before the astonishing flood of exaggerated or false "German atrocity" stories came to Ministers' aid,[2] mass-recruiting of volunteers for "Kitchener's Army" had begun on the greatest scale. And before long, it was possible boldly to deny, at recruiting meetings and elsewhere, that the Serbian Government had any responsibility for the war[3] and to associate Serbia with Belgium as yet another "small nation" to be rescued from invasion, rapine, and murder by Britain and her Allies, pledged as they were, to defeat "Kaiserism", "Prussian Militarism", and all the Habsburg and other tools these had procured. War-fever was soon such that a "halter for the Kaiser" was being demanded since "shooting him would be to give him the honourable death of a soldier".[4] And instead of asking what manner of ally the Russian Tsardom

[1] Cf. Caroline Playne, *Society at War, 1914–1916*, p. 31: "But although many people distributed the 'Appeal of the Neutrality League' on the eve of the war, few stood by it. The storm of heated patriotic fervour swept over the Leaguers, swept their arguments out of date. Perhaps some of them took up the position disclosed in a four-page leaflet. . . . *Is This War Justifiable. . . The Point of View of an English Anti-Militarist.* . . . The compromise reached by the writer, put briefly, comes to this. Our country hates bloodshed and would, if it could, choose the path of reason and righteous arbitrament. But 'this time it has been driven along the old barbarian track, by an enemy who took the decision into his own hands. For us this time there was no choice. . . .' " And of Lansbury's *Herald*, much extremer doubtless than Neutrality League Radicalism, it has been written: "the *Herald*, like nearly all the rest of Britain, assumed at first that nothing else could have been done but declare war and fight it to the end" (R. Postgate, *Life of George Lansbury*, p. 153).

[2] Cf. Lord Ponsonby, *Falsehood in War-Time*, p. 79: "Babies not only had their hands cut off, but they were impaled on bayonets, and in one case nailed to a door. . . ." Even *The Times* had its part in quoting refugees to this effect though it refused credence to the "Mutilated Nurse" story, later thoroughly exposed in Court.

[3] Cf. Lord Ponsonby, *Falsehood in War-Time*, p. 44, for Mr. Lloyd George speaking at the Queen's Hall on September 21, 1914: "If any Servians were mixed up with the murder of the Archduke, they ought to be punished for it. Servia admits that. The Servian Government had nothing to do with it. . . . The Servian Prime Minister is one of the most capable and honoured men in Europe. Servia was willing to punish any of her subjects who had been proved to have any complicity. . . . What more could you expect?" In point of fact, the whole Servian Cabinet seems to have known of the plan of assassination though it was later claimed that a tardy attempt to stop the assassins had been made.

[4] Cf. *Daily Mail*, September 22, 1914, in a letter from the painter, Sir W. B. Richmond. It was Sir James Crichton-Browne, the distinguished doctor, who was there assigned the credit for having called "at Dumfries" for the Kaiser's halter.

was likely to make in a war against militarism and on behalf of small nationalities, the British public insisted on believing, with passion, that huge numbers of Russian troops had crossed Britain to take part in the defence of France and Belgium.[1] In short, there was credulity, ignorance, and prejudice enough to promise unexampled profit and power even to Horatio Bottomley's *John Bull* if only a more ruthless and vulgar anti-Germanism was affected than any other newspaper found the stomach for.[2] By 1918, Horatio Bottomley, despite a notorious swindling record which he was actually engaged in surpassing with *John Bull*'s own readers as the victims, was so much the hero of the trenches that, when the demobilization troubles arose, there was talk among the troops of putting him in Downing Street by force.[3]

It is just possible that if Morley and Burns, the Cabinet

---

[1] Cf. Amber Blanco White, *The New Propaganda*, p. 17, for the view that the rumour had been set going by the British Intelligence Service. "Their first great *coup*—the story that a Russian Army was being transported through Britain to reinforce the Western Front—was apparently started in order that it might be transmitted abroad by spies, but its reception in this country should have been, and to Intelligence doubtless was, an object lesson in human credulity." Lord Ponsonby's *Falsehood in War-Time*, pp. 84–7, would apparently have attached greater importance and greater blame to the false ascription to the Kaiser of the Army Orders "to exterminate first, the treacherous English, walk over General French's contemptible little army".

[2] Cf. Julian Symons, *Horatio Bottomley*, pp. 164–6: "Within a fortnight of the outbreak of the war, Bottomley, forgetful of the words that had so recently been written about Servia, was proclaiming that Germany 'must be wiped off the map of Europe' and her colonies and navy divided between France and Britain. The Kaiser received attention in such articles as 'The Potty Potentate of Potsdam' and 'No Mercy for the Berlin Butcher'. . . . He advocated hanging all German sailors or letting them drown. He said that the Zulus or Basutos should be armed and allowed to run amok on the enemy's ranks. He suggested the use of poison gas (this was before the Germans had used it) and said that no prisoners should be taken. He had always believed that the war would be a short one, and these measures would certainly end it in a few weeks."

[3] Cf. *Ibid.*, for a painstaking examination of Bottomley's swindling technique, going right back to his "promotion" of the Hansard Publishing Union and the Anglo-Austrian Printing and Publishing Union which resulted, in 1891, in his first petition in bankruptcy. His later exploits in the "Westralian" boom of the middle 1890s must have put millions of a trustful public's money into his hands for "developing" West Australia's gold-mining but nothing he touched seems to have brought anything but loss or ruin to investors. Since founding *John Bull* in 1906 he had introduced fraud into the allocation of competition prizes and whether or not he meant the Premium Bond Scheme and the Victory Bond Club of 1918–19 to be run differently, his planning proved woefully deficient and the itch to fraud over-powering. Yet this was the man whom some had been trying to push into a key-position even in 1916. According to Julian Symons, *Horatio Bottomley*, p. 179: "Just before Asquith's resignation at the end of 1916 the *Evening News* bore the words 'Bottomley Wanted'. . . . Soldiers on leave carried these placards through the streets, cheering Bottomley and demanding his inclusion in the Cabinet."

Ministers who had resigned rather than share responsibility for the war, had undertaken a vigorous and persistent campaign to explain their reasons, some of the more undesirable sides of Britain's war-mentality might not have developed so soon and so dangerously. But they knew better than the public what dangers their Cabinet colleagues and the British Army and Navy were facing and resolved not to add to their difficulties by giving any countenance to the kind of anti-war campaigning which it seemed, at first, only the Independent Labour Party was prepared for.[1] Yet Charles Trevelyan, the third Minister to resign, though, like Morley and Burns, averse to increasing the immediate difficulties of Army, Navy, and Cabinet, did not intend to stay muzzled for very long. Regarding it almost as his mission to organize a popular movement to prevent any further "secret diplomacy" of the kind that could already be blamed for Britain's entanglement in what were virtually war-alliances, uncommunicated to the people and Parliament till the last possible moment, Trevelyan was allying with Ramsay MacDonald and the two famous publicists, Norman Angell[2] and E. D. Morel,[3] to found the organization soon "notorious" as the Union of Democratic Control. As it was this U.D.C. that gradually prepared some of the country's most strenuous Radicalism to break from Liberal War Ministers, committed to an ever-more implacable armed struggle, and to seek admission, instead, into MacDonald's I.L.P., something should be said here of the organization's declared aims.[4] The

---

[1] Cf. *The Labour Year Book, 1916*, p. 18, for the I.L.P. Manifesto of August 13th concluding: "Across the roar of guns, we send sympathy and greetings to the German Socialists. They have laboured unceasingly to promote good relations with Britain, as we with Germany. They are no enemies of ours, but faithful friends. In forcing this appalling crime upon the nations, it is the rulers, the diplomats, the militarists who have sealed their doom. . . ."

[2] His *Great Illusion* of 1910 had already been extensively translated. As Manager of the Paris *Daily Mail* since its inception in 1905, the pre-war Norman Angell, destined though he was to bloom into a Labour M.P. by 1929, would hardly have been counted among the "advanced".

[3] Cf. F. S. Cocks, *E. D. Morel, The Man and his Work*, pp. 200–8, for Morel's adoption as Liberal candidate for Birkenhead in 1912 after a remarkable career in exposing the horrors associated with King Leopold's management of the Congo Free State, later the Belgian Congo. Morel laid down his candidature after war came in August 1914 but did not join the Independent Labour Party till March 1918.

[4] Caroline Playne's two books, *Society at War, 1914–1916* and *Britain Holds On, 1917–1918* will be found very revealing of feeling and thinking in the "progressive" camp. By contrast, *John Bull*'s attacks on the failing "Kur Hardie" and MacDonald reached the point where the demand was made for a court-martial on the "two traitors within our gates". *John Bull*'s violence defeated its own ends, however, for even the pro-war Labour majority rallied

letters sent out, in September 1914, to possible supporters ran thus:[1]

There are very many thousands of people in the country who are profoundly dissatisfied with the general course of policy which preceded the war. They are feeling that a dividing-point has come in national history, that the old traditions of secret and class-diplomacy, the old control of foreign policy by a narrow clique, and the power of the armament organizations have henceforth to be combated by a great and conscious and directed effort of the democracy. . . .

The objects we have in view are:

(1) To secure real parliamentary control over foreign policy, and to prevent it again being shaped in secret and forced upon the country as an accomplished fact.

(2) When peace returns to open direct and deliberate negotiations with democratic parties and influences on the Continent, so as to form an international understanding depending on popular parties rather than on governments.

(3) To aim at securing such terms that this war will not, either through the humiliation of the defeated nation or an artificial arrangement of boundaries, merely become the starting-point for new national antagonisms and future wars.

When the time is ripe for it, but not before the country is free from danger, meetings will be organized and speakers provided. . . .[2]

This is not the place to go into the detailed story of how the U.D.C. became merely the first of a number of war-born protest organizations including, finally, a No-Conscription Fellowship, a Fellowship of Reconciliation, and a Stop-the-War Committee. Nor is it even the place to illustrate how the U.D.C. was ultimately able to produce sufficient effect in key industrial areas like South Wales, Clydeside, and parts of the North of England to cause some anxiety even to War Cabinets apparently all-powerful at Westminster. Here it is necessary to turn back to some of the immediate difficulties war brought to a people and a Government far from fully prepared to participate in full-scale continental hostilities or even to have their normal financial and commercial

to MacDonald's defence, knowing, of course, of such things as his attempt to join in Ambulance work in Belgium, ended by an insulting arrest and deportation at British military request.

[1] Cf. H. M. Swanwick, *Builders of Peace, Being Ten years History of the Union of Democratic Control*, pp. 31–2.

[2] Cf. *Ibid.*, pp. 32–3, for some original troubles: "This private letter came into the possession of the *Morning Post* which published it together with an editorial claiming to have unearthed a conspiracy. . . . Other papers took up the cry. . . . It was therefore considered advisable very quickly to make the whole movement public."

routines exposed to major disturbances. Ministers, for example, had been so disquieted by the increased unemployment obvious even before August 4th that, at considerable financial cost, they made it almost a major aim of the war's first weeks to prevent the distress arising which, apart from anything else, might very quickly have turned the war from a "popular" to an "unpopular" one.[1] And it was possibly, not without guile, that they virtually invited all sections of the "Labour Movement" to co-operate with them as spokesmen for the "workers", finally allotting almost a privileged position to the War Emergency: National Workers' Committee which resulted.[2] Naturally, even if they half-expected some Socialist pressure in the shape of draft suggestions that would nearly all bear traces of Sidney Webb's hand,[3] they were confident of finding tactful means of evasion while yet keeping Labour's co-operation in the task of holding mass-unemployment at bay. Meantime, they won from "Labour" such important decisions as those by which full co-operation was promised for Army and Navy recruiting and full participation in a war-time "political truce".[4] In regard to recruiting, indeed, some of Labour's spokesmen almost matched Bottomley for the violent anti-Kaiserism they were prepared to employ,[5] and even Ramsay

---

[1] Cf. *Beatrice Webb's Diaries, 1912–24*, for some revealing entries, August 1914.

[2] Cf. *The Labour Year Book, 1916*, p. 39: "The Committee . . . is in constant touch with many Government departments on questions arising from the effects of the war, and is the recognised channel by which the workers' grievances and complaints are brought to the notice of the departments."

[3] Cf. *Ibid.*, pp. 32–5, for a very full-blooded thirteen-point programme including such items as "the inauguration of a comprehensive policy of municipal housing," "national care of motherhood, by the establishment of maternity and infant centres", and "the compulsory provision of meals and clothing for school-children, three meals a day, seven days a week".

[4] *Ibid.*, p. 19. There was even talk of an "industrial truce" as Unions, in dispute, found it wise, when mass-unemployment seemed to be threatening, to offer to submit to arbitration. Matters, of course, became very different in this field when labour-shortages began to develop.

[5] Cf. Ben Tillett, *Memories and Reflections*, p. 256, for other matter which strikingly recalls the kind of material that Bottomley was wont to announce in such notorious placards as "What Haig Told Me". Tillett, who liked to think of himself as having played an important part in the war, told this of Kitchener: "One incident in my talk with Lord Kitchener will remain in my memory as long as I live. I can see the great figure . . . shaking hands with me as we parted. He said gruffly, 'What are you going to tell the public, Mr. Tillett?' I replied with some emphasis, 'The truth, Lord Kitchener.' His cold eyes looked down into mine as he made his answer, 'Would to God I could tell the truth. Good day.' " And as Bottomley's recruiting efforts were later found to have yielded him very large sums of money, it must be presumed that the war-efforts Tillett described did not go completely unacknowledged. Indeed, good Socialists like the Webbs, pro-war though they were, could, by 1915, speak of the average Trade Union officer as having become almost Government-corrupted not only

MacDonald thought fit, in response to a Mayoral invitation to a great recruiting effort in his Leicester constituency, to write a message of qualified approval.[1]

Meanwhile, Ministers, despite their heavy war-commitments, had, perforce, to devote much attention still to what had been their principal constitutional problem since 1911—the enforcement of the Parliament Act of that year and the placing on the Statute Book, under its provisions, of the Home Rule and Welsh Disestablishment Bills as passed by the Commons, despite rejection by the Lords, in 1912, 1913, and 1914. On July 30th, in view of the possible war-emergency then approaching, Ministers, disregarding the impatience of some of their more "advanced" supporters, had refrained from counter-attack upon the Lords for their sweeping alteration of the Home Rule Amending Bill as well as for their hold-up of the Home Rule Bill proper. After war came, the need for a party-truce was seen to be very urgent, and Ministers made considerable efforts, before setting the machinery in motion for winding up the Session, to convince the Opposition Leadership that they were prepared to go farther in compromise than would be at all to the taste of Redmond's rank-and-file or their own Liberal and Radical "advanced men".[2] There were Ulstermen, of course, who tried to get Bonar Law and Lord Lansdowne to accept nothing less than the complete dropping of the Home Rule Bill till the war was over. Even by normal Opposition standards this was too much, and Ministers were offered, instead, Opposition's readiness for legislation that would freeze the existing constitutional situation as it was till after the war, "the Parliament Act Bills" not going to the Statute Book but not losing, either, the relative proximity to it which a favourably-disposed Government, if such a one was in charge at the end of the war, might still seek to use.

by the hope of getting a highly paid official post, but by the more insidious method of fat allowances for service on Committees. (*Beatrice Webb's Diaries, 1912–1924*, p. 45.)

[1] Cf. L. MacNeill Weir, *The Tragedy of Ramsay MacDonald*, pp. 63–4: "My opinions regarding the causes of the war are pretty well known, except in so far as they have been misrepresented; but we are in it. . . . I want the serious men of the Trade Union, the Brotherhood, and similar movements, to face their duty. To such men it is enough to say 'England has need of you'; to say it in the right way. They will gather to her aid."

[2] Cf. Sir Charles Petrie, *Life and Letters of Austen Chamberlain*, ii, 1–14, for evidence that Harcourt, Lloyd George, and Winston Churchill were all in contact, during August and the first half of September, with Opposition's ex-Chancellor of the Exchequer on Irish questions.

To judge from the articles on the Irish question which "A Radical Member" had been contributing to the "advanced men's" favourite weekly, *The Nation*,[1] there would have been a Back-Bench revolt against any Minister or Ministers prepared even to parley on such a basis. Ministers, too, knew better than the Back-Benchers their desperate need not to antagonize the powerful communities of Irish Catholic descent living in the United States and the Dominions at a time when, as at the end of August and the beginning of September, the fall of Paris looked more likely than not.[2] And the amount of rage that could be generated even in the British House of Commons by the suggestion that Home Rule should now be abandoned for the duration of the war, the ex-Prime Minister, Balfour, was made to feel in person on August 31st.[3] It was on September 9th that the Opposition Leaders got their last chance of coming to terms with Ministers when they met in order to come to a decision on a Memorandum from Mr. Asquith in which two alternative ways of winding up the Session were suggested though they were told, in advance, that "it was very doubtful whether the second would be acceptable to his followers". The Prime Minister, in short, was prepared, if assured of Opposition co-operation, to try his utmost to press upon Redmond, the Radicals, and the Labour men a solution, obviously unpalatable even to his own Cabinet and only envisaged as a means of making a striking display of national war-unity to the world. And the Opposition Leaders, while rejecting Mr. Asquith's first alternative which commanded more assured support from his

[1] Cf. *The Nation*, July 25, 1914, for the "Radical Member" voicing his objections strongly even to the "Royal interference, however technically constitutional" which had taken place when the Buckingham Palace Conference had been called by the King and an invitation sent "to men who had taken up an attitude of open rebellion against the Government of the day". The "London Diary" for the July 25th number of *The Nation* suggested that Ministers' following would break up if they consented, under "Court" or other pressure to a General Election with Home Rule uncarried or, if nominally carried, unenforced. An interesting examination of the three brands of British opinion behind Home Rule spoke of "the Labour Party watching keenly and sullenly a State palaver to which they are not invited. . . . The Liberals have remained loyal, but they are very uneasy, and the Radicals resentful of the implied slighting of Parliament. Why, they ask, should the Prime Minister shoulder full responsibility for a speech which he did not initiate and did not even draft?"
[2] Cf. *Life and Letters of Austen Chamberlain*, ii, 11, for Mr. Winston Churchill's appeal to Austen Chamberlain.
[3] Cf. *The Nation*, September 5, 1914, on "the dismay, amazement, and anger that swept over the House as the wrecking intention of the performance became manifest".

following, decided, not without reluctance, to accept the second, based on the following principles:[1]

(1). The Home Rule Bill to go on the Statute Book, but not to come into operation for, say, six months.

(2). Six Ulster counties to be provisionally excluded for three years.

(3). At the end of three years the Imperial Parliament to determine the whole question of exclusion, and the six counties not to be included until this had been done.

(4). Sir Edward Carson, Mr. Redmond, and their friends to accept the decision "until another new Parliament".

Unfortunately, as it proved, Mr. Asquith finally had to tell the Opposition Leaders that the plan which they had accepted was not welcome "either to his colleagues or to the leading members of his party", and that as a result, the Cabinet would, on September 14th, have to proceed with the alternative plan. Briefly, that plan was for:[2]

(1). The Irish Bill to be put on the Statute Book.

(2). Its operation to be suspended by a provision that it was deemed to be passed on a date one year later than the date of the Royal Assent or the end of the war, whichever was the later.

(3). The Government to undertake in the next session to introduce an Amending Bill, and to prosecute this until disposed of either by acceptance or rejection.

There are some strange stories as to how the final Cabinet decision was reached,[3] and no doubt there was sufficient anti-Carsonism

---

[1] Cf. *Life and Letters of Austen Chamberlain*, ii, 5.

[2] *Ibid.*

[3] Cf. David Garnett, *The Flowers of the Forest*, pp. 11–12, for one of the strangest, based on reports given to Garnett by Francis Birrell, son of the Irish Secretary. According to the younger Birrell, Kitchener, Asquith, and Grey were all originally opposed to the course ultimately taken, and the issue was decided after the Irish Secretary determined to resign rather than have a large retreat from the Government's Home Rule commitment. Three important Ministers finally rallied to Birrell's side though for different reasons. Churchill accepted the contention that powerful military forces would be immobilized in an antagonized Ireland; Lloyd George feared that a Cabinet and Party split, following on Birrell's resignation, would force Asquith to ask the Conservatives into a Coalition Government and that he, in the existing Conservative temper, would be excluded; and Grey, who had, at first been opposed to Birrell changed his mind after the arrival of a private secretary from the United States who told him that American opinion would be more influenced by Redmond than by any number of White Papers. But, according to Garnett's report from the younger Birrell: "It was a very near thing. Asquith had already made tentative proposals to the Conservatives on paper and Bonar Law waved them in the Prime Minister's face before the Unionists walked out of the Commons. They were not however divulged." There is here obviously some basis of fact.

still rabid on the Radical Back-Benches to turn the scale against giving Sir Edward even an incomplete Six-Counties victory over that "faithful ally", Mr. Redmond. It was known, moreover, that the Irish Leader had pledged himself to help in a recruiting drive in Catholic Ireland directly Home Rule was on the Statute Book unaccompanied by a precise Six-Counties "surrender" to Carson. Nevertheless, Mr. Bonar Law's angry comparison of Mr. Asquith's standard of honour (in withdrawing the original commitment) to that of the German Minister, responsible for tearing up the Belgian Treaty, did little good abroad[1] even if Radicals felt the satisfaction of the righteous at the spectacle of Bonar Law, Lansdowne, and Carson all temporarily worsted.[2]

In point of fact though Redmond, amid the cheers of virtually all the "progressives",[3] attempted to persuade Ireland that it was now Irishmen's duty to help Britain, whose democracy had behaved so honourably,[4] it was plain, before long, that he was failing against the efforts of Sinn Fein and other "extremists".[5] It tooks years for it to become plain what all this might portend and, meanwhile, Ulster could claim to have an increasing case for declaring that, whereas all its young Protestant manhood had streamed out to fight, the Irish Volunteers were staying behind in a way that seemed ever more menacing. Of course, there were sections of "progressive" thought which, even after the Rebellion

[1] Accompanied as it was by the Unionist walk-out of September 15th, it gave the world notice that there were still some very serious rifts in Britain.

[2] Cf. *The Nation*, September 26, 1914, for an end-of-the-Session demonstration that Redmond contrived to make less partisan than some Radicals would have had it.

[3] Cf. *Ibid.*, September 26th, October 3rd, and October 10th, for judgements on the situation preceding and following the Dublin Mansion House meeting of September 25th in which Asquith had called for an Irish Army Corps from the Volunteers and Redmond had endorsed the appeal.

[4] Cf. *Ibid.*, September 19th quoting Mr. Redmond's Manifesto just issued: "The democracy of Great Britain listened to our appeal and kept faith with Ireland. It is now a duty of honor for Ireland to keep faith with them."

[5] Cf. *Ibid.*, October 3rd, for some early realization that matters would not be easy. "We must not," said a somewhat chastened *Nation*, "expect too great a rush of Irish Volunteers to the colors until Mr. Redmond has had time to settle the question of the control of the organization and its funds. This he has had no chance to do while the centre of the Irish battle for Home Rule lay at Westminster. Now that he and Mr. Devlin are in the field, the overwhelming strength of the Irish Nationalist Party will no doubt bear down its rivals. But what student of Irish politics ever expected to exorcise its secular anti-Englandism at one wave of the Home Rule wand? Behind the organized parties in Ireland lies a loose body of opinion . . . with some power of giving trouble to the orthodox leaders . . . Sinn Feiners . . . Larkinites, pro-Germans, National Volunteers, and disgruntled politicians . . . there may be some intimidation practised on Volunteers who are anxious to enlist."

in Dublin at Eastertide 1916, could contrive to blame Kitchener
and the War Office[1] rather than their own shallow Utopianism,
for the beautiful Liberal dream of permanent Anglo-Irish reconciliation having failed of realization. But many other lovely dreams
had failed by then—a decisive "pursuit" of the Germans, for
example, who had been checked at the Marne,[2] a relatively speedy
collapse of Austria under Russian assault,[3] or of Turkey under
the menace of the Dardanelles expedition[4] and, finally, the kind
of dream that began, even before the end of 1914, to see signs of
growing financial and economic difficulties in Germany.[5]

It was not Asquith but Lloyd George who was the first Cabinet
Leader to detect that there might be something basically unsound
in the way even Kitchener was thinking about the war, especially
in the field of Munitions Supply. Much of Asquith's attention
was doubtless distracted by such problems as the best type of
reprisal to take in retaliation for the German "submarine
blockade"[6] or what to do about Welsh Disestablishment and the
Plural Voting Bill which should not antagonize his Radicals on the
one hand or, on the other, give the Opposition, bitterly critical on

[1] Cf. David Garnett, *The Flowers of the Forest*, p. 12: "Birrell was also furious
with Kitchener for having an article published in Ireland saying: 'Lord Kitchener
is disgusted at the poor response in Ireland to his appeal for recruits; unless you
enlist, Territorials will be sent to Ireland which will be a humiliation etc.' In
point of fact 18,000 Irishmen had by then enlisted of whom 14,000 were
Nationalists. Birrell and Kitchener were by then not on speaking terms and
were soon fighting over another matter. Birrell asked that a large proportion of
'Kitchener's Army' should be trained in Ireland."

[2] Cf. *Field-Marshal Sir Henry Wilson, His Life and Diaries*, i, 177–8, for this
high Staff Officer's discussing with equally over-confident French generals
whether it would be three or four weeks before the Anglo-French forces were
on German soil. And even after the Germans had halted their retreat on the
Aisne, he was still confidently predicting "that the war will be over in February
or March".

[3] Cf. *The Nation*, September 19, 1914: "Austria's ruin (with the Serbs still
successful in the South) is not to be averted."

[4] Cf. *Ibid.*, March 13, 1915, for discussion of how the arrival of the powerful
Anglo-French bombarding squadrons in February had already tempted Greece
towards the Allied camp and might yet be made to tempt Rumania and Bulgaria.

[5] Cf. *Ibid.*, September 26, 1914: "One must not make too much of the stories
of economic distress in Germany. To some extent Germany resembles us, only
more so. The huge draft which the army makes on her male population has cut
away a great mass of unemployment, and has also set the industries which supply
the soldiery going at full speed. . . . She has gold in abundance—she had a
special war reserve of one hundred millions—and her internal loan has been
fully and rapidly taken up. Unemployment there is, and both Berlin and
Hamburg are centres of distress. But not till next spring, think the well-
informed, will the great pressure come, and then with terrible severity, so terrible
that an end of the war about that period is rather confidently hoped for."

[6] Cf. *Hansard*, March 1st, for Asquith's announcement of the form reprisals
would take. There had been long consultations with Russia and France.

his Home Rule decisions of 1914, added ground of complaint in 1915. The Prime Minister doubtless guessed already that the Opposition might soon have to be invited into a Coalition Government, and his decision that there would be no Government Plural Voting Bill in 1915, and that therefore "One Man One Vote" was to gain nothing from the Parliament Act during the war but might have to start again, from the very beginning, at the war's end was certainly a considerable concession to Bonar Law and Lord Lansdowne. And Welsh Disestablishment, on the Statute Book though it was already, saw a further concession which came near to provoking a Welsh Radical revolt. Here is the Radicals' favourite weekly, *The Nation*, rebuking the Prime Minister in March 1915 when his principal concerns were, doubtless, the U-Boats and American objections to Britain's retaliatory programme:[1]

The Government have so far bowed to the Opposition in the Lords and the Duke of Devonshire's Bill on the Welsh Church as to give the Establishment a further *moratorium*. Disestablishment is not to take effect till six months after the war. On their side, the Opposition pledge themselves not to agitate for the repeal of the Act till the expiration of that time. Of course they can begin the day after it. The chief effect of this extension of the truce is to improve the terms of compensation for life interests. And the measure itself would seem to be imperilled, for a General Election will now almost certainly precede the time fixed for its operation. The concession was also made without consultation with the Welsh Liberal Members, who are furious. . . . Meetings of the revolters have been held, and addressed by Mr. McKenna, but without apparent effect. The Prime Minister has been told that the Welshmen consider that there has been a breach of the pledge to introduce no controversial matter, and that they will speak and vote against a second reading. They have also appealed for Nonconformist help in the House, and have obtained it. It is a pity that the Government acts so often without taking its followers into its confidence and carrying them with it. In the Welsh case, only one party, and that the opposition, was consulted.

Two Ministers who counted as quite combative Radicals capable, in peace-time, of having very much to say on a Prime

---

[1] *The Nation*, March 13, 1915. The same number contained a piece of intelligence probably not wholly unconnected with the need for meeting Opposition: "The Opposition in the Commons opened on Thursday a tentative attack on the administration of the War Office, led by Mr. Walter Long. The chief charges were the bad selection of sites for camps, confusion in methods of recruiting for the two kinds of army—'Kitchener's' and the Territorials; the poor payment of regimental officers even when wounded. . . ."

Minister's going too far in meeting the views of Opposition and the House of Lords, were Lloyd George and Dr. Addison, both now occupied with major problems against which the Disestablishment "grievance" doubtless sank to its true proportions. Addison had gone as Under-Secretary to the Board of Education in Trevelyan's place and, before long, even in that Department apparently so far removed from war-issues, had been brought up against Britain's marked inferiority to Germany in many fields of technology, an inferiority which was soon to threaten disaster in the field of Munitions Supply to the Services. He was encouraged by his chief, Pease, and by Lloyd George to remodel the "educational reforms" of the 1914 Budget, virtually laid aside when war came, so that they had an obvious relation to Britain's actual problems. And as some of the results of Addison's work were important for the future, it might be well to let him tell the story of how he was occupied before being chosen by Lloyd George as his Under-Secretary in a completely new Ministry of Munitions. Mentioning "some proposals I had prepared for Lloyd George before the Budget for increasing the facilities for technical and higher education",[1] Addison continued his diary account of how he was authorized, on December 2, 1914, to set up a Board of Education Committee which might revive and readapt the original plans. By January 19, 1915 he was giving Britain's first two heads of a yet uncreated Munitions Ministry, Lloyd George and Edwin Montagu, his view of the critical dearth of trained British scientists and technologists which war-events had already revealed in dye-making, explosives manufacture, the glass industry, and many other fields. An impression was obviously made, for ten days later Addison was asked to see Lord Haldane and consultations began on possible foundations for what ultimately became the National Council of Scientific and Industrial Research.

Meanwhile the more direct work needing to be done to secure an adequate flow of talented students to British science and technology continued, by May 4th Government approval had been obtained, and, on May 13th, Pease as President of the Board of Education revealed the details in an official statement on a State Scholarship plan. Gifted students at secondary and technical schools were to be given the means to continue their training, and the universities and similar institutions were to be aided in

[1] *Politics from Within, 1911–1918*, i, 48–52.

providing the additional facilities necessary. The scheme was to begin with 120 whole-time selected technical students and provision was to be made for the number to rise to 300, while a parallel stream would flow, not from technical schools or classes, but from the secondary schools.

This account should undoubtedly be read in conjunction with the story of the remarkable raids into the Munitions field which Lloyd George had meanwhile been making. Within six or seven weeks of the opening of the war, it became obvious that the danger of massive Unemployment Distress was largely passing and that the flood of war-orders for everything from muskets, greatcoats, and hutted camps, to transports, battle-ships, and tinned foods was likely to bring on, before long, a number of labour-shortages.[1] By the winter-months of 1914–15, indeed, there were already colourful reports of many kinds of pay-packets, much swollen by continuous work at over-time rates, and often misspent on drinking-bouts with their own calamitous after-effects on war-production in centres like the engineering shops and the ship-yards. Of course, these accounts often omitted to stress such facts as that the swollen pay-packets were still confined to very specialized kinds of craftsmen,[2] that the employers' profits, in such cases, tended to be even more grossly swollen and that, finally, there were still very considerable classes of labour—especially women's labour—whose earnings had been diminished by the war, while the price of their food and coal had risen steeply.[3]

[1] Cf. *The Nation*, September 26, 1914: "West Yorkshire is booming. Immense orders for blankets and shirts have been received, and the mills are working at the highest possible pressure. It is not only the custom of the army but of our allies which makes for this tremendous output. Russia and France have both lodged orders for boots and other necessaries which tax our productive power, great as it is, to the utmost." Even cotton, which had been hard-hit was beginning a recovery while, before long, farmers in some parts of the country were reported to be aghast at the wholesale volunteering of married farm-labourers, attracted by the—to them—generous Army allowances for wife and children.

[2] Cf. *Ibid.*, December 26, 1914: "A very large proportion of the million a day expended directly on the costs of war goes in demand for labor in the engineering, shipbuilding, cutlery, leather, woollen and other clothing trades, as well as in those trades directly engaged in making arms and ammunition. Even the building trades in many districts are kept in full activity by war-contracts for military huts."

[3] *Ibid.*: "Professional, clerical, and distributive employment must have been subjected to large shrinkages. . . . The case of women-workers also deserves grave attention . . . a far larger proportion of women are occupied in small businesses and in those fashion, luxury, and other less organized trades which have suffered most through the economies which all classes of the consuming public have been impelled to practise. . . . After the preliminary panic of early

Yet when Lloyd George entered the field of major Munitions propaganda in a Sunday address at Bangor on February 28, 1915, there were generations of Radical Temperance tradition behind his readiness to assign such weight to the drinking-stories from the Munitions centres as to justify the announcement that the Government was considering how to counter the "lure of drink". The fact that Russia could be quoted as having suppressed the sale of vodka and France the sale of absinthe apparently increased the strength of the Chancellor's case for something parallel in Britain.[1]

Though the Temperance advocacy of Lloyd George eventually produced the war-time Control Board despite "Labour" protests that he was maligning the British workman, it was his urgency that the public, the Trade Unions, and the employers should realize how much peace-time productions patterns needed to be changed if Munitions Supply was to suffice for the needs of Britain and the Allies which proved more historic. He was, doubtless, aware when he spoke at Bangor on February 28th that the Amalgamated Society of Engineers had given a cold reception both to an employers' approach of December[2] and to a War Office appeal of February 8th in Parliament,[3] and that, as a result, the

August food prices fell to a level of about 10 per cent above the July figure. But since September they have been gradually rising, and at the beginning of this month they stood at 17 per cent above the July level in large towns, and 15 per cent in the small towns and villages. Now this a movement of serious import." By the time of the debate in the Commons on February 11, 1915, food and fuel prices had risen further.

[1] Cf. *The Nation*, March 6, 1915: "Now, no one acquainted with what is going on can give his charge a point-blank denial. Mr. George insisted that in many of these absolutely vital trades there are men who 'refuse to work a full week's work for the nation's need' and it is 'the lure of the drink' which leads these men astray. . . . But because we are not prepared to go so far as Russia, or even France, may we not go a little farther than we do? . . . If all places where liquor was for sale were prohibited from opening before eight a.m., a stoppage would be placed upon the practice of early morning 'nips'. If again, all public houses and clubs were closed for the sale of alcohol at nine o'clock, in accord with our general curfew policy, such restrictions would, no doubt, with some grumbling at first, soon settle down into a serviceable usage."

[2] Cf. *Ibid.*, February 27, 1915, for a contribution from G. D. H. Cole in defence of the engineers' rejecting the employers' approach on ending, for the duration of the war, the Amalgamated Society's restrictions on the manning of machines and hand-operations, the demarcation of work between trades, the employment of non-union and female labour, and the whole question of the limitation of over-time. One of the engineers' fears was a vast post-war surplus of trained labour in their trade.

[3] Cf. *Ibid.*, February 13, 1915, for Kitchener's Under-Secretary in the Commons, Tennant, making "an appeal to the Labor Party to help the Government by relaxing trade union rules that interfered with the dispatch of Government business, and particularly in connection with work on armaments" and getting "some sharp retorts from Labor Members".

first considerable Munitions strike of the war had begun on Clydeside with a demand for an increase of 2*d*. an hour for engineers. Of course, all sorts of justification could be advanced for the engineers, the rise in their employers' profits, for example, and the increased cost of living,[1] and possibly the Chancellor was not altogether diplomatic when, alongside his demand for compulsory arbitration in war-time industry, he declared it "intolerable that the lives of Britons should be imperilled for the matter of a farthing an hour". Certainly, the Radicals' own weekly, *The Nation*, to whose thinking J. L. Hammond brought the sometimes over-indulgent pro-Trade Unionism of the *Town Labourer* and the *Village Labourer*,[2] took a surprising line in its next number with an editorial entitled "WHY LABOR IS SUSPICIOUS" which can hardly have been wholly to the Chancellor's liking. Here are significant passages:[3]

> Nothing is gained by abusing the workmen on the Clyde, or by telling them that they are betraying Great Britain, or Europe, or civilization, for the sake of a sordid five-farthings an hour. Nothing is gained by wild dreams of coercion and martial law. . . .
> Now the main fact about the temper of a great body of working people is that it is full of suspicion . . . but there is a special element in the suspiciousness of very many of the younger workmen. They do not merely suspect the employer. They suspect Parliament and they suspect their leaders . . . we must remember that the last few years have been marked by a number of prosecutions of working men, and a conspicuous refusal to persecute rich and powerful men for similar offences. The House of Commons was not struck by the spectacle of Mr. Mann serving a sentence for sedition, while Privy Councillors were allowed to be as seditious as they pleased, as many working men were struck by

[1] Cf. David Kirkwood, *My Life of Revolt*, p. 89, for the leader of the Clydeside strike claiming, with some exaggeration: "By this time prices of necessaries had risen so much that sixpence an hour would have been more reasonable than twopence an hour." Kirkwood admitted in his autobiography that he was an I.L.P. stop-the-war man but argued also that he had put forward the 2*d.* demand before the war and that a squad of engineers brought in from America were being paid a good deal more than the strikers were asking. He was, in fact, ready himself, in February, to settle for an advance of a penny an hour, one farthing more than the employers had offered.

[2] Cf. F. A. Hayek (ed.), *Capitalism and the Historian*, for a distinct reaction against the type of economic history Hammond wrote as over-biased against Capital. Yet its influence on the "progressive" thinking of the time is very obvious as when Arnold Bennett defending workmen in the *Daily News* in February against charges of under-production is summarized thus: "He cannot forget that the workman is not merely a citizen helping his country: he is a combatant in a struggle, a century old, against the power of capital. It is right and proper for him to remember this, and to maintain the strength of his class. . . ."

[3] *The Nation*, March 6, 1915.

it. Politicians think the trouble has blown over, but some day the nation has to pay for it.

The element of suspicion is not going to be eliminated at a moment's notice and represents the habitual outlook of a great number of men and women on the life of the society to which they belong. . . . War has merely revealed the extent of its influence. But this is not to say that this temper is quite unamenable. Why should not Mr. Lloyd George . . . go to one of the big industrial centres and speak plainly and openly on the facts. . . . He has the power that no other man possesses of making this great human tragedy a real influence in the daily lives of men and women.

When the Chancellor made the next important move for increasing the Munitions supply by introducing a new Defence of the Realm Bill on March 9th and urging its immediate passage through the House, the Radicals of *The Nation* still had some criticism even though it was not the rights of Labour but those of Capital that were under threat in a Bill permitting the taking-over of many types of factory never contemplated in the original Defence of the Realm Act. Though accepting the Government's word that the new measure was not a mere manœuvre to ease the way for what some were already calling the "conscription of Labour", *The Nation*, among other things, asked why the armament firms were still left to their own devices though they could already have been taken over under the 1914 Defence of the Realm legislation. It complained of the way Ministers were treating Parliament when hurriedly summoning it to pass legislation at top speed and almost undiscussed, and it made a real grievance of a Defence of the Realm Bill, already before Parliament, to extend the scope of military jurisdiction. But to indicate what Radical thought was busy with at this time, it might be best to let *The Nation* of March 13th speak for itself in the following passages from an article entitled "On Government by Persuasion":

"Even in time of war," urged *The Nation*, "the Government exercise no divine or prescriptive rights. They must satisfy the nation. . . . They should trust to persuasion and debate. . . . They should keep Parliament at work instead of summoning it for a series of brief and breathless Sessions and then dismissing it. Above all they should trust and freely employ the best forms of capacity . . . that is civil capacity. We cannot say that these qualities are conspicuous in the Government's treatment of the two Defence of the Realm Acts. Act No. 1 has thus far been presented in both Houses of Parliament without, as far as we can ascertain, one argument which really appeals to the civilian. The

Government has not yet explained why a military court . . . should be given authority to judge all Englishmen. . . .

"Act No. II may be described as a measure of emergency Social-ism. . . . It gives the Government leave to take over and control any factories or workshops capable of producing munitions of war. This tremendous proposition was not submitted to the House of Commons in the shape of a printed Bill. . . . Nevertheless Mr. George invited the House to pass it at a single sitting. . . . A second day was given . . . the capitalist's right of property and direct management is swept away. He will be entitled *ex gratia* to indemnification but this will not, it appears, be a statutory right, or cover indirect losses. It was natural for a Radical member to ask whether this ukase was also to be applied to labor. The Chancellor insisted that martial law was not to be applied. . . .

The Government have for months had power to take over the businesses whose equipment and management are specially designed for the manufacture of war material. What has happened to the great armament firms? We do not believe that on any question concerning the war a stronger public opinion exists than that the manufacture of munitions for private profit should cease. The general reason of policy is obvious. An enormous stimulant to the existence of this world-war has been supplied by the co-operative activities of these firms.

Some of the characteristic limitations of the doctrinaire Radical are very obvious in this passage. Thus, the whole question of Armament production is discussed in what might be called an anti-armament spirit at the very time when shortage of munitions had become critical. Then, the necessity for enlisting the practical knowledge and experience of the armament firms, and even their enthusiasm, is totally ignored—and this, too, at a time when heavy taxation, if not total confiscation, of their "excess profits" was in question as the one thing which might tempt the unions to surrender their right to strike and their restrictive craft-practices for the duration of the war. Certainly when, on March 9th, Lloyd George announced the Government as on the look-out for a "man of push and go" to put in charge of the whole arrangements for Armaments production,[1] he was undoubtedly cutting loose from much of the characteristic thinking on Armaments on his own side of politics. And by the time he had used the "emergency Socialism" of his new Defence of the Realm Act as one argument to secure the assent of over thirty trade unions to a maximum war-

[1] Cf. *The Nation*, March 13th, for a convenient summary: "Mr. Lloyd George's opening speech was too brief . . . but in supplementary speeches he explained that the Government was looking for a capable business man who would be at the head of a Committee for pushing through the organization and mobilization of engineering and the allied industries. . . ."

production programme, and the coming "excess profits" taxation
of their employers as another, it was doubtless beginning to
emerge that the man of "push and go" might have to be Lloyd
George himself.[1] A last Temperance Budget with extra taxation
of spirits and beer was, probably, very much on Lloyd George's
mind already even if it was not introduced till May 4th;[2] the
probable necessity for a speedy Coalition, involving a drastic
reconstruction of the Government, was out of no one's thoughts
who was enough behind the scenes really to know how unsatisfactory had been the results of the first Anglo-French offensives
of March 1915, results which the British Command in the field
was soon, in a notorious Press campaign, trying to ascribe to the
Kitchener régime at the War Office;[3] and a Ministry of Munitions
under Lloyd George was, doubtless, not a pure improvisation, to
be dated wholly after Navy troubles added to those of the Army,
forced on Government reconstruction by May 17th.[4] But the
political, Press, and Service backgrounds of the Government
crisis of May 1915, that ended Britain's last purely Liberal
Administration, need detailed treatment in a new chapter if something of the uniqueness of the situation is to be recaptured.

[1] Cf. *The Nation*, March 27th: "The conference at the Treasury between Mr.
Lloyd George and the representatives of the trade unions lasted three days last
week, and they reached an agreement which the representatives of some thirty-
three trade unions undertook to recommend to their members. . . . The A.S.E.
at first refused to agree, but at a further conference 'signed on'. They have consented to relax some of their restrictions, on condition that the Government
limit private profits to the advantage of the State."

[2] Cf. *Hansard*, April 29th, for the introduction of the proposals for increased
Liquor taxation in advance of the Budget proper on May 4th, "the most
stupendous in our financial history," as the journalists were soon calling it, with
estimated revenue of £270,332,000 and estimated expenditure of £1,132,654,000
(on the assumption that the war lasted to the end of the financial year). The
war's daily cost was now £2,100,000.

[3] Cf. *Field-Marshal Sir Henry Wilson, His Life and Diaries*, i, 214: "After
7½ months of war we have exhausted all our available ammunition in an attack
by three divisions." The bigger offensive of May 9th went just as badly, and
the Commander-in-Chief, Sir John French, taking advantage of Kitchener's
having asked for some of his inadequate ammunition for the Dardanelles, sent
two A.D.C.s to London to see Bonar Law, Balfour, and Lloyd George. In his
book *1914* this figures as the main cause of the reconstitution of the Government
as a Coalition.

[4] *Life and Letters of Austen Chamberlain*, ii, 22, for Asquith's putting a first
list of names before Bonar Law on May 17th.

CHAPTER VII

HOW COALITION CAME, 1915

The Nation, May 1st: "*The Times* seems to make a rather fumbling business of its policy of deposing the Prime Minister and setting up a semi-demi-Coalition . . . the attacks on Mr. Asquith are conducted with such a multitude of reserves that one would suspect either an unconvinced writer, spurred on by a whole-hearted proprietor, or a campaigning scribe checked by a doubting over-lord. . . . With as little definite statement as possible, it is hinted that certain Ministers—the Prime Minister, Lord Haldane, Mr. McKenna (at times Sir Edward Grey)—are inferior to their colleagues in wisdom, energy, resourcefulness, and power of organization; that other Ministers —such as Mr. Lloyd George and Mr. Churchill—are not open to these criticisms and that the nation might do well to replace its less efficient servants by others. The list varies from time to time, one Minister stepping down from the pillory and another taking his place. An obviously slighting treatment of Lord Kitchener is a recurring feature of these manœuvres. In effect the movement is one for dispossessing the present Government . . . in favour of a Coalition of which Mr. Balfour would be the most conspicuous member though Mr. Law and Mr. Chamberlain are added as an emergency afterthought. An index finger is usually pointed at Mr. Lloyd George— notably in *The Pall Mall Gazette*—as the governing spirit of such an Administration."

> Lord Northcliffe mounting an attack on the Asquith Government.

The Nation, October 30, 1915: "The country will welcome the announcement that, on Tuesday next, the Prime Minister will address Parliament, and through it, the nation, on the state of the war. Mr. Asquith is bound thus to speak to the nation, for he is its supreme representative. In that capacity he is directly assailed—his policy, his judgement, his personality. By a hundred bye-paths of suggestion, the people have been invited to conclude that he is unfitted to direct their destinies. . . . Mr. Asquith is, we suppose, the ablest head of a Cabinet that the country possesses. None of his colleagues would dispute this title. . . . Are all these gifts, and the capacity of right and orderly government with which they are associated . . . so outweighed by other defects that Mr. Asquith ought to give way to some undiscovered genius? To be quite plain—is

Mr. Lloyd George this man? And, if we may put the consequent proposition, is either or any political party, among whom admirers of Mr. George's attractive gifts abound, prepared to propose him as an alternative head of Government? We wish to utter no disparaging comment when we say that such an exchange is unthinkable. What other presents itself? Mr. Balfour is a statesman of the same rank and quality as Mr. Asquith but he is an older man. We search the field of Cabinet politics in vain for a third possible Prime Minister, and we conclude that the country would be indisposed to place its fortunes in the hands of Lord Curzon. . . ."

A defence of Asquith's Prime Ministership against continued criticism.

I T was doubtless folly for the average British citizen to expect better results from the war than he got between August 1914 and May 1915, seeing the petty army he had started with and the tremendous expansion called for in its numbers, training, and supplies before it could even hope to be in a position to alter the face of things in Western Europe. Yet better results than he was getting the British citizen certainly did demand by the spring of 1915, it having been a specially painful surprise to him to find the considerable enterprise and dash of Germany's naval and air forces ("dastardly" though their methods might be), unmatched apparently by anything similar on the British side. British counter-measures as the full financial, economic and man-power resources of a tremendous Empire were brought to bear were privately recognized by the enemy leaders as full of peril to themselves but they could never, even if more fully grasped by the "public" than they were, evoke the same emotional response as a Zeppelin raid,[1] a cruiser sortie,[2] or a submarine foray.[3] In these circumstances what Radicals called the "baser parts of the Press", with *John Bull* conspicuous from the very beginning, were already busy, during the winter of 1914–15 finding their own reasons for the "un-satisfactory state of the war". Spies and secret agents were claimed to exist in large numbers among the unfortunate German and Austro-Hungarian nationals caught by the war in Britain[4] and all

[1] Cf. *Whitaker's Almanack, 1915*, Diary of the European War, pp. 486–8, for mention of various English and French attacks on Zeppelin installations, raids on London and Paris having already become an unpleasant possibility. It was on December 26th (*Ibid., 1916*, Diary of the War) that the first intervention of Zeppelins in naval fighting is mentioned and for January 19, 1915 the report is: "Zeppelin raids on Yarmouth, King's Lynn, Snettisham, and other Norfolk towns and villages; four persons killed."

[2] Cf. *Ibid., 1915*, Diary of the European War, for the *Emden's* raiding among others, not to mention the decisive appearance of the *Goeben* and *Breslau* at Constantinople, which helped the Germans to bring Turkey into the war on their side, and Von Spee's naval victory off the coast of Chile on November 1st. The *Emden* entries are these; September 20th: "The German cruiser *Emden* captured six British merchantmen in East Indian waters, and shelled the oil tanks at Madras; September 29th: "German cruiser *Emden* sank four more British steamships; October 21st: "The sinking of five further British steamers by the *Emden* was announced"; October 28th: "The German cruiser *Emden* entered Penang disguised and sank a Russian cruiser and a French destroyer." It was on November 10th that the *Emden's* destruction by the Australian cruiser, *Sydney* was announced.

[3] *Ibid.*, under September 22nd for the first really serious news: "German submarines torpedoed the cruisers *Aboukir*, *Hague*, and *Cressy*, the loss of life amounting to about 1,400 officers and men, 900 being saved."

[4] Cf. Lord Ponsonby, *Falsehood in War-Time*, p. 152: "Almost every foreign governess or waiter in the country was under grave suspicion, and numberless

had their special part to play, it was claimed, if a German force were ever landed. "Intern them all" became, in fact, a demand to which Ministers ultimately had to give way a good deal further than some of them deemed wise.

But matters did not stop there, for soon the hunt was up against the naturalized Germans, Sir Edgar Speyer included, and the enemy Royalties whose Garter banners were still displayed in St. George's Chapel, Windsor. What was, perhaps, more insidious than all this, by the spring of 1915, was the readiness of some portions of the Conservative Press to attribute pro-Germanism, at least in the past, to the whole Cabinet, and this despite the fact that it was the same Cabinet which had taken the grim responsibility of declaring war upon Germany. Lord Haldane's polite phrase to a pre-war German visitor, "Germany, my spiritual home," became the pretext for a campaign to drive him from public life and blacken the Cabinet in which he sat, just as the pre-war Asquithian phrase, "Wait and See" was ultimately to be worked up to imply that Asquith, by his own confession, delayed every move for "a more vigorous conduct of the war". Malicious rumour had, indeed, already begun to weave the most fantastic stories about the private life of the Asquith family and if the full height of the later venomous slanders[1] was not to be reached for some time, it is none the less significant to find that some of the Conservative Leaders would have liked to make it a condition of Coalition bargaining that Asquith should lose the Prime Ministership.

were the stories invented about them" [especially the high-explosive bombs in the governess's trunk]. Then any concreting done for hard courts, paved back gardens, and roofs was suspect as presumed siting for German invasion guns and, finally, there was the really dangerous story, implying apparently that, in April 1915 (the month was gradually shifted forwards) Zeppelins would drive the population of London to the Tubes where German agents would be able to destroy them *en masse*. This story was so dangerous that Scotland Yard took the trouble to trace it to its source, the second mistress of a London boarding-school, who claimed she had got it from a school-cleaner (cf. Sir Basil Thomson, *Queer People*).

[1] Cf. *The Autobiography of Margot Asquith*, ii, 168–74, for some of the rumours already in the course of building-up: "The D—ss of W— and others continue spreading amazing lies about me and mine . . . Elizabeth is in turn engaged to a German Admiral or a German General; Henry has shares in Krupps; I 'feed Prussian prisoners with every dainty and comestible' and play lawn tennis with them at Donnington Hall. . . ." Though Mrs. Asquith eventually obtained £1000 damages from the *Globe* newspaper when it ventured a manner of indirect publication, that did not stop the rumours rising to the later monstrous heights of "The Hidden Hand" and their publication too. More of this will have to be given later.

Perhaps, this filling-in of the background may explain why the Cabinet, already in trouble owing to German successes in Flanders achieved by surprise "poison gas" attacks, was quite unable to stand up to the series of dangerous shocks it received between May 7th and 17th. On May 7th took place the notorious sub-marining of the *Lusitania* as it arrived off the Old Head of Kinsale on its way from New York. The death-roll of 1134 was appalling, and Mr. Churchill had to admit, for the Admiralty, that no special protection had been provided though a course had been set. On May 10th Zeppelins dropped some one hundred bombs on the Southend district and, if the actual results were not startling, notice had certainly been served on London as to what might be next expected. There followed, on May 12th, the serious anti-German riots all over the country which had hardly any parallel in British history,[1] and the same day, as Ministerial ill-luck decreed it, there occurred yet another naval loss by torpedo at the Dardanelles, H.M.S. *Goliath* sinking with a loss of some five hundred officers and men. Nor would the issue of the notorious Bryce Report on alleged German outrages do anything to help the Government to restrain the rabble-rousers, seeing the dangerous exaggeration of its finding that "Murder, lust and pillage prevailed over many parts of Belgium on a scale unparalleled in any war between civilised nations during the last three centuries."[2] It was, in fact, on May 13th, the day after the *Lusitania* rioting, that the Government made its most conspicuous surrenders yet to mob-feeling. The King was advised to give way on the Garter question on which a much louder clamour had arisen than that which had forced him, the previous October, to accept Prince Louis of Battenberg's resignation as First Sea Lord and nominate

---

[1] Cf. E. Sylvia Pankhurst, *The Home Front*, pp. 170–1, for the East End rioting. She claimed: "The meanest elements among the jingoes worked up the first of the anti-German riots. These were deliberately organised, in no sense a spontaneous popular outburst; but the prospect of looting without fear of punishment made its appeal. . . . Many a home was wrecked; many a peaceable working family lost its all."

[2] Cf. Lord Ponsonby, *Falsehood in War-Time*, p. 128, for such views on the Bryce Commission as that its Chairman had been chosen mainly to influence American opinion and that: "Affidavits of single witnesses were accepted as conclusive proof. At best, human testimony is unreliable, even in ordinary circumstances of no consequence, but where bias, sentiment, passion, and so-called patriotism disturb the emotions, a personal affirmation becomes of no value whatsoever." It might be added that, by this time (Cf. *Hansard*, May 8th), a case was being worked up on Germany's maltreatment of British prisoners-of-war and that the Prime Minister thought fit to accept it almost unchallenged.

Lord Fisher, whom he distrusted, instead.[1] And orders went out for the arrest and internment of all enemy aliens of military age.

It was at this stage that Lord Fisher, furious, doubtless, at the heavy Naval losses that he held Churchill's Dardanelles policy to have been responsible for, insisted on resigning. He could hardly have been unaware that his action might endanger not only Churchill, who was in trouble already at the Admiralty,[2] but the Government itself.[3] It was, in fact, to try and prevent an immediate political crisis from arising before Italy's dear-bought adhesion was secure, that the Prime Minister contrived to enlist the King's support in demanding the return to duty of the First Sea Lord, who had quitted his post without leave and before he had been replaced. But Lord Fisher put forward such intolerable demands for a species of Naval dictatorship that the Prime Minister considered him to be on the verge of insanity.[4] By May 17th, at any rate, the crisis at the Admiralty had become known to the Opposition and when Bonar Law communicated to

[1] Cf. Harold Nicolson, *King George V*, pp. 249–52, for the King's stand on both these subjects which certainly showed courage. It would have been interesting to have an assessment of the Royal mind as divided between contempt for the mob-Press, anxiety to prevent mob-intervention in affairs of the Royal House, and desire not to break down the last bridges that might have been of some use, in certain circumstances, for peace-making. The eight names removed from the Garter roll were those of the German Emperor, the German Crown Prince, the Emperor of Austria, the King of Württemberg, the Grand Duke of Hesse, Prince Henry of Prussia, the Duke of Saxe-Coburg, and the Duke of Cumberland. And if the King's advice against Lord Fisher as ageing, vacillating, and writing and talking too much had been taken by Churchill, Fisher would not have been in a position to force on the crisis of mid-May, when Asquith thought him half-deranged.

[2] Cf. *The Nation*, May 15th, on the revelation that the First Lord had been absent in France the previous Saturday and Sunday, the days immediately following the *Lusitania*'s torpedoing: "there is very strong feeling over the revelation that he was absent from the Admiralty in France during Saturday and Sunday, and that he was not there on Admiralty business. . . . The First Lord is not always fairly criticised. But the country as a whole would like to think that he adhered to his own department, and was present at it in moments when his co-operation was vital."

[3] Cf. *Ibid.*, May 1st, for the "movement" it noted in the Conservative Press "for dispossessing the present Government . . . in favour of a Coalition of which Mr. Balfour would be the most conspicuous member. . . ."

[4] Cf. Harold Nicolson, *King George V*, p. 263 for quotations from the Royal Archives indicating Asquith's view that "signs of mental aberration" appeared in Fisher's demand, among other things, for "complete professional charge of the war at sea, together with absolute sole disposition of the Fleet and the appointment of all officers of all ranks whatsoever and absolutely untrammelled command of all the sea forces whatsoever". "The King", we are told, "was shocked" as, indeed, every responsible politician must have been, important enough to be given, in confidence, the full story.

Lloyd George the certainty of grave political consequences, he found the Radical Chancellor almost as furious at Lord Kitchener's alleged mismanagement at the War Office as Lord Fisher was reported to be at Churchill's behaviour at the Admiralty. Thereafter things moved very fast for a space, and the first Coalition discussions at 10 Downing Street between Asquith, Lloyd George, and Bonar Law took place on May 17th itself, turning, to some degree at least, on Balfour's replacing Churchill at the Admiralty and the Exchequer's going to Bonar Law if Lloyd George replaced Kitchener at the War Office. And when reporting to his senior Conservative colleagues next day, Bonar Law made it plain that he had ventured with Lloyd George the private suggestion that Asquith too might go and be replaced as Prime Minister by Balfour, by Grey, or by Lloyd George himself. He had been told that the Liberal Parliamentary Party would not have a Conservative Prime Minister, that Grey's failing eyesight, as well as other things, made him impossible and that the Radical Chancellor was not prepared to face the storm of jealousy and obloquy that would arise against him as Prime Minister in place of an ejected Asquith.[1]

Before a "National Ministry" faced Parliament on June 3rd, there had been some tough bargaining and many disappointments. The Conservatives, for example, had insisted on forcing out Lord Haldane altogether and in driving Churchill from the Admiralty if not from the Government. The accession of "Labour" had been won at the price of one Cabinet seat for Henderson and two lesser posts for Brace and Roberts, but the attempt to bring the Irish Nationalists into the Coalition had failed.[2] Irish opinion would not have forgiven Redmond if he had joined Bonar Law in Cabinet, and Nationalist self-exclusion became the more certain when Carson, too, entered, leaving "Galloper" Smith as his principal assistant just outside.[3] Of course, as fair a face as possible was put on the matter with a claim that Redmond had promised "independent" support and had, meanwhile, successfully insisted that whoever else might move, Birrell must stay at the Irish Office where he had established such confidence among

---

[1] Sir Charles Petrie, *Life and Letters of Austen Chamberlain*, ii, 26–7.

[2] Cf. *The Labour Year Book, 1916*, for Henderson as President of the Board of Education, Brace as Parliamentary Under-Secretary at the Home Office, and Roberts as a Junior Lord of the Treasury.

[3] Carson was Attorney-General with a Cabinet seat. Smith was Solicitor-General and succeeded Carson in Cabinet when Carson resigned.

Ireland's representatives during the stormy history of the three Home Rule Bills. But Back-Bench Radicals, who had been in Redmond's confidence since 1906, knew very well how provocative, especially to Ireland, he considered a situation in which the most notorious promoters of "Ulster rebellion" had been metamorphosed into "Law and Order's" leading representatives as Attorney-General Carson and Solicitor-General Smith. In fact, when Ireland's own legal posts were being mapped out as part of the Coalition bargaining, and the Irish Lord Chancellorship was claimed for an ally of Carson's, the Irish Nationalists had to threaten to end the "political truce" before Conservative and Ulster pressure could be terminated.[1] Meanwhile, it had been rank-and-file Conservatives who had been most shocked by another aspect of Coalition bargaining and manœuvre—the attempt to oust Kitchener from the War Office as an ineffective administrator, especially on the Munitions side,[2] and to replace him by Lloyd George, from whose war-zealotry Conservative leaders and Press proprietors were now expecting a "Compulsory Service" call. The tremendous public revulsion in Kitchener's favour and against the "Northcliffe Press", notably the *Daily Mail*,[3] which had been preparing his destruction, was decisive,

[1] Cf. *The Nation*, June 5th: "The new Ministry is almost complete, though a grave political difficulty threatens the Irish appointments in it. It has been proposed to make Mr. Campbell, a strong backer of the Ulster rebellion, Lord Chancellor. Mr. Dillon, writing to the *Manchester Guardian* declares that such an appointment would be an 'outrage', and, so far as the Nationalists are concerned would break the political truce. This is a grave warning, which will be echoed by the whole Liberal Party. . . ."

[2] Of course, the manœuvre would have been partly disguised by the offer, it might be, of the Commander-in-Chief to Kitchener and a high decoration though, perhaps, hardly the Garter which he had to be offered when the manœuvre was found to have revolted the general public.

[3] Cf. *The Nation*, May 29th, for this interesting commentary: "The public burning of a newspaper is not a common event in England. . . . Yet that scene was enacted in the London Stock Exchange. . . . It was repeated in the 'Baltic' and the Corn Exchange. It was imitated in the Liverpool Stock Exchange. The Manchester Stock Exchange passed a resolution solemnly excluding both *The Times* and the *Daily Mail* from its precincts. The Newcastle-on-Tyne Exchange recorded its preference to be wrong with Lord Kitchener rather than right with the *Daily Mail*. . . . But what was it all about? What caused so violent a revulsion in the public mind. . . ?

"The immediate occasion was merely an article upon ammunition. The headlines were not much more startling than usual. 'The Tragedy of the Shells', 'Lord Kitchener's Grave Error'. Lord Northcliffe's readers are well accustomed to . . . such incitements to perusal. "Scare Heads" serve as finger-post or index to the idle or busy reader. . . . To be sure, the information to which attention was directed stood on a very different level from the old discussions about Standard Bread and Sweet Peas. To inform readers that 'Lord Kitchener has starved the army in France of high explosive shells' is a terrible piece of news.

and Kitchener remained War Secretary in the "National Ministry" while adding a K.G. to his other decorations. Yet Lloyd George, at the head of a new Ministry of Munitions, could not be prevented from annexing large War Office responsibilities, and, simultaneously, the War Secretary's prerogatives were cut down, from another side, in favour of the Chief of the Imperial General Staff.

It is quite plain that "advanced opinion" in the shape of the Radical Wing of the Liberal Party and its organ *The Nation*, had little love for the Coalition and feared the speedy raising of the Conscription and Protection issues by the Conservative politicians who had been admitted into the Government in replacement of the less-securely seated of the Asquithians. *The Nation*'s comments on the admission of Carson and Smith were acid, and it refused, too, to believe that Asquith's surrender of his old Ministry, to permit of its replacement by the Coalition, had been either inevitable or advantageous. Here is *The Nation* on May 29th:

The Coalition Cabinet has been formed. It consists of twenty-two members—two more than its predecessor—including twelve Liberals, eight Conservatives, one general, and one representative of Labour. . . .

The broad reason for a device of this character is national necessity. In our view, no such necessity existed, or has been disclosed. Had the Prime Minister waited, the gust of poison gas which threatened Lord Kitchener would have been swept down the wind, the personal trouble at the Admiralty settled to the national satisfaction by the retention of Lord Fisher and the dismissal of Mr. Churchill, and a deficient organization of warlike supplies changed and extended. . . . The Coalition is not a stronger organization than that which preceded it. It is essentially and inevitably weaker. The strength of a party Government lies in

Everyone saw in it . . . information which the enemy might put to hideous use. One member of Parliament wrote, publicly denouncing Lord Northcliffe as worse than a German spy. . . . It was suspected also, that the knowledge, whether true or not, had been obtained and passed through the Censorship by underhand means; that Lord Northcliffe's correspondents had been specially favoured abroad. . . . And then there was the prestige of Lord Kitchener's name. An attack upon that prestige was dangerous for . . . an army confronted by an immensely powerful foe.

"Lord Northcliffe has a dangerous record. . . . We believe the fear of this danger to have been the real reason at the back of people's minds when they began burning Lord Northcliffe's papers. They were resolved at last to stop the stampedes he sets going. . . . Readers had watched Prince Louis of Battenberg stampeded out of office. They had watched one stampede after another set going against various statesmen in turn, sometimes with success, always with some loss of national confidence. When they saw a stampede against Lord Kitchener started, they felt that, whether the particular charge were true or false, government by newspaper stampede must be stopped. . . ."

loyalty to its chief and in the close comradeship of its members, in the maintenance of a disciplined party in Parliament, and in the enthusiasm, organized and unorganized, of its soldiery. . . .

All these bonds of strength, being either absent from the Coalition Government, or existing to an attenuated degree, we must look for it to supply some intellectual quality which its predecessors lacked, or to secure some finer adjustment of characteristics and abilities, or to draw out some fresh source of national energy. The last purpose is hardly attained . . . by restoring to office a number of gentlemen from sixty-five to seventy years of age whose last conspicuous service in the organization of a campaign dates from the Boer War. . . . The sacrifice of Lord Haldane is a grave national loss. . . . A jest of a grimmer order is the appointment of a self-confessed offender against the law as head of the English Bar. . . . Not many months have passed since our Attorney-General announced that "he intended when he went there [to Ulster] to break every law that was possible'. . . ' he was as good as his word, for he established, in the congenial company of his new Solicitor-General, a reign of lawlessness in Ireland. . . .

Justifiable as some of this very unenthusiastic comment was, it clearly under-rated the dangerous loss of prestige by the old Government,[1] and the virtual certainty that, even if the Fisher and "Shells" "scandals" had been lived down, war-events would have brought new "scandals", at short intervals, during the many months which even victory-optimists foresaw as necessary to draw level with the Germans in war-making capacity before passing them irretrievably. Indeed, in *The Nation*'s very next number of June 5th, there was plain anxiety as to whether the Conscriptionist attitude Lloyd George was adopting as the new Minister of Munitions did not forebode quick new political shocks, and the ability of the Northcliffe Press to make a very rapid recovery from its Kitchener defeat was one anxiety the more. Lloyd George, speaking at Manchester on June 3rd, had ventured to assert that the British, given the munitions which had just allowed the Germans to assist the Austrians to complete victory over Russia at Przemysl, would already have ejected the Germans from Flanders and have penetrated into Germany. And as the *Daily Mail*, which had resumed the lead of the Northcliffe pack, treated Lloyd George's speech as its own vindication, *The Nation* uttered

---

[1] Which, for example, had encouraged *The Times* to play for an Asquithian resignation, pure and simple, when announcing that "the time for a Coalition had gone by". Yet Pound and Harmsworth's *Northcliffe* (p. 480) seems to show that *The Times* writers disliked the attacks on Kitchener the public revulsion from which, of course, strengthened Asquith temporarily.

this loud warning on the call that was going out "for forced Service, military and industrial":[1]

> The newspaper organization which has just failed to rush out Lord Kitchener is seeking to mend its shattered repute by rushing in conscription. . . . Early in the history of the war, a magnificent feat of British arms was represented in *The Times* as an effect, of demoralization and disaster. One paper of the syndicate refused to publish a War Office advertisement for recruits. Others sneered at it. A campaign of personal and professional disparagement was opened on the great soldier and great man who was responsible for the supply of men and material, and had continued to resort to the voluntary system for them. These efforts to create uncertainty and depression in the national mind have had a certain effect. This is more spiritual and political than military. The Liberal Government, the chief bulwark of voluntary service is discouraged and bewildered and finally throws up the sponge. A mixed administration takes its place, containing a definite conscriptionist element. There is a constant renewal of the attacks of suggestion and implication. No facts are stated, only the old insinuations of distrust and failure. The vital issues—whether, for example, it is possible to mix a conscript and a voluntary army, whether forced service could be applied to Ireland, whether at any moment there has been a deficiency of men . . . are ignored, for the simple reason that the answer would destroy the conscriptionist case. . . . We hope that we are not too late in warning the Government and the country of the grave danger to national unity arising from the campaign to which the new Minister of Munitions has now lent his aid.

Of course, *The Nation* and its Radical supporters were asking almost a God-like liberty for the individual English citizen when claiming that it must be left to his own conscience how he was to serve his country in the war. As the casualty-lists among the first hundreds of thousands of eager volunteers grew ever longer and more tragic,[2] it was inevitable that *Daily Mail* and *John Bull* campaigns for sweeping all "slackers", and especially all "single slackers", into khaki should grow in compulsive force. Yet there was sufficient moderation even on the Conservative side of the Cabinet to accept, despite the *Daily Mail*, some of the Radicals' contentions as temporarily true. It was agreed, for example, that volunteering had hitherto supplied virtually all the man-power that could be adequately trained and armed and that it was unwise, too, after seeking to impress the whole world by the formation of

---

[1] *The Nation*, June 5th, under the heading "Forced Service and Forced Labour".

[2] Vera Brittain's *Testament of Youth* gave, in 1933, a significant and moving private account.

a harmonious Coalition, to break it up almost at once by the demand for conscribing many hundreds of thousands of young men before the country's industrial and financial apparatus could organize their replacement and the War Office their military training. And so, for weeks and even months longer, Radicals could report occasional rebuffs for over-eager Conscriptionists and rejoice that the "Voluntary Principle" was still entire. Thus the very Bill, setting up the new Ministry of Munitions was significantly altered, under what was described as "Liberal, Radical, and Nationalist" pressure, so that "the chance of using it for the compulsion of labour" might be eliminated.[1] A little later there was pleasure both at the tone on Coalition matters that the Prime Minister had taken in the House of Commons and the tone that Lloyd George had taken in the country when making Munitions appeals at Cardiff and Bristol.[2] Too soon, as it proved, was *The Nation* affirming: "At home it has been a week of recovery. Conscription, Forced Labour, a Khaki Election, Boulangism (English style)—have all been carried down stream. . . . Mr. George is now on the right tack, and is sailing it with his usual vigour. The Treasury, too, is in thrifty hands."

The next big news of Munitions plans to beat the enemy production of 250,000 shells a day was given to Parliament on June 23rd and still seemed to show Lloyd George content to bargain with the Trade Unions whether for recruiting a mobile Munitions labour-force or for getting compulsory war-time arbitration of labour-disputes accepted in return for the heavy taxation of Capital's war-time profits. But soon a new cloud was reported on the horizon in the shape of a National Register Bill to be moved by the Conscriptionist President of the Local Government Board, Mr. Walter Long, for the alleged purpose of ascertaining the national resources of man- and woman-power but plainly capable of providing a master-plan for industrial and military conscription. Before long, *The Nation*, while congratulating the

---

[1] Cf. *The Nation*, June 12th.

[2] *Ibid.*, June 19th: "On Tuesday [June 15th] the Prime Minister gave the House of Commons an unexpected and remarkable account of the formation of the Coalition. In effect, it was an extremely skilful appeal for the confidence of Parliament, and its success was evident . . . he had come to believe in the necessity of an overwhelming demonstration of national unity. . . . We welcome Mr. Lloyd George's speeches at Cardiff and Bristol, for it is a special satisfaction to those who know and value his mobilizing power to see him appealing to his fellow-countrymen for the kind of service they can and will give with enthusiasm. . . ."

Radicals on winning Lloyd George's attention for that scheme of "fixing fair rents in munition areas" which eventually blossomed into full-scale rent-control,[1] was giving this emphatic warning to Register Bill Conscriptionists in the Cabinet or outside:[2]

The Government must expect some plain speaking on the National Register Bill. Most Liberals (and some Conservatives) think it a piece of gratuitous folly and I can't imagine its passage through the Cabinet was a smooth one. It will meet rougher waters in Westminster. Practical administrators who know what the organization of a Census (or of an Insurance Bill) means, ridicule it. They denounce the use of amateur collectors and local busybodies, predict endless blunders, countless omissions, and declare that the mere problem of removals will destroy the value of this ramshackle census, whose results will not be available for months to come, and will be worthless when they are. . . .

Meanwhile the Conscriptionist case is pretty well finished, as far as this Government is concerned. The minority must by this time know that if they press it, the Cabinet will break up, and the country will have to find another Prime Minister and another set of men—with a *Daily Mail* Premier at the head of them—to do the work of splitting the nation in two in the midst of a struggle for its existence. That consideration may not stop Lord Northcliffe. But it means that if things come to a push, the blow which the anti-Kitchener crusade inflicted on the Harmsworth press—and it was a heavy one—will be repeated.

In view of this loud Radical warning, the history of the vital Parliamentary stages needed to put the National Register Bill on the Statute Book, on July 15th, is worth giving in *The Nation*'s own words. And it is, perhaps, worth noting that a new Northcliffe campaign was being worked up alongside,[3] a fact that

[1] By the 5 & 6 Geo. 5, c. 97, The Increase of Rent and Mortgage Interest (War Restrictions) Act, 1915, whose most epoch-making section ran: "No order for the recovery of possession of a dwelling-house to which this Act applies or for the ejectment of a tenant therefrom shall be made so long as the tenant continues to pay rent at the agreed rate as modified by this Act and performs the other conditions of the tenancy." There was a plentiful background of charges—not always justified—of "landlord-profiteering" because of occasional rent-raising by house-owners who, on Clydeside, Tyneside, Merseyside, and other munition and camp-areas, had been known to find several lodgers or two and even three families living—destructively—in premises originally let to one. But, naturally, there was also the occasional case of "totally unjustifiable" rent-increase or ejectment which provided the banner behind which all tenants could rally.

[2] *The Nation*, July 3, 1915.

[3] Cf. *Lord Riddell's War Diary, 1914–1918*, for some of the activities of Northcliffe, who used Riddell, proprietor of the *News of the World*, when he wanted private interviews with Lloyd George whom he was hoping to break away from Asquith. Thus, on July 2nd, Riddell reported lunching with Northcliffe and finding his host prophesying great disasters (such as the "probable" loss of all the British troops at the Dardanelles) with outbursts of public fury to follow at home. And after the meeting of Northcliffe and Lloyd George had

probably decided some of the "advanced" to accept Asquith's assurances and refrain from open opposition, if not from private criticism, of a measure that did, after all, pave the way for Conscription.

"The second reading of the forcible-voluntary National Register Bill," said *The Nation*, "was carried on Monday by 253 votes to 30. . . . On the Liberal side the prevailing attitude was either hostile or critical. . . . Mr. Asquith prefaced the debate with a reply to Mr. Alden that no action in the way of conscription or forced labour was contemplated and Mr. McKenna reduced its compass to that of a 'statistical' or new Census Bill. Sir Thomas Whittaker's attack was based mainly on the folly and impropriety of dividing the nation for so small a result, and Mr. J. M. Robertson's on an analysis of its complete futility. In Committee, the element of secrecy was properly imposed, but attempts to make the Bill voluntary, to exclude women, and to reduce the age limit to more practical proportions, were all rejected."[1]

Despite the assurances given by Asquith and McKenna (Chancellor of the Exchequer and the most vigilant of the Cabinet section already on guard against Lloyd George's ambitions and Conservative-Conscriptionist alliances),[2] Radical anti-Conscriptionists were soon uneasy once more. Walter Long, President of the Local Government Board, who was in charge of the National Register Bill and would be responsible for its enforcement, refused to accept the view that anything that had been said from the Front

taken place on July 4th, Lloyd George reported to Riddell that Northcliffe had again indulged in the gloomiest prophecy of an impending national disaster, within the next two or three weeks, which would sweep away the detested Asquith and his Cabinet though Northcliffe had professed himself as anxious to save Lloyd George from the flood. It is difficult to refrain from seeing signs of incipient insanity both in Northcliffe's persistent vision of the "great disasters" which would give him a complete triumph over Asquith and in his efforts to persuade Lloyd George to throw over all alliances but Northcliffe's even while making it plain that he was reserving the right, on Munition shortages, to blame Lloyd George as equally, if not more responsible than other Ministers. And how relentlessly a Northcliffe attack was pressed, the Riddell diary entry for July 8th makes plain. Haldane had just tried to come to the rescue of the chief of the Ordnance Department of the War Office who, because he stood in the way of a further expansion of Lloyd George's Munitions Ministry, had been subjected to a surprise attack by another newpaper ally of Lloyd George, Sir Henry Dalziel, proprietor of the Radical *Reynolds's Newspaper*. On this occasion, after forecasting Asquith's downfall within six weeks, Northcliffe, whose renewed campaign against Haldane had opened in that morning's *Times* and continued in that afternoon's *Evening News*, left Riddell early to prime the next morning's *Daily Mail*.

[1] The 5 & 6 Geo. 5, c. 60, as the Bill became with the short title of the National Registration Act, prescribed that "A register shall be formed of all persons, male and female, between the ages of fifteen and sixty-five" with certain exceptions, and prescribed penalties for refusal or neglect to register.

[2] Cf. *Lord Riddell's War Diary, 1914–1918*, under June 11, 1915.

Bench prevented the Government from proposing Compulsion and announced, in fact, that he would resign if there was hesitation about adopting it as a necessary measure. Lord Lansdowne, too, when moving the Bill in the House of Lords, announced his belief, that the country would no longer tolerate voluntary service "with its present injustices and anomalies" and was charged in the Radical Press "with a gross breach of the understanding under which the measure was framed and submitted to Parliament".[1] Indeed, during an increasingly anxious summer, when the North-cliffe Press whipped up a new campaign against a spiritless Asquith at Downing Street and "slackers" tolerated everywhere though unparalleled disaster threatened in Poland, throughout the Balkans, and much nearer home too,[2] some Radical anti-Conscriptionists, aware that intrigues to procure a call for Conscription even from a Radical minority were succeeding,[3] began to put more and more reliance on a hoped-for Trade Union ban. Certainly, the South Wales Miners had brought the Government to terms resoundingly in July when they called their vital coalfield out on strike and successfully defied what they considered a forced and unjust interpretation of the Munitions Act.[4] And early in

[1] Cf. *The Nation*, July 17th.

[2] Cf. *Ibid.*, August 7th, summarizing the current Northcliffe "denigration" thus: "Our manhood had failed; the country was full of 'slackers'. We were in the hands of a listless, spiritless Premier; a Government only redeemed from contempt by the genius of Mr. Lloyd George; a sham and idle Parliament; and administrators so criminally careless as to starve the army of shells and overfeed Germany with cotton. . . . The danger of this slap-dash indictment was that through the excellence of the Continental organization of the Harmsworth press, it fell on the ear of our Allies. . . . Disjoint the Allies, discourage the Army, disunite the nation—what can one make of such a campaign but that there are anti-voluntarists who would rather lose the war than win it without conscription." On August 21st, *The Nation's* continuing uneasiness was thus expressed: "Lord Northcliffe's new Conscriptionist League is so much a piece of *Daily Mail* organization . . . that I don't regard it in itself as a serious step in the movement. And it would not be in the least serious if it were not one of the many signs of the sapping and mining which is constantly going on. . . . It is disconcerting to think of the existence of a cabal which speaks together and acts together, and is using the Registration Bill for the end which the Prime Minister ruled out of its operation and under which the Liberal Party yielded it an unwilling assent. . . . And yet what true force lies behind this faction? . . . Certainly not the working people, who so far as I gather regard conscription either with a dull fear and aversion, or in the organized and most political sections, such as the miners, with fiery revolt."

[3] Cf. *Ibid.*, August 14th: "Two Liberal Members of Parliament [Mr. Ellis Griffith and Sir Leo Chiozza Money] have sent a letter to the papers in favour of conscription."

[4] Cf. *Ibid.*, July 24th: "The failure of the renewed conference . . . brought the nation and our allies into a situation of acute anxiety. There were 200,000 men out on strike. The Government having launched its unhappy proclamation bringing the industry under the Munitions Act had nominated a tribunal . . .

September, the Trades Union Congress fulfilled some of the hopes of the anti-Conscriptionists when adopting unanimously so apparently resounding a resolution of its Parliamentary Committee as the following:[1]

We, the delegates to this Congress, representing nearly 3,000,000 organized workers, record our hearty appreciation of the magnificent response made to the call for volunteers to fight against the tyranny of militarism.

We emphatically protest against the sinister efforts of a section of the reactionary press in formulating newspaper policies for party purposes and attempting to foist on this country conscription, which always proves a burden to the workers and will divide the nation at a time when absolute unanimity is essential.

No reliable evidence has been produced to show that the voluntary system of enlistment is inadequate. . . .

We believe that all the men necessary can, and will be, obtained through a voluntary system. . . .

Of course, the Radical anti-Conscriptionists tried to assert that so decisive and "unanimous" a pronouncement from all the skilled and organized workers of the country definitely disposed of the Conscription "peril". But T.U.C. resolutions are not always what they seem, and the keenest-sighted observer present at the Bristol T.U.C. proceedings of September 1915, Mrs. Beatrice Webb, had a more involved story to write into her famous *Diaries*.[2] According to her, the T.U.C.'s Parliamentary Committee and the bulk of the senior Union officials were "conventionally warlike" and the "pacifist" element only a tiny minority. If unable, because of the deep emotional antagonism still stirred up by the mere mention of Conscription as "the accursed thing", to prevent the anti-Conscription resolution from going through with enthusiastic applause, the Parliamentary Committee nevertheless saw to it that an antidote was forthcoming in the arrival of Lloyd George to give an insinuating and flattering address.[3] Mrs. Webb, indeed, but the proclamation had no other effect than that of confirming the suspicions and resentment of the workpeople. . . . A change of policy was adopted on Monday when Mr. Lloyd George, Mr. Runciman, and Mr. Henderson travelled down to Cardiff and entered into new negotiations. . . . The new terms of settlement are an improvement on the old from the men's point of view."

[1] Cf. *The Nation*, September 11th.

[2] *Beatrice Webb's Diaries, 1912–1924*, under September 9th.

[3] Cf. *The Nation*, September 11th: "He told the delegates that the war had resolved itself into a conflict between the mechanics of Germany and Austria on the one hand and the mechanics of Britain and France on the other. The problem was almost entirely a Labor problem, and the country was not at the present moment doing its utmost. An addition of 80,000 skilled men and

went so far as to conclude that the average Trade Union official seemed to be insidiously "retained" by the Government both through tempting allowances for services on Committees and through hopes of more permanent Government appointments.

It is obvious from Beatrice Webb's account that she considered that no effective lead against Conscription would come, at a crisis, from the Parliamentary Committee of the T.U.C.—and particularly if Lloyd George were to claim that there was no other method of achieving victory or even avoiding defeat. In point of fact, it was not long before the Radicals of *The Nation* ruefully admitted both that Conscription pressure was no less[1] and that Free Trade, too, was in danger from Conservative moves almost as "insidious" as those that were sapping and mining the principle of "Free Service". Since McKenna had become Chancellor of the Exchequer on Lloyd George's going to the Munitions Ministry, there had been a growing Radical reliance on him to counteract Lloyd George's obviously vaulting ambitions and the increasing hugeness of the demands he was held to be putting forward to make his Munitions Ministry a well-advertised success.[2] Yet

200,000 unskilled men and women was required for the new additional arsenals. Only 15 per cent of the machines for turning out munitions were working night-shifts. . . . Turning to the employers, Mr. George said that practically all the engineering works in the country had been taken over and controlled by the State. Profits had been limited . . . the Government had power to determine wages as well as hours and conditions of labour. This was the greatest step that had ever been in the direction of controlling the industries of the country by the State, and it prevented unfair profits from being made at the expense of Labour. Piece rates had been maintained, and if a single case were brought to his notice where the Government's bargain had not been adhered to . . . he was prepared to remedy it within twenty-four hours. Mr. Lloyd George then gave some instances of the way in which, he said, trade union restrictions had interfered with work. His last appeal was to beg the delegates not to put the country against organized Labor."

[1] Cf. *Ibid.*, September 8th: "The Conscriptionist agitation goes on. . . . I find Labor members holding up hands of horror at the lightheadedness of its leaders and agents . . . behind it stands a really sinister movement to force a dissolution on the top of a resignation of the conscriptionist group in the Cabinet. . . . I believe it would stop to-morrow if Mr. George were not judged to be at its back, and able to stem the Labor opposition."

[2] Cf. *Whitaker's Almanack*, *1916*, pp. 188–9, for Lloyd George, before his Ministry was two months old, reporting on the sixteen national and three special factories that had been set up and the further "new and great programme which would tax the engineering resources of this country for some months. To meet this gigantic demand, it would be necessary to set up immediately ten large national establishments. . . . The necessary machinery had been ordered, and steps were being taken to erect the buildings." No wonder *The Nation* considered that a good way to check Lloyd George's overweening ambitions might be to contrast his Exchequer thriftlessness in "having borrowed practically all the money to pay for the first year of war" with McKenna's determination to begin some real war-taxation.

McKenna, too, in his first War Budget, had caused some Radical disappointment even though announcing, on September 20th, more effective new war-taxation than Lloyd George had ever attempted, taxation estimated to bring in 102 millions in a full year and balancing 77 millions from higher taxes on income (including 30 millions from a new war-profits tax) against indirect taxes principally affecting sugar, tobacco, and tea. According to *The Nation*, the case for a supplementary income tax on landlords' incomes now that the war was raising both urban and rural rents notably had been disregarded; the case for Death-Duty increases, to match Income-Tax increases, had not been pressed; and even the Spirit duties had been left alone though there was the strongest justification for raising them.[1] And, if to account for all these Budget deficiencies, it was easiest for Radicals to lay the blame upon Conservative influence in the Coalition Cabinet, there was one section of tax-increases, calculated to yield only comparatively trifling amounts, behind which Radicals feared they saw a compromise with the most Machiavellian Conservative calculations of all.

There was, it was true, a strong exchange-case already for restraining luxury-imports especially from neutrals and, above all, from neutral America. That was why a Chancellor, now more trusted on the Radical Back-Benches than Lloyd George, claimed that he had put import-duties upon motors, films, clocks, musical instruments, plate-glass, and hats. But Radical suspicions fastened, from the first, on the fact that, as no countervailing excise-duties were proposed on British-produced articles in these classes, the manufacturers concerned were, in effect, being awarded, at the expense of the consumer, the first instalment of Protection for which Conservatives, and the Tariff Reform Union had been campaigning so long and so ardently. It came, in fact, to a not unrewarding struggle in the House of Commons, thus cheerfully recorded in *The Nation*:[2]

[1] Cf. *The Nation*, September 25th: "The rent of land is, of course, taxable as general income. But there is every reason why in the present emergency it should be subjected to special taxation, especially at a time when both agricultural and many sorts of town rent are rising. Again, in the revision upward of the income-tax, it is sound policy to make similar additions to death duties. . . . As for the exemption of spirits from increased taxation, it will probably be defended not by the presence in the House of a hundred watchful Irish votes, but on the ground that the limit of productive taxation had been reached. . . . But the case for repressive taxation is overwhelming in face of the great increase in the consumption of spirits in the first half of this year. . . ."

[2] *Ibid.*, October 2nd.

The new import duties were very roughly handled in the House of Commons on Wednesday and Thursday nights . . . on Thursday the motor tax was just saved by the intervention of the Prime Minister. But two other duties—those on plate-glass and hats—fell before the Free Trade assault. On a third, the duty on musical instruments, it was shown that British piano manufacturers had already raised their prices by its amount.

Meanwhile, the Conscription issue had been raised on the floor of the House of Commons in what was regarded as a manner personally offensive to the Prime Minister, and the more so, perhaps, because a nominal Liberal had been responsible.[1] It became increasingly obvious, in fact, that if the Franco-British offensive, preparing for the end of September, on the Western Front, yielded disappointing results, the pressure for Conscription might well break up the Cabinet. Unfortunately, as it proved, the Franco-British attack, carefully prepared and adequately munitioned though it had been,[2] failed to produce what the neutral world considered as adequate gains. By contrast, the Austro-German assault on Serbia mounted just afterwards, seemed so much more effective that Bulgaria, with justifiable grievances against Serbia, joined the enemy and the Greek Court, despite ex-Premier Venizelos, declined, with greater determination than ever, to allow itself to be bribed,[3] cajoled, or forced on to the Allied side.

When the complete ruin of Serbia seemed approaching, despite

---

[1] *Ibid.*: "In the House of Commons on Tuesday there was an unpleasant revival of the spirit of undisciplined intrigue which lies behind the Conscriptionist movement. Captain Guest, its Parliamentary leader, asked the Prime Minister whether he would, early next week, make a statement on National Service. Mr. Asquith not only refused this request but appealed to the House to abstain from debating the question because we were at what he described as 'a very critical moment in the history of the war . . .' this appeal was contemptuously disregarded. Captain Guest made his Conscriptionist speech, and was followed by Mr. Amery, Sir Griffith Boscawen, and Sir Frederick Banbury. The House received it with marked disfavour."

[2] Cf. *Whitaker's Almanack, 1916*, Diary of the War, under September 25th: "Great allied advance in France after a bombardment of German positions for 25 days. . . . German trenches captured [by British] and lines penetrated 4000 yards . . . in Champagne, the French penetrated the German lines on a front of $15\frac{1}{2}$ miles and depth of $2\frac{1}{2}$ miles."

[3] Cf. *Hansard*, October 26th, for the British Foreign Secretary stating, in the Commons, that Greece had refused the offer of Cyprus which had therefore lapsed. It may be mentioned that there were circles in London and Paris eager to use force to compel the Greeks to help in the rescue of Serbia, according to what it was claimed were their Treaty obligations. And the deposition of King Constantine, the Kaiser's brother-in-law, would have delighted the war-zealots despite its harmful effects on much neutral opinion.

the rescue-plans of an Anglo-French force that had been summoned to Salonika while Venizelos had still been Greek Premier, Britain's Coalition Government faced its first dangerous test. Another Press "stampede" was threatened on account of the alleged delays, hesitations, and general ineffectiveness of Asquithian Government which, it was said, failed to use Britain's sea-power adequately to prevent neutrals from provisioning and supplying Germany[1] and which, just as culpably, still set its face against using Britain's man-power properly by instituting Compulsory Service. Nor would the unsatisfactory position at the Dardanelles, the serious London Zeppelin raid of October 13th,[2] or even the infuriating news of Nurse Cavell's execution in Belgium have done much to help the Prime Minister and his immediate supporters. If, indeed, Sir Edward Carson was ultimately the only Minister to resign, that was merely because important concessions were already being made, with more in prospect, to those pressing towards what today would be called "total war", with all its risks.[3] On October 11th, for example, Lord Derby, at the War Office, began a recruiting drive, which was soon to "prove", as many intended it to from the first, that nothing short of Conscription would now do.[4] And on October

[1] Holland, Denmark, Norway, and Sweden were all credited by the war-zealots with helping, for the sake of profit, to keep Germany supplied not only from their own resources but from what they imported from the Americas and other overseas areas. There were even occasional calls for extending the virtual blockade of Germany to include those countries, calls which no Government, professing the slightest regard for international law, could follow though, in point of fact, the overseas trade of all four countries mentioned was put under ever closer controls and surveillance.

[2] Cf. *Whitaker's Almanack, 1916*, Diary of the War: "Zeppelin raid over part of the London area: 59 killed, 114 injured, and damage done to property."

[3] Cf. *The Nation*, October 2nd, for the construction of a War Committee of the Cabinet as a sop to those who had been demanding a small War Cabinet with dictatorial powers: "Too much should not be made of the new War Committee of the Cabinet. . . . It is in no sense a concession to the Little Cabinet-makers. . . . It was necessary to have a smaller consultative body, for the Cabinet itself is really a debating assembly whose power of *conclusion* varies inversely with the preaching powers of its members."

[4] Cf. *Ibid.*, October 9th, for Derby's own opinion running apparently, on, these lines too: "Lord Derby has been placed at the head of the recruiting department for the Army, and though he opens his office with the improper declaration that he goes in as the receiver of a bankrupt concern (i.e. voluntary-ism), his practical ability and his sense of honour give him claims on public confidence. His first act has been to bring about the withdrawal of a clumsy circular issued by the War Office." Of course, the Radicals of *The Nation* had soon cause to protest bitterly against the immediate Conscription-forcing tactics of the Northcliffe Press as when they reported *The Times* thus: "Everyone is agreed to regard it [Lord Derby's crusade] as the final test of the voluntary system. Everyone desires a plain statement to this effect from the Government,

12th Sir Edward Grey announced what neutrals considered to be a further harshening of British "blockade" measures at sea. Yet it was because he was almost openly contemptuous of expedients like these at a time when Serbia was being overrun that Carson, on his resignation, became so much the hero of the Tory Back-Benchers and the Conservative War Committee that he was regarded as a possible Prime Minister in certain circumstances of Coalition collapse.

Perhaps the story of the "Derby Scheme" and how Conscription was pushed on behind it had better be reserved for the next chapter. This chapter may well be closed by quotations to illustrate how Radicals tried to prevent the Northcliffe Press from stampeding the British public into panic-decisions whether on "rescuing Serbia" or destroying the Coalition. Here is writing on Serbia from *The Nation*, the Radical weekly with a strong and merited following among "progressive" professional men, ministers of religion, City and County Councillors, Parliamentary Back-Benchers and, it was known, Cabinet Ministers too:[1]

We can decide this thorny question only if we are clear about the objects we pursue in this war. There is much we might do if we were omnipotent. The whole world would stand a certain amount of reconstruction from Belgium at our doors to distant China. Our resources, however, are restricted. There is some time-limit even to our financial endurance, and a still more obvious limit of our reserves of men. In such a position we must ask ourselves to whom do we owe the clearer obligation? Our sole tie of treaty was with Belgium. Our tie of sentiment and affection is with France. We have not yet recovered a square mile of Belgian soil; we have even lost some part of the fragment which we held. Our part in recovering the occupied portions of France, very gallant, very splendid, very hopeful as it is, is still a limited one. Can we afford . . . to launch into fresh enterprises in the Balkans? Are we so strong in Flanders and France that we can lightly throw our hundreds of thousands into Macedonia? Our military position is neither a matter for despondency nor for wild hopes. But will it bear the indefinite multiplication of overseas expeditions— Salonika, Gallipoli, Mesopotamia?

This was fine, balanced writing and sound sense too. But when it came to dealing with what *The Nation* considered to be the

together with a pledge that they will introduce compulsion if the six weeks' trial fails, and arm themselves meanwhile with the necessary powers to do so. If the Government takes this course, there seems no immediate reason why Sir Edward Carson's resignation should be followed by any others."

[1] *The Nation*, October 9th.

reckless incitements of the Northcliffe Press (it rarely condescended to notice what it would have classed as the "gutter-Press", headed by Bottomley's *John Bull*) even *The Nation*'s writers could become angry and shrill. Here is *The Nation* of October 16th, denouncing, under the title of "THE PERIL WITHIN", the current line of depression imposed by Lord Northcliffe's orders on the readerships, among others, of *The Times*, the *Daily Mail*, the *Evening News*, and the *Weekly Dispatch*:[1]

It would be well for the British people to divert their eyes for a few moments from the danger from without in order to realize how grave a peril threatens them from within. . . . If the Harmsworth journalism is in the last resort brainless, it is clever enough to lead the weak and to impose on the ignorant. It has destroyed one Government, and now threatens another. But its real attack is on the spirit of the nation. This it saps by singling out one of our leaders after another, and suggesting their incapacity, or their treachery to the national cause, or both. In this fashion it has already treated Mr. Asquith, Sir Edward Grey, Lord Haldane, and Lord Kitchener. . . . The other day one of these journals published a political map which might well have issued from Berlin, to illustrate the world-triumph of German arms. . . . An article from another of these prints was recently translated into Arabic . . . in order to show the failure of the cause of the Allies . . . the selection of anti-conscriptionists as the Ministers who are thus sniped at in every stiff corner of the country's fortunes reveals the main design of the Harmsworth Press. Now it is Sir Edward Grey, and now Mr. Runciman. The depression of the public mind, the spreading of disunion at home and want of confidence abroad are all effects incidental to the grand aim of forcing conscription. The country must be conscripted—therefore it must be shown to be in a bad case. . . . But if conscription wins the victory, it will be Lord Northcliffe's, not Lord Curzon's, Mr. George's or Mr. Churchill's.

[1] Cf. Lord Beaverbrook, *Men and Power*, p. 59, for one view of Northcliffe's power: "To-day no parallel exists to Northcliffe's domination of newspaper sales in the metropolis. The circulation of my newspapers is the nearest approach to it. Beaverbrook Newspapers hold one-fifth of the London newspaper market. But Northcliffe held one-half." Naturally, the Beaverbrook fifth of 1956 accounts for three times as many copies sold as the Northcliffe half of forty years before.

CHAPTER VIII

CONSCRIPTION

"This quality of mind seems to us inherent in the nature of a Coalition. The Prime Minister oppressed, as no statesman of our time has been oppressed by the sense of a very imperfect loyalty inside his cabinet and a highly strenous opposition without, reflects this dualism, and indeed regards himself as its interpreter. We are therefore in the region of perpetual compromise. . . . There is one obvious cure for this indecisiveness, so fatal to the conduct of a war. This is that we should return to the older and more familiar condition of a homogeneous Government.

"Of this resource only one of two forms is possible. The Liberal Party is broken beyond the hope of immediate repair. The Tory Party remains intact in face of the immediate issue of Conscription, and no one can doubt that in policy it represents the dominant wing of the Cabinet. In individual talent it is inferior to its rival, and it is without a majority in the House of Commons. It is also falling under the domination of a personality of force and sincerity but little wisdom or breadth of view, whose career as the late leader of our internal sedition may be held to justify him in the conduct of external war. A Carson Ministry, damning consequences, neutrals, and the Foreign Office with equal vigor, would doubtless conduct the most tremendous politico-military transaction in our history to an end as visible as the Fire of London. But personally, if change is to come, we should prefer it in the less drastic alternative of a Conservative Government, under its regular rather than guerrilla chieftains, taking courage and responsibility in its hands, producing a policy and offering it in frankness to the nation. . . . For it seems to us that Liberalism has almost reached the last trick in the game of a Coalition in which one view of life and policy is deliberately staked over a table against another, and the Liberal and Democratic card is always the loser. Free service is gone; free trade is going; one figure after another disappears or is marked down for discredit; principle after principle falls. . . . This process of surrender cannot proceed much further. . . .

"Is it not the business of the leaders of the Liberal Party to retire from a position from which honor and power have departed, and form a moderate, patriotic, helpful, but critical opposition. . . ?"

The Radical *Nation*, January 22, 1916, wants Asquith to consider going into Opposition rather than making further concessions to Conservatism.

"The House will be aware that, in January 1916, in order to secure the necessary supply of labour by means of the policy dilution, the Ministry of Munitions appointed three Commissioners to represent him on the Clyde. . . .

"In the course of the past week, however, a number of strikes have been organized . . . sometimes on the most trivial grounds, by a self-appointed body known as the Clyde Workers' Committee. This Committee . . . has repudiated any connection with, or allegiance to, established trade unions, and decided about a fortnight ago to embark on a policy of holding up the production of the most important munitions of war in the Clyde district, with the object, I am informed, of compelling the Government to repeal the Military Service Act and the Munitions of War Act, and to withdraw all limitations upon increases of wages and strikes. . . .

"The present series of strikes commenced on the 17th of March, when one of the chief members of this committee insisted that he should be entitled during working hours, without the permission of the management, to leave his work . . . and go into any other department . . . for the purpose of investigating what was being done with unskilled labour, interviewing the women introduced. . . . The man . . . and his associates, in breach of their own agreement, declined to place the matter before the Clyde Commissioners, and succeeded in bringing out about 1000 men from these works.

"From that time the series of strikes appears to have proceeded upon a systematic and sinister plan . . . to bring out on strike workmen engaged upon the production of a particular heavy gun and gun-mounting for which we are receiving the most urgent demands. . . . The Executive Committee of the Amalgamated Society of Engineers, on the matter being reported to them . . . immediately issued a statement repudiating the strike . . . and calling upon the men to return to work. . . .

"These efforts were unfortunately unsuccessful, and on Friday last . . . my right honourable friend requested the military authorities to remove under Section 14 of the Defence of the Realm Regulations six of the ringleaders, who were found, with others, to be contemplating a further extension of their operations. . . ."

> From *Hansard*, March 28, 1916; Dr. Addison reporting the Clyde deportations for Lloyd George's Ministry of Munitions.

"Monday, April 17, 1916.

"On Sunday morning I was informed . . . that the account of the Cabinet meeting published in *The Times* on Saturday was substantially correct. It is really too scandalous that *The Times* should be able to publish these accounts of Cabinet meetings. But seeing that the whole of the recent daily discussion and negotiations between Carson, Curzon, Northcliffe, Lloyd George, and others are probably at the disposal of *The Times* through various intermediaries, this publication is scarcely to be wondered at.

"According to Davies' account, the mood of L.G. on Friday was, that if the Staff would stick to him, he would resign. A closer examination of the facts makes me sceptical whether with the present confessedly incompetent machinery of the War Office, we should be any more likely to get the men we want by bringing in the unattested married men than with those at present available. They are not getting the men who are available . . . the important thing is to put men of brains in command of the War Office recruiting machinery. Macready and some others answer the description, but they are not given a proper chance . . . if L.G. were to go out, he would be in company with the Carsonite party and a very small section of our own party. Loyal as I am to L.G., I feel considerable hesitation. . . . His idea appears to be that he would go out and conduct a campaign in the country. Personally, I think that if he did go out, the Government could not last. There would therefore be no Bill giving soldiers votes and I doubt whether the state of affairs, from the point of view of beating the Germans, would not be worse than it is now. . . . Robertson is very stiff and unyielding in his demand, though it cannot be part of the duties of the Staff to say how the men shall be obtained."

> The Radical Dr. Addison shows some initial distate for the intrigues in which Lloyd George is involved. (From his *Four and a Half Years*.)

A BREAK-UP of the Coalition Government was avoided in October 1915, when war-news was very depressing and the most powerful forces in mass-journalism still intent on driving out the Asquithians, by the device of putting Lord Derby in charge of a great new recruiting drive. By the end of the year, Conscriptionists expected to have figures which would give them an irrefutable "patriotic" case for resigning, even in war-time, and forcing an election, too,[1] unless Asquith and his Cabinet group accepted, at least, a limited Conscription—perhaps, of single men only in the first case. The Derby recruiting campaign of the autumn of 1915 differed from the Kitchener campaign of the previous year in laying its main emphasis on bringing system and method to securing a planned increase, by stages, of Britain's Army, the recruiters dividing their human material into 46 classes, 23 age-groups of single men and 23 age-groups of married men between eighteen and forty-one years of age, who would be summoned to the colours by classes. As events turned out, the greatest rush to "attest" under the "Derby Scheme" came from the older groups of married men after Lord Derby was understood to have given a pledge that they would not be called upon till single men, especially in the younger age-groups, had been summoned to do their duty. There was something in the cynical view that numbers of the older married men hardly believed that they would be called upon if they provided the justification for conscripting the single men by "attesting" their own readiness to serve and by displaying, in great numbers, the khaki armlets, bearing the Royal Crown, which were soon available as proof of their patriotic attestations.[2]

The final Derby recruiting figures, available early in January 1916, may be set forth as follows:[3]

[1] By allowing the Lords' Conservative majority to decline passing the Act necessary to extend the sitting Parliament's life into 1916.

[2] Cf. E. Sylvia Pankhurst, *The Home Front*, pp. 258–60 for a revealing if somewhat exaggerated account, of the way in which employers, including Government Departments, pressed men, almost on pain of dismissal, to attest. The result was that "amongst the unwilling pressed men who were fathers of little families, the cry that the single men should be the first to go was apt to receive a fervent welcome".

[3] Lord Derby's Report was issued as a White Paper on January 4, 1916. A full account of Lord Derby's activities at this stage will be found in Randolph Churchill's *Lord Derby*, pp. 184–208.

Number of men enlisted, attested, or rejected: 2,950,504.
Number of single men presenting themselves: 1,150,000.
Number of married men presenting themselves: 1,679,213.
Number of single men remaining: 1,029,231.
Number of married men remaining: 1,152,947.

Of the 1,029,231 single men not presenting themselves for attestation, Lord Derby assumed that 651,160 were "unstarred" and therefore not engaged in essential trades or work of vital national importance. The Cabinet, of course, must have had preliminary figures before it several times during December when the final arguments were proceeding for and against a Conscription Act to be placed on the Statute Book early in 1916. But it might be well, before proceeding to deal with the Cabinet position of December 1915 and the Parliament position of January 1916, to outline what attitude the country's "progressive" forces had been taking up since the possibility of Conscription had become plain during the summer of 1915.

Of legislators, it may be said that, whereas almost the entire Conservative Party was assumed to be Conscriptionist, it was still · believed that the Radicals, Liberals, Labour men, and Irish of the old governing majority of 1906–14 would show a heavy preponderance against Conscription. Yet though Redmond's entire block of over eighty Irish votes was still solidly to be relied on if there was the slightest question of conscripting Irishmen, anti-Conscriptionists in politics were soon to be made aware that provided the effects of a Conscription Bill were confined to Britain, as they ultimately were, the Irish instinct would be to stand aside from a British quarrel. Then, if there was still a seemingly heavy majority against Conscription among the Radical "advanced" men on the Asquithian Benches, it was plain, too, that Lloyd George's advocacy of Conscription as the only way to enforce the democratic principle of "equality of sacrifice" and the only way, also, to win the war, was having a considerable effect. This was specially true of some Radicals who had cause to fear disastrous electoral defeat if the political truce were abandoned and they were branded as half-hearted about victory and even, perhaps, as pro-German because of some pre-war Peace and Disarmament activity. As for Asquithians, "moderate" enough to question a good many of the "advanced's" Radical principles, a "ginger" Conscription group was developing amongst them, almost more troublesome to the Prime Minister than the larger group of belligerent Conservatives who had put themselves under Sir Edward Carson's leadership.[1] Even the whole-heartedness of the Labour men's objections to Conscription was open to question, after the capture of the deceased Keir Hardie's Merthyr seat by a Labour man, who held it to be his duty and the Party's to wage the war against "Kaiserism" and "Prussian Militarism" to the death.[2] On many war-matters, indeed, C. B. Stanton, Merthyr's new Labour M.P., hardly seemed to differ essentially from Horatio Bottomley.[3]

It has, perhaps, been made obvious why the Parliamentary situation of the mid-winter of 1915–16 was shaping itself towards the adoption of a limited Conscription Bill with some safeguards, conceded to Asquith and his wing of the Cabinet, partly in order to avoid a Government break-up and partly in order to have the Bill moved by the long-reluctant Prime Minister himself. Outside Parliament, meanwhile, there were powerful Trade Union forces apparently ready to join in any Radical-Labour struggle against Conscription and, the more so, because it appeared impossible that the results of a Conscription Act would not spread widely and quickly to Industry in many ways deemed adverse to "Labour". The heckling and mobbing on "Dilution of Labour" that Lloyd George himself underwent in Glasgow on Christmas Day, 1915, with the reports virtually suppressed under the Defence of the Realm Act,[4] seemed proof of strong "Labour" feeling, and, to the

[1] Captain F. E. Guest, who represented East Dorset, had already given the Prime Minister serious trouble, but during 1916, it was Sir F. Cawley, Bart., M.P. for Prestwich, whose name was applied to the "Cawley group". He had lost a son, also a Liberal M.P., earlier in the war.

[2] Cf. *Whitaker's Almanack*, 1916, p. 198, for the voting in which Stanton defeated the candidate who, under the party-truce, held himself entitled to the seat: "C. B. Stanton, Labour, 10,286; J. Winstone, Labour 6080."

[3] Cf. E. Sylvia Pankhurst, *The Home Front*, p. 418, for episodes in 1916: "A conference advocating peace negotiations held by the National Council for Civil Liberties in Cardiff and attended by 415 delegates, was raided with great violence by a mob organized by the jingo, Stanton, Member for Merthyr, and the notorious Captain Tupper."

[4] Cf. David Kirkwood, *My Life of Revolt*, pp. 111–12: "He agreed to meet us in St. Andrew's Hall on Christmas Day if I could organize the meeting, and on my telling him that the men would lose a day's pay . . . he said they would get their wages. What a meeting it was! The hall was packed. . . . Girl workers dressed in khaki were brought up from Georgetown and set on the platform. The Union Jack covered the table. A choir sang patriotic songs. Dozens of police were in the hall. Everything which the men regarded as 'kidding' was there. As Mr. Lloyd George entered, the choir started *See the Conquering Hero Comes*. Then pandemonium broke loose. As Mr. Lloyd George sat down, a lock of hair strayed over his brow. Shouts of 'Get your hair cut' came from all quarters. . . . The meeting ended as a fiasco. . . . Next day newspapers had only an official report of the meeting. On New Year's Day *Forward* contined a full

end, Radical "progressives" like the writers of *The Nation* expected a more powerful resistance from the Trade Unions than was actually forthcoming. Doubtless, they did not make sufficient allowance for the effect of all manner of counter-measures open to the Conscriptionists from stressing the need for help and reinforcement to the lads already in the trenches, facing a cruel and relentless foe, to giving unofficial assurances to Trade Union officials that they would certainly be treated as "starred" and "reserved" men when Conscription came into force, Of course, the Conscriptionists, too, made their miscalculations when over-rating, for example, the effect of the blare from the greatest Press megaphones yet known in British history or under-rating the effect still producible in "progressive" England by "advanced" minority organizations like the No Conscription Fellowship or the National Council against Conscription.[1] Ultimately, the "conscientious objectors", who had often been forced into khaki against the plain intention of the Conscription Act itself, must have caused the War Office more detailed trouble[2] than even the Clyde Workers' Committee.[3]

But it is time to deal systematically with the gradual disillusion

report. Before noon the offices were in control of the military. Every available copy was impounded, the machines were dismantled . . . and the paper was suppressed indefinitely."

[1] Cf. *The Ploughshare*, A Quaker Organ of Social Reconstruction, for monthly issues after February 1916, largely occupied with such "news of progressive movements". The September number was marked by an article eulogizing Clifford Allen, the founder of the No Conscription Fellowship, quoting from his defence before a court-martial and giving the reader a striking full-page portrait. The June number of *The Ploughshare* in reporting the erection of a Peace Negotiations Committee quotes the following: "progressive movements" as playing a part: "The Peace Society, U.D.C. [Union of Democratic Control], Women's Labour League, I.L.P. [Independent Labour Party], W.I.L. [Women's International League], N.C.F. [No Conscription Fellowship], Friends' Peace Committee, Friends' Service Committee, etc." Meanwhile a weekly periodical *The Tribunal*, was being set up to report the treatment given to claims for exemption from military service, more especially the claims of "conscientious objectors", by the local Tribunals set up under the Military Service Act.

[2] Cf. *The Ploughshare*, July 1916: "As we go to press the news arrives of the death sentences on four conscientious objectors in France. This was commuted to ten years' penal servitude. . . . Seven other C.O.'s have received one year's hard labour . . . and all these men were during the week ending June 24 in Rouen Military Prison. . . . Fourteen men of the first seventeen sent abroad from the camp at Felixstowe were interviewed at a No. 1 Field Punishment Prison . . . they were undergoing periods of bread and water diet and had been subjected to 'crucifixion'."

[3] Cf. David Kirkwood, *My Life of Revolt*, p. 101: "The Clyde's reply to the Munitions Act was the Clyde Workers' Committee, which had its representatives in every workshop . . . the leaders met every Saturday afternoon to evolve new methods of self-protection against the Act and against the employers who, to us, seemed to be exploiting the patriotic sentiment."

of some of the most representative and influential Radicalism in the country as the Asquithians of the Cabinet, albeit reluctantly and under heavy pressure, allowed continental-style Conscription a quick advance to the Statute Book early in 1916 with Sir John Simon's the only resignation and Simon's prompt replacement as Home Secretary by a brother-Asquithian, Herbert Samuel. One Radical organ reported thus on the opening Parliament-exchanges of January 5 and 6, 1916:[1]

The first Conscription Bill ever presented to Parliament was outlined by the Prime Minister on Wednesday, January 5th. Mr. Asquith's main object seemed to be to minimize its scope and importance. It was limited to the unattested single men (number unknown) and to the redemption of his pledge to the married which was given to avert the breakdown of the Derby Campaign. The pledge came in force when it was made clear that more than a negligible minority of single men had abstained from attesting. Under the Bill, all unattested single men of military age will be treated as if they were attested. . . . Ireland is excluded, and there are to be many exceptions and exemptions. Among the former are the whole body of the clergy, conformist and Nonconformist. The latter are to include workers in the national interest, those with absolute dependents or who are sole supports of a parent, the physically unfit, and conscientious objectors to "combatant" service.

The case for the Bill was brilliantly contested by Sir John Simon, who has resigned the Home Secretaryship mainly on the ground that it was a case of Verdict First and Trial Afterwards. His criticisms clearly shook the "friendlies" of the Labor Party, who expressed their doubts in the person of Mr. Hodge, and strengthened the Liberal and Radical Opposition, while Mr. Redmond refused Irish support even for the first reading.

The second day's debate was overshadowed by the immensely important fact that the Labor Conference of the same day decided to throw over the official resolution, which, though opposing conscription, left the Labor members free to vote as they pleased, in favor of an uncompromising amendment pledging the conference to use "every means in its power" to "oppose" forcible enlistment. This was carried on a card vote by 1,715,000 to 934,000. . . .

The first reading . . . was opposed by 105 members against 403. . . . The minority included 60 Nationalists, 34 Liberals and 11 members of the Labor Party. . . .

At this stage, the cause of "Voluntary Service" was obviously not yet regarded as a completely lost one even though there was

[1] Cf. *The Nation*, January 8, 1916.

loud enough lamentation on the fate that was overtaking Liberal principles and the Liberal Party.[1] But before long, disillusion became more complete as skilful management was applied to the Labour position[2] and Redmond's Nationalists were persuaded, since Ireland had been excepted, to keep out of a British Conscription debate which, if they meddled, might arouse unnecessary enmities for Home Rule. Moreover the high proportion of the Liberal Party that had already been persuaded to abstain, where it could not positively support Asquith in his difficulties, became apparently more significant by the time the Second Reading Division came and produced a majority of 431 against a mere 39, 27 of them Liberals, 10 Labour men, and 2 "Independent" Nationalists. On the face of it, such a triumphant Division must certainly have served to convince Conservative Leaders, despite Lord Northcliffe, of the continued indispensability of an Asquith Premiership. But Conservatives and Radicals alike were also busy studying the abstentions which might obviously come to have their importance if a Cabinet split should develop on Asquith's refusing to go more than a certain way with the Conservatives in war-time. The Radical reading of Division and abstention figures which brought them most encouragement was this:[3]

We are glad to note that the opponents of the Conscription Act in the House of Commons, rejecting the counsels of the *Westminster Gazette*, have maintained their resistance up to the final stage of the measure . . . the vote on the third reading [353 to 36] of the Bill completes the testimony of the divisions that at no stage has it secured the support of the majority of the Parliamentary Party which seated

[1] Cf. *Ibid.*, January 15, 1916 under the heading "THE FRUITS OF CONSCRIPTION": "Within a few hours of its introduction this Bill has divided the Liberal Party. It has divided the Government, and with Mr. Henderson's resignation, stripped it of its character of a national administration. It has divided the Labor movement. It has divided Ireland . . . it threatens to sunder, to adulterate, to confuse the purpose born of indignation, pity, and the national peril under which the whole community sprang to arms in August 1914."

[2] *Ibid.*: "The Prime Minister has used his gift of diplomacy with great skill. . . . Addressing the Labor members, he induced them to give Mr. Henderson and his two Labor colleagues a kind of ticket-of-leave to re-enter the Ministry, pending a review of the situation by the Labor Party's conference which meets at Bristol. . . . 'Securities' and 'safeguards' were to be inserted, and the Parliamentary draughtsmen set to work to frame them. . . . Under this pledge Mr. Henderson returned to the Treasury Bench and defended the Bill. . . . A small number of Liberal members withdrew their opposition, and one or two Labor representatives."

[3] Cf. *Ibid.*, January 29, 1917.

Mr. Asquith in power. On the first reading, 155 Liberal and Labor
Members voted for the Bill, while 224 Liberal, Labor, and Irish
members abstained. On the second reading, 181 supporters of Mr.
Asquith voted for the Bill and 201 voted against it or abstained. On
the third reading, 156 Liberal, Nationalist Irish and Labor men voted
for the Bill while 266 resisted it or abstained. Nor is this all. The list
of voters for the Bill includes many members to whom its principles
were entirely repugnant, and whose decision was governed by the fear
of a harsher measure following the rejection of the limited Bill, or of a
General Election affirming the principle, and seating in power, not a
divided and half-resolute Administration, but a whole-hearted Conscriptionist Government.

Undoubtedly Radicals, who bargained with the Asquithian
Whips on the Conscription limitations which would induce them
to abstain from a hostile vote, played some part in securing that it
was a relatively "limited" Conscription that was put on the Statute
Book as the Military Service Act of January 27, 1916.[1] No doubt
those Radical bargainers hoped that a political or military situation
might yet arise which would permit them to assert their principles
more openly and courageously. But war-events were hurrying
Britain into ever greater war-expenditure in life and money and
towards ever clearer "proof" apparently that unless a decisive
victory were obtained, "at whatever cost", the post-war world
would be full of the most insoluble problems, moral, political,
financial, and strategic. Accordingly, so far from any retreats from
the Conscription principle proving possible, the War Office was
soon to decide to call up all the attested men of the "Derby
Scheme", married[2] as well as unmarried, and then, in justice to
the attested married men, to call for that speedy and compulsory
enlistment of all the "slackers" of forty-one years of age or under,
for which the more war-infected part of the Press had already
begun demands.

Perhaps discussion on the new Radical agonies over the second
Conscription Act of 1916—the Military Service Act of May 25th
—should be delayed and attention concentrated on the ever-
keener problems of conscience that every month of intensified
warfare was, meanwhile, bringing with it to those who had really
believed in the "principles of freedom" which seemed to be

[1] As the 5 & 6 Geo. 5, c. 104.
[2] The Attested Married Men's Protest Societies, that were set up in consequence, were one curious feature of the times. They held that the "married
slackers", who had not attested with them, ought to be conscripted first.

increasingly laid aside in the presumed interests of victory.[1] Thus "freedom of the Press' (like habeas corpus and Free Speech already) was being drastically curtailed, it was claimed, in a totally unexpected direction when the Defence of the Realm Act was applied not merely to confining reports of Zeppelin-raid damage, it might be, or Western offensives to official or sponsored material but to suppressing a perfectly truthful account in *Forward* of disorder at a Lloyd George meeting and then proceeding, for good measure, to close down the paper too. Free Trade, also, was under threat from a variety of different directions, for war had certainly increased Tariff Reformers' propaganda opportunities whether to preach tariffs as a ready way to meet much of the cost of the war or to argue the necessity for high post-war tariffs to keep out the enormous export-dumps that Germany was asserted to be building up from materials unsold because of hostilities. A totally new threat to Free Trade was even expected to develop from an Allied Economic Conference for which preparations had begun with the specious aim of systematizing mutual inter-Allied economic aid for the war- and the post-war periods. By the time Radicals and Free Traders had done comparing and collating the hopes that British and Dominion Protectionists, not to mention French, Italian, and Russian Government and business circles, were placing in the Conference, they saw reason to fear that, unless extreme vigilance were shown, Britain might well emerge from the Conference pledged to a four-tier tariff, combining Protection for "home industries" from German post-war dumping with first preferential rates for Dominions and Colonies, second preferential rates for Allies, ordinary rates for neutrals, and penal rates for Germany.

Then, suddenly, towards the end of March, with Asquith away for War Conferences in France and Italy, another full-scale Conscription crisis was, in Radical opinion, precipitated by the powerful Conservative War Committee on the subject of the

[1] Cf. *The Nation*, February 26th: "There is a type of Liberal whose idea of patriotic duty during war consists in throwing to the wolves one after another of his Liberal principles . . . Free Speech, Free Press, Habeas Corpus, Voluntary Service, Free Trade—let them all go in this war for Liberty! The process is called 'making sacrifices to win the war'. But it has become so automatic and indiscriminate as to threaten alike the safety and the sanity of the nation. The reactionary elements in this country utilize it with the plain intent of recovering all their 'lost causes' and establishing new forms of political and economic privilege. . . . Just now they are gathering themselves together for a frontal attack on Free Trade. . . ."

unattested "married slackers" who had not thought fit to volunteer at Lord Derby's call.[1] The great German attack on Verdun was already well under way, air activity against Britain was most marked,[2] and, altogether, Conservative all-out Conscriptionists, with so many propaganda advantages in their favour, would doubtless have preferred to have an excuse for driving out the Asquithians instead of reopening parleys with them on exceptions to be allowed in a second and more far-reaching Conscription Bill. The rumours the all-out Conscriptionists' Mayfair friends were now circulating against Liberal Leaders and Conservatives who worked closely with them had, by now, certainly reached a stage of credulous ferocity that today seems hardly believable. Five of the rumours, collected with scorn and published in a Radical weekly at mid-April, were actually these:[3]

1. That Lord Haldane's son has been shot as a spy.
2. That Miss Asquith is engaged to the son of Count Zeppelin.
3. That Mr. Asquith has Sir Edgar Speyer to dinner every night and shows him the private telegrams, which, of course, Sir Edgar telegraphs at once to Germany.
4. That, of course, Mrs. McKenna is German, and that is why she is so fond of German music.
5. That "the Alkali Company" of which Mr. Gerald Balfour is Chairman has made millions selling chemicals to Germany.

Fortunately, there was still enough sense of honour and responsibility on the Conservative side of the Cabinet to set aside the temptation to climb back to formal political supremacy by the aid of panic-rumours or the political tactics propounded for the party by Carsonite Back-Benchers. In regard, for instance, to the panic-

[1] Cf. *The Nation*, April 1st: "It was a stiffish proceeding to choose the Prime Minister's absence on a War Conference in France and Italy to spring a mine on his Government but that is the openly-avowed strategy of the hour. The newly formed Slackers Brigade may not be much of a weapon against the Germans, but it has its guns quite openly trained on Parliament. . . . To suggest that the use of such tactics and such instruments is an open dishonour to the country, conveys no reproach to certain minds, who are forming their new Carsonite Administration on the calculation that when the time comes the Unionist members of the Cabinet, led by Mr. Law, will desert and so force an election. . . ."

[2] Cf. *Whitaker's Almanack, 1917*, Diary of the War, pp. 466–7, for February 21st as the opening day of the Verdun attacks and March 19th as the day when the Germans used seaplanes against Dover, Deal, Ramsgate, and Margate, as a variation from Zeppelin attack.

[3] Cf. *The Nation*, April 15th, which did not, perhaps, need to comment on the significant omission of Lloyd George from the rumour-mongers' attentions. It had been very different in the "Marconi" season of 1912–14.

mongering of their own side, they must have had an even better idea than the Radical journals of the serious food-plight and the many blockade difficulties already overtaking Germany[1] despite the great military position established since August 1914. Moreover, at the very height of the all-out Conscriptionists' manœuvres after mid-April, when, with the help of the "patriotic" Press and some cheerless war-news, they had produced a situation allowing the Conservative side of the Cabinet, accompanied by Lloyd George, to be reported as preparing to resign,[2] there occurred, on April 24th, the notorious Dublin rising of Sinn Fein and the associated German attempt to provide arms, ammunition, and Sir Roger Casement.[3] It was inevitable, in such a situation, that the Cabinet should immediately close its ranks, and though Radicals were to complain before long that, as usual, virtually all the concessions, whether on Conscription or the Allied Economy Conference, were made by the Asquithians, the dethronement of the Asquithian Cabinet majority was certainly postponed for a space. In fact, Asquith and Lloyd George were given a last chance of almost cordial co-operation in the effort to snatch some good from the Irish bloodshed by exploring, for months, the possibility of an agreed installation of a pro-war and anti-German Redmondite Administration at Dublin in charge of the more domestic aspects of government in the Twenty-six Counties. When the Army and Conservatism blocked the modest instalment of Home Rule thereby contemplated and turned the temporary anti-Sinn Fein swing of Irish opinion back towards the Sinn Fein "martyrs"

[1] Cf. *Ibid.*, April 1st: "I counsel a course of reading of the German newspapers to any man who wants a rest from the nightmare of a German economic 'dump' at the end of the war. He will read there of the closing of spinning mills for lack of cotton; complaints of 'pasteboard' shoes put on the market because of the scarcity of leather . . . admissions of the failure of the meat supply in Berlin; suggestion of an extension of meatless days for households in Leipzig—already three a week; confessions of a 100 per cent to 200 per cent rise in food prices . . . of the shutting of cake and biscuit factories; of the setting-up of an 'Imperial Office' for supplying poor civilians with clothing; of great numbers of German women parading the streets of Berlin shouting for 'bread and peace'. . . . Does this look like a great organized spring on the world-markets?"

[2] Cf. *Ibid.*, April 20th: "The Government is on the verge of disruption though a final effort of reconciliation or an intervention of the King may avert it. The form of severance will probably be the resignation of the Unionist members, accompanied by Mr. Lloyd George as the protagonist of the out-and-out Conscriptionists."

[3] Cf. *Whitaker's Almanack, 1917*, Diary of the War, under April 24th: "A German auxiliary, disguised as a neutral merchant vessel, and a submarine attempted to land arms and ammunition on the Irish coast. . . . Taken prisoner on shore was Sir Roger Casement, who had been trying to induce Irish soldiers imprisoned in Germany to join a German Irish brigade."

again,[1] there was even a chance that Lloyd George might throw over that collaboration with Conservatism and the Northcliffe Press that was, before long, to put him in Asquith's place.

But this is to outrun the day-to-day and week-to-week development of events as Radicals of the spring and summer of 1916 anxiously watched them. Here, for example, is *The Nation*, at the end of April, commenting bitterly on the Prime Minister's new surrenders to the Conscriptionists:[2]

We live in a world of make-believe. The Prime Minister, driven by internal difficulties to reverse his policy on Conscription, and to pronounce for that general policy of compulsion which he and Lord Kitchener declared to be unnecessary, has used the ingenious method of a Secret Session . . . to announce the change and make it palatable to the Labor members. The further device was used of a secret conference between Mr. Asquith, Lord Kitchener and Mr. Law, on the one hand, and the trade union leaders on the other. The secrecy was defended by one of the most sweeping Orders in Council ever promulgated. . . . The plan took shape in two Bills. . . . The minor Bill . . . extended the service of time-expired men to the end of the war, empowered the military to transfer the Territorials to other units . . . made exempted men liable for service as soon as their Certificates expired, and, above all, conscripted all boys after their eighteenth birthday.

The major proposal decidedly conflicts with the Prime Minister's assurances as to the finality of the first measure of Conscription. It gives the unattested married men four weeks grace (ending with May 27th) to enlist, and provides that if 50,000 men are not then enrolled, and less than 15,000 in any ensuing week, the whole class shall be taken by force . . . 200,000 recruits in fourteen weeks. . . . How can there be any justification for fixing upon a number of these dimensions? . . . The case becomes aggravated when one examines the scheme of financial relief which is proposed to help the fathers of families to go forth to battle gladly. . . . How does this scheme pretend to relieve middle-class men whose rent and rates alone may come to more than the £104 limit, and who may pay another £100 in insurance premiums? . . . The Ministry can only, with decency, propose the conscription of men by adding the conscription of wealth, i.e. by making the people who stay at home maintain those who go to war.

Radical laments of the next few weeks on England's having "become a conscript nation", on the Coalition's having passed under Conservative domination, and on the certain loss of a

[1] Cf. *Whitaker's Almanack, 1917*, Diary of the War, under May 8th: "Casualties in the rising—military and constabulary: killed 124, wounded and missing 397; civilians: killed 180, wounded 614. Of the rebels, 14 had been executed, 73 sentenced to penal servitude, and six to imprisonment." Many of the listed civilian killed and wounded were, doubtless, "rebels" too.

[2] Cf. *The Nation*, April 29th.

possibly last chance in Ireland if a halt was not called to court-martial executions of young Irish "rebels" who had only been following Sir Edward Carson's example—all this must largely be left without illustration in chapter and verse. So must the Radical protests as to the misuse and misinterpretation of their powers, especially in regard to "conscientious objection", undertaken by many of the local Military Tribunals—Tribunals whose juris-diction was now being extended to mere lads of eighteen and to the middle-aged fathers of families, without any security that they would observe the law better in the future than in the past.[1] Of course, the Secret Sessions on Conscription and the hurrying through of a second Conscription Act were connected, just as were Mr. Asquith's visits to France and Italy earlier, and a visit to Russia just being arranged for Lord Kitchener, with the hopes of staging simultaneous Allied offensives in the high summer of 1916 which would break German and Austrian resistance and end the war. The Conscription Acts allowed Britain to promise that there would be reserves to replace the heavy initial losses to be expected as well as to exploit the projected break-through on the Somme, and, in point of fact, other inducements, too, proved necessary to get full assurance that Allied offensives would match the British effort.

As ill-luck would have it, the British nation was fated to receive two very severe blows to its *morale* before it could be informed that its Army was preparing to launch an offensive on which very high hopes were placed. At the very end of May came the Naval battle of Jutland which was, at first, so awkwardly reported that pessimists suspected that it really was the German victory claimed by Berlin[2] and, if not marking the end of British Naval power,

[1] Cf. *The Ploughshare*, May 1916, for Clifford Allen: "All schemes to impose alternative service so far outlined only affect the few men who have been deemed to be conscientious objectors by the Tribunals. Now it is admitted that there are hundreds of men, whose sincerity is beyond dispute, who have failed for geographical and other reasons to convince the Tribunals. These men are being daily arrested and deprived of any opportunity of accepting alternative service, even if they should be willing. . . . The Government have been able to slur over the hopeless breakdown of the machinery of the Act, to persecute its victims, and then give the public the impression that it is most conciliatory by trifling with the granting of alternative service for a few fortunate conscientious objectors who have been lucky enough to emerge from a Tribunal with a certificate."

[2] Cf. *Whitaker's Almanack, 1917*, Diary of the War, under June 7, 1916: "Mr. Balfour declared that the German Navy was relatively inferior to what it was before the Battle of Jutland. The Kaiser, speaking at Wilhelmshaven asserted that the British fleet was beaten." Mr. Balfour's declaration was an effort to undo the harm done by the Admiralty's original announcement of June 2nd which *The Nation* of June 10th treated thus: "It is a great feat for the British

might very well dangerously reduce the future effectiveness of the British blockade. Only a few days later came the report of the destruction of H.M.S. *Hampshire* with heavy loss, loss that included Lord Kitchener who had been dispatched on a special mission to Russia.[1] The general public almost reeled under the second shock, and those who thought they knew how it all happened were soon busy scandal-mongering on rumoured information leakages from Britain to Germany in a fashion that seemed strikingly to confirm the "Hidden Hand" explanation of every war-misadventure—the "Hidden Hand" of traitors, German agents or, perhaps, merely blackmailed Britishers whose secret vices, that spelt ruin if revealed, had become known to Berlin.[2] Nor can it be pretended that the news that Lloyd George had been appointed War Secretary in Kitchener's place brought much original reassurance even if Northcliffe's Press had worked long and assiduously to build up, in the public mind, a picture of the founder of the Munitions Ministry as the country's greatest hope for success in the war. The contrast between the wily politician and the massive and trusted soldier was certainly startling, and though Northcliffe and Bottomley doubtless considered that a war-excited populace could be quickly persuaded, by the Press, to believe that the change at the War Office was for the better, it is hard to find evidence that, when the great British offensive on the Somme was attempted, it was the newly-appointed War Secretary who bulked largest in the public eye. Doubtless, a fair proportion, even of the readership of the *Daily Mail*, must have been aware that if, as was being reported, Lloyd George was hard at work on finally vain negotiations for an agreed Irish settlement, the running of the War Office, like the running of the Somme offensive, must have been largely left in the hands of the Staff and the Generals.

Admiralty to win a battle on the sea and lose it in a dispatch." *The Nation* commented severely, too, on the "distrust and dismay that spread through the country" on June 2nd and its opinion is the better worth noting as it surmised correctly that the Germans were making a sustained attempt to conceal their true losses and that the German Navy might "never emerge again, save for unsubstantial raids".

[1] Cf. *Whitaker's Almanack, 1917*, Diary of the War, under June 5, 1916, for the number of survivors as twelve only.

[2] Cf. Arnold White, *The Hidden Hand*, p. 241: "Year after year minute details of all the scandals were added to the Potsdam archives. And so, with unceasing assiduity, there was placed in the Kaiser's hands a monumental aggregation of secrets imperilling the reputation—aye, and, perhaps the liberty or even the life—of just the very political schemers in whose hands, as the all-Highest hoped, might be the elaboration of British policy during a war with Germany."

These, meanwhile, had been taught that if Lloyd George had been useful to them when it was a question of forcing Kitchener's hand or Asquith's,[1] it was going to be much less comfortable to have him as Secretary for War. He had begun by demanding much wider powers already[2] and, before the end, as is well known, he seemed, to some, to be fighting, with the aid of his "newspaper lords", not so much the Kaiser as Robertson and Haig on Army matters, Jellicoe on Admiralty business, and Trenchard on Air organization.[3]

Of the British offensive, which opened on the Somme at the beginning of July, it may be safely stated that there is hardly a military authority in the world today, who would consider that its results justified the terrifying casualties involved. But the real truth was carefully concealed from the contemporary "public", by arrangement, almost, between the War Office and the newspapers, and for months there were exaggerated hopes that the heavy pounding of the German trenches and the subsequent "British breaks-through" might bring a victorious end to the war conspicuously nearer. How Lloyd George endeavoured to annex part of the credit for what was still regarded, on August 1st, as a hopeful enterprise may be judged from a farewell speech he gave that day to the Ministry of Munitions staff—though, of course, other glittering, if indirect, advertisements of his record were introduced as well as an anti-German pugnacity worthy of Horatio Bottomley himself. Here is part of the speech which took him a great step on the road to the "Knock-Out Blow" rhetoric of September 29th that finally clinched his claims to the Premiership with the bellicose:[4]

I well remember what the Department was like when I entered it. . . . There was a table, I forget whether there was one or two chairs,

[1] Cf. Dr. Addison, *Four and a Half Years*, for such diary entries of April 1916 as this: "I told L.G. that I thought he ought to have a good deal more information before he acted on Robertson's document, which meant universal compulsion. The Army wasted great numbers of competent fighting-men in all kinds of unessential non-military jobs, many of which could well be done by women or by men who were unfit. . . ." The greatest political intriguer among the Staff Generals, Wilson, was eventually used to replace Robertson.

[2] Cf. *The Nation*, June 24, 1916, on "THE WAR OFFICE AND THE WAR."

[3] Cf. Lord Beaverbrook, *Men and Power, 1917–1918*, for one of the "newspaper lords" in attempted justification of himself and Lloyd George.

[4] Cf. Dr. Addison, *Four and a Half Years*, i, 244–7 for a fuller reproduction of the speech-copies distributed in the Munitions Ministry which are here requoted by permission of Messrs. Hutchinson.

but there was no carpet allowed by the Board of Works. . . . Then I do not think we had annexed Lord Moulton. He had a very complete staff and establishment. . . . Subsequently we annexed him and annexed Woolwich. At the time I am speaking about, Sir Hubert Llewellyn Smith, Dr. Addison and myself, and my private secretaries, Mr. J. T. Davies and Miss Stevenson, with that simple furniture, constituted the Ministry of Munitions.

Now here you are, one of the greatest Departments not merely in this country, but . . . in the world. I had had some experience of starting another new Department, and that is the Insurance Department, . . . that was a Department which administered about 20 millions a year, which I thought a very big thing. Here is a Department, which administers between 400 and 500 millions a year, set up in the middle of a great war. . . .

You cannot realise what you have done. Just look where we were! That story has not been told altogether, but it must be told one day. Just look where we are now! . . . I could tell you where we were, if you wanted to know, but as to where we are now you must ask the Kaiser. Ask the Kaiser what has happened. . . . You can ask those who are muttering curses under the shower of shell which has been manufactured or you can ask those gallant fellows of ours whose bravery is now the talk of the world and the terror of the foe. Just you ask them how you helped them to get through barbed wire and shatter the dug-outs and concrete. . . .

You have left your mark in the history of this country. They cannot write the history of this country without telling the story of the Ministry of Munitions. . . . Every little child for centuries to come . . . will read that there was a Ministry of Munitions, and that people came from every quarter, from every trade . . . and threw themselves into the salvation of their country. . . .

You have no idea what an alteration you have made in the industry of the country. . . . You have helped to resurrect the old country as well as protect it and save it. When people write about capital and labour there will be a new chapter beginning, "Ministry of Munitions, Advancement, Social Welfare, New Ideas, Improved Condition of Workers, New Discoveries. . . ."

I will tell you what I want to say to you finally—Keep it up! Keep it up! Shower brimstone upon the murderers of Captain Fryatt. Help to call them to account!

I want you to keep it up until we win: Keep it up until we rid the earth of this cruel monster of Prussian militarism. When you have done it, you will feel to your dying day . . . "I helped to slay the beast".

It was towards the end of August 1916 that the dearly-bought adhesion of Rumania to the Allied cause was obtained, and almost simultaneously Italy's declaration of war upon Germany was announced.[1] Though it is true that promises of territorial gain had been conceded which made the "Secret Treaties" involving Rumania and Italy perhaps the most indefensible of those revealed to a shocked world in 1917,[2] those two countries must have kept a fair amount of confidence in the result of the concerted offensive of Britain, France, and Russia still proceeding. According to one claim made, in fact, in Paris just after mid-September, the combined captures of Britain, France, Russia, and Italy numbered 490,688 prisoners and 1131 guns.[3] As it happened, German help to Austria and German retribution upon Rumania and Russia were about to descend with hammer force in the famous Mackensen drive which resulted in such spectacular enemy successes in the closing months of 1916.[4] But, perhaps, it would be well, before attempting to assess the results of the new war-disappointments upon British politics towards the end of 1916, to make a brief review of Radical preoccupations after the deep chagrin of seeing a second Conscription Act placed on the Statute Book in May 1916.

Ireland was, of course, constantly in Radical thoughts especially after the Dublin Rising with its heavy toll of policemen and troops who had, in the military view, often been needlessly done to death by the rebels. Radicals made efforts, not altogether fruitlessly, to get the court-martial executions stopped quickly[5] and the lamentable Skeffington murder adequately investigated.

---

[1] Cf. *Whitaker's Almanack, 1917*, Diary of the War, which gives under August 27th, "Roumania declared war on Austria-Hungary" and under August 28th, "Italy declared war on Germany." Italy had bargained hard, territorially, before declaring war on Austria in the spring of 1915 and had been raising her terms whenever opportunity offered afterwards.

[2] It must be held that the serious losses of France and Russia gave them, in the eyes of the British Foreign Office, the right to insist on getting relief even on terms so exorbitant as those conceded. But, in point of fact, France and Russia were committing themselves more and more to a complete break-up of the Habsburg Empire.

[3] Cf. *Whitaker's Almanack, 1917*, Diary of the War, quoting the *Journal* of Paris under September 19, 1916.

[4] Cf. *Ibid.*, under September 18, 1916, for this opening report: "The Russo-Roumanian forces in the Dobrudja, under pressure by General Mackensen retired. . . ." And under October 2, 1916, for "The Roumanians suffered a reverse in the Herrmannstadt region at the hands of Falkenhayn."

[5] Cf. *The Nation*, May 13th: "The severity of these proceedings created a sharp revulsion in Liberal circles . . . Mr. Redmond and Mr. Dillon both called for a pledge that shootings by the military should cease to which Mr. Asquith responded only with a hint of mercy in the near future. . . . Mr. Asquith's second announcement of his visit to Dublin was much more cheering."

They even tried to save Sir Roger Casement[1] from the gallows on the ground that his execution would poison Anglo-Irish relations at a critical moment when Redmond needed every possible help to swing Irish opinion into accepting a very limited instalment of Home Rule, confined to the Twenty-six Counties, as a provisional settlement entitling Britain to expect full war co-operation for the remainder of the struggle against the Central Powers. Moreover, Radicals took Redmond's side almost unreservedly when, after a tripartite negotiation between Redmond, Carson, and Lloyd George had yielded an enactable provisional settlement, Lord Lansdowne, followed ultimately by the Conservative side of the Cabinet, insisted that the handing-over of limited authority in the Twenty-six Counties to Irish Nationalism must be accompanied by Irish Nationalism's own surrender of the strangle-hold established at Westminster in virtue of Ireland's 103 members. In point of fact, by the standards of 1916, there seemed so much justification for the view that 103 Irish members at Westminster, in combination with a Dublin Nationalist Government, would be able completely to dictate the "permanent" Irish post-war settlement, that Asquith and Lloyd George, not without reluctance, decided to ask Redmond to accept a reduction of the Irish contingent at Westminster, after the next election, to 42, the figure fixed by the Home Rule Bills of 1912–14. When Redmond refused this till there was a "permanent" settlement and the negotiations were broken off, *The Nation*, regarded almost as the voice of the Radical groups in Parliament, denounced Redmond's treatment under so startling a heading as "THE VIOLATED TREATY" and had little use for any of the counter-arguments employed and especially that which urged that, at any rate, the break-up of the "National Ministry" had been prevented.[2] Here is the tone of *The Nation* on the subject:[3]

[1] Cf. *The Nation*, July 1st: "There will be a petition promoted both in this country and in Ireland for the commuting of the death penalty on Sir Roger Casement. Many will sign who feel no personal sympathy . . . the moral power of magnanimity . . ought to count heavily for clemency. And there is something to be said about the trial. . . . The prosecution should never have been conducted by Sir Frederick Smith. It is not enough to urge that the Smith rebellion stopped with the war, and the Casement rebellion did not. . . ."

[2] In point of fact the strongest Unionist of the Cabinet, Lord Selborne, had resigned towards the end of June in a fashion that would have spread but for the concessions finally made to Lord Lansdowne.

[3] Cf. *The Nation*, July 29th, for this treatment of events in the Commons on July 24th which should also be studied in *Hansard*, 1916, lxxxiv, 1427–70.

... there was much in Monday's happenings to disgust everybody with the Coalition and its works. Ireland was the chief victim, and this time nearly everybody sympathises with her. . . . To make an offer of a settlement, to get Mr. Redmond to back it at all but the cost of the life of Irish Nationalism, and then to raise the terms over his head—how could any statesman . . . associate himself with such a method in such an hour? Honeyed words and a flattering manner were used. . . . But Mr. George's *apologia pro missione sua* left none of its worst points unrevealed. . . .

What were these unauthorised, unrevised additions to the pact to which Sir Edward Carson, Mr. Redmond and Mr. Lloyd George were parties? The first established the permanent character of the severance of the six Ulster counties. . . . The Irishmen did not want the idea of permanency stamped too deeply into the fabric of the Bill. . . . They were out for their lives, and it was a callous business for Home Rule Ministers to ignore the fact. Even so, I doubt whether this new "permanent" clause would have wrecked the Bill. But it was accompanied by one serious and admitted breach of the agreement. This provided for the retention of the Irish members in full strength at Westminster until a permanent settlement had been reached. . . . Why change it? The one reason assigned was that the Unionist members of the Cabinet had joined Lord Lansdowne's revolt and, headed by Mr. Bonar Law, insisted that the full Irish contingent should go. After the next election, their representation was to be reduced to 42, and only restored to its full complement, when the question of a final settlement came up. The meaning of this was plain. The Unionists feared that the election might give the Irishmen the balance of power: in other words that it might unseat a Unionist Government or prevent its formation. . . . Was it necessary to bow to Lord Lansdowne, a *démodé* politician whose head the *Daily Mail* demanded as a disturber of the national unity? The Prime Minister had the country with him. He had almost the entire Press . . . above all, he had the Carson-Redmond agreement. Were these cards not strong enough for . . . a course of absolute fidelity to the compact with Mr. Redmond even if it had involved the tender of resignation by the Prime Minister and Mr. Lloyd George? These contrasted figures, so often in dissonance, were closely united in Monday's defence of the broken covenant. They sat together, making joint avowal of their abiding Home Rule faith, encouraging and applauding each other, deprecating the rupture even at the eleventh hour, but hinting not dubiously that the responsibility for it would lie with Mr. Redmond.

The Radical attitude towards Asquith on other matters than Ireland was hardly more enthusiastic. Though, for example, a policy was slowly being evolved to put a stop to some of the disturbing results flowing from the prejudiced decisions of numbers of Tribunals set up under the Military Service Acts, there were

Radicals who complained of the Prime Minister's still cautious attitude towards imprisoned "conscientious objectors" whose claims had been rejected by a Tribunal.[1] Nor was Asquith really trusted to safeguard Free Trade adequately from the interested clamour of those who, on the pretence of preventing Germany from ever again dominating "key industries" in the Home, Colonial, Allied, and Neutral Markets, had devised the suspect Resolutions of the Paris Inter-Allied Economic Conference and plans to implement them that no pre-war Tariff Reformer would have ventured.[2] Radicals, in fact, were increasingly reluctant to accept further "sacrifices of principle" to keep Asquith's Coalition together and sometimes tended to forget the heavy burden the Prime Minister held himself to be carrying in the effort to secure any respect at all for "Liberal principles" at the height of the grimmest war Britain had ever fought.

It was not only that Northcliffe, in command of the greatest newspaper power ever known, was plotting, day-in and day-out, to "stampede" Asquith from power, that Lloyd George had barely been kept from resigning and starting a stampede of his own,[3] and that large sections of the Conservative Back-Benchers, and even

---

[1] Cf. *The Nation*, July 22nd: "In an answer to Mr. Snowden, the Prime Minister has confirmed the more pessimistic interpretations of the new policy towards Conscientious Objectors. Those who refuse to perform any kind of alternative service are to be handed back to the military authorities . . . we suppose that they also come under the general threat made by Mr. Asquith, that men who are sent back to the Army after the process of sifting will be treated 'with the utmost rigor'. For our part, we think that men who refuse to do such remedial work as ambulance duties or forestry are pushing the logic of their position to an unsocial excess. But to deny them on that account the relief provided . . . is to stultify the whole spirit of the Act. They are facing every kind of social and civil penalty, and risking physical ill-treatment and degradation. . . . They are exactly the extreme rare cases for which Parliament has now twice provided the possibility of 'absolute exemption'. . . . It is time to make an end of this folly."

[2] Cf. *Hansard*, August 2nd, and *The Nation*, August 5th, commenting thus: "Mr. Asquith did not absolutely commit himself. . . . The most ominous feature of the speech was the affirmation of Free Trade orthodoxy in the peroration. Experience teaches that it is always by such declarations as this that the great Parliamentary mesmerist endeavours to send his own party to sleep when he surrenders its fundamental principles. . . ."

[3] Cf. Dr. Addison, *Four and a Half Years*, i, 189–90, for some of the diary entries of April 1916: "I told him that it was to court failure if he went out solely with the backing of the Harmsworth Press, the wild men among the Tories and only a small following of Liberals. . . ." As the contemplated crusade was against "incompetence, whether at No. 10 or the War Office", or in other words against both Asquith and Kitchener, Addison was right in warning Lloyd George that he might wll ruin himself instead of his two Cabinet colleagues.

of the Army chiefs, were bitterly hostile.[1] The Prime Minister
had had to submit to some Conscriptionist blackmail in January
to get the House of Lords to accept the Bill which extended the
sitting Parliament's life for eight months beyond the quinquennial
term fixed in the 1911 Parliament Act, and there was more trouble
and even humiliation to be faced in July and August when, a
General Election still being deemed impossible, a further Parliament Extension Bill had to be suggested.[2] Lloyd George, too,
was acting, when he was so minded, in virtual independence of the
Prime Minister, and in the notorious "Knock-Out" interview,
published on September 29th, he took one of the crucial decisions
of the war without having been invited thereto either by the
Prime Minister or by Grey, the Foreign Secretary. An American
journalist had sought him out, and Lloyd George, suspecting that
President Wilson of the United States, not to mention the Pope,
was anxious to offer mediation and that some of his own colleagues
were not to be trusted to make an outright refusal,[3] announced,
almost in Bottomley language, Germany's complete military defeat
as the war-aim from which the Alliance would not allow itself to
be diverted. There is no doubt but that History will hold that
those colleagues of Lloyd George, like Lord Lansdowne,[4] who
were already beginning to suspect that there would have to be a
change of course unless the whole familiar world of 1914 were to
be allowed to go for ever, showed greater ultimate wisdom than

[1] Cf. *Field-Marshal Sir Henry Wilson, His Life and Diaries*, i, 274–80, for the
views of one who would, before long, become Chief of the Imperial General
Staff. Of an interview with Bonar Law late in April 1916 he wrote: "Bonar Law
really believes that the Coalition is the best possible Government at this time.
I told him that if we did not get rid of Asquith, we should lose the war but he
remained obdurate."

[2] Cf. *Hansard*, August 14th, for the Prime Minister's introduction of the
"Prolongation" Bill and his explanation of the Government's difficulties in
planning the Registration Bill to fix the Registers for the next Election, difficulties
that had already caused serious trouble in the Commons on July 19th. One of
the problems was how to poll millions of soldiers and sailors all over the world;
another, the measure of Women's Franchise to be allowed; and a third, how to
poll the munition-workers, living away from home. Ultimately the device of
an all-Party Speaker's Committee was hit upon to recommend the new electoral
arrangements necessary but, meanwhile, Asquith had to accept a "Prolongation"
Bill reduced to a seven-months period.

[3] Cf. *Lord Riddell's War Diary, 1914–1918*, under October 1st.

[4] Cf. Lord Beaverbrook, *Men and Power, 1917–1918*, xxxvii, for Lansdowne
"having already submitted a Peace Plan as a Cabinet paper to the Asquith
Government in 1916" with Lord Robert Cecil voicing the objection "that any
such peace would bring final disaster to Britain." According to *Lord Riddell's
War Diary, 1914–1918*, under October 7th, Lloyd George believed "his recent
interview was none too soon and that there had been 'peace talk'. Also that
Asquith and some of his associates are in it."

Lloyd George and Northcliffe in Britain, and the even wilder plungers of Petersburg,[1] Paris, and Rome. This chapter must conclude with some of the more "popular" sections of the "Knock-Out" interview, followed by an angry Radical commentary.

"Britain," said Lloyd George,[2] "has only begun to fight. The British Empire has invested thousands of its best lives to purchase future immunity for civilisation. This investment is too great to be thrown away. . . .

"The British soldier is a good sportsman. He enlisted in this war in a sporting spirit—in the best sense of that term. He went in to see fair play to a small nation trampled upon by a bully. He is fighting for fair play. He has fought as a good sportsman. . . . He played the game. He didn't squeal, and he certainly never asked anyone to squeal for him.

"Under the circumstances the British, now that the fortunes of the game have turned a bit, are not disposed to stop because of the squealing done by Germans or done for Germans by probably well-meaning but misguided sympathisers and humanitarians. . . .

"He [the British soldier] saw the Allied causes beaten all about the ring. But he didn't appeal either to spectators or referee to stop the fight on the ground that it was brutal. Nor did he ask that the rules be changed. He took his punishment, even when beaten, like a dog. He was a game dog.

"During these months, when it seemed the finish of the British Army might come quickly, Germany elected to make this a fight to a finish with England. The British soldier was ridiculed and held in contempt. Now we intend to see that Germany has her way. The fight must be to a finish—to a knock-out. . . ."

The Nation, aware both of Germany's growing economic plight[3] and, yet, of the Fight-to-a-Finish Party's dangerous determination to throw in new masses of conscripts, whether procured from Ireland or from the extension of the Conscription liability to Britishers of forty-five[4], was angry both with Lloyd George's

---

[1] Cf. M. Paléologue, *La Russie des Tsars*, for the Tsarist régime, on the very eve of its collapse, still supporting France, during February 1917, in plans for detaching not merely an enlarged Alsace-Lorraine from Germany but an "autonomous" Rhineland State as well.

[2] Cf. *The Times*, September 29th.

[3] Cf. Sir Almeric Fitzroy, *Memoirs*, ii, 635, under October 16, 1916, for an interesting confirmation of what *The Nation* had been proclaiming for some time: "Captain Hall, of the Intelligence Department of the Admiralty, calculates that, if Germany waits till her economic resources are exhausted before suing for peace, she will be face to face with a period of absolute starvation . . . he therefore looks to her showing the first official symptoms of having had enough in the course of the ensuing February. . . ." The collapse of Rumania and Russia was, of course, to interfere with the calculation.

[4] Cf. *The Nation*, September 30th: "Looking about for further opportunities of subjecting the British people to compulsion, the party of conscription

manner and matter. Echoing, perhaps, the opinions of the McKenna-Runciman Cabinet wing with which it shared some views *The Nation* held that Lloyd George, instead of stimulating war-passion to rise higher, should have turned his mind to such definable war-aims as "the withdrawal of German troops from the invaded territories, the reinstatement of all the threatened nations, the satisfaction of France, the contentment of Russia, the fair settlement of Italian claims, above all the framing of a measure of international security". All these aims were attainable—especially if mediators were allowed to smooth the way for the yielding side —without a "knock-out, i.e. a point of complete subjugation, such as Louis XIV or Napoleon never attained over their greater adversaries". Besides what right had Lloyd George, who was not even the official expositor of British Foreign policy, to commit Britain, let alone the whole Alliance, to "interminable war"? And as for the "sporting terms pretty well understood wherever English is spoken", which had made the interview so welcome to mass-circulation proprietors like Riddell of the *News of the World*, *The Nation* had this biting comment to make:[1]

To Mr. Lloyd George . . . the tragedy of our time, which turns Europe into a stage littered with the corpses of young men, presents itself . . . as a kind of dog-fight. Our soldiers, who conduct it, . . . are "game dogs". . . . When they seemed to be losing, they "hung on without whining" and "endured without wincing". Even when reinvested with humanity, they appear chiefly as "good sportsmen" . . . asking for themselves no more than a "sporting chance". In this temper they "play the game" neither "quitting" nor "squealing". The end they elect for themselves. The spectators have no right. "At this stage," says Mr. George, "there can be no outside interference"; the fight must be to a finish—to a knock-out. Till that is reached, the British Army knows "neither clock nor calendar", for time, which wastes the lives of men, is the "least vital factor". Peace can only come when the victor determines that it brings with it "the final and complete elimination of the cause of conflict."

Now, it may be enough to say that if the war can truthfully be described in these metaphors of the kennel and the prize-ring, we ought never to have entered it. . . . The soldier fights and suffers, the statesman does neither, save in his conscience when he possesses one. . . . In no sense, therefore, is it his task to exasperate feeling. . . .

But there are other limitations to the strife . . . of which Mr. Lloyd

hesitates. It may raise the age of obligatory service to forty-five, or it may fasten its system upon Ireland. The former alternative is not attractive as a military policy; the latter would be a crime. . . ."

[1] Cf. *Ibid.*, October 7th.

George's American interview takes no account. There are neutrals, and neutrals have their rights. Nearly all suffer something, the weakest most of all . . . when the society of nations is as deeply convulsed as ours, it is one of the small alleviations of the hour, that behind the passions of the belligerents and as a way of escape from complete deadlock, there exists something or somebody in the shape of a mediator. He may not be wanted, but then he may, and he may come to do the world the service of giving the victor all that he substantially wants and the vanquished the chance of accepting defeat without the extreme humiliation of formal surrender to his foe. . . .

CHAPTER IX
LLOYD GEORGE SUPPLANTS ASQUITH

"Nov. 27. I saw Robertson. . . . The Cabinet had asked him for his views as to when the war would be over, and what chance there was of winning it. On this Robertson wrote a most admirable paper . . . and said that no one but 'cowards, cranks and philosophers' could doubt the final result, provided we did what we ought to do, and did it in time.

I dined with Fred Oliver, also there, Milner, Carson, Geoffrey Robinson and Waldorf Astor. . . . Carson asked what he should advise Lloyd George and Bonar Law to do, as a crisis was coming. Our unanimous advice was that he should get Lloyd George to smash the Government."

From *Field-Marshal Sir Henry Wilson, His Life and Diaries* to show the anti-Asquith forces "plotting" late in 1916.

"A day or two after the [German] Chancellor's speech the *Westminster Gazette*, in reviewing what it called the unanimous rejection of the German proposal, used the significant term, 'An all-round bad Press for the Kaiser.' 'Bad Press,' it seems, is a term used to describe the unfavourable reception by the journals of anything, from a novel to a revue . . . so low and false is the scale of values now current among the makers of public opinion that anything really good and hopeful is sure to have a 'bad press'. . . . The *Westminster* gave no rebuke to any of these contemporaries who during the fateful days were inoculating us all with the inevitable poison. When the mischief was done, it wrote on December 18th as follows:

" 'We are strongly of opinion that, whatever its motive or intention, any overture from the Central Powers should receive a serious reply from the Allied Governments. . . . We are engaged not in a mere partisan recrimination but in a conflict of flesh and blood, in which an immense number of lives are at stake. Germany would have us believe she is moved by considerations of humanity to make proposals which she thinks will provide the basis for an honourable peace . . . it is clearly incumbent on her to produce her Bill and to show us at least in outline the scheme of pacification. . . .'

"Those who are anxious to think rightly in these terrible times will now turn to see what the German proposals are, and will realise what an ill turn the 'bad press' has done the world. . . ."

From *The Ploughshare*, January 1917, an organ of Quaker "cowards, cranks and philosophers" to use General Robertson's phrase above.

English Radicalism: The End?

"I noted on April 10 the lines of a general conversation I had with a foreman of electric works. . . . The things he said thousands were saying. . . . He had been a Socialist before the war and had been on deputations but he didn't believe in international Socialism any more. The German Socialists had voted money against us. He would not care ever again to meet them. His blood boiled at things Germans did. He said his own relations who had 'been out' told of their finishing off our wounded. Then he proceeded to lay it all on the Kaiser, who never liked King Edward. He welcomed the Russian Revolution and thought our Royal Family would be nowhere after the war. . . . He would like peace but 'we must end this business first'. He repeated twice—'we have got to go through with it'. Then suddenly he said he knew whose fault it all was. Asked who this might be, he said 'Queen Victoria'. The Kaiser was her favourite grandson; he never could do wrong, and he had a claim to the English throne. When asked how, he said through something back in English history. He persisted that if the Kaiser had come to the throne we never should have got rid of him. . . . This man's talk apparently summed up a good deal of public-house talk. . . . Certain prejudices, hatred of the Kaiser, general feeling against royalty and a vague belief in Lloyd George 'because he was active and knew religion' were underlying sentiments."

From Caroline Playne, *Britain Hold On, 1917–1918*.

I T is just possible that if the war-news from Rumania in the autumn of 1916 had been a little better, Lloyd George's seizure of power in December would have been harder to accomplish. Since becoming War Secretary in June, he had several times interfered in France and at the War Office in a way that had led to open complaint on the Conservative Benches and in the columns of the Conservative Press. Already, in August, Haig, in command in France, was reported to be in danger[1] and, by October, Haig's General Headquarters was receiving information of the trouble Lloyd George was making for Robertson, Cowans, and others in the War Office, the warning being sent that it had been Lloyd George's invariable practice, when taking over a new Department, to kick out those he found installed. Additional information, too, was forwarded of the new War Secretary's plans to withdraw certain types of responsibility from professional soldiers altogether, and the appointment of the railway manager, Eric Geddes, as a sort of General Officer Commanding Lines of Communication was instanced as a revealing case in point.[2] By the time the *Morning Post* had undertaken one counter-offensive on behalf of the harassed military chiefs[3] and Northcliffe was reported as ready even to turn to Asquith against Lloyd George's improper presumptions at the War Office,[4] Asquith's danger might well be presumed to be diminishing.

Yet the great Rumanian disasters, if really ascribable to Russia, and the increasing Greek imbroglio, if really ascribable to France, were bound to strengthen the hands of all those calling for a change of war-system in London, and, by the beginning of

---

[1] Cf. *Field-Marshal Sir Henry Wilson, His Life and Diaries*, i, 292, for Foch reporting to Wilson how Lloyd George had complained of the heavy British losses for disproportionately small gains of ground and prisoners in comparison with the French. Haig had been supplied, according to the angry Lloyd George, with all the artillery and shells he could make use of and yet nothing effective had been accomplished. Though Foch told Wilson that he had stood up for Haig, pointing out that Haig's men, in contrast to his own veterans, were "green soldiers", he passed on the information, nevertheless, that he thought Haig's position was not very safe. It is now known, of course, that it always proved just too politically perilous for Lloyd George, even as Prime Minister, to undertake Haig's outright dismissal though the difficult relationship between the two men is illustrated by the anecdotes that give "cur" as Haig's occasional way of referring to the Prime Minister and "butcher" as Lloyd George's occasional appellation for Haig. [2] *Ibid.*, p. 295.

[3] Cf. *Lord Riddell's War Diary, 1914–1918*, under October 1, 1916, for Lloyd George's threatening, in reply, to tell the country the true measure of British losses under their leadership. [4] *Ibid.*, under October 14th.

December, Lloyd George had obtained the approval not only of Carson, the unofficial Conservative Leader, but of Bonar Law, the official Conservative chief, for a species of ultimatum to Asquith.[1] A War Committee of Four, meeting daily, was to be set up with supreme control of hostilities, and the suggested members were to be Carson, Bonar Law, Lloyd George, and Henderson as representing Labour. Though there were many Conservatives who questioned the feasibility of excluding the Prime Minister or the desirability of some or all of those nominated, an enormous Press clamour was organized in favour of Lloyd George's War Committee. Of course, what seems in retrospect, an unscrupulous amount of plotting had been going on against Asquith for a long time, and under the cloak of "patriotism" and "determination to win the war", a dangerous array of private ambitions, resentments, frustrations, rascalities, and veritable manias had aligned themselves to throw caution to the winds and "fight to a finish". Northcliffe may be taken as a specimen of one who was already suffering from a species of mania, more ultimately dangerous than that which induced hundreds of thousands of the resentful and frustrated to see "the Hidden Hand" in every British miscalculation or set-back. Bottomley is the leading specimen of the arrant rogues and swindlers who were flourishing on the war and on professions of a super-patriotism which allowed him to suggest, at one later stage, the hanging of Mr. Asquith. And if Lloyd George,[2] Max Aitken,[3] and Mr. Hughes, "the great Prime Minister of Australia" would probably need books and psychologists to themselves if a proper analysis were to be attempted of their patriotic professions, a word may here, at least, be said of General Sir Henry Wilson whom Lloyd George would, before long, appoint Chief of the Imperial General Staff. From his place at the War Office he had intrigued against the Asquith Govern-

[1] Cf. *Life and Letters of Austen Chamberlain*, ii, 59: "I certainly would not have served under such a Committee nor would Curzon or Cecil. We have little confidence in Bonar Law's judgement and none in his strength of character. Carson was a great disappointment in the three months during which he sat in Asquith's Cabinet. . . . Henderson on all the larger issues . . . would have been a cipher. . . ."

[2] Cf. Lloyd George, *War Memoirs*, for a massive account, by himself, of his own activities which would, of course, have to be the psychologist's main quarry.

[3] Cf. Lord Beaverbrook, *Politicians and the War, 1914–1916* and the much later *Men and Power, 1917–1918*, for his own accounts. It is in Volume II of the first book that the Nigerian Debate of November 8, 1916 is shown to be a turning-point in the developments that were coming. That debate is mentioned below.

ment even before the war, and the "Ulster Pogrom" was his picturesque way of describing the abortive attempt of that Government in March 1914 to put a stop to the most defiant aspects of "Carsonism". Now he was demanding "two Sommes at once" in 1917 and, in view of expected casualties of "at least a million between April and October" 1917, a Government which would promise to draft out 1,700,000 men over the next twelve months including 200,000 to 300,000 "good Irish soldiers" who would, of course, have to be conscripted.[1] If, indeed, Wilson's prescriptions for victory had been known to the whole nation, instead of to tiny cliques of Tory politicians meeting Lloyd George in secret,[2] the revulsion of public feeling would have been immense.

But it is time to turn to the Nigerian Debate of November 8th, the reconciliation of official and unofficial Conservatism that followed, and the creation, thanks to Max Aitken's assiduity, of the Law-Carson-George Triumvirate to drive Asquith from control of the war. The question at issue on November 8th, was the disposal of sequestrated German properties in Nigeria, and the "ginger" Tories under Sir Edward Carson were furious because the decision had been taken of "open sale" which would doubtless yield a better price but would allow even suspect neutrals to bid. The German properties, according to the "ginger" group, had been a conspicuous example of the Germans' infiltration into the heart of British territories and commercial interests, and now Dutch and Americans, whether acting for themselves or the enemy, were being permitted to attempt the perpetuation of foreign control. And though Bonar Law did his duty, fighting strenuously for Conservative votes and finally winning a majority of them for the Government's Nigerian decision,[3] he was aware

[1] *Field-Marshal Sir Henry Wilson, His Life and Diaries,* i, 294–6. The demand for "at least 1,700,000 men in drafts in the next twelve months" was made in response to Lloyd George's query as to whether Wilson thought the Germans could be beaten.

[2] Cf. Lord Beaverbrook, *Politicians and the War, 1914–1916,* ii, 99, for one piece of assumed "slimness" on the dangerous Division-night of November 8th which angered Bonar Law. Lloyd George made no appearance at the House that night and, perhaps, would rather have had the Government defeated. Beaverbrook reports that "Lloyd George was dining that night with Lord Lee of Fareham at his house in Abbey Garden where several meetings had already taken place between Lloyd George, Carson, and Milner . . . it is claimed, the question of the Nigerian debate never came up at all."

[3] Cf. *Ibid.,* p. 92: "Bonar Law made a powerful statement of his case—but he was subjected to much interruption. . . . The feeling between the two Tory sections was very strained. . . ."

that it had been a near thing[1] and that he himself shared some of the objectors' feelings. In fact, while instructions were being given from the Colonial Office to outbid any foreign offer at the Nigeria sale,[2] the Conservative leader was being persuaded, despite his strong suspicions of Lloyd George's ultimate motives,[3] to begin discussion of virtual Conservative backing for a Lloyd George ultimatum to Asquith. And it suffices to read the typical Asquithian and Labour comment on the Nigerian Debate to see why it could only have hardened the heart of Bonar Law against the political interests still presumed to be insisting on Asquith's retention of undiminished prerogatives as Prime Minister.[4] Here is some typical "Radical humbug", as many Conservatives would have considered it, from *The Nation*'s comments on the Nigerian Debate:[5]

The German properties in Nigeria are to be sold. A great agitation springs up against the resolve of the Government to make this sale an open transaction. The proper course would, in our view, have been for the State to take over these concerns, and either lease them or work them itself. . . . But it would not have suited the Ring, which by its association with the shipping companies, controls 80 per cent of the available cargo space, and now sees its way to grasping the whole trade by purchase, to the exclusion of competitors—American, French, Dutch, or British—neutrals and Allies alike. . . . The difference between the cost of the palm-kernels, paid to the native producer, and that charged to the British consumer at Liverpool, has gone up since the war from £4 to £14 while the prices realized by the native growers (our subjects) have gone down. . . . Mr. Law's palm-kernel tax is one instrument of that monopoly. But in view of the agitation among the native growers and British traders outside the dominant combine, he has decided to maintain at least the form of competition. . . .

Now it is clear that if the war for Liberty is to be turned into a war for profiteering and Protection, the democracy of Britain will have something to say. Blood in rivers has been poured out; not for these

[1] Cf. Lord Beaverbrook, *Politicians and the War, 1914–1916*, ii, 93, on "the critical nature of the situation".

[2] Cf. *Ibid.*, pp. 126–7 on how "Bonar Law himself was full of the sale of enemy property in Nigeria. . . . He was anxious that no foreigners should buy."

[3] Cf. *Ibid.*, pp. 127–8: "Bonar Law had formed the opinion that in matters of office and power Lloyd George was a self-seeker . . . when the Government was formed Lloyd George had seized on munitions for himself and joined in the intrigue which relegated Bonar Law to the Colonial Office. Then he had insisted on retaining the Deputy Leadership of the House of Commons as well. . . ."

[4] Cf. The hostile tone towards Tory notions of Imperial Trade manifest in *The Nation* quotation below.

[5] Cf. *The Nation*, November 11, 1916, under the heading "WAR AND THE PROFITEERS".

ends . . . Sir Edward Carson pinned his colours to the mast under the strange device "War for the sole advantage of this country" . . . this is a plan of profiteering devised in the interest of selected and powerful groups of monopolists. The native producer, the independent British trader, the British consumer are equally sacrificed to it. It is foreign to the idea that we hold our overseas possessions as a trust rather than in absolute ownership. The subjects of that trust are, first, the colonists themselves, white or black, and secondly, the whole family of industry as it exists in great European and extra-European nations. For such an Empire scores of thousands of British workers have died. . . ."

It was at the beginning of December that Asquith was facing the virtual ultimatum from Lloyd George, demanding the creation of the small War Council. It seems possible, that despite the crisis atmosphere raised by Lloyd George's newspaper friends,[1] a compromise would have been reached especially as Bonar Law's Conservative Cabinet colleagues hardly relished the extent to which he had committed himself. In fact, by Sunday, December 3rd, they were so incensed by the fresh proofs of Lloyd George's Press intrigues, illustrated apparently anew in that morning's issue of *Reynolds's*, that they favoured the extreme measure of a complete recasting of the Government, after universal resignation, so that he could be brought to heel or expelled. If Bonar Law had made the situation plain to Asquith, instead of leaving him with the impression that Conservative resignations would have been in Lloyd George's support, the course of the next few days would have been very different.[2] As it was, Asquith felt himself largely constrained to accept Lloyd George's plan leaving details to be decided on Monday, December 4th. That day, however, was to bring him apparent proof that majority opinion among Conservative members of the Cabinet was in his favour against Lloyd George; that every Liberal Cabinet Minister except Lloyd George would side with him to the point of pledging himself to take office from no one else if there was a crisis; and, finally, that that morning's *Times* revealed anew the extent of his subordinate's malice and untrustworthiness.[3] Accordingly, after some probing of the Conservative side as to whether the Cabinet could be recast without universal resignation, the Prime Minister decided to go to the Palace and announce the end of the Government. The

[1] Especially in the *Evening News* placard "LLOYD GEORGE PACKING UP", broadcast throughout London and the Home Counties on Saturday, December 2nd. There had been a "crisis" tone that morning both in the *Daily Chronicle* and the *Daily Express*.
[2] Cf. *The Life and Letters of Austen Chamberlain*, ii, 58.   [3] Cf. *Ibid.*, p. 59.

chances still seemed to be that Bonar Law would be unable to form a Cabinet, since Liberals and probably Labour would decline to co-operate, that Lloyd George's attempt, next to be expected, would break down even sooner[1] and, finally, that Asquith would have to be commissioned again.

Bonar Law's attempt to form a Cabinet was soon, indeed, given up though Asquith was destined to suffer for the rest of his life for his refusal to co-operate when Lloyd George was ready to do so. Of course, Asquith was bound in honour to stand by the ten Liberal Cabinet Ministers, who were risking their political lives, to help him to beat off what they, doubtless, all considered to be the reckless and unjustifiable political plotting that had been going on. But Lloyd George's Cabinet-making negotiations with the Conservatives, that followed, might not have gone as smoothly as they did if there had not been his "patriotic" readiness to serve under Bonar Law to allege. Then Northcliffe's attempt to dictate the disappearance not only of Lansdowne,[2] but of Balfour and Walter Long, from the Conservative side of the new Cabinet was quickly abandoned. More surprising to contemporaries was the unexpected success of Lloyd George in winning away from Asquith a fair proportion of the Liberal strength in the House of Commons once he had received a commission to form a new Government. A fascinating story will, no doubt, be told some day of how Welsh Radicals welcomed the thought of a Welsh Prime Minister,[3] of how Dr. Addison, placed by Lloyd George at the Munitions Ministry, plied the English Radicals[4] and of how, finally, a Parliamentary band, numbered at eighty or even more, were free, if they were so minded, to begin speculations as to how ten vacant Asquithian Cabinet places, and more minor appointments, might come to be distributed among themselves.

[1] Cf. Lord Beaverbrook, *Politicians and the War, 1914–1916*, ii, 207, however, for some consideration of Lloyd George, "even if all forsook him and fled", trying to form an Administration out of the Tory Back-Benchers which would be "more alert and able than its predecessor".

[2] Cf. *Ibid.*, p. 19: "It is now known that before the political crisis of 1916 Lord Lansdowne had sent to the Prime Minister his memorandum advocating Peace without Victory; and that the Prime Minister circulated it to the War Cabinet. . . ."

[3] The adhesion to Lloyd George of such Welsh notabilities as David Davies, M.P., and Lord Rhondda, both, too, be it noted, in the "millionaire" class, was essential to his success. Then there was J. M. Lewis, M.P. for Flintshire, and Parliamentary Secretary to the Board of Education, and Sir Alfred Mond, M.P. for Swansea, who went straight into the Cabinet.

[4] Cf. Dr. Addison, *Four and a Half Years* and *Politics from Within* for two books in which there are revealing extracts from the diaries he kept.

But what set the seal on Lloyd George's Cabinet-making success was his surprising capture of "Labour" from Asquith. Asquith had certainly fought hard and risked his political life to meet, as far as he could, "Labour's" many objections to the Conscription Acts of 1916. Right up to the crisis of December 1916, the three Labour Ministers, headed by Henderson, were supposed to be insisting on Asquith's indispensability as head of the Government. Yet when, on December 7, 1916, Lloyd George, addressing a joint meeting of the Parliamentary Labour Party and the Labour Party's Executive, offered what seemed a large increase of Labour's share in Government, with Henderson in the War Cabinet and office in the three new Departments of Labour, Pensions, and Food Control allotted, as it proved, to Roberts, Hodge, and Clynes, he won "Labour" over without giving the kind of guarantees that Sidney Webb, for one, demanded.[1] As the new Prime Minister was simultaneously inviting into much more vital positions in the Government "outside experts", especially from "big business",[2] there is something, besides disappointment, in the diary entry that Sidney Webb's wife made next day.[3] She was trying to explain, and not uncharitably, why there had been a majority of 18 against 12 for what was virtually an unconditional acceptance of Lloyd George's "cynical" offer of an increased quota of Labour places and why the majority had included some who had been opposed to Lloyd George's seizure of power only, it seemed, a few hours before. She admitted, frankly, that the temptation of six official salaries of a size which would, in a year or two, confer "personal independence for life" on those accustomed to living at the very frugal standards of Trade Union officers had, doubtless, something to do with the decision. So, too, in some cases, had the desire for a thorough beating of the Germans. But the dominating motive in the Labour majority's action was, she felt, the notion that the increased quota of Labour offices was, in itself, a species of democratic advance and, then, there was Clynes's naïve belief that a say would be obtained in the Peace

[1] Cf. *Beatrice Webb's Diaries, 1912–1924*, pp. 72–3.
[2] Notably Sir Albert Stanley as President of the Board of Trade, Sir Joseph Maclay as Shipping Controller, and Sir Eric Geddes, soon to blossom into First Lord of the Admiralty. Moreover the Food Controller was to be Lord Devonport with Clynes as his spokesman in the Commons. Another "outside expert", whom the Webbs had less distrust for, was Fisher as President of the Board of Education.
[3] Cf. *Beatrice Webb's Diaries, 1912–1924*, under December 8, 1916.

English Radicalism: The End?

Terms. Accordingly, in Mrs. Webb's view, a mixture of pecuniary interest and class-illusion had led to success for Lloyd George and to Labour's accepting responsibility in advance "for every plan which a majority of reactionaries" might undertake instead of laying down conditions under her beloved Sidney's direction.

Lloyd George, then, succeeded in constructing an apparently powerful Government, resting on a great House of Commons majority, much more easily than many of the political experts had expected. Moreover, even some of those who knew or guessed the unsavoury intrigues that had long gone on behind the scenes to blacken Asquith's reputation and undermine the position of all his leading supporters allowed themselves to be persuaded that the new Prime Minister's administrative vigour was indispensable for winning the war.[1] Indeed, helped by a great welcoming Press roar extending from the *Morning Post* on the political Right to *Reynolds*'s on the political Left, the new Government seemed, for a few brief honeymoon weeks, to be almost beyond the possibility of serious challenge. Of course, the time would come when Lord Northcliffe, the *Morning Post*, and the Generals would have their taste of the new Prime Minister's "slimness" and when all his administrative agility would fail to halt German triumphs on sea and land greater than those of Asquith's day. But such things still lay in the future, and, for the time, with the entire Tory strength behind him, some, at least, of the new Prime Minister's attention was devoted to posing, to the other side of politics, as the super-democrat, more entitled than Asquith to Radical and working-class support. Here is Sylvia Pankhurst's sardonic account:[2]

Though Lloyd George had become the instrument of the extreme Tory conscriptionists, the legend that he was a liberty-loving democrat still in certain quarters survived tenuously from his land-tax days, and was industriously propagated. Press paragraphs asserted that he was about to democratise the Government of the country by setting up

[1] Possibly C. P. Scott of the *Manchester Guardian* is the best single example, and it is an example the better from the fact that Scott wanted to keep clear of the honours and peerages which Lloyd George was prepared to shower on newspaper controllers in return for their support.

[2] Cf. E. Sylvia Pankhurst, *The Home Front*, pp. 423–4. The democratic "writing-up" of Lloyd George, instanced above, seems to bear some resemblance to the tone which Sir Henry Dalziel, Radical M.P. for Kirkcaldy Burghs since 1892, strove to give to *Reynolds*'s, which he controlled, and, later, to the *Daily Chronicle*, when interests behind Lloyd George helped him to gain control of that, too. His rewards came in the shape of an enhanced Fleet Street fortune and a peerage.

Parliamentary Committees of the French model, for dealing with finance, foreign affairs, and so on; that he was pledged to the conscription of wealth, in order that the rich and not the poor, should pay for the War; to the nationalisation of shipping, mines, railways, and the food supply in the interests of the masses. In actual fact some measure of Government control was now exercised over railways, mines, and shipping. There was a 50 per cent increase in railway fares, trains were fewer and slower, but the workers discovered no improvement in their lot. Despite the appointment of a Food Controller food difficulties increased. Women stood in queues for potatoes, sugar, meat, butter and other fats, cheese, jam, etc. In February 1918, when rationing was at long last introduced, the police estimated that 1,300,000 people were standing in the food queues in the Metropolitan area. . . .

But, perhaps, it is rather the great opinion-making weekly of all the "progressive" politicians of that day, *The Nation*, that should be examined for indications of what the "advanced" thought of the new Government. There was, of course, little welcome for the great "trick-rider's" proposal to career round the circus of British politics with one foot on the Tory horse and the other on the "Labour" animal; there was some suspicion of the new formula developed in reply to a German peace-overture, "complete restitution, full reparation, effectual guarantees"[1] though it was, at least, better than the "Knock-Out Blow"; and there was alarm when a later Allied Note added "Liberty for the Czecho-Slovaks" to the list of war-aims.[2] Even in February 1917, when the growing menace of shipping losses and the folly of prolonging hostilities for a myth like the Czecho-Slovaks could have been used with

[1] Cf. *The Nation*, December 23, 1916: "It is obvious that each of these three words is capable of a maximum or a minimum interpretation. Restitution means first of all the restoration of occupied territory, and difficulties begin when one asks if it applies to old acquisitions like Alsace-Lorraine, if Poland must be restored to Russia or to the Poles, and whether we will restore the German colonies or their equivalents. Reparation means chiefly an indemnity to Belgium but Mr. George seems also to include in it satisfaction for other outrages. Guarantees may be either material or moral. Some would include under this word any conceivable measure for the weakening of German power including the 'break-up' of Austria, strategical demands and even the confiscation of the fleet. . . ."

[2] Cf. *Ibid.*, January 20, 1917: "The Note of the Allies . . . is a statement of maximum terms. . . . Britain did not go to war to break up the Austrian Empire or to construct an entirely new set of strategic frontiers. It is possible to hold that the note commits us to the first . . . by its pledge to release 'Czecho-Slovaks' from 'foreign domination' and to the second by its demand for 'territorial conventions' 'so as to guarantee land and sea frontiers from unjustified attacks'. . . . Such objects are worth no British bones: our armies . . . would justly regard a pursuit of them as a breach of our earlier covenants with our living and our dead . . . [in] the scheme for relieving Europe of the direct rule of the Turk . . . every Liberal must feel that he reaches the goal of a long and honourable aspiration."

English Radicalism: The End?

advantage, *The Nation* still refrained from an outright declaration of war on the new Premier. It invited him instead to use his admitted qualities for reducing the intensity of war-passions and for helping forward President Wilson's plans for a new and better International Order. Here is *The Nation* of February 17, 1917 on "The Opportunity of the Prime Minister":

In a few weeks or days, all the greater European societies will open the greatest gamble in human life and well-being they have ever known [Spring Offensives]. The merely cynical observer of the game sees in it the old stake of power, distributed on the system of balance between the half-dozen Empire-States. But the statesmen who play it have themselves introduced a new element in this speculation of death. They have promised the youth who have gone to the shambles in millions the definite creation and maintenance of a new international order. If we may judge from the spirit of our own soldiery, of the French armies, and even of the idealists in the enemy's ranks, this vision was a real marching presence with the hosts of 1914; thousands had their deaths illumined by it. But since there has been a change. There have been the secret territorial agreements of the Powers, and now, so far as the ambiguous voice of the oracle enlightens us at all, it speaks in the old terminology of conquest. An insidious scheme of substitution goes on. Austria is to go down, Russia is to go up. "War for the Tchecho-Slovaks," "War for a Russian Constantinople," "War on German Trade," slip into the place . . . of "War for a Free Belgium," "War for a Reunited Europe," or "War to end War". . . .

Now Mr. George enters on this confused and tragic scene in the embarrassing company of Tory Imperialism and the Northcliffe Press. . . . He has attained his ambition, broken up two Governments, broken Liberalism, broken with old friends and his old self. . . . Mr. George is not what some flatterers name him, an organizer, a strategist, a planner of victories. Lord Northcliffe's phrase will serve—he is a "vitalizer". He has been wrong in cutting himself off from the best forms of British government, from its more habitual moderation of tone and thought. . . . But the human problem remains, and that is whether the Prime Minister has the power of returning on himself, looking on war as he would have looked at it ten years ago and yet assimilating the new and ameliorating idea which American statesmanship has struck out. He may have lost this power, if so he has lost himself. But we should still suppose that, if Mr. George left himself a few moments for thinking his mind would turn to means of slaking down the vast conflagration of this war. There and there alone, can his true gift and art, which is that of management appear. . . . Opportunity contracts for him—but he has his chance. . . .

Considering what the new Prime Minister had been guilty of in his climb to power, this was hardly spiteful—and, in fact,

Asquith himself was successfully endeavouring to prevent the most incensed of his deposed colleagues from undertaking the systematic Front Bench opposition which could be decried as "unpatriotic". There was some magnanimity in Asquith's attitude, but also the fore-knowledge that he and his team would thus return to power more easily in the not improbable event of a great war-misfortune overtaking the new Government despite its boasted character of a "business Administration".[1] But magnanimity had a hard task of it when meeting Lloyd George's characteristically "slim" political tactics and the outrageously misleading and provocative writing of his Press supporters, shady or otherwise. Thus, for the new Parliamentary Session begun on February 7, 1917, the dangerous policy was adopted, with loud approval from the *Daily Mail*,[2] of keeping the Prime Minister almost outside and above Parliament. Of course, the pretence could be advanced that he was too busy countering the revived submarine menace and securing the efficient conduct of the war but the effect sought, by some at least, was to discredit, in advance, a possible "Opposition of Talkers" whose manifold crimes of "commission and omission' had produced the grave consequences now needing the undivided attention of the Prime Minister and his ablest assistants. Then there was, at least, one unscrupulous attempt to put the blame for the unsatisfactory record of the Salonika expedition, a very heavy user, to little apparent profit, of shrinking Allied tonnage, on Mr. McKenna, Lloyd George's most determined opponent in the late Government.[3] And, finally, an

[1] Cf. *The Nation*, February 24, 1917, for one sardonic writer to this effect: "Men used to govern are thrust aside, and those unused to it taught to think that they alone possess the grand secret. People in 'business' are presumed to know politics, or to be full of meaning because they have never learned to say what they mean. The Press discovers a totally new standard of merit. The people who ruled the country up to the end of last December (except Mr. George) were corrupt and effete; the men who now rule it (though they are mostly the same people) are Spartans of energy and brimming over with intellect."

[2] Cf. *Ibid.*, February 17, 1917: "The House of Commons which was informed by one member of the Northcliffe Press that the Prime Minister proposed to absent himself from its opening councils is now, I see, warned by another to abstain from criticism of that Imperial gesture. The *Daily Mail* will not hesitate to 'name' an 'Opposition of Talkers' guilty of various unstated crimes of 'commission and omission'."

[3] Cf. *Ibid.*, February 24, 1917: "I notice a statement in the *Daily Mail* which fixes on Mr. McKenna the responsibility for the despatch of the expedition to Salonika. The motive for this monstrous suggestion is clear; and if every Cabinet Minister whom a newspaper desires to discredit for purposes of its own is to be held responsible for a policy he notoriously disliked and opposed, it is hard to see where the remedy lies. . . . And there can be no doubt as to the source of the main support of the Eastern school of strategy. . . ."

advance Interim Report, on the Dardanelles Expedition, was put into print, ahead of the qualifying evidence, for little other reason, or so Asquithians suspected, than to give the Northcliffe Press and *John Bull* more plausible insults with which to bespatter the ex-Prime Minister.[1]

In point of fact, by mid-March 1917, the public's welcome for the new Government was already felt to be evaporating and Mr. Asquith's credit to be reviving, especially in Parliament, where many outside his half of the Liberal following felt him to have been disgracefully treated by his supplanter.[2] Indeed, at one Parliamentary stage of March 1917, with all Lancashire excited on the subject of new Indian duties proposed against its textile exports, the ex-Prime Minister was supposed to have the Government's fate in his hands though he finally forbore from bringing it down.[3] Perhaps the skilful German withdrawals to stronger prepared positions in France had something to do with it, for Ministers and their Army chiefs certainly resented bitterly the suggestion that they had been outwitted by the enemy and all their offensive plans for 1917 brought to nought.[4] Moreover,

---

[1] Cf. *The Nation*, March 17, 1917: "The point of curiosity in the Dardanelles debate is to discover whether Mr. George will array himself in the white sheet with which he has generously enveloped Mr. Asquith. Mr. George's association with the expedition was close and constant . . . he may well have wished to tack the Salonikan project to it . . . the story of the Report becomes a piece of arbitrary editing. Why then was it allowed to appear? It is admittedly a preface . . . and it has no relevance to any issue but a purely political one. One may think as ill as one pleases of the workmanship, political and military, which it half discloses, and, yet, after last week's orgy of malice, conclude that the country has more cause to be ashamed of the appearance of the Report, and of the uses to which it has been put, than of all her losses and disappointments put together."

[2] Cf. *Ibid.*, March 24, 1917: "It is, I think, an excessive compliment to Mr. Asquith to say that his speech on the Dardanelles Report killed it. That is the truth, but it is not the whole truth. The House of Commons felt itself bound to 'assist', as the French say, in an act of reparation. . . . But what can be said of a Minister who, owing, what he owes to Mr. Asquith sought or permitted this assault on him?"

[3] Cf. *Ibid.*, March 17, 1917: "Had the ex-Premier raised his hand on Wednesday, the Government would have been lost. On Sunday the opinion was that its fate was sealed, that Mr. George must go and either dissolve or take his seat in an Administration headed by Mr. Bonar Law. The stroke was never delivered. The Liberal leaders wavered, and finally swayed to their chief's Fabian counsels and his sense of the overshadowing issue of the war."

[4] Cf. *Ibid.*, March 3rd, for the article, entitled "The Meaning of the German Retreat", which later was given as one of the causes that induced the Government to apply its Defence of the Realm powers to banning *The Nation*'s foreign sales. It was, by no means, the strongest article that could have been written even if its general theme was, "we have little reason to congratulate ourselves". But the Prime Minister was to pay dear for his war on *The Nation* which, as the best-written "progressive" weekly, was a dangerous enemy for the rest of his Administration.

Germany's reply to the Allied refusal to negotiate for peace, in the shape of the de-restricted submarine warfare announced on February 1st, was instantly felt to be a serious matter even though it made an American breach with Germany probable in the near future.[1] The efficiency of German war-planning was known, from painful experience, to be such that it was rightly assumed that the Germans had allowed even for the contingency of an American declaration of war and had still assumed that the new submarine warfare would prove decisive. And had not the Food Controller first, and the Prime Minister afterwards, given the gravest warnings of the urgent steps that would be necessary to prevent hunger?[2]

Here is one disparaging description of the Lloyd George Government, when merely in its fourth month, from the Radical columns of *The Nation*:[3]

War is a study in disillusionment; and our people have already sustained a swift revulsion from their first feeling about their new Government. That impulse was generous and confiding. Every art of journalism was used to prepare the country for a fresh infusion of energy into the conduct of the war; it accepted this advance advertisement; and even those who disliked the web of intrigue from which Mr. George's Administration was woven, were prepared to take its very mixed material for what it was worth. How has this trust been fulfilled? Brief as Mr. George's tenure of office has been, half-a-dozen purposes have been allowed to come athwart the prosecution of the war. The premier trade of England has been attacked without warning or Parliamentary process, and a bitter and dangerous controversy opened between it and the Indian Empire. Protection has been inaugurated not in England's favor but against her. Mr. Redmond's support of the war has been rewarded by a challenge to the doctrine of Home Rule . . . and his party

[1] Cf. *Whitaker's Almanack, 1918*, p. 411, for even this bare summary: "Feb. 1st. United States officially informed that Germany 'must abandon the limitations she had hitherto imposed upon herself in the employment of her fighting weapons at sea', and proposing that the U.S. Government should warn their vessels against entering the dangerous zones. Great indignation in America, and alarm in neutral countries; Danish and Dutch vessels stopped their sailings. . . . Feb. 2nd. Appeal to the nation by Lord Devonport, Food Controller, to economise in food to avoid compulsory rationing. . . ."

[2] Cf. *Ibid.*, p. 129: "The Prime Minister on Feb. 23rd announced that drastic restrictions would be imposed on imports not essential to the prosecution of the war, while production at home would be stimulated to its utmost capacity by State assistance. As stocks of food were lower than they had been within recollection, it was imperative that more food should be grown at home. To overcome the farmers' timidity they were to be guaranteed minimum prices for wheat, oats, and potatoes; while agricultural labourers were to be given a minimum wage of 25s. a week, and landlords were not to be allowed to raise rents. . . ."

[3] Cf. *The Nation*, March 17, 1917, p. 792.

driven into opposition . . . Parliament has been affronted by the Prime Minister's withdrawal from its councils, and a slight put upon the Civil Service by his interposition of a screen of ambitious amateurs between it and the great administrative departments. Daily a new locust-swarm of officials descends on the land . . . until the number of "controllers" threatens to exceed that of the controlled. . . .

The Government bids men serve their country, without finding them places to serve in; "combs out" farm labourers from the land and "combs" them in again; tells farmers to grow and not to grow; and raises a stentorian call for ships, soldiers, and workers, in the same breath. In mere efficiency it has already fallen so far below the not extravagant level of its predecessor that men may well begin to long for a more intelligent stewardship. . . . Concentration is essential and yet new and distracting elements continually appear. The Dominions are summoned to a "War Conference", and this again shapes itself into a Committee on Imperial Preference, while *The Times* suggests a further plunge into an Imperial Constitution. . . . The Government thus begins to drag an increasing load of irrelevancies, at a moment which calls for direct and simple thinking on the problems of war and peace. For the conflict develops; it approaches a period of dreadful sacrifice. For what ends? America invited us to define them. Mr. George's speeches offered her every discouragement. . . .

There is a certain exaggerated piling of Pelion upon Ossa in this indictment by an angry journalist, aware of the long history of newspaper misrepresentation on which Lloyd George's war-fortunes had been built. But the indictment would have been much more severe—and much more justifiable—if more could have been known at the time of what occupied the Prime Minister's agile, if superficial mind. Thus, his low view of the British Army leaders virtually led to the subordination of Haig and Robertson to a new French Commander-in-Chief, Nivelle, with that policy of a ruthless "spring offensive", which, in April, came near to breaking the French, instead of the German Army.[1] Possibly, when the Nivelle offensive had first been discussed with the French, the need for encouraging the Tsar's Ministers to stand firm against "separate peace" offers from the enemy had been very much in mind. But the Tsar's Government had fallen in mid-March, and when "the greatest tyranny in the world" was replaced, on the Allied side, by the "advanced Liberalism" of its successor, the last American hesitations in declaring war on Germany vanished early in April. Yet a military observer, summoned from France at the end of April, found the Prime Minister against the

[1] Cf. *Field-Marshal, Sir Henry Wilson, His Life and Diaries*, i, 323, under March 5th.

offensive which Haig had prepared to launch,[1] and the War Cabinet, a couple of days later, pessimistic enough about Russian developments for peace possibilities to be mentioned. The Prime Minister, meanwhile, seems to have been pondering longingly on how a mere fraction of the men and the armament, earmarked for the relative stalemate in France, could, if diverted to the Levant, bring even Jerusalem into jubilant, prestige-bringing headlines and sermon-passages at home.[2]

The War Office, which was convinced that the ultimate decision would be in France, managed to prevent a premature singing of Hallelujahs for Jerusalem's capture. But the Prime Minister, though finding one road for adding powerfully to his prestige temporarily blocked, was not to be prevented from undertaking a number of other manœuvres to strengthen his political position. Thus, he desired to increase the number of Liberal Ministers of Cabinet rank to give himself a better standing over against the Tories, and by July he was ready to announce the appointment of Dr. Addison as Minister of Reconstruction, of Edwin Montagu, enticed from the Asquithians, as Secretary for India, and of Winston Churchill as Minister of Munitions. There were considerable risks in Churchill's nomination, for many were still inclined to lay the main blame for the great Dardanelles failure on him. But Churchill's war-criticism was proving exceptionally acute; Lloyd George wanted him away from the dangerous company of the Asquithians on the Opposition Front Bench; and, finally, the owner of the great Press megaphones, who could have aroused the loudest outcry, had just been flattered into heading Government's "Northcliffe Mission to America".[3] The considerable Ministerial reshuffle of July 1917 also involved Sir Edward Carson's nominal promotion to the War Cabinet from the

---

[1] *Ibid.*, p. 344, under April 29th, for Lloyd George on possibly waiting until 1918 before putting in the British blow. It is worth remembering that, in private, British Government circles had discussed the advantages of having their forces as strong as possible at the war's climax, Lord Kitchener, for example, assuring Lord Derby that the reservation of conscription until 1916 meant that Britain would then have the most important man-power reserves and a corresponding influence on the Peace. But if Haig exhausted British man-power in 1917 (especially as France, after Nivelle, and Russia, after the Revolution, could not be relied on for parallel efforts) it might be the Americans who, thanks to the blood-sacrifices of France, Russia, and Britain alike, would be able to dominate the anti-German side.

[2] *Ibid.*, p. 361, for resistance at the War Office to Lloyd George's notions.

[3] Cf. Lord Beaverbrook, *Men and Power, 1917–1918*, for very full treatment of all the topics mentioned.

Admiralty where he was succeeded by Sir Eric Geddes. In politics a mere creature of Lloyd George, Geddes was not likely to stand up for professional Admiralty opinion against the Prime Minister as Carson had done.[1]

Possibly the most successful and least justifiable of the Prime Minister's activities for strengthening his personal position in a Government of mainly Tory composition, were those undertaken to fortify himself for the inevitable General Election. The life of the sitting Parliament should constitutionally have run out at the end of 1915 but was being renewed by short-period Acts till the war should end or elections become possible under a new Franchise Extension Bill actually under debate during the 1917 Session. Of course, an unsatisfactory General Election, with the Expeditionary Forces, the women, and many munition-workers in lodgings deprived of their votes, might have been found "necessary" by the Prime Minister on the old system and before the "generous" new Franchise plans became law. Indeed, such an Election was under discussion during the new Government's first shaky period in March and, to some extent also, during several shaky periods later. Possible Election strategy, too, was canvassed, and how best to put the blame for the "unsatisfactory election" and the disfranchisement of half the country, on the "unpatriotic" fault-finding of the Asquithians, who not content with nearly losing the war themselves, were trying to prevent their successors from winning it. Of course, other claims would have been made, too, of the benefits the country would receive from the new Fisher Education Bill, from the great Reconstruction programme to be planned by a special Ministry or, in the rural areas, even from the Corn Production Bill. Yet Asquithians controlled the Liberal Party Chest, and Lloyd George and his "Coalition Liberals" had also to make allowance for the not impossible event of part of the Tory Party forcing an election by objecting to his courses, even if on different grounds from the Asquithians.[2] A Lloyd George Political Fund, then, was regarded as an obvious strategic necessity, and the accumulation began of the vastest political treasure-chest ever gathered in Britain under virtually one-man control. To judge from the "Honours Scandals" already under

[1] Lord Beaverbrook, *Men and Power, 1917–1918*, pp. 144–85, for the long chapter entitled "The Ulster Pirate".
[2] Cf. *Ibid.*, pp. 137–9, for the near-crisis caused in July 1917 when Churchill was made Minister of Munitions.

discussion in August 1917,[1] what opponents were later to call the hawking of Knighthoods, Baronetcies, and even Peerages must have been set on foot by the Coalition Liberal Whips' Department fairly early in the life of the new Government.[2] And, doubtless, the creation of the new Orders of the British Empire and of the Companions of Honour, announced on June 21st, owed something to the desire of having more favours and distinctions to bestow.[3]

To return to the 1917 Session is to notice that a good deal of its time was necessarily devoted to a new Representation of the People Bill conceding many of the electoral reforms demanded for two generations—Women's Suffrage for an estimated six million women over thirty; a reduction of residence qualification to six months, calculated to add hundreds of thousands of hitherto disqualified, because constantly shifting, "general labourers" to the rolls; special registration arrangements for Service personnel; all elections, at a Dissolution, on one day; and a vast reduction in the scope of Plural Voting if not, yet, its entire abolition in favour of "One Man, One Vote".[4] Truth to tell, the all-party Speaker's Conference, set up towards the end of Asquith's day, on whose

---

[1] Cf. *Hansard* (Lords), June 22, 1922, for Lord Harris, when initiating the famous debate on the full range of "Honours Scandals", reminding the Peers of their debate of August 1917 and their Resolution, then accepted on behalf of the Government by Lord Curzon, asking that the reasons for conferring any Honours should be made public and that the Prime Minister should satisfy himself that there had been no payment of money or the expectation of it.

[2] Cf. Sir Charles Mallet, *Mr. Lloyd George: A Study*, pp. 250–1: "The Chief Coalition Liberal Whips, Captain Guest and his successor, Mr. McCurdy must, it seems, share the main responsibility between them. They had junior Whips in their offices, and the junior Whips had their correspondents or agents, and the agents had . . . something analogous to travellers or touts. At each stage . . . no doubt, there were details left to the subordinates . . . details on which a Chief Whip would not ask for information, and with which a Prime Minister could have no concern. It is always easier to disavow what one has not been told."

[3] Cf. *Whitaker's Almanack*, *1918*, pp. 155–6, for the use to which the new Orders had been put by the end of the year 1917. Lord Burnham of the *Daily Telegraph* and General Smuts were the most serviceable of those who had been awarded the Companionship of Honour but its award also to Lady Lansdowne and Miss Elizabeth Haldane was a gesture towards the home circle of two Peers, with reasons for resentment; three pro-war Labour men in Gosling, Wardle, and Wilkie were also deemed worth gathering in among others; and, finally, there was even an award to the irate Mrs. Asquith's sister-in-law, Mrs. Tennant, wife of the M.P. for Berwickshire, who had been his brother-in-law Asquith's last Secretary for Scotland.

[4] Conservative opinion had been ready to compromise on a basis of ending the possibility of using more than two votes—one, the residential and the other, the University or the "business premises" vote. From the Radical point of view, this was somewhat more justifiable than a system that had produced electors, registered, in respect of branch businesses, in a dozen constituencies or more and, under the old system, when a General Election was capable of dragging on for many days, with special facilities for exercising every vote.

recommendations the Bill was largely based, would have been prepared for a large infusion of Proportional Representation in big multi-member constituencies to be arranged for at Redistribution. On the whole, Radical opinion, if regretting the limitations still imposed on Women's Suffrage and on the abolition of "Plural Voting", had felt that the necessary compromises, made at the Speaker's Conference, had been well worth while. But opinion was to change when both in the 1917 Session, and in the subsequent one of 1917–18, which continued with much detailed Representation of the People discussion, both Proportional Representation in multi-member constituencies and the "alternative vote" in single-member constituencies came to be denied.[1] There was already some dim fore-vision of the electoral fate in store for Liberals, even of the most Radical kind, if they came to be caught between the upper millstone of Conservatism and the nether millstone of "Labour" without the slightest safeguards. The "progressive" way of putting that fear in 1917 and 1918 was, of course, to point out the many industrial constituencies likely to stultify themselves at the next Election by putting in Conservatives on a minority vote while the majority divided itself between Liberal and Labour without the power the "alternative vote" would give of indicating a second preference when the first was hopelessly at the bottom of the poll.

It cannot be pretended that the "public" was greatly interested in much of the Radicals' case on Electoral Matters or, for that matter, in their views on the Corn Production "ramp",[2] the

---

[1] Cf. *Hansard*, July 4, 1917, for the first vital defeat of Proportional Representation by 201 to 169 on a "free vote" of the Commons, a considerable part in the decision having been played by Austen Chamberlain's view that majorities ought to be over-represented Parliamentarily in order to obtain a strong instrument of government. Persistent attempts continued into 1918, especially among the Peers, to get at least a trial working for P.R., as it was called (Cf. especially *Hansard* (Lords), January 21 and 22 and February 4, 1918), but all were doomed to failure. Meanwhile, the Liberal and Labour interest in the "alternative vote" had won for it (Cf. *Hansard*, August 9, 1917) the not very impressive majority of 125 to 124, a majority not calculated to intimidate the Peers when rejecting so anti-Conservative a device a first time on January 22, 1918 and again on February 4, 1918 when the Commons' majority for rejecting the Peers' excision of the "alternative vote" could only be raised to 8.

[2] Cf. *The Nation*, July 28, 1917: "Who represented the laborers? . . . the Corn Production Bill represents a bargain between the Government on the one side and the landlords and farmers on the other—a bargain in which the vast majority of the people engaged in agriculture are at once vitally interested and absolutely ignored. And who, we may ask, represents the consumer? For our part we believe that . . . when the Army returns it will abolish by one method or another the land system which has reduced the country to its present plight."

"reckless extravagance" of Government Departments, the War Office mania for driving even the unfit out of essential industries into the Army, and the many similar topics that made the "progressive" politician's round. The great and still unfolding wardrama, as interpreted or misinterpreted by the "sensation Press", obviously absorbed the "general public" to the virtual exclusion of most normal subjects of discussion. And occasionally, if "murderous Hun air-raids" or the alleged devilish cunning of the enemy's use of the "Hidden Hand" whether to light up strikes in the British munition areas or find victims for the submarines, then making food scarcer and dearer, did not suffice, the wardrama and the British war-spirit could be enhanced by the sudden discovery of a new and even more sensational "Hun" atrocity. And so it came about that, during April 1917, when the War Office had begun using the Censorship in a way not ventured before,[1] turning even against so responsible if critical a paper as the Radicals' *Nation*,[2] the most extreme "Hun atrocity" campaign yet attempted was launched. As there was obviously a good deal of official connivance and approval behind the scenes, it might be best to end this chapter with the view of one of the most careful contemporary students of war-psychology. Caroline Playne's account of the "atrocity" propaganda of the spring and summer of 1917, and its results, is phrased thus:[3]

[1] Cf. Caroline Playne, *Britain Holds On, 1917–1918*, p. 59: "The Nobel endowment in Norway, founded to encourage the scientific study of Peace, and the similar Carnegie endowment in the United States had instructed the National Peace Council and others to collect for them publications on peace representative of all opinions. The War Office Censor, on March 31, forbade the dispatch of the collections made and notified the collectors 'that it is considered undesirable' that the following publications be included: Any publications of the National Labour Press, of the Union of Democratic Control, publications containing writings by Messrs. Bertrand Russell, Arthur Ponsonby, E. D. Morel, C. P. Trevelyan, Norman Angell, Philip Snowden, C. R. Buxton and Lowes Dickinson. Also certain specified publications, *Common Sense, The Herald, The Tribunal, War and Peace, What are we fighting for?, Peace this Winter, The Socialist Review, Towards Ultimate Harmony*."

[2] *Ibid.*: "*The Nation* was by no means an anti-war journal; Massingham and his writers cherished above all things the great liberal idea of freedom. For them the war was fought against the principle of military force, to purge the world of the military rule known as Prussianism. . . . It was therefore all the more surprising when, on April 7, 1917, the overseas circulation of *The Nation* was prohibited by the Army Council." If, as Massingham suspected, the War Office's ill-will, due to his disregard of the official hand-outs of the Press Bureau, had found an ally in the Prime Minister's resentment of Massingham's fierce hostility to the "Knock-Out Blow" policy, *The Nation* had certainly made itself some dangerous enemies.

[3] Cf. Caroline Playne, *Britain Holds On, 1917–1918*, pp. 72–5.

English Radicalism: The End?

The British War Propaganda Department evidently thought that depression and discouragement must be countered by some special stroke if bellicose ardour were to be maintained, so they did not combat a terrible rumour which emerged. In April 1917, the Northcliffe Press spread the news of a most shocking business.[1] The world had got used to horrors, but this was so vile and nauseating that it was calculated to rouse afresh unbounded wrath and indignation. . . . In Germany and Austria there were factories which treated the carcases of animals as described [extracting fats for lubricating oils and crushing the rest for pig-food or manure]. But it was the unholy inference of soldiers' bodies being thus desecrated which circulated among the Allies and stirred up hatred of the loathsome Hun. The stunt answered its purpose till the myth was explained and exposed. . . . In Britain in order to keep up wrath, this moment was chosen to publish a White Paper about the use of police dogs in prisoners' camps in Germany. It was said that these dogs were trained to set on prisoners who had given no cause for such treatment. Complaints of the use of police dogs . . . had been made since 1915 but now the methods and abuses of the system were described in a manner calculated to keep awake the popular anger. . . . Other terrible accounts of the sufferings of naval and military prisoners in German camps also excited great indignation. *The Daily Chronicle*, which now represented the politics of the *Knock-Out Government* had, on June 1, on the first page, the exciting heading "Australian Prisoners of War obliged to eat grass."

Some notes of a conversation during a call I made on a woman show how the flame burnt. In answer to a suggestion that there must be give and take among nations when peace should be made, she replied that there must be no give. Germany's claws must be drawn for generations. She herself could never trust the word of any German ever after. They must not keep Kiel. They must give up Holstein and Schleswig, Alsace and Lorraine. If a peace by negotiation were attempted, the people of England would make a revolution.

[1] Cf. *The Times* and the *Daily Mail* for April 16, 1917. Needless to say, the full exposure of what has acquired notoriety as the "Kadaver stunt" was not possible till the war was over (Cf. *The Nation*, October 31, 1925). That *The Nation* itself should have had some original doubts is the best measure of the "stunt's" success.

CHAPTER X

1917

"There were present Bonar Law, Curzon, Carson, Henderson, Barnes, Bob Cecil. At this meeting Henderson said that he was going to Paris with four Russian Socialists . . . and with Ramsay MacDonald to make arrangements for the Socialist gathering in Stockholm. . . . Henderson wanted a destroyer to take the party across the Channel the following day.

Bonar Law said, in Lloyd George's absence, that he did not know what to do; . . . and Bob Cecil asked if he was to issue passports. Henderson said that of course he was to issue passports and to order a destroyer . . . the party went over yesterday. This is a shocking business."

> One description of a War Cabinet, late in July 1917, from
> *Field-Marshal Sir Henry Wilson, His Life and Diaries*, ii, 7.
> Henderson was dismissed in August.

"Rumour has run a wild course through the week. From one mouth she has blown peace in forty-eight hours, from another two or three [more] years of war. She has settled the Treaty and the men who were negotiating it. She has taken the Germans out of Belgium in October—next spring—and set them back again. She has made several new Governments. She has invented a great number of air-raids. The nation, being in the dark . . . reaches out naturally to these half-lights of gossip. But the interest shown in Mr. Asquith's speech, and the almost wild enthusiasm of his reception at Leeds, are evidence of how welcome would be the advent of an open, honest, rational, practical statesmanship. . . . The air raids were not badly borne. They try the nerves of mothers, children, the young and the excitable. . . . They depopularize the Government, brutalize the war. . . ."

> *The Nation*, September 29, 1917, portrays vague popular restlessness.

"It is not at all surprising to hear that the Army is democratic. . . . For the most part they believed, and may still believe, in the moral purpose of the war. But they know, too, that the State they left behind was, for them, a City of Destruction, whose secret and exclusive polity . . . had ensnared their youth. They will require a change. . . . The new electorate . . . will never settle down on the blood-soaked [National Party] ground of Protectionism, Nationalism, Imperialism, Militarism and

Conscription. . . . The framework of a true National Party is more likely to emerge from the exploring work of the Sub-Committee of the Executive of the Labour Party than from any enterprise of General Page-Croft and his friends. . . . We are not in the secret of the movement of re-organization of which Mr. Henderson is the centre. But we can readily divine its spirit. . . . The Labour Party had never established a broad basis in the life and thought of the constituencies. . . . It had never called on middle-class brains to supply its deficiencies of knowledge. . . . Now, as we understand, it will fling a net over the whole political and electoral surface, abolishing its exclusive industrial tests, accepting middle-class candidates . . . aiming to capture the intellectuals. . . . Doubtless it will join forces with the Liberals in driving out the Georgian bureaucracy, restoring the power of Parliament. . . . But its special ambition must be to lay down at least the framework of a new industrial order. . . ."

The Nation, October 13, 1917, "ON THE NEW DEMOCRATIC PARTY".

To study the "popular Press" on the Russian Revolution of March 1917 or on the American declaration of war against Germany shortly afterwards is to become markedly aware of the full meaning of the phrase, "blind leaders of the blind". Hardly an instance is to be found for months of a warning to the nation that the Russian Revolution could bring great profit to the Germans. Instead, all the busiest and most plausible pens were occupied proving that the Russian people had revolted because they were sick of the pro-German intrigues of Court circles, anxious to sign a separate peace. Now that the Tsar had been deposed, the nation was told, and a Provisional Government installed, faithful to the anti-German Alliance, something like a full-scale Russian war-effort might be expected to bring speedier and complete victory. And the notion that the American President and Congress had come into the war for any other purpose than helping to defeat and abase the Germans is also hard to find in the "popular Press" of the spring of 1917. Obviously, the British "man in the street" was hardly well-prepared to understand why, before long, St. Petersburg was demonstrating for a "peace of no annexations and no indemnities" and why the United States, declining the status of an Ally, set itself, as an Associated Power, a very different set of war-aims from those of the "Secret Treaties" discovered in the Tsarist Chancellery.[1]

The chagrin may be imagined of the predominant Government circles at Paris, Rome, and London who saw a defeated Russia, still leaning heavily on them for help of every kind and yet, as they held, trying to snatch the diplomatic initiative with high-sounding phrases that spelt the doom of all their war sacrifices and cherished, if largely concealed, war-ambitions. Nor did "progressive" American "phrase-mongering", on occasion, cause them much less concern seeing the possibility that American man- and money-power, held back till others were exhausted, might come to dominate the end of the war. But this is not the place to study such questions in detail, but rather to let a leading British Radical

[1] Cf. *The Nation*, May 12, 1917, p. 130, for the struggle proceeding inside the first Russian Provisional Government as to whether it was right to abandon any or all the covenanted gains for which so much Russian blood had been shed and whether, whatever Russia decided, it was right to publish the "Secret Treaties" against the wish of Russia's Allies: "The Russian Provisional Government has just contrived to survive a grave crisis. . . . M. Miliukoff defended his adherence to the various secret treaties . . . and maintained his refusal to publish them . . . however, the triumph of the No Annexation Party is complete."

organ, bitter against Lloyd George and his Press, air its suspicions
of how the British public had been misled about Russia and was
still being systematically misled about almost every other war-
topic. Here is *The Nation* of May 19, 1917:[1]

Take, for example, our first news of the Russian Revolution. It
cannot have been by accident that all the early accounts represented it
as a patriotic revolt by the Duma leaders in the interests exclusively of
a more energetic prosecution of the war. That legend was gradually but
effectively dispelled but it revealed the bias that colors all news that
is allowed to reach us. Take, again, the news which one may pick up
here and there in the foreign press of the Rome meeting—that its chief
result was the assignment to Italy of an immense sphere in Turkey, the
Smyrna, Aidin, Konia region. That news, if true, ought to be authoritatively known here. It defines one of the more important aims of the
war; it is for such aims good or bad, and not for phrases that we are
fighting. . . . There can be no free discussion and no informed discussion in these conditions. A calculated and interested view, evolved
by the official mind for narrow propaganda ends, is imposed upon or
suggested to the whole Press at each turn in the rapid march of events.
We are nearing the plight of what used to be called the "reptile Press"
of Germany. . . .

Before long, the Russian Provisional Government, moving
steadily to the Left under a variety of pressures, was causing new
anxieties to the Allied Cabinets. Here is that Government's
position, as reported during June, in two successive numbers of a
leading and sympathetic Radical weekly:[2]

The Revolution retains its suspicions of the Imperialism of the
Western Powers, and the habitual argument of its press is that there is
little or nothing to choose between Britain and Germany. . . . Until
we say plainly, "We do not ask you to go on fighting in order to enable
us to add Mesopotamia, Palestine, and the German Colonies to our
Empire, nor to establish Italy in Smyrna, nor yet to dismember Austria-
Hungary," we shall not succeed in convincing them of our sincerity
elsewhere. It does not help us, when in the midst of this argument,
Italy, of her own motion, proclaims a protectorate over Albania. . . .

The Provisional Government now proposes that an Allied Conference
should be held at an early date to revise all the agreements binding the
Allies, excluding from revision only the Pact of London which provides
against a separate peace. . . . The telegrams from Russia are much more
optimistic in tone, and all convey the impression that Lenin's faction is
losing ground.

If Lenin's faction, the Bolsheviks, was optimistically reported
on as losing ground, that was due, possibly, as much as anything

[1] Under the title, "The Frustration of Opinion".
[2] Cf. *The Nation*, June 16th and 23rd.

else, to the widespread suspicion, even in Russia, that he had accepted, and was still accepting, from the Berlin Government much more than the famous permit to cross Germany, with his followers, in a sealed train. But some, at least, of the greater optimism reported from Petrograd arose from growing hopes of what might be accomplished in the direction of a just and speedy peace at a projected Stockholm Conference of the Socialist International where the representatives of the neutral States would be ready and eager to mediate between the Labour and Socialist parties of the contending belligerents.[1] If, for example, the "Majority Socialists" of Germany and France could, by Dutch and Swedish mediation, be brought to some exchange of views on the Provisional Government's peace-basis of "no annexations and no indemnities", a great step forward might well have been taken. Even the futile Russian offensive, begun on July 1st and evoking Leninist protests that soon became insurrection,[2] was apparently intended to forward peace by showing Germany that Russia was not powerless and the Allies that they were not deserted. And though a German counter-offensive annulled the Russian results so speedily[3] as to profit Lenin within Russia and the German General Staff outside rather than the German Opposition,[4] hopes

[1] Cf. *Whitaker's Almanack, 1918*, Diary of the War, under May 9, 1917: "Resolution of Russian Soviet in favour of the international Socialist Peace Conference at Stockholm. British Labour Party decided not to associate itself with Stockholm Conference; Mr. A. Henderson deputed, with two colleagues, to go to Petrograd to impress upon Russian Labour and Socialist representatives the necessity of avoiding a separate peace." Under May 28th is reported, "French Socialists decide to attend the Stockholm Conference," and under June 1st both the French Government's refusal to grant passports for Stockholm and some change in the British Labour attitude.

[2] Cf. *Ibid*, under July 16, 1917: "Disbanding of recalcitrant regiments and a mutiny in barracks, due to Maximalist and Leninist intrigue, caused serious disorders in Petrograd"; under July 17th: "Mutineers and workmen from Kronstadt arrived in Petrograd, where disorders continued; mutiny denounced by the Soviet"; and July 18th: "Disorder at Petrograd quelled by arrival of several military units, who used artillery. . . . Letter from the Russian Chief of Staff revealed M. Lenin as . . . supplied with funds by an intermediary of the German Legation at Stockholm."

[3] *Ibid.*, under July 19th: "Germans counter-attacked Russian N.E. Galician front, and pierced positions . . . on a wide front. Certain Russian regiments, influenced by extremist agitation, disobeyed orders and abandoned their positions; similar indiscipline occurred further south on General Korniloff's line."

[4] *Ibid.*, under July 6th for the most promising stage hitherto reached in Germany though, of course, before the success of the German counter-attack: "Crisis in Germany resulting from Herr Erzberger's demand in the Reichstag for far-reaching reforms, and peace without indemnities or annexations." The fall of the German Chancellor, Bethmann von Hollweg was reported under July 14th.

of Stockholm were certainly not over till some sensational developments in August.

Before these developments are dealt with, it might be well to give an informed view of the Russian scene of July as it appeared to a sympathetic Radical weekly, much read in Labour circles, whom, indeed, it was urging to Stockholm. Few pieces of the journalism of the time stand historical scrutiny so well as this extract from *The Nation* of July 28th:

> The current diagnosis seems to be that Lenin and his faction, seduced by German gold, tried to upset the Provisional Government in the interests of Berlin, and succeeded in spoiling an otherwise promising offensive. The prescription which follows on this diagnosis is equally simple: arrest the traitors, expose their plans, put Kerensky at the helm, and all will be well. This is to reduce a grave and complicated chapter of contemporary history to mere melodrama . . . Leninism is a doctrine of long standing . . . if an armed proletariat is strong enough to overthrow Tsarism, it ought also to be able to overturn Capitalism. That is the central Leninite thesis. . . . Starting from this fundamental position of hostility to any compromise with the "bourgeoisie", the Leninites found confirmation in each turn of events. For them Anglo-French-Italian Imperialism is as dangerous as the German variety, for in each they see only a phase of capitalism. They predicted that the Provisional Government would fail to induce the Western Allies to follow Russia's example and abandon Imperialist aims. . . . They backed their arguments with an unceasing stream of "revelations". Now they divulged the alleged terms of secret pacts among the Allies for annexations that defied every principle of nationality. Next they drew attention to the alarming indebtedness of Russia. Finally, they attributed the offensive itself to direct financial pressure from one of the Allied Governments. . . . The plain fact is that Russia has to face an economic collapse. . . . Her present standing in the world's markets is measured by the fall of the rouble from 2s. to 11d. The drop in its purchasing power is still more serious; one rouble before the war was worth eight to-day in real values. . . . The land question awaits solution. . . . The peasants are bent on having the land of the nobles, the monasteries and the Crown; they have, indeed, taken it already. . . . Is it to be expropriation without compensation. That means gross injustice to individuals. Some order must be introduced into what the peasants have done, often with violence. But where is the machinery that can impose order? The police and civil service have disappeared. Hardly less serious is the question of nationalities. . . . The salvation of Russia depends on an early general peace. . . .

History may well come, one day, to say, if it has not done so already, that the most vital policy-mistakes of the war were made

218

during the summer of 1917 in the Russian field. The Prime
Minister was almost as ignorant of the Russian situation as it was
possible for one in his high position to be—and, in any case,
tended to become too absorbed in the day-to-day political
manœuvring he doubtless thought necessary to prevent serious
anti-Government feeling from arising on the perilous German air-
raids of the time,[1] the growing Sinn Fein problem in Ireland,[2]
the merciless War Office call-up of the patently unfit,[3] and the
food and price difficulties which had so much to do with industrial
unrest.[4] Then, there were such things to prepare for as the war
anniversary of August 4, 1917 with a Westminster Abbey service
to be attended by the King and Queen and a "great patriotic
speech" to be made at the Queen's Hall afterwards by the Prime
Minister. Meanwhile, the British Army had been committed to a
great Flanders offensive in unfortunate weather[5]—and intricate
manœuvring from the Prime Minister's office was proceeding
intended not only to effect great changes in Britain's Land and
Sea efforts but even to reorganize the Air effort in such a way as
to take the blame for anything that should go wrong in future in
London's air-defences off the Prime Minister's shoulders and put
it on to those of a "Press Lord".[6] It was plainly not a situation
that allowed Mr. Arthur Henderson, the only member of the
War Cabinet with some personal experience of the Russian
Provisional Government's tremendous difficulties,[7] to persuade

[1] Cf. *Whitaker's Almanack, 1918*, Diary of the War, under June 15, 1917, for
the most serious of the summer: "Raid by 15 German aeroplanes on the City
and E. London: 104 killed, 432 injured; one hostile machine brought down."
For some time the Prime Minister's prestige was felt to be reeling.

[2] *Ibid.*, under July 25, 1917. for a new manœuvre: "First meeting of the Irish
Convention in Dublin; Sir Horace Plunkett appointed Chairman."

[3] *Ibid.*, under July 24, 1917: "Agreement by the Government to the suggestion
of the Committee on the Military Service Acts that the whole system of [medical]
examination and re-examination should be transferred to the Local Government
Board."

[4] Cf. *Ibid*, under July 23, 1917, for the Publication of the Report of the
Commission of Inquiry into Industrial Unrest. It may be mentioned that by
this time the food and price position had brought down the first Food Controller, Lord Devonport, who had been succeeded by Lord Rhondda, a more
enterprising figure.

[5] Cf. *The Nation*, August 4th: "The new British offensive began on Tuesday
morning . . . in indifferent weather. . . . The ground was wet. . . ."

[6] The "Press Lord" ultimately aimed at was no less a personage than Northcliffe, and when he evaded repeated attempts at enlistment, his brother, Lord
Rothermere consented to become President of the Air Board.

[7] Cf. *Whitaker's Almanack, 1918*, Diary of the War, under May 29, 1917:
"Mr. A. Henderson's departure for Russia on a special mission announced,
Mr. G. Barnes taking his place, in his absence, in the War Cabinet."

the Prime Minister to take a Stockholm decision in defiance of the Northcliffe Press. And as the long-term consequences of Henderson's subsequent dismissal proved singularly important in the history of British party development, a little attention to the immediate circumstances seems justifiable.

Here is the leading Radical weekly of the day on Henderson's attempt, after he returned with a Russian party from Petrograd (where the Socialist, Kerensky, was now head of the Provisional Government) to unite all sections of the British and French Labour movements with Petrograd, first, for an Inter-Allied Socialist Conference and, then, for a Stockholm meeting of the International where it was, doubtless, hoped to turn the German "Majority" Socialists against the "Kaiser's War":[1]

The visit of Mr. Henderson and Mr. MacDonald to Paris in company with the delegate from the "Soviet" (Council of Soldiers' and Workers' Delegates) has resulted in an agreement between the French Socialist Party and the British Labor Party (subject to ratification by its Conference) to attend the Stockholm Conference and to make no further objection to a meeting with the German Socialists. On this point, Mr. Henderson's stay in Petrograd has been educative, and he now realizes that something is due to the Russian Revolution. The decision is a compromise however. Mr. Henderson has carried his point that there shall first be a separate Allied Socialist Conference, and that the American Labor Delegates (who are non-Socialists) shall attend it. The Conference will be a very difficult adventure. . . . The extreme Tory group in the House with the backing of *The Times* is using this visit to Paris to assail Mr. Henderson's position in the War Cabinet. Three charges are made, (1) that Mr. Henderson went without the Cabinet's knowledge; (2) that he associated with Mr. MacDonald; and (3) that his position as Secretary of the Labor Party is incompatible with his membership of the War Cabinet. . . . Why must Mr. Henderson cease to be an official of the Labor Party while Mr. Bonar Law may continue to lead the Tory Party?

It does seem that Mr. Henderson obtained Mr. MacDonald's passports for Paris by allowing the Foreign Office to assume that the absent Prime Minister understood and approved his plan; but, it is true also that Prime Ministers have a habit of not desiring to know too much when they want a test made of "public opinion" without becoming personally committed. The fact that Mr. MacDonald had just led a mixed "Pacifist" band of Radical and Labour men in asking the Commons to approve a late "peace

[1] *The Nation*, August 4, 1917.

resolution" in the Reichstag did not, of course, help Mr. Henderson.[1] Nor was he helped by the united resolve of the Foreign
Offices of London, Paris, and Rome to give their own Socialists,
"ignorant of foreign affairs", no chance of falling into "German
peace-traps" nor the German Socialists the chance of claiming,
if they turned against the Kaiser, that they had been promised a
"peace of no indemnities and no annexations". Mr. Henderson's
last sin was committed when, after being provided with a misleading message from Petrograd,[2] which would allow him to
claim, at the Labour Party Conference, that the Kerensky Government was no longer insistent on Stockholm, he chose still to
affirm his conviction that Labour delegates should go and carried
his motion by 1,846,000 votes against 550,000. The Prime
Minister decided to believe that he had been wilfully misled;
Henderson was dismissed in anger and replaced by Barnes; and it
was announced in Parliament that, in accord with the Governments of the United States, France, and Italy, Britain, too, would
refuse passports for Stockholm.[3]

As Secretary of the Labour Party, with his hands on an important
and growing political machine, Mr. Henderson was to prove a
more dangerous enemy than the tricky Prime Minister doubtless
supposed. There were other enemies, too whose belief that the
Lloyd George régime could not last long seemed to be upheld by
the difficulties and heavy losses of the Flanders offensive and by
the Prime Minister's apparent inability to stop the serious German
air-raids of September and October.[4] The war-hate Press seemed,
indeed, to be his main reliance, and his eagerness to enlist Lord
Northcliffe as first head of a new Air Ministry[5] and his readiness,

[1] *Hansard*, July 27th. The defeat was by 148 votes to 19.
[2] Cf. *The Nation*, August 25th: "Two new facts have emerged this week. . . .
One of them is Mr. Henderson's definite statement that Mr. George was last
May in favour of the Conference. The other is the explanation of the famous
'Kerensky' telegram . . . it was our Government, or perhaps Mr. George
personally who at least inspired the telegram. . . . Mr. George's misuse of
M. Kerensky's name has exposed the Russian Prime Minister to somewhat
violent attacks. . . . He is suspected in Petrograd of double-dealing, while all
the while the duplicity was in London."
[3] *Hansard*, August 13th, Mr. Bonar Law.
[4] Cf. *The Nation*, September 8, 1917: "Another night air-raid took place on
this country on Tuesday, the third in three days. . . . It is not pride but stupidity
and incompetence to ignore the fact that the new tactics create a serious
situation."
[5] Cf. *Ibid.*, November 20, 1917, in jocular vein under the heading "MASTER
AND MAN": "However the nation will earn with relief that the door of the War
Council . . . closed on Sir William Robertson, as that of the Cabinet on Mr.

despite a humiliating public rebuff, to take Rothermere, his brother, instead, must serve to illustrate his anxiety not to let the "Press Lords" part company from him.[1] Meanwhile, the Radicals' *Nation*, which had its own quarrel with Lloyd George and had gleefully reported in August that Tories, disgruntled by Churchill's reappointment, were talking of a Balfour-Asquith Government or a Lansdowne-Cecil-Asquith combination,[2] gave, in mid-September, a picture of opinion in the country hardly flattering to the Prime Minister or his Press claque. Here it is:[3]

A series of country visits leaves me with a clear impression of the difference between the private speech of the people and the forensic view of their minds which one obtains from the London daily press. The only theme of the latter is the war; the former, when it quits the subject of the crops, the prices and the all-pervading and most depressing topic of Government Beer, breathes an unreasoned, but deep and universal aspiration for peace. . . . The feeling I record was quietly though firmly expressed among civilians; much more strongly by civilians on leave. . . . The political view surprised me. A good deal of politics is talked and thought and the revival of a free kind of Liberalism, joined with not a little rather naïve revolutionary sentiment, is a distinct strain in it. The one party of which I could find no trace is a Georgian party. With the average Liberal, the Prime Minister's personality is sunk in the Carson-Milner association. . . . For a few brief weeks he might have shone in a reflected light of victory; but that vision has faded. . . . In the world of medium Liberalism the hero is still Mr. Asquith. He is thought to have kept the right tone and the right policy and to be the safest guide available for the difficult times ahead. . . . The idea of a crushing military success, or that war on the modern scale lends itself to such an issue hardly exists. . . . The Young Liberal is a League of Nations man. . . . He leans to an understanding with Labor . . . I believe him to be staunch to Free Trade. . . .

The picture here given has some of the elements of the truth in it, and, in addition, there had already been tendencies among

Henderson, one or the other portal has long been widely, even imploringly, held open to receive Lord Northcliffe. There can be no doubt on this point, for Lord Northcliffe hastens to tell us so. He has, it appears, decided to refuse Mr. Lloyd George's repeated and urgent offers to assume the Ministry of the Air, proposals so precipitately conveyed that (by some inadvertence) they preceded the invitation to Lord Cowdray to quit it. . . . We do not know whether a British Prime Minister was ever so addressed. . . . Founding himself on the most ambitious and least responsible force in Britain, he has given ambition and irresponsibility the power to wreck him with a word."

[1] Rothermere as controller of the *Daily Mirror*, the *Sunday Pictorial*, and other properties was, of course, a formidable Press power in his own right, and there was the added expectation that his brother's writers would hardly attack a Government of which he was a member.

[2] *The Nation*, August 4, 1917.   [3] *Ibid.*, September 15, 1917.

Conservatives to abandon Lloyd George as a slippery and none too successful mountebank and substitute a Conservative Prime Minister. Yet *The Nation*'s picture hardly makes sufficient allowance for the ring of Press magnates soon enlisted in the work of preventing a possible Lansdowne-Asquith-Henderson coalition from displacing Lloyd George and the "Knock-Out Blow",[1] nor for the apparent ability of the baser fry of journalism, headed by Bottomley, to threaten almost a revolutionary situation if "pacifism" and the "Hidden Hand" were allowed to return to Downing Street. Then, increases of Army and Navy pay, made necessary by the galloping paper-money inflation (like Old Age Pensions increases earlier), could be represented almost as the Prime Minister's personal largesse to Britain's brave fighting-men. The alleged discovery, too, of Germany's "Hidden Hand" in Paris, in the person of Bolo Pasha with £320,000 from the Deutsche Bank to distribute, was a veritable godsend to the Prime Minister and his backers[2] during the dark autumn days of 1917 when, amid the ribaldry of the unfriendly, it was Germany who seemed to be delivering the "Knock-Out Blows" at Italy and Russia in turn. Perhaps nothing would do more to illustrate how

[1] It appears to have been widely known in Fleet Street, even before the famous "Lansdowne Letter" appeared, that the Tory ex-Foreign Secretary disliked the "Fight to a Finish" basis on which Lloyd George had taken his stand. He was repeatedly mentioned as a possible Prime Minister, with Asquith as his Foreign Secretary, and Henderson as his Home Secretary, if the "Fight to a Finish" school lost ground and it was resolved, instead, to test Germany's readiness to evacuate and compensate Belgium as well as to negotiate on Alsace-Lorraine.

[2] The *Daily Mail* and the *Evening News* quickly snatched at the chance of a new "stunt", and the Prime Minister himself, in the words of one of his tartest critics, "groping for a watchword in Carmelite Street, has picked up Boloism and waves the shining emblem aloft". Of course, the critics noted that Boloism, in crossing the Channel, had apparently undergone a sea-change for while Bolo's alleged crime in France was to seek to influence the Chauvinist papers, in Britain the "British Bolos" all seemed concerned with "Pacifism". According to the *Daily Mail*'s leading article of October 8, 1917, on the theme of "Who is the British Bolo?", "The question of supreme importance for Great Britain is now whether Bolos exist in Great Britain and, if so, who they are. There is every surface indication that they are active here. We have pacifists who behave precisely as though they were employed by some British Bolo; and we know that they have large funds. Whence do they get these funds? . . ." And if this was the *Daily Mail* tone, when treating of the few thousands raised with difficulty to throw in for "A Peace of Reconciliation" against the millions spent on Government War Propaganda in many different disguises, the *Evening News*'s was headier still. It had heard, it claimed, that "Germany through numerous agitators and agents operating in certain centres has been preparing to launch a desperate pacific campaign among the civilian population. . . . It is stated that by means of colossal bribes the German Government sought to control various enterprises with a view to undermining public opinion on the prosecution of the war."

English Radicalism: The End?

his Praetorian Guard of Press magnates prevented Lloyd George's being driven from power than a study of the kind of treatment they instructed the Sunday newspapers, say of October 14, 1917, to take into a majority of the homes of the country. The subject was handled thus by one mocking observer:[1]

> In the *Weekly Dispatch*, Mr. Arnold White, high priest of the Hidden Hand, is led astray by the new mystery of the Bolo Man. . . . He feels he is on Bolo's track. . . . One is surprised to find that in the *Illustrated Sunday Herald* Mr. Robert Blatchford misses his chance with Bolo and is forced back upon that dear old "Hidden Hand". He tells us he is not alarmed by the revolutionary scare, but will say "plainly and frankly, that he will sleep more soundly, when he has been convinced that the country has not been sold to the enemy".
>
> The Mystery Prize, however, must be equally divided this week between the *Weekly Dispatch* and the *Sunday Pictorial*. In the *Sunday Pictorial* (which boasts a circulation of 2,529,740) Mr. Horatio Bottomley, our old champion of the Bulldog Breed, gets his teeth into mysteries Divine. Like other guests of the Army's generously undiscriminating hospitality, he has been running about in France. Owing to these peregrinations, Mr. Bottomley has become even more profanely intimate with theology than he was before. He is hand-in-glove with the God of Battles . . . he does believe that "God has summoned the Anglo-Saxon and the Latin races to His banner" while "the Devil has called the Kaiser and the Sultan and their savage hordes to do battle for him". It is a daring heresy, and a fine "Armageddon" (much-tried but blessed word) is likely to ensue. Mr. Bottomley declares that to him "Armageddon has been a revelation as well as a shock" but when he calls upon his readers to embark with him upon a spiritual voyage of discovery, we must politely decline. A man with Mr. Bottomley's record is not the fellow-passenger we should choose for that.
>
> After all we are inclined to back the *Weekly Dispatch* for the Mystery Stakes. Its column on "A Spirit Prophecy of the War's End" by "A Messenger" is hard to beat. It comes from *Private Dowding*, a book by Mr. W. Tudor Pole, who, while walking on the sands at Bournemouth had the good fortune to meet an invisible spirit "anxious to communicate". This sociable spirit turned out to be the ghost of Mr. Dowding, "since found to be a Suffolk schoolmaster killed in action". The extract is from spirit-writing taken down from "A Messenger" called by the spirit of the aforesaid Dowding. . . . Mr. Max Pemberton calls it a masterly prophecy. . . . "Few kings will be left in Europe, or, for that matter, anywhere. . . . The drinking of alcohol will cease . . . climates will improve, disasters caused by earthquakes, sea and air will diminish." When the spirit begins to soar . . . W.T.P. (author's initials) sensibly brings him down with the question, "What about

[1] Cf. *The Nation*, October 20, 1917, under the heading "LORDS OF THE SABBATH".

food?" "Grossness will disappear" is the immediate answer. . . . On America "we must expect revolutions of a peculiar sort at no distant date". He tells us "Armageddon" (glorious word again) must be fought out, and he is inclined to think that will be done in 1919; but he admits pathetically, "I am not a very high being, and to me is not revealed details of all these wonderful happenings."

Yet despite "all this trashy slush—this literally infernal non-sense—poured out upon the people Sunday after Sunday", some facts, inconvenient for the Prime Minister, could not always be talked or "explained" away. The formidable blows struck at Russia in mid-October, which gave Germany control of the Gulf of Riga, obviously brought a Russian break-away from the Allies nearer. And there followed, in the second half of October, even greater defeats inflicted by the Austro-Germans on the Italians, defeats already permitting the enemy, by October 31st, to claim 120,000 Italian prisoners and over a thousand captured guns. By November 7th, when 250,000 Italian prisoners and 2300 captured guns were claimed and a formidable invasion of Venetia had begun, major diversions of British and French forces, in aid of Italy, had had to be ordered to prevent a complete Italian military collapse.[1] To make matters worse, the French Government of the day fell on November 12th, the Bolsheviks triumphed at Petrograd on November 13th, and Lloyd George's dash to Rapallo, Rome, and Paris, to set up a Supreme Allied War Council, seemed to those who knew him best, merely another appallingly dangerous move in his struggle to impose his personal war-policies on the protesting Haig and Robertson. His critics, indeed, objected as much to what he had said abroad in disparagement of British Army achievements as to what he had done in placing the troops under outside control, and Tory censure, if it had not been muzzled by Bonar Law, might well have gone farther than this venom from the Radical *Nation* of November 17th:

The momentous announcement of the creation of a Supreme War Council . . . was made from Rome on Saturday. . . . The tone and circumstance of the Prime Minister's speech were unexampled in British war and statesmanship. Never, we suppose, has a revolutionary change in our military and civil government been announced from a foreign capital. And the policy itself was developed in sentences which gravely disparaged the major strategy of the campaign, including his

[1] Cf. Hugh Dalton, *With British Guns in Italy*, for one account of the British effort in Italy by a participant who became a Chancellor of the Exchequer.

own share in it. He denounced the neglect to send a great expedition to the Balkans in 1915 as "an inconceivable blunder", ignoring the crushing military evidence against that adventure, and coupled with his censure a hit at the policy of hammering with all our might at "the impenetrable barrier" in the West. The Russian and Rumanian failures he also set down to want of unity though they had nothing whatever to do with it. Recurring to the theme later on, he compared Germany's advance by fifty kilometres in Italy and her capture of 200,000 men with our advances of a single kilometre and our success in "snatching" a "shattered village" and "capturing a few hundreds" of her soldiers. All these disasters he set down to want of "real unity" in command. We are not allowed to hear what France thought of this extravaganza. British opinion was hostile almost to a man. Mr. George's speech has not crushed Germany. But it has helped to bring down the French Cabinet.

The bitterly hostile Radicals of *The Nation* once again considered that Lloyd George had put himself into grave danger, and, to controvert the argument that there was no alternative Ministry for the time being, they claimed that there were half a dozen, "all of them incomparably better than the unstable and disorderly thing that exists". *The Nation* certainly gave one remarkable Cabinet list to show the alternatives there were, and as such a Government remained a distinct possibility until the tide turned definitely against Germany in the summer of 1918, the list might be worth repeating. Here it is:[1]

Prime Minister,	Lord Lansdowne.	War Secretary,	General Smuts.
President of the Council,	Lord Rosebery	First Lord, Minister for Education,	Mr. Runciman. Mr. Fisher.
Foreign Secretary,	Mr. Asquith.		
Minister of Munitions,	Lord Robert Cecil or Mr. Churchill.	Minister of Labor,	Mr. Thomas or Mr. Anderson.
Colonial Secretary,	Mr. Balfour.	President of the Board of Trade,	Mr. Pringle.
Chancellor of the Exchequer,	Mr. McKenna.	Lord Chancellor, India Secretary,	Sir John Simon. Viscount Grey.
Home Secretary,	Mr. Henderson.	Lord Privy Seal,	Lord Buckmaster.
Chancellor of the Duchy,	Mr. John Burns.	President of the Local Government Board,	Mr. Long.
		Minister of Reconstruction,	Mr. Sidney Webb.
		Minister for Ireland,	Lord Gladstone.

[1] *The Nation*, November 17, 1917.

The name of Lord Lansdowne, a one-time Governor-General of Canada, Viceroy of India, Foreign Secretary, and Leader of the Lords, was repeatedly mentioned, during 1917, as that of a possible "Elder Statesman" Prime Minister to inaugurate a departure from the emotional and diplomatic crudities of the "Knock-Out Blow". For one thing, such a nomination as Lansdowne's would have been a neat evasion of the whole spurious mythology of the "Hidden Hand", which had been built up largely to prevent Asquith's return to power and could hardly have been used as effectively against Lansdowne though, no doubt, the "Press Barons" and *John Bull* would have made the attempt and Pemberton Billing have endeavoured to find Lansdowne's name alongside Asquith's and Haldane's in the "Berlin Black Book".[1] Lloyd George, however, though in undoubted danger,[2] was not brought down in mid-November. And the Viscounty, conferred later in the month on Lord Northcliffe,[3] and the Cabinet place on

---

[1] Cf. *The Imperialist*, January 26, 1918, for Pemberton Billing's first "revelations" of the "Black Book": "There have been given many reasons why England is prevented from putting her full strength into the war. On several occasions in the columns of the *Imperialist* I have suggested that Germany is making use of subtle but successful means to nullify our effort. Hope of profit cannot be the only reason for our betrayal. All nations have their Harlots on the Wall, but those are discovered in the first assault, and the necessary action taken. It is in the citadel that the true danger lies. . . .

"Often in this column I have hinted at the possession of knowledge. . . . Within the past few days the most extraordinary facts have been placed before me which co-ordinate my past information. There exists in the *Cabinet noire* [*sic*!] of a certain German Prince a book compiled by the Secret Service from the reports of German agents who have infested this country for the past twenty years, agents so vile and spreading debauchery of such lasciviousness as only German minds could conceive and only German bodies execute. The officer who discovered this book while on special service briefly outlined to me its stupefying contents. In the beginning of the book is a précis of general instructions regarding the propagation of evils which all decent men thought had perished in Sodom and Lesbia [*sic*!]. . . . Then more than a thousand pages are filled with the names mentioned by German agents. There are the names of forty-seven thousand English men and women . . . Privy Councillors, youths of the chorus, wives of Cabinet Ministers, dancing girls, even Cabinet Ministers themselves, while diplomats, poets, bankers, editors, newspaper proprietors and members of His Majesty's Household follow each other with no order of precedence." To cull other choice extracts on listed public-houses and bars, "comfortable flats furnished in an erotic manner", the corruption of engine-room staffs at Portsmouth and Chatham, the "Lesbian ecstasy" in which Prime Ministers' wives betrayed State secrets and the "sexual peculiarities of members of the peerage" is to understand why some thought Billing a more dangerous rascal than Bottomley.

[2] Cf. *Lord Riddell's War Diary, 1914–1918*, under November 27th, for Lord Derby, Secretary for War, to Riddell: "The Army Council were on the point of resignation. Had they resigned, I think the Government would have fallen."

[3] Cf. *Whitaker's Almanack, 1919*, Diary of the War, for Northcliffe's step in the peerage ("for services" in his "mission to the United States") dated at

Lord Rothermere represent, doubtless, two of the means by which it was hoped to strengthen the Prime Minister's somewhat shaken position.

Lloyd George certainly needed all the fortification that could be procured for him. At the end of November and early in December came the deep disappointments connected with the complete and speedy German reversal of all the much-lauded results of the Cambrai tank-offensive.

Almost as disappointing and much more ominous was the opening, at Brest-Litovsk, of German-Bolshevist Armistice negotiations which might free scores of German divisions for action on the Western Front. Both these dangerous set-backs gave extra point to Lord Lansdowne's famous letter, published in the *Daily Telegraph* of November 29th and discussed throughout the world for months afterwards. The pertinent sections of the "Lansdowne Letter" deserve quotation since they were adopted, almost as a manifesto, by the very strong sections of British "public opinion" which ached for a lead away from the mass-incitements of Bottomley and Billing or even Northcliffe and Lloyd George.[1] And Lloyd George himself, at this rather cheerless stage, was, in private, hardly objecting, on "Knock-Out" grounds, to the "Lansdowne Letter" in itself, or to the notion of negotiating with Germany but only to Lansdowne's timing.[2] The "Lansdowne Letter" ran thus:

We are now in the fourth year of the most dreadful war the world has known; a war in which, as Sir W. Robertson has lately informed us, "the killed alone can be counted by the million, while the total number of men engaged amounts to nearly twenty-four millions." Ministers continue to tell us that they scan the horizon in vain for the prospect of a lasting peace. And without a lasting peace we all feel that the task we have set ourselves will remain unaccomplished. . . .

November 23rd and Rothermere's appointment as President of the Air Council dated at November 26th.

[1] The "Tank Bank" campaign, organized in Trafalgar Square from November 26th—and rather spoiled by the victorious German counter-offensive—represents almost the circus element that was now being introduced into war- and war-Loan propaganda.

[2] Cf. *Lord Riddell's War Diary, 1914–1918*, under December 3, 1917: "Of course the time will come when it will be necessary to open the question of peace, but the moment is unfavourable. . . . It will be a big task. The pacifists favour Asquith because they believe he will be more likely to make peace than I shall be, but they are mistaken. . . ." By this time, Lloyd George was becoming aware that circles inside his own Government had not discouraged Lansdowne, and that Colonel House, President Wilson's personal representative in Europe, was supposed to have asked for a mention of the "freedom of the seas" on which subject not only Germany but the United States was at odds with Britain.

In my belief, if the war is to be brought to a close in time to avert a world-wide catastrophe, it will be brought to a close because on both sides the peoples of the countries involved realise that it has already lasted too long. . . .

An immense stimulus would probably be given to the peace party in Germany if it were understood:

(1) That we do not desire the annihilation of Germany as a Great Power.

(2) That we do not seek to impose upon her people any form of government other than that of her own choice.

(3) That, except as a legitimate war measure, we have no desire to deny to Germany her place among the great commercial communities of the world.

(4) That we are prepared, when the war is over, to examine in concert with the other Powers the group of international problems, some of them of recent origin, which are connected with the question of "the freedom of the seas".

(5) That we are prepared to enter into an international pact under which ample opportunities would be afforded for the settlement of international disputes by peaceful means.

Lansdowne was, doubtless, not unaware that the "patriotic" Press would try and shout him down by allegations ranging from the accusation that he had, for years, been an out-dated and useless survival to suggestions that, if he had been paid, he could not have done the Kaiser's work better. After all, as its "pacifist" critics alleged, Fleet Street was doing very well out of the war, and its "patriots", who had never known such emoluments, influence, and power as they were enjoying, were the reverse of eager for a "premature peace". Just the same was true of some of the loudest "patriots" among the Labour leaders, and, all in all, the average London crowd in Trafalgar Square, Hyde Park, and the music hall could (especially with some stimulus from Colonial or British Khaki and Hospital Blue) be worked up to orgies of delicious if vicarious sacrifice for a "Fight to a Finish" as was noted in his angry war-poetry by Captain Siegfried Sassoon.[1]

[1] See the poem called *Blighters* for searing anger:

"The House is crammed: tier beyond tier they grin
And cackle at the Show, while prancing ranks
Of harlots shrill the chorus, drunk with din:
'We're sure the Kaiser loves the dear old Tanks!'

I'd like to see a Tank come down the stalls,
Lurching to rag-time tunes, or 'Home, sweet Home',—
And there'd be no more jokes in Music-halls
To mock the riddled corpses round Bapaume."

Trafalgar Square, indeed, with its Tank-Bank for selling War Bonds, was being organized just then into a species of open-air war propaganda circus, and the newspapers duly reported the constant succession of exciting novelties: ten girls who had lost their sweethearts in the war as the Tank-Bank's first customers; George Robey with his music-hall wit adapted to the War Savings movement; lovely actresses reciting and buying; Havelock Wilson with a legless sailor to illustrate the horrors of U-Boat warfare and to condemn Lord Lansdowne; and the famous preacher, the Rev. R. J. Campbell, proving that unless the Allies prevailed, the whole world would become Prussianized.[1]

Despite the vigour and ingenuity of the attempts to discredit and shout down Lord Lansdowne, success was very far from complete. The Radicals of *The Nation*, for example, whose correspondence columns were filled with pro-Lansdowne material, reported not only that the Asquithians of the ex-Cabinet were in private agreement with Lansdowne but that the politicians would find it "impossible to go back to the world as it existed before his letter appeared". For the next eight months, certainly, the name of Lansdowne remained in many minds as that of one who might finally have to be called in, and, indeed, in March 1918, there was a second "Lansdowne Letter" of marked importance. But it might be worth while, at this stage, to give a view of the British Press as it reacted to the strong stimulus of the "Lansdowne Letter" of November 29th. Here is one pro-Lansdowne view from a leading Radical journalist:[2]

I have seen the Lansdowne Letter compared to a bombshell, and that word fairly describes the scattering effect it has had on its critics. It has just sent Mr. Garvin sprawling over leagues of slatternly prose, and *The Times* ranging between anguished attempts to represent Lord Lansdowne first as a man of no importance, then as a world-incendiary, and finally as so much of a nuisance that the sooner the lid is clapped on him and his letter the better. Add to this an ingenious attempt to concoct a hostile American opinion, an outraged England, and a horrified Alliance, the whole liberally served with personal abuse growing hotter as the Northcliffe Press descends from Printing House Square to the gutter.

It would be a great mistake to suppose that even, taking our journalism

---

[1] Cf. Caroline Playne, *Britain Holds On, 1917–1918*, pp. 173–4. Similar methods were taken to other parts of London and to the greater provincial centres.

[2] *The Nation*, December 8, 1917 (Wayfarer in his famous "London Diary").

as it stands, subject to the lure and threat of the Northcliffe Press, its verdict has gone against Lord Lansdowne. I take the following list of daily journals which can be described as pro-Lansdowne:

Daily Telegraph, Daily News, Westminster Gazette, Evening Standard, Star, Manchester Guardian, Western Daily Mercury, Sheffield Independent, Birmingham Gazette, Daily Mirror, Aberdeen Free Press, Edinburgh Evening News, Leicester Post, Darlington Echo, North Eastern Daily Gazette, Freeman's Journal, Irish Independent.

Add to these such journals as the *Scotsman*, the *Yorkshire Post*, the *Liverpool Daily Post*, the *Glasgow Herald*, the *Dundee Advertiser* whose criticism is moderate and balanced. Where is the anti-Lansdowne movement? Outside the mechanics of the Tory caucus and the froth of the Jingo Press it hardly exists. . . .

One of the manipulated Press-points that, doubtless, hurt Lansdowne's cause most was the alleged "proof" that American opinion was strongly against him. Of course, America, ablaze with war-prosperity, free from air-raids, and still quite immune from the appalling trench-massacres that made Lansdowne, despite all official discouragement, the private hope of many a British "Tommy", only had its opinion canvassed by the "Jingo Press" when it could be made to supply ammunition against Lansdowne and the "Pacifists". Even President Wilson had been freely bespattered with abuse as long as he stayed neutral and now, in private, plentiful suspicions were still aired as to what he might contrive to do, whether in war or peace, to the British Empire's detriment and to America's advantage.[1] But, truth to tell, President Wilson, whose representative, Colonel House, had given Lansdowne, at one stage, some encouragement,[2] now found himself irked by the British Peer's presumed readiness for an Anglo-German settlement under five headings instead of waiting for the President's world-programme under fourteen. Certainly the Northcliffe Press did its best to torpedo the "Lansdowne Letter" by using President Wilson's Message to Congress of December 4th with its affirmation that "our object is to win the war" and that the American people were "deeply and indignantly impatient" with those desirous of peace by compromise. But, naturally, it was no business of the *Daily Mail* to point out simultaneously that, as the

[1] Cf. *Lord Riddell's War Diary, 1914–1918*, under December 9, 1917, for Lord Riddell to his intimate, Lloyd George.

[2] *Ibid.*, under December 3, 1917, for Lord Burnham of the *Daily Telegraph* telling Riddell not only that the British Foreign Office had not objected to the "Lansdowne Letter" and "on the whole thought that publication would be advantageous" but that Lansdowne "had also discussed the letter with Colonel House on several occasions, and that he was favourable to publication".

Americans had not yet a man in the firing-line despite well-advertised plans for millions in 1919 and millions more in 1920, the British blood-tax to the war, during 1918, might prove more terrifying even than those paid at the Somme in 1916 and in Flanders during 1917.[1]

Yet, despite the efforts of what Radicals called the "Jingo Press", there is plenty of evidence that Lansdowne's courageous initiative had altered the political climate considerably both at home and abroad. At Brest-Litovsk, for example, the Russo-German Armistice and Peace negotiations were noticably affected; at Berlin, readiness for a general Peace Conference was expressed and this, in turn, during the political manœuvring that followed, led on, early in January, to a new British statement of War Aims; and, then, on January 8, 1918, came President Wilson's famous "Fourteen Points". Meanwhile, at home, a stronger stand had been encouraged against the "Never Endians" who refused to contemplate any cessation of the slaughter, it seemed, till Berlin had been occupied and the Kaiser and Crown Prince made captive. The spirit being brought to the fight against the "Never Endians", after the "Lansdowne Letter", may be gauged from two successive numbers of the Radicals' *Nation*, those of December 15 and 22, 1917. On December 15th, confidence was expressed in the Allies' ability to secure Germany's admission of defeat and the signature of suitable terms if only a clear and reasonable definition of such terms were to be had. But no such detailed definition was available; there was merely a babel of the most varied demands. As *The Nation* put it:

> The war, says Mr. Asquith, was made to secure a "clean peace". The war, says Sir Edward Carson, exists for the bombing of Hun businesses. The war, says the *Daily Mail*, is an excellent profiteering investment. The war, says *The Times*, is for dismembering Austria and giving French capitalists a good slice of industrial Germany. The war, say the authors of the Non-Ferrous Metals Bill, is for setting up a British corner in spelter. The war, say all the Protectionists, is to put down our Hun competitors. The war, said the Tsar, was for a Russian Constantinople and a Russian mastery of Turkey. In substance, all these pleas are excuses for a prolongation of the war. But a needlessly prolonged war is a lost war, and each stroke in it is a blow at British interests. . . . And that is the kind of war which Liberalism has the duty, the right and the power to bring to an end.

[1] Cf. *Field-Marshal Sir Henry Wilson, His Life and Diaries*, under October 16, 1917, for some even of the fire-eaters of the General Staff growing worried.

On December 22nd *The Nation* not merely expressed hostility
to the latest Lloyd George war-pronouncement, the last as it
proved before that weather-cock politician decided to veer round
towards less bellicosity,[1] but claimed also that the Prime Minister's
speaking had been deeply and widely resented. Here are some
passages:

> Mr. George has added a fresh speech to his knock-out. The last of
> them points to an end of the war in 1919 rather than 1918. Describing
> Germany as a "criminal" and "bandit" nation which had committed
> "murder, arson, rape, burglary, fraud and piracy"—he declared that
> such states would always exist until their crimes were made un-
> profitable. . . . The unprofitability of war is, we imagine, a lesson that
> has been equally impressed on all the nations. . . . Meanwhile the nation
> must strip barer for the fight and "grousing", i.e. criticism of Mr.
> George, must be discouraged. . . . The Gray's Inn oration seems quite
> in the natural order of events. Its audience heard it with coldness; in
> the country, apart from the gramophone echoes of his press, it is widely
> and profoundly disapproved.

[1] Cf. *Lord Riddell's War Diary, 1914–1918*, under December 1917, and
January 1918, for some intimate pictures of the Lloyd George circle which
help to explain how he came to the War-Aims speech of January 5, 1918, of
which its author, said "I went as near peace as I could", though, as he claimed
in private, "with a view of appealing to the German people and detaching the
Austrians".

CHAPTER XI

THE WINTER OF 1917–18

"President Wilson, in an address to Congress yesterday, dealt with the peace proposals of the spokesmen of the Central Powers as presented to the Russian representatives at Brest-Litovsk . . . the Central Empires had again challenged their adversaries to state their war aims . . . . But he accepted the challenge, and put forward what he conceived to be the peace programme of the world. The points of this programme were:

(1) Open covenants of peace and no secret diplomacy in the future.

(2) Absolute freedom of navigation in peace and war outside territorial waters, except when seas may be closed by international action.

(3) Removal as far as possible of all economic barriers.

(4) Adequate guarantees for the reduction of national armaments.

(5) An absolutely impartial adjustment of Colonial claims, the interests of the people concerned having equal weight with the claims of the Government, whose title is to be determined.

(6) All Russian territory to be evacuated, and Russia given full opportunity for self-development, the Powers aiding.

(7) Complete restoration of Belgium in full and free sovereignty.

(8) All French territory freed, and the wrong done by Prussia in 1871 in the matter of Alsace-Lorraine righted.

(9) Readjustment of Italian frontiers on lines of nationality.

(10) Peoples of Austria-Hungary accorded an opportunity of autonomous development.

(11) Rumania, Serbia, and Montenegro evacuated, Serbia given access to sea, and relations of Balkan States settled on lines of allegiance and nationality.

(12) Non-Turkish nationalities in the Ottoman Empire assured of autonomous development, and the Dardanelles to be permanently free to all ships.

(13) An independent Polish State.

(14) An Association of Nations affording guarantees of political and territorial independence for all States."

The Times, January 9, 1918.

"Some war posters exploited morbid sentimentality. Some presented the most horrible misdeeds of the Huns in the most revolting way, thus renewing war-hatred. Many appeals were

234

based on partial truths and war-lies [as] READ THE WORDS OF RUDYARD KIPLING.

We are fighting for our lives, the lives of every man, woman and child, here and everywhere else. We are fighting that we may not be herded into actual slavery such as the Germans have established by force of their arms in large parts of Europe.

We are fighting against eighteen hours a day forced labour under the lash or at the point of the bayonet, with a dog's death and a dog's burial at the end of it.

We are fighting that men, women and children may not be tortured, burned and mutilated in the public streets, as has happened in hundreds of towns.

And we will go on fighting till the race who have done these things are in no position to continue or repeat their offence.

As you read each morning the breathless story of our stern resistance to Hun onslaughts backed by all the devilry of high science, do you not feel how eagerly you would help our men if you could? You *can* back *their* blood with *your* money. Put every pound you can possibly spare into

NATIONAL WAR BONDS."

Caroline Playne in *Britain Holds On, 1917–1918* on what official war-propaganda had become by the spring of 1918.

"The Battle of Armentières.
The position of the British Army is now graver. Mr. George has had power such as a Caesar might envy. How has he used it? . . . men hold their breaths as they open their morning or their evening newspaper. Mr. George would have no thought or talk of peace, either from the Pope, or from the Austrian Emperor, or from Stockholm. How has he conducted the war? He cannot escape responsibility. . . . The country is undergoing a rapidly intensifying strain, which he has demonstrably produced and his ineradicable deficiencies of character and judgement hourly aggravate, and it is time for her to be done with him."

The Nation, April 20, 1918.

I T might be well, before going on, in this chapter, to treat of the effects in Britain of Brest-Litovsk or the "Fourteen Points", to dispose, first, of a purely British political development of great importance for the future. Since 1914, Mr. Sidney Webb had been supplying more and more of the tactics and strategy of the Labour Party—and as he seemed to look for no reward save the privilege of being consulted behind the scenes by those who would get the public credit for all he planned and did, confidence in him at the Labour Party Headquarters had become almost complete. Even the most shortsighted Trade Union leaders and Labour politicians had come to appreciate something of the value to their cause of the Fabian Tracts and the Fabian Research apparatus, and, besides, where else was Labour to find, for its foreign contacts in preparation for peace, one who had learnt his spoken French and German on the Continent as a boy and could read and interpret documents in a number of other important languages besides? At any rate, in May 1918, when a Labour Party, ambitiously reconstituted on plans which Sidney Webb had helped to draft, was being widely discussed as the possible principal source of an alternative Government after peace should have come, Beatrice Webb added this note to her account, in her famous *Diaries*, of Arthur Henderson's dismissal from the War Cabinet the previous August:[1]

We none of us realized the enormous importance of Henderson's ejection. . . . He came out of the Cabinet with a veritable hatred of Lloyd George, who insulted him at their last interview. . . . From that day Henderson determined to create an independent political party, capable of becoming His Majesty's Government—and he turned to Sidney to help him. . . .

A sub-committee of the Labour Party's Executive was, indeed, soon busy on plans, to attract into the Labour Party, the considerable Radical elements, discontented alike with Lloyd George and Asquith. Local and constituency Labour parties were to be provided for, to which individual adhesion by "workers with hand or brain" would be open, and rather specious arrangements were offered to allow those local parties some influence on the determination of national policy alongside the "block votes" of the

[1] *Beatrice Webb's Diaries, 1912–1924*, p. 94, as the note under the entry for August 12, 1917.

affiliated Trade Unions and Socialist propaganda societies. The "intellectuals" were especially aimed at, their professional status and financial means being expected to make them more suitable candidates for many types of Parliamentary seat than the normal Trade Union official. And there were already a number of Radical M.P.s and journalists, so antagonized by Lloyd George's reckless aggravation of the war-spirit and Asquith's inability or unwillingness to stop him that they were ready to abandon their traditional allegiance[1] if "Democratic Party" could have been substituted for "Labour Party" as the party-name and the Trade Unions' "block votes" surrendered. But no adequate financial basis even for the existing small-scale Labour Party seemed possible without the Trade Unions, which not only declined to consider a change of name or a surrender of "block votes" but often showed some dislike of the whole Fabian tactic of annexing the "brain-worker" middle-class intellectuals. Indeed, early in 1918, it took considerable management by Henderson to prevent the new constitution from being voted down by a Trade Union combination which feared for its hold on the Party if professional men, with political ambitions, gained a firm footing.

It is Beatrice Webb's memorable *Diaries* that again supply the indispensable description of the hesitations in the Labour camp before the new Constitution was accepted and the chance taken of beginning the absorption of much middle-class Radicalism. Of the Nottingham Labour Party Conference of January 1918,[2] Beatrice Webb reported that Henderson was originally nervous that his new Constitution might be rejected by Union block-votes wielded by hostile Trade Union secretaries mobilized by Tom Shaw. Shaw certainly had his own Cotton Unions lined up against the Constitution, the Miners were doubtful, and the Leftists of Syndicalism and the I.L.P. had, of course, some special objections to becoming the possible tools of political opportunists from the middle and professional classes. Mrs. Webb thought she detected in Henderson the ambition of becoming, through the marriage, in his new Constitution, of the Trade Unions and the middle-class "brainworkers", the first Prime Minister of a Labour or

---

[1] Cf. *The Nation*, February 2, 1918, for a letter from C. P. Trevelyan which was significantly printed under the headline, "CAN RADICALISM AND SOCIALISM UNITE?" It contained such assertions as that "Many Radicals are already openly joining the Labor Party. Others are hesitating. . . ."

[2] *Beatrice Webb's Diaries, 1912–1924*, under January 21, 1918.

predominantly Labour Cabinet. MacDonald she reported as trying to sit on the fence; the Labour Leadership generally as concerned at the uncritical acceptance accorded by the rank-and-file to what she called "the lurid doings in Petrograd"; and the I.L.P. leaders as not knowing whether they wanted an English Revolution or not.

As Beatrice Webb realized, the actual strength of the Labour Party could be greatly exaggerated by those who neglected its tumultuous cross-currents and the fact that, as "the new thing", it might be attracting some support that would not prove lasting. Yet Henderson and Webb certainly pushed their advantage audaciously and were helped by the fact that "Labour" could claim to be free of all blame for Asquith's "Secret Treaties" and Lloyd George's "Knock-Out" follies, not to mention the long and sorry history of Tory entanglement with "Carsonite Treason" in Ireland. And so it was that the new draft Constitution was followed by a War-Aims Memorandum that got much of the credit for bringing back the Prime Minister to the comparative moderation of his War-Aims speech of January 5, 1918[1] and, then, came "Labour's" "Message to the Russian People" welcoming their formula of "No annexations, no punitive indemnities", repudiating the "Secret Treaties" and, finally, for good measure, accepting and defining how the most debatable part of President Wilson's programme—"the right of self-determination"—would be applied in the British Empire. Yet there were Radical writers, prepared to risk their Asquithian proprietors' displeasure, by describing this "Labour" exercise in Utopia-building as "making policy for the country and for the world".[2]

Of course, the swelling vogue of Utopianism suffered some deflation when the German authorites made it quite plain that all the wooing of the "German people" with Wilsonian phrases, that ignored Germany's case against the "Secret Treaties" and the *status quo* of 1914 at sea, would not be allowed to talk the German Armies unconditionally out of occupied territory and out of Alsace-Lorraine, Danzig, Thorn, Posen, and the sovereignty of

[1] Cf. *The Nation*, January 12, 1918: "There are some points of tone and manner in the Prime Minister's speech to the trade unionists which are relatively so good that we wish the speech as a whole had been a different and a better one . . . it was nearly time for statesmen to begin extinguishing the flames instead of fanning them. . . ."

[2] Cf. *Ibid.*, January 19, 1918. The proprietors of *The Nation* must already have begun to view with some doubt the increasingly pro-Labour tone of Massingham and his famous team—Hobson, Brailsford, Nevinson, Hammond, etc.

the German colonies too.[1] Indeed, on January 24th, the Reichstag heard the German Chancellor, Count Hertling, make a very forthright reply to Lloyd George and Wilson in which the full German case was maintained and the counter-suggestion advanced that the "freedom of the seas" would be better secured if Britain gave up her fortified Naval bases in Gibraltar, Malta, and elsewhere. Of course, the German Chancellor had to pay a price for his "firm stand" both in the industrial unrest reported from Germany's sorely-tried civilian population[2] and in the apparent justification given to the Allies' Supreme Council, assembled at Versailles between January 30th and February 2nd, to return to the old talk of "the vigorous prosecution of the war, and particularly the closer and more effective co-ordination of all the Allied Powers".

Yet there was plenty of industrial unrest in Britain, too, which was certain to rise steeply as Government's suggested Man Power Bill was pushed through Parliament so that hundreds of thousands, hitherto reserved, might be withdrawn from industry and agriculture and fed to the War Office for what would presumably be the bloodiest campaigning yet.[3] Moreover, the British Prime Minister's busy tacking, as the wind changed, between comparatively moderate and "Knock-Out" War-Aims declarations, excited anger and contempt against him in some political quarters at the very time when others were thoroughly antagonized by his treatment of Jellicoe, Haig, and Robertson.[4] Here is one damaging

[1] Cf. *Ibid.*, February 16, 1918, for one interpretation of what Lloyd George might be held to have demanded even in the "moderate" speech of January 5th —"that the Central Powers should give up Alsace, Posen, Galicia, Trentino, Transylvania, Syria, Palestine, Arabia and Mesopotamia". President Wilson's "Fourteen Points" of January 8th were themselves interpreted in this sense at Versailles.

[2] Cf. *Ibid*, February 2, 1918: "The men's demands are not yet Bolshevik in scope . . . a prompt peace without annexations, the participation of Labor in the negotiations, the abolition of the state of siege and the censorship, democratization of the German Empire, and universal suffrage (including women) for Prussia. . . ." The previous week's *Nation* had reported that "a strike for peace broke out last week in Vienna, and spread rapidly throughout Austria".

[3] Cf. *Ibid.*, February 2, 1918: "Here, too, the heather is on fire. Great meetings of engineers and allied workers have been held in Liverpool, on the Mersey, at Coventry and on the Clyde, rejecting the Man-Power Bill, and demanding either an armistice or the immediate opening of peace negotiations."

[4] Cf. *Lord Riddell's War Diary, 1914–1918*, under December 25, 1917, for Lloyd George congratulating himself on having brought about Jellicoe's resignation and under February 16–18, 1918, for the "secret or unworthy methods" (including the "Northcliffe attacks on Haig and Robertson") which the public suspected the Prime Minister to be using against the Service chiefs.

Radical indictment, calling for a change of Government, and after offering a Lansdowne-Asquith-Henderson combination, venturing to suggest, despite the almost certain doubts to be expected from the Asquithian proprietorship, that a Labour alternative might be preferable for several reasons:[1]

I do not know what impression the manifesto of the [Versailles] War Council . . . has made upon the enemy, but I can testify to the anger and revolt in Liberal and Labor England . . . the idol of the knock-out blow [is] set up again on its blood-soaked pedestal and millions of boys drummed back to slaughter. For what? For the peace of the secret treaties . . . which no statesman dares put to his people, no general to his armies? For the peace of President Wilson, which all the world wants? None know. . . .

The effect of this levity and duplicity [of the Prime Minister] is to convince a body of men in all parties that an end must be put to it. . . . The Government is the object of almost universal fear and distrust. It is neither honest nor able. . . . But the Paris Manifesto is a last straw. . . . But what is the alternative?

Broadly speaking, there are two. A Lansdowne-Asquith-Henderson combination is, I imagine, always possible. It could be instantly manned, and should not lightly be dismissed. The nation, looking as Mr. Holt suggests in a letter to *Common Sense*, to a united demonstration of its most trusted advisers against the policy of the knock-out blow, might virtually insist that the secret treaties, instead of being played with as they are to-day, should be definitely repudiated, and the statesmen who negotiated them given a new mandate for a League of Nations peace. As things stand, they may feel themselves bound to French Nationalists and Italian Imperialists, however much they disagree with them. But a new political situation here would bring a measure of release. The question is whether, in spite of its availability, this device is really adequate to the situation.

There are three strong reasons for the growing feeling in favour of the more drastic alternative of a Labor Government. The first is that Labor leaders, and they alone, may be able to control the fast-growing menace of the industrial situation. The second is that the formation of a Labor Government here would almost inevitably lead to its establishment in France and Italy. The third that a Labor Government alone can at once tear aside the serpent coils of the Secret Treaties and inaugurate a free diplomacy, certainly with a Liberal-Socialist Austria, perhaps with a Parliamentary Germany. . . .

But the great force which drives towards a Labor Government is moral. . . . Doubtless the problem is more complicated than that—the Red Revolution of one mass of workers crosses the Pacifism of another; the Pacifists themselves shade off into varying colours; workmen, like other parties, have their Left and Right Wings, and many workmen

[1] *The Nation*, February 9, 1918.

have slight or no political ideas. But there in the main lies the great body of innocence, of non-responsibility for the war, and there, too, is the visible effort at reconciliation. That we may be quite sure will not cease. . . .

Obviously, *The Nation* writers, in their disgust with the "Secret Treaties", were in danger of adopting a somewhat uncritical cult of Labour, quaintly reminiscent of that of Rousseau's followers for the "Noble Savage". The belief, for example, that a minority Labour Government could hold strikes and wage-demands in check was to prove the purest fantasy in 1924. The fatal weakness, too, that Continental Governments of the Labour brand might be expected to show in the face of the revolutionary minorities that existed in France and Italy was overlooked despite what had just happened in Russia. Moreover, the working-class mobs who had undertaken the *Lusitania* riots, who gave Bottomley fifty times the circulation of Morel, who swallowed every malignant rumour of the "Hidden Hand" and the "Berlin Black Book" and who, by pre-war standards, had done quite heavy war-wage profiteering themselves while girding incessantly at the profiteering of others, were not "the great body of innocence" that middle-class senti-mentalists sometimes chose to believe. Yet the extract is worth giving for the light it throws on the spirit and motives which were already influencing many 1914 Radicals towards the Labour camp.

But, perhaps, the time has come to turn from the topic of international war and peace to follow how "progressive" opinion was trying to prepare the ground, early in 1918, for post-war political "advance" at home. There still seemed considerable chances that short-term "advance", at any rate, would primarily be determined by Asquith, Henderson, and their followers, and Lloyd George was certainly driven, on occasion, to meditate on how he might outbid Asquith in offering "to do a deal" with Labour.[1] Here, at least, is one account of January 1918 intended to show how reconcilable and even parallel the Radical and Labour post-war policies really were:[2]

Mr. Runciman's article in the January *Contemporary* is a spirited statement of Radical policy after the war. It will be interesting both to state his programme and to compare it with that of the Sub-Committee of the Labour Party's Executive.

[1] Cf. *Beatrice Webb's Diaries, 1912–1924*, under March 1, 1918.
[2] Cf. *The Nation*, January 5, 1918.

1. *Agriculture:*

Free Food [i.e. free of tax], and scientific aid to production, and a wide State plan of allotments and co-operative small holdings. The Labour Party proposes a great scheme of land reclamation, and road, railway and harbour development.

2. *Wages:*

The extension of the minimum wage (the Labour plan proposes a national minimum of 30*s*.), the restoration of trade-union privileges, a State building scheme of 600,000 houses.

The Labour Party proposes to re-build a million houses, at a cost of £300,000,000.

3. *Education:*

Better schools, more open-air schools, more training and money for teachers, an enlarged system of care and medical treatment for the children, municipal milk and midwives.

The Labour Party proposes a scheme for the development of higher and secondary education, supported by a further shortening of the hours of labour for young persons.

4. *Temperance:*

Continued State control.

The Labour Party propose local option and prohibition.

5. *Taxation:*

The burden to be laid mainly on the well-to-do, but no repudiation of the Debt.

The Labour Party proposes a capital levy to pay off a "very substantial part" of the National Debt, and a new scale of graduated income-tax, rising from a penny in the pound to 16*s*. or even 19*s*. on millionaire properties.

Programme-construction of this type appeared very much to the point when the great Western Front battles of 1917 had been brought to a standstill by the oncome of winter and when major peace-negotiations seemed under way at Brest-Litovsk. But signs and portents began multiplying fairly early in 1918 that the German authorities considered that another great military effort from themselves would be necessary before they could hope to have what they deemed a tolerable peace. There were troublesome air-raids on London and Paris late in January;[1] and in February,

---

[1] Cf. *Whitaker's Almanack, 1919*, Diary of the War, under January 28, 1918, for the worst raid on London for some time, with an admitted casualty list of 58 killed and 173 injured. The London raid of January 29th was less serious—10 killed, 10 injured—but the Paris raid of January 30th, with an admitted 49 killed and 206 injured, was the most serious ordeal the French capital had had for a long period.

there were not only reports of heavy German massing on the Western Front but the disturbing Bolshevik tactics at Brest-Litovsk were finally countered by Germany's breaking off the Armistice and helping (often with merely skeleton forces) great additional territories to free themselves from Red control and put themselves under German guidance and protection. By March 2nd, when the rapid and practically unresisted advance of numbers of German and even Austrian columns had forced the Bolsheviks to sign an ignominious peace,[1] Germany had apparently obtained her biggest and cheapest success of the war. And there are accounts of Lloyd George, after "going moderate" early in January with President Wilson and reverting to "Knock-Out" at Versailles some weeks later, veering round again, on receipt of the sensational Russian news, to thoughts of whether a "deal" with Germany might not be possible after all. Certainly Beatrice Webb seems to have spent eight or ten anxious days after a private opportunity of hearing the Prime Minister in person, on February 28th, wondering whether Germany was not going to be offered the opportunity of keeping much of her new "sphere of influence" in Eastern Europe, stretching, as it did, from Finland to the Ukraine, in return for concessions elsewhere to Britain, France, and Italy. She realized, moreover, that the Prime Minister might find a good deal of support, from numbers of quarters hitherto strongly opposed to him, if he could manœuvre himself into a position which would allow him to suggest the "cynical peace" he seemed to be considering.

It might be well, before passing on to the great German offensives of 1918, to have the "cynical peace" possibilities related as Mrs. Webb saw them. After setting the scene round Lord Haldane's dining-table on February 28, 1918, with the Webbs, Haldane, and the Prime Minister as the only four present, Mrs. Webb committed to her famous *Diaries* her impression that one of the Prime Minister's aims had been to test whether there had been any Labour response "to the Asquith touting for coalition". But she claimed also that she had had to evade "distinct advances" when he "pressed us repeatedly to come and dine with him and

[1] *Ibid.*, under February 18th for the Germans' breaking off negotiations and under February 21st for their Peace demands, the surrender of Poland, Lithuania, the Baltic Provinces, the Ukraine, and Finland; demobilization of the army; disarmament or internment of warships, including those of the Allies: resumption of Russo-German Commercial Treaty of 1904.

meet Milner—apparently to discuss the terms of peace".[1] Then Mrs. Webb continued with an interesting reappraisal of the Prime Minister as seen for the first time since the beginning of the war. She was not favourably impressed by his readiness for a deal with anybody who could be used and, while admitting his patriotism and executive energy, found all his ways crooked and the craving for power his overmastering obsession. She suspected that the Prime Minister and Milner were considering possible Peace-Terms at Russia's expense since Lloyd George emphasized repeatedly that Britain and France could not be expected to fight on to restore Courland, Lithuania, and the Polish provinces to a Bolshevized Russia. She gathered that Haldane, too, was thinking of a possible reconciliation of British and German Junkerdom and, indeed, with the Russian Empire to cut up, there could be the means of effecting compromises which would allow not merely the British and German Empires but those of France, Italy, and Japan to emerge from the war stronger than before. There were the obstacles, indeed, presented by the presumed dislike of Washington and the "democracies" for such arrangements but Mrs. Webb hardly seems to have felt confident of their ability to stop a "cynical peace" from going through.

On March 3rd the *Diaries* still show Mrs. Webb worried about the "cynical peace" while, by March 7th, her thinking had even advanced to considering the personal and party alignments that might be expected if and when it was proposed.[2] She had no right, she felt, to blame Haldane and Milner for favouring it for they really believed in German civilization while the Prime Minister's

[1] *Beatrice Webb's Diaries, 1912–1924*, under March 1, 1918. An Inter-Allied Socialist Conference had concluded not long before, which had been accepted as an "outstanding success" and at which Sidney Webb had been Chairman of the Commission on Territorial Adjustments.

[2] Cf. *The Nation*, March 9, 1918, for a second effort by Lord Lansdowne: "Lord Lansdowne has sent a second letter to the *Daily Telegraph* which will serve to keep the idea of a negotiated peace alive. . . . He rebukes the tone of the Versailles communication and seconds Mr. Runciman's proposal, which Count Hertling adopted, for 'conversations in an intimate circle'. . . . Lord Lansdowne . . . distinguishes again, and even more sharply, . . . between our demands for the restoration of occupied Allied territory, which admit of no compromise, and our demands for the improvement of the Allied position (Alsace, Trentino, etc.). These latter, he thinks must be left to the Peace Conference with the question of the African Colonies—an obvious hint of accommodations and exchanges and compensations. This is a shrewd and moderate proposal . . . its weakness is that it ignores the East. We do not suggest the return of the Borderland to Russia (much of it may not desire that solution). But the Entente, if it aims at anything better than Imperialist barter, must insist on securing here the reality of independence and self-determination."

attitude would be decided by pure opportunism. The peace party would able to rely, too, on those "Tolstoyans" whose hatred of war had all along led them to call for "peace at any price" and the far stronger forces, represented by Lord Lansdowne, whose objections to a continuation of the struggle rested mainly on the prohibitive material price that would have to be paid. And while Henderson, the Webbs, and the popular forces represented in the International Socialist Bureau would try harder to prevent the surrender of a struggle for "democratic equality between man and man and race and race", the Radicals of *The Nation* would condemn, with equal vigour, those who refused to negotiate and those who showed any symptoms of readiness to sign conditions which the Germans would accept.

In point of fact, it would have been very difficult even for one with Lloyd George's comparative lack of scruple to act as Mrs. Webb feared for he had just given hostages to the "Knock-Out" school when appointing Lord Beaverbrook to take charge of British Propaganda, with Lord Northcliffe directing the flow to enemy countries.[1] At any rate, by March 18th, the Allies had decided to refuse all recognition to the Brest-Litovsk Treaty, and, by March 21st, "Imperialist barter" with Germany was put still more out of the question by the opening of the great German assault on the British positions in France. It was an assault, moreover, that began so successfully for the Germans that by March 24th ("Black Sunday") the possibility of a major catastrophe was being faced and the stream of appeals for quicker American action had already begun.[2] Yet great as was the loss,

[1] Cf. *Ibid*, February 23, 1918, for the kind of attack the Prime Minister had exposed himself to: "He has got rid of our best strategist [Robertson] and he has put the worst journalism in Britain in control of our case for the war. The two transactions give an accurate guide to the mind of their author. Sir William Robertson has saved the country from innumerable follies; he has not been able to save himself from the inevitable consequence of averting them. . . . However, if the England of Mr. George seems a bad place for honesty and competence, it resembles an earlier Empire in being a good one for janissaries and sycophants. It may have lost the services of Mr. Asquith, Mr. Henderson, Sir John Jellicoe, and Sir William Robertson. But it is the richer for their executioners, and when Lord Northcliffe, Lord Rothermere and Lord Beaverbrook have been joined by Mr. Bottomley, the "stunt" Press will stand as one wall against the over-estimated power of Prussianism." More immediately dangerous were the strong Conservative objections voiced by Mr. Chamberlain (*Hansard*, February 19, 1918) who, if he had been so minded, could apparently have overthrown the Government on the issue.

[2] Cf. *Lord Riddell's War Diary, 1914–1918*, under March 24th, for Lloyd George himself: "Things look very bad. I fear it means disaster—unless President Wilson hurries up, he may be too late. He has wasted too much time. . . ."

disorder, and disorganization behind the lines that the new German break-through tactics achieved, they could not, in view of the vast defence-resources available, win the war at one stroke. Further blows would be necessary in different directions and, meanwhile, the Allies would have the chance of detecting how the Germans built up, in concealment, powerful assault-forces and how these were trained for break-throughs so complete as to threaten whole Allied Armies with encirclement. The Allies, too, would have some chance, before the next blow came, of endeavouring to complete their arrangements for unity of command, mutual aid, and the building-up of still further strength in France.

It might have been expected that when the Prime Minister, facing a none too friendly Parliament on April 9th, asked for such extraordinary supplementations of the drastic and unpopular "Man Power Comb Out" already operating[1] as was represented by the extension of conscription to men of fifty and to Ireland,[2] the doom of his Government was near at hand. Few politicians, certainly, would have been willing to prophesy a long life for the Administration, the more so as the very day of the new proposals saw the launching of a second great German offensive which seemed to underline all the contentions of Robertson and Haig with the Prime Minister to the effect that the war would be won or lost in the West and not at Baghdad, Jerusalem, or Salonika. But as a situation developed in which Viscount French, now in command at home, expected a second Sedan and began to prepare to repel invasion,[3] the very magnitude of the peril gave the Prime Minister some protection from the grosser forms of political opportunism. Though the Radicals of *The Nation* had, for months, been urging Lansdowne, Asquith, and Henderson to combine to drive out the reckless, extravagant, and incompetent

---

[1] Cf. *Hansard*, January 14, 1918, for Sir Auckland Geddes explaining how it was hoped to make some 420,000 to 450,000 available for military service by a Bill abolishing the two months' exemption given to certain men and allowing the authorities to withdraw any exemption certificates granted on occupational grounds. The Bill became law at the same time as a second for adding to the National Register lads who had attained the age of fifteen after August 1915, and men discharged from the forces.

[2] Cf. *Ibid*, April 9, 1918, for the Prime Minister not merely asking, in general, for leave to take any suitable man under fifty-one but, in certain specified cases such as medical men, confining exemption to those over fifty-five. Even ministers of religion, in the first draft, were to have been liable to non-combatant service. There was, of course, constant interruption from the Nationalists on the Prime Minister's Irish proposals.

[3] Cf. *Lord Riddell's War Diary, 1914–1918*, under April 1918.

Government, established and maintained by newspaper intrigue and corruption; though, after Austen Chamberlain, temporarily out of office, had protested strongly about the Press position, *The Nation* favourably reported on some Conservative readiness to make him Prime Minister;[1] though, finally, a Government of Lansdowne, Asquith, Grey, and Henderson was suggested,[2] after Prince Lichnowsky's striking vindication of Grey's Foreign Secretaryship,[3] the proposed ejectors of Lloyd George proved far more scrupulous than he himself had been. They certainly refrained from rash caballing; they declined to take the responsibility for further discouraging the imperilled troops in France by a display of personal political ambition; and, doubtless, they expected what was already described as a "tottering Government" to fall, of itself, on the receipt of the half-expected further bad news from France. The emergence of new Service troubles, this time at the Air Ministry and between General Trenchard and Lord Rothermere,[4] did nothing to help Lloyd George nor did the revelation that secret Peace talks with Austria had been allowed to break down owing to the extravagant demands of France on Germany and of Italy on Austria.[5] The Government's position

[1] Cf. *The Nation*, March 9, 1918: "Nothing has done Mr. George more harm than his addition to the stately [Government] pile of an *annexe* of newspaper proprietors. I think the Unionists were angrier than the Liberals. The breach with tradition, with seemliness, struck them more. If they could have voted on it, they would have deposed Mr. George solely on the strength of the Northcliffe and Beaverbrook appointments, and put Mr. Chamberlain in his place . . . Mr. George's Government is more unconstitutional than George III's, and now it avowedly rests, not merely as before on an *entourage* of doubtful journalism— Lord Northcliffe, Lord Beaverbrook, Lord Rothermere, Sir George Riddell, Sir Henry Dalziel, Mr. Donald . . . but . . . a janissary guard is formed round his person; and honours, titles, salaries, dignities, great powers of forming opinion and directing policy are showered on its officers. . . ."

[2] Cf. *Ibid.*, May 11, 1918.

[3] Cf. *Whitaker's Almanack, 1919*, Diary of the War, under March 15, 1918: "Publication by Swedish *Politiken* of the document written by Prince Lichnowsky, former German Ambassador to St. James's for private circulation; a telling indictment of the German policy which led to the war." Lichnowsky's readiness to admit Grey's consistent conciliatoriness, despite the troubles made for them both in Berlin, proved an acute embarrassment to the German Government which held that Lichnowsky's *pique* at the failure of his mission had distorted his judgement and announced the resignation of his Ambassadorial rank on March 19th.

[4] Cf. *The Nation*, April 20, 1918: "Britain's . . . fate trembles in the balance . . . the Press that records it happens also to relate the virtual supersession of General Trenchard by Lord Rothermere. General Trenchard is the creator of the Air-Service . . . Lord Rothermere is or was the director of the *Daily Mirror*. That is an epitome of the Government of Mr. George."

[5] Cf. *Ibid.*, May 4th: "The exchange of views, conducted through Prince Sixte of Bourbon-Parma [brother-in-law of the Austrian Emperor] began in

would have been worse than it was if Austen Chamberlain had not decided that it was his patriotic duty, in the existing emergency, to abandon his doubts of the Prime Minister's dubious relations with the Press and accept, instead, his pressing offer to join the War Cabinet.[1]

But it is time to give some picture of how the Radical attempt, generalled by *The Nation*, to bring down Lloyd George and end the apparent policy-dictatorship by the questionable "Janissary band" of Press proprietors and controllers round the Prime Minister, was put to the politicians and the country in April and May 1918. The culmination of *The Nation*'s dangerous attacks on the new Man Power Bill (as certain to cause immeasurable trouble in Ireland and profound industrial disturbance in Britain for the relatively small yield of middle-aged recruits fit for the front-line and likely to reach it in time for the decision) came on April 27th in an article entitled "The Responsibility of Mr. Asquith". Here are extracts:

The country has before it the immediate results of Mr. George's conduct of Irish affairs. In a single fortnight he has made a united Ireland—against himself. . . . Apply this unique strategy to the war and the diplomacy of the war. Mr. George deducts from our fighting force enough British soldiers, it may be, to decide the pending battles in our favour, while he shuts out all hope of Irish recruitment. He tears to fragments the conciliatory work of two generations of Liberalism and puts in grave jeopardy the American Alliance. . . . This is his offence. No British Minister ever committed a greater one. The Liberal leader, whose policy he has brought to nought, has, in grave error, consented to pass it over. Parliament will next week go through the mockery of discussing a Home Rule Bill in sittings which Nationalist Ireland will not even deign to attend. Why should she? The Bill was not brought

March 1917, and went on into July. There is a second (unpublished) letter from the Emperor, and one from M. Poincaré which demands not merely Alsace-Lorraine but the frontier of 1814 [including the Saar] and 'guarantees' as to the whole left bank of the Rhine. If Italian demands were on a similar scale, the marvel is not that the negotiations were fruitless, but that they lasted so long. The most startling fact which emerges from these documents is that . . . America, Russia and Belgium were neither consulted nor informed. . . . The *dossier* contains some further facts about the German offer through M. Briand in August 1917, and the two later series of meetings in Switzerland in the autumn of 1917 and the early months of 1918. A chance of an honourable peace, which would have included some concessions over Alsace-Lorraine was rejected. . . . Is our House of Commons content to leave the whole task of investigation to the French Chamber? Has it any sense of responsibility left?"

[1] Cf. *Life and Letters of Austen Chamberlain*, ii, 114: "My distrust of these appointments was not wholly allayed by the explanations and assurances. . . . But the circumstances of the time are very grave. I do not think that they admit of a change of Government. . . ."

The Winter of 1917–18

in to redeem any hope or aspiration of hers. It was introduced, on Mr. George's confession, because a naked act of Irish conscription, without a pretence of consulting a single Irishman, would not have looked nice in the eyes of America or of British Labour. . . . Mr. George has got the shadow of his Bill and lost the substance, and has dealt his country a worse blow than the Germans struck it at St. Quentin. . . .

This is the measure of Mr. George's statesmanship. That he is a public danger, as his Government is a public scandal, and that for the sake of England and Ireland, of the war, and the peace, he should be got rid of, at the earliest possible moment, is the prevailing sentiment, uttered or unexpressed, among men of good sense and good feeling, who love their country and her cause, and see them in imminent risk of perdition at his hands. . . .

What of his administration? His extravagance no man can describe. His own career as Minister of Munitions was a carnival of financial disorder and profligate expense. . . . And if economy is one test of a good government, stability in its ordering and *personnel* is another. But with Mr. George the waters are always troubled. . . . Three men of high character, ripe in experience and unsurpassed at their work . . . Jellicoe . . . Robertson . . . Trenchard . . . all are gone and their places given to inferior men. . . . The indictment of Mr. George is that he has introduced into politics a class of men who, while they are the foundation of his power, are unfit to govern England. Lord Rothermere is known as the director of a low type of journalism, and is known for nothing else in the world. He has now resigned his office, but the results of his brief administration remain. It is possible to argue that he had a good case for getting rid of Sir Hugh Trenchard and Sir David Henderson. But considering what the work of these men has been, the importance of the Air Service, and the alarm and discouragement that prevail in it at a most critical hour, the matter is one for a close inquiry. . . . Now there is one man to whom a demand for inquiry into the management of the war . . . cannot be refused. That man is Mr. Asquith. . . . He might have stopped Irish conscription. . . . He held his hand. It was a grave error, for the country waited for a lead. . . . It is not too late for Mr. Asquith to intervene in the grave case of Ireland. It can never be too late for him to protect the war services from unreasonable and unsettling treatment. . . .

In our view the time has come for the House of Commons. . . . It is not possible to deny an investigation into the cause of the breach which the Germans made in our line in the area of St. Quentin. That event has changed the whole course of the war. . . . For that defeat . . . and all it involved, Mr. George must be called to account . . . there are at this moment four men on whose wisdom and courage the restoration of the threatened power of this Empire largely depends. They are Mr. Asquith, Lord Grey, Lord Lansdowne and Mr. Henderson. These statesmen represent the forces from which, in the main, the work of rescue must come. . . . They should be ready to take office to-morrow. . . .

English Radicalism: The End?

A powerful and talented alternative Government *in posse*, of course, existed—but its advent would have ruined the political career not only of Bonar Law and Lloyd George but of their close associates and the "Press Lords". Resignation and political ruin was not yet in their minds, and the "Press Lords", more especially Northcliffe,[1] had it in their power, if they were prepared to face the risks, of stirring up the gravest mob-trouble against the mere possibility of the reappearance of the "Old Gang" and the "Hidden Hand" at Downing Street. The danger of perilous street-brawls developing at the height of possibly decisive fighting in France was, doubtless, one of the factors inducing some members of Parliament to caution before turning out the Government, and the astonishing demonstrations, early in June, in favour of Pemberton Billing and his absurd "Berlin Black Book" libels[2] are convincing enough proof that the return of Asquith and Lansdowne could and probably would have been critically challenged. Asquith himself undoubtedly realized this, and since his fall in December 1916, had taken the greatest pains to keep himself and his associates clear of every possible charge of indulging in merely "factious opposition" or even criticism. In fact, he had always claimed, to the disappointment of some of his more Radical followers, to be lending the Government's war-effort "independent support" and had just gone so far, in that respect, as to allow the extreme Man Power proposals of April through with no more

[1] *Life and Letters of Austen Chamberlain*, ii, 117–18, for the effrontery of the Northcliffe Press's efforts to ban even Austen Chamberlain's return.

[2] Cf. *The Nation*, June 8th: "A fuddled indictment of our public men is dragged into a law case, turned for the moment into an entertainment of Colney Hatch. The enemy is credited with a supernatural knowledge of these people's abnormal weaknesses and vices. There is not a scrap of evidence that such knowledge or such vices exist. The supposed German 'list' includes some of the most honoured names in England. . . . Nevertheless rounds of applause greet the chief accuser and acclaim his acquittal, and he becomes the interpreter of the popular discontent and unbelief. . . . A sufficiently strong appeal to fear or hate is hard to resist. . . . A Carson, a Northcliffe, a Bottomley, a Tupper, or a Billing—it is all one to the war-mind. This war-mind has taken four years of training on German spies, concrete emplacements, Donington Hall, Bolo hunts, pacifist conspiracies, camerillas, and Berlin 'Black Books' to get it to its present maturity. . . . The Black Book turned out a much more interesting stage 'property' than 'Salomé'. There was only one copy of it; but it turned up in Albania, London and Berlin; and though it was a dead secret, it was always being seen. . . . An ex-Whip (since honourably dead in the field) shows it casually in one hotel. . . . He even points out his chief's name in it (which happens to be the Prime Minister's), and mentions at another hotel-meeting that it has gone back to Berlin. There are 47,000 Britons (or 53,000, the exact figure is doubtful) holding the most important positions in society, prepared to sell their country and addicted to unnatural vice. . . ."

vital challenge from himself than expressing his conviction that
Irish Conscription was unenforceable, which Ministers themselves
ultimately admitted, and that a lower Conscription age-limit was
called for than one of over fifty. It was, indeed, the Back-Bench
Unionist, Sir John Spear, who had taken the responsibility of
dividing against the Government for an age-limit of forty-eight
and had obtained, despite the usual flow of soothing Government
assurances, customary on such occasions, the surprising Division-
list of 152 against 262.[1]

Before going on to deal with the noteworthy "Maurice Letter"
of May 7th and the epoch-making Maurice Division that followed
upon it, something should, perhaps, be said on leading Sessional
topics of 1918 not yet discussed. The Bonar Law Budget of
April 22nd, for example, with its estimated expenditure of
£2,972,197,000 and estimated revenue of £842,050,000, aroused
considerable Radical criticism because of its proposal to raise only
£67,800,000 per annum in new taxation (not, it was claimed, very
wisely or justly distributed) while leaving the immense sum of
£2,130,147,000 to be borrowed and added to the already stupendous National Debt. One Radical member, Mr. Sidney Arnold,
estimating the post-war National Debt as likely to reach eight
thousand millions, put forward the most drastic Capital Levy
proposals yet heard outside Socialist circles when suggesting that
the whole national future would be distorted and imperilled by
the effort to pay interest on so vast a sum, which must be quickly
and firmly scaled down. Perhaps the tone on Budget and finance
matters, which had been reached by the "advanced" schools of
Radicalism, at any rate, can be gauged from the following comments in *The Nation*:[2]

The debauchery of borrowing, in which ever higher prices are paid
for loan money furnished for a large part out of swollen war-profits and
for the rest out of bank-inflation, is to continue, and on a larger scale
than ever. For out of the estimated expenditure for this year, close

[1] Cf. *Hansard*, April 11, 1918. One of the Government's assurances was that
only seven per cent of the men between forty-two and fifty would be taken from
civil life. But suspicion emerged, before long, in view of the high medical
grades that were assigned to these ageing men and the apparent reluctance to
reject outright, instead of placing in Grade 3, those with admitted and grave
disabilities like club foot ("if able to walk fairly") and eczema ("of moderate
severity").

[2] Cf. *The Nation*, April 27, 1918, for the articles headed "ANOTHER YEAR OF
BAD FINANCE" and "THE CAPITAL LEVY AS A BUSINESS PROPOSITION".

upon 3,000 millions, 842 millions is to be furnished from revenue, leaving much more than 2000 millions for fresh borrowing. And, if experience teaches anything, the actual figures of expenditure will far exceed the estimate. . . . It can never be repeated too often that a really rigorous taxation, begun in 1914 . . . would have left us in a far sounder condition both for conducting the war and for facing the peace finance. The money and the goods are there. We get them. But we get them by crooked and expensive methods of borrowing which inflate prices, oppress the poorer purchasers, put huge war loot into the pockets of contractors and financiers, and fail to restrain expenditure on luxuries.

As for the patchwork of new taxation, it contains one major and many minor vices. The major vice is its preference for indirect taxation. Why is no more than $23\frac{1}{2}$ millions out of 135 to be taken out of increased income taxes? Not less flagitious is the failure to put even a penny more on the Death Duties. . . . Why this tender regard for accumulated property? Or can it be that Mr. Bonar Law postpones immediate action in order not to reduce the size of the body upon which he reckons that a capital levy may be raised? He made, indeed, no response to Mr. Sidney Arnold's powerfully urged demand. Does this silence mean assent? . . .

With Mr. Arnold's preliminary estimate of the National Debt after the war as not likely to be less than eight thousand millions few will disagree. His proposal is that not less than three quarters of this sum should be raised by two levies, the first to take place as soon as possible after peace, and the second some two years later. Each levy should raise some three thousand millions, all forms of property being valued as for death duties. . . . The option, as Mr. Arnold presents it, is between a capital levy with an income tax of 2s. 6d. and no levy with an income-tax rising in its higher super-tax level to 12s. 6d. The proposed levy would be so graduated as to leave untouched properties of less than a thousand pounds, would reach $4\frac{1}{2}$ per cent at about £5,000, $7\frac{1}{2}$ at about £20,000, and $12\frac{1}{2}$ at £60,000, rising to a much higher figure for great individual aggregations of wealth. . . .[1]

Other sets of debates were going on, the decisions upon which would condition the post-war world in important ways but, here, the final rejection of Proportional Representation, for example, the

---

[1] Cf. *The Nation*, April 27, 1918, for other aspects of the Capital Levy discussion: "There is the further contention that such a confiscation of capital would be a dangerous deterrent to thrift. This is met by pointing out the emergency character of the measure. In point of fact, high income tax which is the sole alternative would be likely to be a far more effective interference with productive industry than the levy. . . . Finally there are two important arguments of a more general character . . . the first is the urgent necessity of paying back . . . while the inflated condition of the currency and other abnormal financial circumstances maintain high prices and high levels of monetary income. . . . Finally the strong and growing public sentiment among the working classes . . . cannot safely be ignored. The well-founded belief that large fortunes have been made out of the havoc and misery of war by smart or fortunate business men is a source of deep and dangerous indignation."

Housing ideas of the Local Government Board and India Government Reform shall be passed over in order to allow a few more words each to Second Chamber Reform, as discussed in 1918, and the somewhat altered basis of the perennial argument on Free Trade versus Protection. Radicals were suspicious of an attempt, as responsibly urged as Lord Bryce's Chairman's Report from a mixed Conference of Lords and Commons, to produce a Second Chamber to which a stronger veto on ordinary legislation and even increased Budgetary powers could be allowed. The attempt finally came to nothing but Radical fears of "diluting democracy" and Radical suspicions that costly post-war Housing and Land-Settlement schemes might run greater risks in the proposed Second Chamber hardly seemed very responsible to some who remembered how near Civil War Britain had come after a mere two years in the hands of the unconvincing yet uncheckable Commons majority of 1912–14. And Radical suspicions, this time on the score of Free Trade, were still more strongly excited against the Final Report of the Committee to whom the "Paris Economic Resolutions" of 1916 had been remitted and which now proposed "Protection", it was claimed, not merely for "key industries", and "trades of a special or pivotal kind" supporting munitions or other essential industries but for "any industry of real importance . . . exposed to undue foreign competition, inadequate supplies of raw materials or any other cause", notably "dumping" and "sweated goods". There certainly seemed room here for almost every industry to claim a protective tariff or an alternative subsidy.

It is time to end this chapter with the sensations of the "Maurice Letter" of May 7th and the Maurice Debate of May 9th. Perhaps the "Maurice Letter" had better be treated in phrases from a contemporary source. Here is the leading Radical weekly on the subject:[1]

Major-General Maurice, lately Director of Military Operations on the General Staff, has launched a thunderbolt at the Ministry. This able and well-informed soldier has written to the papers charging Mr. Lloyd George and Mr. Law with misrepresenting the military situation in three important particulars; first by denying that the taking over of the St. Quentin line had been "dealt" with by the War Council at Versailles; secondly, by falsely claiming that Sir Douglas Haig's fighting strength on the eve of the battle of March 21st had not been diminished; and, thirdly, by wrongly limiting the diversion of force to the East to

[1] *Ibid*, May 11, 1918.

one white infantry division in Mesopotamia and three white divisions in Egypt and Palestine. All these assertions General Maurice declared to be "incorrect" and known to be so by a "large number of soldiers'. The result of this knowledge of Ministerial untruthfulness bred distrust of the Government in the Army and must impair its *moral*; therefore he spoke. . . .

It is now known that the military statistics used by the Prime Minister in attempting to clear himself of responsibility for the large-scale British disaster at St. Quentin came, indeed, as he claimed, from General Maurice's own deputy though a further communication from the General, revising those statistics in important particulars, had been sent on afterwards. As it happened, the second communication had never been handed on to the Prime Minister owing to an oversight by his Secretaries who ultimately destroyed this second message, when discovered, rather than risk new troubles by its production.[1] On the facts as they stood before the House of Commons on May 9th, Mr. Asquith was well within his rights when claiming that an inquiry was called for but the Prime Minister, while admitting, perforce, that Sir Douglas Haig had been against extending the British lines to St. Quentin, had the priceless advantage of having the original communication and figures from General Maurice's Department in his possession though the General could not explain why the revised figures from himself had failed to reach the Prime Minister similarly. When Mr. Asquith declined to accept Mr. Bonar Law's offer of a Court of Honour of two Judges to investigate the highly secret material involved but claimed a small House of Commons Committee of, perhaps, five instead, as more politically adequate, the entire Tory Party turned against him in a way which, for many months, he had been painstakingly trying to avoid. Mr. Lloyd George, too, apparently made one of the great speeches of his life in marked contrast to Mr. Asquith's, whose Parliamentary strategy, also, was deemed to be at fault.[2] As the Irish Nationalists, offended by the ex-Premier's failure to do more than criticize Irish Conscription in the Man Power Debates of April, were not available on his behalf,[3] a crisis, which some had foreseen

[1] Cf. Lord Beaverbrook, *Men and Power, 1917–1918*, for the important section on the "lost Box".

[2] Cf. *Lord Riddell's War Diary, 1914–1918*, under May 11, 1918, for Lloyd George himself.

[3] Many seem to have been over in Ireland organizing resistance to Conscription. And Redmond's death in March had certainly not helped Asquith either.

as bringing down Lloyd George, ended in a division in his favour by 293 votes against 106. And the unfortunate 106 may well have had a presentiment of the political fate intended for them in following a lurid new Press campaign ordered against Asquith by Lord Northcliffe. As one journalist put it:[1]

This is an age of advertisement; and the Prime Minister is its most conspicuous beneficiary. Apparently his monopoly is now disputed. I am not at all surprised that the Northcliffe Press should resent any attempt to counter its campaign of abusive suggestion. Mr. Asquith has his faults with the rest of us. But he is perhaps the most placable, temperate, dignified figure in our public life. This is the man whom the Northcliffe Press, in the course of its swift descent from Printing House Square to the gutter, has made the daily target of its insults. Why? He is out of office, and probably no politician in England has a greater dislike to resuming it. But I suppose this contingency hourly presents itself to Lord Northcliffe's guilty conscience.... Anyway, the stream of abusive insinuation never stops. In my knowledge of journalism I have never seen anything so coarse and so malignant. Anti-Asquith cartoons, epithets, headlines, all the flash coinage of the vulgar mind, are unceasing. Under Lord Northcliffe's monopoly, and at his command, this poisoned gas shell explodes daily and hourly over a vast surface of journalistic Britain. It is a great scandal and a great abuse of power, for which sooner or later its author will pay the penalty he so richly deserves....

[1] Cf. *The Nation*, May 25, 1918. One of the special reasons for Northcliffe (and Government) anger was the alleged detection of anti-Government propaganda disguised as advertisement.

CHAPTER XII

VICTORY

"The abdication of the Kaiser was announced by Prince Max on November 9th. . . . The united Socialist parties have taken complete control. . . . The Emperor Karl of Austria proclaimed his abdication on November 12th. The Armistice was signed early on Monday morning. . . . The naval clauses are even more drastic than the military ones. . . .

"The Prime Minister has taken sudden advantage of the end of the war. The Election has practically been fixed by him for mid-December . . . and he will then appeal for the return of the predominantly Tory Coalition Government which he formed out of the ruin of the first Coalition. That Government was built up for the purpose of the war. It is now to snatch a vedict on reconstruction. For this purpose a programme was necessary, and Mr. George sketched its outlines in a brilliant impressionist speech delivered to a select gathering of his 'Liberal' friends. Its conception is progressive. Mr. George's attitude was: 'I am a Liberal, the child of Liberalism.' The war was to end in a tolerant peace. The German example of 1871 was to be avoided, revenge banished as an impossible basis for European politics, and its society founded on disarmament and the League of Nations. At home, land reform —Mr. George scoffed at the pettiness of the once famous Budget—housing, the minimum wage, the raising of the physical and intellectual standard. Ireland was to have Home Rule, subject to the condition of no coercion for Ulster. . . .

"This was very well, but it was presently made clear that the Liberal wine was to be mixed, more or less plentifully, with Conservative water. Mr. Bonar Law, addressing a meeting of Unionists, secured their adhesion to the Coalition on his own speech and on an undisclosed letter from the Prime Minster. This letter, according to *The Times*, qualified Free Trade with Colonial Preferences, the protection of 'key' industries and a veto on 'dumping'. In other words a perfect model of Protection (for no one taxes food nowadays) may be built on Mr. George's formula of Free Trade. In the same way Ireland may be coerced in the name of freedom for Ulster. . . .

"The Army which saved the country will be largely disfranchised in fact and can in no sense give a serious vote. The contest will be one of hypocrisies and reserves. . . . The Labour Party has formally broken with the Coalition. . . ."

The Nation, November 16, 1918 on "snatching a verdict".

Victory

The Social section of a Draft Liberal Programme prepared for Lloyd George in July 1918, when a General Election before the end of the year seemed certain. (From Dr. Addison's *Four and a Half Years*, ii, 554–5.)

"1. LAND.

(*a*). Extensive arrangements for the acquisition of suitable land on fair terms by simple machinery for established needs as for:

The provision of gardens, allotments and small holdings;
Housing and reclamation;
Sites for factories and works.

(*b*) A State scheme of Afforestation on a definite and progressive programme.

(*c*) Agencies in counties for the assistance and promotion of good cultivation, the improvement and regeneration of village life and of rural industries.

"2. HOUSING.

(*a*) A Housing Scheme to come into operation immediately after the war.

(*b*) Removal of the injustices of the leasehold system.

(*c*) Town planning powers for the promotion, where needed, of industrial suburbs and for dealing with overcrowded areas.

"3. SAILORS AND SOLDIERS.

(*a*) Adequate Pensions and care for the Disabled.

(*b*) Preference for Government Employment.

(*c*) Absolute right of sailors and soldiers to an opportunity of settlement on the land.

(*d*) Provision of proper facilities for training and priority of opportunity for re-employment in former occupation.

"4. LABOUR.

(*a*) Full and adequate recognition of the pledge given to restore pre-war Trade Union rights.

(*b*) Organized machinery in the different industries for securing to Labour a proper voice in determining the conditions of employment and the well-being of the industry and the provision of added security against unemployment. Good wages and greater output.

(*c*) The provision of minimum wages and proper working conditions to women and unskilled workers.

"5. HEALTH.

(*a*) The establishment of a Ministry of Health.

(*b*) The development of a health programme especially directed to the preservation of the lives of mothers and infants and the care of children.

(*c*) The prevention and early treatment of disease and the improvement in the standard of health and strength.

"6. POOR LAW.

(*a*) Abolition of the present Poor Law system with Health Services, the care of children and unemployment dealt with by the appropriate authorities.

"7. EDUCATION.

(*a*) Passing of the Education Bills.

(*b*) The development of technical and university training so as to make them available for all those found suitable for it.

(*c*) The encouragement of Industrial Research.

"8. WOMEN.

(*a*) Equality of laws as between men and women.

"9. DRINK.

Appropriate parts of the control of liquor developed by the war to be continued by statutory enactment."

I F the Prime Minister had overcome serious dangers in the Maurice Debate and Division of May 9th, his position remained still very far from secure. He had, for example, promised both the General Staff and some of his Ministerial colleagues that provision for Irish Conscription should not be left out of the draconian Man Power Bill of April,[1] and the measure did, therefore, contain a clause allowing the extension of Compulsory Service to Ireland by Order in Council.[2] The Irish Nationalist members had fiercely resisted the plan, though it had been baited with an accompanying promise to proceed immediately afterwards to legislation empowering the setting up of a Home Rule system at once instead of waiting for the end of the war. It was the obvious Irish case to argue that, if an Irish Parliament was soon to be set up (without further waiting, for the Catholic-Carsonite compromise which had evaded the now defunct Irish Convention, initiated by Lloyd George a year before) Conscription should be left to that Irish Parliament. And the Irish members did not confine opposition to Westminster for, abandoning Parliament, they hurried over to Ireland to join the almost nation-wide preparations there for mass-resistance, preparations that not merely set Sinn Fein growing like a prairie-fire, but so obviously presaged troubles of the worst kind that the largest military precautions had to be ordered at once. Indeed, with Viscount French moved from the Horse Guards as the new Viceroy and "revelations" of a new German-Sinn Fein "plot" to justify numerous arrests and internments, matters in Ireland, during May, seemed to be moving straight towards another explosion. And yet the Prime Minister, immediately after surmounting the Maurice trouble and under continuing heavy pressure, though he was, from the land peril in France and the submarine peril at sea, had under pledge, to produce a quickly-enforceable Home Rule Bill that should not antagonize America,

---

[1] Cf. *Field-Marshal Sir Henry Wilson, His Life and Diaries*, ii, 76, 79, and 81, for proof that the Prime Minister had not been easy to commit. Of one very characteristic Lloyd Georgian effort, a telephone message to the effect that President Wilson had promised to send 120,000 American infantry a month for four months "but asked that conscription be not put on Ireland, as his task would be rendered very difficult", his new Chief of the Imperial General Staff remarked suspiciously, "The whole thing sounds a little fishy." How the Prime Minister ultimately succeeded in evading his promise, on terms, is mentioned later.

[2] Cf. Clause 2 of the Military Service (No. 2) Act, 1918, 8 Geo. 5, c. 5.

on the one hand, or British Conservatism and Ulster on the other.

How and why, therefore, Lloyd George was still attacked with some hope of bringing him down and substituting another Government may be illustrated from the writing of the Radical weekly, which was said to be President Wilson's favourite among British newspapers.[1] Here is *The Nation* on the "impending calamity" in Ireland:[2]

> Against the advice of every Irishman able to speak for her . . . he has passed an edict for conscripting her youth. Without one word of Irish approval, North or South, he is devising a totally new kind of government for her and for us. He has sent in a soldier to act as the vice-gerent of the Crown, the first since the rebellion of '98. . . . He has lost the services of the Lord-Lieutenant, the Irish Secretary, the Irish Attorney-General and the Irish Commander-in-Chief, every one of whom was opposed to his policy. He has created a Convention to frame a Constitution, has destroyed its work in a week, and been informed by its Chairman . . . that his method is madness. He has set all Ireland seething with anger and fear. . . . He has given us a new war front on the Liffey, and drawn to it the troops that we can ill spare from the Aisne and the Somme. . . . Now there is one force in politics which can mitigate or even arrest the impending calamity in Ireland . . . and that is the united protest of Liberalism and Labour. . . .

Writing of this kind, in truth, was one of the factors which finally helped Lloyd George to free himself from his double commitment on Ireland without breaking up his Government. A first cautious step was taken, in instructing Viscount French, when "proclaiming" the plotting with Germany, to appeal for Irish assistance and announce a resort to voluntary recruiting. And, by June 20th, Lord Curzon was declaring that the Government had come to the conclusion that it would be a folly, and almost a crime, in existing circumstances, to proceed with the preparation and introduction of a Home Rule Bill, and that policy would accordingly be adjusted both in regard to that and to Irish Conscription. A few days later the new Irish Secretary was blaming the "plot" for the fact that the dual policy of Home Rule and Conscription was in abeyance and the Prime Minister finding another cause, which would have made it folly to proceed, in the

---

[1] Cf. *Life and Letters of Austen Chamberlain*, ii, 123: "I am told that his favourite among English newspapers is *The Nation*, and that he is really a typical Gladstonian Liberal. . . ."

[2] *The Nation*, May 18, 1918.

attitude of the Irish Catholic hierarchy. In short, the year 1918 saw neither a new Home Rule Bill from the Government nor yet an Order in Council extending Conscription to Ireland under the Military Service (No. 2) Act of 1918.

Meanwhile, a number of factors were moving to Lloyd George's support—a fresh onslaught, for example, on the Asquithians by Northcliffe, a successful new "atrocity" campaign based on the alleged "deliberate" bombing of British hospitals in France,[1] and the revelation both in the Pemberton Billing "Berlin Black Book" case and in the vigorous renewed agitation being whipped up against aliens, naturalized and unnaturalized,[2] of what mob-folly could do to prevent the return of the "Old Gang" to power. But Lloyd George was, doubtless, helped most by the gradual revival of confidence in the outcome of the war when, after the sickening apprehensions of early spring,[3] it gradually became plain that the German Armies, for all the technical competence of their continued offensives and advances,[4] would be unable to force a decision before the Americans, already numbering 700,000 in Europe by mid-June,[5] increased the odds against Germany still further. And so, if in April, even *John Bull* had seemed to be

---

[1] Cf. the *Observer*, May 26, and the *Daily Express*, May 29, 1918. According to the *Observer*: "All questions of truce or stay have passed. Last Sunday the enemy carried out the reddest of all his unforgivable crimes since the sinking of the *Lusitania*" in allegedly launching two large aerial squadrons against British hospitals. "There was no possibility of mistake. The hospitals were chosen . . . just because their character was all too plain. . . . The casualties mounted up to several hundreds, and the whole episode was more barbarous than any raid on London." Of course, punishment had been "swift and memorable" and the *Observer*'s readers had the satisfaction both of enjoying righteous indignation and hearing of eight days of retaliatory raiding on Cologne, Saarbrucken, Coblentz, Landau, and Mannheim. Yet, according to Caroline Playne (*Britain Holds On, 1917–1918*, p. 312) "about the middle of June it became known that the military authorities found no evidence to show that these air attacks on hospitals were deliberately planned. In their view hospitals were found to be placed near military objectives and had to suffer the risk of being hit when these were being attacked. It is, however, impossible to obliterate a state of mind once it has been created."

[2] Cf. *Whitaker's Almanack, 1919*, Diary of the War, under June 20, 1918, for Lloyd George's unseemly readiness to offer "his personal attention to the question". The sequel shall be related later.

[3] Cf. Caroline Playne, *Britain Holds On, 1917–1918*, p. 307: "People had been horribly scared when the enemy broke through and gained ground. But when the Entente armies held the line generally and went on fighting as before, they rallied their spirits . . . the further German advance to Soissons and the Marne at the end of May did not have the same effect as previous German successes."

[4] Cf. *Field-Marshal Sir Henry Wilson, His Life and Diaries*, under June 1, 1918, for the apprehension still being shown by the General Staff.

[5] Cf. *Whitaker's Almanack, 1919*, Diary of the War, under June 12, 1918.

preparing to turn against Lloyd George,[1] two months later an Imperial War Cabinet, joined by the Canadian and New Zealand Prime Ministers,[2] could be confidently set to planning the 1919 campaigns while a leading opponent of the Prime Minister, in bitter jest, advised the following reconstruction of the Ministry in Britain:[3]

Prime Minister, Generalissimo and Admiralissimo,	Mr. Lloyd George.
Chancellor of the Exchequer and Keeper of the Privy Purse,	Mr. Bottomley.

[1] Cf. *John Bull*, for an April editorial: "What is the game? Only a week ago I warned Mr. Lloyd George that the country was not prepared to give him a blank cheque. . . . When the old Asquith Government was removed from office . . . Mr. Lloyd George was welcomed as Premier by general acclamation . . . we forgot everything save that he was all for the war . . . that he personified the knock-out blow." Now, according to Caroline Playne's summary, doubts arose. "In the hour of our greatest peril . . . when our splendid sons are holding the long thin line which divides safety from surrender . . . the Prime Minister severely shakes our confidence and gambles with our trust." Among other complaints Bottomley attacked the appointment of Lord Milner as War Secretary because of his German connections, announced an Albert Hall meeting to permit "a spontaneous outburst of the People's Will", and indicated that he might "feel justified in drawing aside the veil which at present hides many scandals a revelation of which . . . would set the country ablaze".

[2] Cf. *Field-Marshal Sir Henry Wilson, His Life and Diaries*, ii, 108, for an Imperial Conference listening, on July 11th, to an introductory account of the position in France.

[3] Cf. *The Nation*, June 8, 1918, for this list of Massingham's introduced thus: "I confess to being a little chagrined at the indifference which greeted my suggestion of a Lansdowne Government. . . . But I expect a warmer welcome for an alternative Government—an appropriate tribute to the emotions of the hour." An understanding of the ironies implicit in the list would, in fact, explain some of the under-currents of politics and propaganda in 1918: the Prime Minister's growing opinion of himself as a strategist; Mr. Bottomley's notorious swindling record; the Harmsworth Press's vital part in keeping Lloyd George Prime Minister; Mrs. Pankhurst's propaganda in the W.S.P.U. and *Britannia* which, even in 1916, had risen well beyond "Traitor Haldane" and "Traitor Asquith" towards "Traitor Grey"; Father Bernard Vaughan, the famous Jesuit preacher ot the Catholics of Belgravia, whose sermon-series, *The Sins of Society* had, as early as 1906, given him a sensation-making authority, beyond Pemberton Billing's reach in normal times, as to what was corrupt in fashionable circles; Captain Spencer, Pemberton Billing's main informant of the contents of the alleged "Berlin Black Book"; the Bishop of London, who had carried "official Christianity's" not uncriticized self-identification with the war to the point of declaring in his St. Paul's sermon on Easter Day, 1918 that a Government Department had asked him that day to appeal for 30,000 more women for the land; and Mr. Garvin, who, in the *Observer*, was strenuously supporting a policy which the Ministers themselves found it wise to abandon. The *Daily Mirror*, of course, was Lord Rothermere's main contribution to the nation's education while, in making the *Sunday Pictorial* almost Bottomley's pulpit for recounting how the War had converted him from Atheism to belief in God and God's support for the Allies, its editor could doubtless claim to be doing something for "religion".

Victory

Secretaries of State, Home and Foreign Affairs, Colonies, India, Press Stunts and War	The Harmsworth Family.
Ministers of Propaganda: (a) Secular,	Mrs. Pankhurst.
(b) Sacred,	Father Vaughan.
Director of Intelligence,	Captain Spencer.
Director of Peace Offensives,	The Bishop of London.
Minister of Education,	The Editor of the *Daily Mirror*.
Minister of Public Worship,	The Editor of the *Sunday Pictorial*.
Attorney-General and Director of Prosecutions,	Mr. Billing.
Irish Secretary and Commander-in-Chief of the Forces in Ireland,	Mr. Garvin.

During June and July 1918, despite occasional flurries of nervousness, Allied Governments began slowly reaching the firm conclusion that the continuous series of German offensives would not only force no decision but could ultimately prove dangerously exhausting to the Germans' own fighting- and will-power. Indeed, the Allied counter-offensive, begun on July 18th under General Foch's orders, almost seemed to have proved this by the end of July when 33,400 German prisoners, including 674 officers, were claimed, much lost ground had been regained, and the major British counter-offensive, timed to begin on August 8th (Ludendorff's "Black Day of the German Army") was yet to come.[1] By August 5th a fleeting idea of a possible major weakening of German military power seems to have crossed the almost incredulous mind of the Chief of the British Imperial General Staff[2] but, for months yet, official assumptions were still that the war could not be won till 1919. The kind of discussions taking place in the highest circles during the summer of 1918 is well-mirrored in a shortened account of a meeting of the Imperial Cabinet on July 31st and August 1st which was held to allow the Dominions to participate in advance war-decisions for 1919.[3] Lord Milner,

---

[1] General Ludendorff's *My War Memories, 1914–1918* show that Ludendorff, though impressed by August 8th, and urging an offer of peace, still thought in almost a victor's peace-terms. Things were very different by the end of September when he had decided to press the political authorities to ask for an immediate armistice.

[2] Cf. *Field-Marshal Sir Henry Wilson, His Life and Diaries*, ii, 120: "I am puzzled by the Boche, and think that he must be more tired than we have been giving him credit for . . . it is an amazing business. They are falling back. . . ."

[3] *Ibid.*, pp. 118–19.

as War Secretary, was apparently very definite that the Germans would not be broken in the West and favoured a major holding operation there which would release ten British divisions for more fruitful operations elsewhere. Hughes of Australia wanted the Germans smashed in France. Borden of Canada argued the case for attack from the air and for organizing, against Germany, the economic war after the war. And Smuts of South Africa apparently still considered the Germans strong enough to be able to mount one more attack in France and one more in Italy. Smuts's view was, like Milner's, that the German Armies would not be broken in the West even in 1919 and he favoured, therefore, the use of spare British divisions against Austria. Even on September 23rd, when Milner as Secretary for War, discussed Haig's plan of breaching the Hindenburg Line with the Chief of the Imperial General Staff, there was still a very wholesome respect for German military prowess in Milner's cautious disapproval of Haig's "ridiculous" optimism and his fear that Haig might "embark on another Paschendaele".[1]

The "Home Front", too, took some time to adjust itself to the notion that Germany's power might be waning, and some of the unloveliest, if most characteristic, manifestations of the temper of the "public", as agitated by the "gutter Press", took on the shape of an anti-aliens "movement" whipped higher than ever. In accordance with a promise given by the Prime Minister in June, a small group of M.P.s was appointed to "make a thorough investigation of the enemy alien problem, and to advise him what action should be taken to allay public anxiety". And, on July 2nd, the probing Members just nominated were given an idea of what the "public" expected of them when a conference, representing seventeen London City and Borough Councils, called for the internment even of naturalized British subjects of enemy alien origin. Thus smartly prodded on, the Parliamentary investigators had a Report ready for the Prime Minister by July 8th and Government proposals were announced by the Home Secretary on July 11th.[2] Of course, over-obsequious though these were to "mob-opinion", Government proposals can never, from their nature, satisfy the loudest anti-alien rant, based as this often was

[1] Cf. *Field-Marshal Sir Henry Wilson, His Life and Diaries*, ii, 126.
[2] Cf. *Hansard*, July 11th, for Sir George Cave. On July 12th the Commons gave the British Nationality and Status of Aliens Bill a unanimous Second Reading.

on strong, if completely unfounded suspicions, that secretly
conveyed information from aliens, some of them naturalized
British subjects in Government employ, helped German air-raids
and submarine sorties and was possibly even responsible for the
great munition-factory explosion in the Midlands on July 1st.[1] A
"great demonstration" in Trafalgar Square on July 14th brought
fresh concessions to the anti-alien campaign which were to be
further increased before the new legislation was safely on the
Statute Book by August 8th.[2] But still the anti-alien vigilantes
refused to be satisfied with anything short of the revocation of all
naturalizations granted in the past to Germans, Austro-Hun-
garians, Turks, and Bulgarians and the internment of all de-
naturalized in consequence, even to the women and children,
until they could be deported with all "enemy aliens" *sans phrase*
at the end of the war. Indeed, as some remnants of conscience
still prevented the Government from ordering the internment or
deportation of numbers of unnaturalized women- and child-
"enemy aliens", a few of them bed-ridden old ladies who had been
resident in Britain for fifty years and more, the vigilante roar went
up once more. On August 24th took place a great Hyde Park
demonstration, in support of the "Intern Them All" campaign,
called by a new party of Imperialist super-patriots which, in
appropriating the name of National Party in readiness for the
General Election, had unwittingly crossed the plans of some
round the Prime Minister who would have liked the name left
available for the Coalition. The street-procession from Hyde Park,
on this occasion, included thousands of discharged soldiers, smart
women, Dominion soldiers, men of the Baltic and the Stock
Exchanges, and members of the British Empire Union, all
marching to the patriotic strains of several bands. The most
notable of the many flags and banners carried was a great white
sheet which called for "A Clean Sweep" of the enemy alien, and
the deputation, which went to 10 Downing Street, with the "Intern

[1] Cf. *Whitaker's Almanack, 1919*, Diary of the War, under July 1, 1918, for
the 100 lives lost and the 150 injured.
[2] Cf. *Hansard*, July 11th, for Sir George Cave's original concessions: A
review of the list of men exempted from internment and of women exempted
from deportation; a review of all certificates of naturalization granted to enemy
aliens during the war, with revocation in proper cases; no persons, not natural-
born British subjects, to be allowed to change their names without licences or
to be employed in Government offices during the war except for urgent reasons;
enemy businesses and banks, still functioning as sequestrated properties to be
wound up.

Them All" petition claimed that over a million signatures had been appended.[1]

If there was a good deal of Radical disgust at the whole sorry history of the agitation and the Prime Minister's connivance, politicians did not feel as free to air their views in public, as say, the writers of *The Nation* who spoke boldly of a "stunt" Cabinet subject to a "stunt" Press and remarked of one Lloyd George passage that "such sheer demagogy has never been uttered by a Minister within the walls of Parliament—or outside it".[2] There was constant exposure, too, of the weaknesses of the "Press Lords", and now that Beaverbrook had become Lloyd George's Minister of Information a very dangerous attack on the questionable way in which he was running his Department.[3] Yet essentially the course of events during the summer of 1918 disappointed Radicals of *The Nation* school more and more. The United States, for example, on whom they had been relying to moderate the savage European rivalries, rending the Continent, had itself become infected with a mass war-hysteria that left public and private rights more at mob-mercy—and the War Administration's—than was the case even in Britain or Germany.[4]

[1] Cf. *Evening News*, August 24, 1918.

[2] Cf. *The Nation*, July 20th, which held that, thanks to a section of the Cabinet readier to face the anti-alien uproar than the Prime Minister, a measure "mostly camouflage" had been offered. As for Lloyd George "in a speech which fully disclosed his slavery to the Northcliffe-Hulton, Rothermere-Beaverbrook Press" he had "complimented it on its choice of 'good copy' . . . implored the House 'to keep the Government up to the mark' and spoke of this obvious 'stunt' as a matter closely connected with the prosecution of the war".

[3] Cf. *Ibid.*, August 3rd: "The *Westminster Gazette* in a very powerful article gives a description of the character of Lord Beaverbrook's appointments. . . . It shows that this gentleman, whose name . . . was 'familiar' enough in Canada, though it was barely heard of here till it blossomed out in one title or another, has chosen as his head employees and 'directors' of propaganda in Scandinavia, Spain, Switzerland, Asia and the Far East a choice band of financiers, financial secretaries, and agents of various shipping, rubber, tobacco and railway trusts. These are the persons whom he assumes to be the proper spokesmen of the democracy of Great Britain. . . . Others belong to the Northcliffe branch of the firm or are associated with enterprises in which Lord Beaverbrook has also played a part. . . . We shall see what Parliament has to say to this method of turning a great political trust into a kind of commercial combine."

[4] Cf. *Ibid.*, July 6, 1918, for disquiet at American complacency with the fact that not only " 'we have muzzled the disloyal Press and the disloyal orator' but public opinion is organized to bring pressure upon persons suspected of peace sentiment, persons who have failed to contribute to the Red Cross . . . or who, in the opinion of their neighbours, have not bought as much war-loan as they ought. In some towns 'hyphens' [German-Americans] have been lynched by 'loyal mobs'. . . . Freedom of speech, press and meeting has been stamped out far more rigorously than in this country or Germany. . . . The cause of reaction there, as here, plucks up courage. . . . Labour's hands are bound tighter in America than ever. . . ."

And when the United States Government, joined with those of Britain and France, in according quasi-recognition to the "Czecho-Slovak Government" of Dr. Masaryk and committed itself, therefore, to the break-up of the Austrian Empire, the agonized *Nation* feared a possible prolongation of the war by years.[1] The characteristic eagerness, too, of the Prime Minister's circle and the Northcliffe Press to stage a "Khaki Election" as soon as the war-news became more reassuring, was a subject of deep Radical concern.[2] It seemed likely that a public temper could be whipped up, not merely against the "tumbling into enemy peace traps", denounced by the *Daily Mail* whenever a German or Austrian or British Radical-Labour suggestion of negotiations was made,[3] but even against any end to the war that did not involve the further frightful massacres implied by the resolve not to stop fighting till Berlin was reached or, perhaps, the whole of Germany occupied. Even the official Labour Party—as apart from the belligerent wing which had lately taken to dining, in furtherance of the Empire's war-effort, with Dukes, Marquesses,[4] and Mr. Hughes, the super-belligerent "Labour" Premier of Australia[5]—seemed, to some, to

[1] Cf. *Ibid.*: "On the basis of the total dismemberment of Austria, there can be no negotiated settlement with the Central Powers. The Pichon and Lansing telegrams commit the Allies to a 'Bitter-Endian' settlement. It is a moderate and optimistic reckoning which looks for this after much less than a seven years' war. . . ."

[2] Cf. *Ibid.*, July 27, 1918 for comment on forecasts in *The Times*

[3] Cf. *The Times*, August 9, 1918, for comment on the last effort of the previous day when Parliament had adjourned until October 15th. There is an editorial entitled "The Vanity of Negotiations", and mockery of the "doleful speeches" of the "pacifist group" who, in complete disregard of British navalism, had been solemnly told by Balfour, the Foreign Secretary, that "German militarism" was the great obstacle to peace. Meanwhile another "peace trap" was being avoided when passports were refused to a Labour delegation anxious to consult the Dutch Socialist Leader who was, doubtless, in touch with German Socialists.

[4] Cf. *Sunday Times*, July 28th, under the headline "A NOTABLE DINNER PARTY": "A significant illustration of the new and better relations between capital and labour that the times are developing was to be seen at the dinner of the British Empire Producers' Association last week under the presidency of the Marquis of Londonderry. Side by side at the principal table sat representatives of the classes and the masses, Mr. Hughes by the Duke of Northumberland, Mr. O'Grady by Lord Cowdray, Mr. Ben Tillett by the Marquis of Bute, Mr. Havelock Wilson by Sir Vincent Caillard; and I may add that, to judge by the animated conversation, an evening has seldom gone better." Sir Vincent was a Director of Vickers and an authority on "Imperial Fiscal Reform".

[5] Cf. *The Nation*, July 27, 1918, for anger at the interventions of Mr. Hughes (who was apparently on indefinite leave in Britain, presumably guarding Australian interests in war and peace) in British politics: "I suppose there is some use (and some fun) in seeing Mr. Hughes run by the *Daily Mail* as a kind of super-George but I find a great number of Liberal and Labour men think it time to end Mr. Hughes's gross and deliberate abuse of the hospitality of these shores. We have had a great many Australians here. . . . None of them have ever

be too ready to avoid awkward debate and dispute on War and Peace by concentrating instead on blissful vistas of Reconstruction.[1]

By the latter half of August, with the Germans in full retreat and obviously not the Army they had been in March, the Prime Minister's plans for a General Election towards the end of the year were known to be ripening.[2] Though, too, he was suspected of a fixed determination to extract an immense political dividend from the efforts and sacrifices of the troops, it could be plausibly argued for him that, as the sitting Parliament should have expired at the end of 1915 and had only been prolonged by a succession of short-term emergency Acts, now that the emergency was passing the justification for another emergency prolongation had gone. Parliament, then, would assemble on October 15th, the date fixed at the Adjournment, indispensable business would be hurried through, and then would come the Dissolution. By that time, it might be November, the military position in France and Belgium would have improved much further, and the issue, it was expected, that would be put to the country was whether Lloyd George's hands were to be strengthened to deliver the "Knock-Out Blow" and to give the signal, thereafter, for benevolent planned Reconstruction to begin in Britain.[3] As was natural, the Asquithians and Henderson, whose political annihilation was already being half-meditated,[4] had many objections. Victory was not an Election issue, they claimed, for all of them desired it, and how, too, were four millions of men in arms all over the world to be canvassed

interfered with our politics or attacked the principles and even the personalities of our public men. Mr. Hughes . . . commits and repeats this offence without the excuse of speaking for Australia. His career there is finished, and all parties have his measure. [He had lost a referendum on Conscription for Australia]. . . . He can say what he pleases when he has resigned his office. . . . Then he can join Mr. George or the staff of *John Bull* or any other statesman or 'stunt' that wants him. . . ."

[1] Cf. *The Nation*, July 6th: "In the view of the *New Statesman* the problem of the 'reconstruction' of the economic order is to supersede the vital debate of its rescue from the grand assault of the war. That is impossible: and the mere thought of it is treason to mankind. . . . For the war is the capital world-event, and the Labour Party cannot pass it by as if it were an unpleasant acquaintance. Still less can it deny its special and vital concern for Labour. . . ."

[2] Cf. *Lord Riddell's War Diary, 1914–1918*, under August 13th and 14th, for the point matters had already reached then.

[3] Cf. *Ibid.*, under August 1918: "The issue at the election will really be who is to run the war. Is it to be L.G., Bonar Law, and their associates, or Asquith, McKenna, Runciman, and others who act with them? L.G. spoke again of his domestic programme. . . . L.G. said . . . 'It is useless to fight this war unless the condition of the poorer classes is to be improved.' "

[4] Cf. *Ibid.*, under August 1918: "L.G. . . . commented upon the obvious fear of an election on the part of Henderson and the Asquithians."

and polled in the middle, it might be, of military or naval operations?

September 1918 was a month in which the indications became clearer as to how events, national and international, were likely to move. A Lloyd George speech at Manchester, on September 12th which the Prime Minister had been preparing for some time as a kind of advance manifesto of his zeal for working-class betterment and war-efficiency, made the claim that the worst was over and that the advances taking place in France were costing only a fifth of the casualties that the same ground had cost in 1916. Meanwhile alternative plans were being discussed, in private, as to how this democratic Prime Minister, who was winning the war, might get command of his own party for the General Election. The purchase of the *Daily Chronicle* in Lloyd George's interest was being negotiated though few could have guessed that vast political funds accumulated by what the uncharitable called "the sale of honours" were a main factor in the transaction. And, for months, debating in the Prime Minister's circle turned on whether to try a mixture of cajolery and electoral blackmail on the larger Asquithian half of the Liberal and Radical members[1] or, alternatively, whether it might not prove possible to cajole Asquith himself to end the unfortunate divisions in the party by re-entering the Government as Lord Chancellor. There were even schemes under consideration to remodel the Coalition to allow not only Asquith to re-enter but an Asquithian contingent, headed by Runciman and Samuel,[2] but, doubtless, these were frowned upon not merely by Lord Northcliffe[3] but by the Conservative Whips. These had a very different idea of a desirable future and, despite the case that could be made out for a broader-based Coalition to carry greater authority both in peace negotiations abroad and growing industrial troubles at home[4] (in which the nervous

[1] Cf. *Ibid*, under August 1918: "L.G. proposes to hold a meeting of the Liberal Party. . . . He also proposes to make an arrangement with the Tories as to the seats which are to be left to their candidates. . . . He hopes to carry with him 120 of the Liberals. . . ."

[2] Cf. *Ibid*., under September 27th: "Lord Murray and Lord Rothermere appeared . . . yesterday, with the proposal . . . that . . . Asquith would become Lord Chancellor, and Runciman and, I think, Samuel, would enter the Government together with half a dozen of the younger men. . . . I am told that Mrs. A[squith] approves. . . ."

[3] *Ibid*., under October 3rd, for Northcliffe's hardly cordial acceptance of Asquith but not apparently the rest of "the Old Gang".

[4] Cf. *Whitaker's Almanack, 1919*, p. 424, for such items as: "July 8, 1918. Spread of strike in aeroplane factory at Hammersmith: 40 works affected. . . .

detected almost "revolutionary" under-currents)[1] it was the Conservative Whips, as will be seen, whose action finally secured the elimination of Asquith and his entire team not merely from Administration but even from Parliament.

Meanwhile, Germany's military set-backs and retreats, though still being conducted well away from the German frontiers, sounded the knell of doom to Germany's despondent Allies, the hard-pressed Turks, facing a new offensive in Palestine and on the Hejaz railway, the Bulgarians, called upon to meet a confident Franco-Serb advance in Macedonia, and, above all, the Austrians, aware that all the Allied Governments had now committed themselves very far towards a break-up of their Empire.[2] It was the Vienna Government which, in mid-September, offered almost a semi-capitulation when, in Notes addressed to all belligerent and neutral Powers as well as the Papacy, it proposed "non-binding" peace discussions among the belligerents. It was rebuffed by America and insulted by Britain and France amid yells of delight from those who had been christened the "Never-Endians" by the Radicals of *The Nation*. Two Northcliffe headlines of September 17th must suffice to picture the ugly state of mind that was being fostered—*The Times*'s "Deaf Ears in U.S. to Peace Chatter" and the *Evening News*'s "Nothing Doing. Austrian Peace Trap a Dismal Failure".[3] In point of fact, the greatest Trafalgar Square "war stunt" yet attempted was being organized to promote the sale of another thousand million pounds' worth of War Bonds, and while the fate of the world was being decided at the end

August 18th. Strike of London women tramway and omnibus workers . . . for the same bonus as that given to the men. . . . August 22nd. 40,000 miners in Rotherham district out on strike. . . . August 30th. Strike of Metropolitan and City police. . . . September 16th. Strike of Lancashire cotton spinners: letter from Mr. Lloyd George appealing to workers' patriotism. September 24th. Spread of South Wales railway strike. . . ."

[1] Cf. *Lord Riddell's War Diary, 1914–1918*, under August 1918, for a strike of the Metropolitan Police, who assembled in "great force" in Downing Street and assumed a "very menacing" attitude, reported to have made the occupants feel that they really were face to face with a revolution.

[2] Cf. *The Nation*, September 7, 1918: "On September 3rd the Czecho-Slovaks were recognized as a *de facto* belligerent nation by the United States. . . . Mr. Wilson still preaches his idealism. But . . . American policy may find itself committed to a wide scheme of European partition. . . . *Delenda est Austria*. Three new States, a Greater Poland . . . Bohemia and Yugo-Slavia, would join with Italy and hold out a forbidding hand to German trade with Russia and the Near East. That is the New Europe to which Professor Masaryk and his friends are prepared to devote the lives of unnumbered British, French, Italian, and American boys."

[3] *Evening News*, September 17, 1918.

of September and early in October, London's eyes were more often turned on the "Feed the Guns" campaign proceeding in a Trafalgar Square transformed into "a ruined French village".[1] The religious service which inaugurated the campaign makes strange reading, with the Bishop of Kensington and the Mayor of Westminster presiding on the gun platform of a 9·2 howitzer and massed choirs ranged behind the guns which needed feeding.[2] All in all, it must be assumed that the publicity consultants of the War Savings Committee had learnt much from American "Liberty Loan" pushing and even from that "great new war film", D. W. Griffiths's *Hearts of the World*, with its "faked" scenes of sentimentality and horror.

There was some Radical effort to stop the country's slide into the bellicose vulgarity which was, before long, to produce the clamour to "Hang the Kaiser" and "Squeeze the Huns till the pips squeak". Here is one call to Asquith to take a firm stand:[3]

We think that the time has come for the Liberal leaders . . . to make a bold stroke for the future. The war, as an agent for repelling a German supremacy of Europe, is substantially won. The task remains of restoring sanity and security to a society it has almost destroyed. What are to be the character and cement of the new structure? If it is to be built up of the old scheme of Power-balances, the conscript nation . . . then youth has been cruelly deceived. . . .

It is the business of Liberalism to stand between the living and the dead, and firmly uniting itself with the American President and the Labour Party, to throw the weight of its experience into the fight for a new and better management of the world. It would not, of course, withhold its support from the Executive force so long as the war promised any success for Germany. But it should be equally clear in repudiating the wrong kind of peace, a punitive peace, a territorial peace, a peace of trade preferences and trade boycotts, any kind of peace, indeed, save a true peace of the League. That a good peace carries with it the fall of the militarist autocracy in Central Europe and of its doctrine of might, we have no doubt whatever, and it is a prime object of Liberalism to see the dark idol overthrown. It is also its object to shake this country free of complicity with the European and the British reaction—Prussianism has fought Prussianism; it has been a War Office war; and if the present Coalition holds, it will be a War Office peace.

[1] Cf. *The Times*, October 1, 1918, however, for the more seemly official opening of the "Feed the Guns" campaign at the Guildhall by the Chancellor of the Exchequer.
[2] Cf. Caroline Playne, *Britain Holds On, 1917–1918*, p. 383.
[3] Cf. *The Nation*, September 14, 1918.

English Radicalism: The End?

It will have been noticed that, after several years of agitation, mainly by Anglo-Saxon Liberal influences on both sides of the Atlantic, "a peace of the League" had emerged as a major war-objective, a peace, that is, that would set up a League of Nations as an international authority to enforce peace by strong measures against future would-be aggressors. Those, who had begun the propaganda, indeed, belonged largely to "pacifist" Radical sections[1] who felt that Germany had not been without a case in 1914 and who hoped, too, to avoid the sickening bloodshed of a "Fight to a Finish" solution by a resolve, on both sides, to abandon the War, Armaments, and partial Power-Alliances in favour of an impartial League of Nations to guarantee future Peace, Security, and Justice to every nationality. Yet, if by the autumn of 1918, a considerable measure of Allied lip-service was already being paid to a League of Nations peace, it was always a pre-condition that victory must come first and the downfall of "Prussian militarism". This pre-condition, of course, ultimately entailed the meanness and folly of Versailles peace-making with a League of Nations installed to enforce, it seemed, for ever the crying injustices of exceptionally short-sighted and vindictive Treaty-writing by a combination of Marshal Foch, the British Admiralty, and all the Allied Exchequers. As will, perhaps, have been noticed, the Radicals of *The Nation* were not unaware of the danger of an Allied "Prussianism" seeking to dictate a "War Office peace" but they, too, were moving some way, at least, with the stream when implicitly accepting the "fall of the militarist autocracy in Central Europe" as almost a pre-condition of negotiation. That formula might certainly be held to cover what President Wilson was doing during October 1918, when after receiving the offer to negotiate on the basis of his Fourteen Points from a new German Chancellor pledged to democratization, he succeeded in making the difficulties of October 8th, 15th, 19th, and 24th,[2] which brought down the

[1] Cf. A. J. P. Taylor, *The Trouble Makers*, p. 141: " 'the League of Nations' had become common currency since Lowes Dickinson coined it in August 1914 ... it was used more persistently, and emphatically by those who regarded the League as a substitute both for the defeat of Germany and for traditional foreign policy".

[2] Cf. *Whitaker's Almanack, 1919*, Diary of the War, under these dates: "Oct. 8th. President firmly refuses an armistice until all the territories occupied by Germans have been evacuated by them. ... Oct. 15th. Pres. Wilson's reply to Germany. The Allies and U.S. must judge about 'the process of evacuation and conditions of an armistice'. Germany warned to expect no armistice while German outrages on sea and land continue. The ruling power in Germany, too, is an arbitrary power. ... Oct. 19th. Reply of Pres. Wilson to the Austrian

Austrian Empire by October 31st[1] and the German Empire
shortly afterwards. It turned out that President Wilson had thus
unwittingly handed over Central Europe to the unbridled
Nationalism of France, Italy, Poland, Serbia, Rumania, and the
Czechs. But, thanks to reported expenditure on arms and subversion of a million pounds by the Bolshevik Embassy in Berlin,
it remained doubtful for a considerable time whether German
"Reds" in the Fleet,[2] in the Berlin garrison, and in the dislocated
industrial areas might not put Central Europe under a Germano-
Russian Bolshevism instead.

Meanwhile, in Britain, as it became increasingly certain that
Germany was going down to irretrievable defeat, the "Fight to a
Finish" school, headed by Northcliffe and Bottomley, tried hard
to commit the nation to refuse all parley with Germany till Berlin
had been reached and occupied by Allied troops. Bottomley's
John Bull, as might be expected, was particularly ferocious and
irresponsible, insisting that 'I don't want any more talk about not
being out to destroy the German nation—that is just what I *am*
out for." That was on October 12th when Mr. Bottomley's
Peace Terms were an indemnity "if it takes a thousand years to
pay it, and we'll annex the German colonies. And next, if you
please, we'll have the German Navy . . . there will be darker days
unless the British nation makes it stand from now henceforth until
we have dictated a bitter and remorseless peace in Berlin." Later
in the month, *John Bull* was accusing the War Secretary, Lord
Milner, of "Lansdowneism" because of his readiness to stop

Note published; mere autonomy for Czecho-Slovaks and Jugo-Slavs no longer
an adequate basis for peace. . . . Oct. 21st. Reply by German Government to
Pres. Wilson dealing with the evacuation of North France and Belgium, and
the charges of illegal and inhumane actions . . . and the status of the German
Government. . . . Oct. 24th. Reply of Pres. Wilson to Germany, demanding
'extraordinary safeguards because the present war is not under the German
people's control'."

[1] Cf. *Ibid*, under October 31st: "End of Dual Monarchy; revolutionary outbreaks at Vienna and Budapest; demonstrations against the Hapsburgs;
Hungarian National Government, at Budapest, . . . proclaimed a Republic.
Bosnian National Council, at Sarajevo, proclaimed the amalgamation of Bosnia
and Herzegovina with the kingdom of Serbia. Austrian commander-in-chief
on Italian front applied to Gen. Diaz for an armistice." A Czecho-Slovak State
had already been proclaimed at Prague the day before, and the Agram Diet,
too, had announced the independence of Croatia and all the Southern Slav
territories.

[2] Cf. *Ibid.*, under Nov. 7th: "Kiel and Hamburg reported to be in the hands
of Committees of Workmen and Soldiers . . . part of the German Fleet flying
the Red Flag. . . ."; under Nov. 8th: "Resignation of Prince Max of Baden,
Imperial Chancellor. Spread of revolutionary movement over Germany," etc.

fighting short of Berlin and was warning the nation to "beware or the gentlemen of the black coats will let the blonde brutes of Middle Europe loose upon the world once more, to procreate their lustful and bloody breed and pollute the human race with their lewd, coarse and savage strain. . . . The People's Mandate is —Destroy the Beast. And that is the purpose of my present campaign." The handing over the Kaiser to the Allies was first to be insisted on; then the sentencing of the German people to redeem by the sweat of their toil the "precious treasure we have poured out in this struggle for Freedom and Right"; and, next, "their War Lords must pay with their heads for the blood we have lost". A list of twenty "Huns to be hanged", headed by Hindenburg, was printed with the chief "crimes" alleged against them.

Despite Bottomley's now enormous readership—in the trenches as elsewhere[1]—his despicable private character was well enough known to the politicians to ensure that he had no direct influence but only the attention given to one who could mobilize ugly mob-suspicions and, perhaps, a good deal of troublesome heckling at the coming General Election. It was a very different story with Lord Northcliffe and, at one stage in October, there was, among Radicals, something almost akin to despair at the efforts of the Northcliffe Press to prevent the Armistice negotiations for which Germany had asked. Here is one Radical picture of the situation:[2]

> The forces both of folly and wickedness are at work to confuse men's minds . . . every device of an unscrupulous press is being used to make chaos of our dawning sanity. . . . We could have the military surrender of Germany to-morrow if we proclaimed our acceptance of the fourteen points. But every effort is being made to make it appear that we will not pay the price. . . .

[1] Cf. Caroline Playne, *Britain Holds On, 1917–1918*, p. 378: "In October, *John Bull* was busy exploiting grievances as usual. The curious righteous indignation aroused by many *John Bull* revelations of gross injustice done to women, to soldiers at home and at the front, to all and sundry, which are plumped down between revengeful demands for reprisals and unconditional surrender as the only reply to the Huns' overtures. all this showed amazing insight regarding the popular mind. . . . So the popular paper was delivered by wagonsful in the midst of fighting, in victorious pursuit, finally in occupied Germany." Caroline Playne's summaries of 1918 journalism (and especially of *John Bull*'s more notorious writing) has been of great use for this chapter.

[2] Cf. *The Nation*, October 26, 1918. It was one of the few papers which foresaw the Bolshevist danger in Germany, and its comments over the next few months on German Spartacism, the German Councils of Workmen's and Soldiers' Delegates, Karl Liebknecht and Rosa Luxemburg emerge as among the wisest of the time. So do its comments upon the Kurt Eisner régime in Bavaria and the Bela Kun version of Bolshevism in Hungary.

Let us be quite clear as to the actual consequences of the folly of demanding that Germany should surrender to unknown terms. The Independent [Left] Socialists have already proclaimed that they will support a "war of defence enforced by necessity". . . . If the Independent Socialists [of Germany] are forced to line up in national defence, the war will become a war of annihilation. . . . Lord Milner plainly thinks that the Germany we shall then meet will be a Bolshevist Germany. One would have said that every reasonable man would shrink from such a consummation. Yet when Lord Milner most cautiously suggested that even from considerations of the most severely practical expediency anarchy in Germany was undesirable, his words were smothered by the Northcliffe Press. It revealed them only after four days while *The Times* correspondents were collecting "evidence" with which the leader-writers could, with an appearance of objectivity, assert that Lord Milner was misguided. Now Lord Northcliffe in person denounces Lord Milner's "Lansdownisms". If any man of authority dares to suggest that any action of a reformed German Government might conceivably be something other than the basest trickery, slander and contumely is his portion. Whether the voice of sanity will ever be heard, we do not know: but we do know that if it is not heard now, the world will be rushed into disaster. . . .

In point of fact, the Armistice negotiations, though delayed sufficiently for a Central European Bolshevism to be given dangerous and unnecessary chances to take over the succession of the two Kaisers, were not finally prevented. But plentiful counter-concession was apparently deemed necessary by the Prime Minister to the spirit of revengeful unreason. This is not the place to illustrate why virtually all Germans considered that they were continuously tricked and cheated out of the protection of the Fourteen Points in the long series of negotiations for the original Armistice, the Armistice extensions, the Peace, and the post-Peace (not to mention the pre-Peace) "settlements" demanded of ever new claims under threat of military action. Lord Northcliffe, of course, shouted fervent encouragement to Marshal Foch, and Hitlerism was to be one of the eventual results. But here the question treated must not be the long-term continental results of the lengthy course of Quai d'Orsay chicane practised against Germany, with the British Prime Minister's gradually diminishing approval, but rather that Prime Minister's exploitation of Germany's defeat in the sphere of British politics. He had begun preparations for a triumphant Election as the "man who won the war" directly military news began to improve during the summer. But even in October, he was still listening to those who favoured a reconciliation with the Asquithians[1] and the admission of an Asquithian contingent into an enlarged Coalition which would be able to take a more authoritative stand at the Peace Conference and, at home, organize a General Election without serious risk to the traditional party-pattern and without special need to truckle to the mob. But he was far more the prisoner of Bonar Law and the Tory Whips than many realized; he claimed, too, to have special reasons for gratitude to the Tory Leadership; and Election preparations, moreover, were far advanced for a campaign largely based on the case that, taking over a losing war from Asquith, his Coalition had won it. When the Prime Minister finally decided against the risks of opening up a quarrel, on the Asquithians' account, not merely with Northcliffe but with the Tory Party organization, he took, as events proved, one of the most fateful steps in British party history.

As far back as July both main party-wings of the Coalition had drafted Election-programmes,[2] and in the first half of November, while the inevitable bargaining over constituency maps was proceeding between the Lloyd Georgian organization and the Tory Whips, there were still Liberal optimists who believed that, since Asquith was prepared to accept a Lloyd George policy-speech lately made at Manchester[3] as a Liberal programme, no mass-Coalition assault on the hard-pressed Asquithians would be authorized or encouraged. In point of fact, the Lloyd Georgian "Coalition Liberal" organization seems to have put forward claims of its own to every Asquithian seat for which it could find candidates and to have agreed, in return, to accept properly sanctioned Conservatives as the Government candidates where no "Coalition Liberal" could be put into the field. The deadly political sin, specially fixed upon as deserving to bring political annihilation on its committer, was to have voted with Asquith on the Maurice Debate some six months earlier.

Meanwhile, a mixture of blandishment and blackmail had almost brought the Labour Party, through its office-holders, into the Coalition arrangements, and though, thanks to Henderson, the attempt was largely blocked, the Coalition's ability to claim all the

[1] Cf. *Lord Riddell's War Diary, 1914–1918* under September 27th and October 3rd.

[2] Cf. Dr. Addison, *Four and a Half Years*, ii, 553–6.

[3] Cf. *The Nation*, November 2, 1918: "At Manchester he talked like an ardent Liberal, panting to rejoin his lost comrades, and speak once more the language of Limehouse."

credit for Britain's victory did not leave him particularly optimistic as to the polling results. In pressing the inadvisability of going into Opposition before the peace was made, Clynes repeatedly urged that those who refused the "Coalition ticket" faced political annihilation. In the end, Clynes, Hodge, and Brace obeyed the call of the party and resigned but Barnes headed a group of four who decided to stand by the Government and (according to the malicious) their salaries, seeing no reason why Henderson's feud with Lloyd George, made use of by Fabians, intellectuals, and "extremists" of every kind, should completely decide their course. Mrs. Webb's *Diaries* show Henderson and Webb, directing Labour's Headquarters effort, much less hopeful than they once had been, Henderson rightly doubting whether he could now win his own seat and Webb estimating that only sixty Labour members would be returned at best, and from "massed trade union constituencies" exclusively. As Mrs. Webb admitted, the glamour round the Labour Party when, in the spring of 1918, it seemed a main hope of rescue, nationally and internationally, from "Knock-Out" had gone; the quarrels as to staying in the Coalition had made matters worse; and the "professional rebels" were another source of distraction to a party that finally entered the electoral struggle, in Mrs. Webb's vivid phrase, "a distracted, divided and depressed rabble of some three hundred nondescript candidates".[1] In point of fact, however, the great bulk of a much-strengthened "Labour movement" obeyed the party's central direction more unhesitatingly and polled more strongly than Henderson had feared in his more depressed moments. It was different with the Asquithians for a number of reasons, and these will have to be investigated in the next chapter.[2]

[1] Cf. *Beatrice Webb's Diaries, 1912–1924,* pp. 134–5, under November 4 and 7, 1918.

[2] Though here it may be said that the Asquithian "advanced", impatient of the apparent immobility of their Front Bench as it waited, finally in vain, for a fatal mistake by Lloyd George, had announced, in July, the formation almost of a breakaway Radical Council because "great numbers of Radicals throughout the country feel that their opinions are not being voiced by the leaders to whom they have hitherto been accustomed to look." If the war had ended less triumphantly for Lloyd George, greater importance might have to be ascribed to the "advanced" thirty-two point programme from the Radical Back-Benches including as it did Capital Levy. Retention of Excess Profits Duty, "in an appropriate form", State Ownership of Railways, Mines and Munition Factories, Old Age Pensions of increased amount to become payable at an earlier age, Abolition of the Workhouse and Disappearance of Titles and of the House of Lords.

BOOK THREE
Asquith and Lloyd George, 1918–26

CHAPTER XIII

THE COUPON PARLIAMENT

"HOW FAR CAN GERMANY PAY FOR THE WAR

"The demand for a huge indemnity to be exacted from Germany makes a powerful appeal. . . . Germany is no doubt a country with some very rich natural resources. A recent article in the *Fortnightly Review* estimates that 'the Rhenish-Westphalian coalfield alone contains considerably more coal than the whole of the United Kingdom and that the coal in that district represents a value of £1,067,830,000,000. . . . But difficulties arise when we look beneath . . . that majestic figure. This coal can only be got out and made available piecemeal. The whole German output for 1910 amounted to a little over 150 million tons, or a value of £75,000,000. . . . Most of this value would be absorbed in labour and capital expenses. . . . The same reasoning applies to the other industries of Germany. . . . But could even this limited indemnity be got without grave perils to the economic interests and social order of Europe . . . an Allied Army of Occupation in Germany, backed up by the retention of conscription. . . ? The indemnity must take corporeal shape in a flood of German goods . . . the biggest and most dangerous form of 'dumping' that the world has ever witnessed. . . ."

The Nation, November 2, 1918, gives a warning that electioneers and electors alike ignored.

"THE MINERS' SHOCK TACTICS.

"A threatened strike of colliers in the depth of winter would be a serious enough matter in an ordinary year. In our present situation, with narrow rations, and in many parts of the country complete failure of delivery, the prospect . . . brings anxiety to every home. There is the still graver menace of a stoppage of manufactures for lack of fuel. Thus the miners make full employment of their position of economic vantage to enforce their claims . . . they act as does every monopolist. . . . There are, however, one or two considerations. . . . There is a risk lest a monopoly of mining Labour . . . may seek to demand 'more than the trade will bear' with damaging reactions on themselves. Again, even supposing that general industry can adapt itself to the higher price for coal which their demands entail, their fellow-workers in other industries will be mulcted in the purchasing power of their wages to pay for dearer coal. . . . Is there no solidarity of Labour, save in Conference rhetoric? . . .

English Radicalism: The End?

"Nor must we neglect the part which coal itself plays directly in our export trade and in our shipping economy. . . . Have these interests really been weighed in the new policy of the miners? . . . At present there is in some Labour quarters a hardening suspicion against all proposals for increasing productivity, on the assumption that the capitalists must get the increased product. . . . But it is fundamentally unsound. Unions that are strong enough to hold up the whole trade of the country to-day are strong enough to see they get their full share from increased production . . . a mere recovery of pre-war productivity will not yield to the workers of this country a sufficiency of wages and of leisure for a life worth living. . . . It cannot be got by each industrial group playing for its own hand. . . . For if the miners were to succeed for the moment . . . imitations by other well-organized workers would soon filch away from them the substance of their gains by similar reductions of output and rises of price."

A Radical economist warns the pitmen in *The Nation*, January 25, 1919.

T HE downfall and flight of the Kaiser,[1] the acceptance by the enemy of catastrophic conditions for a mere short-term cease-fire,[2] and, finally, the tremendous Armistice rejoicing on November 11th for the victorious end of so long a period of heavy war-strain[3]—all these made it certain that a "snap election" could be used to destroy, at least temporarily, the political position of the Prime Minister's best-known critics and opponents. And though Lloyd George had given some occasional consideration, at least, to the problem of whether it was wise to risk leaving himself so completely the prisoner of the Tory Party as the General Election of December 1918 was to make him, the Election machinery that had been set in motion almost necessarily moved at a pace that brought nomination-day on December 4th and polling-day on December 14th before second and third thoughts could be acted upon. Doubtless, the Prime Minister could contrive to put the blame on others that so many constituency Liberal Associations, refusing the suggestions of his Whips and maintaining their loyalty to Asquithian candidates (even when those had "unpatriotically" voted against him on the critical Maurice Debate of May) were bringing their fate on their own heads. Certainly, in nearly all such cases, the Tory Whips secured the issue of the notorious "coupon" of Government sponsorship for their own man, such numbers of traditionally "Liberal strongholds" passing into Tory hands that the final Election returns gave a mere 28 of "Independent Liberals" against a vast Coalition host of 478, 334 of them Unionists, 133 Liberals, and 11 Labour men. Even

[1] Cf. *The Times*, November 12th: " 'Empires and Kingdoms and Kings and Crowns are falling like withered leaves before a gale,' Mr. Lloyd George said at Guildhall on Saturday night, but the Prime Minister spoke of the monarchs and countries that made the war. The Kaiser, the Austrian Emperor, and Tsar Ferdinard are fugitives. King George, the Constitutional Sovereign of Great Britain, who is not clad in 'shining armour' and has never rattled a sabre, . . . was acclaimed by his people . . . in dense streams they made their way to the Palace to cheer. . . ."

[2] Cf. *Lord Riddell's War Diary, 1914–1918*, p. 379, for Riddell quoting the Prime Minister on the German envoys nearly dumb with astonishment at the severity of the Armistice terms.

[3] Cf. *Manchester Guardian*, November 12th, for the Manchester area, the *Yorkshire Post* of the same day for York and Newcastle where "a general holiday was almost immediately taken", and *The Scotsman* for Edinburgh and Glasgow, in which last place demonstrations of surprising fervour took place. Despite Clydeside's "Red" reputation, "crowds paraded the streets, singing and cheering; soldiers and sailors were made the centres of demonstrations . . . and rejoicing was general." (Partly Re-quoted from H. C. Dent, *op. cit.*)

Asquith, McKenna, Sir John Simon, Herbert Samuel, and Runciman went down in the struggle, Asquith's seat held, since 1885, passing to a Conservative who, for shame's sake, had not been formally authorized by a "coupon". There were, indeed, to add to the 334 Coalition Unionists, 48 others, including the Ulstermen and those who had campaigned without "coupons", described as Unionists and, sometimes, like Bottomley[1] of the Independents and Page Croft of the National Party, plainly purporting to be made of far sterner stuff as far as dealing with "barbarous Huns" or traitorous Sinn Feiners was concerned. As those same Sinn Feiners swept Catholic Ireland to the tune of 73 seats to 7 for the less revolutionary Nationalists, there would obviously, in the Ulster view, be much need for sterner stuff in Ireland than pure Coalitionist expediency.

The fate of Asquithianism, of course, had not merely been decided by Coalition dislike but, often enough, by Coalition dislike aided by a Labour attempt to supplant. And it is strange to find how much Labour was helped by many who had hitherto described themselves as Radicals and who still flinched at the thought of Marxian formularies or a Trade Union domination of the national life.[2] If Lloyd George's war-record seemed detestable to these men, they found it hard, too, to forgive the last Asquith Government its continual surrenders to the Conscriptionists, the Protectionists, and the foreign "statesmen" who had been allowed to drive the hard and immoral bargains of the "Secret Treaties". In this mood of revulsion from the baseness of "practical politics" as hitherto practised, it was easier for many to swallow their doubts, if only temporarily, and to accept the skilful Webb-designed Labour propaganda, based on over thirty Fabian years of "ensnaring Radicals", as offering the best hope of a better Britain and a better world. It might be well, here, to quote from a review of the Election campaigning dated December 14th, the day when Britain voted though the results were not to be made known until December 28th—after the last voting-papers from

---

[1] Cf. *Whitaker's Almanack, 1919*, under the House of Commons, for this rascal's return for South Hackney by the triumphant majority, over a Coalition Liberal, of 11,145 votes against 2830. In Asquith's contest in East Fife the voting had been: Col. Sir A. Sprot, Unionist, 8996; Rt. Hon. H. H. Asquith, Liberal, 6994, and W. P. Morgan, Independent, 591.

[2] Among these were Lees-Smith, C. P. Trevelyan, and Noel Buxton, all members of the late Parliament and ultimately destined to sit as Labour Ministers alongside men like Dr. Addison and Josiah Wedgwood who were still "Coalition Liberals" at the elections of December 1918.

the men abroad would have been added to those awaiting the counting clerks. The quotation is the better justified as coming from the leading Radical weekly of the day which persisted, for several successive numbers,[1] in throwing more weight and enthusiasm behind the Labour opposition to the Coalition than behind that of the Asquithians'. Here is *The Nation* of December 14, 1918:

The election has ended as it began, in an orgy of sops and sophistry. Mr. George has let passion ramp, and fed it. . . . Need he cannot satisfy. But he can give everybody a little cheque on the future, and pay in bribes and hints the debts he knows he can never discharge. . . . The [Coalition] Liberals will not let him say "Conscription", or the Tories "No Conscription". So he says both and neither. I suppose he will win through. None the less he is lost . . . . And he won the war! One man's word drove tens of millions of boys hither and thither (about one in five to their death), and a mass of them to victory. An attractive and ingeniously adherent FLY sat on the mighty wheel and guided its whirl. How comforting! . . . Mr. George did bad things and good things and usually irrelevant things. But how could a good military decision come from such a mind as Mr. George's, "slim", intuitive but ill-furnished and careless of detail? The event showed that his coquetry with minor adventures was wrong; and that his neglect of the Western Front might have lost the war if the British soldier had allowed him to lose it. . . .

The enthusiasm has been for Labour and for those free Liberal candidates with a personality and a programme. . . . And the main intellectual drift is Labour-wards. Take the really formative writers— Wells, Shaw, Bennett, Zangwill, Masefield, Carpenter, Olive Schreiner, Hewlett, Havelock Ellis, Jerome, Bertrand Russell, Graham Wallas, the Webbs, Hobhouse, Hobson, Cole, the mass of the younger poets, artists, essayists, and last but not least, the soldiers. There is the same drive in the ranks of the Civil Service. There the intellectuals are divided between the eclective Imperialism of the *Round Table* and the Foreign Office and the ideal vision of internationalism. The movement to democracy is the most dramatic I have known since Fabianism and is much more radical. In five years its political equivalent will be in full power.

This, as time proved, was to rush matters far too fast, and to assume that over a century of Liberalism and Radicalism could quickly be disposed of even with the assistance of a Great War, a disastrous "election betrayal", and the "drift Labour-wards" of

---

[1] Cf. *H. W. M.: A Selection from the Writings of H. W. Massingham*, p. 99, for the view that "at the General Election of 1918 . . . four issues of *The Nation* [were] powerful electoral pamphlets for the Labour Party".

considerable sections of the "intelligentsia". It was not 1924 but 1945 before command of the House of Commons was obtained, and even then by less than fifty per cent of the votes cast. And, indeed, not merely Massingham, the Radical, but Webb, the Fabian, was disconcerted by the way in which the masses had sent over three score of uninspiring and virtually useless Trade Union officials to Parliament while allowing the Coalition to butcher, alongside the Asquithian ex-Ministers, such essential members of a Labour Front Bench as Henderson,[1] MacDonald, and Snowden.[2] Before long Massingham was recoiling from the spectacle of ineptitude presented by the Parliamentary Labour Party as the "official Opposition" under the leadership of Adamson, the Fife ex-pitman.[3] And if Massingham took to unceasingly imploring Liberal and Labour to work together to oust the Coalition, it was because, as he repeatedly admitted, Labour would long need the professional talent and experience which Liberals and Radicals possessed in such embarrassing plenty. The Webbs, of course, were in closer daily contact with the manifold deficiencies of the Parliamentary Labour Party of 1918–22 than Massingham, and at one stage, early in 1920, when a breach between Lloyd George and the Tories seemed on the way, they were driven to their much-criticized public contemplation of the notion of annexing Lloyd George, complete with personal following and Million Pound Election Fund, to the Labour Party or, at least, to the "steering" headship of a Labour-Radical Coalition.[4]

[1] Cf. *Whitaker's Almanack, 1919*, p. 172, for Henderson at the bottom of the poll for East Ham South: Edwards, Coalition Labour, 7972; Hamlett, Unionist, 5661; Henderson, Labour, 5024.

[2] *Ibid.*, p. 171, for what the charge of "pacifism" did at Blackburn: Norman Coalition Liberal, 32,076; Dean, Coalition Unionist, 30,158; Snowden, Labour, 15,274. At Leicester West, MacDonald was defeated by 20,570 against 6347.

[3] Cf. *The Nation*, November 15, 1919: "Trade union experience needs to be supplemented and reinforced by other kinds of knowledge and ability in a party that is to govern an Empire. . . . There is still a danger that the Party will be composed of trade union secretaries. . . . The Labour Party . . . does not pull half its weight. There are in its ranks three or four men of conspicuous ability; it has behind it a great and growing body of opinion in the country, and yet it makes comparatively little impression—less, on the whole, than the much smaller body of Free Liberals."

[4] Cf. *Ibid.*: "I read with some astonishment an article by Mr. Sidne Webb. . . . The Premier will probably come to a breach with the Tories, retire from office, and from the Opposition Benches 'cultivate friendly relations' with Labour. Out of this will grow an electoral understanding which will give the 'Labour Party and the Lloyd George Party four hundred members between them'. 'A combination to take office' would then be inevitable, and it would matter very little whether Mr. George, or Mr. Henderson, Mr. Thomas or Mr. Clynes was actually Prime Minister. The division of work, however,

It is, perhaps, at this stage worth giving Mrs. Webb's ironic picture of the man who had been allotted the task of coping with Lloyd George, Bonar Law, Arthur Balfour, Austen Chamberlain, Winston Churchill, Edwin Montagu, and the rest. In her famous *Diaries*, Mrs. Webb had much to say of her husband's problems in beginning the tutoring of one who had claimed from the Speaker the full prerogatives of Leader of the Opposition. She had seen Adamson at Labour's Albert Hall meeting before the General Election and had not thought much of his pompous platitudes.[1] She surmised, of course, the industry and trustworthiness which had taken him up the scale from pitman to checkweighman and from checkweighman to Miners' agent and Miners' M.P., but found in him, despite such other estimable qualities as abstemiousness and pious family life, no real driving force either emotional or intellectual and none even of the managing ability of Henderson. And in the discussion that arose on how the Webbs and the Fabian and Party apparatus could help him, he put most emphasis on the three clerks, the two typists, and the messenger that he and his fifty-eight M.P.s would like and had to be prompted to recognize the manifold uses that could be made of the Labour Party Executive, its staff, and the Advisory Committees. In short, Mrs. Webb's private conscience found Adamson as Opposition Leader almost as absurd as Barnes in the War Cabinet and at the Peace Conference. Adamson, it should be added, had, after six years in Parliament, blossomed into Chairman of the Parliamentary Labour Party when all usable men, not out of the running as "pacifists", had been invited to take office. Though three of the Labour Ministers had reluctantly obeyed the party call to quit the Coalition in November 1918, Adamson was not, after all, replaced from among them partly, perhaps, because he had never received office from Lloyd George and partly because a Parliamentary Labour Party containing 25 pitmen out of a total of 59 could hardly be expected to ask a pitman-Chairman to make way for any late associate of Lloyd George.

It was, of course, a thousand pities that, at such a fated turning-point of European and world history as the first six months of

would be thoroughly arranged; the Labour Party would supply the 'policy' and Mr. George would do the 'steering' . . . it hardly seems worth while beginning a Labour Party for it to be 'done in' so soon and so effectually. . . .'' Yet a "deal" of this kind remained a subject of political gossip for years.

[2] *Beatrice Webb's Diaries, 1912–1924*, pp. 142–3.

1919, the vast Coalition majority was able to depise the calibre of the "official Opposition" and to deride the scanty numbers of the Liberal and Radical "Wee Frees" led, in Mr. Asquith's absence, by Sir Donald Maclean. Much that went wrong with the peace-making might have been avoided if Lloyd George, instead of being driven by the Coalition masses farther in Clemenceau's direction than even he thought it wise to go, had been able to make of the presence of two vigilant and experienced Opposition groups in Parliament a reason for greater caution and moderation in the terms being drawn up for dictation to the infant German Republic. Great and relatively speedy as was the national revulsion from the more dubious aspects of Lloyd George's "coupon" strategy, its relatively scanty chances of manifesting itself at occasional by-elections proved far below the true need. Yet the remarkable series of by-election shocks administered to the Government, and in a measure to "Labour" also,[1] in the spring of 1919 undoubtedly had its uses. Perhaps the voting figures at West Leyton's by-election of March 1, 1919, at Central Hull's of March 2, 1919, and at Aberdeen and Kincardine Central's of April 30, 1919 should be instanced before attempting to draw conclusions. At West Leyton, where the Coalition Unionist had, on December 14, 1918, polled 10,956 votes against the Liberal Newbould's 5288 a mere two and a half months sufficed to reverse the General Election verdict and to give Newbould 7934 votes against a Coalition Unionist's 5915.[2] At Central Hull, the change-over was even more remarkable for whereas the General Election had given 13,805 votes to a Coalition Unionist against 3434 for an Asquithian, the by-election gave the Liberal the seat by 8616 votes against

[1] Cf. *Whitaker's Almanack, 1920,* pp. 414–15, for a Labour chronology of 1919, showing the forcing tactics being widely employed in the industrial field, in virtually total disregard of the views and interests of the public at large. Pitmen were confidently leading the way in a mid-winter world, starved of coal, and the nature of the demands they were putting forward can be gauged from the following entries: "Feb. 12th. Miners' Conference rejected Government's offer. Feb. 13th. Conference decided to take ballot on question of national stoppage to enforce miners' demand for 30 per cent increased wages, six hour day and nationalisation, and to recommend men to vote for a strike. . . . Feb. 24th. Miners' strike ballot resulted 611,998 for strike, 104,997 against." The tactics of the National Union of Railwaymen were not very different from this "Bolshevik" pattern.

[2] Cf. *The Nation,* March 22, 1919: "The West Leyton election came as a bombshell in the world of politics." This was in an article on "The Party of the Coupon" which charged Lloyd George's Coalition Liberals with cowardice and selfishness in not having sought to protect their Liberal comrades from the political "assassination" which had been temporarily enacted but was already being avenged.

7699. In Aberdeenshire and Kincardineshire, finally, where the General Election had permitted a Coalition Unionist to eject the old Asquithian member in a poll of 6546 against 5908 and where it had been feared that a Labour intervention might spoil the chance of reversing this result, a new Asquithian won the seat by polling 4950 votes against the Coalition Unionist's 4764 and Labour's 3482.

If one thing emerged plainly from such a series of results as these, it was that "Independent Liberalism" was still a much stronger force than the quick talkers of the political clubs and the glib leader-writers, who had hurried forward its burial service, had made allowance for. Such a series of results, too, was a special encouragement to those Asquithian politicians who were striving hard to avoid being bustled into approval for all manner of social and economic "advance" on the ground that no party could keep touch with the "people" unless the "people's" alleged demand for such "advance" was accepted. Massingham's Radical weekly, *The Nation*, which had certainly rendered them great service in the past, was till the spring of 1923 to be unwearying in its efforts to commit them to Nationalization of the Mines and the Railways[1] despite their not unfounded fears that there would be a loss of efficiency, productivity, and discipline, capable, in view of the basic character of Mines and Railways, of doing infinite harm to the whole National Economy. By the end of the war, however, Massingham's younger and more "advanced" contributors, helped by the Bolshevist outbreak with its later extensions to Germany and Hungary, had convinced him that Society's most urgent task, unless worse was to befall, was to secure a wholesale revision of the economic order or, in Massingham's own words, "to revise the industrial contract without destroying it".[2] And his answer to Asquith's objection that the Mining Industry could not be efficiently run by a bureaucracy— the "Guild Socialism" of letting the mining workers and technicians run the mines themselves—ignored, in the Asquithians' view, the even greater danger that, after the State had, presumably

[1] Cf. *H. W. M.: A Selection from the Writings of H. W. Massingham*, p. 99, for the 1918 General Election programme, advocating in Home Politics, the "national control of the land and its supporting industries of mines, transport and electric power".

[2] Cf. *The Nation*, April 28, 1923, for Massingham's farewell statement to *The Nation*'s readers on behalf of "the company of journalists who founded it more than sixteen years ago, with their more recent associates".

against compensation, procured the handing over of Mines Control to the Mining Guilds, it would be ceaselessly exposed to tough bargaining that might soon become blackmail. It was obviously not for nothing that Massingham had ultimately to be displaced from control of *The Nation* and that Keynes, the keenest economic thinker in the country, played some part in ending a Massingham régime which had allowed increasing scope to the economic propaganda of the "Left" and even the "Extreme Left".

But all this is to peer some way into the future, and here it must suffice, abandoning the hope of detailed attention even to such first-class politico-economic debates of 1919 as those on the Bills for setting up a Ministry of Health and a Ministry of Transport, for increasing the Housing effort, for amending the law on compensation-assessment for compulsorily-acquired land, for dealing with "profiteers", and for prolonging Rent Restriction, to concentrate on developments in the key-controversy of the day on Mines Nationalization. On all the other subjects mentioned, there were plenty of divergences and difficulties of principle between the Lloyd George and Conservative wings of the Coalition as when, on the Ministry of Transport Bill, the Government had to surrender the proposed right, in certain circumstances, to take possession of docks and harbours and content itself with the right to require improvements[1] or as when, on the Housing Bill, the Lords insisted on an amendment making it necessary to specify the total estimated cost of local authorities' schemes, the estimated rent obtainable, the estimated deficit resulting, and the portion to be charged on the rates. On the Rent Restriction and Profiteering Bills there were also occasions when something like the old Radical-Labour alliance of 1906–14 showed signs of reappearing as when numbers of Lloyd Georgians, Asquithians, and Labour men united to condemn and reverse amendments carried in the Lords for reducing the period of Rent Restriction and increasing the standard rent.

But on all these subjects, as well as on the Budget debates concerned with the absorbing controversy on Capital Levy or no (to permit the scaling down of the gigantic National Debt and the crushing weight of Debt-interest), there was never the prospect of the first-class political and economic crisis which repeatedly

[1] Cf. *Hansard*, July 1st, for Joynson-Hicks announcing that a group of members had come to an agreement with the Government. Hicks was already very prominent among Conservative private members, especially on transport.

seemed to threaten on Mines Nationalization. Nationalization of the Mines had, of course, been a demand of the Miners' Unions for many years, and in the Syndicalist period just before the war, veritable industrial sabotage had been preached, especially in South Wales, in the hope of making "capitalist" ownership and direction of the mines so unprofitable as to procure almost a "capitalist" abandonment of the "pits" which would then be run by the "pit-workers".[1] Naturally, such serious trouble-making as occurred, if it failed to end the "capitalist system", certainly did not fail to raise coal-costs for the "public"—and even Fabians, for all the Syndicalists' professions of zeal for the general good, were not unaware that uncontrolled occupation of the pits by the pitmen might come to have some unfortunate effects for the entire nation.

There had, in fact, been many occasions during the war when the "public" considered itself to have very legitimate complaints against the pitmen[2] and now, in Feburary 1919, with Britain, the Allies, and the world desperately short of coal, the pitmen, it was said, under the guidance, doubtless, of the more "Bolshevik" of their leaders, had chosen to attempt a supreme piece of blackmail. They, who had done better out of the war than almost any other class of workers, had voted for a national strike unless accorded thirty per cent more pay, a working-day cut down to six hours, and nationalization of the mines. The world-economic position was, however, under such strain that the Prime Minister, on February 20th, thought it wise to temporize with the offer to consider an advance of wages and to appoint a Royal Commission on Hours. His presence, too, on February 27th, at a National Industrial Conference to consider the causes of unrest in industry,

---

[1] Cf. *The Miners' Next Step* of 1912 with a "Policy" whose Clause 10 mentioned the "more scientific weapon of the irritation strike" by which pitmen were to contrive "to make the colliery unremunerative" and whose Clause 13 was this: "That a continual agitation be carried on in favour of increasing the minimum wage and shortening the hours of work until we have extracted the whole of the employers' profits." The ultimate objective, as stated in Clause 14, was "to build up an organisation that will ultimately take over the mining industry and carry it on in the interests of the workers". *The Miners' Next Step* was produced by "the Unofficial Reform Committee of the South Wales Miners Federation" but special responsibility was ascribed to A. J. Cook and Noah Ablett, whose views were certainly absorbed by the militants of every area, with a special welcome for Clause V's: "The old policy of identity of interest between employers and ourselves be abolished and a policy of open hostility installed."

[2] Cf. J. R. Raynes, *Coal and its Conflicts*, p. 152, for pitmen's large part in forcing up living-costs.

may have helped him further, for many leaders of other trades there represented, certainly had good reason to fear the results of intransigence among the pitmen. At any rate, on February 28th, it could be announced that the Miners' Conference had decided to postpone the threatened strike and take part, instead, in the suggested Commission of Inquiry into their trade. But, meanwhile the pitmen's "Bolsheviks" and Labour's "intellectuals" had combined in another piece of "blackmail" as the Prime Minister considered it. Though he had attempted, he claimed, to take counsel with Labour's intellectual tutor, Sidney Webb, in making proper arrangements for the Coal Commission,[1] his reward was to be pulled out of the Industrial Conference and have a ten-minute ultimatum presented to him. It is Mrs. Webb's *Diaries* that give something of the full flavour of the story.[2] The Prime Minister had finished an acceptable and not inappropriate address to the Industrial Conference when he and Adamson left the platform. He was back in half an hour, extremely angry. The miners had brought their terms for postponing their strike and co-operating with the Mines Commission—the right to nominate half the Commission with Chiozza Money, Tawney, and Webb named on the spot. The Prime Minister was allowed ten minutes to accept their terms or face a strike for, according to Smillie, the delegates had to catch the five o'clock train. Even Mrs. Webb was sufficiently taken aback to write into her *Diaries* the comment, "But where is parliamentary government?"

The resulting Inquiry, under the Chairmanship of Mr. Justice Sankey, is one of the most curious in British official records for, as the pitmen had merely postponed their strike till March 22nd, they eventually succeeded in getting vital proceedings, only begun on March 3rd, terminated by March 17th. And the Sankey Inquiry, if unique for the haste enforced under miners' ultimatum, must also be unique in the fact that the members nominated to the Commission by the Miners' Federation had almost more to say than all the witnesses. Yet there can be no doubt but that, in the sheer technique of propaganda cross-examination, the Employing side was completely overborne (both in the March proceedings

---

[1] Cf. *Beatrice Webb's Diaries, 1912–1924*, p. 147, for the Prime Minister's meeting with Sidney Webb, contrived by Lord Haldane. This was on February 22nd when Webb skilfully began the work of breaking down the Prime Minister's resistance to the kind of Coal Commission that he ultimately accepted.

[2] *Ibid.*, pp. 151–2, under February 28th.

and those arranged later) by the six Commissioners out of thirteen nominated to demand Nationalization, Smillie, Herbert Smith, Frank Hodges, Chiozza Money, Tawney, and Webb.[1] Everything was pressed into service by a remarkable team, set on "proving" that colliery exploitation, on the existing basis, was shortsighted, greedy, and backward, inevitably accident-prone, slum-spreading, and profiteering. Ultimately pit-village legend, too, was invoked against dead royalty-owning grandees of the past[2] to supplement the effects of the hostile cross-examination of a Lord Durham or a Duke of Northumberland. Indeed, in the temporary elation produced by their obvious propaganda successes against less agile minds and slower tongues, untrained to platform work, "Bolshevik" pit-leaders, Fabian theorists, and "extreme" Guild Socialists, aware of the effect they were producing on the Commission Chairman with the casting-vote, began to dream of other Nationalization fields to conquer by similar methods. Even Mrs. Webb, who, despite her beloved Sidney, had been somewhat taken aback by the notion of a pitmen's ten-minute ultimatum to a British Prime Minister showed a much-altered tone in her diary entry for March 12th. She had gone, earlier that day, to the House of Lords Robing Room to see the Royal Commission on the Mining Industry at work but found it behaving more like a revolutionary tribunal, listening to charges against the coal-owners and their managements. It was the superior skill of the miners' representatives that was turning the proceedings, she thought, into a species of State trial. The result was that "public opinion" which, only a week before, had been hostile to the pitmen had

[1] Cf. J. R. Raynes, *Coal and its Conflicts,* p. 162, for the Commission of thirteen enumerated as follows: The Hon. Mr. Justice Sankey (Chairman). Mr. Arthur Balfour, Sir Arthur Duckham, Sir Thos. Royden (nominated by the Government). Mr. Evan Williams, Mr. R. W. Cooper, Mr. J. T. Forgie (nominated by the Mining Association). Mr. Robert Smillie, Mr. Herbert Smith, Mr. Frank Hodges, Sir Leo Chiozza Money (nominated by the Miners' Federation). Mr. R. H. Tawney, Mr. Sidney Webb (agreed upon between the Government and the Miners' Federation by arrangement).

[2] Such as a dead Duke of Hamilton, alleged to have squandered a great fortune while tolerating medieval housing conditions in the pit-villages that provided the money. It seems doubtful whether Mr. Justice Sankey ought to have allowed Smillie, for example, quite the incessant running commentary he undertook, in addition to propaganda speeches phrased as questions. In truth, Mr. Justice Sankey himself appears to have realized this for a comparison, say, of *Reports and Minutes of Evidence of the Second Stage of the Inquiry* with journalistic comment day by day, seems to afford evidence of some editing. And he had certainly been appealed to (p. 622), not very successfully, to keep Smillie within his proper province.

now been turned against the owners and the apparent scale of their profits at the coal-consumer's expense. And more than that, she found a precedent was being set for putting the management of other industries in the dock before a court half-composed of "the prosecuting proletariat".[1]

Of course, this was going too far and too fast besides leaving out of account the ability of most men of affairs to guess that, though pitmen might come to be very much better off under the plausible new schemes their advocates were suggesting,[2] the coal-using industries and the coal-using public might well end up by being much worse off than under the existing dispensation. Asquith, for example, might very well have forwarded an electoral *entente* with Labour and earned the temporary gratitude of the "advanced" Radicals, represented by *The Nation* if he had consented even to consider Nationalization. Yet, despite Mr. Justice Sankey, Asquith proved hostile from first to last to anything more than the Nationalization of Mining Royalties with, of course, the added pay, hours, housing, pit-head baths, welfare fund and organizational benefits that were offered in the Mining Industry Act of 1920 after Cabinet consideration of the three separate Interim Reports and the four Final Reports from the fractions into which the Sankey Commission had split. And though there was unending complaint (capped by the disastrous strike of 1921) from the pitmen's leaders on the score of the Government's declining to enforce the alleged Nationalization majority-verdict returned by six miners' advocates and (in a less biased Report) Mr. Justice Sankey, public attention had, by then, long been diverted to fresher fields, unstaled by the unsatisfactory controversy that pitmen seemed to have raised for so many years. Even in April and May 1919, it must have been an exceptional member of the public and, perhaps, also an exceptional pitman who found the Miners' Federation's *Facts from the Coal Commission*[3] more

[1] *Beatrice Webb's Diaries, 1912–1924*, p. 152.

[2] Cf. *Minutes of Evidence, Sankey Commission*, p. 324, for Straker of the Northumberland Miners opening with the assumption that "the mere granting of the 30 per cent and the shorter hours demanded will not prevent unrest, neither will nationalisation with bureaucratic administration". What apparently was needed was Nationalization under a "Mining Council of ten members, five . . . appointed by the Association known as the Miners' Federation of Great Britain."

[3] Smillie and Hodges contributed a Foreword, dated April 21st, to this pamphlet compiled by Page Arnot. "A lurid light", they claimed was thrown on "the economic rottenness of the present system of capitalist ownership of one of our greatest national assets."

exciting reading than, say, discussion of the draconian Peace Terms handed to Germany on May 7th, surmises on the possible effects of the complete breach obvious between the Prime Minister and Lord Northcliffe or, it might be, illustrated accounts of such pageantry as the Australians' Anzac Day march through London on April 25th and the similar march of Overseas' troops on May 3rd. And there followed all manner of other exciting topics to divert even the normal pitman—what counter-proposals, for example, the German Government might vainly seek to offer and what terrible means of coercion—including the unlimited bombing of Berlin—the Allies might threaten to use unless the German acceptance of the Allied terms were speedy and complete.

But, perhaps, an attempt should be made to picture more fully the issues before the public as they were presented by an "advanced" Radical weekly when Germany, early in June 1919, was facing the demand for a virtually unconditional acceptance of very harsh and, indeed, inexecutable Allied Peace Terms.[1] Reports from Berlin were held to warrant the belief that "the present Government will not sign the Treaty, even under protest, unless there were changes which can be represented as substantial", and attention was drawn in another part of the paper to a report in the *Daily Mail* which seemed to suggest that consideration was being given to day and night bombing of Berlin and the possible use of particularly deadly poison bombs.[2] Notice, too, was taken of the first unsuccessful French attempt to stage a "Rhineland" breakaway from Prussia and Germany, and of the crying injustice of the Austrian Peace Terms. The alleged Allied terms for recognizing Admiral Kolchak in Russia, the pogroms sweeping the great areas of Central Europe which the Allies were trying to set up as a Polish Republic, the intensity of anti-Bolshevist feeling in the United States and the hope of the

---

[1] Cf. *The Nation*, June 7th.
[2] Cf. *Ibid.*: "Sir William Robertson, it was said, and the General of the American Army at Coblentz had been talking over what should be done in case the Germans refuse to sign. . . . It was decided that it would be quite practicable to bomb Berlin both by day and night. Further, it was said, the Americans had ready for the purpose a new kind of poison which would 'wipe out every trace of animal and vegetable life'. All this may or may not be, at the moment true. . . . The writer of the passage in the *Daily Mail* is certainly no monster. . . . And to him it seems quite natural after five years of war, that the whole population of a great city should be extinguished by bombs because a Government has refused to do what his Government wants them to do. . . ."

Montagu Reforms for India[1] make up other overseas parts of the week's story. And even at home, Asquith's crushing retort to the monumental ingratitude of Viscount French's final chapter in *1914*[2] seems to have ranked as more important than the principal news that week from the extended inquiries of the Coal Commission—three pitmen's wives decrying their housing and demanding pit-head baths at all collieries while owners regretted what was called "their failure to institute educational efforts to remove the prejudices of the miners themselves".

In view of many things during the summer and autumn of 1919 —the increasing realization, for example, of the mischievously unrepresentative character of the Parliament that had been placed at Westminster by Lloyd George's "Victory Election", the growing awareness of the dangers of a "Peace Settlement" whose revision had become a matter of urgency even before it could be ratified, and above all, perhaps, the seemingly never-ending upward move of prices—the return to the Front Opposition Bench of figures, nationally and internationally important enough, to give some prospect of a change had become plainly desirable. The fact that Lloyd George had publicly committed himself, in July, to a new "stunt" and a new distraction in a "Trial of the Kaiser" to be staged in London[3] carried implications that appalled even the Royal Family and some of his Conservative colleagues.[4] In these

---

[1] There was no realization yet of the appalling follies General Dyer had committed at Amritsar in the Punjab, even the Secretary of State himself apparently being denied, at this stage, his own opportunity of making an independent judgement of the full facts.

[2] Cf. *The Nation*, June 7th: "Mr. Asquith's speech on Tuesday last, forced from him by the charges made against him . . . ends the controversy. The *Daily Express* says what most people think: 'the next move is up to the soldier, and if he is wise, he will disappear'. . . . Mr. Asquith concluded his speech by quoting from a letter written to him by Lord French from France on May 26th 1915 . . . 'no General in the Field has ever been helped in a difficult task by the Head of his Government as I have been supported and strengthened by your unfailing sympathy and encouragement'."

[3] Cf. *Hansard*, July 3rd. It might be well to quote even so brief a summary as *Whitaker's Almanack* to convey the Prime Minister's tone: "all the territorial adjustments were restorations, and he challenged anyone to point to a single clause which was not in accordance with the stern and highest demands of justice and fair play. The only limit to the justice and wisdom of the reparation claim was the limit of Germany's ability to pay. Those who were responsible for plotting and planning the war would be tried, and he announced, amid loud cheers, that an inter-Allied tribunal would sit in London for the trial of the ex-Kaiser. . . ."

[4] Cf. Harold Nicolson, *King George V*, pp. 336–8, for a few indications of George V's attitude. And by the time the Bill for carrying into effect the Treaty of Peace was debated in the Lords, Curzon was bold enough to venture a semi-

circumstances, the return of Asquith to the Front Opposition Bench should, it would have seemed, have made an appeal to almost everyone in the country. Despite the slow drift Labour-wards from his camp of "advanced men" that had already set in because, in a distracted world, he declined to lead passionate crusading against the Peace Terms or favour revolutionary changes in pit and factory which, as he saw them, would decrease produc-tivity,[1] his dignity and integrity were very widely respected in a nation that still had reproaches of conscience for having allowed him to be "plotted" out of Downing Street in 1916 and even driven from Parliament in 1918. Yet as Asquith's return to the Front Bench would be a danger-signal both for Lloyd George and Labour, and great efforts to prevent it might be expected, unusual caution had to be exercised in selecting his by-election opportunity. Ultimately, despite the dangers of delay, Asquith waited until the beginning of 1920, when the Paisley Liberal Association deter-mined to invite him to fill the place left vacant by the death of one of the thirty or so "Independent Liberals".

The Paisley election certainly decided some of the history of the 1920s though, of course, the over-long deferment of Asquith's return strengthened the position of Labour as the main alternative to the Coalition, the more so as it could claim to have done better in by-elections than the "Independent Liberals".[2] Yet there were still undoubted chances for Asquith in the occasional fury against Labour, called out, in the "general public", by some particularly obnoxious or irresponsible strike-action or strike-threat—the abortive "lightning" police strike, for example of August 1919 with a sympathetic London Tube strike in support;[3] the "lightning" railway-strike of September-October 1919 which, thanks to eager "volunteer labour", quite failed to effect the

repudiation of the Prime Minister to the effect that it by no means followed from the Treaty that the trial of the ex-Kaiser would take place in London.
[1] Cf. *The Nation*, July 5, 1919, for one acid comment from the "advanced": "Mr. Asquith's speeches at Leeds with all their lucidity and felicity of language, make depressing reading. . . . Liberal prophets who are dumb upon the character of the peace, who have no condemnation for the Russian crime, no programme of social reconstruction for the people of this country, and nothing but the ancient verbal rotundities for Ireland ('a full, a prompt, and an adequate settle-ment') had best say as little as possible. The betrayal of every Liberal principle, including Free Trade, by Liberal Ministers during the war is not and cannot be forgotten."
[2] Cf. *Whitaker's Almanack, 1921*, p. 465, for "the strong position on borough councils" also established by Labour in November 1919.
[3] *Ibid.*, 1920, pp. 414-15.

hoped-for paralysis of the country;[1] and, finally, the continuous manœuvring of the pitmen's leaders to impose Nationalization upon an unconvinced country by threats of "direct action" on the part of a Triple Alliance of pitmen, railwaymen, and transport-workers, backed by the entire weight of the T.U.C.[2] Against the Coalition, too, a very massive case, in the Asquithian style, could be made out, and if the ex-Prime Minister appreciated to the full the damning indictment provided in Maynard Keynes's *The Economic Consequences of the Peace*, his own experience led him rather to stress such things as the increasingly dangerous aspect of affairs in Ireland and the perilous financial position, due to vast Government expenditure and enormous military commitments from Murmansk and Archangel to Jerusalem and Baghdad. Paisley electors, too, complaining of the never-ending problem of the cost of living, could be warned that the position, aggravated already by some subtly-concealed Protectionism, would become much worse if the full Protectionist plan, cherished among the great Conservative majority of the Coalition, were imposed.

By the end of January 1920, Asquith's candidature, opposed by a Labour nominee and by a Coalition Unionist, was fast becoming the leading topic of the political commentators. The Radical *Nation*, whose editor was committing himself ever more completely to Mines and Railway Nationalization, was not at first enthusiastic for one whom it had failed to prod in its own direction.[3] Even its third weekly comment of January 31st, on Paisley issues, could hardly be called rapturous:[4]

Mr. Asquith has made two important speeches at Paisley which, with his answers to hecklers, outline a Liberal policy both of criticism and construction. He declared a break with the Coalition, to which he left the choice of execution or *felo de se*. And he has also pronounced for a revision of the Treaty, and for peace with Russia. The Treaty was,

[1] *Whitaker's Almanack, 1921*, under September 29th: "Considerable numbers of volunteers came forward and restricted train services were started. Distribution of food and milk proceeded smoothly with aid of fleets of motor lorries."

[2] *Ibid.*, under September 10th: "Trades Union Congress at Glasgow decided by 4,478,000 against 77,000 to reject Government scheme for management of collieries, and to take steps to compel Government to adopt scheme of majority of Coal Commission."

[3] Cf. *The Nation*, January 17, 1920: "Mr. Asquith's willingness to contest Paisley, if Liberal Paisley asks him, is, no doubt an event. . . . But even so, is an Asquith candidature wise?", and *Ibid.*, January 24, 1920: "if a fight with Labour is engaged, we strongly hope that Mr. Asquith's part in it will be both critical and constructive".

[4] *Ibid.*, January 31, 1920, under "WHAT MR. ASQUITH CAN SAY".

he said, "impossible" to carry out, and we assume therefore that Mr.
Asquith will actively promote the business of re-drafting it. The ideal
of foreign policy he described as the conversion of the old State system
into a "true international democratic polity" based on "self-determination". That language carries far. It, among other things, means that
Liberalism must give Egypt and Ireland the power to decide their own
form of State life. . . . Mr. Asquith also pronounced against Conscription, favoured a "drastic reduction" of armaments, and supported the
withdrawal of our troops from Russia. . . . On constitutional and Home
policy Mr. Asquith proposed . . . a small consultative Second Chamber
proceeding partly from the Commons and partly from nomination. . . .
He favoured proportional representation, or the alternative vote, and
was against an "Imperial Parliament". In taxation he was willing to
inquire into the case for a capital levy, . . . accepted the special dealing
with war fortunes and declared for the taxation of land values, now, as
always, the passionately pursued ideal of Scottish Radicalism. He
opposed protective duties. . . . The programme, though incomplete on
its social side, is Radical, and it is safe to say that Scotland would not
have looked at anything less. . . . Mr. Asquith spoke of land nationalisation as a red herring—a rather perilous phrase. But for the moment,
men's eyes are fixed on the more restricted problems of mines and
railways.

It was, indeed, peevish, to say the least, for a nominally Liberal
journal to try and force an ex-Prime Minister, endeavouring to
reconstruct his party's fortunes and his own from the lowest
point of abasement for generations, to take on not merely the far-
reaching Radical commitments he had accepted but all manner of
further sweeping commitments at home and abroad. It might be
easy for a Labour candidate, with no real expectation of having to
take personal responsibility for the consequences of his most
"advanced" policies, to accept everything *The Nation* desired and
much more. But one who had been a British Prime Minister for
nearly nine years and might be charged with heavy responsibilities
once more had not merely to be cautious about Mines and Railway
Nationalization. He had to remember that to shout for an instant
and unconditional recognition of the blood-stained Bolshevik
Dictatorship was to abandon the hope of obtaining some compensation for confiscated British property, some acknowledgement
of Russian war-debts, and some security against the advance of
Red execution-squads to Archangel. But even *The Nation* was
finally overcome by the spectacle of the ex-Prime Minister, aided
by his remarkable daughter, battling with sustained courage and
equanimity against the most formidable odds, a spectacle, indeed,

that was arousing nation-wide sympathy for him. On February 14th, two days after the polling had ended though the result was not to be available until February 25th, *The Nation* printed this report of the contest:

> Mr. Asquith conducted his campaign with great energy. It was the hardest electoral battle of his career, and he fought it with a courtesy and serenity of temper that won admiration from friend and foe. The Paisley programme which he unfolded in a series of masterly speeches is admirable on the critical side but weak constructively. . . . He is out of sympathy with the new economics, and to nationalization of the mines he was adamantine. . . . But he wants labour to have a share in the control of what he called their "joint adventure". . . . After a week's campaigning Mr. Asquith, helped by his brilliant daughter, had made a great impression . . . the Labour workers were very depressed. Then came a Labour revival . . . with the decision of the United Irish League to support Mr. Biggar; it was strengthened by three trenchant speeches from Mr. Ramsay MacDonald, deepened by a profoundly moving speech by Mr. Smillie. Up to the close of the poll Labour men were very confident. . . . The possibility of a Labour victory must not be excluded. . . . Great efforts were made by Labour and the Tories to create prejudice [among the "16,000 women on the register"] against Mr. Asquith on account of his former antagonism to women's suffrage. . . . Mr. Asquith's policy is sound but it is not inspiring. His demeanour in "this dark and difficult adventure" was irreproachable.

The polling results for which the politicians had to wait anxiously for almost a fortnight (owing to the need, soon to be ended, of getting in the Service men's votes from abroad) were thus declared: Asquith, 14,736; Biggar (Labour), 11,902; McKean (Coalition Unionist), 3795.[1] Asquith's convincing victory, won against such odds, made a number of things relatively certain. It was plain, for example, that Labour's attempt to annex the Liberal vote without the slightest consideration even for "Independent Liberal" politicians as eminent as Asquith would not succeed either as rapidly or as completely as some Labour optimists had been hoping.[2] Indeed, if Labour wanted to have its professions

---

[1] Cf. *Whitaker's Almanack, 1921*, p. 228.

[2] Cf. *Ibid.*, pp. 226 and 463, for the Spen Valley by-election of December 20, 1919, whose result announced on January 3, 1920, had apparently showed Labour's ability to exclude even the Asquithian ex-Home Secretary, Sir John Simon, if suitably helped by the Coalition. The figures were: Tom Myers, Labour, 11,962; Sir John Simon, Liberal, 10,244; Col. Fairfax, Coalition Liberal, 8134. But these figures, despite the jubilations of the *Daily Herald*, did not prevent Sir John Simon from ejecting Labour in 1922 and remaining Spen Valley's member till 1940.

of anxiety to turn out the Coalition at the first possible moment taken seriously, there would be no alternative to the establishment of some kind of co-operation with Asquith. What made this thought the more disturbing to Labour stalwarts was the fact that Asquith's return was bound to have a profound effect on the bulk of the Coalition Liberals in the House, whose constituency Associations, if not always the members themselves, were aching for a "Liberal reunion". And, of course, if Liberal reunion were arranged even on a part of the field of politics, Liberal members would count as over 160 against Labour's 70 or less, and all the rejoicing over having achieved the position of alternative Government as "His Majesty's Opposition" would seem to have been premature. Meanwhile Lloyd George and Bonar Law, it was plain, would have to consider the effects of Asquith's achievement from another angle. To prevent Coalition Liberalism from flowing back to the parent stream, the notorious "Fusion" plan for fusing Coalition Liberalism and Unionism into a new "Centre Party" was pressed with determination for some time. But "Fusion" shall wait for the next chapter, and this chapter shall end with *The Nation*, in gratitude for Lloyd George's thorough discomfiture, almost ready to support Asquith again. Here are short extracts from its issues for February 28th and March 6th:

Mr. Asquith bearing on his back the fortunes of the Liberal Party has accomplished his Aeneid, "with a bit over". His great poll of 14,736 votes . . . was reaped from many quarters. . . . Mr. Asquith and the Liberal Party thus avenge themselves fully for the trick of the Coupon . . . and the Coalition which then drove every rival from the field, is already reduced to "freak" candidates unable to poll an eighth of the electorate, and compelled to forfeit their deposit of £150. From "freak" candidates to a "freak" Prime Minister is only a step as things go in these days. . . . In the House of Commons, no doubt, the Coalitionists will huddle together like frightened sheep. But frightened sheep are easily stampeded. Little moral force attaches to Mr. George's personality, and there is universal speculation on what he will do next and what port he may seek in a storm.

Mr. Asquith's return to Westminster was turned into something of a triumphal progress by the crowds. . . . Mr. Asquith's presence at Westminster can work no miracles but it will, we have no doubt, correct some of the grosser faults which Mr. George has added. . . . The force of experience and authority will have weight. . . . There is a third feature of Georgian politics. That is the appalling traffic in "honours" . . . in two years, Mr. Lloyd George, the ex-democrat, has created over eighty new peerages—a little House of Lords in itself. Some of these new magnates of England are men of extraordinary wealth, and of no record at all in politics, science, the arts, or even the constructive side of industry. Why then do they appear in the legislature? What is the nature of their "services" and to whom are they rendered? As for the House of Commons, what corner of it remains unvisited by the unceasing deluge of Privy Councillorships, baronetcies, knighthoods and orders? . . . The course which the country pursues depends on the will of one of the most variable of the race of opportunists. And that is why Mr. Asquith has been called back again.

CHAPTER XIV

1920

"The feature of the Turkish Treaty is the unmeasured aggrandisement of Greece, Her Empire in Europe will now stretch unbroken from the Adriatic to the Black Sea, and will include a big amalgam of subject races, Albanians, Bulgarians and Turks. Even more dangerous to her and to us all . . . is the attribution to her of Smyrna with a big hinterland. . . . The Turkish Treaty is said to be a success for Great Britain because (1) the control of the Straits will be chiefly naval and (2) because we have set up a puppet Government at Constantinople. . . . The only result, however, is that this palpably foreign régime in Constantinople wields power no further than our naval guns can carry. Signor Nitti, fresh from presiding over the Supreme Council, has stated his views frankly. He predicts a war in Asia Minor to which Italy will contribute neither a soldier nor a lira."

> *The Nation*, May 1, 1920, reports a prophecy ominous for Lloyd George.

"After the Prime Minister's speech to Mr. Thomas's deputation, the people of Great Britain have no excuse for misunderstanding the meaning or the gravity of the Government's quarrel with the people of Ireland. It is no longer necessary or indeed possible, to pretend that it is merely to protect policemen—victims of a cruel and depraved vendetta—that we ship soldiers, tanks, aeroplanes . . . across the Irish Sea. These are military measures, the reply to the successful campaign of Sinn Fein . . . the policemen are to the Government an incident in the larger issue of our claim to rule Ireland. We are moving . . . to war."

> *The Nation*, June 26, 1920, infuriates many by making too light of Sinn Fein "Murders".

"We are by no means disposed to join in the conventional attack on the *Daily Herald*. It has had a hard road to hoe. . . . Its method has often been below its mission. . . . Its director has indeed professed ideal aims. . . . But these were rarely reflected in the columns of his journal. The *Herald* was not over-candid about its news. . . . It was not merely for this strike or that strike, it was for all strikes; and it was impossible to dissociate these tactics from its uncritical attraction for Bolshevism . . . it should not have given its enemies the chance to say that, in

allowing Zaghlul Pasha and the Indian Home Rulers to subscribe heavily to its funds, it had taken a fee for their advocacy.
. . . Still more unwise were Mr. Meynell's and even Mr. Lansbury's deals with the Russian Government."

The Nation, September 18, 1920, on Lansbury's *Daily
Herald.*

FOR many years Liverpool had represented an important element of Conservative strength. Even in the crash of 1906, when every one of the nine Parliamentary seats in Manchester and Salford had been lost, though eight had been held previously, five of Liverpool's seats had been retained. And by the end of 1910, Liverpool's Conservatism held eight of the nine City seats besides having helped to regain others, like Bootle and Birkenhead, in Liverpool's sphere of influence. The reason for Conservatism's strength in Liverpool was hardly lack of money or suitable candidates among their Merseyside opponents—such Liberal names and fortunes as those of the Holts, Rathbones, Booths, Muspratts and, above all, W. H. Lever (from 1917, Lord Leverhulme) were ample testimony to that.[1] It would seem, indeed, that the never-ending stream of "poor Irish" who, for a century and a half, had entered England by Liverpool and often enough contrived to stay there, as the Irish Nationalist representation of the Scotland Division since 1885 appeared to show,[2] had something to do with the phenomenon. Certainly, labouring Liverpool of the native and Protestant brand, rallying to defend its standards, its religion and, on occasion, it claimed, its very livelihood, had little use for "Irish agitation" and Home Rule and much inclination, instead, to Orangeism, anti-Ritualism,[3] and the powerful Conservative Workingmen's Association.

Here is not the place to discuss how the remarkable "Boss" Salvidge, joining this Association in 1885 at the age of twenty-two and becoming its Chairman in 1892, built up, in the course of becoming Managing Director of Bent's Brewery, a unique political machine, with twenty-six branch-clubs and eight thousand members, that gave him a controlling voice in Liverpool's local and Parliamentary life for many years. Eschewing

---

[1] Cf. S. Salvidge, *Salvidge of Liverpool*, p. 19, however, for what the Home Rule split had done: "in Liverpool such traditionally Liberal families as the Brocklebanks, Gaskells, Ismays, Browns, Gambles, and Oultons transferred their allegiance to Chamberlain's Liberal Unionists".

[2] Cf. *Who's Who, 1914*, p. 1571, under T. P. O'Connor, for the Irish Nationalist, who represented the division, often unopposed, from 1885 to his death when "Father of the House" in November 1929.

[3] Cf. S. Salvidge, *Salvidge of Liverpool*, p. 46, for the astonishing strength of the feeling against the "Romanizers" of the Church of England by 1903: "Organizations with titles such as the Protestant Thousand, the Independent Protestant Party, and the Protestant Electoral Federation sprang into existence and put forward their own champions at the City Council elections. . . ."

Parliamentary honours himself, if not those of the Liverpool City Council and the National Union of Unionist Associations, Salvidge had yet been able to render indispensable constituency services to such prominent colleagues of the Prime Minister as Lord Chancellor Birkenhead, a Liverpool M.P. from 1906 to 1918, and Bonar Law, M.P. for Bootle from 1911 to 1918, while the Prime Minister, too, had received his help in the matter of War Liquor Controls. If, therefore, the idea of "Fusion" was put to Salvidge at a small private gathering in February 1920 of Birkenhead, Austen Chamberlain, Winston Churchill, the Prime Minister, and himself, it was as to one who was regarded as holding a key-position in constituency Conservatism and some special claims to Bonar Law's attention. Salvidge's own account of his contribution to the discussions, and what followed, is worth some quotation:[1]

> When it came to my turn, I opened by stating that whether the proposed fusion was or was not accomplished at the present time, I was certain that in the years ahead governments would necessarily partake of a coalition character. Socialists would coalesce with extreme Radicals, Irish Nationalists and Sinn Feiners. Unionists would find it necessary to coalesce with moderate Liberals, and perhaps with patriotic Labour . . . if fossilized Toryism continued to dominate the Party to which I belonged, it was doomed . . . with tact and firmness a permanent combination could be brought about. The last time I had talked with Bonar Law his mind had been moving in the same direction. . . .

Ably engineered as the "Fusion Plan" was, and with the strategic advantage of having obtained Salvidge's important assistance from within the heart of constituency Conservatism, it had, before long, to be temporarily laid aside. Bonar Law and his Chief Whip were far from convinced that the surrender of Conservatism's special identity should be conceded in the interests, presumably, of the political future of Lloyd George, his Coalition Liberals, and "patriotic Labour". If the external situation had been more immediately threatening than it was—with Germany, perhaps, still representable as a menace, Russian Bolshevism nearer real ability to make bad trouble for "British Imperialism" and the two seeking, with some prospect of success, to fish in Ireland's troubled waters and those of Trade Union extremism, "Fusion" might have come nearer success than it did. But anxious

[1] Cf. S. Salvidge, *Salvidge of Liverpool*, pp. 181–2.

though the situation might be in many quarters,[1] some Conservatives did not see how it would help matters to break up their own party by provoking a "Die-Hard" revolt against "Fusion" under Lloyd George. Their own party, they held, should be ready and united to take over from the Prime Minister directly he claimed, as he sometimes seemed inclined to do, that the Coalition in its existing shape was too much for him or directly he sought to impose policies which Conservatism could never accept.

The heavy attack on "Fusion", too, from all "progressive" quarters did not help. It was specially disconcerting for some of the Prime Minister's backers to find the effects of a hostile Press bombardment, ranging from the Asquithians of the *Westminster Gazette* to the "Reds" of Lansbury's Bolshevik-defending *Daily Herald*, forwarded from among the Coalition Liberals themselves. Here is the mocking *Nation* on the plight of "Fusion" though irritated Asquithians claimed it was often busy on a "Fusion" of its own, a melting down of Radicals into the Socialist mass:[2]

"Check" has been administered to Mr. Lloyd George's proposal to turn the Coalition into a party for himself. . . . At first all went well. Dr. Addison, that Radical stalwart, seems to have led off with the brave decision to dare all for a party devoted to "our great Prime Minister". Dr. Addison's brick was well and truly laid, and Mr. Churchill and Sir Gordon Hewart added others of a similar quality. But from that point the plan of turning Liberalism into a Trust House for Mr. Lloyd George went no further. In fact a frost set in. There were references to principles, to benighted beings who had been Liberals all their lives, to the chance of a revolt among those grovellers, the Liberal Associations, and even to such degraded people as constituents.

But if the idea of "Fusion" and a Centre Party, standing between the "fossilized Die-Hards" of Toryism to the Right and the alleged predatory Triple Alliance near-Bolshevism to the Left,

[1] Cf. *Field-Marshal Sir Henry Wilson, His Life and Diaries*, ii, 219, for the anxieties as the Chief of the Imperial General Staff had seen them at the close of 1919: "The Frocks [leading statesmen in frock-coats] have muddled everything . . . the coming year looks gloomy. We are certain to have serious trouble in Ireland, Egypt and India. . . . At home, those who know best say we are going to have a strike of the Triple Alliance and the Post Office." In January and February 1920, he was bitterly critical of the Cabinet's lack of spirit and decision in face of the "Triple Red Revolutionary strike" and, by April 1920, having learned, perhaps, that while "Fusion" had been discussed by Lloyd George with Conservatives, unofficial discussions with Labour had been attempted, too, he wrote: "I become increasingly suspicious of Lloyd George and whether he is not trying to shepherd England into class war."
[2] Cf. *The Nation*, March 20, 1920, which also gives the information that "the secret was betrayed to *The Times* and the *Glasgow Herald*".

was to be revived, *The Nation* itself bore some of the responsibility. It was not merely Coalition Liberal big-industrialists but Asquithians of the most Radical pre-1914 brands who objected strongly to Massingham's allowing some of his Guild Socialist contributors to go on campaigning for a Nationalization which was, by market-standards, semi-confiscation or more. Of course, quite a number of the Radicals of 1906–14 had begun moving into the Labour camp. Chiozza Money had left a junior Ministership under Lloyd George to fight and lose for Labour in December 1918; Josiah Wedgwood, elected as a Coalition Liberal in 1918, had taken himself and his seat into the Labour camp by joining the I.L.P. in 1919; C. R. Buxton, Noel Buxton, and Charles Trevelyan were three more ex-Radical politicians prepared to fight the next election as Labour men; and, finally, there were those moving in the Labour direction, if not yet arrived, like H. B. Lees-Smith and, as it turned out, Dr. Addison himself, the "Fusion" advocate of 1920.[1] Yet defections like these could be plausibly explained by personal frustrations or personal ambitions,[2] and the bulk of the old party machinery, in the shape of the Liberal and Radical constituency Associations and the Provincial and National Federations, seemed suitably manned, in working order, and capable of making a real struggle to reacquire a powerful political position for "Independent Liberalism". But even the stalwarts of "Independent Liberalism", dreaming of another Asquith Cabinet, were inclined to see some good in Coalition Liberalism after indignantly reading *The Nation*'s "new economics" in which railway-shareholders and colliery-proprietors were told that they were fortunate, indeed, to be offered Nationalization compensation, equivalent to their pre-war dividends, instead of seeing the "organized attack of the Triple Alliance" end some dividends altogether and greatly reduce others. Of course, the fact that the pre-war dividends would buy less than half of what they did in 1914 was not lost on the Asquithians any more than it was on Guild Socialist pitmen and railwaymen. And there was the

[1] Cf. *Who's Who, 1914*, and *Who's Who, 1931* for the careers of all these men as summarized at two important turning-points.

[2] Cf. Lord Wedgwood, *Testament to Democracy*, p. 106, for one of these men confessing this in 1942: "The perpetual preoccupation of every Member of Parliament is the retention of his seat. . . . I pretended to myself that I joined the Labour Party in 1919 in order to teach a more responsive crowd, both inside and outside the House, the immortal doctrines of Henry George; but I was always secretly aware that I wanted also to save my seat in the collapse of the Liberal Party."

further provocation of reading *The Nation*'s semi-approval for the pitmen's notion that they were entitled to forbid the payment of any compensation whatsoever to mineral royalty owners though they were willing to consider "compassionate allowances" in cases of exceptional hardship.[1]

Whether the Triple Alliance of railwaymen, transport-workers, and pitmen would or would not attempt, against virtually all the advice from political Labour, to call a paralysing strike in order to force Society to concede—as a first step—Coal Mines Nationalization on the pitmen's own terms, was not fated to be decided until the spring of 1921. Meanwhile, amid constant wage-forcing moves, justified till the turn of prices sharply downwards at the end of 1920 on the ground of the rising cost of living[2] (though, of course, pitmen, railwaymen, and dockers had learned to keep their wages well ahead in the race, Mr. Ernest Bevin, for example, in a famous case before the new Industrial Court, claiming £4 8s. 0d. a week with "certain other advantages" as the dockers' basic pay),[3]

[1] Cf. *The Nation*, March 20, 1920, reporting, altogether apart from the Nationalization demand, that "the movement of the miners for an increase of 3s. per day for men and 1s. 6d. for boys has progressed rapidly to a critical stage . . . the South Wales men threaten to strike on their own for £2 a week [extra]", and yet upbraiding Lloyd George for preparing "in alliance with the Tories and the Central Liberals" what it called "a naked encounter between Capital and Labour". "Mr. Lloyd George," it affirmed, "has declared that the miners' demand is pure Syndicalism in its least attractive aspect. He gives the suggestion, apparently widely held, that this is an indirect attempt to obtain ownership of the mines and to confiscate all the profit derived from them. Nothing is further from the truth. Mr. Hodges' calculations . . . provide for the full payment to the mine-owners of the guaranteed pre-war dividend . . . both in the mines and railways, the shareholders are receiving dividends which they would have no chance of receiving but for the Government guarantee and . . . the war. Had the peace prevailed, the organized attack of the Triple Alliance would have transferred a substantial proportion of those dividends from profits to wages. . . . The miners do not believe in any moral right of the royalty owners. . . ."

[2] Cf. *Whitaker's Almanack, 1922*, p. 839, for a convenient tabulation of the Cost of Living statistics issued monthly by the Ministry of Labour. The percentage increase above July 1914 had reached 100 by May 1918, 150 by June 1920, and 176, the high-point, by November 1920. The figure for December 1920 was down to 169 and for January 1921 to 165. Then came the very sharp falls to 151 in February, 141 in March, and 133 in April though, of course, a dangerous growth of Unemployment since the autumn of 1920 was a far less satisfactory symptom, than the cost of living falls, of the powerful deflationary forces internationally at work.

[3] Cf. *The Nation*, February 7, 1920: "The first public sitting of the Court of Inquiry appointed to investigate the claim of the dock and riverside workers for a minimum daily wage of 16s. was interesting for several reasons. No one knew definitely whether or not the question of shipowners' profits would be admitted as relevant. . . . As to profit in the transport industry, Lord Shaw, the Chairman of the Court, argued plausibly for the elimination of this thorny question. . . . But it was clear from Mr. Bevin's reply that when the employers pleaded

a variety of the most difficult political issues was constantly threatening, not merely to raise "popular" outcries against the Coalition, but even to break it asunder into its component fractions. Thus a biographer of Austen Chamberlain, the politician whose attempts to prevent the Coalition's break-up in 1922 were to cost him the Conservative Leadership and the succession to the Prime Ministership, has held that the first warning cracks came on July 8, 1920 when the Coalition Liberal in charge of India, Edwin Montagu, infuriated the many Conservatives who, disregarding the Hunter Committee's condemnation of General Dyer's conduct at Amritsar in April 1919, persisted in believing, despite the 400 dead and the 1200 injured, that his conduct had saved India from another 1857. The storm of anger that went up from the Conservative Benches when Montagu, thinking, perhaps, rather of India than of Westminster, condemned Dyer outright without even a word of sympathy on his broken career, was certainly phenomenal.[1] And the angry, not content with promptly defeating the Government in the Lords,[2] went on to organize the two years' vigil against what they considered the culpable sacrifice of British interests that was to play so big a part in bringing the Coalition down.[3]

Perhaps, before turning to the Irish situation where the Prime Minister was well aware of a Conservative readiness to revolt against himself if he allowed "advanced" opinion to dictate a "surrender" of Ulster to Sinn Fein "gunmen", a short notice should be given to the long controversy still proceeding on a British Government's proper attitude towards the Russian Bolsheviks. The "advanced" were undoubtedly too ready to make

inability to pay and suggested that the consumers must bear the burden, profits must be examined. . . . Mr. Bevin opened brilliantly . . . with a ruthless exposure of the notorious failure of shipowners and dock authorities to realize their social and human obligations."

[1] Cf. *Life and Letters of Austen Chamberlain*, ii, 152–3. Of course, Montagu reaped some praise from the "advanced" but his relations with the Prime Minister and the Conservative side of the Cabinet never seem to have recovered after this—to them—"maladroit" handling.

[2] Cf. *The Nation*, July 24, 1920, for a comment on the voting, 129 to 86: "The division was on a vote-catching resolution, which, without expressly acquitting the General, censored the 'conduct' of his case as 'dangerous' to the 'preservation of order in face of rebellion'. This virtually accepts the legend of Dyer as the saviour of India and is therefore well calculated to do the maximum of harm to our rule there."

[3] Cf. *Life and Letters of Austen Chamberlain*, ii, 153: "This debate was the first step in the break-up of the Coalition, and . . . the critics of Mr. Montagu, began to act together on other questions."

or accept excuses for the Bolshevik Dictatorship—and, perhaps, the sense that, in doing so, they were striking blows against what they considered to be the worst aspects of British and French Imperialism did not prove a deterrent. At any rate, by the spring of 1920, when the Bolsheviks had crushed those internal enemies[1] who, on the score of their readiness to hold to the British and French alliance and to acknowledge war- and other debts, had obtained some British and French support, the case for establishing a *modus vivendi* with the Bolsheviks, if it were possible, had become overwhelming. A first tentative step in this direction had been taken on February 24, 1920 when it was announced that the liberated "Border States" would be supported in war against the Bolsheviks only if they were attacked in their own territory and that trade with Soviet Russia would be encouraged even if recognition were denied until Bolshevik methods and diplomatic conduct conformed "to those of all civilized Governments".[2] Since the "advanced", at any rate, took this as a Government admission that Winston Churchill's anti-Bolshevism[3] was being abandoned and presumed too readily that the Soviets would honour, when the fortune of war was with them, all the guarantees for the "Border States" they had offered when defeated, the summer of 1920 was destined to be a time of some disillusion.

Reluctant, of course, as the "advanced" were to admit it, the Bolsheviks outdistanced everybody, even the Prime Minister, when it came to "lack of scruple" though it must be confessed that the Soviets had had a good deal of provocation from Poland's ruling classes and their almost incredible ambition to take their Polish State hundreds of miles east of the ethnographical frontier of the "Curzon Line".[4] Relying on French moral and material

[1] Cf. *Whitaker's Almanack, 1921*, p. 470, for a section on Russia and the "Border States" with entries like these: "(1919). Nov. 15th. Omsk, seat of Admiral Koltchak's Government, captured by Bolshevists. . . . Dec. 13th. Reds captured Kharkoff and Poltava from Denikin. 17th. The Reds captured Kieff. . . . (1920). Jan. 9th. Bolshevists reported that remnants of Koltchak's armies had surrendered. 27th. General Yudenitch arrested. . . . Feb. 7th. Admiral Koltchak and his Prime Minister shot at Irkutsk by Revolutionary Committee. 8th. Bolshevist troops captured Odessa. 12th. Red armies opened offensive against Whites on Archangel front. . . ."

[2] Cf. *Annual Register*, 1920, pp. 193–4, for this pronouncement from the Supreme Council of Allied and Associated Powers meeting in London which, in regard to trade, had already been anticipated in Lloyd George's speaking in Parliament.

[3] Cf. *Ibid.*, for the typical anti-Bolshevik tone, almost as depressingly partisan as that of the pro-Bolshevik "advanced".

[4] Cf. *Ibid.*, p 197, for the admission even of an anti-Bolshevik source.

support, the Poles had actually undertaken a deep advance into Soviet-controlled territory when the Bolsheviks began the massive counter-attack which, during some July and August weeks, seemed likely to take them to Warsaw and to Sovietize Poland. It was, naturally, not by pure chance that the Kamenev-Krassin Mission was most active in Britain during the whole manœuvre, Krassin seeking to persuade British businessmen, as well as British Labour, of their vast export opportunities in Russia and Kamenev aiming, with the *Daily Herald*'s help, to make it as difficult as possible for aid from the West to reach Poland in time to avert Sovietization.[1] Probably the most notorious episodes in the whole strange story were Kamenev's attempt to hoodwink Lloyd George as to the true nature of the terms the Russian invaders were trying to dictate; the *Daily Herald*'s busy whipping-up of a Council of Action, ready, it appeared, to threaten a general strike rather than permit intervention against Russia; the astonishing allegations that followed against the *Daily Herald* itself;[2] the subsequent termination of the Kamenev Mission; and, finally, the complete Polish triumphs against the over-extended Russians that certainly left some exponents of the Council of Action with much to explain. Nor were matters much improved for the "advanced" when the *Daily Herald*, despite its previous indignant denials, asked its own readers to decide whether it should accept an offer of £75,000 in Russian gold to guarantee its continued publication.[3]

The "Irish question", of course, it was, producing, on both sides, brutalities such as had not been known within the British Isles for over a century, that gave the politicians their toughest problems of 1920. In retrospect, it seems difficult to agree that, given the 1920 balance of forces in Britain and the world, Lloyd George was in a position to offer Irish national sentiment a more generous compromise than Dominion status for the Twenty-six Counties with some tenuous links left with the Six Ulster Counties, capable, if there was good management, of becoming something more. The subsequent career of a Michael Collins or a de Valera

---

[1] Cf. *Annual Register*, 1920, p. 209.
[2] Cf. *Ibid.*, p. 97.
[3] Cf. *The Nation*, September 18, 1920, on "THE CASE OF THE *DAILY HERALD*" for grave criticism from the most influential of the "advanced organs", beginning: "The directors of the *Daily Herald* have finally refused the subsidy of £75,000" and revealing that the Egyptian Zaghlul Pasha and the Indian Home Rulers had already been permitted to subscribe heavily to its funds."

is ample proof that, soon or late, the Sinn Fein claim, on the ground of "self-determination", to order the unconditional surrender of British authority in Ireland and to abet, if not to organize, violence, bound to culminate in wholesale arson and assassination, had to be compromised. Yet if the facts of political life gradually penetrated the dourest Sinn Fein fanaticism, not much of the credit can be given to Britain's "progressive" and "advanced" politicians and journalists anxious, it was complained, as always, to emphasize the shortcomings of their own Government and the merits of Britain's opponents. Even Asquith, in calling for an all-Ireland Dominion, went well beyond the immediate possibilities and ultimately, under pressure from behind, he went so far as denouncing the unofficial anti-Sinn Fein reprisals, undertaken by the police,[1] as constituting "the most deplorable and scandalous chapter even in the annals of Irish Government". "Labour", meanwhile, had been even more inclined to slur over the deplorable murder-record of Sinn Fein's revolver-desperadoes when not laying the entire blame for their existence on the original "High Treason" of Carson and Smith, backed by the whole Conservative Party. And while giving some countenance to the anarchy on the Irish railways and in Irish industry, fomented by Sinn Fein, Labour nevertheless loudly claimed that, if entrusted with power, it would find the best solution of the Irish problem, thanks to the mutual trust and confidence of British and Irish trade unionists.[2]

---

[1] Cf. *Ibid.*, October 9, 1920. This "advanced" organ had been attacking the R.I.C. recruits and auxiliaries, obtained mainly in Britain, and christened "Black and Tans" by their enemies. It hardly made sufficient allowance for the "murders" of policemen by Sinn Fein.

[2] Cf. *Annual Register*, 1920, pp. 66—9, for some typical "bounce" from J. H. Thomas, at the head of a N.U.R. delegation of June 3rd, as he averred that the Irish problem would be solved from the industrial side rather than the political. The Prime Minister retorted that Trade Unionism was entering an entirely new sphere when trying to affect political decisions by threatening to disorganize the country's industries and gave 48 as the number of recent police murders and 120 as the number of attempted murders. Some time later, Thomas reappeared with the whole N.U.R. Executive and an Irish Railwaymen's delegation to propose that the Government should stop sending further troops and munitions to Ireland (for the railwaymen to carry) and, in return, the railwaymen would appeal to the Irish people to turn against crimes of violence and, during the truce interval that might be expected to result, there could be a meeting of the British and Irish T.U.C.s. The Prime Minister naturally refused to abdicate in favour of Mr. Thomas, making it plain that the Irish railways (and railwaymen's pay) would be closed if troops and their supplies were refused transport but offering to "meet anybody representing Irish political thought" including Sinn Fein.

But, perhaps, instead of dealing with J. H. Thomas's "bounce" on behalf of his Irish N.U.R. members or Mr. Henderson's "peace mission to Ireland", it would be most revealing of "advanced opinion" to quote *The Nation*'s view of Ireland in the autumn of 1920. It was to play into the Government's hands to wax so indignant about the "misdeeds" of the Auxiliary Police (the "Black and Tans") as to forget the numerous Sinn Fein "murders" that had provoked them. But the most authentic "advanced Radical" voice in Britain shall be allowed to speak for itself:[1]

For every hour this barbarian force remains in existence, the British Government remains outside the civilized order. It can say nothing about Lenin's Chinese executioners. . . . For it has come to this, that we have raised a mercenary force in England—it being no longer possible to recruit for the R.I.C. in Ireland—among demobilized officers out of a job, that we give these men a sovereign a day with their keep, and let them understand, by one kind of *sous-entendu* or another, that as soon as they find themselves on the other side of the Irish Sea they may kill, wound, burn and loot as they please. . . . The Government have deliberately recruited for service in Ireland a body of men to whom Ireland means nothing more than the opportunity for violence. . . . They are called the "Black and Tans" but their real name is the "Black Hundreds". . . . The Government claim the right to act in Ireland precisely as Germany acted in Belgium and France. But they have never proclaimed war on Ireland or asked Parliament to sanction such an enterprise. If this claim is tolerated now, where is it to stop? To-day it is the peasants of Balbriggan or Fermoy who watch their homes burn, while their children cry in the street from terror of bayonet and bomb. Whose turn will it be to-morrow? There is no reason why Mr. George's Government, seizing the occasion of an unpopular or a violent strike, should not let loose such a force in this country. . . . Are the murders and burnings of Fermoy, Tuam, Balbriggan, Trim, Mallow, and scores of towns and villages, are the midnight raids on houses from which men and boys are taken to be bayonetted and shot, at the caprice of this or that scoundrel in uniform, are the evictions of hundreds of peasants at the point of the bayonet, are all the hideous methods of terrorism and espionage known to a political police bidden by its employers to forget the law—are these methods repugnant or not to "the humanity and the justice and the democratic principles of the English people"?

In certain circumstances, this eloquent if unbalanced fury from Massingham and J. L. Hammond, repeated week after week and widely requoted in anti-British publications abroad, might have

[1] *The Nation*, October 2, 1920.

had dangerous consequences for the Coalition. But Sinn Fein's revolver-gangs could always be trusted to supply their opponents with appropriate counter-matter, and never, perhaps, more than in the notorious Dublin murders of November 21st when fourteen Army officers and ex-officers were done to death in their lodgings, some in the presence of their wives.[1] The landing of the unfortunate men's bodies in England, and the solemn funeral processions of November 26th to Westminster Abbey and Westminster Catholic Cathedral fortified general anti-Sinn Fein sentiments further, and a climax seemed to be reached by the end of the month when the newspapers of successive days reported unprecedented anti-assassination precautions at Downing Street, the bloodiest Sinn Fein ambushing of Auxiliary Police yet effected, and the extension of Sinn Fein incendiarism to the Liverpool area.[2] The Radicals of *The Nation* still, indeed, ventured to persist with palliation and counter-attack which even the mass of the *Manchester Guardian* readership found it difficult to stomach. The fourteen murdered men of "Bloody Sunday", it was asserted, were largely concerned with British "intelligence" and courts-martial; there had been the most barbaric reprisals yet when fire had been opened on a great Dublin football-crowd at Croke Park; incendiarism at Liverpool was only Sinn Fein's retort to military incendiarism in Ireland where, indeed, it reached a notorious height at Cork after a bloody new ambush on December 11th.[3] This line of argument was too extreme altogether for Asquith who, however, persisted with less provocative and ultimately more dangerous criticism, backed by the *Manchester Guardian*, the *Daily News*, the *Westminster Gazette*, and an increasingly representative and influential Peace with Ireland Council.[4] Yet, for the

---

[1] Cf. *Annual Register*, 1920, p. 134.

[2] Cf. *Field-Marshal Sir Henry Wilson, His Life and Diaries* for the irate comments of the Chief of the Imperial General Staff, who wanted the "Black and Tan" reprisals stopped but Martial Law proclaimed instead: ". . . Downing Street's answer to outrage was to build a fortification round the place, whereas they ought to arrest the Council of Action, kick out Krassin and his vile brood, declare martial law in Ireland and stamp the vermin out." The full story of Sinn Fein's relations with Soviet Russia has not, of course, been published, and both parties to the transaction had, and have, very good reasons for secrecy.

[3] Cf. *Whitaker's Almanack*, 1922, p. 475, under December 11, 1920, for a succinct account: "Twelve cadets wounded, one fatally, in ambush near Cork. Series of reprisal fires later occurred in Cork, principal public buildings and business premises being destroyed and damage estimated at £3,000,000."

[4] Cf. *The Nation*, November 27th, for this organization calling its first mass-meeting at the Albert Hall with Asquith as one of the speakers, billed for

time, Asquith himself could be attacked and even derided by both Bonar Law and Lloyd George, and the great Coalition majority assume the appearance of being more firmly knit than ever. It was in the November proceedings on the Government of Ireland Bill for setting up two Parliaments in Ireland that Bonar Law condemned Asquith roundly for pouring ridicule on a measure which went farther, he claimed, in according genuine Irish self-government than the pre-war Asquithian measure. And when Lloyd George, speaking on December 3rd, at a dinner given in his honour at the great Conservative shrine of the Constitutional Club, denounced not only the "murder campaign" but Asquith's attitude towards it, he gave such unbounded pleasure that prospects of a Conservative breakaway from the Coalition seemed to vanish. As one summarizer put it:[1]

He said that a well-organized, highly subsidized murder campaign was going on in Ireland . . . but he heard of no demonstration to be addressed by Mr. Asquith to denounce it. All the execration was for the victims and their avengers. For the honour of his party he declared that faction did not represent Liberalism. Slander always had a big circulation. . . . .

Of course, it hardly proved possible to persist on this line very far into 1921. But, perhaps, the time has come to turn, for a space, from Ireland in order to examine the political contentions of the autumn and winter of 1920–1 on economic matters. It will be remembered that pitmen, after a war which had greatly improved their bargaining power, had found immediate post-war conditions in a coal-starved world even more favourable. By a species of strike-ultimatum, they had forced the Prime Minister's hand in February 1919 and had secured the heavy packing of the Sankey Commission with their nominees and ultimately what they claimed was a "majority award" for Nationalization which the Prime

Saturday afternoon, December 4th. The mere half-dozen other names available to impress the public show the infant character of the organization when compared with the long string of famous names already available for advertisement in *The Nation* of January 6, 1921, names mainly Liberal, Radical, and Fabian, but including also Chesterton, Belloc, and General Gough as well as the invaluable names of two Conservative M.P.s to flaunt in the most conspicuous positions—those of Lord Henry Cavendish Bentinck as Chairman and of Oswald Mosley as Hon. Secretary. Bentinck had shown much personal sympathy for the Asquiths, and Mosley's break with official Conservatism must already have been a possibility.

[1] Cf. *Annual Register*, 1920, p. 139

Minister, it was alleged, refused to honour. By the summer of 1920, more self-confident than ever, they not only had no use for the species of Mines Decontrol for which Ministers were trying to prepare the way by offering the large advantages of the Mines Industry Act, but were planning another ultimatum and obtaining the blessing of the T.U.C. and of their transport and railway confederates of the "Triple Alliance". This time the Government was required to share the alleged sixty-six millions of surplus profits on coal-exports—a figure which the fast-approaching collapse of coal-prices was about to render more than absurd—and allow twenty-seven millions for increased miners' pay and thirty-three millions for lower coal-prices to the home-consumer. In the final negotiations before work ceased in all mines on October 16th, the affectation of public-spirited concern for the poor consumer at home was abandoned[1] though, in point of fact, the first pinch of nearly forgotten winter-distress had already arrived. This was made plain by the Unemployed demonstration of October 18th, the Downing Street rioting that followed, and the assurance that was given to London's Mayors that an elaborate scheme of winter-relief works was being planned.[2]

Throughout the negotiations of September and October 1920, a good deal of "advanced opinion" was taken aback, not merely by the miners' eagerness to budget permanently on the assumption of vast export profits representing the bitterest privation, say, in starving and shivering Vienna,[3] but by their ultimate readiness to refuse the home-consumer even the limited concession of accepting their pay-increases conditionally on firm obligations to increase shrinking output. Indeed, when the railwaymen decided to show their power, too, by ordering the resumption of negotiations with

[1] Cf. J. R. Raynes, *Coal and its Conflicts*, pp. 178–9, for a bitter comment on the mounting tendency to abandon the altruistic pose of Mr. Smillie.

[2] Cf. *Whitaker's Almanack, 1921*, under October 18, 1920. In London, according to *The Nation* of October 9th, "bitter privation" was already being suffered by the dockers while the motor-trade slump at Coventry had created five thousand unemployed there, some of whom were carrying on a "Soviet" agitation. Apart, too, from serious unemployment existing or expected, it was anticipated that "short time will be widespread in the textile and engineering trades".

[3] Cf. *The Nation*, September 4, 1920: "The miners are not demanding that the price of coal shall be reduced to the populations of Europe . . . we are still to drive a hard bargain with the workers of other countries, living in cold and famine. . . .", and *Ibid.*, September 25th: "Do people here realise what a coal famine means for Vienna? . . . thousands of people, having exhausted their dole of fuel, which just cooks a mess of potatoes, will practically give up their chance of life. . . ."

the striking pitmen on pain of a railway stoppage,[1] *The Nation* warned both sets of over-confident operatives that some Ministers were so convinced that the "public" had been hopelessly antagonized that they desired to make this a "fight to a finish".[2] In point of fact, the Prime Minister thought it wise to forward a short-term compromise which granted 2s. per day until January 3, 1921, a temporary sliding-scale of day-increase after that depending on output and ultimately a National Wages Board to operate (in the light of the experience gained during the experimental period) a permanent scheme after March 31st. The price for which peace in the mines for five months had been bought turned out to be unexpectedly severe owing to the collapse of coal-export prices during the period. One set of figures, ultimately presented by the coalowners as evidence for their view of the complete unacceptableness of the men's ideas for the National Wages Board, showed the following f.o.b. export prices: Last quarter of 1920, 83s. 2d.; January 1921, 65s. 4d.; February 1921, 49s. 1d.; March 1921, 43s. 6d.[3] Some official figures to hand by April 1921 showed the guaranteeing Exchequer to have lost on the coal-working of the previous month £5,259,209 even before allowance was made for guaranteed dividends, depreciation, or loan-interest.[4] It was certainly not the kind of calculation with which Ministers felt able to meet the swelling "Anti-Waste" chorus that was becoming one of their principal preoccupations.[5]

But "Anti-Waste" must wait till the next chapter, and here

[1] Cf. J. R. Raynes, *Coal and its Conflicts*, p. 179, for the ultimatum of October 21st from the N.U.R. announcing that the miners' "claims are reasonable and just and should be conceded—forthwith".

[2] Cf. *The Nation*, October 30, 1920: "We believe that the Prime Minister was pressed to accept this as a challenge to constitutional government, and to fight the issue out on a grandiose scale. Happily the temptation to regard the N.U.R. decision as the beginning of Bolshevism was resisted."

[3] Cf. J. R. Raynes, *Coal and its Conflicts*, p. 182, for Mr. Evan Williams, Chairman of the Mining Association, giving these figures to the Prime Minister during the long April conferences at the Board of Trade after the men had called their 1921 strike.

[4] *Ibid.*, pp. 186–7, for the Chancellor of the Exchequer during the same proceedings: "No system, nationalised or otherwise, could carry on upon that basis." And the Statistical Summary of the Mines Department seemed to show that the loudest nationalizers of them all, those in South Wales, had, even in January, such a high wages cost per ton, that 14s. 5·77d. was being lost on every ton they produced.

[5] The surrender in November 1920 of the Wrekin seat to an "Independent", backed by the Northcliffe-Rothermere-Beaverbrook-Bottomley chorus was followed by the more resounding and more humiliating loss of the Dover by-election of January 12, 1921.

attention shall be given to the Emergency Powers Bill of 1920 which was drafted in the summer of 1920 to be ready for passage should the oft-brandished Triple Alliance strike-weapon or even the "general strike" of the "Council of Action" come to be essayed. It was a Bill designed to give the Government emergency powers to make provision for the whole population's elementary needs for food, fuel, water, light, and transport, and in view of the N.U.R.'s aggravation of the already perilous, nation-wide pit-strike of October 1920, it was pushed through fast. Yet sufficient attention was paid to Liberal and Labour criticisms for very important modifications of the original plan to be accepted. Parliament's approval of the declaration of the emergency and the steps taken under it had to be obtained within a week instead of a fortnight; the right to call a strike and to picket was safeguarded; and there was to be no conscription of labour. These were formidable concessions even if Ministers declined to make the Act a short-period, temporary one only, or to accept the delays incident on a Select Committee examination of their proposals or, finally, to take seriously such arguments as that the passage of the Bill would ruin the influence of the moderates in the Labour movement. As it happens, every subsequent Government, including some containing leading critics of the Emergency Powers Act of 1920, has had good reason to be thankful that its principles were placed on the Statute Book without a time-limit and that the pressure for confining it to the actual emergency of the autumn of 1920 was resisted. Yet the "advanced" certainly raised a hostile enough clamour. Here is *The Nation* of October 30th:[1]

The Prime Minister, who has accepted full responsibility for the death of the Lord Mayor of Cork and for the official defence of Irish reprisals, has now appeared as the parent of the Emergency Powers Bill. We dare to say that for three hundred years no British Monarch has asked for such powers to override the law. . . . The title itself is a trick. The Government call it an "Emergency Bill". That would seem to mean that it was framed under the pressure of these anxious days. . . . Nothing of the kind. The Government admit that it was drafted months ago. . . . Yet it was thrust on Parliament at the most critical hour of a great strike, when an effort was being made to compose it, and to create the atmosphere—of peace. It was then forced at top speed through the Commons—a body consisting mainly of capitalists. . . .

[1] In the article entitled "THE LIBERTIES OF ENGLAND" and bearing marks of the hand of J. L. Hammond.

English Radicalism: The End?

Under such a law . . . any striking trade union, or any co-operative society in sympathy with a strike, can be broken up, its funds sequestrated, and its officers put under arrest. In the critical hours of a miners' strike, Mr. Smillie can be . . . tried . . . the *Daily Herald* can be suspended. . . . We imagine that a man talking in a club in favour of a strike of transport workers might be held to be impeding the supply of the necessaries of life, and fined £100 for doing it. Whatever powers the Government might fail to secure under the clause which places the "essentials" of life under their control would descend to them under the general powers they also take for the "preservation of the peace". . . . There need only be a threat of action or an apprehension in the mind of some timid or despotic official . . . to set this tremendous engine going; and, for a week—the original term was a fortnight—their agents may operate it without a word in Parliament to say them nay. . . .

This manner of protest was doubtless too shrill and too un-balanced for most of the "advanced" who had not yet deserted the Asquithian banner. But if they found ever more to complain of in Massingham's conduct of *The Nation*; if they considered he erred in allowing Hammond to pen passages like the above and Brails-ford to stress, often disproportionately,[1] what could be said in favour of Soviet rule in Russia, they, nevertheless, cordially approved his consistent efforts to forward a Liberal-Labour electoral understanding which could be trusted to smash the Coalition at the next Election. Massingham, of course, like many others among the controlling Radical groups of 1906–14, considered that Lloyd George's record from 1916 to 1920 had been a world-disaster. More than that, he feared further disasters yet to come if power were not decisively wrenched, at the first possible moment, from the small group of politicians who had conspired, with Lord Northcliffe's aid, to seize it in December 1916. In Massingham's eyes, every major question in politics had already been seriously mishandled, and matters could only grow worse under the Coalition. A wicked chaos, according to Massingham, had already been made of Anglo-Irish relations; the flagrant injustices of the Peace Treaty and of the monstrously-inflated Reparations demands threatened continuous German crises which would drive Germany ultimately to a desperate throw for Bol-shevism or for a military dictatorship of the Right; Palestine and Mesopotamia were an unceasing drain of British money and men;

---

[1] Cf. *The Nation* of October 30, 1920 for "A FACTORY IN SOVIET RUSSIA" and *Ibid.*, November 13, 1920 for "A SOVIET IN SESSION".

and the rising Nationalisms of Egypt and India had been dangerously antagonized. There were many other perils that faced the world—the Serb-Italian contentions on the Adriatic; the undesirable inflation, thanks to French domination of the Paris Peace Conference, of Poland and the "Little Entente"; the swelling Greek ambitions in Asia Minor faced by the defiant Kemalist Young Turks of Angora with some countenance from Russia; and, finally, the likelihood that a Europe, that had by now departed so far from the high production and exchange standards of 1914, would be unable to set up an adequate peace-time demand for British goods. Only the removal of the Coalition, still lectured and hectored by the "Press Lords"[1] who claimed to have put it into power, would make the beginnings of salvation possible.

It was not, Massingham averred, from the Asquithian Liberals and Radicals that the difficulties came in attempting the electoral arrangement that would spell the doom of the Coalition at the polls. While refusing to make way for Labour, except by agreement, in the numerous rural, residential, and mixed constituencies in which a Liberal still normally stood more chance of winning a Coalition seat, they were virtually ready to negotiate on a basis almost certain to leave Labour in the lead of the victorious anti-Coalition forces in the next Parliament. But it was Labour, according to Massingham, that either would not or could not negotiate the balanced electoral arrangement necessary for routing the Coalition. Locally, of course, there were the scores of miners' agents, trade union secretaries, and Labour leaders in Town Councils, District Councils, and Boards of Guardians, who, if they had not already contrived a candidature in 1918 which they could now profess to be confident of pushing to success, had since staked out electoral claims. Such men asserted and, doubtless, often half-believed that they were moved by nothing more than zeal to serve their "fellow-workers", though *The Nation* claimed that many of them would be of little or no use in Parliament in comparison with those better-equipped Radicals or Socialists whom they endeavoured to shoulder aside by use of their local connections. Readers of Mrs. Webb's famous *Diaries* will not need to be reminded how even Sidney Webb's candidature, warmly

[1] *Supra* for the "Anti-Waste" cry, already loud and destined, during 1921, to extort one concession after another, notably, of course, the "Cuts", sometimes mistaken or socially harmful of the "Geddes Axe".

English Radicalism: The End?

pressed though it was from within the Seaham constituency, was almost blocked by the Durham Miners' Union claim to the seat.[1]

Apart, however, from the difficulties made by local Labour ambitions, the central direction of the party was always dominated by the anti-compromise section, and so thoroughly, that the case for the "electoral arrangement" was normally dismissed with contempt. It proved altogether easier to carry Labour conferences for the view that electoral bargaining with the Asquithians, besides antagonizing the Socialist stalwarts of the I.L.P., would only weaken the case for asking the "people" for as clean a sweep as possible of the "old gangs" of politicians, responsible, it could be claimed, for so many of the ills afflicting Britain and the world. Naturally, the smug careerism that sought to veil itself and its own crying deficiencies, moral and intellectual, under such a formula provoked some angry retorts from Radicals not yet minded to take a J. H. Thomas or a Ben Tillett as their political exemplars. But here is the very pro-Labour *Nation*, too, regretting Labour's successful exclusion (at the Penistone by-election of March 5, 1921)[2] of "the most brilliant of our younger Parliamentarians", W. M. R. Pringle, who, during the years 1916, 1917, and 1918 had been Lloyd George's most persistent and most dangerous critic on the Radical Back-Benches:[3]

the plain truth is that Mr. Pringle was not only a more practical politician than his Labour rival, but his platform was more advanced and democratic. Mr. Gillis made his appeal as "a delegate to the Yorkshire Mining Council, for thirty years". He stated that two questions dominated all others, "Unemployment and Ireland". He asked for a representative League of Peoples. He condemned reckless waste. He demanded a capital levy on accumulated wealth of over five thousand pounds. He made no mention at all of the nationalization of mines and railways, of "Capitalism", or of Socialism. Mr. Pringle, putting Ireland, Unemployment, Waste, and Foreign Policy in the fore-ground, demanded peace with Russia, the restoration of the economic situation in Central Europe and a capital levy. He also advocated the public ownership of mines and railways, a close supervision of rings and trusts, and a representative organization in industry, giving the workers a share in the control of the conditions and a minimum standard of real wages. To these vital matters the Labour candidate

[1] Cf. *Beatrice Webb's Diaries, 1912–1924*, under February 18, 1920.
[2] Cf. *Whitaker's Almanack, 1922*, p. 232, on what happened when the Asquithian, Sidney Arnold, resigned because of ill-health and Coalition Liberals would not have so redoubtable an antagonist of Lloyd George as Pringle. Gillis (Lab.), 8560; Pringle (Ind. Lib.), 7984; Hinchcliffe (Co. Lib.), 7123.
[3] *The Nation*, March 12, 1921.

322

made no allusion at all. . . . That the country is moving towards the Left is undoubted. But no Left party can make a success of its great venture if it be limited to manual workers and their most respected representatives in the conduct of trade union politics, and if a broad and reasoned policy is not presented for Europe and the Empire. And it remains open for the consideration of the far-sighted on both sides whether it is not possible to devise a method whereby not only this "Left" may get the majority it can fairly claim, but may marshal a force of ideas and criticism adequate to encounter, in the House of Commons, the leaders of the Coalition.

CHAPTER XV

1921

"The other night, I was at a big West London music-hall. All the topical references were disrespectful to the Government, to the Prime Minister, and to Mr. Churchill. . . . The time, therefore, seems ripe for an attempt at reconstructing politics. It is no use merely generating anti-Georgian hot air. There is plenty about; but there are solid masses of voters to be collected and given an object for their discontent. So long as the Opposition is split up into warring Liberal and Labour sections this process of . . . intellectual organization cannot be set up. . . . But the moment these parties come to an electoral understanding, the lethargy will disappear, and the disapproval become active and concrete. Hope will bloom again, even in Ireland; and industry revive, for it realizes that under a free trade administration the hated shackles will fall from it. . . . The Liberals are placable, for though they gain ground in the constituencies they don't look to a pure Liberal majority. And I dare aver that four out of five of the men in the front ranks of Labour would like to see a 'business' arrangement with Liberalism. . . ."

Massingham of *The Nation* as "Wayfarer", February 26, 1921.

"The high, and in some instances, preposterous demands put forward by the unemployed must not be allowed to obscure the vital facts of the situation. In the existing cost of living, it is probable that the compromise offer of the Woolwich Guardians of 30s. for man and wife, with £3 as a maximum for a family, represents the necessary expense of providing a true economic subsistence. Anything less probably means letting the family down into ill-health and inefficiency, an ultimately costlier process. But if this be so, two almost insoluble problems arise: raising the money so as not to injure trade and worsen unemployment, and furnishing relief without offering a bonus to shirking. . . .

"So far as the problem consists in finding the money, the rich districts, and in those districts appreciating property must be made to pay. . . . Not only are poor London boroughs, but poor industrial cities in various parts of the country, quite unable out of their separate local resources to meet the dimensions of such a disaster as confronts us. . . . The other practical problem, that of reconciling adequate relief with sound habits of industry, presents equally grave difficulties. If enough provision is made for decent maintenance, the cost at least equals the normal earnings of an unskilled labourer. If that provision is secured unconditionally and continuously for an unemployed family, must it not sap all incentive to work in a considerable number of workmen?"

The Nation, September 10, 1921, begins a Radical discussion on the Unemployed.

"Big Business and the 'Anti-Waste' newspapers appear to be keenly alive to the possibilities of this [Geddes] Committee.... Big Business first fought the highly-skilled and highly-paid trade unions and has beaten them. It has got down the wages of the coalminers and the railwaymen. It will probably get the $12\frac{1}{2}\%$ bonus off the engineers. These reductions may be necessary, and in any case the warfare was between the unions and the employers with no destruction of State machinery.... But employers are not likely to be content with this attack on the post-war standard of skilled labour.... Lord Rothermere ... declares this week for the thorough overhauling of the National Insurance Act.... A coach and four has already been driven through Mr. Fisher's Education Act . . . the joyful announcement is made that 150 Labour Exchanges are to be suppressed . . . the attack beats up fierce against money spent on Insurance, against Trade Boards, inspection, against all machinery operating for the protection of the poor."

The Nation, October 1, 1921, voices Radical disquiet on "Anti-Waste".

THE gloomiest features of Britain's situation during the opening months of 1921 were the unsolved and blood-soaked Irish problem and the rapid growth of serious unemployment with 925,000 already registered at the Exchanges by January 14th. On the Continent, moreover, the inevitable consequences of Versailles and the inflated Reparations demands were hurrying Europe on to a series of crises between the Allies and a "defaulting" Germany, certain to depress the markets for British exports and to increase America's distaste for the notion of cancelling inter-Allied War Debts as a contribution to Europe's revival. Labour, too, according to Government critics, sought to strike every manner of righteous attitude on Ireland, Germany, Russia, and much else without any serious regard to the consequences and, while denouncing Government "waste" furiously, called for a scale of Unemployment Benefits that would leave many working-class families better off without work and go far to bring down in ruin the already over-loaded taxation system.[1] The Prime Minister made a specially revealing appeal to Welsh Liberalism, on February 8th, to stand by him and national unity and to disregard, at the critical Cardiganshire by-election of the time, the strong temptations to "party faction" presented by the Radical candidature of one of the best-known Welsh "Independent Liberals". One summary of his eloquence noted his emphasis on the critical conditions that existed in a world still reeling from the most terrible blow it had ever received. And danger was not over, affirmed the Prime Minister, for if it were, he would resign forthwith. The Press, it seemed, knew better than he did his alleged General Election plans and was marking out his course over the next six months. Did any "Independent Liberal" really expect Asquith to return with as many as a hundred followers from the next Election, and if, meanwhile, the existing Government was overthrown by a combination of opposites, including Asquith himself as well as Northcliffe and the "Die-Hards", on what issue would Lloyd George himself be found wanting in Liberalism? The surest way, in fact, to destroy Liberalism, according to the Prime Minister, was to convince England's forty millions that, at a time

[1] Cf. *Annual Register*, 1921, English History, p. 3, for the demand for 40s. per week for each householder, 25s. for each single man or woman, and dependents' allowances in addition in a programme drawn up by the special Conference, called for January 27th, by the T.U.C. and the Labour Party.

of great national difficulty, Liberals, instead of helping, would only criticize and denounce.[1]

The Cardiganshire seat was saved in polling which, by the Coalition standards ruling of late, was not unsatisfactory.[2] Some two weeks later, when Ramsay MacDonald just failed to retain Will Crooks' Woolwich seat for Labour after envenomed opposition,[3] which brought him much sympathy on his own side, a Coalition gain could even be claimed. But then followed a series of by-election misfortunes, inevitable, no doubt, when Unemployment was still rising,[4] when Government's proposed Unemployment Benefits were sometimes less than half those Labour suggested, and when, too, the unpleasant necessity of wage-cuts was being faced even by grades of workmen who, like pitmen, cotton-workers, and engineers, had been in the strongest of bargaining positions for four or five years. In point of fact, owing to the powerful deflationary forces internationally at work, the cost of living was falling so fast that the reduced wage-scales put forward by employers as necessary to keep their industries going at all were not nearly as catastrophic as Union negotiators liked to represent and, indeed, formed the settlement-basis on which most industries readjusted their affairs without major disturbances.[5] But workmen, grown accustomed to forcing through regular wage-advances year after year, were in very ill-humour none the less and very ready to take part in the intense Labour propaganda in preparation for the next Election which was adopted as the party plan instead of the general strike, pressed for

[1] Cf. *Ibid.*, p. 11.

[2] The Coalition Liberal polled 14,111 against 10,251.

[3] Cf. L. M. Weir, *The Tragedy of Ramsay MacDonald*, p. 90, for the activities of the hooligan group known as "Bottomley's Circus".

[4] Cf. *Annual Register*, 1921, Chronicle, p. 4, for Labour gains at Dudley, Kirkcaldy, and Penistone in rapid succession. The Unemployment figure had risen to a total of 1,108,000 by the beginning of February.

[5] Cf. *Whitaker's Almanack*, *1922*, p. 479, for such items as: "April 19th. Reduction of wages in shipbuilding industry agreed to. . . . May 6th. Agreement reached in building trade for reduction of wages. . . . June 6th. Cotton mills in Lancashire ceased work through refusal of operatives to accept reduction of wages of 5s. in the £. June 7th. Engineering employers posted notices of proposed wage reductions. June 15th. Terms of settlement of cotton wage dispute reached. . . . Notice of wage reductions in engineering trades suspended, and modified terms offered by employers, which were eventually accepted on a ballot. . . . July 20th. Agreement for reduction of dockers' daily minimum wage of 16s. by 3s. in two stages reached. July 21st. Agricultural Wages Board decided on reduction in farm labourers' wages with minimum of 42s. a week. Aug. 9th. Railway managers came to agreement with men's leaders on subject of reduced wages for railway shopmen. . . ."

by the still-resisting pitmen. As for the unemployed, they were in peril of becoming, it was claimed, not so much the tools of a Labour Party avid for power but of the more sinister "Unemployed Workers' Movement" dreaming of British Soviets and, like the British Communist Party founded in 1920, in unavowed touch with Moscow.[1]

If all these matters were very much in the Prime Minister's mind even when Sinn Fein activity seemed to rise, in the effort to stop court-martial executions, to the bloody heights of March[2] and when, too, a dangerous new epoch in continental developments began with the Allies' decision to occupy new areas of a Germany in alleged wilful default with Reparations,[3] it was an unexpected new difficulty that brought the gravest peril to the Coalition. This is not a reference to the great pitmen's strike, begun at midnight on March 31st and with the added new dangers imported into the situation by the resolve to call out the "safety men" too, so threatening the coalowners and the nation with the submergence of the pits beneath the flood of waters to be expected when the pumps were left unmanned.[4] In fact, Government calculations that the "public", and even some of the colliers' own fellow-workers, had grown very weary of never-ending pit-troubles proved to have some foundation, and, besides, Whitehall was prepared to use the new Emergency Powers Act of 1920 in a way that upset many presumptions of the Miners' Federation. But two weeks before the pitmen aimed their blow at the Coalition and its policy of ending a Mines Control that was costing the Exchequer well over five millions a month, chance had struck it a blow that, in the long run, proved deadlier. On March 17, 1921 had been announced the resignation, through illness, of Mr. Bonar Law, Leader of the Commons and head of the Conservative Party for nearly a decade.

As it was very widely known that, without Bonar Law's cordial

[1] Cf. Wal Hannington, *Unemployed Struggles, 1919–1936*, for the avowed part of the story. The unavowed may be guessed from the Labour Party's declining the affiliation of the Communist Party at the 1921 Conference.

[2] Cf. *Annual Register*, 1921, English History, pp. 20–1, for the six men executed in Mountjoy Gaol, having been found guilty of murder and high treason.

[3] Cf. *The Times*, February 7th, for Lloyd George on Germany's ability to pay the bill presented if she had a mind to. He was speaking at Birmingham.

[4] Cf. J. R. Raynes, *Coal and its Conflicts*, p. 187, for the miners' executive meeting of March 30th and a majority of ten to eight, acting against the advice of the acting-president and secretary.

assistance, Lloyd George could never have become Prime Minister in 1916 or remained so for over four years afterwards, political speculation became rife. But Ireland, Unemployment, the Reparations crisis, and the difficult wage-negotiations proceeding in almost every industry, presented such a ring of problems that Austen Chamberlain, Bonar Law's unanimously-chosen successor, so far from desiring to end the existing Prime Ministership in his own favour, tried, for the time, to slip as unostentatiously as possible into his predecessor's place. Yet Lloyd George's critics and opponents realized that the beginning of the end might well have sounded for the Coalition, and for more reasons than that the new Leader's hold on the great Tory mass in the Commons promised to be less secure than Bonar Law's.[1] The exultant *Nation* even ventured to forecast "The Coming Downfall of the Coalition" in a special article under that heading and to urge on, once more, the Radical-Labour *entente* necessary to bring it about.[2] Another *Nation* article, finding pleasure in the Prime Minister's increased problems and urging on an Asquithian-Labour agreement from another angle, had this to say of the new political position:[3]

Mr. Law was under the Georgian spell; Mr. Chamberlain is a rather stiff and independent character. . . . Mr. Law had no marching orders. . . . Mr. Chamberlain is under a kind of commission to do things, e.g. to set the House of Lords up again, to maintain the liquor traffic, and to bring in Protection. Obviously there are more thorns than gems in the crown that is being rather firmly pressed on the Prime Minister's brows. . . . What therefore will he do? . . . He is a good political soldier and he knows the value of attack. Like Napoleon in the Waterloo campaign, he has to face the fire of two hostile forces, and it will be his natural strategy to strike before they unite, and then beat them in detail. If no such union is possible or contemplated, then

[1] Cf. *The Nation*, March 26, 1921: "While Mr. Law remained leader of the Commons, his smooth carpentry gave the [Coalition] structure an appearance of firmness it never really possessed. Mr. Chamberlain has no such arts, and he lacks Mr. Law's quick responsiveness to the master hand."

[2] *Ibid.*, for: "Of course, if the Labour Party is bent on setting up Marxianism in Great Britain *uno ictu*, it must set about that task in splendid isolation, and may calculate on achieving it about the time when Lenin has become President of the Liberty and Property Defence League. But if it means business, we suggest that it declare first for a practical electoral programme, and secondly for a practical electoral strategy, and having thus cleared the ground to an almost certain victory, set to work to destroy Mr. George's power for evil in Ireland, in Europe, and in the United Kingdom."

[3] *Ibid.*

indeed there is no such hurry. . . . Nationalism, Imperialism, Capitalism, Protectionism will be the substance of his electoral appeal. But the form is bound to be demagogic and anti-revolutionary. . . .

For good measure, *The Nation* added the kind of junction of forces it considered capable of destroying Lloyd Georgism at the next General Election, and this time it played into the hands of its critics at Labour Party Headquarters by not confining its case to the Radical-Labour *entente* (which had some concealed friends there) but by dragging into the argument, and into the next Government", a couple of leading Tory opponents of the "Black and Tans". Lord Robert Cecil, Lord Henry Bentinck, and even young Oswald Mosley might have their uses in discrediting the Coalition's Foreign or Irish policy—but to dream of seating them in a largely Labour Government, when place for Asquith, Grey, and McKenna, if it proved indispensable from the Parliamentary viewpoint, might well split the Labour movement from end to end, was to romanticize politics, it could be held, in a way that deprived the proposer of all serious claim to attention.[1]

Lloyd George, of course, was not got rid of quite so quickly or satisfactorily as Radical and Labour prophets of the Coalition's doom would have liked. For one thing, the Coalition's enemies also made their mistakes, notably the pitmen, when attempting to intimidate the owners, the Government, and the nation by the "destruction" resolution of March 30th, for withdrawing the "safety men" too, from the pits when the strike began at midnight, March 31st. By contrast, the Government, though making large use of its emergency powers to defeat what it claimed were threats to the nation's vital interests, showed moderation enough in offering to find a total of ten millions to ease the transition-stages into Coal Decontrol for the miners that the Triple Alliance broke up and the miners were left to fight a losing battle alone.[2]

---

[1] *The Nation,* March 26, 1941. The suggested Government list, however, has its importance as indicating the rating that a skilled Fleet Street eye gave to the politicians most under discussion. The Labour Cabinet Ministers were apparently to have been Clynes, MacDonald, Henderson, Sidney Webb, Thomas, and, perhaps, Bevin or Gosling while, among junior Labour Ministers, the names of Snowden, Noel Buxton, Spoor, Ponsonby, Maclean, Graham, and Wedgwood are seen.

[2] Cf. *Whitaker's Almanack, 1922,* p. 478, for a succinct account: "a state of emergency was at once proclaimed . . . coal exports were prohibited, and consumption regulated. Effort to resume negotiations on April 6th failed because miners refused to restart pumping as a preliminary to meeting owners, and upon

In Ireland, too, extremism was finally fated to shock its own public when taking so inexcusable a step as the destruction, on May 25th, of the Dublin Customs House, one of the country's best and most prized architectural monuments.[1] The anger and dismay excited among the country's more moderate elements, strongly represented in the Catholic Church, seems to have had its part in forwarding the project of a Truce for allowing negotiations with the British Ministry in conditions by no means to the taste of many of the Sinn Fein extremists. By this time, moreover, the unfortunate politicians in the uneasy Coalitions ruling a Germany, plunging into ever more catastrophic inflation, had allowed Lloyd George what could still be represented as a particularly striking success. The Germans had apparently hoped that a firm stand on their part in February and March for something like Keynesian Reparations only might bring Britain round to the conviction that it was time to stop defying all economic laws in estimating the amount of transferable assets available as Reparations.[2] But Lloyd George, with *John Bull*, the *Daily Mail*, and much else to think of, including his Government's own election rhetoric of December 1918, could not move nearly as fast as the Germans knew to be necessary to prevent a complete financial crash. Instead, after the first coercion of March, in the shape of the occupation of Dusseldorf, Duisburg, and Ruhrort, he joined in the further coercion represented by the ultimatum of May 5th, threatening the extension of Allied occupation to the whole of the Ruhr. It can hardly be doubted but that, by this time, Lloyd George was fully aware of the dangerous game France was playing and possibly, in private, would have defended what he was doing as hanging on to the coat-tails of France to prevent a worse thing befalling.[3] Yet when, on May 11th, he reported Germany's

threat of Triple Alliance to call a general strike, Government called out reserves and formed Volunteer Defence Corps. On April 10th men's executive agreed to allow steps to be taken to save the mines, and negotiations were opened the following day. The conference broke down, but threatened strike action of Triple Alliance was postponed until the 15th. A few hours before the time fixed, railwaymen and transport workers cancelled the general strike because miners disavowed proposal made by their secretary, Mr. Frank Hodges. . . . Miners' delegates, on April 28, rejected Government's offer involving grant of £10,000,000. . . ."

[1] Cf. *Annual Register*, 1921, English History, p. 50.

[2] Cf. *Ibid.*, p. 45, for the German offer of thirty thousand million gold marks in full settlement.

[3] *Ibid.*, p. 47, for the French "concession" of putting off the occupation of the Ruhr.

complete acceptance of the ultimatum, the righteous self-satisfaction of the Coalition Press was loud.

Before dealing with the Coalition's problems of the summer of 1921, it might, perhaps, be wise to note some of the more significant changes in the composition of the Coalition Ministry. In February 1921, for example, there had departed one of the original War Cabinet of December 1916, Viscount Milner, and Winston Churchill had moved over to the Colonial Office from the War Office, bringing with him plans for cheapening British military costs in Palestine, Transjordania, and Mesopotamia by organizing native levies and native authorities. A whole series of Cabinet changes had been precipitated by the departure of Bonar Law in March, and though no one would have foretold it at the time, the most critical for Lloyd George's personal fortunes was the appointment of Stanley Baldwin to the Presidency of the Board of Trade after several years as Financial Secretary to the Treasury. But possibly the best illustration of Lloyd George's constant need to study the problem of Cabinet balance concerned the difficult case of his old Radical comrade, Dr. Addison. When, in January, another old Liberal crony, Lord Reading, had been elevated to the Viceroyalty of India,[1] the gnashing of teeth in certain Anglo-Indian circles must have been immense, and it, doubtless, needed a good many reminders of the dangers he would be facing from the hostility of Hindu and Moslem alike to prevent louder criticism from arising than there was.[2] But there seemed much less need for discretion when Addison, a reputed total failure with Housing as Minister of Health, emerged from the Cabinet transformation, after Bonar Law's departure, as Minister without Portfolio at £5000 a year with another Lloyd Georgian, Sir Alfred Mond, at the Health Ministry, enjoying a similar salary. The "Anti-Waste"

---

[1] Cf. *The Nation*, August 28, 1920, for the first names canvassed: "The competition for the Viceroyalty of India is brisk; since Mr. Montagu was ruled out, three illustrious men have entered the lists or had their names inscribed there—Mr. Chamberlain, Lord Birkenhead and Mr. Winston Churchill." Mr. Chamberlain declined the definite offer in October; Birkenhead's friends affected to fear the loss of a possible chance of the Premiership in the future; Churchill was almost "counted out at the first ballot".

[2] The *Morning Post*, the stoutest organ of old-fashioned Conservatism, tried to make the appointment impossible by treating the nomination of a Jew as an affront to Indian Mohammedanism, already antagonized by Britain's part in bringing down the Khalifate of the Turkish Sultans and in accepting, in Palestine, part of the Jewish case. The most eloquent Anglo-Indian of them all, Rudyard Kipling, had already made a ferocious attack on Reading's Marconi record on the occasion of Reading's being made Lord Chief Justice.

clamour was already of a size and ferocity to make one of the Government's main problems with its own side,[1] and by June 23rd, Lloyd George, scenting real danger, agreed to the eventual sacrifice of his old ally despite the latter's Chairmanship of four important Cabinet Committees and membership of six others.[2] The aggrieved Addison soon resigned after Mond, in the interests, it was claimed, of economy made formidable cuts in the Housing programme, drawn up if not executed by Addison, who, indeed, went on to make a formidable anti-Government intervention when Asquith moved to reduce the Ministry of Health's vote in order to give expression to the dissatisfaction with the Government's Housing record.[3] Lloyd George might claim that not a single house less would be produced in Britain over the next eighteen months or in Scotland over the next two years but made the awkward revelation, all the same, that heavy expenditure in Mesopotomia had produced the change of plan as far back as February.

Meanwhile, despite a Budget, open to "advanced" criticism for its abandonment of Excess Profits Duty,[4] and a Safeguarding of Industries Bill, alarming to Asquithian and Labour Free Traders alike,[5] the Coalition's future depended primarily on whether

[1] Cf. *Whitaker's Almanack, 1922*, p. 476, for four successive by-election successes of "Anti-Waste", two of them involving the defeat of the orthodox Coalitionist Conservatives and two representing the "Anti-Waste" triumph of having forced on the victorious candidates the abandonment of the Coalition ticket and the adoption of the style of Constitutional Anti-Waste instead. The four by-elections were: June 6th, St. George's, Westminster; June 17th, Hertford; June 26th, Abbey, Westminster; Sept. 13th, West Lewisham.

[2] Cf. *Hansard*, June 13th. The *Annual Register*'s comment makes it plain that something like a revolt of Back-Bench Conservatives was imminent in view of what it called "widespread criticism among those who had adopted the watchword of economy".

[3] Cf. *The Betrayal of the Slums* (1922) for Addison's continuation of the debate in book-form. He put the blame for the disappointing House figures so far achieved on the War Cabinet's neglect of his warnings of 1918 in regard to such basic needs as the extension of brick-making capacity and the expansion of the output of all building accessories. He hardly, however, made sufficient allowance for Mond's case, that to contract, too far ahead, at a period of steadily-falling prices was to help to keep prices higher than they would otherwise be.

[4] Cf. *Annual Register*, 1921, English History, p. 9, for Austen Chamberlain's announcing this in advance of the Budget and justifying it on several grounds —that Excess Profits was a war-tax, that it operated against new business enterprise, and that it encouraged extravagance in order to reduce tax-liability.

[5] Cf. *Whitaker's Almanack, 1922*, p. 239, for a succinct summary of proceedings that began with the resolutions of May 9th, for imposing an import duty of 33⅓ per cent to safeguard certain "key industries" at home and others threatened by imported articles offered below the cost of production in Britain. The first challenge came on May 10th, with an Independent Liberal amendment to reduce the period of operation from five years to one, and it needed an all-night sitting to complete this preliminary stage and clear the way for the Bill

English Radicalism: The End?

Lloyd George could find a way out of the Irish impasse. A Catholic Conservative had been appointed Ireland's last Viceroy early in May, and in his name the election machinery of the 1920 Government of Ireland Act had been set to work to produce a Twenty-Six County Parliament at Dublin and a Six-County Parliament farther north. The Sinn Feiners obtained 120 out of the 128 seats for the Dublin Parliament, virtually uncontested, but then blocked the further implementation of Dominion Status under the Crown. In the North, meantime, the election procedures of May 24th produced a House of Commons of 40 Unionists, 6 Sinn Feiners, and 6 Nationalists, and, next day, Sinn Fein extremists undertook the Dublin Customs House destruction which brought so marked a revulsion against them. Yet, in the North, Sinn Fein continued spasmodic outbreaks intended, apparently, to spoil the inauguration of a new system there and, above all, to make it too dangerous for the Coalition to bring the King and Queen over to Belfast for a Speech from the Throne, certain of world-wide attention and not always of a kind welcome to Sinn Fein.[1] The tremendous reception given to the Royal couple in Belfast on June 22nd, and the moving personal appeal made by the Sovereign for "an end of strife" were, in fact, a good deal more effective than some of Lloyd George's "advanced" critics forecast.[2] They certainly permitted him to offer South and North renewed negotiations in London, and when de Valera tried to substitute a North-South meeting in Dublin which the North declined, pressure on de Valera to explore the new possibilities in London apparently became too much even for one whose ideas of negotiation seemed limited to an endless round of argument on

proper which was fought with some persistence during June, July, and August, Sir Donald Maclean leading the fight on Second Reading and Mr. Asquith himself on Third Reading. As Mr. Baldwin claimed, the Bill was one to protect employment in this country, employment specially threatened by depreciated continental exchanges, and as food, drink, and raw materials were to be excluded from its operation, the Labour members normally found it wiser to leave opposition to the Asquithians.

[1] Cf. *Annual Register*, 1921, English History, p. 61, for some of the Belfast disorders of mid-June, excited, according to the Coalition's Irish Secretary (see *Hansard*, June 14th) in the hope of making the Parliament of the North impossible. Belfast, of course, has a large Catholic minority, and Irish immigrants in Britain were doubtless used for the June "outrages" there, intended to "scare" British opinion.

[2] Cf. *The Times*, June 23rd: "I speak from a full heart when I pray that my coming to Ireland to-day may prove to be the first step towards an end of strife amongst her people. . . . In that hope, I appeal to all Irishmen to pause, to stretch out the hand of forbearance and conciliation, to forgive and to forget. . . ."

the theme of Irish self-determination. By July 8th it could be announced that an Irish Truce had been arranged, and on July 14th began Lloyd George's long and wearisome attempt to convince de Valera that he could not expect to swallow the North, declare a Republic, and have the British blessing too. An Irish Free State within the Empire was, however, possible and if he accepted the wisdom of meeting some of the Empire's strategic needs, it might prove the first step in a reconciliation with the alienated North which the London Government was anxious to forward. It was an insinuating Radical line which a majority of de Valera's party, if not de Valera himself, ultimately found it impossible to resist though much was to happen first.

The Prime Minister entered upon the Irish negotiations with better hope in that his toughest British problem had just been settled by the capitulation of the defeated pitmen who returned to work on July 4th after having inflicted great privation on themselves, their families, and many workers in the coal-using industries. Moreover, it could be argued that, considering the harm the initial over-confidence and ultimate obstinacy of the pitmen had inflicted, the Prime Minister and his majority showed reasonable generosity in agreeing not to withdraw any part of the ten millions that had been offered in March to avert the strike by easing the pitmen's wage-position in the initial stages of De-control.[1] In point of fact, the pitmen's thorough defeat helped downward wage-adjustments in many other trades to be negotiated without strikes, especially as the cost of living was falling at a rate which permitted many classes of labour, in assured work, to suffer no fall at all in real wages.[2] Yet a strike of nearly fourteen weeks by over a million men in a basic industry affecting almost all others, and some very disastrously, had to be paid for. Over the next few years, of course, the pitmen themselves paid a grim enough price for having permitted valuable export-markets in Italy, Holland, and Scandinavia to be lost to cheap competing

[1] J. R. Raynes, *Coal and its Conflicts*, p. 129, for the Miners' Federation officers claiming that the principles of the agreement under which the men were returning "will provide a more just method of fixing wages and profits than we have ever had in the industry". Lloyd George was simultaneously claiming in Parliament (*Hansard*, June 28th) that no such large and scientific application of profit-sharing had ever before taken place in the history of any industry in any country, and certainly not in this country.

[2] Cf. *Annual Register*, 1921, Chronicle, under October 1st, for the official figure of the cost of living standing at about 110 per cent above that of July 1914, having fallen 10 points during September.

coal,[1] but other sections of the working population in the unskilled and semi-skilled class suffered even more. By the autumn, indeed, with Unemployment figures reaching one and three-quarter millions and the percentage of workless in some branches of the metal trades standing at seventeen,[2] the employment situation had become almost as critical as at any time within living memory. Nor was it being helped by the rival schools of dogmatic politics. The mass of the Coalition, capitulating to the "Anti-Waste" movement of the "Press Lords", had demanded and obtained a Geddes "Axe" Committee to cut Government costs and enforce a not always discriminating "economy";[3] Labour and the "advanced", on the other hand, were not nearly critical enough of the swollen out-reliefs for unemployed and unemployables associated with Lansbury's sentimental "Poplarism";[4] the tiny Communist clique that officered the "National Unemployed Movement" set on foot demands for a super-"Poplarism" calculated to bring the day of British Soviets nearer[5] and, finally, the "Independent Liberals" urged that true economy could not be expected from a Committee headed by one with the alleged war-spending record of Geddes.[6] To remember that Lloyd George was simultaneously wrestling with the rival Irish dogmatisms of Sinn Fein and Protestant Ulster is to appreciate something of the strains under which he and his Coalition were labouring.

Meantime the Irish negotiations had been taking a unique course, sometimes picturesquely crossing paths with "Poplarism" as when Lloyd George and part of the Cabinet, resting in Scotland

[1] Cf. *The Nation*, April 9, 1921, for the dangers developing, even before the strike began, in Holland, Scandinavia, and Italy from surplus Reparations coal from Germany offered by French interests. Before long the Poles were offering the Continent coal even cheaper from ex-German pits in Upper Silesia, transferred to them under the Versailles Treaty.

[2] Cf. *Hansard*, October 19th, for the Prime Minister admitting the seriousness of the problem to a Parliament just reassembled to deal with four remedial Bills before the Session closed.

[3] Cf. *Ibid.*, August 16th, for the names and functions of the Committee whose drastic recommendations on economies in the Armed Services and Education, in preparation for the 1922 Session, were unexpectedly far-reaching and severe.

[4] Cf. *Whitaker's Almanack, 1922*, p. 479, for the Poplar defiance which helped to make "Poplarism" the term applied to all over-indulgent relief expenditure: "Sept. 1st. As a result of High Court decision several Councillors of Poplar were arrested for refusing to levy rates to meet demands of London County Council and Metropolitan Asylums Board. In all 25 men and women were confined in prison until Oct. 12th."

[5] Cf. Wal Hannington, *Unemployed Struggles, 1919–1936*, pp. 28–44.

[6] Cf. *Annual Register*, 1921, English History, pp. 85–6, for Sir Donald Maclean criticizing "not only the functions of the Committee but the personality of the Chairman".

and waiting to see whether a renewal of Irish conferences might prove possible, faced an invasion of London Labour Mayors come to demand more help with their unemployed. London working-class boroughs had, indeed, like a number of other places, seen hitherto unparalleled mob-scenes at their Town Halls and Poor Relief Offices, and attempts, sometimes temporarily successful, had been made to dictate relief-scales of a generosity that threatened them all with bankruptcy in a matter of weeks.[1] Despite medical objections on behalf of an exhausted Prime Minister, who had just had the heavy chagrin of cancelling a care-fully-prepared Inverness conference with Sinn Fein because of de Valera's demand to be treated as representing a Sovereign State,[2] the London Mayors were eventually allowed to put their case to the Prime Minister in person. Some assurances were given them, and, before long, while the Prime Minister and the Cabinet waited for de Valera's colleagues to bring him to reason, a minia-ture industrialists' conference was gathered to advise the Prime Minister on possible ways of reducing Unemployment. The reassembly of Parliament, on October 18th, for a few last weeks of the 1921 Session did not, therefore, allow the type of debate on a proposed settlement with Sinn Fein which had at one time seemed possible. It was the four Government Bills, drafted to deal with Unemployment and the Unemployed, which made the big party debates of the 1921 Session's closing weeks. But it naturally helped the Prime Minister that a Sinn Fein negotiating party, from which de Valera had been flatteringly persuaded to exclude himself,[3] was once again in conclave with the Government by October 11th, and that de Valera chose to break in on the

---

[1] Cf. *Ibid.*, pp. 105–7, for the scenes of violence at Dundee, Bristol, Liverpool, and London. In the London area, it was the Labour Boards of Guardians who seem to have been subjected to the worst pressure (sometimes by means of unemployed processions and demonstrations in which ex-Service men took a prominent part) and to have weakened most before the clamour for relief-rates virtually equal to a full working wage. The Ministry of Health found it necessary to decide that such relief-scales as those proposed, for example, at Islington were illegal and to issue a circular directing that relief should always be on a lower scale than earnings; should not be given without full investigation; should be given largely in kind and, possibly, on a loan basis.

[2] *Ibid.*, pp. 96–7.

[3] There are indications that some leading Sinn Feiners, in despair at de Valera's rigidity, had combined to persuade him that it would diminish Ireland's international status if he, as "Head of State", undertook to bargain with mere Ministers. Ulster was even repeating stories that de Valera was beginning to expect others to back away from his presence, face towards him, as in the case of Royalty.

negotiations, from Dublin, in a way that many Irishmen could not forgive him. There had been a friendly exchange of telegrams between the Pope and King George V on the occasion of the resumed talks with Sinn Fein, and de Valera, without consulting the Sinn Fein negotiators in London, chose the moment to instruct the Pope by public telegraph on how not to be misled by the rulers of Britain.[1]

Of course, the two "progressive" Oppositions had plenty of fault to find with Ministers during the mainly economic discussions of the 1921 Session's closing weeks between the reassembly date of October 18th and the prorogation of November 10th. Thus Mr. Clynes, who was giving Labour considerably more effective spokesmanship than Adamson had done, chose to complain that Government's four Bills on Unemployment and the Unemployed were to be hurried through in a fortnight and demanded two or three times as long for their consideration.[2] Mr. Asquith, for his part, regretted the delay in introducing Government's measures and claimed that the return of Free Trade and a great lowering of Government expenditure, permitting large reductions of the crushing load of taxation, would have gone far, in themselves, to put right what was wrong. And the irate Dr. Addison, who had once been a principal assistant in rallying from Asquith to Lloyd George a large Liberal contingent, denounced the futility of Government's measures and especially the increase of Unemployment resulting from the abandonment of his Housing policy.[3] Naturally, the Unemployed Workers' Dependents' (Temporary Provisions) Bill and the Local Authorities (Financial Provisions) Bill allowed those berating Government better opportunites than their measures to help ex-Service men to emigrate and to find aid for the export-trades by loan-guarantees that would permit great development in the Dominions. Ministers might claim that their difficult Budgetary position did not permit their placing upon the national accounts the wives and children of the Unemployed at anything like the figures demanded by Labour, and that to propose to take more than 1s. 2d. from every employed man per week and more than 1s. 3d. from his employer

---

[1] Cf. *Annual Register*, 1921, English History, p. 120.
[2] Cf. *Hansard*, October 18th. It had been Austen Chamberlain as Leader of the House who had suggested a fortnight.
[3] Cf. *Ibid.*, October 20th, who claimed that, in one case, ten times as many men could have been employed as were now engaged.

was dangerous from several points of view. Yet when it left them not merely declining to take the 5*s*. per week grant for the wife any nearer to the Labour demand for 10*s*. or to increase the child-grant from 1*s*. to 2*s*. per week,[1] there seemed to be ample room not only for Labour indignation but even for some from more financially orthodox Liberals. And on the Bill to cope with "Poplarism" for the future, by allowing somewhat more generous help from the Metropolitan Common Poor Fund indeed,[2] but coupling with that the Ministerial right to appoint a rating official to do what a defiant rating authority declined, Government earned but little thanks. For the Liberals, Sir Donald Maclean blamed Ministers for their delay in extending the scope of the Metropolitan Common Poor Fund; Labour and the "advanced" found the extension quite insufficient to relieve working-class boroughs of an intolerable burden; and, finally, there arose a demand from all over the country for some plan, similar to London's, for asking better-off districts to share, in part, the Poor Law burdens of their workaday neighbours.

Yet despite such difficulties and disappointments as those narrated above, the Prime Minister's fate, and the Coalition's, turned above all on the measure of his success in effecting an Irish "solution" which he could persuade both Sinn Fein and his Unionist colleagues to accept. Already the Prime Minister had scented the possibility that, without de Valera, the Irish negotiating team would be prepared to accept an Irish Free State within the Empire. And he had been much encouraged to find himself emerging, on October 31st, from an attack in form by the Conservative "Die-Hard" section anxious to break up the Coalition and break off the talks with the "murder gang", possessed of the huge majority of 439 against 43, and the qualified approval of Mr. Asquith and Mr. Clynes. The electioneer, who had emerged

---

[1] The Labour demand was for 7*s*. 6*d*. per week for the first child and 6*s*. a week for the rest, and the Government's refusal to consider the serious Budgetary burdens involved had already led to angry scenes, the Chairman's order to two Labour members to leave the House and a marchout, in sympathy with them, by many others. The more moderate demand for 2*s*. (*Hansard*, November 1st) rallied so many Liberals and Coalitionists that the Government majority fell to 33 despite a strong intervention in aid of the unfortunate Minister in charge, Dr. Macnamara, by the Chancellor of the Exchequer.

[2] A Royal Commission on London Rating was just being appointed but, pending its Report, the Metropolitan Common Poor Fund would do considerably more than in the past for boroughs like Woolwich, Limehouse, Stepney, and Poplar.

more powerful from each of the last three General Elections, was not unaware that if the Sinn Fein negotiators finally agreed to end the "Irish troubles" on terms that Mr. Austen Chamberlain could be persuaded to accept, the stage could be set for another triumphant General Election. The "man who won the war" against Germany would now be represented, perhaps more truly, as the man who won the peace with Sinn Fein, and, despite the "hard times" being suffered, a great majority seemed certain, if not the overwhelming figures of December 1918.

Spurred on by such a prospect, the world's smoothest and most beguiling negotiator, after a world of difficulties,[1] procured the Sinn Fein signatures on December 6th. Perhaps some little attention should be given to the obstacles that had been overcome, for Lloyd George's principal Conservative colleagues were the first to recognize that there was not another figure in public life capable of what he had done. The Oath of Allegiance, finally agreed to by the Sinn Feiners, is a special case in point and is worth quoting in full:[2]

I do solemnly swear true faith and allegiance to the constitution of the Irish Free State as by law established, and that I will be faithful to His Majesty King George V, his heirs and successors by law, in virtue of the common citizenship of Ireland with Great Britain and her adherence to, and membership of, the group of nations forming the British Commonwealth of Nations.

Of course, the Sinn Fein delegates knew that the immense Irish communities in Great Britain and the Dominions would gain greatly, in legal security for the future, from a Free State rather than a Republican settlement; many important Irish interests, too, notably those of the Old Age Pensioners, could be more adequately safeguarded. Yet Republican propaganda against the British Royal House had been so rampant for generations that, to explain the Sinn Fein signatures, recourse has often been had to another part of the Treaty under which a Boundary Commission of Three, with a representative of the British Government in the Chair, was to have the right to determine boundary rectifications as between

---

[1] Cf. S. Salvidge, *Salvidge of Liverpool*, pp. 194–219, for the great risks that had been run at the November meetings of the National Unionist Association at Liverpool where the Conservative "Die-Hards" made much use of Ulstermen's known dissatisfaction with the character of the terms being discussed. The Sinn Feiners were simultaneously trying to turn the Council of Ireland of the 1920 Government of Ireland Act into an All-Ireland Parliament.

[2] Cf. *Annual Register*, 1921, p. 139.

the Dublin and Belfast Governments. It may well be that Lloyd George, or some of his staff, did convey the impression that the Boundary Commission could do much in the future to effect considerable "rectifications" in Tyrone and Fermanagh but the assertion that something akin to binding pledges was given can be safely dismissed. The mere suspicion of such a possibility would have ruined Lloyd George and the Coalition, for Ulster and its "Die-Hard" friends, hostile enough already to some aspects of Lloyd George's bargaining,[1] would have won over the bulk of the Conservative Party.

If Lloyd George could now have had the General Election he craved, British politics would certainly have taken an unexpected turn. The Prime Minister's prestige, temporarily re-established, thanks to the Irish Treaty and the Washington Conference on Naval Disarmament, even with some of the "progressive" and "advanced", would not merely have ended the dreams of sweeping the Coalition from power but might have necessitated considerable downward revision of the 150 Labour members and 80 Asquithians whom political calculators, of a soberer kind, had been expecting in the next Parliament. But the Prime Minister was balked of his chance of continuing the domination of national politics in a new Parliament. For one thing, the disgruntled "Die-Hards" seem to have made some impression on the Conservative organizers who, in their advice to the Conservative Leaders,[2] stressed the danger of a "Die-Hard" break-away if an election were arranged on a basis of lavish praises to a Prime Minister who, in the "Die-Hard" view, "had sold out to Irish gunmen". The Conservative Whips, too, were tired of the company of the almost totally discredited Coalition Liberals and had no mind to carry them on their backs for another Election especially as they could not be relied on for help in realizing Conservatism's ambition of restoring a powerful veto to a somewhat remodelled House of Lords. Then, the Conservative organizers, far from sharing Austen Chamberlain's general pessimism as to what, in the shape of revolutionary perils, might come from a Coalition break-up, were beginning to acquire the conviction that, coming in the

[1] Cf. *Hansard* (Lords), December 14, 1921, for Carson's bitter speech on the theme that "the people of Ulster are expected to be the complacent puppets of the Government, and without demur to take off their hats to the Foreign Secretary [Curzon] and the rest who had done everything which they had previously said would ruin the United Kingdom".
[2] Cf. *Life and Letters of Austen Chamberlain*, ii, 169–70.

right circumstances, it could free Conservatism from the contumely and derision, beginning to be evoked by the mere mention of Coalition, which contumely and derision could be left burdening the unfortunate Coalition Liberals alone.[1] But what apparently ended the Prime Minister's last chances was the unsatisfactory scene at Dublin where the Sinn Fein Treaty signatories were opposed by de Valera and the Republican zealots, who if defeated by scanty majorities in the Dail, were rightly suspected to be in control of much of Sinn Fein's war-apparatus and capable of attempting to start up the "troubles" all over again, especially in Ulster. Possibly there was something in the chagrined Prime Minister's view that a decisive popular pronouncement, in his favour, in Britain might have been of service in Ireland. But the story of his vain attempt to leave Conservatism, rather than himself and his following, burdened with the odium of the Coalition's record must wait till the next chapter, which shall deal early with his offer of February 1922 to retire from the Prime Ministership in Austen Chamberlain's favour.

[1] Cf. W. A. S. Hewins, *Apologia of an Imperialist*, ii, 247: "The striking thing about the last fortnight is the disintegration of the Coalition. . . . Every day weakens the position of the Co. Libs." This is Hewins's diary entry for January 19, 1922, and Hewins had been the Coalition's Under-Secretary for the Colonies.

CHAPTER XVI

1922

"The Prime Minister is making a large and imaginative effort to undo the disaster which he helped to bring on Europe at Versailles. It needs some self-control to refrain from pointing out that it was he and his allies and his colleagues who made the wreck. . . . We believe, however, that the present effort is entirely sincere, and, as we read this mercurial character, the part of saviour is more congenial to him than that of wrecker. The new departure, though its outlines are still vague and uncertain, has a sweep and range of thought and intention which inspire respect and hope. . . . He has put the economic question in the foreground. But even the slight sketch of what he wishes to achieve which he laid before the Cannes Council . . . shows that he aims at something less restricted than an economic settlement, important though that alone would be. The mere admission of Germany and Russia carries us far beyond anything that the League of Nations has yet attempted. . . . In the realm of politics the proposal that every country at the Conference shall guarantee its neighbours against aggression opens up an even wider prospect. . . . We see no reason to doubt the *Manchester Guardian*'s statement that Mr. George originally intended (and may still intend) to make a pact of this kind between Britain, France, and Germany, with an inviolable and demilitarized Rhineland as the object to be guaranteed. That, if it meant the ending of the Allied Occupation, would be perhaps the most brilliant gift which statesmanship could confer on Europe."

The Radical oracle, Massingham, almost ready to forgive Lloyd George, *The Nation*, January 14, 1922.

"Mr. Lloyd George's part in the matter of Reparations is the most discreditable episode in his career. . . . I say this although his present intentions appear to be reasonable. . . . The right solution, the solution we are bound to come to in the end, is not complicated. We must abandon the claim for pensions and bring to an end the occupation of the Rhinelands. The Reparation Commission must be asked to divide their assessment into two parts—the part that represents pensions and separation allowances, and the rest. And with the abandonment of the former the proportion due to France would be correspondingly raised. If France would agree to this—which is in her interest anyhow—and would terminate the occupation

343

it would be right for us to forgive her (and our other Allies) all they owe us, and to accord a priority on all receipts in favour of the devastated areas. If we could secure a real settlement by these sacrifices, I think we should make them completely regardless of what the United States may say or do.

"In declaring for this policy in the House of Commons yesterday, Mr. Asquith has given the Liberal Party a clear lead. . . . But no one must suppose that, even with such a settlement, any important part of Germany's payments can be anticipated by a loan. Any small loan that can be raised will be required for Germany herself, to put her on her legs again, and enable her to make the necessary annual payments."

J. M. Keynes at the Liberal Summer School, August 1922 (From *Essays in Liberalism*, pp. 57–8).

The resignation of Lloyd George has greatly changed the electoral scene. . . . Had the late Prime Minister been able to make the election, all would have been clear. The Coalition would have gone down to a crashing fall . . . leading, maybe, to a Lib-Lab control of the coming Parliament. A very different landscape now meets the eye. The Tory Party needs no allies from any quarter. . . . They are in the hands of a quietly astute man, undistinguished, but able, it is clear, to play a Fabian game against a general of genius whose luck was out. The bulk of the middle-class vote is theirs. . . . Reaction will come, but it will not be preached. The workmen's party will not be affronted, only undermined, and peace, retrenchment and no reform in particular will be the mottoes. . . . Electoral prophecy runs a rather monotonous course. It is always assumed to be only a question of how large the Tory majority will be. . . ."

The Nation, October 28, 1922.

I N the first two or three weeks of January 1922, when a General
Election calculated, at least temporarily, to restore Lloyd
George's tarnished prestige seemed more likely than not,
there was understandable anxiety among Labour and "Independent Liberal" critics of the Coalition.[1] Labour probably had
considerable reason to be thankful that its confident prophecies of
great electoral gains were not put to the test just when Lloyd
George would have been able to flourish such "democratic"
achievements as the seven treaties and declarations towards which
the Washington Conference on Naval Disarmament was moving
and such picturesque benefits to Ireland, from his Treaty, as the
handing over of Dublin Castle on January 16th and the postal
services on January 19th.[2] Possibly the "Independent Liberals"
had even more reason than Labour to be thankful that the Conservative Right had blocked Lloyd George's path to the polls for,
in the Election mood expected to be reigning, the Coalition
Liberal speaking of the Prime Minister, Mr. Churchill, Sir
Gordon Hewart, and their friends seemed likely to carry more
weight than for some time.

Perhaps the shape taken by politics as it became increasingly
certain that Lloyd George would not be allowed his Election can
best be gauged from the "Independent Liberal" retorts of Asquith
and Grey to the Prime Minister's address of January 21st to a
National Liberal Conference of his supporters. On January 23rd,
Grey, whose return to the political arena in support of his old
chief Asquith had some importance, was not only critical of the
Anglo-French tensions that had been allowed to develop but
affirmed the necessity of a reversion to straightforward politics in
Britain and asserted the existence of more than one alternative to
the Coalition. To the same meeting, Mr. Asquith announced that
320 out of England's 400 Liberal organizations had declared for
Independent Liberalism; that Free Liberals had no fear of an
Election; that it was a piece of political effrontery, after the
Coalition's methods in Ireland, to claim, in virtue of the Treaty,

[1] Cf. *Life and Letters of Austen Chamberlain*, ii, 175, for the Prime Minister's
view of the original panic among Opposition politicians.
[2] *Annual Register*, 1922, English History, p. 10. De Valera had, by that time,
been defeated in the Dail and his place as President taken over by Arthur
Griffith who installed a Government prepared to carry the Treaty and work a
Free State system.

to be in the Gladstone tradition; that ruthless economy was now preached by a Government guilty of profligate expenditure and vast and hopelessly incompetent bureaucratic experimentation, and that electors should see if Coalition Liberals could promise the instant repeal of the Protectionists' Safeguarding of Industries Act. In Mr. Asquith's view, the nation's first need was to get rid of the Coalition and return to Governments based on coherent principles and, in a reference to the House of Lords, he made it plain that he would resist current Conservative notions of restoring something like the old Veto powers to a Second Chamber even if it was a considerably remodelled House of Peers. All in all, it was a straightforward enough party declaration though Asquith can hardly have been aware how little his order of ideas now attracted nearly two million unemployed, their dependents, and the politicians who claimed to be acting for them.[1]

The Parliamentary Session of 1922, begun on February 7th, was soon dominated by the issue of the First and Second Sections of the Geddes "Economy" Report on February 10th.[2] The Geddes Committee had apparently likened its functions to those of a City Board of Directors, in charge of a concern threatened with bankruptcy unless expenses were slashed right and left. And though some of its recommendations appalled even Conservatives, possessed of a social conscience, it has to be admitted that the Geddes Committee was prepared to slash at Army, Navy, and Air Force expenditure as lustily as at that under the aegis of the Board of Education or the Ministry of Health.[3] It was, in fact, the Admiralty that first struck back hard and publicly[4] though it was

---

[1] Cf. *The Holmes-Laski Letters*, i, 312–449, for Laski's increasing despair of achieving anything through Asquith though, in 1921, he had been full of admiration and, in the following January still found the speech noted above "a very great work of art" as "a call to followers to battle" even if "as a speech giving ideas it was nothing".

[2] Cf. *The Times*, February 25th, for a third section of the Geddes Report issued a fortnight later. The large allowance of space in a publication like the *Annual Register* must serve as a guide to the Report's place in "public opinion". Primarily, of course, it was intended as a guide to the Chancellor of the Exchequer in what it was proper to allow to the "spending departments" in such an "Economy Budget" as it was intended to make that of 1922.

[3] Cf. *Hansard*, March 1st, for the Chancellor of the Exchequer, Sir Robert Horne, noting such things as the Navy's finally working to the 21 million "cut" of the Geddes Committee (though that was now to include savings from the Washington Naval Limitation), the Army's accepting a 17 million cut if not the $22\frac{1}{2}$ million recommended, and the Air Force accepting a 3 million cut where the Geddes recommendation had been $5\frac{1}{2}$ million.

[4] Cf. *Annual Register*, 1922, English History, p. 16, for the charge that the Committee had fallen into almost every possible error.

the Board of Education, assured of support from both "progressive" Oppositions, that did, perhaps, better proportionately in emendation of the suggested, savage cuts of the "Geddes Axe". It was, after all, difficult to justify the refusal of public schooling to every child under six or the far tighter restriction of secondary education, especially free secondary education, when, despite the talk of impending Exchequer insolvency, such unbridled luxury expenditure by private British citizens seemed to continue in the West End and the cosmopolitan holiday resorts. It was the Asquithian ex-Cabinet Minister and standard-bearer, Masterman, who in the notable book, *England after War*, warned the rich and especially the "new rich" profiteers, of the political extremism which their lavish displays of wealth would breed in a suffering country. And Asquith himself, who was sacrificing his last chances of returning to power by deprecating, in the interests of maximum productivity, quite a number of "New Liberalisms" and "New Manchester Schools" which he conceived to be based on semi-Socialist fallacies,[1] was almost as emphatic.[2]

Perhaps, at this stage, it might be well to narrate how narrowly the dissolution of the Coalition, from internal strains, was being avoided at the end of February 1922. Bitterly chagrined by the increasingly offensive "Die-Hard" tone towards himself which the

[1] Cf. *The Nation*, January 1, 1921, for the article entitled, "The New Manchesterism", and dealing with the volume, *Liberalism and Industry*, "written by Professor Ramsay Muir, in close co-operation with a little group of business men in Manchester" and "quite evidently moved by the fear lest the nation may be captured by a revolutionary Labour Party,'unless Liberalism can rally to the rescue". The new programme suggested for Liberalism was thus summarized by *The Nation*: "The nationalization of mines and railways, with a representative government by all the factors concerned, a drastic control of trusts and cartels by regulation, taxation, and, if necessary, national ownership, the taxation of land values and increments with large power of public purchase, large public provisions for housing, health and education, public guarantees for minimum wages, leisure, and unemployed pay, coupled with a taxation policy in which indirect taxation (except of luxuries) disappears, and income taxes and death duties on an advancing scale form the sources of normal revenue, with a capital levy, as an emergency measure for reducing the war debt to manageable dimensions—these and other proposals go a fair way in the Socialist direction. Indeed, there is one far-reaching proposal which, we think, may be taken as a test for the surrender of past privileges that is of the essence of the new Liberalism . . . that in all well-established businesses, a limitation should be put upon the amount of profits distributed to shareholders, the excess profits being divided between the State, the workers in the concern, and the shareholders in proportions prescribed by law."

[2] Cf. C. F. G. Masterman, *England after War*, pp. 99–100: "I am speaking quite seriously when I say that in my judgement that gross and growing disproportion between the good purposes to which wealth might be devoted, and the frivolous and worthless, the transitory and unproductive purposes to which it is in fact devoted, is one of the tragedies of our modern English life."

Conservative Leadership seemed unable to stop from spreading, mortified by the way in which his pressure for a Dissolution had been over-ruled, Lloyd George tried hard to recover his liberty of action by resigning in Austen Chamberlain's favour.[1] And the Conservative Leader was doubtless right in assuming that, in the circumstances, a Conservative Ministry under himself would probably inherit the full odium of the Coalition's record, about to be augmented, as it was, by some of the "Geddes Cuts", while Lloyd George, despite the promise of "independent support", would, out of Office, contrive to slough off Coalitionism increasingly for something more "advanced" and popular. It certainly appears to have taken a very considerable effort by Chamberlain to induce Lloyd George to stay after the beginning of March 1922,[2] and, even then, both men were not unaware that their continuance together might bring increasing troubles upon them. Lloyd George's indifferent health of the next few months was, doubtless, not unconnected with the growing difficulties and uncertainties of his political position. Chamberlain, meanwhile, who had endeavoured and failed to enlist Bonar Law's help when the latter's recovery seemed established, was conscious that his predecessor as Leader was alive to the possibility of becoming Prime Minister himself in the event of Conservative feeling against the Coalition passing out of the Leadership's control.[3]

There was, of course, always a danger throughout 1922 that Ireland would provide the occasion for a Coalition break-up, seeing the bloody Civil War that was preparing between the I.R.A. factions which, respectively accepted and opposed Lloyd George's Treaty. Though it was a struggle in which brutal assassinations and violations of Northern Ireland's frontier figured from the beginning,[4] the four British party leaderships, Conservative,

[1] Cf. *Life and Letters of Austen Chamberlain*, ii, 174–8, for the Prime Minister's long letter of February 27, 1922.

[2] *Ibid.*, p. 179, which quotes also from another Chamberlain attempt, at Oxford on March 3, 1922, to bring the "Die-Hards" to reason.

[3] Cf. *Ibid.*, p. 181, for a Chamberlain letter setting out his troubles and mentioning, among them, on February 26th: "Bonar Law tries on the crown, but can't make up his mind to attempt to seize it, won't join us and share the load, but watches not without pleasure the troubles of his friends."

[4] Cf. *Whitaker's Almanack, 1923*, p. 464, for such 1922 events, even before the "Civil War" proper, as these: "Feb. 8th. Armed men kidnapped number of leading Unionists who were taken over border into Southern Ireland. . . . Mar. 3rd. Mr. Max Green, Chairman of Irish Prisons Board [and son-in-law of John Redmond] shot dead in Dublin. Mar. 14th. Sir James Craig announced in Ulster Parliament that Field-Marshal Sir Henry Wilson was preparing scheme

Lloyd Georgian, Asquithian, and Labour, contrived to prevent the "Die-Hards" from forcing a crisis even about the "execution" of Field-Marshal Wilson, M.P., by "Republican emissaries" outside his London home on June 22nd.[1] But, meanwhile, the Government had again been badly shaken by the fall, in March, of the Coalition Liberal, Edwin Montagu, whose expulsion from the India Office had been a "Die-Hard" aim for years. Montagu had finally played into their hands by not safeguarding himself completely, as against Lord Curzon at the Foreign Office, when authorizing the publication of a Viceregal telegram which, in the interests of an India now facing the consequences of Hindu discontent, mobilized by Gandhi, being reinforced by Moslem discontent on the score of Britain's "unrighteous" treatment of Turkey, called for large pro-Turkish changes in the terms of settlement in the Near East.[2] Montagu refused to admit to any error of judgement and, after his virtual dismissal, there was an exchange of recriminations between him and Lloyd George[3] that did Coalition Liberalism even less service than what was regarded as Sir Gordon Hewart's "very indecent haste" to make certain of the Lord Chief Justiceship and £8000 per annum before worse befell. If, indeed, Lord Reading had now resigned the Viceroyalty, as seemed a possibility at one stage, the whole structure of Coalition Liberalism might have seemed beyond shoring up. As it was, with Montagu's Secretaryship now made over to the Conservative side of the Cabinet, Chamberlain felt, for a time, somewhat less anxiety on the subject of the "Die-Hards".[4]

Perhaps the kind of Session that 1922 became, as far as "progressive" politics was concerned, may be gathered from two of the leading challenges made to Government policy. The suggested Geddes cuts on education had been notably marked down in Cabinet but the resolve had been taken, none the less, to continue with the Geddes recommendation to deduct a pension contribution

for restoration of order. Mar. 26th. The prohibited convention of Irish Republican Army took place in private in Dublin. . . ."
[1] Cf. Sir Almeric Fitzroy, *Memoirs*, ii, 784, for "the passionate demonstrations of a mourning people" which had been evoked. The funeral procession to St. Paul's and the remarkable service there, on June 26th, made it plain, as did, indeed, Winston Churchill that night in the Commons (*Hansard*, June 26th) that British patience was being sorely tried.
[2] Cf. *Life and Letters of Austen Chamberlain*, ii, 182–3, for a very intimate account.
[3] Cf. *The Times*, March 10th.
[4] *Life and Letters of Austen Chamberlain*, ii, 183.

from teachers' salaries despite the legal doubts that emerged as to whether the existing Superannuation Act could properly be modified while the current Burnham Scale of salaries was in force. The Government was actually defeated on May 16th by 151 votes to 148, and though a Select Committee came to the conclusion that Ministers had given no undertaking to keep the existing Superannuation Act unmodified for the duration of the current salary-scales, a merely temporary two-year Act for Pension Contributions promised to give Parliament a new chance of discussing the question before long. It was obvious that the "progressive" and "advanced" had stirred up serious doubts as to the validity of "Anti-Waste's" attitude towards Education,[1] and the Asquithian Front Bench later attempted a Free Trade demonstration against what it considered the dangerous Protectionism of Stanley Baldwin's Safeguarding of Industries Act. Possibly it was unwise, in such critical times, to make almost a party pre-Adjournment display on such a relative trifle—except in principle—as the Safeguarding Committee's decision to place an import-duty on fabric gloves from Germany. On July 31st Ministers beat off the Free Trade attack by 277 votes against 113—and though the Asquithian Press and Platform continued to have much to say on the Protectionist perils lurking on the consumer's path, it can hardly be held to have produced much effect on the "general public". Of course, a certain amount of Labour support could still be enlisted against Protectionism's alleged tendency to raise the cost of living for the profit of "Trusts anxious to monopolize the Home Market", and Coalition Liberal consciences, too, could sometimes be stirred by the old Free Trade case. But possibly the demonstration was intended to revive flagging Asquithian zeal and confidence, for private complaints of Asquith's growing lethargy were certainly being heard.[2]

[1] Cf. C. F. G. Masterman, *England after War*, for many passages of sympathy with the teachers' plight as it had been allowed to become during the war—and post-war inflation when, according to Masterman, municipalities had expected to engage teachers at less than the pay Unions contrived to force for dustmen. Masterman, an Asquithian ex-Cabinet Minister, was basing himself largely on often pitiful revelations made to the *Daily News*.

[2] Cf. *Holmes-Laski Letters*, i, 427, 449, for behind-the-scenes discussion proceeding in May as to whether Lord Robert Cecil could not be metamorphosed into a Liberal Leader, "Asquith being now generally recognized as hopeless." In September Laski's gossip was taking another turn: "I lunched with Asquith's chief henchman in the Commons, Donald Maclean. . . . He gave me a melancholy history—Asquith devoted to bridge and small talk, doing no real work and leaving the party leaderless. I gathered that they all want him to go."

The Prime Minister, meanwhile, had been making a bold attempt to turn the course of politics into more favourable channels by remarkable personal efforts at the Pan-European Reconstruction Conference at Genoa. Briand had lost the French Premiership to Poincaré in January for surrendering too easily, it was alleged, to Lloyd George's wiles[1] and agreeing to a Genoa Conference in April at which Germany and Soviet Russia, France's debtors and enemies, would be entitled to full membership and could be expected to combine to her detriment. Of course, Lloyd George had hoped, and despite Washington's refusal to participate,[2] was still hoping that America might be induced to take a more liberal attitude towards the cancellation of Inter-Allied War Debts if proof were given that such a cancellation would mightily forward Europe's recovery by facilitating a just and reasonable solution even of Germany's Reparation liabilities and the compensations demanded of Russia for confiscated foreign assets. Though Poincaré was the most obstinate of negotiators and the suspect Russo-German collaboration materialized in the Treaty of Rapallo, Austen Chamberlain, deputizing for Lloyd George in London, expressed admiration for his work at Genoa in these unwontedly enthusiastic terms:[3]

The Press reports, the official reports, and private letters all show that he is at the top of his form and handling things and people with immense skill. Private letters say that our reputation never stood higher, our influence was never greater, and that the P.M. is unmistakably cock of that dunghill. So far . . . he has had a triumph won by force of conviction, acquired authority and great skill and tact. Even Barthou [French head of the Reparations Commission] feels his mastery and the force of his logic, and meditates asserting within limits his independence of Poincaré. . . .

In the end, of course, Poincaré, with the suspect Russo-German Treaty of Rapallo to quote, was barely prevented from destroying all the hopes raised by Genoa. And if he finally agreed, under

---

[1] Cf. *Daily Telegraph*, Centenary Supplement, p. 55, for a reproduction of the notorious Press photograph of Lloyd George's golf-lesson for Briand on January 10th at Cannes which so infuriated Nationalist France.

[2] *Whitaker's Almanack, 1923*, p. 467, under March 9th has this: "Text issued of United States Note declining to attend Genoa Conference"; and under May 15th this: "Report on Inter-Allied debts to United States gave a total of £2,267,856,000."

[3] *Life and Letters of Austen Chamberlain*, ii, 184.

severe pressure, to a Hague Conference on Russia[1] and to some postponement of a declaration of wilful German default with Reparations, he was not to be stopped from trying to make dangerous trouble for Britain at Constantinople, trouble calculated, among other things, to prevent a British veto on a French advance into the Ruhr. It was, doubtless, natural for all the "progressive" and "advanced" to announce, often with malicious and shortsighted glee, that Genoa, like Cannes, had been a failure and that the Prime Minister's prestige had sunk on the Continent almost as low as in Britain. But that was not the view of the Conservative Leader who, well aware though he was of the deficiencies of Lloyd George's record and character, was becoming, as Bonar Law had been before, almost an admirer. Here is Austen Chamberlain's view of the Prime Minister's troubles with Poincaré:[2]

He has saved Genoa from the burning in spite of Poincaré and brought back an 8 months' truce of God—no mean achievement. D— that fellow Poincaré! At the very moment that I was backing the French alliance, P. was renouncing me and all my ways and repudiating Millerand's undertaking that they would not take action against Germany except in accordance with their Allies. How *can* you work with such a man or with such a people? Wherever they have influence in the East they are using it against us. . . .

The Hague Experts Conference of June–July, if "saved from the burning" at Genoa, finally failed too, boycotted as it was by Washington and treated by Moscow to a request for credits to a total of £322,400,000 without any real readiness to assume part-responsibility for past credits.[3] Meanwhile, the hope that had appeared, for a space, of the Allied Reparations Commission itself leading a retreat from the impossibilities demanded of Germany began fading once more,[4] and the prospect of finding speedy and

---

[1] *Whitaker's Almanack, 1923*, p. 468, under May 13th: "Genoa Conference decided to set up expert commission to continue negotiations with the Bolshevists at the Hague." Pound and Harmsworth, *Northcliffe*, pp. 852–4, give some of the last troubles made for the Prime Minister under the aegis of Northcliffe.

[2] *Life and Letters of Austen Chamberlain*, ii, 184–5.

[3] Cf. *Whitaker's Almanack, 1923*, p. 468, for a succinct summary.

[4] *Ibid.*, p. 467, for some vital dates including: "May 30th. Text issued of German reply to demands of Reparation Commission, financial reforms being promised in return for a foreign loan", and "June 11th. Bankers' Committee of Reparations Commission decided not to recommend international loan to Germany."

productive employment for 1,300,000 British unemployed in re-equipping and re-tooling a war-devastated but re-tranquillized Continent faded with it. Of course, it was no part of Opposition politicians' trade to tell the Unemployed that Cannes, Genoa, and the Hague were something more than the inevitable failures of a discredited Prime Minister and a doomed Coalition, and as Lloyd George's ill-luck would have it, there was a bad, new "Honours Scandal", during the summer of 1922, which greatly added to the "Die-Hards' " chances of wrenching the Coalition apart.[1] Of course, the alleged "Sale of Honours" to raise a huge Lloyd George Political Fund had been under attack for years and, though there was something in the counter-suggestion that the Conservative and Asquithian Party Funds had been acquired in much the same way, there had obviously been a brisker and less guarded traffic since 1917. It had been possible to defend even this till 1920 or 1921 on the ground that every variety of service to the national cause had been sought out and honoured, but that defence would no longer serve to explain why two out of the five Peerages recommended for the Birthday Honours of June 1922, were plainly open to grave objection. The Prime Minister again rode out the storm by consenting to a Royal Commission to suggest an altered Honours procedure[2] but it was already plain that the Coalition could hardly survive another angry Conservative outburst against Lloyd George. Even the reluctant Austen Chamberlain began, in September, to see the likelihood of losing control of his party if he did not begin making some advance-preparations for changing the Coalition into a looser association under a Conservative Prime Minister when a suitable moment should appear to have come. But he was determined that proper consideration should be shown to Lloyd George and that the co-operation of Coalition Liberals should not be needlessly thrown away as some "Die-Hards", he considered, were urging.

Austen Chamberlain was not, however, fated to get the chance of preparing a gradual and seemly end to the Coalition,[3] for the autumn of 1922 brought further Conservative complaints against

---

[1] Cf. The *Morning Post*, June 17, August 28 and 29, September 6, 11, and 18, 1922, for some of the juiciest revelations in the "Die-Hards' " own paper.

[2] Cf. *Hansard*, July 17th. As his critics noted, the Royal Commission was to inquire, not into the scandals revealed, but into "the procedure to be adopted in future".

[3] Cf. *Life and Letters of Austen Chamberlain*, ii, 193–8.

Lloyd George on the score of his large personal responsibility for the dangerous Near Eastern position that had almost brought war already and might do so again despite the Lausanne Conference agreed upon.[1] At the end of August 1922, a great disaster had befallen the Greek Armies of Asia Minor facing the Turks of Mustapha Kemal, and during the first half of September it became plain that all the assumptions of British Near Eastern policy would have to be revised not only in Asia Minor but at Constantinople, the Straits, and even Adrianople. Mustapha Kemal had, in fact, obtained considerable help from Moscow which was anxious to cheer him on against British predominance at Constantinople and the Straits, while France and Italy, too, though nominally co-operating with Britain, had done some dangerous intrigue at Ankara, resentful, as it was claimed they were, of Britain's special encouragement, under Lloyd George, of over-swollen Greek ambitions. By September 24th Mustapha Kemal's cavalry had violated the neutralized Straits Zone at Chanak,[2] and for three weeks General Harington, in command at Constantinople, had to face the likelihood of being overwhelmed on the Asiatic side if Mustapha Kemal chose to give the word and face the consequences. On October 1st conversations with Kemal were arranged at Mudania, which twice broke down with lamentable possible consequences, before Kemal, whose troops had misbehaved abominably at Smyrna and elsewhere,[3] consented to a temporary recognition of the neutralized zones in return for the very advantageous Turco-Greek Armistice Terms of October 11th. And it was because Lloyd George and Winston Churchill were principally blamed for what was almost a war-call[4] to the Dominions and Allies that had gone out in September and caused trouble not

[1] *Life and Letters of Austen Chamberlain*, ii, 196, for the views of the Conservative Chairman.
[2] Cf. Harold Nicolson, *King George V*, p. 368, for one vivid description: "The French and Italians recalled their own detachments to the safety of the European shore. The slender British forces stood their ground in Asia, while the Turkish soldiers spat and gibbered at them across the barbed wire at Chanak."
[3] *Whitaker's Almanack, 1923*, p. 468, has these two succinct September entries: "Sept. 9, 1922. Turkish troops entered Smyrna.... Sept. 14th. Smyrna practically destroyed by fire and thousands of persons massacred."
[4] Harold Nicolson, *King George V*: "On the afternoon of September 17th, Mr. Churchill, in the temporary absence of Lord Curzon, issued a communiqué inviting the Dominions and our allies to assist us.... The British public realised, with sudden dismay, that they were on the verge of a new and totally unwanted war."

merely in Moslem India but in war-weary Canada that some
Conservatives, hitherto prepared to follow their Leaders, decided
that Lloyd George's Prime Ministership must end.[1]

Of course, the "notorious war-call" against Kemal had been
intended largely to frighten him into respecting the neutralized
Straits Zones, and, despite the bad faith of France,[2] especially
under Poincaré, it had not been wholly without effect. Yet how
the matter was promptly treated by "advanced opinion", so
anxious to encourage the Conservatives to bring down Lloyd
George as to evade the moral responsibilities of increasing Kemal's
triumph, may be instanced from the most conspicuous writing in
The Nation of September 23rd.

"What was the excuse?" asked Massingham. "That there was a
prospect of a Turkish return to Europe? If that be a true plea, no man
is more responsible than Mr. Lloyd George. It was his blundering
hand that has given force, and even a certain moral prestige, to the
horde that destroyed East European civilisation. . . . The path of the
Turk to Constantinople has simply been rolled out for him. . . . Constantinople might have been made a great international city. That
dream is over. There might have been a just settlement of Thrace.
That, again, the men and ambitions of Versailles forbade. . . . Politically, and looking at its effect on Imperial politics, the appeal to the
Dominions was the greatest crime of all. There is a fund of sympathy
and help in our oversea communities. But it is to be drawn on in
measure and with care. The British statesman who resorts to it to back
a defeated policy, or to bluff an opponent out of his advantage—as
Mr. George has done—runs the risk of drying it up."

By September 30th, Massingham, who had put his finger so
unerringly on the strongest Empire argument against what Lloyd
George had done, was half-contemptuously inviting the Prime
Minister to resign before the alienated Conservative Majority put
him out. Massingham's case was this:[3]

All Prime Ministers have their hours of unpopularity. It was the lot
of Disraeli, Gladstone, the admired and very "national" Palmerston,

[1] *Whitaker's Almanack, 1923*, p. 461, for a significant succession of 1922
entries: "Oct. 9th. Criticism of Government's Near East policy culminated in
growing demand for resignation of Mr. Lloyd George. Unionist leaders met in
private. Oct. 13th. Mr. Chamberlain defended Government and upheld
Coalition at Birmingham. Oct. 14th. Mr. Lloyd George replied to criticisms at
Manchester Reform Club, and claimed Government had saved Europe from
war in Near East."
[2] Cf. *The Nation*, September 23rd: "The Greeks assert that she supplied both
officers and munitions to the Kemalist armies."
[3] *Ibid.*, September 30th.

to be submerged or fiercely hated over long stretches of their lives. But has the country ever had such reason to distrust its political leadership, and been so eager to repudiate it? Mr. Lloyd George has not only led the Empire into an unfathomable mess; he offers it a wide prospect of injury in the future, directly traceable to his practice of substituting himself for the Foreign Office . . . it is hardly the Government as a whole that is to blame . . . it is his duty to resign. . . . Kemal does not trust him. The French do their best to counterwork him. The Italians have lost confidence. The accumulated weight of this disbelief falls on England and makes a bad settlement of the Straits and the Asiatic boundaries inevitable. In such a pass a patriotic man does not hesitate. He may think himself aggrieved or maltreated but he goes . . . it is now only a question of weeks or months as to when the Conservative revolt against the Prime Minister will be consummated. . . .

The Conservative revolt against the Prime Minister did, in fact, take place less than three weeks after *The Nation*'s prophecy. On October 19th, at a meeting of Conservative and Unionist members of Parliament in the Carlton Club, Austen Chamberlain's advice against dismantling the Lloyd George Premiership and the Coalition Government before the coming Election was voted down by 187 against 87 though the Party Leader was known to be supported by some of Conservatism's best-known figures including those of Balfour, Birkenhead, Horne, and Worthington Evans.[1] The really decisive factor in securing such a heavy vote against the Leadership had not been Stanley Baldwin's first nationally notable speech but Bonar Law's conviction that the time had come to form a homogeneous Conservative Government and that such a Government, by undertaking to abandon some of Lloyd George's more doubtful shifts and expedients, would rally a large majority to its side at a General Election. Events were amply to justify Bonar Law after Austen Chamberlain and his supporters had taken their resignations to the Prime Minister, and he, in turn, had gone to the Palace to notify the break-up of his Administration. Yet when Bonar Law was sent for and commissioned to form a Government, he began under the apparently very grave handicap of inability to use even his own party's most experienced administrators who had sided with Austen Chamberlain. Nevertheless, if the wits were soon calling Bonar Law's Cabinet Conservatism's "Second Eleven", the fall of Lloyd George

[1] Cf. *Life and Letters of Austen Chamberlain*, ii, 206, for the names of two other Conservative Cabinet Ministers and of six junior Ministers who signed Austen Chamberlain's retirement manifesto with him and the four Ministers mentioned.

had eased so many dangerous tensions that had been growing up in Britain's political system that the new Government proved to have little reason to fear the kind of attack that the fallen Premier soon directed against it. For one thing, Asquith, despite the hopes that were emerging of winning back Coalition Liberalism to the parent stream, could not resist the temptation of traversing Lloyd George's account of himself, as having been brought down by the aristocratic cabals of Belgravia "Die-Hards",[1] in a fashion that doubtless proved more convincing than could have been contrived by Lords Salisbury and Derby.[2] Then, as a General Election campaign developed on the Dissolution of the "Coupon Parliament", Bonar Law, simply and without apparent fuss, pushed home a number of points particularly likely to tell with hesitant sections of the electorate. And, finally, before detailing some of Bonar Law's election advocacy, it is worth remarking that Conservative candidates, facing two competing "progressive" rivals— and sometimes three in the shape of Liberal, National (Lloyd George) Liberal, and Labour—were found to have much greater polling advantages[3] than Lloyd George and Austen Chamberlain had allowed for.[4]

Of the nature of Bonar Law's special appeal to the electorate, one acute critic had this to say[5]:

When Mr. Bonar Law talks of tranquillity and freedom from adventure, we think of the warlike utterances of last month, and the summons to the Dominions and the Little Entente to take part with us in another Holy War. Mr. Bonar Law, speaking those soothing words, comes

[1] Cf. *Annual Register*, 1922, English History, pp. 114–15.

[2] Salisbury, son and successor of a famous Conservative Prime Minister and a survivor of the Conservative Government of 1905, had early turned against Lloyd George. Lord Derby, who unlike Salisbury had co-operated with Lloyd George, had, by the beginning of 1922, also decided to turn, declining, for example, to accept the India Secretaryship after Montagu's dismissal.

[3] Cf. *Whitaker's Almanack, 1923*, pp. 198–9, for East Ham North even improving on this with the following polling figures: Crook, Conservative, 7215; Susan Lawrence, Labour, 6747; Edwards, National Liberal, 4775; Osborn, Independent Liberal, 4021; Emery, Liberal, 1504. East Leyton's poll was: Alexander, Conservative, 7866; Carter, Labour, 6300; Gibbons, National Liberal, 4568; Ratcliffe, Liberal, 1650.

[4] Cf. *Life and Letters of Austen Chamberlain*, ii, 193, for a calculation that Labour was likely to obtain 200–250 members. It is possible that the figure of 200 might have been approached if the contest had been against so blackened a name as Coalition, but as against Bonar Law the total was 142.

[5] Cf. *The Nation*, October 28, 1922. Before long *The Nation* was accepting Lloyd George's contention that this "standstillism" of Bonar Law's was itself a form of reaction and worse might be to come on the House of Lords, Free Trade, and the Trade Unions if the polls encouraged it.

before us to turn all these alarming experiences into a bad dream. The nation, grateful for his reassuring phrases, accepts "tranquillity" as a sovereign charm just as it accepted "victory" or "reconstruction". But what does tranquillity mean? . . . Well, Mr. Law has explained his doctrine. "If the country is to recover," says the Prime Minister, "it will be by the work of the people, and my idea of the real method of dealing with it is to leave free play to individual initiative, to avoid attempts at improvement which, at another time, would be very desirable and very necessary. That applies not only to the social schemes that will be advocated by others but it applies to things which I myself would like to see done. I say that what we need is quiet and as little interference as possible, either by legislation or administration." These phrases hit off very well the temper of a great number of voters, of whom some dislike social legislation because it touches their pockets, and others dislike it from mere weariness or pessimism. Mr. Lloyd George has, indeed, done his successors a great service . . . he has helped to discredit "reconstruction" in the popular mind. . . . It is all to the good that Mr. Lloyd George has so discredited foreign adventure. . . . Unfortunately he has discredited good ideas as well as bad. The men who are acclaiming the new Prime Minister support . . . "Leave the nation to itself". A C.3 nation left to itself does not become something better than C.3; it becomes something worse.

By November 4th, well before polling-day on November 15th, it was obvious that Bonar Law could only gain by revealing how much he intended to depart from the late Prime Minister's much-abused methods. He could not undertake, the new Prime Minister declared,[1] to deal personally with every difficult question at home or abroad as Mr. Lloyd George had attempted to do. And then after promising loyally to carry out the Irish Treaty, he turned to Foreign policy and again markedly differentiated his Government's proposed course from that of its predecessor. On the Turkish question, his Government's policy would be based on co-operation with France and Italy so that chaos in Europe might be avoided, and then followed a repetition of his intention to leave the main direction of Foreign policy in the hands of the Foreign Secretary. If pledges of this kind could make him many friends and hardly any enemies, the same was true of the further pledge to summon a conference of Dominion representatives to discuss trade development, for if Free Trade stalwarts had their suspicions, a time of mass-unemployment was hardly the most suitable one for campaigning on the theme that an increase of Empire Trade could be bought too dear. Then he turned to deal with one of Labour's

[1] Cf. *The Times*, November 6, 1922.

main financial proposals, that for a Capital Levy, and while admitting that, during the war, he had considered that it might become a war-necessity, in the changed conditions after the war, the proposal would be "absolute lunacy". Here again, the obvious dislocation threatened to industry and finance by the Capital Levy project and the danger that, whatever its ultimate results, the immediate effects could well be a rapid running-down of commercial and industrial enterprise and a great increase of unemployment, sufficed to bring Bonar Law the approbation of nearly all who prided themselves on their "common sense" and business experience.

Perhaps it might be well to leave to the next chapter detailed comment and reflection on Election results that gave Bonar Law's far from distinguished Cabinet an absolute majority of 79 over all their "progressive" and other opponents put together. Here attention might well be given to what the extremists of the National Unemployed Workers' Movement had set on foot and how the new Prime Minister was eventually induced to turn on them some of the pawky common sense which, coming from one of his great political and business experience, a large part of the electorate had found so irresistible. The summer of 1922 had been spent by the "bolsheviks" in organizing an "Unemployed Workers' Hunger March" on London from several different directions, the first contingent of over three hundred setting out from Glasgow on October 17th and others, from nearer London, at later dates so that a simultaneous entry into the capital might take place on November 17th to the plaudits of the *Daily Herald*'s readership. These plans had been drawn up before it could be foreseen that nearly the entire period of the march would be overshadowed by General Election campaigning but, of course, it was natural that its organizers should claim that the "Hunger March" through the constituencies had had something to do with Labour's improved polling and representation.[1]

The claim was very far from convincing but, true it is, that once the "Hunger Marchers" had been brought to London,[2] a

---

[1] Cf. Wal Hannington, *Unemployed Struggles, 1919–1936*, p. 82, for the claim that the rise of Labour's membership from 61 to 142 owed much to the March.

[2] Cf. *Ibid*, p. 84, for a Communist organizer's account: "Twentieth November was the day fixed for the pompous ceremony of opening the new parliament. Two days later was to be the great day of the demonstration of the hunger marchers to press for an interview with the Prime Minister. During these few days the whole of the capitalist press became hysterical, and news columns were

persevering and even persecuting attempt was made to force them upon a Prime Minister who considered that the offer of the Ministers of Labour and Health to receive their deputation should suffice. Despite the clamour of the *Daily Herald* and part of the Labour Benches,[1] despite the occasionally alarming street-demonstrations attempted for months by the "Hunger Marchers" and their friends, the Prime Minister continued adamant against their obstinately-pressed claim to his personal attention at Downing Street. But when, in his Glasgow constituency, just before Christmas, he did, in his capacity as a Glasgow and a Scottish member, allow a personal interview to representatives of the local unemployed they do not seem to have relished the answers he made to their representations. To suggestions that the Government could help the Unemployed by borrowing the money to set them to work, the Prime Minister replied that that would end in an industrial crash. The notion that Government's halving of the interest paid out on National Debt would be of service antagonized the Prime Minister even more for he found it not only unjust but foolish in that it would destroy all possibility of financial credit in Britain. His own view was that there was an improvement in the Unemployment situation since the figures were half a million fewer than they had been at their worst. Moreover, a report from the Cabinet Housing Committee was expected shortly which would probably recommend a continuance of the State Housing Scheme though his own preference was for a transfer to private enterprise schemes. But whatever plans were adopted, they could not possibly absorb all the unemployed, and it would take the Government all its time, too, to balance the Budget on existing taxation. Yet bad as things were, he was convinced that the bottom had been reached and that a real trade revival would take place unless there was the serious trouble in Europe which he feared.[2]

filled with scare articles about 'Secret meetings of the marchers', 'Bolshevik gold', 'Firebrand leaders', and so on. . . . On the evening of 21st November the *Pall Mall Gazette* had a disgraceful article headed 'The Red Plot'. . . . On the morning of 22nd November one was confronted with newspaper placards everywhere . . . 'Keep away from Whitehall' said one. 'Barricades at Westminster' said another. . . .''

[1] Wal Hannington, *Unemployed Struggles, 1919–1936*, p. 88: "night after night heated debates took place in the House of Commons over the Premier's attitude. Mr. George Lansbury was particularly indefatigable. . . ."

[2] Cf. *Annual Register*, 1922, English History, pp. 143–4. The European trouble the Prime Minister rightly feared was the threatened French advance into the Ruhr.

CHAPTER XVII

THE BONAR LAW PREMIERSHIP

"The new Prime Minister does well. There is almost universal praise of his demeanour, its modesty and candour; of the good intellectual quality of his speech on Reparations, delivered, as usual, without a note, but also with no flaw in the close texture of its argument; above all of his 'style'. In the release from Lloyd Georgism, men are disposed even to exaggerate the unfamiliar blessing of having a Prime Minister with a normal regard for principle. . . . So ingrained had political pessimism grown as to produce a general disbelief in the possibility of there ever being a decent Government of England again . . . all our institutions begin to profit. . . . The degrading Honours Lists disappear and the Civil Service recovers its tradition. Abroad the country gets a chance to repair the damage to its good name. . . . If only Toryism will be moderate! That is the capital question."

The Radical *Nation*, December 23, 1922.

"Demonstrations organized by the official Labour bodies in conjunction with the 'National Unemployed Workers' Committee Movement' were held in many parts of the country yesterday. At each a resolution was submitted demanding the immediate meeting of Parliament to deal with the unemployment problem. The opportunity was seized by the Communists to make a bold display in speeches and banners.

"Many thousands were attracted to the London demonstration in Trafalgar Square. None of the banners were brighter or newer than those borne by the various branches of the Communist Party, who had apparently obeyed in full force the official instruction to identify themselves actively with the proceedings. It was a Communist banner . . . that formed the central feature of the background at the main platform on the Nelson Column. 'The Red Flag' was frequently sung. . . . On the instrumental side the 'Marseillaise' and the Sinn Fein 'Soldier's Song' mingled with the pibrochs. Under the banner of the Stepney Young Communist League a group of foreign-looking youths sang Communist nursery-rhymes.

"The hunger-marchers did not parade separately, but were scattered in small contingents among the various processions. Among those taking part, according to the banners, were men from Liverpool, Newcastle, Sheffield, Edinburgh, Glasgow, and Greenock. Mr. George Lansbury, M.P., headed one of the East-end processions, and among other members of Parliament who were present on the plinth were Mr. Bowerman, Mr. March, Mr. McEntee, and Mr. Saklatvala."

The Times, January 8, 1923, suspects Communist infiltration.

RADICAL opinion of the brand increasingly impatient with Asquith's caution in economic and international affairs, yet unprepared still for the Labour Party or Socialism, had gone through some strange vicissitudes in the course of 1922. During the Genoa period it had come near to forgiving Lloyd George and rallied sharply to his support against the combination of Poincaré and Northcliffe that ruined what was considered a very promising chance of salvaging the Continent from the worst results of the war and of the vindictive post-war policy planned by the Quai d'Orsay. There were times, too, when the traditional itch to put the blame for everything that was wrong in the Empire and the world upon the back of Downing Street was held in check by a sorrowful realization that even Gandhi, not to mention de Valera, could make political mistakes of the most damaging and even culpable kind. It comes almost as a surprise to find a temporarily disabused Massingham, capable, in the spring of 1922, of writing thus on the two personalities then setting the British Empire its most formidable problems[1]:

A man who when asked how, if he governed India he would deal with the wild border-tribes, could answer that he would present them with spinning-wheels is a child. And Gandhi's whole political programme is an excursion in childishness. . . . And it was something worse than childish for a saint of Hinduism to throw himself blindfold into the arms of the savage Moplahs who, says Sir Sankaran Nair, killed thousands of Hindus, skinned many of them alive, and raped their women wholesale. . . . Sir Sankaran Nair says truly that Gandhi, long resident abroad, knew little or nothing of India, and that he has drawn her back to Nationalism and Medievalism at a time when art, science, religion, political philosophy, and the idea of human brotherhood were awakening the mind of her youth to sympathy with the best thought in the West. Gandhi has plunged these boys in a confused dream of primitive life. Its motive was not *Ahimsa* but race-hatred. And its visible sign has been the rapid march of India to anarchy.

Indeed, it is one of the really unmerited hardships of this world of ours that the fate of India and Ireland should even temporarily lie in the hands of men like Gandhi and de Valera. They appear to have a conscience, even a great deal of it. But when it is wanted, it is always somewhere else. Gandhi promises the millennium, and when it fails to appear, promises it for a few weeks later. Later on he so conducts his moral crusade against our imperfect Government that he is in a fair way to make India a promising spoil for Moplahs and Afghans. De

[1] *The Nation*, April 15, 1922.

Valera has his Moplahs too, duly transformed into heroes of the Celtic spirit. Both use the cant of idealism to make havoc of average human living; both destroy without a touch of the creative mind.

The failure of Genoa ended Massingham's temporary urge towards Lloyd George; the "Geddes Axe's" presumed menace to all manner of desirable social expenditure renewed his complete alienation from the Coalition and all its works; and when the vain threat to fight the Turk, if need were, shook Lloyd George's position fatally, no one shouted more lustily than Massingham for Lloyd George's quick departure from Downing Street before worse ensued at Chanak or elsewhere. Yet in confidently affirming that either Chamberlain or Curzon, as the next Conservative Prime Minister, could be counted on to get a better Near Eastern settlement than was now open to Lloyd George,[1] Massingham, rightly regarded almost as the Radical oracle, played his part in nullifying Election hopes that he had been cherishing and propagating for nearly two years. He had announced, with conviction, that if all the "progressive" forces opposing the Coalition merely refrained from getting into one another's way, unprofitably and unnecessarily, the Coalition could be defeated—and much more so if they could be persuaded to make an *entente* for an agreed short-term policy in the next Parliament.[2] Certainly, if Lloyd George

[1] Cf. *The Nation*, September 30, 1922: "The danger of the Chanak situation is that the slightest act—the defiance of a Turkish irregular or the nervous zeal of a young officer—may bring about a collision, and a collision war. . . . Public opinion here must insist that an 'Incident' *shall not mean* war, and that its consequences shall be visited *afterwards* on the head of the Minister who has put so many young lives in peril. . . . In our view, there is a political way out of this situation. Mr. Lloyd George should resign. There is danger in such a step, for the Turk might misunderstand it. But a Prime Minister like Mr. Chamberlain or Lord Curzon would act with more confidence. . . . The Turks would not regard him as pro-Greek, nor the French as anti-French. . . ."

[2] Cf. *Ibid.*, March 4, 1922, for a remarkable article entitled "Thoughts on the Coming Government" in which the Labour strategists were warned that Liberalism would not be quickly killed off by running Labour candidates on any and every occasion, and that the country would have much more confidence if McKenna and Keynes, for example, were at the Treasury in a mixed Government than if a purely Labour Administration, without adequate strength or prestige, tried to lay its hands on everything. The cudgels were taken up again when Sidney Webb, as the year's Chairman of the Labour Party, came out strongly for the "absolute" independence of the Labour Party (*Ibid*,. July 8, 1922). "A situation, for example, might arise," asserted Massingham, "in which the Labour Party, with the help of the Liberal Party, and of detached progressives of the type of Lord Robert Cecil might constitute a majority in the new House of Commons. These parties might agree to a programme, good for a full term of Ministerial years, might agree . . . to a Labour Prime Minister, and might by that means avert the great evil and danger of a reactionary government of England, giving a reactionary voice and vote in the affairs of Europe. No matter: the Webbian formula forbids."

had endeavoured, after Chanak, to face an Election attack on his retention of the Prime Ministership, Henderson, Asquith, and Lord Robert Cecil might very well have been set the problem of constructing a joint Cabinet and programme to last out the life-time of one Parliament. And as Massingham had seen it, if the Coalition was doomed to defeat provided the proper precautions were taken on the "progressive" side, the Conservative Party, fighting alone, could not even contemplate single-handed victory.

Of course, the emergence of Bonar Law to take Lloyd George's place removed many obstacles from the Conservatives' path for, under his Leadership, the blame for most of the errors and failures of the Coalition could more easily be ascribed to the personality and methods of the ex-Prime Minister than would have been possible under one who, like Chamberlain, had persisted in Lloyd George's company to the Coalition's very end. Moreover, instead of the bulk of the profit from the normal "swing of the pendulum" against six years of Lloyd George's Coalition going to the "parties of progress" as had been hoped, the Bonar Law manœuvre diverted most of it to the Conservatism that had revolted against the Coalition, and overthrown Lloyd George. Some parts of the electorate, too, as Massingham had feared,[1] increased the strength of Bonar Law's following by the vigour of their revulsion from such dubious accompaniments of "progress" as "Poplarism" and "ca canny".

Yet though "progressives" had occasional nightmares of Bonar Law's receiving what could have been represented as a mandate for "reaction" in the shape of Conservative House of Lords

[1] Cf. *Ibid.*, May 27, 1922, for an article entitled, "The Poplar Path." Poplar was, of course, only the most notorious of the Labour-dominated areas where a combination of anarchic sentimentality of the Lansbury pattern and lax administration was threatening to produce economic chaos, and to the profit of no one more, it seemed, than the habitual cadger or loafer. "It recalls the worst features of Speenhamland," urged *The Nation*, "It pays people to be idle . . . it enables every Conservative in the country to point the finger of alarm and scorn at Labour administration. And they are justified in holding that if a Labour Government were to administer the national resources upon such a plan, it would spell ruin to every section of the community. . . . For extravagant out-relief, though the worst of the Poplar vices, is not the only one. Waste and extravagance are everywhere manifest in the expenditure of public money. . . . Add to these follies a really criminal slackness in revising cases receiving relief, and a refusal to take legal proceedings against persons for concealing their sources of income, and you have social irresponsibility carried to an extreme. . . . What is our Labour Party doing to dissociate itself from this bad administration and to make clear to the nation that its policy of social-economic reform runs along quite different lines?"

"Reform", further departures from Free Trade and, perhaps, more "Geddes Cuts", the actual voting figures, despite their yielding an absolute Conservative Majority at Westminster of 79, proved very reassuring. Indeed, the "progressive" cry, that went up as soon as the complete Election figures were available, was that Bonar Law, with only two-fifths of the votes cast (representing only one-third of the registered electorate) behind him, had received no mandate at all and possessed not the slightest moral authority to propose anything with the slightest savour of "reaction". Five million votes had been cast for his candidates who, thanks to the division of their opponents between Liberal and Labour, had returned 344 members to Westminster while eight million votes for other candidates had merely sufficed to produce 142 Labour members, 60 Independent Liberals, and 57 "National Liberal" supporters of Lloyd George.[1] Treated another way, the figures could be made to prove that the lack of proportional representation, combined with the unwise Labour-Liberal cross-fighting on the "progressive" side, had resulted in Bonar Law's obtaining one supporter at Westminster for every 18,110 Conservative votes cast though Labour members represented 30,672 voters each and Asquithians 49,244 voters each. Indeed, Independent Liberal and Labour votes alone—to the exclusion of those cast for "National Liberals"—showed a majority of one and a half millions against the Conservatives and could be treated as having given Bonar Law's opponents their own mandate to combine in Opposition against the Ministry until it could be ejected and replaced from among "progressives", sensible enough to substitute a political *entente* for the fratricidal strife which had given Bonar Law his unmerited majority.

Of course, this line of argument assumed that the Labour Party, realizing how near it might have come to dominating a Labour-Liberal Cabinet, would change course and give up its strategy of trying to destroy Liberalism, as an alternative to Labour, for those anxious to turn Conservatism out. But Labour was far from dissatisfied with the profits its course had already yielded, and, certainly, in large parts of the country, Liberalism could be

---

[1] Cf. *Whitaker's Almanack, 1923*, p. 190, for a slightly different version of Parliament's composition which gave the Conservatives 347; Labour 142; Liberals 59; National Liberals 59; Nationalists 2; Sinn Fein 1; Independents 5. Of course, numbers of ex-Coalitionists had given assurances which made them claimable both by Lloyd George and Asquith and, on occasion, by the Conservatives also.

regarded as on its way out to obsolescence while, at Westminster, there was the immensely stimulating process of forcing further concessions to Labour's claim for exclusive recognition as the official Opposition. Other forcing-tactics attempted, under the converging pressure of the new Clydeside group of "extremists", George Lansbury, the *Daily Herald*, and the "Unemployed Workers' Movement" need not here be set out but they certainly resulted, before long, in arousing some dangerous antagonisms. The badgering of Bonar Law to receive, in person, an "Unemployed Workers" deputation; the attempt to keep even Mr. Asquith off the Front Opposition Bench;[1] the opening hiss for Lloyd George—all this may serve as further explanation for "Liberal Reunion's" prompt emergence to offer "progress" almost as large a Parliamentary party as Labour and somewhat more restraint.

The first move for "Liberal Reunion" may be said to have come when Lloyd George allowed it to be known that he was ready to serve under Asquith's orders again and that, in view of the depletion of Liberal Party Funds, he was anxious to come to the rescue from the great political funds under his own control. Asquith, a tired veteran in his seventy-second year, was not unwilling to forgive and forget, especially as it was conceivable that "Reunion" might put him back in Downing Street and give him and his family that signal vindication from the slanders which had so strongly contributed to forcing them out in 1916.[2] Yet he recognized that unless "Reunion" was managed with care, caution, and regard to the proprieties, it might well cause another Liberal schism in view of the intense resentments which Lloyd George's activities since 1916 had excited. In fact, the Radical oracle, *The Nation*, promptly threatened not merely schism but a new hiving-off of younger men to Labour if Lloyd George and some of his

[1] Cf. *The Nation*, November 25, 1922: "It is certain that the Speaker will not endorse the party's claim to the whole of the Front Opposition Bench." In the end, room was made on that Bench for Asquith and for Simon, as his Deputy, while Lloyd George was reported to have "prudently reserved to himself the corner seat below the gangway, immediately in front of the benches to which the Wee Frees resort. Everyone who knows the House of Commons can perceive the advantage of this arrangement. Mr. George will be in close contact with the Liberals. Mr. Asquith will not."

[2] Cf. *Holmes-Laski Letters*, i, 561, for Laski, after a lunch at the Asquiths, in 1923, writing this of Mrs. Asquith: "Her passion to be back in Downing Street is incredible. You would have thought that the hope of the world lay in Asquith's return to power. She cursed all his enemies, laughed at the Trade Unions, sneered at the Tories. . . ."

more notorious Coalition Liberal associates were quickly and automatically readmitted to the fold. As *The Nation* had it[1]:

> And as a consequence of Liberal "reunion", do the Man of the Treaty and the Man of Mesopotamia, the Man who spent a hundred millions on the Russian wars, and the Man who saved a few on the children's school-books, the Man who built the Homes for Heroes, and the Man who thought the single-room system made for the felicity of young married couples; and, above all, that Commander of the Faithful, the Man of the Black-and-Tans, become fit associates in the future enterprises of Liberalism? . . . This is not an argument for a pedantic or a Pharisaic spirit. If there are "National Liberals" who are sick of "National Liberalism", the door of re-entry to the fold is open. But to mingle sheep and goats, to create instead of a Liberal party a promiscuous herd . . . is to bring the mission of Liberalism to an end, and reduce its very name to contempt. In that event, honest Liberals, and we should say most young Liberals, will either feel that the world of politics is no place for them, or range themselves with Labour, as the only party with a scrap of principle left.

This plain warning, repeated again and again, was heeded even if at some cost to the giver.[2] Over the next few months "Liberal Reunion" was allowed to develop tentatively and gradually by co-operation whether against Conservative Protectionism to the Right or the Labour "extremism" to the Left which experimented with obstruction in Parliament, gave some encouragement to the suspect "Unemployed Workers' Movement" and, finally, took to justifying not merely the Clydeside rent-strikes but their possible extension to England. Labour's Front Bench was, naturally, far from happy about the activities of the extremer Back-Benchers partly because they powerfully forwarded "Liberal Reunion" and partly because they might conceivably give "Liberal Reunion" the chance of drawing ahead of Labour at a General Election and forming the next Government. Yet Ramsay MacDonald, who owed his position as Opposition Leader to the Clydesiders'

[1] *The Nation*, December 2, 1922. Lloyd George is the Man of the Treaty of Versailles, Churchill the Man of Mesopotamia and the Man who spent a hundred millions, H. A. L. Fisher the saver on the school-books, Addison the Heroes' home-builder, Mond the advocate of felicity in single-rooms and, of course, Hamar Greenwood the Man of the Black-and-Tans.

[2] Cf. *Holmes-Laski Letters*, i, 475, for the revelation, dated at January 21, 1923, that Massingham's proprietors (long worried by the fact that he had often seemed to be backing Labour rather than Liberalism) had sold control of *The Nation* to a syndicate of Independent Liberals, who were dispensing with Massingham's services. Massingham's last number was issued on May 5, 1923 and thereafter *The Nation* was largely under the control of J. M. Keynes. The Rowntrees, however, had apparently offered Massingham a first option.

favour[1] was hardly in a position to discipline them effectively and, meanwhile, on the Liberals' other flank, Bonar Law, too, had unending troubles. There was a continuous anxiety about Foreign Affairs both because the Near Eastern situation continued explosive throughout the long-drawn-out Lausanne Peace Conference[2] with the Turks and because Poincaré insisted on the French march into the Ruhr, in January 1923, that ended all immediate hopes of effecting a political *détente* which might help a trade revival. To make the strain greater on the unfortunate Prime Minister, American pressure on Britain for a War-Debts settlement induced Baldwin, his second-in-command, to accept American terms[3] which events were to prove ungenerous and untenable and which, in any case, made trouble inside a Conservative camp that three by-election shocks, early in March, on advance-preparations for Rent Decontrol proved to be far less securely placed than had been imagined.[4] When Bonar Law, whose personal prestige was still high, was sent by his doctors on an enforced holiday on May 1st, the possibility of remarkable changes on the political scene was already being privately discussed.[5]

[1] Cf. L. Macneill Weir, *The Tragedy of Ramsay MacDonald*, pp. 104–9, for the majority of 61 obtained for MacDonald as against Clynes's 56.

[2] Cf. Butler and Maccoby, *Development of International Law*, pp. 484–6. The negotiations broke down on February 4, 1923, were renewed on April 24th, and resulted, on July 14th, in a treaty with annexed conventions which, however, still left the Turks claiming the Mosul area and finally attempting the armed invasion, repelled and heavily punished by the R.A.F.

[3] Cf. *Whitaker's Almanack, 1924*, p. 471: "Jan 8, 1923. At first meeting of Debt Commission Mr. Baldwin explained British position. . . . Jan. 20th. Mr. Baldwin and his colleagues left for England. . . . Feb. 1st. British Government decided to accept America's terms for funding of the debt." Lord Beaverbrook was the most dangerous critic of the American Debt Settlement.

[4] Cf. *The Nation*, March 10, 1923: "Never probably has a new Government sustained a political crash like that of the past fortnight. . . . It is evident that the control of the rent of houses falls harshly upon the landlord, and especially the small landlord. . . . The existing Rent Restriction Act of the Coalition ends automatically next June, and there is no doubt that the bulk of the landlords of the country, great and small, were anticipating the prospect of an immediate increase to recoup them for the period when the rent has scarcely covered repairs. . . . Decontrol, say the theorists, will produce higher rents, and therefore will encourage capital to flow into building enterprises, which will supply the houses now needed. And so, by the natural law of supply and demand, rents will reach a just and normal amount. Show us the houses we can go into, is the reply of the panic-stricken citizen, at a just and normal rent, before you hand us over to the caprice of the landlord, who, owing to the absolute monopoly he now enjoys, can charge any sum he pleases. . . ."

[5] Cf. *Holmes-Laski Letters*, i, 501, for Laski reporting the Labour Leaders as all feeling "near office" and *Life and Letters of Austen Chamberlain*, ii, 213, for an approach to that statesman to return to the Government when Bonar Law might conceivably be able to recommend him as successor instead of Lord Derby, Lord Curzon, or Mr. Baldwin.

Changes, of course, came in plenty when Bonar Law returned on May 20th, and an immediate operation had to be arranged which, however, failed to avert his death, on October 30th, from cancer of the throat. The sick man resigned by letter without making any precise recommendation to the King on the subject of a successor, and in the circumstances the King's choice really lay between Lord Curzon, who had been deputizing as Prime Minister and Baldwin, who had been leading the Commons. After taking advice,[1] the King decided that it had become unwise, if not impossible, in the existing state of politics, to choose a Head of Government outside the House of Commons, and despite Baldwin's lack of any long experience of first-class responsibility, it was he who became Prime Minister. There is some evidence that Bonar Law had been anxious enough about the possible effects of Baldwin's comparative inexperience to consider whether Austen Chamberlain could not be brought back into the Government in time to inherit the succession.[2] And certainly Baldwin was destined, in little more than six months, to throw away, it seemed unnecessarily, Bonar Law's Majority and to give "Liberal Reunion" and Labour the chance of competing between themselves for the prizes of Downing Street.

Though the dangerous amateurism of the new Prime Minister was obvious to most experienced politicians,[3] the general public and even part of the Press were either unaware of this or cheerfully prepared to believe that the man, who had led the successful revolt against Lloyd George, was deeper than he seemed. Thus, he made many opening blunders in handling Austen Chamberlain who, of course, had much greater official experience[4] and then plunged from the policy of reabsorbing Chamberlain and his following, temporarily blocked by the "Die-Hards", to that of bidding for Lord Robert Cecil, the mounter of many "progressive"

---

[1] Cf. Harold Nicolson, *King George V*, 375-7. It would seem that the really decisive advice was that of the ex-Prime Minister, Lord Balfour, who, despite his view of Curzon's exceptional qualifications and Baldwin's lack of "any signs of special gifts", still held that in the existing state of politics the Prime Minister ought to be in the Commons.

[2] Cf. *Life and Letters of Austen Chamberlain*, ii, 213.

[3] Cf. *The Nation*, June 2, 1923: "What is the calibre of the new Prime Minister, as compared with Mr. Bonar Law? In the House of Commons, the change is regarded in all quarters as an overwhelming loss."

[4] *Life and Letters of Austen Chamberlain*, ii, 220-4, for the ex-Conservative Leader's anger at "the discourtesy shown me down to the last detail" and the inexcusability of the "attempt to buy me out" of politics by the offer of the Washington Embassy.

platforms, and even for Asquith's last Chancellor of the Exchequer, Reginald McKenna. The McKenna nomination caused endless trouble and finally had to be withdrawn[1] while few party stalwarts had much liking for the more "progressive" part of Lord Robert Cecil's somewhat unorthodox post-war career.[2] Yet here is a laudatory "progressive" view of Baldwin, prepared to rate him higher than Bonar Law because he was believed to be capable of departing from his predecessor's policy of "passivity towards the occupation of the Ruhr" by French troops, an occupation which "progressives" detested as alike oppressive, illegal, and ruinous to every prospect of normalizing Europe's trade and politics:[3]

The Bonar Law Government was composed largely of Die-hards, but its strength lay in the support of *moderate* opinion. . . . It was primarily to this opinion that Mr. Bonar Law, with his quiet manner and promise of tranquillity, appealed. To reassure this opinion, which had latterly become uneasy, was Mr. Baldwin's really essential task. Mr. McKenna and Lord Robert Cecil have helped him more in this respect than Mr. Austen Chamberlain and his chief colleagues could have done. . . . The general benevolence with which the new Government has been received is due partly to a belief that it has been reinforced against reaction, and partly to a vague expectation that it will pursue a more resourceful and constructive policy, especially in foreign affairs. The former impression is not unreasonable. Mr. McKenna and Lord Robert Cecil should certainly constitute additional safeguards against further departures from Free Trade, against a reckless breach with Russia, and against armament adventures of the type of Singapore. But the question of immediate importance is the effect on our European policy. . . . A situation will soon present itself which will require us to take once more an active part in the attempt to restore peace in Europe. . . . The next few years will test Lord Robert's quality, no less than Mr. Baldwin's.

[1] Cf. *Whitaker's Almanack, 1924,* p. 466, under August 27, 1923, for the kind of announcement that had to be made three months after McKenna's provisional nomination: "Mr. Neville Chamberlain appointed Chancellor of the Exchequer . . . Mr. McKenna's health not permitting him to contest a bye-election." It seems obvious that McKenna, who would have been resigning a lucrative Bank Chairmanship, expected the Conservative Whips to arrange an uncontested election for him, by preference to a City seat, but that the two sitting Conservatives refused to budge for one who was making it almost a point of honour not to be classed as a Conservative.

[2] Cf. *Holmes-Laski Letters,* i, 408, for what happened in the spring of 1922 after a Cecilian manifesto, urging that the perilous appeals of revolution on the one hand and reaction on the other, must be resisted by a revived liberalism dedicated to the cause of freedom and committed to international peace and a partnership at home between industry and labour. Underground manœuvres began to force Asquith's resignation and the offer of the Liberal leadership to Lord Robert.

[3] *The Nation,* June 2, 1923.

English Radicalism: The End?

What is the calibre of the new Prime Minister. . . ? In the House of Commons . . . the average member speaks of Mr. Bonar Law as "incomparably the greatest Parliamentarian of our time". . . . Mr. Baldwin is described, by contrast as a man of slow wits and third-class debating powers. . . . Parliament, however, is often mistaken. . . . The intangible qualities of character and personality, so much more important than mere cleverness or even intellectual force, are not usually detected until their possessor has passed through the ordeal by fire. The country knows little of Mr. Baldwin, but it likes what it knows. It feels about him a breadth, a courage, and a buoyant temperament lacking in his predecessor; and is prepared to find him prove the bigger man.

There was undeniable foresight in this view as well as a display of a number of the leading "progressive" anxieties of 1923 not yet touched upon—the possibility of more "safeguarding" or Protection, the heavy and continuing expenditure mooted for the Singapore Naval Base,[1] and the fear that Lord Curzon's resentment of malevolent anti-British propaganda activity by the Soviets in Persia and Afghanistan, against their pledged word as it was, would lead to a cancellation of what Anglo-Russian relations there were. It might be well to give an impression of how the leading "progressive" weekly of the day, *The Nation*, dealt with Anglo-Russian tension. *The Nation* had just been removed from the control of the magnificently eloquent band of writers recruited by Massingham partly, it would seem, because it was felt that their approach to every question paid insufficient attention to hard economic facts and too much to the sentimentalism that always contrived to find some justification, past or present, for every Labour or Trade Union demand. From May 1923 the moving force on *The Nation* was the economist Maynard Keynes, a humanitarian, too, in his way but one who was feeling his way forward to a largely different set of explanations for Britain's economic maladjustments from those normally proffered by *The*

[1] Cf. *The Nation*, May 5th, May 12th, May 26th, and June 9th. The first number praised Asquith's unfriendly criticism and the second gave the Singapore scheme a main article beginning: "No more deplorable step has been taken by the present Government." Though *The Nation* hardly made allowance for the fears of Australia and New Zealand in regard to Japanese expansionism and though it was over-doctrinaire on the "international goodwill" that would be evoked by an abandonment of the project, it also put the financial case thus: "At a moment when our financial position imposes rigid limits on our total expenditure, and when the inadequacy of our Air Force for home defence has been admitted, we are to devote £9,500,000 to creating, seven thousand miles away, a base for the largest capital ships. . . . A garrison must be provided . . . provision against a sudden attack from the air. . . . The upkeep of the new base will be a heavy item. . . ."

Nation in the past. Here is no place for the deflation-inflation controversy but only for the new *Nation*'s contriving to set before "progressive" readers an attitude towards Russia differing at once from Labour's and Lord Curzon's. As *The Nation* saw it:[1]

The Labour Party seems ready to tolerate from the Soviet what it would tolerate from no "capitalist" Government. The seizure of British ships on the high seas, and the adding of fuel to the flames which perpetually flicker on the Indian frontier, lose something of their significance in the eyes of Labour when they are the acts of what it persists in regarding as a "working-class" Government. The Labour Party's present stand for the maintenance of the trade agreement is entirely justifiable, but it is doubtful whether its general attitude towards Russia helps to improve Anglo-Russian relations. The idea that it has powerful friends in this and other countries . . . almost certainly encourages the Soviet to acts of hostility, which it would claim were directed against "capitalism" but which belong in reality to the oldest imperialist tradition.

But if the attitude of Labour is open to criticism . . . that of the Government is even more. . . . Admittedly, most of the issues raised in Lord Curzon's Note are of genuine importance. . . . It is impossible, however, to believe that a Note concerned with such issues would, in the case of any other Power, have been written in the tone Lord Curzon adopted or have been couched in the form of an ultimatum. . . . The clue to the only sound policy in the present crisis is to be found in Mr. Asquith's speech in the debate on Tuesday. He recalled the fact that in Tsarist days "propaganda more widespread and more insidious in its character was carried on throughout the most vulnerable parts, so far as the British Empire was concerned, of Central Asia"; and that it had been put an end to by the Anglo-Russian Agreement. "That has been done before," he said, "and it could be done again and ought to be done again" . . . the denunciation of the trade agreement will not stop Russian propaganda in Asia. It will rather intensify it. . . . The real question before us is whether there is any other way. . . . Mr. Asquith clearly thinks there is. . . .

It seems obvious that Keynes and his collaborators considered Asquith as a possible Prime Minister still—and this quotation, at such length, has been deemed justifiable both for this reason and for the advance light it throws on how the "Russian Question" could and did become a central turning-point in the decisive party-struggles of 1924.[2] As it happened, however, the Soviet

---

[1] *Ibid.*, May 19, 1923.

[2] Cf. *Whitaker's Almanack, 1924*, p. 472, however, for such other items as: "March 27, 1923. Archbishop Ciepliak and Father Butkevitch condemned to death at Moscow. . . . May 7th. Russian Red Church Convention declared the

English Radicalism: The End?

Leaders found it wise, in 1923, to beat a considerable retreat rather than lose the Trade Agreement, and the Baldwin Government, with an apparent modest success to its credit, was emboldened, to put forward a British Reparations plan which, it was hoped, might reduce Franco-German tension and promote a French evacuation of the Ruhr. Though "progressive opinion" of many kinds, outraged by the whole course of French policy in the Rhineland and the Ruhr,[1] tried to cheer on Baldwin to a forthright declaration on behalf, at once, of violated international law and trampled-down British interests, it became apparent, before long, that he was meeting not merely the usual Rothermere Press clamour of "France is right"[2] but serious Cabinet hesitations also. Ultimately the vain hope of placating Poincaré by minimizing every necessary suggestion was abandoned, and Britain asserted its doubts on the legality of what had been done, the injury Britain was sustaining, and the possibility that it would challenge an indefinite Ruhr occupation under the League of Nations Covenant. Despite France's slowly-growing Exchange and Budget problems, Poincaré saw no need to flinch yet before what he must have known was a largely hesitant Cabinet, and, indeed, "progressive opinion" was soon to decide that though Baldwin, personally, might mean well, nothing effective could even yet be expected from his Government. The Cabinet, in fact, was suspected almost of over-eagerness to turn

Patriarch Tikhon unfrocked. . . ." These things tended to help anti-Russianism more than "progressive" politicians allowed for.

[1] Cf. *The Nation*, April 7, 1923, for the worst French "atrocity": "In the past week a barbarous event, which throws eternal disgrace on the French nation, has occurred at Essen. Eleven Germans were killed in a wholly unprovoked attack by a panic-stricken French detachment. . . . All M. Poincaré has achieved is to stop the machinery of Europe's greatest and most complex industrial area, and to convert it into a potential volcano which may blow up and destroy the organized communities of a continent."

[2] Cf. *Ibid.*, August 4, 1923, for the famous "A.G.G.": "It would, I suppose, be agreed by every student of public affairs that the most formidable difficulty that besets Mr. Baldwin in dealing with France is the astonishing dementia of Lord Rothermere . . . the daily columns of imbecile letters on the Ruhr with which the *Daily Mail* has made itself a competitor in silliness with Lord Rothermere's other organ, *Comic Cuts* . . . three British Prime Ministers in turn have been engaged in the most desperate attempt to save the shattered shell of the European system from final wreck, and, incidentally, this country from irreparable economic ruin. . . . And all the time the chief enemy of the Prime Minister, no matter whether it was Mr. Lloyd George, Mr. Bonar Law, or Mr. Baldwin has been in our midst. . . . Day by day the country has been flooded with a torrent of garbled and demented propaganda. . . . M. Poincaré has exploited this fantastic situation to the utmost. . . ." Lord Rothermere, who had now added most of his brother Northcliffe's newspaper power to his own (Northcliffe had died in 1922) was probably rendered more anti-German by the loss of two sons in the war.

374

its back on the unsatisfactory European scene[1] in order to concentrate instead on the two Imperial Conferences for which Bonar Law had issued the invitations and which, almost unprecedently, would associate an Imperial Economic Conference, with the Imperial Conference proper. Conference meetings were to begin on October 1st, and one hardly needed to be a prophet to guess that, in view of the apparently worsening European situation, all manner of means to stimulate inter-Imperial trade would figure on the agenda of the Imperial Economic Conference. Nor was the thought ever absent from the minds of politicians that a season, when heavy Winter Unemployment was expected, in many fields, to grow worse from the consequences of the Ruhr imbroglio, might prove as good a time as any for Conservatives to ask the country to consider wide-ranging Imperial Preference and Tariff Reform as likely means to get many of the workless reabsorbed into productive industry.

It had been Mussolini's first monstrous Fascist display at Corfu on August 31st, when taking advantage of Anglo-French tension, he had committed an international outrage of the first order, that finally convinced the Baldwin Government that it must reconstruct the *Entente* to get the Italians out of Corfu without a war.[2] The

---

[1] Cf. *Ibid.*, September 22, 1923: "Inspired by this country . . . the German Government made its last despairing gesture . . . the German offer is still unanswered. In the four months that have elapsed . . . the German nation has crashed from precipice to precipice. The mark has fallen from hundreds of thousands to the pound to millions and tens of millions and hundreds of millions until this week it has disappeared from the currencies of the world. The strangle-hold on the Ruhr has been tightened . . . the Cuno Government which made the offer has fallen, and the Stresemann Ministry that succeeded it cannot long resist the avalanche that is sweeping Germany into the abyss. The faint hope of some economic deal between the iron and steel magnates of the two countries, which, however vicious in itself, might serve to check the plunge into anarchy, has faded, and the world waits for the final catastrophe. . . . Mr. Baldwin and his colleagues, having made a vain demonstration against the strangulation of Germany and having been snubbed for their pains, dispersed to their several holiday haunts, leaving the consummation of the tragedy to the competent hands of its author . . . M. Poincaré. . . ."

[2] Cf. *Ibid.*, for the famous "A.G.G." stressing, resentfully, the apparent humiliations involved in a policy of renewing full co-operation with Poincaré without getting a single satisfactory assurance on the Ruhr or, indeed, on the French attempts to encourage a Rhine-Ruhr "Separatist" movement to break away from Germany altogether. Baldwin and Curzon had both passed through Paris during the holiday season and both had called on Poincaré. The British Foreign Secretary had been allowed twenty minutes because Poincaré "had a train to catch", and after Baldwin's "courtesy" call, "A.G.G." saw "the crowning humiliation of British policy" in the "issue of the communiqué about 'no difference of purpose and no divergence of principle'." And all this, apparently, to get from the French Premier an imperfect acceptance of the League of Nations claim to intervene, on the Greek appeal, in the Corfu question.

consequences of a Greek–Italian War could have been worse even than the French occupation of the Ruhr, and so, during September, Anglo-French co-operation at the League of Nations and elsewhere was restored sufficiently to permit the Italians to be bowed out of Corfu though on terms grievously unfair to the unfortunate Greeks.[1] On the Ruhr, meanwhile, it seemed that nothing could be done until hard economic facts and Poincaré's French critics convinced the French nation that it was being woefully misled but that Anglo-American counsel and help would be available directly a practical Reparations agreement with Germany was sought. Indeed, once the Imperial Conference had begun, Lord Curzon gave it, in confidence, a very revealing picture of Britain's Foreign policy problems, and an American offer to participate in an investigation of Germany's capacity to pay came in time to figure very prominently in Conference discussions.[2] The final Foreign policy resolutions adopted on Germany and Reparations were, thanks probably to General Smuts, of a quite "progressive" character, reprobating attempts to break up German unity and even encouraging the London Government to reconsider calling its own Conference of interested Powers if current plans to secure, with American aid, an expert re-examination of Germany's capacity to pay Reparations should fail of effect.[3] But by this time the Dominion Premiers, and especially Bruce of Australia,[4] were pushing the London Government, in the Economic Conference, towards Imperial Preference decisions certain to provoke a

[1] *The Nation*, September 22, 1923: "Italy is going out, and few people will doubt that she originally intended to stay in.... On the other hand, Greece gets less than her due. She gets no compensation for the monstrous outrage of Corfu, and no doubt the reason is that she did not dare to ask for it." In fact, it was Greece that was mulcted in damages for the murder of an Italian general on Greek soil, the murder that had been made the excuse for the whole bullying Fascist display.

[2] These were, of course, important milestones on the road to the Dawes Report of 1924.

[3] Cf. *Whitaker's Almanack, 1924*, p. 479: "The Conference . . . felt that in such an event it would be desirable for the British Government to consider very carefully the alternative of summoning a Conference itself in order to examine the financial and the economic problem in its widest aspect. The Conference regarded any policy which would result in breaking up the unity of the German state as inconsistent with the Treaty obligations . . . and as incompatible with the future discharge by Germany of her necessary obligations. The strongest representations on this subject were accordingly made to the Allied Governments.

[4] Cf. *Daily Mail*, October 10, 1923, under the headlines "Mr. Bruce puts it plainly. Empire Markets and Men. It is no use our dodging the great issue." The leading article on the opposite page praised Mr. Bruce as a "young, forceful, energetic man," who "means to get something *done*," and added, "he is perfectly right."

political outcry at home. Indeed, it could be, and was, immediately argued that, at the last Election, Bonar Law had given a pledge that no fiscal changes of any considerable scope would be undertaken without a fresh appeal to the nation.

But Baldwin was under pressure not merely from the Dominion Premiers but from Cabinet Protectionists who conceived that the time had arrived for him to announce that, for the sake of the Unemployed, he favoured a good deal more than a wider range of Imperial Preferences. Indeed, the Prime Minister, a convinced Tariff Reformer since the first days of Joseph Chamberlain's agitation, had himself arrived at the conclusion that, in view of what was now likely to be a very slow recovery of Europe, there was no way of reducing Unemployment and maintaining a balanced Budget save by taxing manufactured imports, and more especially from those foreign countries which maintained heavy duties against British imports. And so, on October 25th, without meaning to force on an immediate Election, Mr. Baldwin, speaking for himself personally, told the Plymouth meeting of the National Unionist Association how he would propose to act against Unemployment, stressing not merely the placing of import-duty on manufactured articles for the sake of industrial workers but a bounty on arable land of £1 per acre to help the countryside to pay farm-labourers a minimum wage of 30s. a week. Without knowing it, as the wits were to say later, he had turned on a tap that he could not turn off, and, even on his own side, it was soon seen to be difficult to go on preparing for a normal Parliamentary Session when the Prime Minister had announced that he could see no remedy but a Tariff Reform, procurable, under the Bonar Law pledge, only after new elections. By November 12th, the Prime Minister, with a party far from happy about the results of his Leadership, was requesting from a reluctant King the right to tell Parliament on the morrow that there would be an almost immediate Dissolution, and a General Election on December 6th.[1]

The first instinct on the part of "progressives", as they watched

---

[1] Cf. Stanley Salvidge, *Salvidge of Liverpool*, pp. 253–4, for the irritation and dismay of some powerful Conservatives: "I hinted to [Lord] Derby that if he cared to come out publicly and give a strong lead he could . . . kill the whole silly business stone dead. But he was not contemplating anything so drastic. Instead he suggested we should both endeavour to gather from Mr. Baldwin some idea of what he actually contemplated doing, and that, if my opinion was invited, I should say how precarious it seemed to us in Lancashire for a Tory Government to give up a comfortable majority in Parliament for the purpose of letting our opponents raise the old 'dear food' cry in the constituencies. . . ."

Baldwin bringing Tariff Reform to the very forefront of politics, was to shout loudly that they were facing an unprincipled Tory manœuvre to take a wicked advantage of the woes of the Unemployed and the general sympathy they excited, to carry, doubtless at a sudden "stunt" election, a policy that would strengthen every manufacturers' ring in Britain in its work of fleecing the home consumer. The immorality of the supporting bribe to the countryside at the expense of the general taxpayer; the dearer prices and the foreign counter-measures that might result from the wider scope of Imperial Preference already promised;[1] the likelihood that Dominion pressure for Preferences on meat, corn, and dairy products had been met by half-promises too—all this made a case which, especially in its work of frightening shopping-wives, was soon seen to be very formidable. And almost as formidable was the argument that a British tariff could not "protect", but only harm, some of the most suffering British industries, shipbuilding, for example, and the engineering trades that exported locomotives, railway rolling-stock, bridging materials, gas and electric industry requisites, and a thousand other things. Before long, as "progressive opinion" saw Baldwin sliding uncontrollably forward to an Election, undesired by the bulk of his own unprepared party and at which little better than neutrality was to be expected from the Rothermere and Beaverbrook Press organizations,[2] the conviction grew that the Cabinet Tariff stalwarts, marshalled by Amery, had dug a pit into which they themselves, and not the Opposition, would fall. Indeed, well before the end, Baldwin was being pityingly treated as a well-intentioned bungler,[3] much below nearly all previous Prime Ministers in his

[1] Cf. *Whitaker's Almanack, 1924*, p. 481, for the better terms allowed to Empire Dried Fruit, Sugar, Tobacco and Wines, and the proposal to begin wholly new Preferences on the import of Raw Apples; Canned Salmon and Lobster, Crayfish and Crabs; Honey and Lime, Lemon, and other fruit juices. Nor was this all for the obligation had been assumed of giving effective preference, in all Government Contracts, to Empire foods and materials.

[2] Cf. *The Nation*, December 1, 1923, on "the manœuvres of the Rothermere and Beaverbrook papers", Lord Beaverbrook "damning with faint praise" while Lord Rothermere's "abuse of the Government is unconcealed, though he is in difficulties as to what to recommend".

[3] Cf. *Ibid.*, November 24, 1923, for "A.G.G." on "Mr. Toots in Office": "He is an amiable, almost lovable man, honourable in business no doubt, and blameless in private life; but, apart from his qualities of character, there has never been a Prime Minister so deficient in the essentials of statesmanship, so naïve, so thoughtless, so irresponsible, so ludicrously unworthy of the task of directing the affairs of a great nation. He has turned on a tap that he has been unable to stop, and the best we can hope is that the flood will wash him away.

standards of ability and whose rise, by a chapter of accidents, to the Leadership of his own party would bring it to ruin.

The most sensational feature of the Election campaign was certainly the rapid completion of "Liberal Reunion" with Asquith and Lloyd George agreeing to campaign together against the Tariff, and Liberal and Radical Clubrooms, throughout the land, again humming with activity and the hope that a Liberal return to office was far from incredible or impossible. Here is how one famous Radical organ put the relative merits of Liberal and Labour Opposition to the Government[1]:

> The Party struggle is not an ignoble instrument for the advancement of human affairs. Old associates have joined their ranks again under their old leaders, by general admission the most famous and experienced body of statesmen in the world, with clear issues before them and with great hopes of winning much ground. Coalition has failed; and Toryism has failed. We too would like to try our hand at mitigating the moral and economic disorders of the stricken modern world.
>
> We have not mentioned Labour. Does this invalidate our argument? We think not. An underlying current of weakness in the inner life of the Labour Party is obvious to any observer. It is possible that they may have some electoral success. But in power and in action, there is no likelihood of their accomplishing in the near future any part of their programme which is peculiar to themselves . . . which is not on Liberal rather than on Labour lines, and is not carried through with Liberal support. . . . In the short run it will be Liberal strength which will be most potent to check Labour excesses; and in the long run nothing but Liberal weakness can cause the eventual reaction from Toryism to play into the hands of extremists.

As Election day and the Election counts drew nearer, the belief that Labour had again handicapped itself by pushing the Capital Levy on an electorate primarily interested in other things,[2] sent Liberal hopes to their height. It not only seemed probable that the Tories would lose heavily but that the big anti-Tory majority expected in the new House might be almost equally divided between Liberal and Labour. In such circumstances, commentators were prepared to allow that, in view of Labour objections

Mr. Toots, in fiction, is a delightful figure; but Mr. Toots in power is a jest that no nation can afford."

[1] *Ibid.*, November 17, 1923.

[2] Cf. *Ibid.*, December 8, 1923, for one of the extremer flights of Tory electioneering from McNeill, Foreign Under-Secretary: "If the Government's present policy were successful, then from the revenue they would get they intended to reduce, and in a short time to knock off altogether, existing duties on such things as tea, tobacco, sugar, and possibly beer."

to a Liberal-Labour Coalition or a Labour Government, dependent on Liberal votes, a possible outcome was a new Asquith Government with Grey again at the Foreign Office, using the great prestige of his name both in France and Germany to secure a Ruhr and Reparations settlement, while Lloyd George, again at the Exchequer, took charge of an energetic attempt to break the housing *impasse* and make public credit available for neglected capital enterprises. But this interesting if difficult experiment was never fated to be tried, since the Parliamentary Labour Party, returned from the elections at 192 against the Liberals' 159, resolved, despite some internal criticism, to form a Labour Government after all if the Liberals' votes helped it to eject Mr. Baldwin.

CHAPTER XVIII
THE LABOUR GOVERNMENT OF 1924

"A great Socialist leader said to me in 1918 that his policy was to prevent any co-operation between his party and the Liberals on the matters where they were agreed, in the hope of prolonging Tory rule till Liberalism was squeezed out; then he and his friends would form their own Government. 'And suppose in the meantime, through that lack of co-operation, Europe is ruined?' 'It will be worth while,' he smilingly replied. . . . One does not much like to trust the country to rulers of that type. . . .

"At the present time it looks as if Democracy and Progress were parting company. They have already done so in the colonies, where the Labour Governments on the whole may be said to aim at a standard of civilization which need not be high or progressive but must be comfortable to the working class. The British Labour Party is a great amalgam. . . . Its ablest champions still carry with them the idealist tradition which they learnt as Radicals. Many of its new recruits are keen Liberals, who have left their party because in the turmoil of war it seemed to have forgotten its Liberality. Some are the mere extremists of the Left. . . . But . . . the vast masses who take drink and love betting; who think it silly to stop bribery in elections; who hate 'idealists' almost as much as Lord Birkenhead does, are now voting Tory or Labour, with an increasing drift towards Labour. . . . Democracy, the mere desire of the mass, broken loose from Progress, the will for better life: the break has, of course, not yet come about, at any rate in England. But already the rift is shown. . . . If organized Liberalism dies, the nation will be divided by a simple struggle between rich and poor, in which the Labour Party will probably keep some steadily dwindling traces of the ideals derived from Liberalism, while the Conservatives will wish to stand for civilization and good government, but will inevitably confound these good things by the old lust for big profits, class ascendancy and coercion. If organized Liberalism continues . . . the split will not come between the rival greeds of rich and poor, but the opposing principles of those who stand for the higher or lower elements of human nature and organization, for Progress or for reaction. . . ."

The great academic Liberal, Gilbert Murray, in *The Nation*, March 15, 1924.

"Those among the members of the Labour Party who were opposed to its taking office were soon justified by events.

381

Without a majority in the House it was in an impossible position. Neither of the two opposition parties sought immediately to butcher it outright, but they continued to place upon it every humiliation. . . . The relationship between the Labour and Liberal parties quickly became acute and strained. Mr. Asquith was majestically patronising, and his followers were waspishly critical . . . they exploited every device of parliamentary obstruction to keep the House sitting until the last trains had gone, and the tired and penurious Labour men had to walk to their lodgings. . . . The Tories were less adept and used blunter weapons. . . ."

A Labour member of 1924 shows special resentment of Liberalism's Parliamentary efforts to secure more consideration (Lord Snell, *Men, Movements and Myself*, p. 215).

I T is said that Mr. Baldwin's first instinct on receiving the results of the General Election of December 6, 1923 was to resign forthwith though, of course, his party comprising well over two-fifths of the Commons would heavily outnumber either Labour or the Liberals taken separately. He was persuaded to hold on, partly because there were excellent constitutional precedents for putting the onus of turning out a Government in the position of his own on the new House of Commons itself. There were, besides, all manner of other relevant considerations[1] though, perhaps the principal was the hope that a considerable section of the Liberals—if not the party majority—would flinch before the prospect of putting a minority Labour Government into office which, though it had only obtained thirty-one per cent of the votes cast at the General Election, might well, under extremist Clydeside and Poplar pressure, seek to make improper use of the Government Departments as party vantage-grounds. Indeed, it was the prospect of pushing Socialist Housing and Rent Bills from the Government side of the House as well as what their opponents denounced, in advance, as a "rabble-rousing Budget" with a propaganda Dissolution to follow which induced the "extremists" to agree to the distasteful compromises of minority rule,[2] and there were, besides, such delectable expectations as those opened up if Labour were to take charge of the Foreign Office and recognize the Soviet Government unconditionally. Yet if there were some undeniable Liberal qualms as to what a Labour Government, under "extremist" pressure, might connive at, there was no apparent hesitation in Asquith's announcement at a meeting of Liberal M.P.s on December 18th. The Baldwin Government would go, and "go with a short shrift", and if a

---

[1] Cf. *Hansard*, January 15, 1924, for the King's Speech which, intimating as it did, that proposals would be submitted to Parliament for implementing the Imperial Conference's conclusions in favour of extending Imperial Preference, shows, perhaps, that Mr. Baldwin held himself morally bound, if he could do so constitutionally, to honour, to the best of his ability, the draft engagements he had made with the rest of the Empire.

[2] Cf. Harold Nicolson, *King George V*, pp. 389–92, for the problems made by appointments in the Royal Household and the further problems made by Court Dress for Ministers on State occasions. It should be noted, perhaps, that Nicolson claims for George V the main responsibility both for the decision that Baldwin should carry on till defeated in Parliament and the further decision that, when that occurred, there was no alternative to the summoning of Mr. MacDonald.

Labour Government then took office, "it could hardly be tried under safer conditions".[1]

If Asquith's tone was resented as patronizing, a veritable storm was brought about his ears by his further claim that any Labour Prime Minister, taking office in existing circumstances, would acquire no automatic right, from the moment of his installation, to request a premature Dissolution until other efforts had been made to provide an alternative—Asquith meant, of course, a Liberal—Administration. Instead of the ideal picture, painted by some Liberal optimists, being realized of a MacDonald Cabinet taking office with general Liberal support and consenting, in its turn, to support a Liberal Government if and when it lost control[2] —all this as part of a process of building up a gradually unifying "Party of Progress" to face "Tory Reaction"—Labour vituperation and insult rent the air at the trickery and insolence that was being attempted by a dying party which was merely cumbering the ground and preventing the real struggle against "Reaction" from even being begun. This was, perhaps, a somewhat high line to take by a party which the Proportional Representation Society estimated to have been supported by 4,681,496 British voters against the Liberals' 4,555,320[3]—there were other estimates which even gave the Liberals the superiority by a different treatment of the unopposed returns—yet a powerful section of the Tory Press, in the hope of frightening the Liberals, also chose to take up the cry that, once Baldwin was defeated and MacDonald sent for, the road not only to a Dissolution but to Red ruin was thrown wide open.[4]

---

[1] *Daily News*, December 19, 1923, which also gave Asquith's further claim that the Liberals, if smaller in numbers than either of the other parties, were yet the only one whose policy had not been "decisively and derisively rejected" by the electors as Protection and the Capital Levy had been.

[2] Cf. *The Nation*, December 15, 1923 under the heading, "THE SEQUEL TO THE ELECTION".

[3] Cf. *Ibid.*, for the long communication from John H. Humphreys who gave these calculations for the 590 County and Borough Seats for England, Wales, and Scotland excluding Derby, Western, and, of course, the University and Northern Ireland seats. On Humphreys' proportioned figures, Liberal members should have numbered 178 and Labour 182. The total Conservative vote for the 590 seats Humphreys calculated as 5,786,247, and the proportionate quota of members as 225.

[4] Cf. *Ibid.*, January 5, 1924, for the famous "A.G.G.": "The storm that beats about Mr. Asquith gathers violence every day.... In the last weekly convulsion of the *Observer*, Mr. MacDonald's right to demand a dissolution was defended. In the Rothermere Press the motive is to compel the Liberals and Conservatives to unite against the red flood. . . . The attempt to represent the matter as

The Labour Government of 1924

The shattering din of the combined Labour–Tory onslaught on Asquith's positions of December 18th seems to have confirmed some bold political theorizers in their calculations as to what might be expected to prove the next stage of British party development. Under the combined squeeze between Left and Right, already begun, the Liberals' prospects would grow steadily darker, and the next General Election, whether called by Labour or by Conservatism, would be so arranged as to promise the maximum fallaway of Liberal votes, Tories hoping that every owner of a cottage or a hen-coop would move to their side while Labour's calculations would be concerned with the three to four million working-folk who had still voted Liberal on December 6, 1923. One last development in Liberals' favour, however, took place in the first half of January 1924 while the new Parliament was preparing to swear itself in and begin the debate on the Address. There had been a considerable flight from the pound and near-panic in the City from the moment, in November, when a Government under possible Clydeside and *Daily Herald* domination, had emerged as a possibility,[1] and MacDonald had, in fact, already thought fit to denounce the "wangle" that he believed to be proceeding to deny Labour "fair play" and its alleged constitutional right to be called on to form a Government even if Office, without power, was hardly Labour's wish. It was the City of London Conservative Association, indeed, representing great and alarmed banking, insurance, and merchanting interests which tried to arrange an agreed departure of Baldwin, in favour of Asquith, from Downing Street,[2] MacDonald's alleged right to a summons being evaded by Baldwin's consenting to support the formation and maintenance of an Asquith Government for which, in such circumstances, a majority of well over 400 against 192

involving the relation of the Crown and Labour is peculiarly mischievous and offensive. . . . It is not likely that Mr. Asquith will be shaken by all this sound and fury. . . ."

[1] Cf. *Ibid.*, January 12, 1924, for the view, as the decisive meeting of Parliament approached, that "if foreign holders of sterling balances and securities are frightened into selling in order to buy dollars, there is nothing much in the existing position on the Stock Exchange to withstand the strain". Prices, which had somewhat recovered from the steep November falls, now sank lower than before.

[2] Cf. *The Sunday Times*, December 16th, for Lord Birkenhead early putting forward, such a plan which would have been based on an agreed programme, involving the Conservative promise to suspend their Tariff propaganda and accept the Alternative Vote from which Liberals were expected to be the greatest gainers. There were other plans to form a new Coalition under Asquith with Baldwin leading a Tory wing.

might have been claimed. But there were almost insuperable difficulties, not the least of them, it seems, at the Palace,[1] to the realization of the plan, and so it was the Baldwin Cabinet that was still in Office when Parliamentary proceedings proper began with the Speech from the Throne on January 15th.

It was on January 17th, that the constitutional machinery was finally set in motion for ejecting the Baldwin Government when Clynes moved a Labour Resolution of "no confidence" in the Ministers. Asquith announced that he and his friends would give support owing to the confusion, vacillation, and impotence, both at home and abroad, which had been displayed by the Baldwin Administration, but gave the warning that his party was pledged to give no more countenance to Socialistic experiments than to Protection. The closing speeches were made on January 21st, Baldwin declaring that his party, if critical, would indulge in no factious or fractious opposition and MacDonald undertaking that the Labour Party would do their best to allay the fear about a Labour Government's policy. The Division that followed showed the Government defeated by 328 votes against 256.[2] Next day the Government's resignation was announced, and the Houses adjourned until February 12th to permit the construction of a new Government.

The Liberals of the would-be moderate wing of the "United Army of Progress" were fated to have some sorry experiences during the next three weeks of waiting. They were kept at arm's length by the triumphant Labour Cabinet-makers; neither the personnel nor the policy of the new Government was discussed with them; and, as Labour was short of suitable lawyers, Haldane, already won from Asquith and Lloyd George by the promise of the Lord Chancellorship,[3] was used to try to make similar con-

[1] Cf. Harold Nicolson, *King George V*, pp. 383–4. On January 5, 1924, George Lansbury, at a notorious Shoreditch Town Hall meeting, was regarded as having indirectly threatened the King if he consented to co-operate with Conservative and Liberal leaders in denying Labour the fruits of its "victory". "Some centuries ago," he said, "a King stood against the common people and he lost his head." George V was not afraid of this kind of ranting but was most anxious to avoid giving Labour even the semblance of a legitimate grievance.

[2] *Hansard*, January 17th and 21st. Ten Liberals were included in the 256, and obviously they were "moderate" enough to prefer Baldwin to MacDonald. It is possible that more Liberals of the "moderate" variety would have declined to follow Asquith in clearing the way for MacDonald but for the warning against "Socialistic experiments" issued by their Leader.

[3] Lord Haldane, *An Autobiography*, pp. 307 ff., makes it plain that his "affectionate letter" of political farewell to Asquith was not written until MacDonald had approached him in flattering terms.

versions from Liberalism and even from Conservatism. Meanwhile, if the thrills of Office increased the strenuousness of the Labour claim that Liberalism was already a dying creed whose best men had passed or were passing into Labour's camp, Liberals were more taken aback by a sudden *volte-face* on the part of the Conservative Press. After busily prophesying "Red ruin" if Asquith allowed MacDonald in, the Conservative editorial offices, finding their readers very curious about the personal histories of Britain's new Ministers,[1] decided to give them a good deal of friendly publicity on the assumption, doubtless, that the new Cabinet needed to be helped to keep their extremists in check and the pound sterling from falling. As one half-irate, half-amused Liberal ex-Minister put it, not wholly unaware that a Conservative-Labour *rapprochement* meant mortal peril for his own party:[2]

For a week we had listened in Parliament, with humility, and, I suppose, in some cases, with terror, to prophecies from the late Government Benches of what would happen if we kept our promises to our constituencies and voted the Conservatives out of office. It would mean the end of all things. It would mean the "Reds" triumphant. It would mean the destruction of Society; the coming of Socialism; the abolition of God. Above all, we were moved by the extraordinarily unexpected solicitude of these orators for the future of the Liberal Party. Metaphorically they took black-bordered handkerchiefs out of their silk hats and wept salt tears over the fact that we were committing political suicide. . . .

Since that date the Conservative Press has been pouring butter from a lordly dish over this singular aggregation of revolutionaries [the MacDonald Government]. Mr. Garvin, who was denouncing its advent, less in journalism than in delirium, now emits calm and succinct praise condensed into three columns, with the titles, "A Ministry of Work", "The Premier and Big Plans", "A National Cabinet". Another Sunday paper which has been raving like a madman now encourages its readers with the information that Mr. J. H. Thomas is a "regular diner-out" . . . and that Lord and Lady Chelmsford have had experience of entertaining on a scale of magnificence which is "only inferior to that of Buckingham Palace". A third is also reassuring in its statement that Lord Haldane has entertained seventeen of the

[1] The *Daily News* and *Manchester Guardian* of January 23, 1924 show, however, that the Liberal Press, too, found it necessary to give the gossip-writers their head, the *Daily News* sending an interviewer to the twenty-year-old Ishbel MacDonald and the *Manchester Guardian* reminding its women-readers of the dead Mrs. MacDonald whose means, be it mentioned, had certainly contributed to her husband's political career.

[2] Cf. *The Nation*, February 2, 1924, for C. F. G. Masterman as "M.P." deriding the MacDonald Government under the heading, "The Proletarians".

Cabinet at once with his usual princely hospitality. Lord Rothermere has abandoned his scares. . . .

It is a Cabinet of old and ageing men. . . . It is a Cabinet . . . in the main of dullish men. . . . It is a Cabinet largely of rich men . . . of men who, if they appear on a Liberal platform, are described in the rich vocabulary of Glasgow and Glasgow's disciples, as "peers", "plutocrats", "plunderers", "profiteers", or "parasites".

It is a Cabinet which has no claim to call itself "Labour" . . . the majority of it, at least during adult life, have had no direct experience of the conditions of poverty. . . . The country is obviously reassured. The sight of Lord Haldane on the Woolsack again . . . should send up the Funds by at least ten points. Lord Parmoor's name but thinly disguises the Mr. Cripps who in all my time in the House was the most dreary and most reactionary of all Tory opponents of social reform. . . . It is the "Reds" who have been "dished". . . .

A very considerable price, of course, had to be paid in these circumstances to avoid a mutiny of the "Reds". One element in the price which MacDonald was himself anxious to pay, because he thought it would yield big propaganda profits, was the immediate and unconditional recognition of the Soviet Government, with compensation and other negotiations to follow instead of preceding the recognition. But for all the momentary Labour propaganda made of the decision, there never resulted the great trading and diplomatic advantages, which had been confidently foretold if Britain took the lead among the Great Powers in according recognition.[1] Instead, MacDonald's Government was sucked further and further into the bog of a Russian Loan Treaty which did so much to destroy Labour's first Administration. Another concession to the "Reds", that almost wrecked the Cabinet in its first weeks, was the appointment of the Clydesider, Wheatley, to the Ministry of Health, and Wheatley's over-prompt decision to annul the "Poplar Order" which had served as some check on the extravagances of a "Poplarism" that had frightened and antagonized cautious people all over the country. And a particularly

---

[1] Cf. *The Nation*, January 12, 1924, for "A.G.G." the very experienced Liberal journalist, falling into the same type of commercial credulity. "I am told," he wrote, "on good authority that there is trade in sight, only awaiting favourable conditions for release, which amounts in value to not less than a hundred millions. The French are besieging Moscow for orders." And, on February 9th, "A.G.G." even ventured on this perilous dithyramb: "It is tolerably certain that the countries of the world will be tumbling over each other in their eagerness to follow the British lead, but nothing can rob Mr. MacDonald of the distinction of having set the fashion. It is the boldest and best act done by this country since the war, and the December election was worth having if only to substitute this plain business acceptance of facts for the pompous obstinacy of Lord Curzon."

heavy part of the price paid to secure "Red" acquiescence in what MacDonald had done, in Cabinet-making, to reassure the *bourgeoisie*, was the Prime Minister's acceptance of the notion of the Committee of Fifteen—twelve private members and three Ministers—to serve as liaison between the Parliamentary Labour Party and the Government.[1] Before the end, this Committee seemed capable of demanding, and even enforcing, changes of policy upon the Government and certainly played its part in bringing about MacDonald's ultimate fall. The Parliamentary Labour Party, after all, was much more under the influence of Labour eminences like Smillie, Lansbury, and Morel even if, for one reason or another, they were not in the Government, than it was under the influence of the bulk of the Cabinet.

All manner of other pitfalls for the MacDonald Government could be instanced as, for example, the increased industrial unrest that became manifest as soon as a more favourable atmosphere for "Labour" was supposed to reign at Westminster and Whitehall. Indeed, a Locomotivemen's strike, in defiance of an award of the industry's National Wages Board, was antagonizing the public at the very time when the Labour Ministers were taking over their Departments and further trouble was rightly forecast at the docks,[2] in the pits, and elsewhere, most notably, as it proved, on the London trams and buses where Bevin's conduct of the strike, in March, was widely condemned. Yet all this and more notwithstanding,[3] MacDonald and the inner Cabinet ring[4] were not wrong

---

[1] Cf. Lord Snell, *Men, Movements and Myself*, pp. 215–16, for one of the Committee's private members on such parts of its functions as receiving the suggestions and criticisms of private members and making them known to the Prime Minister or the heads of Departments. Snell almost admitted the unscrupulous use that was made of the Committee by "pressure groups" of every kind.

[2] Cf. *Whitaker's Almanack, 1925*, p. 479, for such typical Labour entries for early 1924 as: "Jan. 20th. Strike of enginemen began at midnight and services throughout the country were disorganised. Jan. 29th. Settlement of strike reached. . . . Conference of dockers decided to strike at all British ports unless their demand for 2s. increase in wages were conceded. Feb. 11th. Employers offered advance of 1s., which was rejected. Feb. 16th. Dockers' strike commenced. . . . Mar. 14th. After negotiations, miners' delegate conference refused terms offered by owners and urged Government to pass Minimum Wage Bill. March 20th. London tramway and busmen came out on strike. . . ."

[3] *Beatrice Webb's Diaries, 1924–1932*, p. 18, at April 3, 1924, show Webb and Henderson, two of the inner Cabinet ring, perturbed at what was resulting from the activities of "little bands of wrecking Communists" and the "unthinking Leftism of some of the minor Trade Union leaders". They feared a vigorous anti-Labour reaction by the general public of which Winston Churchill might take charge as a British Mussolini.

[4] *Ibid.*, p. 28, at May 25th, gives the "inner circle", meeting at Prime

in assuming that his Government had real chances of winning sufficient propaganda successes to facilitate the task of asking the country for an absolute majority, and real power, whenever the next General Election should be precipitated by what could be represented as an immoral Liberal–Conservative alliance to turn Labour out. Trade and finance, for example, were both on the mend; Unemployment figures had been falling steadily so that if the trend continued, as expected, "normal unemployment" figures only could be awaited by midsummer; and Housing especially seemed to offer Labour's first Government, if it was, indeed, true that the Building Unions would trust it more with "dilution" than previous Administrations, excellent chances of "proving" to the country all-round superiority to the Lloyd George, Bonar Law, and Baldwin "capitalist" Cabinets. As far as the Empire was concerned, Labour would apparently have the rare good fortune of reaping what its predecessors had sown when planning the tremendous Empire Exhibition at Wembley,[1] an Exhibition that gave the capital some of the atmosphere of an international tourist resort after the State opening of April 23rd. And, abroad, not merely the Anglo-Soviet position but that, at Geneva, in the League of Nations[2] and that in the Ruhr and Rhineland, as between France and Germany,[3] seemed to offer such attractive political prospects that the Prime Minister, at the grave risk of over-loading himself, took the Foreign Office in his determination that they should be fully exploited.

It was on February 12th, some three weeks after MacDonald

Ministerial Monday lunches to discuss the coming week's Parliamentary business, as Henderson, Clynes, Thomas, Snowden, MacDonald, Webb "and usually Ben Spoor" (Chief Whip).

[1] Cf. *Daily Chronicle*, April 24th, for the King saying: "The Exhibition may be said to reveal to us the whole Empire in little, containing within its 220 acres of ground a vivid model of the architecture, art, and industry of all the races which come under the British flag. . . . This Exhibition will enable us to take stock of the resources, actual and potential, of the Empire as a whole. . . . It stands for co-ordination of our scientific knowledge and a common effort to overcome disease, and to better the difficult conditions which still surround life in many parts of the Empire." The King and Queen of Rumania and the King and Queen of Italy visited Wembley during May which also saw, on Sunday afternoon, May 25th, in the Stadium, the tremendous Empire Service of Thanksgiving that the *Morning Post* of May 26th claimed to be "without parallel in the world's history". (Part re-quoted from H. C. Dent, *op. cit.*)

[2] What was once famous as the Draft Treaty of Mutual Guarantee seemed to offer great scope for the beginning of massive disarmament.

[3] The fall of the franc had, by now, convinced many in France that Britain's help should be secured in mediating between France and Germany an agreed evacuation of the Ruhr on conditions.

had been summoned to the Palace, that the new Government faced both Houses of Parliament. Its supporters already claimed positive "achievements" to its credit like the Soviet recognition[1] and a friendly exchange of letters with the French Government which promised to improve on Lord Curzon's record in these matters. And though it was plain from MacDonald's opening policy-statement that the demand of the "Reds" for a prompt Dissolution on a propagandist programme had been eluded, there was still considerable matter for disquiet even to the Liberals. The Capital Levy, it is true, was being remitted for inquiry and so could hardly figure in Snowden's Budget statement of April; there was no word, either, of nationalization of the mines or the railways. But Asquith was antagonized by MacDonald's attempt to treat Wheatley's quite unwarrantable action on the "Poplar Order" as "a merely mechanical operation" of no significance, and Liberals, too, felt that MacDonald's attitude towards Housing, also in Wheatley's Department, showed dangerous signs of propagandism[2] and insufficient regard for such hard economic and financial facts as the steep rises certain in building wages and building material costs directly a big, politically-motivated, and relatively unprepared acceleration of building activity was attempted. As *The Nation* put the Liberal view in its discussion of the danger and the heavy cost of a Labour snatch at propaganda "successes":[3]

The Government have no need to aim at quick returns. The favourable trade outlook, and the signs which have become really

[1] Cf. *The Nation*, February 9, 1924, however, for the first evidence that the results might deceive all the Left's fond expectations: "The Soviet Government has shown no particular haste to acknowledge Mr. MacDonald's Note conveying full diplomatic recognition and inviting Russia to send representatives to clear up outstanding differences. . . . Mr. MacDonald's action, which has encountered singularly little criticism in this country, is not being followed in France. . . . The Italian negotiations have also hung fire . . . while America shows no more sign than she ever did of recognizing the present administration of Moscow. Meanwhile the British Government's decision to recognize unconditionally has had the rather unexpected effect of complicating its negotiations with Mexico, which now declines to discuss conditions which were considered superfluous in the case of Russia. . . ."

[2] *Hansard*, February 12, 1924, for the assertion that where "other Governments have failed, we are going to succeed" with the problem of dilution, and the Prime Minister's seeing "no difficulty" over "the guarantee of continuous work over a certain number of years" which the men demand for "your shortage of houses now is so great". This was, perhaps, all a little too simple as was the underlying assumption of much heavier subsidization for the building of houses to let to people who could afford only nine shillings a week for rent and rates.

[3] *The Nation*, February 16, 1924.

significant of a move towards moderation in French policy, will give them all the prestige of immediate improvement that they require, leaving them free to concentrate on laying sound foundations. The change in French opinion is, indeed, the most remarkable and hopeful event of the month. . . . Evidently M. Poincaré has come round to the view that the achievement or the prospect of a settlement would serve him better at the forthcoming French elections than a record of un-shaken firmness in a policy the futility of which can no longer be con-cealed. It is a rare stroke of luck for Mr. MacDonald; and it was naïve and somewhat ungrateful of him to attribute it to the superiority of his friendly letter to "the beastly clever Notes" of Lord Curzon, whose stand over the Palatinate contributed something to the change.

Of course, MacDonald, throughout his nine months of office, was trying to show every section of his very mixed following— "Reds", "Pacifists", "Moderate Trade Unionists", Co-operators, Dockyard and Arsenal M.P.s and the rest—that he could do some-thing for them all while preparing the way for a, perhaps, far from distant electoral triumph. As might be expected, there was a succession of troublesome incidents—MacDonald himself delaying too long, during the February Dock Strike, a definite assurance that Ministers would not fail to secure the public "the necessary food supplies";[1] Henderson breaking out, during a difficult Burnley by-election, against the Versailles Treaty; the Under-Secretary for Air in an Air Defences discussion implying that the best Air Defence was the Sermon on the Mount; and MacDonald as part justification for accepting the Admiralty's new cruiser programme, challenged by a Liberal section as starting the armaments race all over again, venturing to bring Unemployment into the discussion. Probably, it was due as much to Baldwin's half-amused tolerance as to anything else that Labour's first Government survived its difficult opening weeks,[2] lived to present and carry a Budget and, finally, in conjunction with a new and sympathetic French Government of the Bloc des Gauches, seemed

---

[1] He obviously feared a "Red" charge of strike-breaking.

[2] Cf. *The Nation*, March 1, 1924, for the caustic Liberal House of Commons commentator, "M.P.": "Meanwhile the show blunders on, its survival an astonishment day by day, its continued existence a miracle. . . . Mr. MacDonald . . . did succeed in whipping into the Lobby in favour of the building of five new enlarged and powerful cruisers all the miscellaneous collection of con-scientious objectors, Clydeside Socialists and others, the bulk of whom would have fought the proposal to the point of expulsion if it had been advanced by any other party. But now this miscellaneous collection is being bombarded with protests from the Socialists, from all the constituencies except the dockyard towns, and it must only be a matter of time before a considerable bulk of it turns into open revolt."

to go on to the startling Reparations-Ruhr successes of the London Conference of August and the apparently epoch-making Disarmament-Security business of September at the League of Nations in Geneva. It was not for nothing, indeed, that Labour's politicians and journalists had early taken to praise of Baldwin's chivalry towards Labour's infant Government and stressed, by contrast, the alleged spiteful ill-will of the Liberals.[1]

The Liberals, for their part, held that they had been and were being treated very badly by Labour whom they had helped to office. It was not merely that they were not being consulted in the slightest though their following in the country, as proved at the last General Election, was virtually equal to Labour's; it was the malicious and unending clamour from Labour that Liberalism was already dead and that its politicians' efforts to maintain some footing in public affairs as "progressives" might well delay the inevitable political triumph of the "people" if dupes enough were found. In such circumstances, Liberals saw no necessity to offer Labour Whips their votes in order to allow them to closure Parliamentary debates that dragged on too long for the Labour Cabinet's convenience; nor did they see any reason to shut their eyes to what they considered the impudent "Red" tactics of the Clydesider Wheatley at the Ministry of Health. Asquith had already warned the new Government, on the first day it faced Parliament, that Liberals took a grave view of Wheatley's precipitate dash to "Poplarism's" aid; he received scant satisfaction, and accordingly a motion was put down for Tuesday, February 26th, which showed that Liberals were quite prepared to defeat the Government and face the consequences unless there was a definite repudiation of "Poplarism" instead of the continued evasion so far practiced.

As it happened, Wheatley, when defending what he had done on the "Poplar Order", made possibly the best, if not the most straightforward, speech of the 1924 Parliament and raised his

---

[1] *Ibid.*, March 8, 1924, for another famous Liberal commentator "A.G.G." thus: "There is a distinct tendency to look to the Conservative benches rather than the Liberal benches for sympathy, and in the columns of the *Spectator*, that new and ardent disciple of Labour, Mr. Massingham, contrasts the 'gentlemanly tradition' of the Conservatives with the less gentlemanly conduct of the Liberals. There is undoubtedly a bond of mutual interest between Labour and the Conservatives . . . for if the Liberal Party could be thoroughly wrecked, there would be very substantial salvage for both the residuary legatees of the estate."

Parliamentary stock immensely.[1] Yet Asquith was too old a Parliamentary hand to allow himself to be diverted from his immediate purpose by the frenzied Labour cheering which had greeted Wheatley's audacious string of assertions, capped, as they were, by his claim that he had made a friendly gesture towards Poplar in order to bring Poplar back into "legal ways" and that "I have not surrendered to Poplar and I will not surrender to Poplar."[2] Those assertions possibly helped Asquith to decide that, in the circumstances, there was no need to subject the new Government, put into Office as it had been by Liberal votes, to the humiliating ordeal of facing an outright demand for Wheatley's dismissal or transfer. An immediate faction-fight of the kind between the rival "progressive" camps of Liberal and Labour could only have profited the Conservatives who had, indeed, assembled in great force, on February 26th, to take advantage of what might have proved an unexpectedly early chance of returning to power amid wide-spread jeering for the squabbling, mutually destructive parties of "Progress". Yet the resulting situation, even when reported on by an Asquithian ex-Minister, tended to allow the Conservatives to come off best, seeing the way Asquith seemed to shrink from demanding an outright reversal of what had been done on Poplar and MacDonald, in his turn, seemed to shrink from a straightforward defence or justification. Here is C. F. G. Masterman's account of how, amid open Conservative derision, a Government defeat was avoided, which was not desired, at the time, either by Asquith or MacDonald:[3]

The Poplar debate provided the most dramatic moment of a Parliamentary Session which has hitherto been more like a wild cinema show . . . there was no desire to hunt Mr. Wheatley out of the Government, and certainly no desire that the Government should fall with him. Mr. Wheatley's reply had not touched the main issue, and in the middle of the dinner hour, when the House is usually empty but was then crowded from floor to ceiling, Mr. Asquith challenged the Prime Minister on four points concerning the future policy of the Government. . . . It was one of those moments of tense expectation which I

[1] Cf. *Beatrice Webb's Diaries, 1924–1932*, p. 11, under February 29, 1924, for an insider, who began thinking of Wheatley as Thomas's rival for the succession to MacDonald if the latter, who was obviously strained, broke down.

[2] Cf. *Hansard*, February 26th, for such other assertions of Wheatley as that he was emancipating "my department" from the state of degradation in which he had found it and that he was carrying out a sound Parliamentary doctrine of "continuity of policy".

[3] *The Nation*, March 1, 1924.

have rarely seen in the House of Commons, not because of the intrinsic importance of the points themselves, but because on the satisfactory or unsatisfactory reply to them depended the fate of the Government. In a dramatic silence, unbroken by a cheer from his supporters or an interruption from members of other parties, Mr. MacDonald gave satisfactory assurances on all the points raised, went as far, indeed, as any man could do in acknowledging error and in promising amendment without making the position of his own Minister impossible. The tension was suddenly relaxed, Members streamed out to dinner . . . the Tories were left, with the enormous forces they had beaten up, to cheery gibes and, on the whole, good-tempered criticism of the Liberal attitude; and the "Socialists" were saved by Liberal votes, as they were saved by Conservative votes a week before. The saddest figure in the debate was Mr. George Lansbury who spoke in defence of "Poplarization" amid dead silence. . . .

It seems obvious that even the reddest Clydesiders had decided that some prudential restraint was called for to save Wheatley and the "bold" Housing[1] and Anti-Eviction[2] Bills expected from him, not to mention the Bills, from other Ministers, to increase Old Age Pensions,[3] Agricultural Wages,[4] Unemployment Insurance Benefits,[5] and the other good things, certain, it appeared, if time were allowed, to give Labour its absolute Majority at the next General Election. Nor could the "Reds" have been deaf to the voice of their Whips prophesying, as it proved with some reason, that a few months of the existing situation would ruin a Liberal Party, whose Right Wing, hating Socialism more than Protectionism, seemed ready, with Churchill, to move into the Tory camp leaving the great majority to be absorbed by Labour. And, indeed, the remarkable Abbey by-election of March 1924, in the heart of London's West End, was interpreted by some as already

[1] Cf. *Hansard*, June 23rd, for Wheatley moving the Second Reading of a Bill increasing the subsidy payable to a local authority from £6 for 20 years to £9 for 40 years, and in an agricultural parish by a further £3 10s. if the houses complied with certain conditions.

[2] Cf. *Ibid.*, April 2nd, for Wheatley moving a Bill so biased, in the Liberals' view, that even when somewhat refurbished, under pressure, they helped to defeat it.

[3] Cf. *Ibid.*, June 25th, for Snowden moving a measure to allow a maximum income, including the pension, of 35s. a week (instead of 20s. a week) if 15s. of the first 25s. came from sources other than earnings.

[4] Cf. *Ibid.*, June 2nd, for Noel Buxton moving the Agricultural Wages Bill setting up County Wages Committees under a Central Wages Board.

[5] Cf. *Ibid.*, May 20th, for Shaw, after a February Act to fill the "gap" of three weeks in the benefit and an April Act extending benefit from 26 weeks to 41 weeks, venturing the much-criticized proposal to give, "in genuine cases", full benefits so long as unemployment lasted.

spelling Liberalism's approaching and final collapse at the next Election, seeing the deplorable figures obtained by a Liberal[1] who had come forward to give brother-Liberals a chance to vote for another candidate than Churchill (supported as the latter, in the main, was by Rothermere and Beaverbrook against a caucus Tory) but who had been totally outclassed by Fenner Brockway of the I.L.P. Yet it was a second "Red" Wheatley escapade which, contributing mightily though it did to Wheatley's hold on Labour's most vociferous sections, came very near once more to wrecking all its calculated strategy. A new Rent Restrictions Bill had been introduced by a Labour private member, Mr. Gardner, which proposed to reduce the permitted maximum rent above pre-war from the existing forty per cent to twenty-five per cent and, in addition, to end the landlord's chance of getting an order for possession, even for non-payment of rent, unless "wilful" default on the tenant's part could be established. Choosing to ignore the fact that, to keep pace with the general price-rise, rents should have been eighty per cent above pre-war, Labour's "Red" Minister of Health professed his personal view that a permitted increase of twenty-five per cent was still too much and, in promising Government facilities for Mr. Gardner's measure, virtually challenged Liberals and Conservatives to show, by rejecting a Bill, which was expected to be very popular with tenants, that they had the "courage of their convictions".

It was almost inevitable, in these circumstances, that though acknowledging that Rent Restriction provisions needed to be extended for a further period of years, disappointed or irritated Liberals[2] saw no great need to help the Government to muzzle Tory objections to what Mr. Gardner was suggesting and Mr.

---

[1] Cf. *Beatrice Webb's Diaries, 1924–1932*, p. 17, under March 24.

[2] Cf. *The Nation*, March 1, 1924, for a significant article on "Housing and Rent Control" warning the Government against some of the loose financial notions spreading on the Labour Benches. "From the financial standpoint," argued *The Nation*, "the low level of rents prevailing to-day is the essence of the housing problem. It is really misleading to speak of rents being 40 per cent above what they were in 1914. With the general price-level roughly 80 per cent above pre-war, rents, if we have regard to real values, have suffered a serious decline; and this is the fundamental reason why it is impossible to-day to build working-class houses without subsidies—the problem of housing on its financial side is the problem of bridging the gulf between the 40 per cent advance in rents and the 80 per cent advance in the price-level; and no man who is sincerely anxious to get more houses built will give any countenance to proposals which tend in the direction of widening that gulf, as a reduction of rents must necessarily do. . . ."

Wheatley improving upon. Before long, indeed, proceedings in the Standing Committee that was dealing with the Rent Restrictions Bill were described as having "developed into a confused chaos".[1] Meanwhile an almost unprecedented atmosphere was developing, thus feelingly described by one disillusioned Asquithian ex-Minister:[2]

The House is getting exceedingly tired of "moral gestures". It is also getting exceedingly tired of the Sermon on the Mount. It is also tired of "sob stuff" concerning the sufferings of the poor; partly because it contains too many orators who had ladled out the same sloppy or lachrymose rhetoric on the election platform, each of whom feels he could do it better than the orator who is trying it on them. . . . The House is also getting tired of Mr. Oswald Mosley, who speaks on all and every occasion, and combines carefully prepared impromptu epigrams directed against the Tories with "sob stuff" difficult to accept with patience, and elaborate defences of the Government Front Bench on questions of Procedure, with which . . . he is imperfectly acquainted. . . . But as all the legitimate supporters of that Bench are perforce gagged owing to the congestion of business . . . they seem to resent this "independent" straying, with so frequent outbursts, into their own domain. . . . These followers are, indeed, in some disgruntlement. They have become splendidly disciplined. But they are disallowed speech. . . . The Liberals, indeed, present outwardly the more deplorable spectacle: fissuring into a large centre group, a small but persistent "right" which was waiting for the coming of "Winston" . . . and a left which finds refuge in abstaining from difficult divisions.

This was an atmosphere not without its ultimate perils, seeing the "extreme Left's" hopes of playing for further effects at Westminster and in the Trade Unions,[3] the Government Benches' never-ending preoccupation with manœuvring into a favourable position for an early General Election, and, finally, the "extreme Right's" first serious interest (not wholly unrelated to the Government's alleged readiness to "coerce Ulster" into Boundary

[1] *Ibid.*, March 22, 1924: "On the first day the Tories systematically obstructed (not without reason), and no business was done. On the second day the Labour members occupied the whole time in denouncing Tory obstruction, and no business was done. Mr. Mardy Jones, indeed, the enthusiastic Labour Welshman in charge, in long periods of rhetoric, denounced the landlords as "vultures sucking blood". . . . The whole difficulty is caused by the Government suddenly withdrawing the Minister of Health and the Attorney-General from the Committee. They cannot make up their mind whether they lose least by alienating the sitting tenant on the one hand, or the small owner of cottage property, on the other. Meantime violence continues . . . and no progress is made."
[2] Cf. *Ibid.*, March 29, 1924, for "M.P." (C. F. G. Masterman).
[3] Cf. *Beatrice Webb's Diaries, 1924–1932*, p. 18, under April 3, 1924, for suspected Communist activity.

Revision)[1] in Italian Fascism's possible lessons for Britain.[2] It was certainly not the right atmosphere for Wheatley's Anti-Eviction Bill which, once again, on the plea of protecting the hardest-hit of the "poor", seemed, even to "progressive" Liberals, so rancorously biased as to threaten the Government's downfall once more. And, truth to tell, on the Labour Benches themselves, the prophecy was heard that little more rent could ever be expected in Poplar so long as Wheatley's notion prevailed of refusing possession to owners where arrears of rent were "due to unemployment" and where the granting of possession would cause "greater hardship" than its refusal.[3] Mr. Asquith, at any rate, decided to announce that unless such proposals were withdrawn, the Liberals would vote against the Government. And even when Mr. MacDonald rose, on April 7th, to offer the Bill's Amendment and the provision instead that no eviction order should be issued until a tenant had had a reasonable opportunity of applying to the local Poor Law Authority for relief, sufficient Liberals saw enough guile, in prejudice of sorely-tried cottage-owners' just claims, to join Conservatives in defeating the Government by 221 votes against 212 and destroying the Bill. It was obviously expected that the bulk of Labour would decide that its case was far from strong enough with the "respectable working-man" voter, whom it was hoped to win from Liberalism, to stake upon it all Labour's hopes of an absolute majority.[4] In point of fact, Wheatley's Bill was abandoned and, not without calculation, the Anti-Eviction "struggle" was allowed to return to the less provocative sphere of private member's legislation, backed by the Government. Considerable results were, in fact, thus obtained[4] especially after the

[1] Cf. *Hansard*, September 30th, for the Prime Minister, on the Second Reading of the Boundary Commissioner Bill, denying that Ulster was being coerced.

[2] *Beatrice Webb's Diaries, 1924–1932*, p. 18, already speak of the possibility of Churchill emerging as "a modified and constitutional Mussolini" if the "extreme Left's" manœuvres did not cease. This was at the beginning of April. And one day, perhaps, the background and financing of the Boswell Printing and Publishing Company and *The Patriot* may come to be investigated.

[3] Cf. *Beatrice Webb's Diaries, 1924-1932*, p. 19, for the "inner ring's" chagrin.

[4] Cf. *Whitaker's Almanack, 1925*, p. 166, for a very succinct summary of what followed the Government's defeat: "By a coincidence a private member's bill on the same subject was read a second time on that evening, and on the following day Mr. MacDonald said the Law Officers would co-operate to make this satisfactory to the Government. This measure, which provided that a landlord could only obtain in possession where a dwelling house was reasonably required for his own occupation as a residence and where the Court was satisfied that greater hardship would be caused by refusing to grant the order than by granting

Cabinet had accumulated a sufficient record of "benefits to the poor" and "successes in Foreign policy" to be felt to be ready to challenge an election if "evictions" were not made next to impossible even in the numerous cases where a house-owner desired to arrange to move into his own premises.[1] And decades of experience were to prove that the "sitting tenant" beneficiaries of Labour's anti-landlord rancours were often capable of taking the grossest advantage of the further legislative protection now accorded to them,[2] whether by extracting veritable "ransoms" before giving up possession or by imposing oppressive terms on their own sub-tenants.

Something has been said above of the benefits to the "poor" that were already being accorded under the aegis of the Labour Government in the shape of concessions on Old Age Pensions, Unemployment Insurance, and a new Housing Bill. Nor in assessing Labour's hopes of accumulating a winning hand for a General Election, should Snowden's Budget be forgotten, and its part-fulfilment of the old Radical hope of freeing or part-freeing the breakfast table of Government impost. The sugar-duty reduction of $1\frac{1}{2}d.$ per lb.; the tea-duty reduction of $4d.$ per lb.; the halving of the imposts on cocoa, coffee, and chicory; the dried-fruit reductions; the abolition of the sweetened table-water duties —all these did still not complete the list of Budget "benefits". There was also, for the poor, the abolition or reduction, in places

it, passed through Standing Committee, and on report the Government accepted an amendment limiting the provision to landlords who had become owners by purchase before May 5, 1925. The Lords made certain amendments, with some of which the Commons declined to agree, and the bill was placed on the Statute Book."

[1] Perhaps it is only fair to add here that Labour claimed to be reacting against the socially harmful results that, allegedly, had already flowed from Neville Chamberlain's legislation of 1923 which had allowed a house-owner to regain possession from a tenant not only if he desired the premises for his own occupation but even for a son or a daughter—and without any real comparison of the "hardships" involved. There was doubtless considerable exaggeration in the rumours that began to circulate of house-owners' sons and daughters only nominally taking over occupation from unfortunate dispossessed tenants, the real purpose being revealed when a sale "with vacant possession" quickly followed. But the whole position aroused the most furious passion and prejudice as well as rival political manœuvres to turn them to advantage, and the history of Clydeside's—and even the Cabinet's—attitude towards, say, the "advanced Liberal" ideas of E. D. Simon, in regard to tenant-protection, is a cautionary tale.

[2] And, as events proved, to their quasi-heirs and successors who, especially in the shape of the widows or children of a deceased tenant, became entitled to one further privileged life-tenancy.

of amusement, of the entertainment tax on the cheaper seats;[1] for the Free Trade purists, still strongly represented in Liberal circles, there was the end of the McKenna Duties; and, finally, there was the end of the inhabited house-duty and of the Corporations Profits Tax which, whatever the motive, could hardly fail to please Conservatives. It was no wonder that the ex-Tory Chancellor of the Exchequer, Sir Robert Horne, pronounced Snowden's an excellent electioneering Budget and asked for some recognition of the work of previous Chancellors that now enabled the Labour holder of the post to offer taxation-reductions of over forty millions in a full year. It is plain that he had not missed the electoral import of the closing phrases of Snowden's Budget speech when the Chancellor had claimed that his proposals were "the greatest step ever made towards the near realization of the cherished Radical idea of a free breakfast. They give some relief to every man, woman and child in the country."

But despite Labour's obvious effort to collect an attractive domestic record for Election purposes, the Prime Minister was far from wrong in his estimate that to clinch the success that was being aimed at—nothing less than absolute Majority—it would also be indispensable to display Labour's Foreign policy as both more moral and more successful than that of previous Governments. And, truth to tell, Fortune, as has been seen, seemed to favour MacDonald when bringing down Poincaré and his Bloc National at Paris and substituting a Bloc des Gauches willing and even eager to work with MacDonald for a revised Reparations settlement, a gradual evacuation of the Ruhr, a League of Nations Conference on Disaramament and Security and, it might be, some parallelism between Britain and France in treating with Russia.[2] Labour prospects certainly seemed brighter than ever before when, alongside the Anglo-Russian Conference negotiating in London since April 14th, an Inter-Allied Reparations Conference began on July 16th, attended by the French and Belgian Premiers, and

[1] Cf. *Hansard*, April 29th, for Snowden's Budget speech proposing the abolition of entertainment duty in the case of admission charges up to and including sixpence, and the reduction of such duty in the case of admission charges above sixpence and up to 1s. 3d.

[2] Cf. *The Times*, June 2, 1924, for Poincaré's definite resignation after the heavy losses of his Bloc at the General Election of May 12th. The victorious Bloc des Gauches next enforced the resignation of the President of the Republic, elected a new one more to its taste and, when Herriot had subsequently been confirmed as Prime Minister, rejoiced at his prompt departure for a week-end of discussions at Chequers.

reached decisions under the Dawes Plan which German delegates found themselves able to sign on August 9th. As further wonders yet on Disarmament and Security were being prepared for the League of Nations meetings at Geneva in September, the Russians who, relying on Lansbury, the Clydesiders, and the *Daily Herald*, had bargained so toughly in the Anglo-Russian Conference as to bring it repeatedly near to collapse, had already decided that MacDonald could now afford to allow the Anglo-Russian negotiations to break up if they pressed their full demands uncompromisingly. Apparently the signature of two Treaties with the Russians at the Foreign Office, on August 8th, should have had a special place in the "proofs" being prepared for the electorate that Foreign policy under Labour was at once more benevolent, more enlightened, and more successful than it had been under previous Governments. But, in point of fact, there had already been serious rifts behind the scenes between MacDonald and Russia's special patrons in his Party,[1] the rift spread to Home affairs in the notorious case of the Communist, Jim Campbell, and, during September, both Lloyd George and Asquith no longer hesitated to come out in public against the results of the Russian negotiations. All this, however, should go into a new chapter.

[1] Cf. L. Macneill Weir, *The Tragedy of Ramsay MacDonald*, pp. 170–3, for some astonishing assertions. According to his account, even the prompt and unconditional recognition had needed some forcing on behind the scenes, and later there was more trouble because no Ambassador was sent immediately after the recognition and no move made to bring Russia "within the ambit of the Exports Credits Scheme". It would appear that MacDonald accepted the warning of the Foreign Office that, unless he held these things back till after a successful issue of the Anglo-Russian Conference, he would be surrendering his best means of getting the Russians to make adequate concessions to the British viewpoint.

CHAPTER XIX

THE 1924 ELECTIONS

"Very Secret. Executive Committee, Third Communist International, Presidium. September 15, 1924. Moscow.

"To the Central Committee, British Communist Party.

"Dear Comrades—The time is approaching for the Parliament of England to consider the Treaty concluded between the Governments of Great Britain and the S.S.S.R. for the purpose of ratification. The fierce campaign raised by the British bourgeoisie around the question shows that the majority of the same, together with reactionary circles, are against the Treaty for the purpose of breaking off an agreement consolidating the ties between the proletariats of the two countries leading to the restoration of normal relations between England and the S.S.S.R. The proletariat of Great Britain, which pronounced its weighty word when danger threatened of a break-off of the past negotiations, and compelled the Government of MacDonald to conclude the Treaty, must show the greatest possible energy in the further struggle for ratification and against the endeavours of British capitalists to compel Parliament to annul it.

"It is indispensable to stir up the masses of the British proletariat, to bring into movement the army of unemployed proletarians. . . .

"A settlement of relations between the two countries will assist in the revolutionising of the international and British proletariat not less than a successful rising in any of the working districts of England, as the establishment of close contact between the British and Russian proletariat, the exchange of delegations and workers etc., will make it possible for us to extend and develop the propaganda of ideas of Leninism in England and the Colonies. Armed warfare must be preceded by a struggle against the inclinations to compromise which are embedded among the majority of British workmen, against the ideas of evolution and peaceful determination of capitalism. Only then will it be possible to count upon complete success of an armed insurrection. . . ."

From the "Zinovieff Letter" published by the Foreign Office, October 24, 1924.

QUITE a number of the accounts of the decline and fall of Labour's first Government give some part to the "Biscuits Scandal"—the discovery, during the summer of 1924, that Mr. MacDonald had, some time before, accepted the suggestion of an old acquaintance, Mr. Alexander Grant, Chairman of the biscuit firm of McVitie and Price, to make 30,000 shares over to him, the income from which might provide the running costs for a Daimler car, presented by Mr. Grant to ease Mr. MacDonald's problems of personal transport. If it was not precisely helpful to have the Socialist Prime Minister revealed as a shareholding capitalist, possessed of a fine chauffeur-maintained car, it was worse that Mr. Grant had been awarded a baronetcy on Mr. MacDonald's recommendation. Of course, good and ample justification was claimed in the shape of Mr. Grant's other public-spirited benefactions but, to suspicious Tories, Labour, which had had so much to say on "Honours Scandals", had apparently contrived one itself, and in evasion of the very machinery devised, after 1922, to make such a thing impossible. Mr. MacDonald, too, was temperamentally incapable of doing much to improve his awkward, if not sinful, situation, the mere word "Biscuits", it is said, sufficing for a time to throw him off his balance at a public meeting or in Parliament.[1]

As it was, however, the strange history of the Campbell case, rather than "Biscuits", that brought the Government down, attention should now certainly be transferred to that. On Friday, July 25th, the Communist-controlled *Workers' Weekly* published a plainly criminal open letter of incitement to the fighting forces, and on July 30th, the Home Office answer to questions in the Commons called forth a loud protest from the Conservative Benches. There was a further question next day; a week of silence followed; and then it was the Labour Benches that were agitated by the answers of the Attorney-General, Sir Patrick Hastings, to a private notice question from John Scurr, Labour member for Mile End. The Attorney-General's words were these:

My attention was called by the Director of Public Prosecutions to an article in the *Workers' Weekly*, which, in my opinion, constituted a breach of the law. In consequence, the Director of Public Prosecutions

[1] Cf. L. MacNeill Weir, *The Tragedy of Ramsay MacDonald*, pp. 162–3.

has been engaged in the necessary steps to ascertain the identity of the persons responsible for the article. The Editor has accepted responsibility and has been arrested. The raid and the arrest were carried out on the authority of a warrant granted by a stipendiary magistrate. The Editor is being charged with an alleged offence against the Incitement to Mutiny Act, 1797. I am not prepared to state whether any charge will be preferred against any other person.

The angry excitement on the "Redder" Benches was, indeed, such[1] that an investigation behind the scenes began immediately into the methods that had been used to set the law in motion, from the first complaint to the final police raid. It is said to have revealed that though the appropriate War Office Department (which had evidence that the incriminated number of the *Workers' Weekly* had been taken in some quantity to Army barracks in Aldershot)[2] had approached the appropriate Home Office Department for action, Labour's War Secretary may not have been aware of what was happening. And, at the Home Office too, Mr. Henderson's signature as Home Secretary was not apparently in evidence on any document connected with the case.[3] Facts like these could be used by Maxton and Lansbury to fan the Back-Bench flames, and simultaneously Mr. Maxton was offering Sir Patrick Hastings a royal road of retreat, the proof that Campbell had fought through the war from beginning to end, had been decorated for exceptional gallantry, and still suffered, in his bad limp, from the effects of his war-wounds. It is not difficult to see why both the Attorney-General and the Cabinet decided that if they now, on the eve of the much-longed-for Adjournment destined to last from August 7th to Parliament's reassembly on September 30th, decided to withdraw the Campbell prosecution, they had ample means of justification to hand. In any case, pre-Adjournment Oppositions are not usually numerous or vigilant, and, by the time of Parliament's reassembly, the whole matter might well have blown over. If, however, Liberals or Conservatives chose to raise the matter after Parliament's return, it appeared that Ministers might gain rather than lose by exhibiting themselves as anxious to use their discretion to drop the prosecution of

---

[1] L. MacNeill Weir, *The Tragedy of Ramsay MacDonald*, pp. 175–7.

[2] Cf. John Scanlan, *Decline and Fall of the Labour Party*, p. 75, for a semi-jocular view from the "Left" which the War Office did not share.

[3] Of course the Labour Ministers may not have wanted to know too much.

a badly-wounded war-veteran, however mistaken might be his views on what Service men should do during strikes, whatever their orders.

Truth to tell, the Adjournment came on August 7th, with the Campbell case already seemingly sinking in importance, the "Reds" having turned to complaints that, in the current and parallel Reparations and Anglo-Russian Conferences, MacDonald was always ready to show indulgence to the Germans which he refused to the Russians.[1] Obviously the "Reds" seem to have been unaware that their long and very vocal pro-Russianism might weary or even antagonize important sections of the "floating vote". It is true nevertheless that, during the long August weeks following the Adjournment, the journalists of the "silly season" seem to have been more occupied with the dangerous habits of Alsatian dogs than with those of Russian Commissars or British Communists like Jimmy Campbell. Meanwhile, it has been said, MacDonald, in his anxiety to clear himself in the eyes of an aristocratic Lobby Correspondent of any part in the Campbell miscalculations, made confidential revelations from which his political opponents eventually came to deduce a good deal of the less defensible sides of Labour Back-Bench pressures on the Prime Minister and the Cabinet Majority.[2] At any rate, September found not only Lloyd George and Asquith[3] declaring against such results of Labour's prolonged negotiations with the Soviet Government as a British official guarantee for a Russian Loan— more of this will be said later—but a new outcry from Conservative journalists as to what might be presumed to lie behind the decision to withdraw the Campbell prosecution. When Irish Boundary business brought Parliament together again on September 30th, some of the Conservative Benches were soon revealed to be in a mood to try and force the Government out on the Campbell issue

---

[1] John Scanlan, *Decline and Fall of the Labour Party*, pp. 78–9, for some heavy irony from a "Red".

[2] Cf. *Ibid.*, pp. 79–80. Of course, the Conservative Press already had a good idea of why the "Reds" took pleasure in the thought that, in the 1924 Parliament, it was not Back-Benchers so much who were disciplined as the stream of Ministers who were asked to appear before the Labour Parliamentary Committee to answer complaints and objections.

[3] Cf. *Whitaker's Almanack, 1925*, p. 475, under September 11, 1924: "Mr. Lloyd George declared that Liberals would vote against the treaty with Soviet Government", and under September 22: "Mr. Asquith in a letter opposed guarantee of loan to Russia."

and not to wait for the debates on the Russian Loan. In view of the Liberal and Radical tradition in regard to "Freedom of the Press" Asquith was less ready to make the Campbell case a Government-destroying issue but meant, all the same, to insist on an inquiry into whether anything dubious had been going on behind the scenes.

The Labour Cabinet, for its part, returned to face Parliament, not only unaware that mortal danger was soon to overtake it, but convinced that whenever a General Election should come, it was bound to gain considerably from the "blaze of glory" for the Prime Minister resulting from his apparently successful Reparations and Russian negotiations,[1] and from Labour's ability, in Office, as it was, virtually to choose the Election's occasion and issue. At one stage it was almost hoped to be able to make the immediate Election issue a Peers' rejection of the Irish Boundary Commission Bill for which Parliament had been urgently recalled and the necessity for which J. H. Thomas was believed to have convincingly ascribed to "the guilt of Lloyd George in deceiving alike Free State and Ulster over the boundary clauses of the Peace Treaty".[2] In point of fact, on September 30th, when new Campbell troubles overtook the Cabinet, the Prime Minister was personally preparing to move the Second Reading of the Boundary Commission Bill, and the Peers allowed it to reach the Statute Book unamended, on October 9th, rather than give a Government, falling on the Campbell case, a possible means of extricating itself.[3] The Government guarantee for a proposed Russian Loan was obviously another issue on which an Election might be fought if Conservatives and Liberals combined to reject it, and with it, it was claimed, the hope of work for hundreds of thousands of unemployed. There was even Cabinet thought of the possibility, if not the probability, that Labour would make so many gains as to achieve an independent majority, the Liberals being held to have doomed themselves to very heavy losses on account of their

---

[1] *Beatrice Webb's Diaries, 1924–1932*, p. 40. Mrs. Webb knew, of course, what a doubtful success the Russian affair was and mentions the "committee of the rank and file" as one of the obvious pressure-groups involved.

[2] *Ibid.*, for a possible Election in October when, of course, the Liberals could have been damned with Lloyd George and the Tories with the Peers.

[3] Cf. *Whitaker's Almanack, 1925*, p. 167, for a short summary showing that the Peers even refrained from renewing the Conservative Amendment in Committee of the Commons prohibiting any substantial alteration of Northern Ireland's area. A Liberal-Labour majority had defeated this by 257–201.

attacks on a Russian Treaty which was believed to be proving more "popular" than they had expected.[1]

But, perhaps, a well-informed view of the relative confidence with which the Cabinet had prepared for the reassembly of Parliament on September 30th is worth giving at this stage. Beatrice Webb's diary entry for September 24th noted the Cabinet's "harmonious discussion" on India and the instructions sent in consequence to Lord Reading with regard to his demand for special powers. Then she went on to a revealing passage.[2] As the morning Cabinet was breaking up, the Prime Minister suggested a reassembly at three in the afternoon for general discussion. And the afternoon's discussion turned largely on ultimate Election prospects, the prevailing opinion apparently being that there would be no Election on the Russian Treaty despite Lloyd George and Winston Churchill but that Labour would have its own chance of playing for an Election on a bold programme for the next King's Speech. The Prime Minister made some characteristic observations which Sidney Webb apparently thought worth repeating to his wife and which she thought worth noting down. He said he was sick of the misbehaviour of the Party, of the ever-lasting court-martial attitude of the Party's Parliamentary Committee and of the *Daily Herald*'s constantly queering his pitch. And having asked his Ministers if they would welcome an independent Parliamentary Majority and having received, for the most part, the answer that they would, the Prime Minister declared that such a Majority would be a grave misfortune since the Labour Party was not fit to govern. He, of course, had good reason to fear accelerated force-pacing on the Left if anything approaching a Majority was obtained and was, doubtless, relieved to hear that general opinion was that no such Majority would be won though the Government's standing had improved and seats would be gained.

Yet MacDonald and his Cabinet were fated to find the re-gathering of Parliament on September 30th a much more

[1] Cf. *Beatrice Webb's Diaries, 1924–1932*, p. 44, for one estimate that fifty Liberal seats would be lost by sticking "to damning the Treaty".

[2] *Ibid.*, p. 43. This account, which Mrs. Webb must have got direct from her husband, is interesting as showing MacDonald's growing aversion to the average Back-Bencher behind him. There were other and more obvious indications that he disliked their mentality, and, all in all, an attentive student would find a surprising number of advance indications of the possibilities of the resounding breach of 1931.

dangerous experience than they had imagined. For one thing, most Liberals were very dissatisfied with MacDonald's blustering defence of the more questionable aspects of his Russian Treaty-making, a defence undertaken at Derby on September 27th, round such windy phrases as "the Treaties will bring work to the cupboards of our poor people" and "We shall take no words from the House of Commons or party leaders like 'I am in favour of trade with Russia and peace with Russia, but I am not going to accept these treaties.' "[1] It was too well-known that Snowden at the Exchequer had disliked some of the Russians' financial claims; that the shipping industry had opposed others; and that MacDonald himself had been prepared to see the Anglo-Russian Conference break up until Lansbury had mobilized the Back-Bench "Reds" for mutiny.[2] But it was Sir Patrick Hastings's unsatisfactory performance on the Campbell case that raised the immediate storm of September 30th, for it was not merely unconvincing but "old Parliamentary hands" saw ample reason to suspect that it was designed to conceal the Prime Minister's part in the inception of the prosecution and its subsequent abandonment under the pressure of Back-Bench "Reds". Yet neither Mr. Baldwin nor Mr. Asquith, with such critical business as the Irish Boundary Bill before Parliament, was anxious to make an immediate crisis of the matter, Mr. Baldwin, indeed, expressing his readiness to devote the next few days to the Irish Boundary Bill, to let Parliament then adjourn again and to wait for Mr. Mac-Donald's explanation to come later.

It was, in fact, Mr. MacDonald himself who forced a crisis

---

[1] Cf. *The Times*, September 29th.

[2] Cf. *The Nation*, October 4th, for the Liberal candidate, R. F. Walker, on the Russian Treaty and "the unpleasing story of how it came to be abandoned and rehabilitated". He continued: "I wonder, Sir, what would be thought of a shopkeeper who improved his turnover by lending £100 to an insolvent bankrupt on the understanding that he would spend £60 in the shop. . . . It must be remembered that it is not proposed that the Russians should say: 'We cannot as a practical fact pay our debt, but we admit our liability and will use a portion of your loan to be fairly divided among our creditors.' That would be understandable, however it might be criticised. It is proposed, rather, that the Russian should say: 'I still affirm the right of a new Government to repudiate the debts of the last. If, however, you will accept this (to you) dishonest theory we will pay for your acquiescence by returning some of your loan to some of your nationals. This as a bargain, and to detach them from their fellow-creditors." This anti-Treaty position, widely adopted in the commercial world of Liberal tradition, was moderate by comparison with a Tory cry of "no Treaty with the murderers" which finally had more effect than was at all foreseen by those Labour politicians who are reported to have regarded their "Bolshevik Treaty as an electioneering asset".

forward.[1] Galled by the uncharitable "Biscuits" gossip under discussion everywhere, he seems to have developed almost a "persecution complex" when Campbell case and Russian Treaty gossip added to his troubles.[2] At any rate, instead of taking up Mr. Baldwin's offer, he pressed for a Campbell Debate as soon as possible, and one was arranged for October 8th. It was unfortunate that the year's Labour Party Conference opened in London, on October 6th, for attitudes were struck there and defiant war-cries raised that made it doubly impossible for Labour's Prime Minister to accept "humiliation" at the hands of coalized Liberals and Conservatives in the House of Commons.[3] The Prime Minister's neurotic condition, too, was increased on October 8th by having practically to confess, at question-time, that he had previously misled the House on the subject of his alleged complete lack of fore-knowledge of the dropping of the Campbell prosecution.[4] The Tory jeering that followed and that went on while rigorous cross-examination of the Prime Minister was undertaken

[1] *Hansard*, September 30th, for Baldwin thus: "There is obviously a very deep interest in this matter . . . and it seems to me that the time that could be allowed under the Rule for the Adjournment of the House would be altogether inadequate. . . . I wish to ask the Prime Minister, as we are barred by mutual agreement from taking any business besides the Irish business during this week, whether on the resumption of business at the end of October, he will give us a day. . . ." And MacDonald thus in reply: "I am not at all content to wait for the exposure of this until the end of October (Hon. Members: 'Have it now.') I understand that, in the ordinary course of business, we may have two Parliamentary days at least going blank while the Bill [the Boundary Commission Bill] that I shall move in a few minutes will be under consideration in another place, and I shall be perfectly willing to agree that one of those days . . . will be assigned. . . ."

[2] Cf. *The Nation*, October 11th: "it is accepted that the vanity or (in the psychological term) the inferiority of Mr. MacDonald is less a subject for present controversy than one for the pathologist and the historian".

[3] Cf. *Ibid.*, October 18th, for Masterman as "Ex-M.P." asserting Mac-Donald's "state of neurotic disturbance" and that "the Prime Minister, in part inflamed by the violence of the Labour Party sittings at the Queen's Hall, made a passionate and hysterical speech, which banged the door".

[4] *Ibid.*, for Masterman's plainer language: "Mr. MacDonald had to commence the Government defence by the dismal confession (received in dead silence by his own followers) that he had lied in his statement that he knew nothing at all about the matter. The curious explanation of such mendacity was that he had lost his temper and felt 'resentment' at Sir Kingsley Wood's question. But he obviously wilted under Mr. Austen Chamberlain's elaborately courteous but deadly cross-examination . . . the charge against the Attorney-General ceased immediately that Mr. MacDonald asserted that he had known all about the prosecution, had discussed it with Sir Archibald Bodkin and Sir Patrick Hastings on the fatal afternoon, and later in the Cabinet—a fact which he had previously denied. The men, who according to the vivacious Campbell, had threatened a Labour Party split if the prosecution were proceeded with, although in the House through the whole of the debate, remained absolutely silent. . . ."

by Austen Chamberlain and Sir John Simon could hardly have helped Mr. MacDonald to compose himself for the business which opened with the Conservative Vote of Censure moved by Sir Robert Horne. The Attorney-General replied to Horne and then Sir John Simon moved a Liberal Amendment (later adopted by the Tories too) for a Select Committee to inquire into what had really happened to bring about the withdrawal of the Campbell prosecution.

It is just possible that if Simon had been less contemptuous,[1] MacDonald might either have refrained from making a Dissolution matter of the carrying of the Select Committee Amendment[2] or have been overruled in Cabinet. As it was, after Asquith in one of the best speeches he ever made,[3] had reminded the Labour Party that his own Government and Salisbury's had submitted to Select Committees of Inquiry[4] and had gone on, in answer to MacDonald's claim that the Select Committee would be weighted against him, to offer to waive, in Labour's favour, Liberalism's share of the Committee seats, the decision was nearly taken, on the Government side, to call off the Dissolution threat.[5] But the hope that the Liberals would flinch at the immediate prospect of Dissolution or, perhaps, split in the process of voting rallied what was described as a "tiny majority" to sending in J. H. Thomas to the House to stand by the Dissolution menace. It was known, of

[1] Cf. L. MacNeill Weir, *The Tragedy of Ramsay MacDonald*, p. 181, for what was apparently regarded on the Labour side as brutal and unwarranted "defamation" which the Prime Minister, as was shown in the opening words of his reply, bitterly resented.

[2] Cf. *Hansard*, October 8th: "If the House passes either of the resolutions on the paper, then we go. It will be the end of what has been a high adventure which has contributed to the honour of the country and social stability, and which, when the country has had an opportunity of passing a verdict upon us, will come again."

[3] Cf. L. MacNeill Weir, *The Tragedy of Ramsay MacDonald*, p. 182, for a Labour M.P.'s very high praise of a speech which he found at once pungent, witty, and startlingly unpartisan and detached. The joke he apparently enjoyed best was Asquith's banter on the subject of MacDonald's haste in delivering a funeral oration before the doctor had pronounced Government's life extinct.

[4] *Hansard*, October 8th, for Asquith pointing out, too, that both his Government and Salisbury's (in the Marconi and Jameson Raid Inquiries) had had majorities which could, presumably, have been used against the Select Committee suggestion. Yet Select Committees had been accepted without "whimpering about torture chambers". The Ministers concerned had faced "the boot, the thumb-screw, and the rack, and all the rest of the apparatus of mediaeval cruelty" and found the Select Committee "one of the fairest tribunals in the world".

[5] Cf. *The Nation*, October 18th: "As a result of this . . . there was another long Government consultation, in which bitterness and outspoken words were conspicuous. The decision to resist the inquiry was carried by a tiny majority."

course, that an Election in which Liberal members had to explain to irritated voters why there were continuous political crises as Liberals turned this way or that, was likely to prove fatal to many of them. And, perhaps, there was exaggeration of the possible effects of the rumoured Back-Bench peddling to "advanced Liberals" of offers of speedy reception into the Labour Party if they but supported the Government.[1]

At any rate, Asquith, in his speech, had certainly gone to the utmost limits of concession and could retreat no further without complete loss of face. And if fourteen Liberals still thought fit to support the Government against the Simon Amendment as well as against the Conservative Vote of Censure, that still entailed the Government's heavy defeat when resisting the Select Committee, called for not only by the bulk of the Liberals but by the Conservatives, too, as soon as it became plain that the conciliatory Asquith was prepared to lead a practically united Liberal Party to Labour's support against the Conservative Vote of Censure. Indeed, the fact that the Conservative Vote of Censure was defeated by a Liberal-Labour majority of 359–198 despite Labour's failure the same night, in a Division of 198–364, to defeat the Simon Amendment also, might have provided, if it had been so desired, a final opportunity to reconsider the Dissolution threat. But the Prime Minister, so far from contemplating anything of the kind, was already planning an unusually rapid Election campaign[2] in which he apparently meant to strike with special fury at Liberalism,[3] whose 150 seats certainly offered the

[1] Cf. *Ibid.*, October 18th, for "desperate attempts had been made to woo a number of Liberals from their allegiance to Mr. Asquith", and *Beatrice Webb's Diaries, 1924–1932*, pp. 44–5, for the Labour view, not only that the fourteen Liberal pro-Labour members of October 8th might have become fifty on the Russian Treaty but that the fourteen Liberal members—including their ablest lawyer and Mrs. Wintringham—might join the Labour Party. Obviously Asquith had behaved too well and MacDonald too badly for such a consummation.

[2] Cf. *Whitaker's Almanack, 1925*, p. 167: "On the following day [October 9th] Mr. MacDonald announced that the King had consented to a Dissolution. To avoid the municipal elections and reduce inconvenience to a minimum, the dissolution took place the same evening, and nominations were fixed for the 18th and polling for the 29th." It is questionable whether matters had ever been rushed through at this speed before, and there seems little doubt that some advantages to Labour, as the Government party, were expected to result. That at least was a Liberal charge, several times repeated.

[3] Cf. *The Nation*, October 18, 1924: "In reality the end came because Mr. MacDonald, who confessed a black hatred in his heart against the Liberals ever since he was put in office by their votes, in a state of neurotic disturbance and troubled by many other disputes besides that of Campbell, determined suddenly to destroy this Parliament and to rush the election in minimum time; in the hope that he would find the other two parties imperfectly prepared, and that

most tempting prospect of political booty. And as remarkable combative enthusiasm round a fighting "people's" Premier had lately been evidenced both at the Labour Party Conference and in Parliament, a far-ranging electoral tour by MacDonald played an important part in Labour's political calculations.[1]

It did not take Liberals long to realize that they were in serious electoral danger though the probable outcome was not a continuation of Labour rule but the return of Conservatism to Office, helped by the great faction-fight amongst the rival "progressives" and the weariness of the "public" at being subjected to the third General Election in two years. And it is certain that, though the "march of progress" would presumably be slowed down under Conservatism, most Liberals were not sorry that the vaunting hopes of Labour were likely to be defeated. As their weekly, *The Nation*, put it:[2]

Nothing could be more conducive to a healthy development of British politics than that it should be made plain that such tactics as Labour has pursued during the present year bring it to disaster at the polls. The whole course of the Labour Government during its nine months of office has been determined by the primary aim of destroying the Liberal Party. This statement will not be disputed, we believe, by any serious student of public affairs. The Labour Government when it took office was confronted with two broad alternatives. It could endeavour to realize to the utmost the opportunities for progress afforded by the balance in the House of Commons. . . . Or it could use its term of office primarily as an opportunity for propaganda and party tactics. . . . There were important elements in the Cabinet who would have chosen the former course, but these elements did not prevail . . . the main reason was the calculation, strong in the Cabinet, and stronger still among the rank and file . . . that Labour had only to hammer once or twice more and the Liberal Party would dwindle and disappear, and leave Labour in undisputed possession of the field as sole champion of progressive courses.

The ugly truth revealed in the polls of October 29th was uglier by far than even pessimist Liberals had foreseen. For one thing,

in a dramatic platform campaign he might still retain the leadership of his own." The fact that the Labour Party was mobilized at their Annual Conference seemed to give special chances to this strategy.

[1] Cf. L. MacNeill Weir, *The Tragedy of Ramsay MacDonald*, pp. 184–5, for the arrangements for a great electioneering effort, a triumphal tour of the modern campaigning model, with crowds to meet him wherever the train halted between London and Glasgow. There were short speeches from him at Rugby, Crewe, Carlisle, and other stations, and the tour was to reach its high point at Glasgow from which he was to broadcast.

[2] *The Nation*, October 25th.

the offensive enthusiasm of Labour, and the effect of the Prime Minister's electioneering tour,[1] combined, until within a few days of the Election, to make the notion of an independent Labour Majority altogether less far-fetched than it had seemed at first. And even when the appearance of the "Zinoviev Letter", four days before the polls, shattered all Labour's more hopeful calculations, the results of October 29th were still to leave Labour's voting strength increased by well over a million though, by the accidents of the electoral system, fewer Labour members had to do duty for greatly increased numbers of supporters. It was the unfortunate Liberals, attacked from the Right for having put Labour into power at all and from the Left for having turned finally against the "people's" government, who were the main victims of the polls of 1924.

Perhaps something should be said first of the "Zinoviev Letter". Every serious politician knew that Moscow used a variety of means to try and influence the British situation, and that the Labour Cabinet's lack of enthusiasm for the kind of Anglo-Russian Treaty the Soviet Government desired had led Moscow to make trouble. Apparently it had been agreed for some time between MacDonald and Sir Eyre Crowe, Permanent Under-Secretary at the Foreign Office, that directly reliable evidence was obtained of Soviet interference in British internal affairs, a strong protest should go to the Russian representative in London, the Chargé d'Affaires Rakowsky.[2] As the affair worked out, the Prime Minister was campaigning at Aberavon, his own constituency, when the Foreign Office sent on to him a presumed letter of exhortation and advice, addressed from Moscow to the British Communist Party, and the draft Protest Note to Rakowsky which the Foreign Office had prepared in consequence. There was certainly no disloyalty to MacDonald in Sir Eyre Crowe's action. and, indeed, it would almost seem that he was trying to help him by half-suggesting how the current electoral charges of pro-Russianism might be rebutted. MacDonald must certainly have interpreted matters in this way

[1] Cf. *Ibid.*, October 25, 1924, for instances of the "offensive" spirit carried too far: "the rowdyism organized by the Labour Party in some constituencies seems like an outrage to their own creed. . . . I hear that Captain Wedgwood Benn is having an extremely rough time in Leith. . . . On Monday night a Conservative meeting was broken up at Colchester, and at a Conservative meeting at Kensington the same evening the disorder was so violent that the police had to be called in. . . ."

[2] Harold Nicolson, *King George V*, p. 401.

413

for, after amending the Protest Note in some particulars, he sent it back to Sir Eyre Crowe. At this stage, Sir Eyre Crowe learned that the *Daily Mail* had also obtained a copy of the presumed "Zinoviev Letter" and intended to publish the Communist International's alleged firebrand appeals for such things as the creation of Communist cells among soldiers, sailors, and munition-workers, not to mention the organization of insurrection in Ireland and the Colonies. And so, rather than have the Foreign Office and MacDonald, its political head, revealed as apparently backward in reproving intrusion from Russia into British domestic affairs, Eyre Crowe authorized the immediate forwarding of the Protest Note to Rakowsky and the immediate communication of the whole affair to the Press.[1] But for the Election mentality prevailing on every hand, the matter would hardly have gone forward at such a pace on a document which had not been adequately checked, either by MacDonald or by Crowe, and which was soon under suspicion as a "White Russian" forgery, intended, by Bolshevism's enemies, to make trouble for the Soviet régime.[2]

Yet the fact that MacDonald and Crowe had had such bitter experience of Soviet methods as not to be surprised by any reported subversion attempted (even at a time of Loan and Friendship Treaty negotiation) was to prove decisive with key-sections of the electorate. Hundreds of thousands of voters who might apathetically have stayed at home or voted Liberal decided to vote Conservative as the strongest way of protesting against what Moscow had apparently attempted.[3] The unfortunate Liberals, indeed, who had already lost hundreds of thousands of their working-class supporters to the Labour offensive, were robbed, possibly, of even more by the oft-repeated Conservative charge that, as the party who had put Labour in power, they bore the ultimate responsibility for what had now been uncovered. Roughly summarized,

[1] Cf. Harold Nicolson, *King George V*, p. 402, for Sir Eyre Crowe's explanation to the Prime Minister, as copied and sent to the King.

[2] Cf. L. MacNeill Weir, *The Tragedy of Ramsay MacDonald*, p. 189, for the view that the "Letter" had been rather clumsily patched together from extracts found in Communist speeches and pamphlets and that no one had seen the original letter though the *Daily Mail* had obtained several alleged copies.

[3] L. MacNeill Weir, *The Tragedy of Ramsay MacDonald*, p. 188, for the notorious cartoon which helped so much, the cartoon entitled "On the Loan Trail" and depicting a repellent Russian sandwich-man slouching along the roadway in Whitehall. He wore Russian headgear and highboots. His long hair was unkempt as was his untidy beard. "Vote for MacDonald and Me" was inscribed on his sandwich-boards back and front.

electoral statistics were these: 800,000 more entitled to vote than
in 1923; 2 millions more actually voting; loss of Liberal votes over
a million; increase of Conservative votes 2 millions; increase of
Labour votes 1 million. As the British electoral system worked, in
default even of the partial Proportional Representation which
Liberals had now vainly bargained for with both other parties,
Conservative representation rose from 258 to 413, Labour representation fell from 191 to 150, and Liberal representation fell, if the
severest judgement is accepted, from 156 to the catastrophic depth
of 39.[1] But the effects of all this on party alignments shall be reserved
for a space, and attention concentrated on the personal problems
of the two defeated party Leaders, MacDonald and Asquith.

It was, perhaps, inevitable that MacDonald, when he found
that his Rakowsky Protest manœuvre to prove himself as vigilant
a patriot as any one in the land, was failing, the electorate concentrating instead on the ugly implications of Russian subversion,
should find cause, in the last days of Election campaigning, to
question what had been done by the Foreign Office.[2] Indeed, the
resignation of the Government was held back for some days while
a rapid inquiry was undertaken into the provenance and genuine-
ness of the "Zinoviev Letter" and, in effect, into the related
question of whether there was anything in the Left's whispered
suspicions that there had been a plot between the *Daily Mail* and
certain elements in the Foreign Office. As nothing really decisive
issued from the necessarily hurried inquiry—not even a firm
decision as to whether the "Zinoviev Letter" was genuine or not[3]
—MacDonald's position became difficult and even dangerous. In
the eyes of Clydeside and Lansbury, he had been presented with
the chance of introducing a genuine Socialist policy but had
preferred, sometimes a species of reformist Liberalism and, sometimes, as in the matter of the new Cruiser programme and the

[1] *Whitaker's Almanack, 1925*, p. 168. This figure, admittedly, did not include
Whitley, the Speaker, and a number of members who are described as Constitutionalists and Independents so that some calculations of Liberal strength
go a little higher.

[2] Cf. L. MacNeill Weir, *The Tragedy of Ramsay MacDonald*, p. 194, for the
conclusion of one who was long his Parliamentary Private Secretary, and who
dismissed the Prime Minister's self-exculpation as mere quibbling.

[3] Cf. *The Nation*, November 8th: "Resignation was postponed for a few days
in order that a Cabinet Committee, consisting of Mr. MacDonald, Lord
Haldane, Lord Parmoor and Mr. Henderson might inquire into the authenticity.
. . . In the end, however, they shirked the task, and publicly announced that
they 'found it impossible on the evidence before them to come to a conclusion'." Their successors decided that the "letter" was genuine.

"Zinoviev Letter", an attempt to win the applause and support of Toryism. Efforts were made to find a new Leader for the Session of 1924–5, and when Mr. Henderson declined to stand and imperil party unity, Maxton even tried to push Lansbury into the Leadership though with farcical results.[1] Even when MacDonald returned from a long holiday of recuperation in Jamaica, the effort continued to make his position as Leader in the House impossible and to weary him out by constant fault-finding in the Party's Executive Committee.[2] More than once, the "Right" of the Labour Party discussed what might happen if an open split occurred, and certainly the possibility of working with "advanced Liberals" was repeatedly canvassed.[3] It was most fortunate for Labour that its Right and Left found it indispensable to stay together to beat off such dangers to them both as the 1925 Political Levy Bill of Mr. Macquisten, which would certainly, if passed, have greatly reduced the sums raised as Political Levy by the Trade Unions.

Mr. Asquith's problems were very different in kind from Mr. MacDonald's. Despite the catastrophic nature of Liberalism's political losses, and the private grumbling that had often been heard, from his younger men, as to his lethargy and inability to pretend any vivid interest in "advanced" economic programmes, Mr. Asquith had made a deep impression on the 1924 Parliament.[4] And though he had now lost his Paisley seat and had reluctantly to face the possibility of going to the Lords, his Leadership remained indispensable to the Party. If he laid it down, Lloyd George's claims to the succession were irrefutable and yet, if exercised, would certainly lead to a great schism on the part of those who still dwelt bitterly on their wrongs of 1916–22. Even when the last hope of a return to the Commons was being abandoned in January 1925,[5] and re-entry to Parliament was being

[1] Cf. John Scanlan, *Decline and Fall of the Labour Party*, pp. 85–6. Lansbury's name only raised five votes.

[2] *Ibid.*, p. 85, for MacDonald's gruelling time from the Party Executive both on policy and on the expensive Election tour he had undertaken without proper regard, it was claimed, either to economy or to the plans of the National Organization.

[3] *Beatrice Webb's Diaries, 1924–1932*, pp. 55–6, for one such discussion.

[4] Cf. *Life and Letters of Austen Chamberlain*, ii, 241, for the difficulties in the face of which this was achieved: "The Liberal Party is visibly bursting up. It holds constant Party meetings to decide its course; then 40 vote with the Govt., 20 vote with us, and the rest (including the leaders) walk out or absent themselves."

[5] Cf. *Holmes-Laski Correspondence*, i, 694, 699, for the failure of a plan to

arranged, rather over-floridly, in the style of the Earl of Oxford and Asquith, the position was apparently unchangeable for years to come. Lloyd George's election as Sessional Liberal Chairman in the Commons had not been effected without opposition though Asquith's help was available to keep it within bounds. And when, on January 29th, a special Liberal Convention gathered to begin the uphill work of seeking to restore Liberalism's strength and raise a Million Guinea Fund, the most striking feature of the occasion certainly seemed to be Lloyd George's unreserved acceptance of Asquith's Leadership.[1]

Perhaps, before closing this chapter, the view on the polls should be given of the Radical economist, John Maynard Keynes, who was already playing a part of some importance on the Liberal side and was destined to play a bigger when, despite previous differences, he became almost Lloyd George's economic consultant in the remarkable effort of 1925-9 to put a modernized Radicalism in charge of the Liberal Party machine and make it an effective competitor for power. Keynes was clear-sighted to remind the politicians that it was not their unwavering party-zealots, who decided the issue of elections, but rather the "wobblers"—two million voters, perhaps, of the total twenty millions. Seventy per cent of the electorate, Keynes reckoned,[2] could normally be counted as safe adherents to the respective parties—28 per cent to the Conservatives, 14 per cent to the Liberals, and 28 per cent to Labour, and these figures would only change slowly. Of the remaining 30 per cent, nearly 20 per cent could be expected to abstain from voting, leaving the issue in the hands of the 10 per cent of wobblers. Owing to the geographical concentration of Labour's support in certain parts of the country, Labour's Parliamentary strength was never likely to fall below its actual quarter

recall Fisher to Oxford and seat Asquith in his place for the English Universities. Laski explained "Asquith's surrender—a great pity in every way" by his belief that Asquith "could not stand the strain of another election. . . . But I wish he had not taken so grandiose a title." Asquith was now in his seventy-third year.

[1] Cf. *Beatrice Webb's Diaries, 1924-1932*, p. 56, for some very unsympathetic Labour comment according to which there had been a measure of resentment of Asquith's retention of the party Leadership without re-election (and though he had accepted a Peerage) and that Lloyd George as second-in-command was, to many, not a cheerful prospect. Mrs. Webb doubted whether £100,000 would be obtained now that the party's wealthy men saw no prospect of a return for their money. And though once or twice the possibility seemed near of a millionaire like Lord Cowdray being used to induce brother-magnates to take collective responsibility for a formidable fraction of the desired million, the availability of the Lloyd George Fund always provided those approached for large sacrifices with a counter-plea.   [2] *The Nation*, November 8, 1924.

of the House of Commons but that concentration meant also that it would be much harder for Labour than for Conservatism to win an absolute majority. On the 1924 showing, Labour would have to absorb the entire Liberal Party and all the wobblers as well, to win such a majority but there were many Liberals, who if their party broke up or disappeared, would go to the Conservatives rather than to Labour. Only in the event of a combination of years of Tory misgovernment and a fall in the living standards of the working-masses could Keynes envisage the possibility of an independent Labour Majority, and even then "the tumultuous exploitation of acute distress" was unlikely to prove a safe or happy experience. Was it not better for Labour men to admit that, for many years to come, "a progressive Government of the Left, capable of efficient legislation" was unlikely to come "unless Radicals and Labour men stop cutting one another's throats and come to an agreement for joint action from time to time to carry through practical measures about which they agree".

Keynes concluded meaningfully:

Probably not less than 10 per cent of the British electorate are natural Radicals. Their mentality and their feelings and sometimes their class sympathies are distinct from those of the typical Labour enthusiast. Their proper place is outside the Labour Party. They form a nucleus around which from time to time a substantial body of voters will collect. No important reforms will ever be carried in this country without their intellectual, moral, and numerical support.

But, of course, no party machine, especially one with almost a claim to power by Divine Predestination, will ever admit that the proper place for anybody of use is outside its purview. It will always offer to make room inside and, meanwhile, endeavour to wreck any possible alternative.

CHAPTER XX

BALDWIN, SAMUEL,
AND THE GENERAL STRIKE

"We find ourselves . . . in possession of perhaps the greatest majority our Party has ever had, and with the general assent of the country. Now how did we get there? . . . it was because, rightly or wrongly, we succeeded in creating an impression throughout the country that we stood for stable Government and for peace in the country between all classes of the community.

"Those were the principles for which we fought; those were the principles on which we won; and our victory was not won entirely by the votes of our own Party, splendidly as they fought. I should think that the number of Liberals who voted for us at the last Election ran into six figures, and I should think that we probably polled more Labour votes than were polled on the other side.

"That being so, what should our course be at the beginning of a new Parliament. I have not myself the slightest doubt . . . we believe it is for us in our strength to do what no other Party can do at this moment, and to say that we at any rate stand for industrial peace. . . .

"Although I know that there are those who work for different ends from most of us in this House, yet there are many in all ranks and all parties who will re-echo my prayer: *'Give peace in our time, O Lord'*."

> Baldwin in the House of Commons, March 6, 1925, on the Second Reading of the Trade Union (Political Fund) Bill advocating Peace in Industry.

"The coal mining industry, for more than a century the foundation of the economic strength of the country, has come upon difficult times. This change of fortunes is the result of powerful economic forces. It is idle to attribute it either on the one hand to political unrest or restriction of output among the miners, or on the other hand to inefficiency in the day by day management of the mines.

"At the same time we cannot agree with the views presented to us by the mine-owners that little can be done to improve the organisation of the industry, and that the only practicable course is to lengthen hours and lower wages. In our view large changes are necessary in other directions, and large progress is possible. We agree that immediate measures are indispensable to deal with the immediate position, but the effort ought not to stop there.

". . . the Miners' Federation propose the nationalisation of the mines. We do not recommend the adoption of this policy. . . .

"We are not satisfied that the scheme proposed to us is workable, or that it offers a clear social gain. We perceive in it grave economic dangers, and we find no advantages that cannot be obtained as readily, or more readily in other ways.

"We contemplate accordingly the continuance of the industry under private enterprise, but we make a number of proposals for its re-organisation. . . ."

From the *Summary of Findings and Recommendations of the Royal Commission on the Coal Industry* (1925) as signed on March 6, 1926, by Herbert Samuel (Chairman), H. A. Lawrence, W. H. Beveridge, and Kenneth Lee.

M R. BALDWIN, when summoned to the Palace in November 1924 and requested to form a Government, seemed in an enviable position indeed compared with his rivals. MacDonald's party was badly split by disputes about the leadership he had given; Asquith's had shrunk to two score, and he himself was excluded from the possibility of leading it in the Commons. Baldwin, on the other hand, after having blundered into the fatal Election of November 1923, had received both an unexpectedly early chance to come back with heightened prestige and a huge majority, and the further opportunity to construct a much stronger and more experienced Government than his last. The breach in the Leadership of the Tory Party, occasioned by the manner of the Coalition's break-up two years back, could, it seemed, be regarded as a thing of the past when Austen Chamberlain was invited to take the Foreign Office, Lord Balfour the Presidency of the Council, Lord Birkenhead the India Office, Worthington Evans the War Office, and Gilmour the Scottish Secretaryship. And if the Prime Minister had not invited Horne to return to the Exchequer,[1] that had left him free to appoint Winston Churchill to the vacancy as a portent almost of Conservatism's desire to work with those Liberals or ex-Liberals who regarded "revolutionary Socialism" as the principal peril to Society and the State.

Of course, the political situation bristled with problems of every kind, Egypt, India, the Geneva Protocol, the Irish Boundary, and MacDonald's unratified Russian Treaties prominent amongst them. Yet a relatively enormous Parliamentary majority—the statisticians gave it as 420 in a House of 615—and a far stronger Cabinet than either those of 1923 or 1924, combined to make it certain that overseas opinion would accept the advisability of consulting Britain's interests and even prejudices somewhat more readily than had been the case under MacDonald. Thus, the Egyptian Zaghlulite Nationalists, who had dreamed of forcing on MacDonald almost a British surrender on the Sudan and the Suez

[1] Cf. *The Nation*, November 15th, for Beaverbrook's failure to "create a public outcry" on the matter through his newspapers. And it was noted of Churchill's post: "I fancy there is more approval of that appointment in Liberal circles than anywhere else. . . . In control of the service departments Mr. Churchill would have been a public danger but . . . there is a very widespread belief that at the Treasury the better genius of Mr. Churchill will have full play."

Canal,[1] were promptly displaced by King Fuad when the new British Government determined on strong action after the assassination of the British Sirdar.[2] Nor did the new Government's announcement that it would not proceed with the Russian Treaties do it much apparent harm.[3] And, on occasion, an apparently insoluble problem like that of Boundary Revision in Ireland could take an unexpectedly favourable turn as when the South African Justice Feetham, nominated to sit, in place of recalcitrant Ulster's representative,[4] in the Boundary Commission, took so Ulsterish a line that Free State hopes of Tyrone and Fermanagh were soon over. In India, too, it became plain that a Government with a majority like Baldwin's was not to be coerced by the now seriously divided Swaraj agitation,[5] and as for the Geneva Protocol, biased, it was feared, too much towards the defence of some of the unwisest boundary decisions of 1919, Liberal opinion came promptly to Austen Chamberlain's support when he finally determined, despite Ramsay MacDonald,[6] to lay it aside and work, instead, on what became the celebrated Five-Power Locarno Pact.

[1] Cf. *The Nation*, October 11, 1924: "Zaghloul has come and gone . . . Zaghloul demanded not only complete rights of ownership over the Sudan, but also the withdrawal of all British troops from Egyptian territory, and the abandonment by the Government of its claim to protect the Suez Canal, the withdrawal of British financial and judicial advisers, and the disappearance of all British control over Egypt's foreign relations and over the treatment of foreigners and minorities. In other words, Zaghloul stood out for a hundred per cent of nationalism and for a considerable dash of imperialism besides."

[2] Cf. *Whitaker's Almanack, 1926*, p. 455: "Nov. 19, 1924. Sir Lee Stack, Governor-General of the Sudan and Sirdar of the Egyptian Army, was fatally wounded by shots fired by seven Egyptians in Cairo. . . . Nov. 24th. The Zaghlul Cabinet resigned and Ziwar Pasha formed a new Cabinet which paid fine of £500,000. . . . Dec. 1st. Egyptian Government accepted remaining demands of Britain. . . ."

[3] Cf. *Hansard*, December 15th, for the defeat of a Labour Amendment to the Address being moved in the new Parliament. This Labour Amendment condemning the Government's Egyptian and Russian policy was defeated by 363–132.

[4] Cf. *The Nation*, April 4, 1925, for its irate Dublin correspondent: "The centre of political disturbance in Ireland has shifted for the moment to the six counties. Sir James Craig appears to have set out to prejudice the issue in the Boundary question as far as possible; his method appears to be almost exactly similar to a studied contempt of court for which an individual might be put in gaol."

[5] Cf. *Ibid.*, March 21, 1925: "The accession of a strong Conservative Government to power has undoubtedly had a wholesome sobering effect on India. Her leaders have been forced to recognize that there is no royal road to Swaraj, to rely less on sensational tactics and more on spade work. It seems possible that they may even come to see wisdom in following the route marked out for them by Mr. Montagu. All this is solid gain, as none of the suggested alternatives to the Montagu road appears to be less beset with dangers to ourselves and to India."

[6] *Ibid.*: "At Geneva last week, Mr. Austen Chamberlain announced, as was

All these weighty problems, then, did not vitally affect the basic shape of British party composition and relationship as they might well have done in other circumstances. At home, too, Winston Churchill's first ambitious Budget with the related decisions to inaugurate Widows' and Orphans' Pensions, begin a return towards the pre-war pound-dollar parity and the "Gold Standard", and allow an increase of some Imperial Preferences and the decrease of Income Tax,[1] did not affect party alignments any more than did the Unemployment Insurance[2] and Rent Control Acts of 1925.[3] What, in fact, interested political commentators and observers more than anything else was whether the bitterly-divided Labour Party could continue to function under Ramsay MacDonald's much-criticized leadership or whether it would break into "Red" and moderate factions, the latter capable of allying with the

expected, the definite refusal of the British Empire to ratify the Protocol. . . . The German offer is a new development of first-rate international importance. . . . It is important, above all, that the situation should be considered in an atmosphere reasonably free from party faction. . . . Unfortunately Mr. Ramsay MacDonald has made it clear that he means to drag it in in its crudest form. The protocol, he told his Fulham audience last week-end, was 'one of the great performances the Labour Government had worked for'. The present Government had rejected it 'simply because the Labour Government had agreed to it'. . . . There is one immense advantage in the decision of the British Government to concentrate for the time being on exploring the possibilities of the German offer. It brings in Germany for the first time as a partner in the preparation and authorship of security schemes. . . . The Protocol might in practice have proved an additional and formidable obstacle to Germany's joining the League at all. . . ."

[1] Cf. *Hansard*, April 28th, for Churchill's Budget speaking which was regarded as a very distinguished performance, and, indeed, the commentators noted, throughout the Session, how rhetorically effective the Chancellor was. When Snowden spoke next day from the Front Opposition Bench (*Ibid.*, April 29th) he ventured to declare that the Budget, if shorn of the Pensions scheme, would have been seen by everybody to be what it really was—the worst rich man's Budget ever to have been proposed and he complained, too, of the employers' contributions towards the new Widows' and Orphans' Pensions as imposing a burden upon industry of not less than fourteen millions a year. For the Liberals Sir Alfred Mond condemned the return to the Gold Standard in existing circumstances as well as the new duties on silk, natural and artificial, which the Chancellor had introduced as a species of "Sumptuary Duty".

[2] Cf. *Ibid.*, July 7th, for Sir Arthur Steel Maitland on the Second Reading of this measure which reduced the contribution of masters and men but hoped to save six and a half million pounds a year by taking power to refuse extended benefit to young men living at home and to wives of husbands in work. There were some stormy scenes in Standing Committee before the Bill went through and the Minister finally agreed to some postponement of another Labour-criticized feature of the Bill, the extension of the "waiting period" from three to six days.

[3] Cf. *Ibid.*, March 11th, for Neville Chamberlain moving the Second Reading of a Bill to prolong for two and a half years some existing Rent Control provisions of 1923. At the end of that period he hoped that housing conditions would have been sufficiently alleviated to permit the commencement of a five-year period of partial control.

"advanced" brands of Liberalism represented by such men as Wedgwood Benn and Kenworthy. Here is one instructed comment on the dangerous strains inside the Labour Party as between MacDonald and the "rebels":[1]

> Through Mr. Wheatley they have formally repudiated Mr. MacDonald's official support of Free Trade and claim that the Labour Party is as much in favour of Protection as the Tories. The challenge on the major issue is for the moment eclipsed by the quarrel that has broken out on the subject of the cost of the Prince of Wales's tour to South America in which the whole attitude of the party to the monarchy is involved. And meanwhile the storm of words continues to rage between that "humble follower of Lenin", Mr. A. J. Cook, secretary of the Miners' Federation, and Mr. Frank Hodges, who insists that Mr. Cook's inflammatory appeals to the miners will bring nothing but disaster to his clients. It is obvious that there is no possible accommodation between these violent antagonisms. They represent entirely irreconcilable points of view, and the disorders within the Labour Party will continue and develop until one faction or the other is in indisputable possession of the ship. Mr. Wheatley has the advantage which always belongs to the man who is engaged in bidding highest regardless of consequences, and he has no disposition to spare the old gang. By comparison with Mr. MacDonald, his stock has undoubtedly risen since the election. He is the unchallenged leader of the extreme faction, while Mr. MacDonald's position shows no signs of recovery from the eclipse of the autumn election. There is still much bitterness of feeling in the party in regard to the calamitous strategy of that election. . . .

The situation inside the Labour Party, and the extremist "Red" programmes which continued to be suggested for it as soon as it could get back to Downing Street, undoubtedly gave a good deal of impetus to the notion of a "Liberal Revival". Of course, the record and personality of Lloyd George had produced divisions in the Liberal Leadership which Asquith's utmost efforts failed to

---

[1] *The Nation*, February 28, 1925. When a suggested "Red" programme was unofficially drawn up and published, ultimately, in *Lansbury's Labour Weekly* it is not altogether surprising to find such items as these:

"A Labour Government would be pledged to establish a Socialist State. Its job would be the reconstruction of the State on Socialist lines, and it would be pledged to take on that job and carry it through. There would be no more of the Ins and Outs—no more of the swing of the pendulum . . . it must end the fallacy of national government before everything else; it must cast to the winds the doctrine of continuity with the past. . . ."

"5. Let Labour choose its own Cabinet, down with the dictatorship of the Prime Minister.

"6. A Labour Government should be bound to carry out the policy of the Labour Party Conference and the Trades Union Congress so far as industrial matters are concerned. . . ." More of this egregious "Red" programme will be given below.

close, and the attitude of such Asquithian ex-Cabinet Ministers as Runciman[1] and Sir John Simon, embittered as they were by long years spent in the political wilderness in consequence of what they considered the unprincipled personal manœuvres of Lloyd George, was most hostile to any notion of his having the automatic right to succeed as party chief. Yet they could all agree—and there were other ex-Cabinet Ministers like Grey, Sir Herbert Samuel,[2] and Lord Reading[3] to enforce the lesson—that the country needed to have some better alternative to Baldwin, when the moment came, than a Labour Party always threatening to pass under the domination of "Red" elements, playing with the notion of a "General Strike" industrially,[4] and with what amounted, politically, to an irrevocable dictatorship of the proletariat.[5] Nothing, indeed, could have been more calculated to rally the still powerful forces available for a "Liberal Revival" than some of the shriller slogans of Labour's "Reds", slogans appropriate, perhaps, to Clydeside rent-strikers or East-End dole-drawers but hardly, say, to Liberal ex-candidates doubtful of their future course after the depressing Election results of November 1924. Here shall be given merely three points from a sixteen-point "Red" programme of 1925 to suggest why a good deal of "progressive" professional-class opinion was thoroughly antagonized.[6]

[1] Cf. Charles Mallet, *Mr. Lloyd George*, p. 267, for the formation of a Radical group with Runciman as Chairman. Runciman gave a very indifferent welcome to Lloyd George's Sessional Chairmanship.

[2] Who arrived in Britain, during the year, after a momentous five years as British High Commissioner in Palestine. His influence had been used to heal the Lloyd George-Asquith breach, and after presiding, at Baldwin's request, at a new Coal Inquiry, he was to go on to organize the Liberal preparations for the next General Election.

[3] Lord Reading, who had remained a friend both of Asquith and Lloyd George after 1916, was Viceroy of India, 1921-6. He was in England for consultations during the summer of 1925.

[4] Cf. *The Nation*, January 31, 1925, for "the Bolshevist programme of Mr. A. J. Cook, the Secretary of the Miners' Federation. . . . In declaring himself 'a disciple of Karl Marx and a humble follower of Lenin' he has indicated that his motive is purely political and that the strike to which he invites the railwaymen, the dockers, and other trade unionists is not to be primarily concerned with wages and conditions, but with effecting a revolution."

[5] Cf. John Scanlan, *Decline and Fall of the Labour Party*, pp. 89–90, quoting from *Lansbury's Labour Weekly* a "Red" programme for a Labour Government which insists that such a Government "must be determined to carry through its proposals and stay until it has become impossible to stop them or sabotage them. It must throw over the convention of the alternation of power between the parties. . . . Labour's slogans must be—Get power and keep it. No more of the Ins and Outs."

[6] John Scanlan, *Decline and Fall of the Labour Party*, pp. 90–2. Other slogans in the suggested programme may be quoted as "12. Ration Houses. No Slums cheek

2. Before taking office Labour should receive an assurance that in case of need, a sufficient number of Peers would be created to carry a bill for the Abolition of the House of Lords. These would have to be selected from reliable sources, e.g. every 100th elector of Poplar or every thousandth member of the Miners' Federation. . . .

15. The Right of Every Nation to Live.
Disarmament by Agreement.
Industrial Co-operation with the Workers of the World.
The United Front of the World Working Class.
No Secret Diplomacy.
No Continuity of Capitalist Organization of World Affairs.
Capture the Last Stronghold of the Governing Class—the Ranks of the Diplomatic Service.
Democratize the Diplomat.

16. *The Armed Forces*. The soldier, sailor and airman must be granted full civil rights, including the right to trade union organization. The death penalty must be abolished, as also the system of living in barracks. Soldiers must have the status and rights of a policeman. No officers must be appointed unless they have been through the ranks. . . .

Naturally, if the "Reds" had had, by the standards of that day, peculiar harshness or callous immobility to complain of in the Leaderships of the Tory and Liberal Parties, their chances of giving a revolutionary turn to the masses of their own party would have been better, and MacDonald and the "old gang" more easily forced from control. But the Liberalism of 1924–5, for example, was hardly immobile, and under the impulsion of such men as Keynes and Ramsay Muir had already produced a wide variety of administrative and legislative suggestion at the famous "Liberal Summer Schools"[1] as well as two more official programmes which,

by jowl with Mansions. Invade the Precincts of the Upper Class. 13. Down with Class Education. A Square Meal and a Square Deal for the Children. The Universities for the Workers. . . ." And then there was 7. "No fraternisation with the Enemy. Break the Continuity of Society Tradition. No Court Dress. No Political Accommodations," in obvious criticism of the MacDonald Cabinet.

[1] Cf. *Essays in Liberalism being the Lectures and Papers which were delivered at the Liberal Summer School at Oxford, 1922* for some of the first stages in an activity which still seemed to be increasing in importance when the Summer School for 1925 was being planned to open at Cambridge on July 29th, with an inaugural address from Asquith and to close with a valediction from Lloyd George on August 5th. Between the addresses of the two ex-Prime Ministers, there was to be a wide variety of speaking and discussion, led by internationally respected authorities and presided over by such important party figures as Sir John Simon, Mr. Runciman, and Captain Wedgwood Benn. The scope of the lecturing and discussions shall be suggested by outlining the programme for the two days of August 3rd and 4th. "August 3rd. Morning: An Urban Land Policy, Mr. A. S. Comyns Carr; Liberalism and Modern Industry, Sir Alfred Mond; Chairman: Sir Donald Maclean. Evening: The Education of the Adolescent, Mr. T. E. Harvey; Chairman, Lady Violet Bonham-Carter.

"August 4th. Morning: Some Essentials of Industrial Peace, Mr. B. Seebohm

if too late to affect the surprise Election of October 1924, were to
outlive those polls and markedly influence those of 1929—the
"Cultivating Ownership" plan for Agriculture[1] and, for the mines,
the noteworthy *Coal and Power*. And as for Baldwin, he showed
himself almost pathetically eager to inaugurate a period of peace
and better relations in industry, his Birmingham oration of
March 5, 1925 and his House of Commons speech, next day, on
the Trade Union (Political Fund) Bill being reckoned among the
most important political events of the year. At Birmingham the
Prime Minister, pointing to the million and a quarter still unemployed and to the agitators of suspicion and hate who could
make matters worse,[2] called, instead, for a "truce of God in this
country, that we may compose our differences, that we may join
all our strength together to see if we cannot pull the country into
a better and a happier condition". And some twenty-four hours
later, when vetoing the wishes of his own Back-Benchers
for a Bill that would have prevented the Trade Unions from
raising their "Political Levy" except from members who had
specifically asked for it, he astonished the House and the political
commentators by the effects he succeeded in obtaining from
personal reminiscences of how the tinplate firm of Baldwin's
of Bewdley had functioned happily and not inefficiently[3] on
Rowntree; An Experiment in Profit-Sharing, Mr. G. C. Renold; Chairman:
Miss Violet Markham, Evening: A Liberal Agricultural Policy, Mr. A. P.
Macdougall; Chairman, Captain Wedgwood Benn."

[1] Cf. *The Nation*, October 25, 1924: "The State simply takes over all the land
which is not being farmed by its owners, and with the rents receivable, pays
out the landlords . . . with a negotiable annuity for themselves and their heirs,
equal to the present net revenues. The farmers, whose sole need is freedom
fully to control their land and to utilize all their capital and credit, not on
purchase, but on better farming . . . are given cultivating ownership, for themselves and their descendants subject only to the maintenance of a standard of
good husbandry. . . ." There was, in fact, a considerable element of confiscation
of landlords' interests in these plans.

[2] Cf. Stanley Baldwin, *On England*, pp. 31–9: "And it is at this moment, with
one in ten of the working population unemployed, at this moment when in
some industries there is a faint hope of revival, at this moment when other
industries . . . can but just hold their own, that we witness in England signs of
an industrial storm gathering. . . . Why must we reserve all our talk of peace
and our prayers for peace on the Continent and forget to have our talks and our
prayers for peace at home? It is one of the paradoxes of public life that from
the very lips which preach pacifism abroad we hear the cries for war at home. . . .
Short, too, of any deliberate destruction of our industry, such as we have seen
advocated in a few quarters, I dread that subtle poison of hatred which is
being preached in some quarters. . . ."

[3] Cf. *The Nation*, March 14, 1925: "Friday the 6th was so sensational in its
effects. . . . A speech of Mr. Baldwin, animated either with wholehearted
simplicity or with an astuteness rarely equalled, . . . swept into enthusiasm the
most sentimental assembly in the most sentimental nation in the world . . .

the basis of a sympathetic understanding between masters and men.

In view of the militant preaching of a coal-stoppage then in progress, the Prime Minister did not forget to illustrate the long period of hardship brought to Baldwin's 1000 employees by a past coal-stoppage in which they had had not the slightest concern, or the way the proprietorship, knowing and appreciating its men as individuals, had felt constrained to come to their help just as it had been in the habit of doing when transferring the ageing to light duties.[1] And if Mr. Baldwin freely admitted that in the newer days, when strong unions faced the powerful combines which had absorbed family firms like his own, the old personal relationship was impossible, he still pleaded strongly for greater mutual charity and consideration on both sides of industry. His most powerful closing passage was the following:[2]

I want my Party to-day to make a gesture to the country . . . and to say to them: "We have our majority; we believe in the justice of this Bill which has been brought in to-day, but we are going to withdraw our hand and we are not going to push our political advantage home at a moment like this. Suspicion which has prevented stability in Europe is the one poison that is preventing stability at home, and we offer the country to-day this: We, at any rate, are not going to fire the first shot. We stand for peace. We stand for the removal of suspicion in the country. We want to create an atmosphere, a new atmosphere in a new Parliament for a new age, in which the people can come together. We abandon what we have laid our hands to. We know we may be called cowards for doing it. We know we may be told that we have gone back on our principles. But we believe we know what at this moment the

and, for the first time, assured the Prime Minister's dominance in his own party. Yet it was done with simplicity, with none of the outward arts of oratory . . . when he sat down he was received with tumultuous cheers greater than almost any I have ever heard in Parliament."

[1] Cf. *The Nation*, March 14th, for its Parliamentary Correspondent on the most effective passages: "But he began to take hold of the House when he described "the peculiar circumstances of my own life"—an old family business; an old good tradition; now being crushed to pieces between the organized hordes of capital and labour, manipulated from outside, against which there is no appeal. Gradually he built up the vision of this archaic Paradise, where he had known every man from childhood, talked about the troubles at home and their wives; a place where strikes and lock-outs were unknown, where "nobody got the sack", where grandfathers, fathers and sons all worked together in harmony; where, finally—and this was the oratorical climax—"a large number of old gentlemen used to spend the day sitting on the handles of their wheelbarrows and smoking their pipes". The vision of that Arcadia made even strong reporters weep in the gallery, and from that moment Mr. Baldwin had the House in the hollow of his hand."

[2] Stanley Baldwin, *On England*, p. 51, quoting the Parliamentary Reports.

428

country wants, and we believe it is for us in our strength to do what no other Party can do at this moment, and to say that we at any rate stand for peace.

The Prime Minister's conciliatoriness had important results both in the short term and the long, but for months after his speaking of March 5th and 6th it seemed unlikely that a major industrial clash could be averted in the coalfields with catastrophic possible economic and political consequences. The coalowners of the Mining Association had been pressing the Miners' Federation since November 1924 for urgent joint consideration of what they claimed was the financially disastrous working of a large percentage of the pits under existing legislation and agreements. At some of the joint meetings, indeed, that followed, six coalfields were shown to be working at an actuarial loss despite the gradual closing down of weaker pits and the heavy additions to pitmen's unemployment,[1] additions, it was contended, that might have been avoided if modified agreements and legislation had been accepted. Yet it became obvious, by June and July 1925, that so far from considering a lengthening of the seven-hour day established in 1919 when the coal trade was booming, the Miners' Federation, under such a fugleman as A. J. Cook, was contemplating a counter-offensive, calculated, with the aid of the transport unions, the International Miners' Federation and the T.U.C., to produce a more ruinous stoppage than that of 1921 and one of which would-be revolutionaries might make more use. To read, indeed, how the coalowners' posting of new terms at the pits was to be met, not by the district negotiations to which the men were invited, but by the complete shut-down of coal-production and coal-transport at midnight on July 31st,[2] is to appreciate why the Prime Minister was, towards the end of July 1925, facing one of the critical points of his career. He had begun by refusing to consider the possibility of subsidizing pitmen's wages from the Treasury and had set up,

[1] Cf. J. R. Raynes, *Coal and its Conflicts*, p. 202, for Mining Association statistics ultimately submitted to the Samuel Commission: "Pits were closing with greater frequency, and unemployment rose from 7·9 per cent in January 1925, to 23·2 in September. In January of 1924, 162 collieries were running at a loss, and by June of 1925 that number had increased to 508."

[2] Cf. *Lock-out of Coal-miners, August 1st, 1925. Official Stoppage of the Movement of Coal. Official instructions to all Railway and Transport Workers as agreed unanimously by a joint conference of the National Union of Railwaymen, Associated Society of Locomotive Engineers and Firemen, Railway Clerks Association, and the Transport and General Workers' Executives, and approved by the General Council of the Trades Union Congress.*

under the Industrial Courts Act, the ill-starred Macmillan Court of Inquiry, which was boycotted by the pitmen.[1] As the hour for the complete stoppage approached, Baldwin weakened and finally accepted the pitmen's consent to state their case to a further Inquiry yet to be organized—though without a reduction of wages or increase of hours in the meantime—as a justification for a wages subsidy after all, and one to last for nine months in view of the thorough-going investigations and recommendations intended.

It could hardly be disguised, in view of the loud shouts of triumph that came from the "Red" favourers of "direct action", that the Government seemed to have given way to the mere threat of something a good deal short of the "General Strike".[2] Fair-minded men, of course, were prepared to admit that Baldwin's action was hardly to be ascribed to cowardice, pure and simple, but that it was necessary to make allowance for his sympathy with a class of workmen who had certainly suffered much of late years and for his desire to convince the general public that, if in May 1926, he should finally authorize the use of all Government's resources against still-recalcitrant pitmen, it would not be for lack of patient good-will. Yet even those who gave Baldwin the credit for the best of motives were inclined to fear that it might have been easier for him to grasp the nettle of General Strike in August 1925 than would prove to be the case in May 1926 and that, unless the nine months truce, bought at a cost that could exceed twenty millions, were utilized to investigate something more than the mutual recriminations of coalowners and pitmen, the gravest dangers lay ahead. The Radical *Nation*, for example, had prophesied that the return to the "Gold Standard" would cause difficulties to all the exporting and "unsheltered" trades and, holding that the deteriorating position in the coal and other industries, justified everything it had said,[3] was insistent that the

[1] Though thus deprived of the moral authority necessary to improve the situation, it held a number of hearings and issued a *Report* which the coal-owners, at least, considered somewhat biased in favour of the men if not going all or most of the way with A. J. Cook.

[2] Cf. J. R. Raynes, *Coal and its Conflicts*, p. 214, for the tone taken even by the T.U.C. "Industrial Committee" which had handled support for the pit-men: "The manifestation of solidarity which has been exhibited by all sections of the trade union movement is a striking portent for the future and marks an epoch in the history of the movement."

[3] Cf. J. M. Keynes, *The Economic Consequences of Mr. Churchill*, for a pamphleteering treatment by one who seems to have had much to do with *The Nation*'s economic course though another Liberal Cambridge economist, H. D. Henderson, was the actual editor.

contribution to the coal industry's difficulties from over-valuation of the pound should not be left out of account.

Perhaps "AN OPEN LETTER TO MR. BALDWIN", to which *The Nation* gave the place of honour in its issue of August 15th, will reveal some of the now-forgotten thinking of the time. Mr. Baldwin was thus addressed:[1]

You were faced with a terrible dilemma a fortnight ago. No one who has observed the working of your mind, as revealed in your admirable speeches, will impute the decision you took to cowardice or weakness. You have made it your special mission as Prime Minister to promote the cause of peace in industry. . . . It would have been a tragedy of frustrated hopes if, within five months, the country had been plunged under your leadership into an industrial conflict of unprecedented horror and menace. It is not surprising that you should have thought it wise to purchase a respite at almost any price.

But it is essential that the conflict should not merely be postponed. If we are "to have it out" when the nine months' truce is over, we are in for something immeasurably more dangerous than what we have just escaped. . . . I do not believe that a conflict this month would have been a fatal disaster. But if we plunge into it next spring, it will be Niagara indeed. . . . This class-war atmosphere, which is almost bound to develop, which in fact is developing already, will add enormously to the difficulty of maintaining peace. . . . If the economic situation is no easier next May than it is now, if we have still a huge gulf between the actual wages of the miners and what the industry can afford to pay, with the same thing holding true in a lesser degree of the remainder of the export trades, I can see little hope. Our only real chance lies in a radical improvement in the economic position of the export trades. . . .

You may say . . . "That unfortunately is outside my control". . . . That is not so. . . . You could abandon the Gold Standard and allow the exchange to fall back to its natural level. That would transform the situation for the export trades and make their problems manageable once again. "Impossible," you say. "We have gone back to gold for better or worse. It would never do to run away from it now." I admit the disadvantages of doing so. . . . But they must be weighed against the disadvantages of alternative courses. . . . I am anxious that you should not allow yourself to drift into this struggle, from which I know every fibre of your being will recoil, merely because you have closed your mind on a possible avenue of escape. . . .

A quotation like this—even if it does not include a very significant passage on the possibility of Fascists and Communists endeavouring to use for their own ends the "class-war" preparing

[1] The signature to the letter is "Industrial Pacifist", and the writer warned Mr. Baldwin that the real strength of the Unions had come from the fact that they all felt themselves to be on the defensive together.

on the Coal Question—is worth giving as showing that the public was not left unaware of what might be in store by May 1926. And, indeed, one "Red" historian's praise of the "humble follower of Lenin" Miners' Secretary, A. J. Cook, is that he laboured incessantly to render the General Strike not merely possible but inevitable.[1] Yet great Government efforts had, of course, to be made to use the nine months' subsidization constructively, for Press and Parliament would have turned savagely against a Ministry relying largely on the mere hope that the International Coal Market and coal prices generally would improve, by May, to the point making agreement between owners and pitmen more feasible than in 1925. The Cabinet did not, in fact, find it easy to collect an authoritative Royal Commission, plainly free of bias[2]— but ultimately the Samuel Commission of four, three of them the well-known "progressive Liberals", Sir Herbert Samuel, Sir William Beveridge, and Mr. Kenneth Lee[3]—took charge of the Inquiry in so workmanlike a manner as to make an increasing impression. It was, after all, new for a Coal Inquiry to undertake the twenty-five reported pit visits, divided between Scotland, Lancashire, Yorkshire, and South Wales and to see that the forty-two pits most condemned by the Miners' Federation were thoroughly inspected and impartially reported upon. And then there were the 33 public sittings, the 76 witnesses, the masses of data and information received for checking and further study, and, ultimately, on March 10, 1926, an obviously authoritative Report of 294 pages which, in a cheap threepenny edition, is said to have proved the year's "best seller" and to have continued to sell for years afterwards.[4] It was not for nothing that some saw in the Commission's whole history a public proof of Liberalism's continued indispensability and a very special chance for Samuel to return to an authoritative position in Parliament.

Something of the strength of the unanimous Report of the

---

[1] Cf. John Scanlan, *Decline and Fall of the Labour Party*, p. 102.

[2] Cf. *The Nation*, September 5, 1925: "A month of the coal truce has now elapsed, a month of the subsidy has run its course, at a cost to the Exchequer of not far short of £2 millions, and the Coal Commission is not yet appointed . . . if coal prices should not recover, the position will be far more serious. . . ."

[3] *Ibid.*, September 12, 1925: "There is more than coincidence in this tendency to call in the aid of Liberals, when there is a particularly awkward difficulty . . . despite all appearances Liberalism is still the great nursery of ideas which are at once practical and constructive. . . ."

[4] John R. Raynes, *Coal and its Conflicts*, p. 213. It was made available, before long, at threepence.

Samuel Commission may be suggested by quoting a summary of what it had to say (after dealing hopefully with the Coal Industry's Long-Term Reorganization) of the Immediate Problem facing employers and men:[1]

> To bring any of these measures of reorganisation into effect must need a period of months; to bring all of them into full operation must need years. . . . Meantime the hard economic conditions of the moment remain to be faced.
> The dominant fact is that, in the last quarter of 1925, if the subsidy be excluded, 73 per cent of the coal was produced at a loss.
> We express no opinion whether the grant of a subsidy last July was unavoidable or not, but we think its continuance indefensible. The subsidy should stop at the end of its authorised term, and should never be repeated.
> We cannot approve the proposal of the Mining Association, that the gap between costs and proceeds should be bridged by an increase of an hour in the working day, reductions in the miners' wages, some economies in other costs, and a large diminution in railway rates to be effected by lowering the wages of railwaymen. In any case these proposals go beyond the need, for we do not concur in the low estimate of future coal prices on which they are based.
> If the present hours are to be retained, we think a revision of the "minimum percentage addition to standard rates of wages", fixed in 1924 at a time of temporary prosperity, is indispensable. A disaster is impending over the industry, and the immediate reduction of working costs that can be effected in this way, and in this way alone, is essential to save it. . . . The wages of the lowest-paid men will be safeguarded. . . . The reductions that we contemplate will still leave the mine-owners without adequate profits in any of the wage-agreement districts, and without any profits in most districts. If trade improves and prices rise, a profit will be earned. . . .
> Should the miners freely prefer some extension of hours with a less reduction of wages, Parliament would no doubt be prepared to authorise it. We trust, however, that this will not occur.
> We consider that it is essential that there should be, as there always has been hitherto, considerable variation in the rates of wages in the several districts. But we are strongly of opinion that national wage agreements should continue. . . .
> By a revision of the minimum percentage coal-mining would be saved from an immediate collapse, but it seems inevitable that a number of collieries would still have to be closed. This may give rise to the necessity for a transfer of labour on a considerable scale. We recommend that the Government should be prepared in advance with such

---

[1] In regard to long-term reorganization, Nationalization was firmly rejected though the State's acquisition of all coal likely to be mined or developed was approved, pit-operation, however, being left to private enterprise, as reorganized and provided with better labour relations, under the Commission's plan.

433

plans to assist it as are practicable, and should provide funds for the purpose. . . .

That the Prime Minister offered, within a fortnight of the publication of the Commission's Report, official action on the fourteen recommendations, some of them admittedly distasteful, in which Government was concerned,[1] and offered, also, to both sides of the Mining Industry, temporary assistance in the districts that would be hardest-hit, is merely another proof of the authority so quickly accorded to the Samuel Report. Doubtless, the men would have been well advised to accept Baldwin's offer under protest. Their alignment with the Government and the Commission would certainly have paid them better than their attempt to make a propaganda use of the mineowners' stiff reluctance to abandon notions of increasing hours and reducing pay, a propaganda use in justification, of course, of pitmen's refusal "to surrender any of their present inadequate wages and conditions". But "extremist" activities in the colliery areas had been intense; the slogan of "not a penny off the pay, not a second on the day" was already a surprising force; and, besides, there was the memory of how soon Baldwin had capitulated in 1925 before something considerably less imposing than the "General Strike" for which the T.U.C.'s Industrial Committee had presumably had nine months to prepare. Moreover, a large part of the T.U.C.'s following had been forcibly reminded by the mineowners' criticism of what had been done to the coal industry by rail and dock wages, increased altogether beyond cost-of-living comparison, of the assault that might open up upon all the "sheltered internal trades" unless the "insolent challenge" were resoundingly repelled.[2]

At midnight, then, on April 30, 1926, the Coal Subsidy stopped; the pitmen refused to work on the masters' district terms, posted at the collieries (though these had since been modified in the men's

[1] John R. Raynes, *Coal and its Conflicts*, pp. 223–4, quoting *The Ministry of Labour Gazette*, August 1926.

[2] John R. Raynes, *Coal and its Conflicts*, p. 220, for the coal-owners' submissions to the Samuel Commission, according to which there had been, in the average railway rate on coal, an increase of eighty-three per cent above the 1913 charges. It was forcibly urged what an injustice it was to those, who worked in the "great producing industries", to maintain railway, coal-tipping, and dock charges at disproportionately high levels so that rail and dock wages might be kept well above what it was proving possible for those great producing industries to pay. And local authority rates, too, increased by a hundred and fifty per cent, represented another added burden which had been aggravated by the disproportionately steep increases of local government wages since 1913.

favour under the Prime Minister's pressure); and the nation waited for the mobilized executives of trade unions, affiliated to the T.U.C., to come to a decision as to the final orders that were to be given to 3,653,527 operatives. And though the decision of Saturday afternoon, May 1st, was enthusiastically for strike action on the part of all transport workers, the printing trades, the iron, steel, metal, and heavy chemical group, and the power-supply sections of the gas and electricity industries, the fact that such strike action was planned as from Monday midnight still left a margin of time for negotiation. But the Cabinet, provoked by advance-action on the part of *Daily Mail* operative printers and by the assumption on the part of the T.U.C. Negotiating Committee that it was entitled to claim continued negotiation from the Government even while the last strike-details were being perfected, had now had enough. In the early morning hours of Monday, May 3rd, the Cabinet demanded, before continuing negotiations, a repudiation both of "the gross interference with the liberty of the Press" which had taken place and "an immediate and unconditional withdrawal of the instructions for the general strike". The Cabinet did not get what it demanded and continued developing the emergency arrangements, which it was bringing into force with the help of the volunteer labour it was calling for and obtaining.[1]

On Saturday, May 8th, the fifth day of a General Strike, whose principal victims had so far seemed to be the countless thousands of young women, tramping their weary miles to and from office, shop, and factory, the T.U.C. informed the miners' representatives that the existing position was untenable and that they proposed to find means of reopening the coal negotiations through Sir Herbert Samuel. But the pitmen rejected a first Samuel formula put forward on May 9th; on May 10th, the T.U.C. Negotiating Committee, after bringing Samuel and the pitmen's Leaders together, obtained a second formula; and early on May 11th this, too, was rejected by a Miners' Executive which was not prepared to see market-conditions enforce a worsening of pitmen's pay already, it was claimed, well behind that of comparable grades of worker in other industries. This proved to be the parting of the

[1] Cf. *Daily Express*, May 10th, for 500 volunteers at the docks helping to unload a shipment of flour and the bus-parking arrangements at Regent's Park with the addition of "a complete machine shop and sleeping quarters for volunteer drivers".

ways for many on the T.U.C.'s General Council who, in their own words, "felt that the position was too grave to justify their being tied to a mere slogan". Aware that the strikers, most of whom must have made themselves liable to actions for breach of contract, were growing uneasy at the increasing mastery the Government was establishing,[1] the T.U.C. General Council, after obtaining another Samuel formula, called off the General Strike at noon on May 12th. It was a tremendous triumph for Mr. Baldwin who further distinguished himself by urging on employers his view "that we should resume our work in a spirit of co-operation, putting behind us all malice and all vindictiveness".[2] And the Prime Minister's stature was further heightened when, on May 14th, he sent the Miners' Federation a Cabinet plan which seemed still to contain the essence of the Samuel proposals for effecting a hopeful reorganization of the Coal Industry and, in addition, the offer of three millions to mitigate the effects in the hardest-hit areas of what needed immediately to be done. In refusing the new overture; in relying on the ultimate "stranglehold" they thought they had on British life and industry seeing that the International Transport and Miners' Federations were apparently committed to stop coal-export to Britain, the miners again made a capital mistake, enhanced by their resolve to accept a gift of £260,000 from Russia.

It was not merely the pitmen, and their backers in the T.U.C. and the Parliamentary Labour Party, who hardly stood well with the "public" in the middle of 1926. The Liberals, who seemed at one stage likely to profit considerably from their Coal and Power proposals and the Radical Samuel Report, became involved, as a

[1] Cf. *British Gazette*, May 6th, for the paper which the Government had established to take the place of the strike-bound newspaper-Press on "WHY WALK TO WORK?" Its claim for the Underground and Bus position, even at that early stage, was this: "Central London. Six-minute service. Full service 0-day. Metropolitan. Services still improving. Piccadilly and District Lines. Volunteers standing by. L.G.O.C. 200 'buses on the streets. Independent 'buses. Plentiful supply." And the *British Gazette*'s account of its own circulation, as given in its issue of May 13th was this: May 5th, 232,000; May 6th, 507,000; May 7th. 655,000; May 8th 836,000; May 10th 1,127,000; May 11th 1,801,400; May 12th 2,209,000. (Part re-quoted from H. C. Dent, *op. cit.*)
[2] Cf. H. C. Dent, *Milestones to the Silver Jubilee*, pp. 278–9, for George V's message to the Nation, arranged to repeat the same order of sentiment: "Let us forget whatever elements of bitterness the events of the past few days may have created, only remembering how orderly the country has remained, though severely tested, and forthwith address ourselves to the task of bringing into being a peace which will be lasting, because, forgetting the past, it looks only to the future with the hopefulness of a united people."

result of the General Strike, in another resounding Lloyd George "scandal" with increasingly serious consequences. Lloyd George had been following up the Coal and Power proposals of 1924 by pushing the activities of a Liberal Land Committee in 1925, the "sensational tone" of whose reports on rural and urban land, seriously antagonized considerable Liberal sections.[1] Asquith, now Lord Oxford, had done his best to prevent a new split developing in the party from the Right, just as another seemed to be threatening from the Left on the lack of success in establishing co-operation with the Labour Party.[2] Two ex-Ministers, indeed, were lost Baldwin-wards early in 1926[3]—but a Liberal Land Conference of February 17th and 18th, opened by addresses from Asquith and Lloyd George,[4] was nevertheless deemed of some use in re-attracting farmers' and labourers' votes in the many county divisions forfeited in 1924.

Asquith's over-indulgent attitude towards Lloyd George, as some Liberals considered it, was partly due to his waiting in hope for the conclusion of negotiations under which the official Liberal organization, now much impoverished by its old standards,[5] would get effective help from the huge Lloyd George Political

[1] Cf. Sir Charles Mallet, *Mr. Lloyd George*, p. 269, for Sir Alfred Mond's letter to Lord Oxford in January 1926 when Mond joined the Conservative Party. Runciman, in a speech at Devizes on November 21, 1925, led another section of critics who stayed within the party but had strong objections to the Rural Land Report's "sensational tone, its ill-considered finance, its pathetic belief in State interference, its needless multiplication of public officials—seven new authorities were to be created—a feature almost inseparable from Mr. Lloyd George's political panaceas".

[2] Cf. *Whitaker's Almanack, 1927*, p. 835: "1926. Jan. 10th, Mr. Snowden at Cardiff repudiated suggestion of alliance between Liberals and Labour Party. . . . Jan. 23rd. Lord Oxford denied story of negotiations for working alliance between Liberal and Labour Parties."

[3] *Ibid.*, "Feb. 20th. Mr. Hilton Young, M.P., left Liberal Party owing to land policy." Sir Alfred Mond had gone already.

[4] *The Nation*, February 20, 1926, was critical: "There are disconcerting signs that the land question has become an obsession with him. . . . The keynote of every speech he makes is that we now import some £400 millions of foodstuffs, the greater part of which we ought to grow at home. . . . Indeed the gist of his message seems to be that to increase the size of the agricultural population and to free ourselves from dependence on imported food should be the supreme objectives of British statesmanship to-day. . . ."

[5] Cf. J. A. Spender, *Sir Robert Hudson, A Memoir*, pp. 168–75. As Treasurer of the National Liberal Federation and Secretary of the Liberal Central Association, Hudson played a key-part in the negotiations. It was his complaint that the Liberal Million Fund, the appeal for which had been launched in January 1925, was a failure because of the general knowledge that Lloyd George had a vast political fund in hand which, however, was not being made available. Some of the party activities, at any rate seemed likely to come to a complete halt by the winter of 1926–7.

Fund, accumulated during the years 1916–22 and only scantily available so far for general party ends. But the negotiations dragged on inconclusively and then came Lloyd George's irresistible urge, as many Liberals saw it, to fish for himself once more in the troubled waters of the General Strike. On May 3rd, after attending a meeting of the Liberal Shadow Cabinet, he certainly delivered a House of Commons speech, differing in emphasis from those given elsewhere by Asquith and Grey because contriving to blame the Government equally with the strikers.[1] But it was when he was summoned to attend another meeting of Liberal Leaders to be held on May 10th that he gave most offence both by declining to come and by dissociating himself vehemently from his colleagues in increasing the share of the blame for the General Strike he was now inclined to impute to the Government. As he was simultaneously contributing to the American Press views of a similar kind, accompanied by alarmist forebodings unlikely to be of help to British credit, the resentment of his nominal chief and colleagues is understandable.[2] When the General Strike collapsed early and revealed Lloyd George's miscalculations, the temptation to read him a stern lesson was irresistible though that only promised to make the party's financial plight worse. Obviously a Liberal Party in such straits and preparing for worse was even less of a challenge than the Labour Party, temporarily discredited though that was by its connection with the General Strike. Neither seemed, for the time, in a position to put any serious obstacle in the way of a Baldwin Government which had, to its credit, not merely the defeat of the General Strike, but such things as Locarno (with some evacuation of Germany begun in consequence as well as preparations for a Disarmament Conference and German membership of the League),[3] a settlement of the Irish

---

[1] Cf. *Hansard*, May 3rd, for Lloyd George refusing to commit himself unreservedly to the unconstitutionality of all general strikes though agreeing that such a strike "is a mistake at the present moment. I say also that I think it was a very serious mistake on the part of the Government to announce this morning that they would not negotiate. They will be forced out of that position by circumstances. It is a mistake." By contrast, Asquith, as Lord Oxford, said: "We should have lost all sense of self-respect if we were to allow any section of the community at its own will, and for whatever motives, to bring to a standstill the industrial and social life of the whole nation." Lord Grey's view was: "The issue now is not what the wages of miners should be, but whether democratic Parliamentary Government is to be overthrown."

[2] Cf. Sir Charles Mallet, *Mr. Lloyd George*, pp. 272–8.

[3] Cf. *Whitaker's Almanack, 1927*, p. 843: "1925. Dec. 1st. British troops commenced evacuation of Cologne. . . . 1926. Jan 31st. Evacuation of Cologne

Boundary Clause difficulty, and, at home, an important Electricity Bill[1] as well as the Rating and Valuation Bill which allowed Neville Chamberlain his first major success.[2]

completed amid German rejoicings. . . . Feb. 8th. German Cabinet adopted Note to League of Nations embodying Germany's application for membership. . . ."

[1] This set up the Central Electricity Board and gave hopes of more rapid development.

[2] Cf. *Whitaker's Almanack, 1927*, p. 157: "It was in the charge of Mr. Neville Chamberlain, who displayed a remarkable knowledge of a highly technical subject . . . the Bill aimed at the simplification of the rating system, not a shifting of the incidence of rates, but it contained two exceptions. . . . The relief of farm buildings would be a new burden on other ratepayers, but not on the owners of small house property . . . machinery was disrated, an overdue act of justice, declared the Minister."

BOOK FOUR

*The Last Radical Programmes
of Lloyd George*

CHAPTER XXI

AFTER THE GENERAL STRIKE

"This Labour Poet's Muses, when finished was the fight,
Mineowners versus Miners, commanded him to write. . . .
Of the dictated terms to which the colliers had to come . . .
They told me forced decisions, where Might subdues the Right,
Only suspend, do not decide, the issues of a fight; . . .
Dawes' Plans and the Gold Standard have export trade
    destroyed,
Longer hours will only add to the unemployed,
Three hundred thousand miners must be thrown into the void!

"Two hundred thousand colliers were already on the dole
When seven hours was the limit to toil at howking coal;
An Eight Hours' Day enactment added to the unemployed
One hundred thousand colliers to be cast into the void;
Non-mining 'out-of-works' were a million and a half—
No wonder that the Fates at coal economics laugh,
That supplicating angels the Throne of Heaven throng,
Appealing in this chorus: *How long, O Lord, how long
Must human rights be trampled underneath the hoofs of Wrong?*"

*   *   *

"In Nineteen-ten, when J.R.M. turned down my fiscal scheme,
To sit in Asquith's Cabinet was his daily dream;
He often took his breakfast with Lloyd George at Number Ten,
And Coalition advocated with both voice and pen; . . .
After sixteen years the boot is on the other leg;
Seats in a Liberal Cabinet Mac does not need to beg;
He dreams, with Liberal statesmen, *his* Cab'net to recruit,
And giving, incidentally, Wheatley and Co. the boot. . . .

"Smethwick has MacDonald of Dictatorship bereft;
Oswald Mosley's triumph was a victory for the Left;
When Oswald was a Tory this compliment was paid:
Mosley is the stuff of which Prime Ministers are made.
Mac must either give his Fabian counsellors the knock,
Refusing to be timed by their geologic clock,
Or the Mosleys, the Maxtons, the Wheatleys will supplant
The feeble-hearted coterie who of Gradualness cant,
Whose slogan 'Safety First,' seems to sum up all *they* want."

    Labour's doggerel "poet", Joseph Burgess, in 1927.

D URING the summer and autumn of 1926—and long after the supporting General Strike was over—a great, if slowly declining, pitmen's stoppage continued at alarming cost to the country and to the unfortunate mining families themselves. The phenomenon caused the acutest embarrassment to all the three major political parties. Labour, torn already by fierce disputes as to the responsibility for the "failure" of the 1924 Election, faced a fresh danger of disruption in new quarrels concerning the collapse of the General Strike[1] and the abandonment of the pitmen to the pitiful destitution[2] into which those mining areas were falling that still declined to follow the early Nottinghamshire lead back to work under the Labour M.P., George Spencer.[3] And Baldwin, too, lost much of the credit which he would have gained for his party, if after defeating the General Strike, he had succeeded in getting the pitmen back to work promptly—and on better terms than were ultimately available after several months more of strike-losses. Indeed, by introducing mining legislation to authorize a five years' return to an eight-hour day (against the advice of the Samuel Commission) alongside some of the recommended changes of the Samuel Report, he provided a unifying rallying-point for Labour though it is doubtful whether the pitmen were really helped by the "disorderly scenes" reported from the Commons at the end of June and from the Lords, on July 8th, when the Royal Assent was given there in the presence of protesting "Red" M.P.s[4]

[1] Cf. John Scanlan, *Decline and Fall of the Labour Party*, pp. 103–4, for an angry "Red" view: "On Tuesday [May 11th] . . . I sat in the Gallery of the House of Commons with Mr. A. J. Cook and Mr. Herbert Smith . . . we had come to hear a ringing vindication of the General Council's Action in calling the General Strike and to hear a tribute to the fine courage of the men who responded. . . . Instead we heard a humiliating whine for mercy and forgiveness. Mr. MacDonald and Mr. Thomas were the chief spokesmen."

[2] Cf. John R. Raynes, *Coal and its Conflicts*, p. 262, for the uncomfortable Mr. Baldwin having to reassure American opinion that there was no starvation because the women and children of the pitmen's families could draw Poor Relief, free school-meals could be provided, and "in many places soup kitchens have been opened by voluntary organizations".

[3] Cf. *The Times*, November 23, 1957, for the obituary notice reporting his account to the Commons in 1926 of how "his men had lost confidence in the outcome of the strike, were frightened that they would not get their jobs back, and were drifting back to work. Accordingly at their request he arranged what terms he could, and they were comparatively favourable. . . . For this he was expelled from the Conference of the Miners' Federation, and later from the Labour Party."

[4] Cf. *Whitaker's Almanack, 1927*, p. 159. There had already been a suspension of thirteen Labour M.P.s for persistent obstruction, on April 15th, when Mr.

Probably the pitmen were helped much more, and Mr. Baldwin much less, when sympathetic Christian Leaders, concerned for the destitution threatening not only the mining families in their flocks but those whose bread came from related industries, put forward what became known as the Bishops' Proposals. These Mr. Baldwin felt compelled to reject because they were based on four months more of subsidization to allow work to be resumed on the old wage-rates and hours while new negotiations began. The Prime Minister might be impatient with the "public" for refusing to see that the weakened financial basis of the mining industry, and of the economy as a whole, hardly permitted generous gestures to be made[1] but, obviously, he would have gained more politically from such gestures than from their refusal. And, certainly, by the time the last strikers had given way towards the end of the year, only to find that those for whom work could not immediately be found might suffer from strike-disqualification for unemployment benefit for a considerable while to come, Mr. Baldwin's extra credit, with many, must have completely evaporated. Had not, moreover, the summer witnessed a new contest with the Poor Law authorities of West Ham, a district with chronic poverty exacerbated by the General Strike and its aftermath, where the Guardians, having refused to reduce their relief-scales within the official limits, had had to be replaced under a Bill which would doubtless next have to be held in menace over the Poor Law Guardians of the colliery areas?

But it was the Liberal Party, which should normally have gained most from the grave strike-troubles of its rivals, that appeared, at one stage, to be the most imperilled. The revelation of the wide new rift which had arisen between Asquith and Lloyd George on the General Strike caused the utmost consternation in the ranks of the faithful, and, on June 3rd, the Liberal M.P.s urged reconciliation, followed, on June 11th, by the Liberal Candidates'

Churchill's Economy Bill involving a reduction of Government contributions to the Health Insurance and Unemployment Insurance Accounts was being debated. Mr. Churchill might claim, for example, that there was an estimated surplus of £65 millions in the Health Insurance Fund but Labour M.P.s had many uses to suggest for that amount and even more.

[1] John R. Raynes, *Coal and its Conflict*, pp. 259–60: "I recognise fully the sense of public duty that has led the Representatives of the Churches to intervene. . . . But the proposals . . . seem to rest on a suggestion that the Government should give a further subsidy . . . the disastrous effect of this prolonged stoppage on the national finances has made any further subsidy in aid of wages quite out of the question. . . ."

Association.[1] As Asquith did not ultimately lay down the leadership until October 15th, there were doubtless some last attempts to procure a settlement of the vexed question of the separate Lloyd George Fund and organization but Asquith's final October references to the impossibility of maintaining party unity "under a system of rival authorities, with separate organizations and funds" is proof enough that he failed to get satisfaction. And Asquith's definite departure, leaving Liberalism without a formal Leader and Liberals rent by new disputes between Lloyd Georgians and anti-Lloyd Georgians seemed to make their party's plight far more dangerous than that of their two rivals. Despite the pathos of Asquith's last appearance as Leader in mid-October and of his last invocation to Liberals to keep the faith,[2] few would then have ventured to forecast the great Liberal polls of the next General Election of 1929. Prospects, indeed, looked so different that yet another Liberal M.P., who had worked hard for a Liberal-Labour *entente*, J. M. Kenworthy, decided to resign his seat and fight it as a Labour man in the hope, as he claimed, that this might best help the "spirit of Liberalism" to find a place in a "reinforced, restrengthened Labour Party".[3]

"Public opinion", meanwhile, had been veering strangely during the summer and autumn of 1926 both in regard to the political parties and in regard to the country's whole economic future. As might have been expected after the resounding failure of the General Strike, most people at first considered that Socialism, and possibly the Labour Party too, had suffered a most dangerous

[1] Cf. Sir Charles Mallet, *Mr. Lloyd George*, pp. 278–80, for the depth of the rift, marked, on the one side, by Lloyd George's claim that an attempt was being made to "drum" him out of the party, because he was "on the side of conciliation" in a dispute where millions of British workmen were involved and, on the other, by an anti-Lloyd George declaration of loyalty to Asquith from Lord Grey, Sir John Simon, Mr. Walter Runciman, Lord Lincolnshire, Lord Buckmaster, Lord Buxton, Sir Donald Maclean, Lord Cowdray, Mr. Vivian Phillipps, Sir Geoffrey Howard, Mr. Pringle, and Sir Godfrey Collins.

[2] Cf. *Whitaker's Almanack, 1927*, p. 835, under October 15, 1926: "Lord Oxford delivered his final speech as Liberal Leader to great meeting at Greenock, and urged Liberals to keep their faith."

[3] Cf. *New Leader*, December 3, 1926, for the cool welcome this I.L.P. organ gave to such thinking: "But our joy at Commander Kenworthy's fine victory is considerably tempered after reading an article . . . from his pen in the current issue of *The Review of Reviews*. 'The banner of the spirit of Liberalism,' he says, 'will now be held aloft in the ranks of a reinforced, restrengthened Labour Party, embracing men of all classes and forming a solid National Party able in due course to take over the Government of the country.' . . . Will the new recruit forgive us for saying that this kind of talk just won't do? Labour is not in the mood to inherit the worn-out customs and stale clichés of Liberalism. . . ."

blow that could alter the whole shape of political and economic development in Britain. Here is a typical extract from Garvin's writing in the *Observer* for Sunday, July 11th, under the sensational title of "MARX OR FORD?":[1]

When Henry Ford in 1914 had the idea of a minimum wage of a pound a day for his workers, with profit-sharing on a large scale—terms improved since then—he knocked the bottom out of abstract Marxism. . . . Marxist dogma is the curse of the fairy-tale—the corpse on the back of Labour. One morning the corpse slipped into the well and the man was renewed. To encourage individual power in creativeness and organisation is the first interest of the masses. For highly-industrialised societies like ours, the Bolshevik talk about revolution means suicidal imbecility. Partnership between employers and employed is the sane dream and the real business. Karl Marx, the mid-Victorian Calvin of economics is as dead as the dodo. That practical, original, Henry Ford—as the epoch-making symbol of high wages and profit-sharing—is the real spirit of the morning.

Garvin's Sunday following was immense and from all political parties. Yet it would be easier to dismiss his writing as merely pro-Government were it not for loud complaints from Labour's "Left" that sentiments not so very different were almost simultaneously being put forth by Snowden himself, Labour's ex-Chancellor of the Exchequer. Readers of *Lansbury's Labour Weekly* were given this rendering, astounding, doubtless, to some of them, of what Snowden had just been saying to American businessmen:[2]

A few days ago Mr. Philip Snowden attended a luncheon, given by the American Chamber of Commerce, and made what the daily Press described as "a powerful plea to employers and workmen to get together, abandon old ideas, pool their brains, and restore industrial

---

[1] Cf. *Daily Herald*, August 31, 1927, for Labour's taking the chance of "showing up" Ford when the chance presented itself. "During the past year," *Daily Herald* readers were told, "his production has dropped by more than a million cars. His great works at Detroit have been on short time. Seventy-five per cent of the workers have been working only two and three days a week since November last. Thousands have lost their homes by failing to pay up their monthly hire-purchase instalments. . . . Meanwhile the enemies of the one-time unchallenged motor-car king are, significantly enough, opening Press campaigns against him. . . . Hitherto Mr. Ford's publicity agents have held the field with their 'boosting' of his welfare plans. Organised American Labour has repeatedly exposed his anti-trade union policy, and the speeding-up system which he employs, but the belief still grew that he was a philanthropist. Now, however, that economic and financial interests are concerned, a sudden passion for the truth is revealed by the Capitalist Press."

[2] *Lansbury's Labour Weekly*, July 10, 1926.

447

prosperity." He informed his audience that "they had got to get the workman to realise that they are partners in industry, and that depression in industry hits them probably harder than it hits the employers". He further stated (*a*) "that any progressive expansion of industry will accrue proportionately to their benefit," (*b*) that "in regard to wages and the general remuneration of labour that never more can be taken out of industry than is produced by that industry," (*c*) that he would like to see "the Trade Union policy changed in this respect, that they would not merely be concerned regardless of the condition of industry in getting the highest possible wages they can screw out of it, but rather helping to make the industry thoroughly efficient so that the highest wages can be paid."

Mr. Snowden then paid a glowing tribute to American Captains of Industry who had realised the theory and doctrine of high wages and high production. . . .

If this extract seems to show plenty of "Red" ill-will to the Labour Front Bench, particularly when over-stressing what Snowden had had to say on employers, it is none the less true that the party's Leaders were, in the time of their deep adversity after the General Strike, inclined to favour the new approach to the relations between Capital and Labour which eventually produced the famous Mond-Turner negotiations. Of course, Clydeside and the Socialist purists of the I.L.P. were suspicious and resentful,[1] and, then, a new veering of "public opinion" towards respect for the suffering pitmen's long fight and towards doubt as to the ultimate wisdom of their handling by Baldwin led, in the autumn, to by-election results sufficiently favourable to Labour[2] to make it seem a distinct possibility that, if the Labour Front Bench sat tight and risked nothing, it might yet be returned to Downing Street on better terms than before. It appeared, for example, from the Liberals' sore electoral plight when distracted by the

---

[1] Cf. *Daily Herald*, August 2, 1926, reporting Wheatley (with Snowden almost certainly in his mind): "The sooner Socialists get rid of Free Trade shibboleths the better it will be for the movement. . . . We were living in the most revolutionary period in history. . . . The system was breaking down. . . . Those who sneered at the demand for Socialism in our time should explain how the present system was going to absorb all the unemployed and raise the standard of living for all workers within this generation."

[2] Cf. *Whitaker's Almanack, 1928*, pp. 183, 185, for the Central Hull result of November 30, 1926, and the Smethwick result of December 21, 1926. In the first, Commander Kenworthy, resigning as a Liberal and refighting as a Labour member, scored 16,145 votes against a Conservative's 11,466, and a Liberal's 2885. In the second, Oswald Mosley polled 16,077 votes against a Conservative's 9495, and a Liberal's 2600, declaring, too (*Daily Herald*, December 22, 1926): "It cannot be too strongly emphasised that we won this fight on a programme of uncompromising Socialism; and it is significant that we pulled over a considerable number of voters in the purely middle-class areas."

new controversies turning round Lloyd George, that they
might never again be in a position to veto, as in 1924, Labour's
Nationalization ambitions. No wonder Garvin was depressed, as
he saw what might have been, in his view, a promising turning-
point towards friendlier co-operation between British Capital and
Labour, passed by so that the "Reds" might not be provoked into
the kind of mutiny deemed dangerous for MacDonald's electoral
chances. Here is what the *Observer* was printing, towards the end
of 1926, under the heading, "PEACE OR DECAY":[1]

Newspapers, Labour leaders, and capitalists have taken up the
campaign for industrial peace. . . . Is it all to end again in vain breath
and drifting lethargy? Will anything be done? . . . It is a strange phase
in the fortunes of a great people when we all know the truth but no one
seems capable of acting on it in earnest. . . . Most depends on the coming action of three men—Mr. Ramsay MacDonald, Mr. J. H. Thomas,
and Mr. Snowden. If they repudiate the strike method, if they appeal
for co-operation and stability, if they declare a limited though definite
programme for the next Parliament, they will open the way to a working
understanding with the Liberal Party.

Obviously, Garvin, like most publicists at the end of 1926,
hardly took into account any more the possibility of another
Liberal return to a controlling position in politics, based on a
new Radical programme. The best part he could now find for
Liberalism was as a subordinate ally for those "moderate"
elements in the Labour Party trying to avert the domination of the
"Left" by the forces of Revolutionary Socialism. Yet even as
Garvin was writing, the planning was being done for allowing a
Radical challenge, against both Conservatism and Socialism, to be
made at the next General Election. It was, of course, after
Asquith's departure from Leadership, that negotiations between
Lloyd George and the National Liberal Federation could reach a
stage which promised, thanks to the Lloyd George Fund, that up
to and during the next Election a great party propaganda effort

---

[1] The *Observer*, November 28, 1926, which also contained such passages as:
"What could Labour gain by taking over British industry as a bankrupt
proposition from which all the capital that could escape had fled? . . . Foreign
capitalist systems would be strengthened just as our coal strike has been a
godsend to German interests in the Ruhr. . . . There must be an end of the
printed and verbal caricatures suggesting that the typical employer is a cunning,
heartless, luxurious beast, and that the typical investor is an idle parasite. . . .
So far from being exploiters of society and foes of the workers, the typical
employer and typical investor are work-creating and wage-creating persons
indispensable to the masses in the present state of the world."

would be financed, and sufficient candidates assisted to stand, to make the party's return to Downing Street not an utter impossibility. Indeed, considering the further unpleasantnesses inevitable at Liberal Headquarters, and elsewhere,[1] until the last anti-Lloyd Georgians departed from positions of control, there was justifiable astonishment among the political commentators when, early in 1927, two remarkable Liberal by-election successes after a long period of electoral misfortune, proved resoundingly how eager large sections of the population were to have some other alternative to Baldwin than MacDonald.

It should be stressed, of course, that the long and obstinate coal-strike seemed, by now, to have justified a good deal of Lloyd George's stand, in regard to pits and pitmen, during the previous May. Indeed, a Radical organ so normally loyal to Asquith as *The Nation* had taken the line from the first that it was a mistake in the party Leader to have allowed himself to be pushed by Lloyd George's enemies into attempting his virtual excommunication from the Liberal fold.[2] There had followed, too, the Manchester Reform Club meeting at which Lloyd George had gained a remarkably friendly hearing for his view that, though unfairly attacked and repudiated, he would not be driven from Liberal platforms merely because he was "on the side of conciliation" in a dispute where millions of British workmen were concerned.[3]

[1] Cf. *Whitaker's Almanack, 1928*, p. 474, for such items as these: "Nov. 4, 1926. Sir Godfrey Collins resigned the post of Chief Liberal Whip. . . . Nov. 8th. Sir Robert Hutchinson appointed Chief Liberal Whip. . . . Nov. 17th. Mr. Lloyd George unconditionally offered to place interest on his Party Fund at disposal of central executive of Liberal Party. . . . Nov. 24th. Liberal Administrative Committee decided to renew negotiations regarding Mr. Lloyd George's offer, but several members resigned. . . ."

[2] Cf. *The Nation*, May 29, 1926, for the article entitled "Lord Oxford's Blunder". In the issue of June 19th, *The Nation* dealt with the rumour that it believed to be responsible for the party crisis but which Lloyd George had since disproved. According to *The Nation*, "The story, which was believed by Lord Oxford and his supporters . . . was that on May 7th Mr. Lloyd George met Mr. MacDonald, Mr. Snowden, and Mr. Clynes at Mr. Snowden's country house and agreed to split the Liberal Party and hand over his fund to the Labour Party in return for support of his Land policy and the promise that he should be Minister of Agriculture in the next Labour Government. At the Candidates' meeting last week, Mr. Lloyd George triumphantly disposed of the whole allegation." But not so triumphantly, it seems, as to end all doubts among Asquithians or to prevent the veteran working-man Labour journalist, Joseph Burgess, from pushing the sales of a work entitled, *Will Lloyd George supplant Ramsay MacDonald?*

[3] Cf. Sir Charles Mallet, *Mr. Lloyd George*, pp. 279–82, for an opponent's treatment of this speech of June 5, 1926 and subsequent Lloyd George efforts, made with growing confidence, in a *Sunday News* article of June 13th, and a speech at the National Liberal Club on June 23rd.

Moreover, after well-founded fears had been expressed by Liberal economists as to the ill-advised lines on which coal-owners and the Cabinet were handling the pit-dispute and the pit-settlement,[1] Lloyd George's reputation was sufficiently restored for *The Nation*, for example, to come out strongly on his side when justifying his delay in handing over to the party an income of £40,000 till he was satisfied that it would not be employed against him, his policies, and his party friends.[2] Thus was the road cleared for Liberal Headquarters to be manned by those who had had no part in the Lloyd George excommunication though there was, of course, keen anxiety once more in January 1927, when three such notable Liberal ex-Ministers as Grey, Runciman, and Simon announced their formation of a Liberal Council, independent of a party machine which could now be uncharitably regarded as having been "sold" to Lloyd George.[3] Yet when Sir Herbert Samuel took the lead among those who considered that the anti-Lloyd George vendetta had been taken too far and accepted the direction of a now well-financed party machine,[4] results were produced, which as has been said, confounded the political pundits. Thus, Captain Wedgwood Benn, Liberal M.P. for Leith since 1918, had decided to move into the Labour camp. Yet, at the by-election resulting from Benn's resignation of the seat, the new party organization found in Ernest Brown a candidate who, suffering from almost every apparent initial disadvantage, contrived

---

[1] Cf. *The Nation*, October 23, 1926: "When the Government conspired with the mine-owners to pass the Eight Hours Act as their contribution to beating the miners by district breakaways, they seem to have expected . . . that the process would be smooth and speedy. Their hopes were disappointed; but this did not save them from repeating this month the same miscalculation . . . the damage that is being done is much greater than appears on the surface. The very immunity we have enjoyed from overt disaster conceals the enormity of the national losses which are piling up. . . ."

[2] Cf. *Ibid.*, November 27, 1926: "Those at present in control of the official Liberal machine have left no doubt as to their implacable hostility to Mr. Lloyd George, amounting in one or two instances almost to a Freudian complex. Is it reasonable to expect Mr. Lloyd George to hand over his funds unreservedly to such men . . . ?"

[3] *Ibid.*, January 29, 1927: "Most of the Liberals I meet, whether Georgian or anti-Georgian, think as I do, that the new Grey organization is a sheer misfortune. . . . The country Liberal is sick to despair of the whole business. He wants to get on with the job, if only the disgruntled mandarins would let him."

[4] *Ibid.*, March 5, 1927: "Wherever Liberals foregather there is warm commendation of Sir Herbert Samuel's Eighty Club speech. Much is hoped from his famous efficiency, and still more from his equally well-known independence and his Radical temper. This was a Radical speech, an expression of robust faith in the constructive and forward-looking policies on which all Liberals are hoping to be allowed to unite. . . ."

the astonishing feat of holding the seat against both Labour and Conservative attack.[1] A few days later, on March 28, 1927, there was more astonishment still at the North Southwark by-election caused by the decision of the Labour member, Dr. Haden Guest, to abandon a party whose attitude on Britain's troubles in a China convulsed by civil war and Bolshevik intrigue, he considered to have become, under the pressure of the "Reds", thoroughly irresponsible.[2] Though Haden Guest refought the constituency with some Conservative blessing, and there was a Labour candidate anxious to step into Guest's shoes, it was the ex-Liberal M.P. of 1918–23 who recaptured the seat with ease.[3]

Obviously the nation was coming face to face with a new situation in which large numbers, tired alike of Tory and Socialist prejudice and apparent incompetence, were strongly tempted to turn elsewhere. In regard, for example, to the allegedly foolish preoccupation of the Tory Home Secretary, Joynson-Hicks, with British Communist sedition and Russian Bolshevist incitement thereto, Liberal intellectuals found it, perhaps, too easy to sneer —and too electorally profitable—amid voters trained, for generations, to make ample use of their "godlike freedom" to attack and weaken every British Government in turn.[4] And when the harassed Tory Foreign Secretary, too, Austen Chamberlain, ascribed British troubles in China, at least in part, to the incitements of Borodin's notorious and well-financed mission from the Communist International,[5] the pert rejoinders undertaken by

[1] Cf. The *Observer*, March 27, 1927: "By all the rules Mr. Brown, a stranger, a Southron, and a late-comer in the fight, should have lost. . . . Liberalism is far from dead. It is reviving. . . ."

[2] Cf. *The Nation*, March 5, 1927: "It is not surprising that Dr. Haden Guest has at last found the Labour Party too intolerably uncomfortable. . . . The views with which he returned from Russia are sufficiently well-known. . . ."

[3] *Whitaker's Almanack, 1928*, p. 182, gives the polling thus: E. A. Strauss, Liberal, 7334: G. A. Isaacs, Labour, 6167: Dr. L. H. Guest, M.C., Independent, 3215.

[4] Cf. *The Nation*, October 31, 1925: "Twelve men have been arrested and charged with 'conspiring together to utter and publish seditious libels. . . .' The *Evening News* has already got into trouble for 'contempt of court' by publishing a cartoon and articles . . . the Home Secretary, had himself been dangerously near. . . . Sir William Joynson-Hicks states, however, that he was misreported. It would be interesting to know whether Sir William was also misreported on December 6, 1913 when . . . he said at Warrington: 'The people of Ulster have behind them the Unionist Party. Behind them was the Lord God of Battles . . . I say to the Prime Minister "let your armies and batteries fire. Fire if you dare, fire and be damned" '."

[5] *Ibid.*, March 5, 1927 admitted that "the influence of Borodin is very great. . . . It is reported that Chiang Kai-Shek recently told him that he must withdraw and let Chinese control the movement themselves. The answer was

some Liberals were not very much more responsible,[1] in essence,
than the T.U.C.'s haste to congratulate Chinese "workers",
anxious above all, in not a few cases, to loot the threatened foreign
concessions especially Shanghai.[2] But it was, of course, on the
vexed questions of the pit-stoppage, the General Strike, and the
proposed restriction on Unions and strikes for the future, which
the Government was making its principal legislative objective in
1927, that Liberals seemed to be in the best position to confound
both the rival parties in turn. It was already quite plain that the
Liberals' "Coal and Power" plan, first, and the Samuel Report,
afterwards, had offered pitmen, coal-owners, and the country as a
whole, a far more desirable way through the nation's coal difficulties
than the path which had actually been followed. And, in regard to
the Government's principal legislative measure for 1927, the
Trade Disputes and Trade Union Bill to make a repetition of the
events of 1926, it was hoped, impossible, most Liberals considered
they again had the advantage of both the rival parties. They
agreed that there had been some abuse of the ample privileges
conferred upon Trade Unions by the Liberal Cabinets of 1906
and 1912, and that the Labour Party, instead of resisting the
mischief, had all too readily condoned it or explained it away. But
many Liberals were sure that some at least of the suggested Tory
remedies—and especially the drastic restrictions on the political
levy, on picketing during strikes, and on the type of Trade Union
which Civil Servants might join[3]—could well do much more harm

virtually, 'Return the forty million taels we have advanced'. . . . through China,
he wants to strike Britain to the dust. . . ."

[1] Cf. *Ibid.*, March 5, 1927, for an article entitled, "THE 'SEE RED' DANGER",
which ascribed a "protest and warning" just sent by Chamberlain to Russia as
a concession to the "anti-Reds" of the party. "Our present Government,"
averred *The Nation*, "spends most of its time in making silly concessions to silly
agitators", and then went on to, "We suspect that it is no easier for the Soviet
Government to control M. Borodin than it is for Mr. Ramsay MacDonald to
control Mr. Cook."

[2] Cf. *Hansard*, February 10, 1927, for Labour's objections finally to the
despatch of the Shanghai Defence Force. Chamberlain had claimed that he
was ready to accept "China for the Chinese" as a reasonable cry . . . "but 'Kill
the British' and 'Drive out the British' are the ravings of a mad hatred, and it is
not in that way that you can deal with this country or the British Empire".

[3] *Ibid.*, May 2, 1927, gives Sir Douglas Hogg's explanation of the terms
to which the Tory Cabinet, after long hesitations, finally committed itself.
Picketing at a house, for example, became unlawful as well as picketing elsewhere in intimidating numbers. As for the political levy, contracting-in was
substituted for contracting-out with the Trade Union member apparently
assured of legal protection in his right not to pay the levy unless he desired to.
In regard to Civil Servants, there was a prohibition of their joining any trade
union which was not confined to employees of the Crown, was not independent

than good. For one thing, the wrangling Labour Party would reunite almost enthusiastically, and, for another, Communism's attraction for disgruntled Trade Unionists would increase appreciably.

Even before the hesitant Government had finally decided the character of its Bill to outlaw the General Strike and much else that it disliked in current Trade Union practice, Radical opinion had expressed the gravest doubts and had pointed to the meagreness of the remaining legislation proposed as evidence that no constructive energy or planning, such as the situation really demanded, was any longer to be expected from the existing Cabinet or Parliament. Contrasting Baldwin's ambition of 1925 to bring peace and prosperity back to British industry with the actual facts of 1927, *The Nation*, for example, had this to say, and its comments would apparently have been far more unsparing had it known the ultimate severity of the Government's Trade Union and Strike proposals:[1]

In place of peace and prosperity, we have had two years of trade setback and industrial strife; while ill-feeling between classes is more wide-spread and bitter than it ever was before. Opinions will differ as to how far Ministers are responsible for this state of things. But how do they react to it? . . . Along what lines do they now propose to fulfil their position of "trust" as a national Government? We turn to the King's Speech. . . . The chief measure is to be a bill "defining and amending the law with reference to industrial disputes." Is this likely to promote trade recovery or industrial peace? . . . We view the prospect of this measure with the gravest misgiving. . . . This contribution to social discord is the only measure of the first rank foreshadowed for this session. Mr. Baldwin tells us, indeed, that the Unemployment Insurance Bill will be a very long one . . . it will presumably be a consolidating measure. For the rest we are promised a measure of leasehold reform "to secure for an outgoing tenant compensation for the loss of his good-will and unexhausted improvements", a Bill "to encourage the production and exhibition of British films", "Bills in connection with agriculture" (small Bills as Mr. Baldwin was careful to observe), amendments in the Companies Acts and in the styles and titles of the Sovereign and of Parliament. . . . There is no mention of the Factories Bill, of Poor Law Reform, and none, of course, of such constitutional matters as the House of Lords, or votes for women on the same terms

of outside trade unions or federations of trade unions and was not independent of all political parties. For good measure, local authorities were forbidden to make membership or non-membership of a trade union a condition of employment.

[1] *The Nation*, February 12, 1927.

as men. . . . Well, it is fairly clear that . . . the Tory ardour for social reform has not survived the rough weather of the last two years. . . . The Factories Bill has become a nuisance, calculated to offend employers as another burden on industry. . . .

But, perhaps, a specimen of the species of attack open to Liberalism on both flanks at once should be given to mirror more accurately what were the opportunities of the restimulated Liberalism of the spring of 1927. Here is *The Nation*'s Parliamentary Correspondent even before the Leith and Southwark results of late March announced a formidable "Liberal Revival":[1]

Labour . . . is very content that the Government should bring in a Bill which will alienate the trade unions and thus heal the fissure produced by the general strike. . . . There seems indeed to be a competition in imbecility between the Tory and Labour Parties to give each other battle-cries for election purposes. The Labour amendment, demanding the withdrawal of all British troops from China, was settled by a majority of two only in a half-attended Labour Party meeting by the Socialist Pacifist-Bolshevik rump of the back benches with none of the leaders there. This forced those leaders into speeches delivered with obvious disgust in a tangle of explanation which was too grotesque even to excite anger. If Mr. Baldwin chose to appeal to the country on that issue, he could achieve as big a success as on the Zinovieff letter, and no one knows this better than Mr. MacDonald. . . . The Tories counter this folly by exhibiting a similar folly themselves, and are not likely to appease the members of the unions by their explanations that such mild castigation and torment as they give them are really designed only for their own good. Both—the Government and the Opposition are led by extraordinarily weak leaders without the courage to resist the truculent ranks of their followers when they are playing the fool in the Houses of Parliament and making noises in the country outside. "Time was when brains were out the man would die." But now when brains are out a discredited Government holds on, hoping for something to turn up. . . .

In point of fact, both Labour and Conservatism were destined to antagonize the average uncommitted member of the British "public" a good deal more during the next few months and so promote the "Liberal Revival" still further. Thus when the Labour ex-Foreign Under-Secretary, Ponsonby ventured to initiate a debate in which he recommended the practical abolition of the British Air Force, and indeed of the British Army and Navy also, the Labour Party was subjected to a good deal of ridicule even though only twenty-four of its votes were ultimately cast

[1] *Ibid.*, February 19, 1927.

publicly for a course which most people held would "leave the British Empire open to subjugation by any fourth-rate Power which cares to loot or harpoon this mass of helpless blubber".[1] The trouble, too, that continued to be made from the Labour side on the subject of China, because Chamberlain, despite markedly conciliatory negotiation, refused, in advance of a diplomatic settlement, to allow the massive British interests in Shanghai to be militarily and unconditionally overrun in the fashion Borodin was supposed to have engineered elsewhere, was not likely to arouse any vast enthusiasm for the speedy advent of another Labour Government.[2] The Shanghai Defence Force did, in fact, provide Chiang Kai-Shek and the Chinese Nationalists with the arguments that finally helped them to rid themselves of Borodin and Bolshevism[3] while offering to resume negotiations with Britain and the other Powers having special interests. Meanwhile Liberals had joined Conservatives in criticism of "the grotesque slop talked by so many members of the Labour Party inside the House, and by their funny, silly, noisy little newspapers outside", and Liberals, too, were ready to acknowledge the strength of Conservatism's counter-arguments to this "slop" when they were intelligently put. Indeed, the ablest Conservative counter-attacker was half-gleefully reported in this fashion in a leading Liberal organ, notable for its Radical views:[4]

He blandly informed the House that he had discovered the principles of Socialist foreign policy. The first is that in any dispute with a foreign Power, Great Britain is always wrong. The second is that in investigating the facts concerning any such dispute, you should always trust a foreign revolutionary rather than a British official. The third is that in the matter of research, you should always believe somebody who has never been outside England, instead of somebody who has

[1] *The Nation*, March 19, 1927.
[2] Cf. *Whitaker's Almanack, 1928*, p. 483: "Nov. 29, 1926. Owing to serious anti-foreign feeling at Hankow, new British Minister to China proceeded to Shanghai for conference.... Dec. 18, 1926. British chargé d'affaires at Peking presented to diplomatic corps there Britain's proposals for new policy for reconciliation with China..... Jan. 5, 1927. Serious situation developed in Hankow... British women and children were evacuated.... Feb. 14th. British troops, Gloucesters and Durhams, landed at Shanghai.... Mar. 22. Durham Light Infantry fired on Chinese troops who attempted to enter the British settlement at Shanghai.... April 8th. Soviet Consulate at Shanghai searched by police.... April 10th. Powers presented Note to China protesting against Nanking outrages."
[3] *Ibid.*, p. 484. "April 21, 1927. Government at Nanking dismissed Borodin, Russian agent at Canton, and Communist Ministers."
[4] *The Nation*, March 26, 1927.

spent a life-time on the spot. The fourth is that when the foreign opponents of this country break into two groups, the Socialist Party are in a great dilemma, which they solve by backing the particular group which is most hostile to Great Britain. And finally, when anything happens "of an untoward nature" to our own countrymen, the invariable verdict is "they have brought it upon themselves by their own provocative and arrogant conduct, and anyhow, they are only capitalists and not worth talking about".

If Labour weaknesses of this kind appeared to give further prospects to the "Liberal Revival", there were weaknesses in the Tory record which seemed almost to surpass them. Quite apart from what could be said against Government's performance in 1925 or 1926—and there was much[1]—it was not difficult to "prove", in regard to 1927, that Ministers, in their legislation on Trade Unions and Strikes, were going well beyond the limits of the prudent or the necessary because of the pressure of Home Secretary "Jix" and an extreme Right quite out of touch with the bulk of the nation. And when, on May 12th, the most unprecedented event of its kind in twentieth-century Britain, the police raid, in search of a missing Army document, on the Arcos headquarters of the Anglo-Russian Trading Organization and the Russian Trade Delegation, seemed to show "Jix" and the "anti-Reds" again in charge of Government policy-making, the ultimate effects on "public opinion" proved most unfortunate. It had to be admitted that, despite thorough searches of the premises and the forcing of safes, the missing document had not been found.[2]

[1] To give one example among many, Lord Eustace Percy's Circular 1371, from the Board of Education, had been widely attacked in the educational world for having imposed a financial strait-jacket on local authorities who, it was claimed, would find it impossible, during the triennium 1926–9, to replace any obsolete buildings but financially rewarding to put their under-fives out of the infant-schools "on to the streets".

[2] Cf. *Whitaker's Almanack, 1928*, for a succinct record of the course of events (p. 474): "May 12, 1927. Police raided London headquarters of Arcos . . . taking possession of whole premises and forcing safes. May 16th. Home Secretary informed House of Commons police had been searching for secret War Office document which had been at one time on premises of Arcos but which had not been found. Police evacuated Soviet House. May 24th. Prime Minister announced Government's decision to sever diplomatic relations with Russia and terminate Anglo-Russian Trade Agreement owing to evidence obtained through police raid. Mr. MacDonald arrived home and went straight to House of Commons. May 26th. House of Commons by 367 to 118 approved break with Russia after Home Secretary had revealed remarkable spy system of the Soviet, which would be stopped by Government's action. May 27th. Note announcing severance of Anglo-Russian relations delivered at Soviet Embassy. Addressing National Liberal Federation at Margate, Mr. Lloyd George criticised Government for break with Russia. May 29th. Soviet reply to Note repudiated charges made."

And though it was announced, instead, that the search had revealed an intricate Russian spy-system of a character in such
cynical violation of the Trade Agreement as to warrant the
breaking-off of diplomatic relations, it seems that the mass of the
nation was far from satisfied. It was on May 24th that the Prime
Minister announced the severance of diplomatic relations and the
termination of the Russian Trade Agreement, and the next by-
election took place at Bosworth, Leicestershire on May 31st. The
Conservative majority had been a small one in 1924, and a strong
Government candidate had been obtained in General Spears. Yet
the General was left far at the bottom of the poll, the re-presented
Labour candidate of 1924 was second, and a Liberal friend and
follower of Lloyd George achieved the second Liberal gain in two
months.[1] It was obviously becoming much harder for Labour
and the Government to explain the "Liberal Revival" away.

The "Revival", of course, owed a great deal to the mistakes
both of Tories and Socialists and a great deal also to the effectiveness and ample financing of the new party machine. But much
was due, too, to the rethinking and the rewriting of the problems
of the nation and the party that had been going on for years and
which, in point of fact, had a far wider range[2] than might be
imagined from the concentration of political discussion and controversy on "Coal and Power" and the "Rural Land Report",
promoted and financed as these had been by Lloyd George and
his Political Fund. The Fund, indeed, had another important
Report on the way, that of the Liberal Industrial Inquiry and
there would ultimately be the best-known publication of them all,
We Can Conquer Unemployment, issued in the hope of deciding the
next General Election. Though, of course, the hope of re-
establishing or even improving the position of December 1923
when Liberalism's popular support was virtually equal to Labour's,
was obviously Lloyd George's main animating motive, it must be
supposed that he did not overlook the possibility that such a
consummation might well have become impossible. It appears,
in fact, that his second objective was to require, as a condition of

---

[1] *Whitaker's Almanack, 1927*, gave the Election figures in 1924 as Gee,
Conservative, 10,114: Ward, Liberal, 9756: Minto, Labour, 9143. The figures
of 1927 were: Edge, Liberal, 11,981: Minto, Labour, 11,710: Spears, Conservative, 7685.

[2] The *Daily News* gave wide publicity to some of the best lecturing and
thinking done by the party, especially in the Liberal Summer Schools, in the
form of a well-known series of Sixpenny Booklets, *The New Way* series.

helping to secure Labour in office a second time, a firm promise that
the prevailing electoral system would be "reformed" in a fashion
that would end the existing gross under-representation of Liberal
opinion in Parliament. Since 1918, indeed, both Conservatism
and Labour, happy in concentrated blocks of voting power
allowing them firm control of scores of single-member constituencies, had made use of their advantage to attempt the elimination, as a third political force, of the more scattered elements of
Liberalism, "entitled" on any proportional basis to several times
their actual representation in Parliament.[1]

But, perhaps, the detailed treatment of Election aims and
manœuvres might wait for a space, and this chapter be ended with
a survey of two small corners of the political field in an attempt to
elucidate why it was that, often in the most discouraging circumstances, a strong body of candidates and voters still held together
as the Liberal Party, declining to "desert" either to Right or Left
or to leave politics altogether in despair. Education, Housing,
Rating Law or, indeed, a dozen other subjects might be chosen to
illustrate why Liberals, and especially those of the Radical variety,
considered that they stood for something more genuinely "progressive" than either Conservatism or Labour. Here, however,
shall first be instanced the Exchequer departments concerned with
Inheritance Duties or "Death Duties" to give them the popular
name. Labour had little or no use even for the valid part of the
arguments which Conservatism could bring to show that the
existing Death Duties, even before the great suggested increases,
had already brought some unexpected and unfortunate results in
the dispersion of much constructively-employed capital. Radicals
claimed that they looked to large estates as eagerly, as did Labour,
to provide part of the revenues which would be needed for
"social reform" in the shape of increased educational opportunities,
better health and sanitary services, improvements in the Mines
and Factory Inspectorate and so on. But it was necessary to
remember that all "social reform" depended, basically, on a

[1] Cf. Philip Snowden, *Autobiography*, ii, 756, and 884–9, for the views of the
member of the controlling Labour junta most sympathetic to Proportional
Representation. As he read the figures of the eventual 1929 Election, it took
89,850 Liberal votes to secure a member, 33,845 Conservative votes, and
28,996 Labour. Though this was all to the taste of the Labour Back-Benchers,
who resisted the Electoral Reform Bill eventually offered to Lloyd George till
it was overtaken by the 1931 Election, that Election, according to Snowden,
punished them much harder than would have been the case had they agreed to
Proportional Representation.

progressive increase in capital accumulation, that such accumulation was powerfully forwarded by the expectation that savings could be bequeathed, and that to push the State's taxation of bequests too far would merely result in luxury-squandering of resources during life. Moreover, interesting as were suggestions of the Rignano type as to the possibility of greatly increasing the State's levy as an inheritance passed a second time,[1] it was essential to remember two possible consequences. If the first inheritor were left the full control of the estate, subject, of course, to the payment of a moderate death duty, he would certainly contrive means of dispersing most of it before his death rather than face the certainty that it would be subjected, on his decease, to virtual State appropriation. And what had not been dispersed by the first inheritor, would assuredly be so by the second if, indeed, it was thought fit to allow a testator, in the interests of capital accumulation, to be tempted forward by the hope of being able to do something, it might be, for a grandchild as well as a child. Moreover, if to avoid estate-dispersals in advance of State appropriation, all inheritances were placed in a kind of trust, the result would be that a very large part of the national capital would be virtually frozen and perilously restricted from flowing in the direction of the greatest demand and greatest opportunity.[2]

It was, perhaps, in the field of Poor Relief that Radicals were most critical of the effects of Socialist ideas and Labour administration. As has been seen, the anarchic sentimentalism and profuse, unguarded expenditure, which had made "Poplarism" a by-word in the years 1922–4, had few friends in the Radical ranks. Radicals were not merely antagonized that Lansbury and his like, sometimes in the name of Christian charity,[3] turned a

---

[1] Rignano's *Social Significance of Death Duties* appeared, in translation, for English readers during the course of 1925. The future Labour Chancellor of the Exchequer, Dr. Dalton, had already aroused some interest in Rignano's ideas among his own party, and, of course, it could be strongly argued that the accumulator of capital hardly cared for what would happen after the beneficiaries of his bequests had enjoyed their life interest.

[2] Cf. E. D. Simon, *The Inheritance of Riches*, and Professor Henry Clay, *Property and Inheritance*, for two of the discussions Liberals had heard on this manner of topic at Liberal Summer Schools, and then there was Sir Josiah Stamp's introduction to Rignano in the English translation. It would be, perhaps, fair to add that E. D. Simon was more optimistic as to what might be taken in Death Duties without harm to capital-growth than many other Liberals were, and was also more strongly moved by the hope of reducing extreme inequalities of wealth.

[3] George Lansbury's *Your Part in Poverty*, which had gone through three editions in the first five months of 1917, was one of the best possible proofs of

blind eye to the workshys and "artful dodgers" who flourished on their type of administration. They seemed wilfully blind also to the imminent peril that all businesses, which could do so, would move out of excessively-rated "Poplarized" areas, no new businesses would ever move in, and a permanent quagmire of pauperization would result. Moreover, the continued heavy unemployment in shipbuilding, engineering, and iron and steel areas meant that "Poplarism" of a new type was barely held at bay there, while with the coal-stoppage of 1926, a defiant colliery-area "Poplarism" appeared, completing with that of West Ham, the Government's justification for the Board of Guardians (Default) Act and more. Under the Default Act, elected Guardians, disregarding the statutory and other limitations of their Poor Relief powers could be replaced by nominated officials, but the Government, by 1927, was firmly committed to go further. It was not merely that such an anti-Socialist organization as the London Municipal Society could claim that sixty-four Boards of Guardians, rather than the three actually dealt with under the Act, should have been deprived of their powers for maladministration. It was the fact that hundreds of Guardians areas were too small, too scantily populated, or too dependent on a single industry, liable to serious trade depression, to make them reliable units of twentieth-century Poor Law Administration.[1] Nothing less was planned, indeed, than to hand over Poor Relief responsibility to the County Councils and the County Boroughs.

In all this, Radicals expressed a great deal of sympathy with Neville Chamberlain at the Ministry of Health, who, they noted, not merely had his troubles with the Socialists but also with low-rate Conservative Boards, which did not desire to help bear their "extravagant" neighbours' burdens by higher rates to be collected over much more extended and industrially variegated areas. It was, indeed, the Conservative Boards, especially those in low-rate rural and suburban areas, who whipped up sufficient party support to halt Neville Chamberlain's plans for legislating in 1927. Radicals, of course, had as little patience with the Conservative mixture of selfishness and blindness on the Poor Law as they had with the

what advantages agitation enjoyed if conducted by a professing member of the Church of England, claiming anxiety to put the principles of the New Testament into action.

[1] Under the Poor Law Amendment Act of 1834, nearly six hundred and fifty Boards of Guardians had been constituted in England and Wales.

"Poplar" variety—and they thoroughly approved the plan of eliminating the shortsighted selfishness, say of Kensington and Poplar, simultaneously, by making the London County Council the Poor Law Authority for the whole metropolis. The wealth of London's fashionable boroughs might certainly be drawn on somewhat more freely in consequence, but a County Council, then apparently under firm anti-Socialist control, would have the satisfaction of knowing that the remedy for East-End maladministration was in its own hands.

One fear there was, indeed, which caused some Radicals to suggest that far-reaching as Chamberlain's Poor Law proposals might seem, they might still not be going far enough.[1] *The Nation,* for example, asked whether the West Ham Town Council, even though elected for a much wider range of administrative duties than the West Ham Board of Guardians, was likely to prove a less perilous Poor Law Authority. And if Durham County Council elections came to turn on the rights and wrongs of what the Chester-le-Street Guardians had tried to do for pitmen and their families during the Coal Stoppage, "Red" Poor Law notions might be inflicted on the whole County. In a conclusion, indeed, which would have delighted the Chadwick of 1834 if not the softer democracy of a later age, *The Nation* ventured to suggest that, in view of the increasing mass-bribery attempted by "Red" elective authorities, a very Radical solution indeed was called for. Here is *The Nation*'s warning:[2]

Mr. Chamberlain, after abolishing the Guardians, would be likely to find in many cases that, on the score of poor law profligacy, the new Council was but the old Board writ large. There is, indeed, a real danger that our last state might be worse than our first, that the issue of lavish poor relief might become the leading issue in council elections, and that the sort of demoralization which some Boards of Guardians have exhibited might infect the whole conduct of local government.

The moral, in our judgement, is irresistible. The whole principle of local autonomy is becoming unworkable as the basis of poor law

[1] Cf. *The Nation,* March 19, 1927: "Mr. Chamberlain would doubtless urge that the County area or the County Borough area is usually much larger than the Poor Law Union area; that therefore the burden of poor relief would be spread somewhat more widely, and the risk of irresponsible "Red" majorities somewhat reduced. Under both heads, therefore, he can claim in general terms that his scheme would be some improvement. But he must show more than that, if he is to justify so ambitious and so far-reaching a measure. He must show that the improvement . . . will be substantial, and adequate to the needs of the situation. Can he show this?"

[2] *Ibid.*

administration. The State itself must take over the work of outdoor relief and administer it on a frankly bureaucratic basis, while seeking as far as possible, through local advisory committees, to retain the services of local knowledge and public spirit which the Guardians now enlist. Only so can we secure, in face of the ominously deepening cleavage between the social ideas dominant in one area and those dominant in another, the indispensable measure of uniformity in the scale and system of relief. Only so can we deal satisfactorily with the problem of high rates in the depressed areas, and offer to industry generally the prospect of material relief from that most vicious of all our taxes.

CHAPTER XXII

"THE LIBERAL REVIVAL", 1927-8

"The revival of the Liberal Party in the country was powerfully aided by the appointment, on February 16th, of Sir Herbert Samuel as Chairman of the Liberal Organization . . . since . . . his name [was not] in any way connected with the dissensions which had rent the party . . . Sir Herbert set an example of loyal and whole-hearted co-operation with Mr. Lloyd George which reduced the opponents of that leader to silence. . . . From this time the party had the appearance, if not yet the reality of unity. . . . In the course of the next few months Mr. Lloyd George and Sir Herbert Samuel displayed great activity in addressing public meetings up and down the country."

The Annual Register, 1927.

"The Report proposes to press forward, instead of hanging back, with work of national development which will entail capital expenditure. But this capital outlay should be remunerative outlay, remunerative not only by reference to wide considerations of social welfare, but in the strictest financial sense. The idea which underlies the programme of national development is that there is (1) a large amount of useful work of a public utility character, offering a prospective return of about 5 per cent. which remains undone to-day in Britain because it is not sufficiently attractive to private enterprise and is no one else's business: and (2) much similar work which is not perhaps remunerative under present conditions, but which could be made so, if the increased land values which it creates could be brought into the account by the application of the "betterment" principle. The work of national development contemplated in the Report should be made to pay for itself. Under one heading only does the Report propose additional charges—the heading of the relief of rates. And in this matter, in principle at all events, it appears to have the support of Mr. Churchill."

The Nation of February 11, 1928, on the Report of the Liberal Industrial Inquiry.

A^{T} the close of the last chapter, there was an attempt to show
that, by the spring of 1927, a combatant Radicalism under
Lloyd George was taking charge of the Liberal Party and
offering the nation a great deal of "progress" that should yet be
free of the mawkish sentimentality or plain mass-bribery that
many found to be the principal characteristics of Labour appeals.
But it is necessary to show that, if, on the Radical side, there was
strong criticism of most of the differing groups who had allegedly
banded together to seize power under the denomination of
"Labour", groups ranging from Comrade Mosley and his
"missus", Lady Cynthia,[1] to the "unemployed" Guardians or
District Councillors in local control because of their constant
justification of everything done or left undone by those on the
"Dole" or Poor Relief, there was another and more stimulating
side to Radical activity. It is astonishing, for example, in view of
the part Economy and Retrenchment had once played in Radical
history, to find the vigour with which Economy, for Economy's
sake, and Retrenchment of any social expenditure increases, could
now be disowned by the most authoritative Radical voices.
Nobody, for instance, brought weightier criticism to bear on
Winston Churchill's Economy Bill of 1926 than Radical writers
who claimed almost that it would be wiser to replace the 6*d.* on the
Income Tax, remitted by him in 1925, than to attempt, because
of the unexpectedly heavy cost of the Mines Subsidy, to put a
better face on the 1926 Budget by "Economies" affecting the
Education programme and the Health and Unemployment
Insurance Funds.

Here is *The Nation* on the first reports of a pending Economy
Bill:[2]

We do not want to see the income-tax increased; nor are we accustomed to advocate expenditure irresponsibly in any field. We criticized
strongly, for example, what seemed to us an unnecessary enlargement
of the housing subsidy in Mr. Wheatley's increase of 1924.

---

[1] The gossip-writers of the winter of 1926–7 found Mosley's efforts to fit
himself for proletarian leadership by changes of dress and manner distinctly
stimulating. Lady Cynthia's efforts to help her husband's career in the Labour
Party sometimes produced even odder results but the cynics were amused to
note how many Divisional Labour Parties were eager to have this figure from
the higher aristocracy as their candidate. She joined her husband as Labour
M.P. for Stoke in 1929.

[2] *The Nation*, February 6, 1926.

But we assert deliberately and very seriously the following views:

(1). There is no presumption whatever that the money now spent by the Government and by the local authorities, taking it by and large, is laid out to less good purpose or with less stimulus to trade than it would be if it were left in the pockets of the taxpayers.

(2). It is a gross fallacy to suppose that our high level of direct taxation is an important cause of post-war trade depression, that our trade would derive appreciable benefit from a further reduction of the income tax or would suffer appreciable injury from a moderate increase.

(3). Rather than that the development of education and the public health services, which ought to be a continuous, progressive thing, should be crippled for lack of funds, we would see the standard rate of income-tax restored to 5s. in the £. We do not suggest that the direct taxpayer need be burdened so heavily as this; but, if it were necessary, it would not be an excessive "ransom".

And when the Bill was published and debating began, *The Nation* would have none of Churchill's arguments that he was merely retarding the *growth* of Education expenditure not reducing it; that the Health Insurance Fund's great surplus showed that the Government's contribution could now be safely reduced without the slightest risk to benefits; and, finally, that Unemployment had been falling markedly and continuously enough for some months to permit a reduction also of the Government's contribution to the Unemployment Fund. The educational authorities, it was retorted, would never succeed in dealing with their problems of replacing insanitary and unsuitable school-premises, reducing the size of classes, and attempting a new differentiation between Junior and Senior Schools unless they were stimulated and helped by the Government instead of hampered and repressed. And as for the Health Insurance benefits, long in need of the improvements now made impossible by Mr. Churchill's "economy", and Unemployment Insurance balances, left at the mercy of Mr. Churchill's over-optimistic expectations as to what would happen when Mines subsidization stopped, "public opinion" was apt to be more affected by the cold criticism of Radical economists than by the Parliamentary demonstrations mounted by the Labour Opposition.[1]

But possibly the most Radical line of thinking being undertaken when the "great Liberal Revival" was held to be commencing early in 1927 was concerned with the means of reducing Social

[1] Cf. *Whitaker's Almanack, 1927*, p. 158: "The Committee stage, which opened on March 31st, was marked by several all-night sittings and scenes."

Inequalities by expediting the break-up of estates passing at death. Even that not unsympathetic statistician, Sir Josiah Stamp, considered that there was a distinct lack of the proper scientific caution when a Radical economist, capable of going on record with the warning that "the level of wages and the level of profits are really determined within fairly narrow limits, by forces of so fundamental a character, that you will get into serious trouble if you try to run counter to them" could yet throw caution to the winds when asserting "that the inequality in the distribution of wealth stands out to-day as a gross and indefensible anomaly". Nor was the statistician as convinced as the Radical economist that the Inequalities of Wealth Distribution resulted mainly from traditional Inheritance Laws or that it was necessarily all gain when so Radical a stand was taken as that "It is an indispensable requirement of social justice that there should be a constant erosion of accumulated fortunes, and if the forces which have hitherto done this work are weakening, it is essential to supply others to take their place."[1] The statistician was certainly right, in view of what had happened in the German, Austrian, Russian, and Turkish Empires, and, in a lesser way, in Britain, France, and Italy also, to hold that the economist was considerably overrating the security with which inherited fortunes could be preserved, and even increased, by the investment facilities of the twentieth century.[2] Yet the whole discussion, with the related one on stiff increases of Death Duty, is but one example of the enterprising Radical spirit which was being thrown into the "great Liberal Revival". After reversing discouraging electoral trends (ascribed to the renewed Leadership quarrels of 1926) in the three notable by-election successes at Leith, Southwark, and Bosworth

---

[1] H. D. Henderson, *Inheritance and Inequality* is the source of the paragraph's quotations. It was issued as No. 15 of the *Daily News New Way* Series.

[2] Cf. *The Nation*, November 20, 1926, for Sir Josiah Stamp's reproving caution for such views as that "initial inequality, however caused, tends under our system of inheritance, coupled with modern facilities for investment, to perpetuate itself throughout subsequent generations in a cumulative degree". As Stamp had it: "Having regard to the rapid growth of national wealth in the last two generations, the dispersion due to family diffusion, the disintegration due to natural causes, it is a matter for strong suspicion whether any *considerable* part of present inequality on its 'gross and indefensible side' would be found due to wealth inherited by rich people from accumulations made before 1850 or 1860. Mr. Henderson does not deny that the power to accumulate and the power of disposition may be essential to a modern economic community. He merely says that you must cut off the results immediately the encouragement has had its effect."

during the spring of 1927, the "great Liberal Revival" seemed to get special propaganda chances from three of the main political topics before the public in the spring and summer of 1927. And if the alleged muddled Conservative "follies" of the 1927 Trade Disputes Bill and the Arcos Raid breach with Russia seemed to offer excellent material for platform displays against the Baldwin Cabinet, the Labour extremists' attitude on Britain's Shanghai interests was distasteful enough to the "general public" to make even Lloyd George's qualified support for Austen Chamberlain's mixture of firmness and conciliatoriness "statesmanlike" by comparison. It is even possible that if Baldwin had given way to the temptation of dissolving on Labour's support of the "Chinese revolutionary masses" against so-called "capitalist exploitation", largely British, especially at Shanghai, the result might well have been as devastating to Labour's hopes of a majority as had been the Russian Loan Election of 1924, though, this time, the profit would not have gone entirely to Baldwin but might have been shared by Lloyd George and the Liberals.

At first sight, the Liberal line on the Government's Bill to render another General Strike completely illegal, to restrict the trade unions' rights to make a political levy to those members only who had specifically asked for it, and to undertake various other changes in strike and union law, seemed likely to have many electoral advantages. It was to assert that, though there were, indeed, Trade Union and Strike practices which called for legislative definition, restriction or even total prohibition, the Government's Bill was too partisan and too untimely for the purpose and would do much more harm than good.[1] It was untimely because just when the hard facts of 1926 were teaching the Unions some necessary lessons which they were slowly absorbing,

---

[1] Cf. *The Nation,* April 9, 1927: "Clause 1 seems not unlikely to ban all sympathetic strikes; Clause 3 to ban all picketing whatsoever. We shall not comment at length on the other clauses of the Bill. It is right in principle, we think, that Civil Servants should not be members of trade unions affiliated to political parties or outside organizations. But it is the height of unwisdom to impose a sudden *ukase* to this effect as a feature of a general, partisan onslaught on trade unionism. Clause 6 prohibits local authorities from requiring their employees to join trade unions. The problem of reconciling local autonomy with the practices of certain public authorities of an extreme Labour complexion is serious and difficult enough, without aggravating and confusing it by such a pin-pricking proviso. We take the gravest view of the probable consequences of this Bill. It is the most wanton contribution to social discord that any Government has made in modern times. It emphasizes more urgently . . . the public need for the revival of Liberalism."

a Bill they considered as most biased and provocative would arouse the passionate anger in which all that had been learnt would be swept away. And the political as well as industrial bias of the Bill was such that a Labour Party, which had barely been kept from splitting into two on repeated occasions since Mac-Donald's defeat in 1924, would be furnished with the ideal basis for a complete reunion, loyal and hearty enough to make possible a General Election victory. Yet there was one dangerous flaw in what would otherwise have been a very plausible line of Liberal attack, for it was the foremost lawyer on the Liberal Benches in the House of Commons, Sir John Simon himself, who, according to the Government, was the spiritual father of their Bill. And certainly three speeches delivered by Simon in August 1926 had played a vital part in the defeat of the General Strike for he had held not merely that that Strike had been illegal in itself but that Union Funds, and even the personal possessions of Union leaders and members, could be proceeded against for damages by strike-stopped businesses, without part, lot, or interest in the original coal-dispute. In fact, with Simon as one of the villains of the piece, according to Labour platforms, and Lloyd George, with his allegedly shameless and reckless opportunism, as another, according to Conservative platforms, it may be questioned whether Liberal profit was all that had been hoped. Undoubtedly, by-election results, during the remainder of 1927, were disappointing or positively humiliating after the high hopes aroused by the three successive wins at Leith, Southwark, and Bosworth.[1]

It might be worth while, at this stage, to illustrate the quite Radical line most Liberals were prepared to take on the Arcos Raid and the resulting breach of diplomatic relations with Russia. If not prepared for such outright ridicule of their own Government's views as was manifested by those groups of Labour M.P.s who decided to give the departing Russian delegation a farewell lunch in the House of Commons dining-room and a public

[1] Cf. *Whitaker's Almanack*, *1928*, for the Westbury (Wilts.) by-election result of mid-June where the run of Liberal by-election successes was just halted, and the other two parties, to their immense relief, were once again able to call plausibly to the electorate not to "waste their votes" on a doomed party. The figures at Westbury were Long, Conservative, 10,623; Johnstone, Liberal, 10,474; Ward, Labour, 5396. It was held by some that the Liberal candidate had lost the seat by his preference for working with Viscount Grey's Liberal Council and his declining to call in Lloyd George's help. And once the Liberal "swing" was broken, results began to deteriorate as at Brixton on June 27, 1927, where the figures were Conservative, 10,358; Labour, 6032; Liberal, 5134.

send-off a little while afterwards at Victoria Station,[1] Radical
journalists undoubtedly under-rated what lay behind the so-called
anti-Communist and anti-Soviet "follies" of Joynson-Hicks at the
Home Office. For years they had been turning him into a figure
of fun and ignoring the possibility, or even the probability, that
encouraged by such Liberal manifestations almost as much as by
Clydeside's "Redder" line, the Russian Embassy and Trade
Delegation groups might consider that they had a fair field for a
little espionage, for some planting of Communist "cells" in British
industry and for the establishment of many useful contacts with
anti-British forces ranging from the I.R.A.[2] to discontented lascars
in British shipping. It is probable that if the Arcos Raid had
yielded more damning evidence, Radical journalists would have
seen the seriousness of almost rivalling the Labour Press in discrediting the Home Secretary. But some of the most striking
revelations on the transfer of Russian money for Communist use
and on the Communist penetration of British Trade Unions did
not come until 1928,[3] and, then, Labour tried, at one and the
same time, to take the credit for a patriotic stand and to throw the
blame on a "reactionary" Home Secretary and Government that
Labour and Socialist enthusiasts should have fallen under Russian

[1] Cf. *Whitaker's Almanack, 1928*, p. 832, which has an interesting section also
on Communists and the methods employed by them to penetrate or influence
the more orthodox Labour and Trade Union movements.

[2] Cf. The Home Secretary's White Paper on *Russian Banks and Communist
Funds* on what Russian agents succeeded in effecting even after formal diplomatic relations were broken off. The White Paper, issued in June 1928, was the
consequence of a promise, made to a Parliamentary questioner, after an Irish
gunman, arrested before Easter 1928, was found in possession of two £10 Bank
of England notes which had passed through the Bank for Russian Trade Ltd.
The Irish gunman's £20 was found to have been part of a bundle of notes which
had gone from the Bank for Russian Trade to a Soviet Bank in Berlin, but still
more interesting was the revelation of how the Moscow Narodny Bank Ltd.
transferred money for Communist use in Britain, employing a clerk, Duncan,
in its own offices, who worked with two employees of Centrosoyus Ltd., named
Quelch and Priestley. Twenty-eight thousand pounds was thus transferred
between July 1927 and April 1928.

[3] Cf. *The Nation*, April 28, 1928: "Following upon the revelations by the
Executive of the Boilermakers' Society of the influence which the Communist
Movement had obtained in that trade union . . . comes a similar statement by
the executive of the Scottish Mineworkers' Union. . . . The Scottish miners'
executive, of which Mr. R. Smillie, M.P., and Mr. D. Graham, M.P., are
members states that the Communists have obtained command of the union's
machinery in Lanarkshire, Fife, Clackmannan, and Kinross. The executive has
postponed the meeting of the union's annual conference, and declined to
surrender office until an appeal can be made to a conference fully representative. . . . Mr. Cook has denounced their action as 'the most dastardly undemocratic action in the miners' history'. . . . The sequel will be watched with
interest."

influence at all. Meanwhile Radical journalism, somewhat more responsibly, perhaps, than Labour's, had been harping on the theme of the employment opportunities which had been allegedly lost owing to Russian resentment, and on the hopes that had arisen among continental reactionaries and Fascists that the Baldwin Government had taken the first step in a possible new anti-Communist Crusade.[1]

But it is certainly time to show how, in addition to criticizing the breach with Russia as a graver risk internationally than was warranted by the Arcos revelations, the Radical journalist or Liberal candidate proceeded, for many months to come, to handle the "bread-and-butter" side of the problem. Here is *The Nation*:[2]

Our trade with Russia must be seriously prejudiced, if not virtually destroyed, by the steps which have been taken. Apart altogether from the desire which the Soviet authorities will naturally feel to retaliate ... the very fact that Arcos has been raided and might be raided again, and the general insecurity attaching to Soviet representatives in Great Britain, would tell heavily, from the most prosaic business standpoint, against selecting Britain as the source of supply for machinery and textiles which might be obtained elsewhere, or relying on London as an entrepot centre. It is thus certain that, as the result of the Government's action, our industries will lose orders, and our business houses will lose commissions. What we shall gain is unfortunately not so clear.

It is not generally realized how our trade with Russia has developed during the last six years ... the volume of our direct trade with Russia, in 1925, was twice as large as that of our trade with Brazil or with Japan; £10 millions more than our trade with Sweden; and £5 millions more than our trade with Italy.

Our imports from Russia are mainly foodstuffs and raw materials. . . .
In return, we exported, principally, cotton goods to the value of

[1] Cf. *Ibid.*, June 18, 1927, for a comment on what followed the murder of Voikov, Soviet representative in Warsaw, on June 7th, a comment which, at least refrained from putting the "moral blame" for Voikov's assassination, and the bloody Russian reprisals, on Baldwin or even on "Jix": "By way, avowedly, of reprisal for the assassination of M. Voikov, the Soviet Government has revived the Red Terror and has executed a number of unhappy 'Whites' . . . who have been languishing untried in its prisons. . . . This sickening reprisal indicates the appalling mentality which animates the rulers of Soviet Russia. . . . More serious in their potential consequences are the demands made upon Poland . . . and the working up of a scare of a united bourgeois onslaught on Russia at the instigation of Great Britain. . . ."

[2] *Ibid.*, May 28, 1927. This was, perhaps, somewhat better than Clynes's case for the Labour Party, based on alleged orders that would have been placed by the Russians when expending a ten millions credit from the Midland Bank. Fifty-six thousand men, it was asserted, would have been kept in work for a year though, according to the Foreign Secretary, experience showed that Russian orders vanished into thin air when talk about them no longer served a political purpose.

£1·2 millions, machinery (£1·1 millions), woollens (0·6 millions), and metal manufactures (0·6 millions). Our entrepot trade was very considerable . . . raw cotton (£5·3 millions), hides (£1·3 millions), rubber (£1·5 millions), and tea (£1·0 millions). These figures furnish some idea of the range of interests which will be seriously affected . . . and the matter is the more serious inasmuch as such development as the Midland Bank £10 millions credit indicated the probability that large Russian orders were about to be placed with British firms.

Perhaps if there had been some dramatic worsening of the employment position during the course of the ensuing summer, ascribable, in part at least, to Toryism's anti-Communist obsessions, Liberalism might have gained some tangible electoral profit. Numbers of "floating voters" from the middle classes would have deserted Baldwin for Liberalism once more, as in December 1923, and considerable numbers of working-class families of the "steady" type would have found a Radical professional or business man a more attractive choice, in replacement of a sitting Tory Member, than most of the Labour candidates actually offered. But there was no conspicuous worsening of a strange employment position which showed the co-existence, side by side, of prosperous, newer, industries like motor-manufacture, drugs and chemicals, electrical goods, rubber products, and rayon, executing, as Mr. Baldwin observed, a new "Industrial Revolution" of their own[1] while coal, steel, shipbuilding, and many types of "heavy" engineering remained depressed and suffering from a very high unemployment rate which the unsympathetic were inclined to ascribe to the repeated and inexcusable follies of the men, notably the colliers. Moreover, there was no real proof that the pattern of Russian trade could be dramatically altered to fit in with political rhetoric in Britain so that the election experts finally persisted in believing that both Conservative and Labour organizers might be right in holding that the zeal of their respective party stalwarts had been inflamed by the Arcos issue and its results. "The Liberal Revival", at any rate, would hardly be the gainer from such a consummation, a fact apparently confirmed from the by-elections where deadly use was still being made of the

[1] Cf. *The Nation*, October 15, 1927, for an optimistic, if disputable, treatment of the Board of Trade Returns, by Mr. Baldwin when addressing the Conservative Party Conference at Cardiff: "Quoting with approval Mr. Churchill's statement that 'British industry is once more in full swing,' he declared that 'during the last few months the export of manufactured goods has been slowly growing until, in August, it was 11 per cent greater than it was two years ago'."

taunt that whether Liberals were under fifty in number as in the sitting Parliament or over thrice as numerous, as in 1924, they nearly always split into three and wasted the votes of their supporters. The "moderate Liberals" usually voted with Conservatives, more especially against "Socialism", the Radicals were inclined, if they could, to vote with Labour, and, often enough, a third group, sometimes the largest of all, decided to abstain as unable to commit itself either to Tory or Labour extremism.

Yet the intensity of the effort being made to strengthen the Radical appeal for all those who felt themselves intolerably misrepresented both by the existing Conservative Administration, so largely manned, it was averred by mediocre, C.3 politicians, and by a Labour Parliamentary Party, allegedly capable of disregarding the plainest economic facts if they but conflicted with the supposed interests of a powerful Trade Union,[1] was far too real not to have obvious, and even, conspicuous results. When, for instance, Sir Herbert Samuel was able to announce that there would be over five hundred Liberal candidates at the next General Election, and another Liberal Summer School could be organized, offering many of those candidates and their supporters the best introduction to, and discussion of, "progressive ideas" to be obtained anywhere in the world, the effect was bound to be so stimulating as to make optimists forget the magnitude of the difficulties to be overcome. That scholar-politician, Ramsay Muir, who was, with others like J. M. Keynes, one of the main personal forces behind the "Liberal Revival", the Liberal and Radical Candidates Association and the Liberal Summer School, had already issued a far-sighted warning. Claiming that the new body of Liberal thinking—"their coal schemes, their land schemes, their industrial schemes" so different "from the timidities or negations of Conservatism, and from the inelastic and demoded formulae of Socialism"—represented the most notable intellectual revival in

[1] Cf. *Ibid.*, January 9, 1926, for what happened to possibly the most eloquent man on the Labour Benches in the 1924–9 Parliament, Rosslyn Mitchell, the Glasgow lawyer who had defeated Asquith but was never allowed to sit again because he offended the building unions by advocating the erection of many more Weir Steel Houses: "Mr. Hicks, the Secretary of the Amalgamated Union of Building Trade Workers, has replied with wild abuse of Mr. Mitchell, the Government and the Capitalists, and with the definite assertion—which is more to the purpose—that under a proper housing policy the building trades could produce all the brick houses required without having to fall back on 'substitutes'. Mr. Coppock, General Secretary of the National Federation of Building Trade Operatives, adds that Mr. Mitchell is an 'interfering busybody'."

the country, claiming also that there had been a noticeable return to a still very large Liberal fold by those who had deserted for a time to Right or to Left and been thoroughly disabused, Ramsay Muir still found the general non-political public far from convinced even by Liberalism's ability, "on favourable ground", to win three by-elections in succession. As he put the by-election matter and much else, it was this:[1]

> So far as we are concerned, they have stopped the rot: no more. They show an amazing decline in the Conservative vote. . . . But it cannot yet be said that the pendulum is swinging definitely in our direction. The Labour vote is still growing, in spite of the manifest impotence of the Labour Party in Parliament, its public dissensions, its disastrous blunders, and its lack of any clear policy. It is growing partly because something of the momentum of its rapid rise still survives, but partly because it is still regarded as the practical alternative to Conservatism. The electorate cannot get over the numerical weakness of Liberals in the House of Commons and their incurable habit of cross-voting. Our arguments about the strength of the Liberal vote in the country "cut no ice": that is one of the evil consequences of the present electoral system. . . .
> And there is another reason for avoiding over-sanguine expectations. In too many constituencies the party organization has fallen to pieces; and it is far more difficult to build up a Liberal organization than to build up a Labour or a Conservative organization. For there are Labour fanatics, and paid Trade Union organizers, almost everywhere; and everywhere the respectabilities and the timidities are easily mustered at the Conservative call. Ours is a far more difficult task. Yet it is anything but a hopeless task, if only we can get candidates—and agents —planted in every possible constituency. For the real mind of the country is still Liberal though it does not know it. This country wants "progress without class war" which is the essence of Liberalism. It has condemned the present Government which . . . can be overthrown by a very small electoral turnover. It is dubious and unhappy about the Labour Party. . . .

The summer and autumn of 1927 found both "progressive" Opposition groups anxious to make political capital from a somewhat discredited Cabinet's alleged new mistakes as well as from the old. Thus the failure of an attempt to extend Naval Disarmament to new categories of ships was ascribed principally to London;[2] the resignation of Viscount Cecil became a proof of the

---

[1] *The Nation*, June 18, 1927.

[2] Cf. *Whitaker's Almanack, 1928*, p. 480, for the Geneva Naval Conference, which had opened on June 20th between the United States, Britain, and Japan. A submarine agreement was announced on July 5th, but prolonged discussions

lack of sincerity and zeal in the Cabinet for League of Nations principles; and the Home Office's expulsion of two directors of Russian Oil Products Ltd. was treated as merely another example of "Jix's" costly anti-Communist follies.[1] And Conservative counter-strategy was seen in the resolve to avoid suicide at the polls by resisting "Die-Hard" pressure for making a General Election issue out of Veto restoration to a "reformed" House of Lords and, even, in Baldwin's determination to stand by the pledge he considered himself to have given to equalize Suffrage rights as between men and women by according what the age knew jocularly as the "flapper vote". There may well have been Conservative electoral experts who believed, despite Lord Rothermere's angry Press campaign, that to enfranchise young women of between twenty-one and thirty years of age, relatively free, as the great bulk of them would be, of Trade Union influences, could not but prove an electoral asset for their enfranchisers.

But the "progressive" Oppositions did not merely rely on incessant criticism of the alleged follies and blunders of the Conservative Cabinet. Labour polished up a project for a new surtax of two shillings in the pound which would, it was hoped, yield eighty-five million pounds a year, providing the wherewithal, at once, for much varied social reform and yet a balanced Budget, and, best of all, procuring also, it was asserted, considerable benefits even to the less wealthy surtax-payers themselves.[2] The Liberal economists challenged this account of the new wonder-tax as almost fraudulent[3] and pressed their own panacea for curing Britain's principal economic ills, especially Unemployment. Important, indeed, as were many sides of the Liberal Industrial

on cruisers were finally broken off on August 4th when Britain, in America's view, failed to make a reasonable response to important American concessions.

[1] Cf. *The Nation*, September 3, 1927: "Lost trade will not be conjured back by the inoperative goodwill of the last Baldwin speech. Mr. Baldwin might, at least have a private word with his Home Secretary who is making things needlessly worse by turning out of the country Russian trade experts who are here for our good as well as their own . . . on his mere ukase. . . ."

[2] Cf. *Ibid.*, October 15, 1927, for the tax's eventual adoption at the Labour Party's Conference "with the object of liberating revenue for the abolition of taxes on necessaries, for the development of the social services, and for the reduction of the Debt". Mosley's extremist attempt to let the Debt look after itself and claim the whole of the yield for the social services was defeated for obvious reasons.

[3] Cf. *Ibid.*, August 27, 1927, for complaint of patent miscalculations in Labour's assertions and adding: "Such mistakes are only allowed to pass when they yield results convenient to Labour propaganda . . . whether it be pure carelessness or carelessness which is not quite so pure, it is seriously discreditable to the Labour Party."

Inquiry, which had been proceeding for some time, to supplement and complete the Land and Coal Inquiries, its most sensational outcome, politically and electorally, turned out to be the plan for a National Development Programme to combat Unemployment by undertaking large-scale utility works that were already, in many cases, overdue and that, unlike most Relief works of the past, could and should be made to show a commercial yield. Road-construction, Housing, Electricity, Waterways and Docks Development, Forestry and Land-Reclamation were some of the principal operating fields indicated, and, of course, there were minor fields like the extension of the Telephone Services which seemed to offer the same prospect of contractors being set to work on commercial principles and hiring their labour on normal rather than Public Relief lines.[1] Despite the interested jeerings of Liberalism's rivals, the prospect that an Administration as able as the well-remembered Liberal Governments of 1905–14 would be capable, on such a programme as this, of a rapid clearing of the dole-queues had large and growing electoral effects, and there were, besides, the other striking features of the Liberal Industrial Report. The creation of an "Economic General Staff" to warn Ministers of what lay ahead; the constitution of a Ministry of Industry[2] and a Council of Industry with the duty of advising and stimulating industries towards co-operative action in pursuit of efficiency (rationalization was becoming the operative word, and there were some remarkable results on the Continent); major rating "reforms" to take some "unfair" burdens off the back of industry and redistribute them more justly;[3] Consultative Workers'

---

[1] Cf. *The Nation*, April 9th, sketching a "Liberal Programme for Industry", pointing to the wealth of tried talent available in men like Lloyd George, Lord Reading, Lord Buckmaster, Sir John Simon, Sir Herbert Samuel, and Mr. Masterman besides a new generation numbering Keynes, E. D. Simon, H. D. Henderson, Philip Kerr, and, finally, as between Labour's nationalization and Conservatism's private enterprise, suggesting:

"There are a hundred forms of management and control in which the public interest can be safeguarded without the spur of private enterprise being lost. It should be a primary task of the Industrial Inquiry to search, for each case separately, the best of these systems. But, I would repeat, the ideal system will be different in almost every case. In very few cases will it be Whitehall nationalization; in a diminishing number of cases will it be unfettered private control. . . ."

[2] To be set up by renaming the Ministry of Labour and adding to its functions, the administration of the Factory Acts, the Shop Acts, and the Workmen's Compensation Acts, hitherto under the Home Office, and the administration of the Mines Acts, to be transferred from the Board of Trade.

[3] Cf. *Whitaker's Almanack, 1929*, pp. 843–4, for a conveniently quotable short summary: "Our system of local rating was described as far more injurious to industry than our system of national taxation, and the committee proposed that

Councils for all enterprises with over fifty employees and Workers' entitlement to some distribution of surplus profits as Capital Stock;[1] and the Board of National Investment to take over the functions of the National Debt Commissioners and those of the Public Works Loan Board and, pooling all capital resources accruing to Government Departments, to finance new capital expenditure by public boards and other official bodies. It was all this which apparently led to another electoral shift in favour of a Radicalized Liberalism, during 1928, which, like the previous shift of 1927, that had just averted disaster after the renewed Lloyd George-Asquith split of 1926, aroused unending speculation all over the world as to what was really going to happen at the next General Election.

Perhaps, at this stage, a view from the non-party pages of the *Annual Register* might illustrate what shift there was presumed to be, though it is only fair to add that the 1928 *Annual Register* itself showed a very marked interest in *Britain's Industrial Future* as the Report of the Liberal Industrial Committee was called.[2] Its by-election summary of a period with its own acute anxieties for Lloyd George was that in the five months preceding Easter 1928 there had been some loss of Conservative seats and a more or less heavy reduction in the Conservative vote though, according to Conservatives, only the reduction that was normal to a party in its fourth year of Office. The *Annual Register* certainly accepted the Conservative contention that there had been no such landslide away from the Conservatives as the Oppositions had hoped for

---

the relief of the able-bodied poor should be transferred to the State, that the system of grants-in-aid should be extended, that site values should be rated, and that rating areas should be reorganised." As the Government's own major legislation for the year concerned ways and means for giving Industry Rating Relief, some hot discussion developed as to which plan would be more effective, Keynes, for example, attacking Churchill's Exchequer project as inferior in every way.

[1] *Ibid.*, for this convenient summary: "The committee proposed that workers' councils should be compulsory, their functions being mainly consultative but their assent being necessary for works' rules. These councils should receive annually a statement upon the financial condition of the firm as fully as would be offered to the shareholders, together with an explanation of trade prospects, and they would be consulted in regard to welfare work, and on schemes of profit-sharing or ownership. Describing the distribution of the ownership of property or capital as 'so grossly unequal as to constitute a social danger', the Committee suggested that after existing capital had received an adequate return the balance should be shared with 'employees in the form of capital allotments'."

[2] *Annual Register*, 1928, gave two early pages to the *Report* and noted that like *The Land and the Nation* and *Coal and Power* "it represented the standpoint of the Left or Radical wing in the Liberal Party".

and almost felt entitled to expect in view of what they considered the Government's repeated and conspicuous failures. The *Annual Register* noted also that as Labour had been the gainer from the earlier Conservative losses while Liberal polls had shown a slight fall, there was some reason for Lloyd George's perturbation and the view that the "Liberal Revival" might have spent itself. And then had come the Liberal Industrial Report, the gain of two seats at by-elections with the retention of a third, and the return of a spirit of hope to the Party.[1]

By the time the two new Liberal wins of February and March 1928 had taken place at Lancaster and St. Ives,[2] the 1928 Session was in full course. The great Sessional measures were a Budget, closely linked with proposals for a great lifting of rates from Industry, and the Suffrage Bill for enfranchising millions of new women voters. Of course, there were the usual Sessional "sensations"—a new chance, for example, for MacDonald to lay the blame for his "Zinovieff Letter" troubles upon the shoulders of Foreign Office employees in disgrace in the Courts;[3] occasional suggestions (soon shouted down), even from the Labour side, that Baldwin's Cabinet, thoroughly discredited by mass Unemployment though it was, was still capable of winning a General Election, on a minority vote, if Liberal and Labour candidates opposed one another, to Tory advantage, in over five hundred constituencies;[4] the increasing operations of an Industrial Transference Board, which, under a hail of "Red" criticism, was using Treasury Funds with growing skill in transferring redundant pitmen to other areas and even other trades;[5] and the constant grumbling of the "unco guid" every time a piece of news from

[1] *Annual Register*, 1928, p. 35.

[2] Cf. *Whitaker's Almanack* (for 1928 and for 1929) for the Liberal poll at Lancaster having been raised from 11,085 to 14,689 against Conservatism's 12,860 and Labour's 6101. At St. Ives the Liberal win had been secured despite a rival Labour candidature, introduced since the General Election.

[3] Cf. *Hansard*, March 19, 1928, for a new "Red Letter" debate with Labour almost claiming that their Government had been *sabotaged* by the machinations of the now disgraced J. D. Gregory of the Foreign Office.

[4] Many Labour politicians now believed that they, rather than the Tories, would gain from three-cornered contests in which the middle-class vote divided itself between Conservative and Liberal and left Labour at the top of the poll even if on a minority vote. The 1929 Election proved them largely right.

[5] Cf. John Scanlan, *Decline and Fall of the Labour Party*, pp. 146–9, for "Red" bitterness when the next Labour Government, despite criticism when in Opposition (cf. *Hansard*, April 24, 1929 (Clynes)), adopted at least part of the Industrial Transference and Retraining Machinery. The training schemes to allow boys and girls from the "depressed areas" to train as barbers, waiters, valets, and domestic servants was, as can be imagined, under special attack.

Geneva seemed to show a lack of Cabinet zeal for the latest shibboleth on Disarmament, Compulsory Arbitration, Mandates, and International Labour Draft Conventions. The shortsightedness of some of the "enlightened" opinion of the whole 1919–39 period makes one of History's supreme ironies but, for the time being, it certainly served to raise Liberal polls against the Government, and Labour polls even more. Yet all the busy recitation of the "progressive" case against the Government on its League of Nation failings, its retention of "Jix" at the Home Office to perpetrate new police "blunders" or worse,[1] its alleged complacent acceptance of growing destitution on the coalfields[2] as inevitable, and its complete failure to master large-scale Unemployment—all this might have hurt Ministers less if Churchill's bold Industrial Derating projects had made the impact on "public opinion" that was plainly intended when the Chancellor introduced his fourth Budget, on April 24, 1928, in a speech which admittedly ranked very high as a Parliamentary performance.[3]

To explain the relative failure of Industrial Derating to stay, if only for a space, the declining fortunes of the Government, it is, perhaps, worth remembering that Ministers freely admitted that the first rating reliefs could not materialize before October 1929, and even then only after further legislation and much heavy preparatory work.[4] In a season when the discussion of by-elections and by-election results was becoming almost the main concern of Fleet Street, the political clubs and the House of Commons smoking-room, such an admission was treated by the cynics as virtually ruling out any real Conservative chance of an effective improvement of polling-figures whether at ensuing by-elections or at a General Election almost certain to come before October 1929.

[1] Cf. *Whitaker's Almanack, 1929*, p. 472: "July 2, 1928. Home Secretary announced that Viscount Byng had been appointed Commissioner of Metropolitan Police", an announcement which some affected to consider as marking the beginning of an effort to "militarize" the police.

[2] Cf. *Hansard*, March 26, 1928, for the debate initiated by MacDonald on the distress in the coalmining areas among which South Wales was particularly hard-hit and in no mood to take comfort from Neville Chamberlain's account of the Industrial Transference Board's aims and activities.

[3] Cf. *The Nation*, April 28th: "By common consent Mr. Churchill's fourth Budget speech was admirable as a Parliamentary performance."

[4] *Whitaker's Almanack, 1929*, p. 173, for a convenient summary of this part of the Budget speech: "He proposed to accumulate £20,000,000 to £30,000,000 a year for a great operation upon the rates. A Valuation Ascertainment Bill was to be introduced immediately, a new valuation would be made, and later another Bill dealing with the reimbursement of the local authorities would be brought forward."

Moreover, Snowden and Lloyd George as ex-Chancellors set themselves, in the usual fashion of British Opposition politics, to turn every argument good and bad against the Budget, and the hope of Derating as a Conservative asset[1] must have shrunk considerably after Lloyd George, for example, had finished proving that though it might lead the Federation of British Industries, the Mineowners' Association, and the landlords[2] into the promised land, it would certainly leave the vast majority of the people in the desert. There were, of course, some obvious arguments against a major Derating of all Industry especially as many prosperous trades (Brewing and Distilling were two with particular vexations for most "progressives") would be freed from payments, which they could well bear, for beneficial services directly rendered them by local authorities.

But, perhaps, the time has come to allow Radical critics of the Budget to state their case partly in their own words. Their sharp censures will certainly serve to indicate why Mr. Churchill did not do as much for Conservative electoral chances as he had doubtless hoped. The post-Budget number of *The Nation* will be found especially interesting in this regard. After criticizing what it called Mr. Churchill's "Sinking Fund Wangle" as merely the climax of a whole series of window-dressing wangles in the history of his Budgets and hitting out, too because of its effects on transport, at the new petrol-tax proposed of fourpence per gallon,[3] it gave the word to J. M. Keynes who, as a member of the Liberal Industrial Inquiry, pushed its Derating proposals as altogether superior to Mr. Churchill's. As Keynes put it:[4]

Perhaps this is because Mr. Churchill has not yet thought about the problem or discussed it with competent critics, as keenly as we did on the Industrial Committee . . . this Committee in fact went through a

---

[1] Cf. *Annual Register*, 1928, p. 41.

[2] Farm lands and buildings, but not residences, which had already been relieved of three-quarters of their rates, would now be relieved of the whole, while all other industrial production (transport undertakings included) would be relieved of three-quarters, the Exchequer making good the deficiency to the local authorities.

[3] *The Nation*, April 28th: "It is bound to impede the development of motor-'bus services throughout the country and of road-transport generally. Indeed, this is what Mr. Churchill wants to do in order to safeguard the traffic on the railways. . . . It is the private motorist, however, who has most reason to complain. . . . Moreover, there is a general weariness with the policy of multiplying indirect taxes which has been the one consistent feature of Mr. Churchill's Budget policy, and of which he gives us this year another irritating example in the new safeguarding duty on buttons." [4] *Ibid*.

stage almost identical with Mr. Churchill's present state of mind, a proposal to reduce rates on all industrial establishments by 50 per cent (as compared with Mr. Churchill's 75 per cent) being before the Committee in draft. . . . We rejected it for reasons which may be expected to receive increasing attention as the debate—which is going to occupy the rest of this year—continues.

A relief to industry is plausible at first sight because . . . the distressed areas are industrial. But it is wholly remote from the facts to suppose that areas are distressed in proportion as they are industrial. It is notorious, for example, that the highly industrial areas of Southern England and of parts of the Midlands are amongst the least distressed. Accordingly a far greater effect is produced for a given sum of money, if relief is concentrated on those services which fall on certain areas altogether out of proportion to their average weight throughout the country—in particular the relief of the able-bodied poor. The aggregate cost of this relief is not in fact very great for the country as a whole—not more than £15,000,000 in the worst of recent years. Consequently a comparatively small burden on the National Exchequer is capable of affording very great relief where relief is most necessary. Mr. Churchill referred to the Liberal proposal in his speech and tried to rebut it by the cheap clap-trap, which is the usual stock-in-trade of those opposed to Social Reform, about hordes of officials in Whitehall and the lessening of local responsibility. So far as officials are concerned, the criticism is ill-based, because it forgets that the new plan is to be linked up with the existing local organizations of the Labour Exchanges and Unemployment Insurance, so that there would be a consolidation, not an extension, of bureaucracy. . . . As for the lessening of local responsibility, recent experience has shown that there is no question less suited to local autonomy than the scale of relief to the able-bodied poor. It is astonishing to hear a colleague of Neville Chamberlain defending Poplarism.

And so Mr. Keynes continued, insisting, for example, that there was no case for excusing all and every industry, however prosperous, of its proper proportion of such directly-beneficial local expenditure as that on street maintenance, public lighting and police services; insisting, too, that prosperous industry, at least, had not the slightest claim to the immense rating privileges offered where working-class housing was offered nothing at all;[1] and proceeding to castigate Mr. Churchill for his alleged

---

[1] Cf. *Ibid.*, for Keynes reporting the Liberal Industrial Inquiry Committee thus: "whilst we were impressed by the evils resulting from the burdens of rates on industry, we were not less impressed by the wholly disproportionate burdens on working-class houses. We showed that in the case of a working man with a large family the rates may consume nearly 10 per cent of his income, whereas in the case of the rich man they will usually amount to less than 1 per cent."

predilection for substituting block-grants in place of percentage-grants and other Exchequer methods of aiding local authorities. The block-grant, according to Mr. Keynes, left the development of the Health Services as well as the unclassified roads peculiarly at the mercy of shortsighted local "Economy Campaigners", intent only on low rates.

The final shots in Mr. Keynes's fusillade deserve a concluding paragraph to themselves. According to Mr. Keynes, Mr. Churchill was:

ensuring that, so far as possible, all future increases in expenditure due to progress shall fall on the ratepayer rather than on the Exchequer. His measures—so far from relieving the householder from his present excessive burdens—are, therefore, calculated to increase them in the future above what they would otherwise be. The Liberal plan, of an average all-round reduction in the rates of 33 per cent., concentrated on the areas suffering from abnormal unemployment, is designed in such a way as to promote progress in Health and Road Developments; Mr. Churchill's to retard them. Thus Mr. Churchill's plan, so far as he has vouchsafed it to us, bears the marks—to put it mildly—of haste and of reactionary bias. Incidentally he has not provided this year a single penny wherewith to relieve the rates except by raiding the reserves of the Currency Note Issue. . . .

It is, perhaps, plain why the Labour strategists were deciding that in a larger number of three-cornered fights than ever before, Liberals and Conservatives were likely to knock one another out to the profit of Labour, even where Labour was only capable of raising thirty-five to forty per cent of the total poll. There was, indeed, the growing hope of obtaining an absolute majority in the Commons if further "Red" alarms could be prevented and the "general public" tranquillized by an appearance of increasing economic and political reasonableness. It was hardly pure chance, for example, that both Labour and the T.U.C. gave their approval to the continuation of the Mond-Turner conversations on Industrial Peace;[1] that the days lost through strikes fell to the lowest point for years; and that when, in view of Lloyd George's Green

---

[1] Cf. *Whitaker's Almanack, 1929*, p. 472, under January 24, 1928: "Trades Union Congress Council decided to continue discussions with employers' group"; under June 26th: "General Council of Trades Union Congress defeated motion by Mr. George Hicks and Mr. Cook to terminate industrial peace discussions"; and under July 4th: "Joint committee of employers and labour recommended immediate formation of National Industrial Council, of equal representatives of employers and trade unions for consultation and conciliation boards to act in disputes." Thus was Cook's counter-agitation in the *Sunday Worker* (and *Mond Moonshine*) mastered.

and Yellow Books, MacDonald undertook the production of a
rival and superior prospectus in *Labour and the Nation*, the
moderation of its tone agreeably surprised even the austere *Annual
Register*. And when a much-heralded Cook-Maxton-Wheatley
campaign,[1] calling for something a good deal "Redder" than
Mond-Turner or MacDonaldism, failed to affect either the
Trades Union Congress of early September or the Labour Party
Conference of early October, the Labour Leader's grip on his
party seemed restored in a fashion that would have appeared
incredible either in 1925 or 1926. Some of the "Red" sneerers
ascribed the altered attitude towards MacDonald of large numbers of the hitherto semi-mutinous to the nearer prospect of
MacDonald's having the loaves and fishes of office to distribute
again as in 1924. And, indeed, the Labour victory at Halifax in
July, when all Liberal effort failed to save ex-Speaker Whitley's
seat for the party, was to be followed by a gain from the Tories at
Ashton-under-Lyne, in October, with the Liberals, despite their
Yellow Book, at the bottom of the poll.[2] It was so plain that the
three-cornered contest was now giving Labour more than its
proportional share of seats that the search for special reasons for
each separate Labour win no longer had much point. It might be
true that the Labour poll at Ashton, for example, was the higher
for the unwise belligerence shown by Lancashire cotton-employers
earlier in the year when the lock-out had been threatened in a way
earning the total condemnation of Radical economists. But that
did not make it any the less likely that in the course of the next
twelve months a General Election might take place in which
Labour voters would be markedly over-represented and Liberal
and Radical voters both markedly under-represented and denied
a proper balancing function in a State imperilled by a Minority's
ability to boast a Parliamentary Majority. The one Liberal
consolation was the thought that even Conservatives were becoming aware of the possible advantages of conceding Proportional
Representation rather than relying, it might be in vain, on
sufficient Liberal voters turning to them to prevent a Minority
Labour Vote returning a Parliamentary Majority.

[1] Cf. John Scanlan, *Decline and Fall of the Labour Party*, pp. 101–15 for a
chapter, entitled "The Cook-Maxton Campaign", by an insider.
[2] Cf. *Whitaker's Almanack, 1929*, pp. 182–3. The Halifax figures were:
Labour, 17,536; Liberal, 12,585; Conservative, 10,804. At Ashton they were:
Labour, 9567; Conservative, 7161; Liberal, 6874.

CHAPTER XXIII

THE 1929 ELECTIONS

"TERMS OF EMPLOYMENT.

"We also recommend that every firm should be required by law to give to every man taken into its service a printed or written statement of the terms on which he is engaged, including a statement of the grounds upon which, and the way in which, he may be discharged . . . if any man was discharged without being allowed the safeguards provided for, he would have a ground of action in the courts. . . . In Germany a whole system of local Labour Courts has been set up to deal with cases of this character, and . . . has had the effect of giving a real sense of security. . . .

"We shall probably be told that in these proposals we are descending to minutiae, and that at the same time we are threatening to undermine the proper authority of management, which is indispensable for efficiency. Provisions which safeguard men against injustices that may strike at the very foundations of their lives—injustices, moreover, which have been very prevalent, not through malice but through carelessness—can never be trivial. . . ."

From *Britain's Industrial Future* being the Report of the Liberal Industrial Inquiry, 1928.

"In May 1929, when he took office, the numbers of the registered unemployed were 1,132,297. At the end of the first year of his remedies there were 1,770,051, but by that time nobody expected anything from Mr. Thomas. Behind the scenes there was tremendous activity, of course. Sir Oswald Mosley . . . was bombarding the Cabinet with memoranda. . . . Mr. Tom Johnston, at the Scottish Office, was still trying to make Scotland the world's greatest touring centre. Mr. George Lansbury . . . was being partially satisfied in an effort to transform the Serpentine. . . . It was not a happy time for Labour. Back-benchers were grumbling and even growling. . . . When they found nothing could be done swarms of them went off to the Royal Garden Party in disgust."

A "Red" jeers at MacDonald's Government and majority in John Scanlan's *Decline and Fall of the Labour Party*, pp. 169–71.

"In 1929 the Government was firmly seated and popular in many quarters beyond those of its pledged supporters. In

484

1930 it is unsteady, unhappy, and tired even of itself. How has this arisen? The Government has been unlucky at home, no doubt, in encountering the present economic blizzard. But its fundamental weakness has been a lack of courage, and a desire that all men should speak well of it . . . co-operation with Business, big and little, was essential. Business, to do it justice, was quite prepared to play. Mr. Snowden's Budget changed all that. . . .

"The disillusionment is very great. . . . There is no hope of improvement till the Government decides to sack its hide-bound theorists, to stopper its wild men, to foster in every way that combination of good workmen with good middle-class for which the whole nation is longing. Somebody must form that combination; somebody will form it. . . ."

Walter Elliot, a Tory ex-Minister, in the *Daily Mail Year Book*, *1931*.

DURING the autumn of 1928, Lloyd George certainly had a difficult course to steer despite the success with which he had reanimated and Radicalized Liberalism and taken, more and more undisputedly, its Leadership in Parliament and the country. For one thing, by-election figures were again showing that, if the Conservative vote was still weakening, Labour was gaining more as a result than Liberalism. In striking, often more shrewdly than Labour, at the current infelicities of Tory policy and administration—at the end of the summer Tories had been in special trouble over their inadequate representation at Geneva and their antagonization of America by a "secret" Naval deal with France—Radical journalism, for all its experience, seemed, nearly always to be conferring more benefit on Labour than on its own party. Yet Lloyd George, having spent four or five years on the "Liberal Revival" as well as a good deal of his Campaign Fund, had perforce to continue, trusting to the sudden chances that frequently occur in politics and to his own dexterity and experience in turning them to use. After all, when the Conference of the National Liberal Federation gathered at Yarmouth on October 11th, delegates were well aware that MacDonald's critics, at the Labour Conference of the previous week, had charged him with desiring little more than a patching-up of the existing "capitalist system" and had pointed meaningfully to the family resemblance between *Labour and the Nation*[1] and the Lloyd George programmes for Coal, Industry, and the Land. Accordingly, alongside the main Conference activities in confirming Lloyd George in the party Leadership, endorsing the Coal, Land, and Industry programmes, and making provision for a General Election manifesto (which ultimately took the famous form of *We Can Conquer Unemployment*), there was incessant discussion, especially in private, of Liberal-Labour relations.

The stage reached in these discussions, by October 1928, may be indicated by a meaningful passage in the *Annual Register* on the "many members of both parties" who were suggesting the "possibilities of co-operation after if not also before the General Election".[2] The *Annual Register* found Snowden not unfavourable,

---

[1] Cf. John Scanlan, *Decline and Fall of the Labour Party*, pp. 120 ff. for much "Red" derision of MacDonald's effort and his subsequent ingenuity in finding excuses for evading his alleged pledges.

[2] *Annual Register*, 1928, pp. 90–1.

in theory, to the co-operation suggestion though doubtful whether, in practice, anything could be effected till after the next General Election. MacDonald, too, had not expressed hostility but, to the "Reds", the whole discussion was hateful and Lansbury had done his best to bring it to an end by pouring abuse on the Liberal Party in his opening address at the Labour Party Conference. The Liberal Party heard from Lloyd George its Leadership's decisions, and the *Annual Register* noted that there was no mention of any Liberal-Labour working arrangement before the General Election but a concentration of attention upon what was to happen if no party obtained a working majority over the other two and the Liberals held the balance. Liberals would see to it, Lloyd George declared, that the King's Government was carried on but would resist attempts either to destroy Free Trade or to set up Socialism. Yet there would be a vast Parliamentary field on which men of progressive minds could co-operate though it would have to be on terms different from those of 1924, honourable to all and humiliating to none. The *Annual Register* took Lloyd George to be hinting at some Liberal seats in a Labour-dominated Cabinet.

Obviously, the future of party alignments would depend greatly on whether the Baldwin Government could recover some of the support, from outside Conservative limits, which had given it the great majority of October 1924 and which had not really been withdrawn, in favour of Liberalism or Labour, until the alleged mismanagement of its every opportunity since the defeat of the General Strike. Of course, the "general public", assiduously plied with the propaganda of two Oppositions, made no sufficient allowance for Government's undoubted difficulties nor gave Ministers sufficient credit for what they were undertaking, even though that included the final versions of Neville Chamberlain's highly important Rating and Local Government Bills, which were intended to dominate the legislation of the 1928-9 Session. Indeed, when that Session opened on November 6th, both "progressive" Oppositions were still making abundant play, in alleged support of "Peace" and the League of Nations, with the "secret" though abortive Anglo-French arms compromise with which an angry America and a hostile Geneva had been presented as the Anglo-French specific for success in the Preparatory Commission for International Disarmament. And, besides this, there was Unemployment and Coalfield Distress for the foes of the

Cabinet to exploit so that the last Session of the "Baldwin Parliament" opened while newspaper readers were still studying reports of the previous evening's Albert Hall Labour rally, with its blissful conviction of approaching power apparently justified by the latest by-election figures and by Labour's gains at the Municipal polls.[1]

There were plenty of new anxieties for the Government as the Session progressed. Sir Austen Chamberlain's return to the Foreign Office, after a health cruise had been eagerly awaited because his temporary substitute bore part, at any rate, of the blame for Britain's much-censured Disarmament failings, failings that doubtless had something to do with Lloyd George's seven-day "Liberal campaign for peace", opened, on December 8th, at Manchester by the Liberal Leader himself. Yet Austen Chamberlain, too, if he could not be jeered off the scene like Lord Cushendun, was soon under fire because he presumed to link Germany's Reparations performance, soon to undergo the new expert examination that produced the Young Plan, with any right she might have to request Treaty evacuation of the Rhineland.[2] Worse than this, from the Government's point of view, was Ministers' alleged reluctance to come to the aid of the Lord Mayor's Fund to bring help to the Distressed Colliery Areas. There certainly was a case for the Government's view that its Industrial Transference and Emigration Aid activities were of more importance than they were being given credit for, and that the provision of Charity money might very well be left to non-Government Funds in a country like Britain, whose national wealth continued to grow despite the distress which pitmen's own alleged course of continuous folly had finally brought down upon them and their families. Yet the fact that an uneasy and perhaps conscience-stricken Baldwin retreated, step by step, from a position that many Conservatives considered unwise and ultimately agreed to allow the Treasury and the Prince of Wales to take the lead in a big new

[1] Cf. *Annual Register*, 1928, p. 97, for further claim by MacDonald that there would be almost six hundred Labour candidates for Parliament.

[2] Cf. *Ibid.*, pp. 91–6, for a long and significantly unsympathetic treatment of the Government's (and Lord Cushendun's) Disarmament troubles, uncharitably ascribed largely to "its own bungling methods", followed, too, (pp. 113–14) by a scarcely more friendly treatment of the way Sir Austen Chamberlain had declined to allow Labour badgering to commit him to Germany's unconditional right to demand Rhineland evacuation under the Versailles Treaty. Chamberlain, according to the unusually severe comment in the *Annual Register*, "in the end went to Lugano with a free hand—which meant in effect freedom to support the French demands".

drive for helping the Lord Mayor's Fund shows what the Government must be presumed to have lost and Labour to have gained from the whole episode.[1]

Meanwhile the legislative work of the Session had begun with a Cable and Wireless Bill to carry into effect the recommendations of the Imperial Cable and Wireless Conference on inter-Empire communications.[2] The "pressure of big business" and even its "corrupt influence" accounted, according to Labour, for a plan under which the very reverse of nationalization was to be undertaken with the making-over to a Cable and Wireless merger of the Postmaster-General's (ex-German) Pacific, West India, and two Transatlantic cables (conducted, according to the Postmaster-General, at an annual loss of nearly £40,000 over the past four years) as well as the recently-installed Wireless Beam Service. And, doubtless, when the reader of the *Daily Herald* or the Glasgow *Forward* was told that the transfer was being effected on bargain terms for the Marconi Company and disastrous terms for the nation, his sense of dissatisfaction with the effects of "capitalist government" was suitably heightened. And, of course, suspicion was not lacking either as to the ultimate purposes of Neville Chamberlain's immense Local Government Bill, whose 115 Clauses and 12 Schedules, some of them of considerable length themselves, were destined (with their Scottish counterparts) to bulk so largely in the Parliamentary time-table of the 1928-9 Session. If, indeed, Neville Chamberlain's remarkable two and a half hour speech of exposition, when moving the Second Reading late in November, succeeded in overcoming most of the remaining objections on his own side of the House, the case was inevitably different with the two Oppositions, both aware that £24 millions of Derating, £18 millions of it lifted from the back of what were claimed as really depressed industries, would figure largely, at the General Election, as reasons for supporting the Government.

[1] Cf. *Whitaker's Almanack, 1930*, p. 483: "Dec. 17, 1928. Prime Minister announced that Government would give pound for pound for amount subscribed to Lord Mayor's Fund for distress in coalfields. Dec. 25th. In response to Prince of Wales's (the King was gravely ill) broadcast appeal to Christmas parties for Lord Mayor's Fund gifts of £30,000 and £25,000 were sent by Lady Houston and Lord Rothermere."

[2] Cf. *Hansard*, November 21st (A. M. Samuel), for the Government motion for the Second Reading of what figures in the Statute Book as the Imperial Telegraphs Bill. At one stage the Opposition was moving that not less than two and a half millions should be asked for what, it was alleged, was being valued at a mere £450,000.

Liberals claimed that their Yellow Book's scheme of taking Poor Relief off the rates and making it a nationally administered service would be found to answer better than Ministers' plan, and Labour's search for criticisms and objections went so far as to challenge the setting-up, in Scotland, of County Education Committees. Nor would Neville Chamberlain's separate decision to abolish or reduce housing subsidies for the future (as merely tending to raise house-prices) endear his legislation to the average Labour member.[1]

Mr. Chamberlain's massive and useful legislation must be accepted, then, as tending rather to confirm Conservatives in their allegiance for the General Election than to win over critical sections of the electorate to the Government. There was, of course, still another factor on which the Cabinet was entitled to count, a Churchill Budget in mid-April, resoundingly offered and conferring apparently attractive fiscal benefits as near as possible to the polling-date. But till Budget Day arrived on April 15th, manœuvre and counter-manœuvre were plentiful. On January 22nd, for example, the Prime Minister, hardly, it may be supposed with the undivided blessing of the General Staff, threw into the political ring the possibility of a re-examination of the plan for a Channel Tunnel whose construction was undoubtedly capable of absorbing tens of thousands of Unemployed. Only two days later he was giving twelve Newcastle audiences (eleven of them listening in halls wired for broadcasting) his conviction that further Imperial Preference and Safeguarding could confer great benefits on British Industry. Then Sir Herbert Samuel, who had very little use for price-raising Protectionism, however disguised, warned Labour politicians, too, that the Liberals would on no account put them into office again as they had done in 1924. Yet Labour's growing confidence in a remarkable victory seemed justified by two successive by-election gains in late January and early February[2]

---

[1] Cf. *Hansard*, December 12th, for Chamberlain, as Minister of Health, explaining his order for abolishing the 1923 subsidy and for reducing by £25 the subsidy payable under the 1924 scheme. His reasons, he claimed, were not so much the savings entailed as his conviction, derived from experience, that house-prices rose and fell with the subsidy so that subsidy-reduction would make no difference to the rate of house-building. This was, of course, immediately challenged from the Labour side, and a fall in house-prices, after a previous reduction of subsidy in 1926, was ascribed to other causes such as the fall in wages.

[2] Cf. *Whitaker's Almanack, 1930*, p. 484: "Jan. 29. 1929. Labour won North Midlothian from Government. Feb. 7th. South Battersea by-election resulted in another gain to Labour."

and by a number of unrelated events that all spelt increased anxiety for an already troubled Government—a sudden tightening of credit necessitating a Bank Rate of $5\frac{1}{2}$ per cent, a Back-Bench Conservative mutiny compelling an increase of Irish Loyalist compensations, an Employers' mutiny against the Mond-Turner Council of Industry,[1] and, most serious of all, the return of grave disorder to an India[2] aggrieved by the whole manner of leaving her leaders virtually unconsulted when the all-party Simon Commission was appointed in 1927 to consider lines of further constitutional advance.

It was Lloyd George, however, who was to begin setting the electioneering pace from March 1st onwards. Addressing Liberal candidates that day, he asserted that the party was ready with schemes which would "reduce the terrible figures of the workless in the course of a single year to normal proportions" though they would "not add one penny to national or local taxation". In point of fact, Keynes and Henderson of *The Nation* had been occupied for some time in pushing a National Development Plan, capable of absorbing the workless on capital equipment schemes for increasing houses, roads, bridges, electricity supply, telephone supply, land-drainage, and afforestation. Some of the Plan's features had already appeared in the Yellow Book of the Liberal Industrial Inquiry but the Orange Book, as published on March 13th, was virtually a Radical electoral appeal on the theme of *We Can Conquer Unemployment* by the bold policy of National Investment and National Development advocated. There can be no doubting the appeal's political effects, the more so as it was accompanied and supplemented by newspaper-advertising and by what Lloyd George's opponents denounced as "a deluge of pamphlets, adorned by Lloyd George's portrait and financed by his fund". Here is one of the ex-Premier's most formidable Liberal critics on what he considered the over-favourable reception

[1] Cf *Ibid.*, p. 488: "Feb. 13, 1929. Grand Council of Federation of British Industries and Council of National Confederation of Employers' Organizations rejected Mond-Turner proposal for National Joint Industrial Council."

[2] Cf. *Ibid.*, p. 490: "Feb. 12th. Casualties in Bombay riots announced as 112 killed and 400 injured. . . . Mar. 4th. Gandhi and other Nationalist leaders arrested at Calcutta. . . . Mar. 20th. Number of Communists arrested in Bombay and other parts of India. . . . Apr. 8th. Two bombs thrown from public gallery of Indian Legislative Assembly. . . . Apr. 11th. President of Indian Legislative Assembly ruled out of order Public Safety Bill giving Govt. authority to remove non-Indian Communists from India (etc.)."

accorded to the misleading promise, as he saw it, to end exceptional unemployment, within twelve months, "without adding one penny to national or local taxation":[1]

So weak are logic and electioneering human nature, and so credulous are political agents . . . that it was widely thought that this preposterous pledge would "catch on". Politicians who cared for sincerity were quick to dissociate themselves from it. But the Stock Exchange—possibly not the best representative of Liberalism—was said to be greatly impressed. In speculative circles Mr. Lloyd George's stock went up. Liberals of weight and character, while avoiding a pledge which they did not believe in, thought that something might be made of Mr. Lloyd George's proposals. . . . For they felt that he at least rendered a public service in concentrating attention once again on the urgent problem to be solved.

Yet *We Can Conquer Unemployment* obviously had something to do with the by-election gain from Government at Eddisbury on March 20th, followed as it was two days later by a second Liberal gain in Holland with Boston which accompanied a Labour gain from Government in North Lanark.[2] On March 26th, therefore, Mr. Lloyd George could explain his National Development and Investment Policy to an Albert Hall rally in particularly stimulating circumstances while when, on April 8th, Sir Herbert Samuel opened, at Land's End, a campaign destined to take his party's appeal to John o'Groat's, it would seem from Cornwall's later pollings, awarding all five Cornish county seats to Liberals, that there was still plenty of stimulation in the air. A week later Mr. Churchill made his Budget speech,[3] announcing fiscal plans promptly decried as a "bribery Budget" by Mr. Snowden and as

---

[1] Sir Charles Mallet, *Mr. Lloyd George, A Study*, pp. 296–7.

[2] Cf. *Whitaker's Almanack, 1929*, pp. 186, 187, 192, for the 1924 majorities it had been necessary to reverse. At Eddisbury the Conservative vote had been 11,006 against the Liberals' 9,337; at Holland, the voting had been Conservative, 15,549; Labour, 10,689; Liberal, 6413; and North Lanark had given a Conservative vote of 13,880 and a Labour vote of 11,852.

[3] Cf. *Hansard*, April 15th, for Churchill endeavouring to make his Budget speech a message of good cheer. "We all dwell to-day," he asserted, "in a more powerful, more wealthy, more securely founded and more numerous community than we did five years ago." He was much concerned to rebut the charge, frequently levelled against him by the Radicals' *Nation* that, in returning to the Gold Standard in 1925, he had made a major mistake responsible, in itself, for a good part of the troubles of the Export trades. The fall in the cost of living which the restoration of the Gold Standard had permitted was equivalent to a remission of one hundred and sixty millions a year in indirect taxation, according to the Chancellor, while the permanent annual cost of the Debt had fallen by eleven millions.

"electioneering" by Mr. Lloyd George because they provided for the total abolition of the tea-duty, immediate, instead of October, Derating for Agriculture and an end of Railway Passenger Duties in a fashion intended to be both popular and helpful to railway enterprises meeting, for the first time, perilous road-transport competition.[1] Less than a month afterwards, an interim Finance Bill (to be supplemented later) was receiving the Royal Assent so that Parliament could be dissolved and a General Election take place on May 30th. Electioneering, of course, avowed or unavowed, had been proceeding for a long time before the Dissolution of May 10th.

It seems that both Conservatives and Labour men found it necessary to spend a good deal of their energies in explaining away Lloyd George as a political huckster, distrusted by large sections even of his own party, and in explaining away his Unemployment plan similarly, as part piracy from official projects already under consideration and part, risky speculation for electoral ends. It might be wise to give a summary of the objections that were made for, if they failed to prevent Liberalism from winning a huge mass of electoral support, they certainly proved effectual in reducing the gain of seats so low as to destroy any hope of compelling either of the other parties to agree to a sort of Lloyd George-Keynes joint operation against Unemployment. It was, in fact, to be that transatlantic Radical, Franklin Roosevelt, who first obtained a popular mandate enabling him to undertake the mighty campaign to reverse Deflation and stimulate Employment which opened so resoundingly in 1933. Meanwhile Lloyd George's chance of inaugurating something similar in Britain, though only on the far smaller scale that would have sufficed in 1929, was lost in face of criticism from many directions.

It was urged that the Orange Book programme was a mere recapitulation, though one spiced with "crisp rhetoric, lively partisanship and curious calculations", of many schemes, considered by successive Governments over the past few years, to increase housing, expand the provision of roads, bridges, electricity and telephones, and push drainage, afforestation, and other plans. Mr. Lloyd George's experts, it was claimed, had found nothing

[1] *Hansard*, April 15th. The remitted railway passenger duties were assigned a capitalized value of six millions and a half, and the railways were to be expected to spend this sum in developing and modernizing their systems in a fashion expected to appeal to railway-users and railwaymen.

new except how to make political capital out of ideas which the Government could show were in operation already to a considerable extent. And how, too, were 350,000 men to be put quickly on to Road Development when, quite apart from the problem of their housing or that of the ultimate effect of the development on the railways, the surveying work had not yet been done nor the road materials provided for? What, too, of the huge masses of unemployed from indoor occupations, clerks, shop-assistants, printers, textile and pottery workers, and even waiters, unfit for navvying work? And, finally, what was to happen to the huge numbers recruited and paid from Development Loans when a halt was called?[1]

Perhaps the results of the pollings of May 30, 1929 should at once be given. The electorate, now that women had Equal Suffrage, numbered 28,850,000; there had been a seventy-nine per cent poll; 8,669,469 Conservative voters had returned 260 members; 8,416,469 Labour voters had returned 287 members; and 5,260,050 Liberal voters had returned a mere 59 members, only a third of their due on any Proportional system.[2] Amid Labour exultation, Mr. Baldwin resigned and MacDonald, forming his second Cabinet on a much stronger Parliamentary basis than the first, seemed not only in a strong enough position to ban his most formidable "Red" critic, Wheatley,[3] but to have the means of announcing, during the Government's honeymoon period with the Press and the public, a whole series of apparently striking new measures. And while the political gossip-columns concentrated on the new men, their wives, their daughters, their

---

[1] Cf. Sir Charles Mallet, *Mr. Lloyd George, A Study*, pp. 298–300. Mallet, a Liberal ex-Minister, was one of Lloyd George's most persistent critics inside the party. And he was prepared, as is obvious, to accept almost entire the Government's case against Lloyd George as issued in the *Memorandum Prepared by the Treasury under the Direction of the Chancellor of the Exchequer on the Financial Effect of a Development Loan Programme.*

[2] Cf. *Whitaker's Almanack, 1930*, p. 179, for these figures. There are some unimportant variations in other sources due, doubtless, to a different treatment of such things as the unopposed returns.

[3] Cf. Viscount Snowden, *An Autobiography*, ii, 759–60, for MacDonald's decision against the advice of Henderson and Snowden. Lansbury it was decided to put in but only in a position where "he would not have much opportunity of squandering money", the Office of Works. On p. 762, reporting MacDonald's meeting with the National Executive and the Parliamentary Executive, Snowden expressed his surprise at the free hand that MacDonald was allowed in Government-making, not a single question being asked. "Everybody there who was an M.P.," he commented, "evidently hoped that he would be in the new Government, and was afraid to speak."

climb upwards and their presumed policy, the Orange Book seemed to have become merely a speculation that had failed and the Liberals, still holding the balance of power though they did, a party that had tried but not succeeded in expunging a sentence of ultimate doom.[1] What made the Liberal position seem much worse than it was in reality was the consent of one of their best lawyers, Jowitt, to go over to Labour immediately after the General Election and become MacDonald's Attorney-General. When the transaction, moreover, was submitted to Jowitt's constituents at a by-election, the honeymoon spirit, in regard to the new Administration, was still such that Lloyd George apparently decided against putting forward a fresh Liberal candidate in opposition to Jowitt and left the stating of what moral case there was against the new Attorney-General to a Tory and to an Independent.[2] And that the wise course had been chosen at Preston, in July, became obvious in August, when the Liberal candidate, who had polled respectably if not gloriously against "Jix" in suburban Twickenham, tried again after "Jix's" elevation to the Peerage in Baldwin's winding-up honours. His figures were a disaster, many of his General Election supporters having obviously gone over to Labour while all was still ringing "as merry as a marriage bell" for the new Administration.[3]

Of course, *in foro conscientiae*, it was open to Jowitt and the Twickenham Liberals to plead that MacDonald's Government, heavily tilted against the "Reds" as it was,[4] could be accepted as a Radical Government in all but name and that Lloyd George himself could welcome nearly all the policies it was announcing on Unemployment, Disarmament, Free Trade, the School Leaving Age, Colonial Development, Egypt, India, and much else. The pleading could be taken even farther and the case made that, if some Radicals came inside the Labour fence, Radical causes could

[1] Cf. *The Fruits of Folly* (by the author of *The Pomp of Power*), pp. 13–14, which while admitting that Lloyd George had used the soundest tactics, took the result as implying that "everything points to the gradual extinction of the Liberal group".

[2] Cf. *Whitaker's Almanack, 1930*, p. 184. The General Election figures had been: Shaw, Labour, 37,705; Jowitt, Liberal, 31,227; Howitt, Conservative, 29,116; Emmott, Conservative, 27,754; Holden, Independent, 2111. On July 31st, the voting was Jowitt, 35,608; Howitt, 29,168; Holden, 410.

[3] *Ibid.*, p. 188. The General Election had been: "Jix", 21,087; Mason, Labour, 15,121; Paterson, 7246. On August 8th, the voting was: Ferguson, Conservative, 14,705; Mason, Labour, 14,202; Paterson, Liberal, 1920.

[4] Cf. Viscount Snowden, *An Autobiography*, ii, 767, for one treatment of the Government as "overwhelmingly" anti-Red.

be promoted better, revolutionary Socialism combated nearer its source and, finally, the way prepared both for a friendlier Liberal-Labour co-operation than had been achieved in 1924 and for an amendment of Electoral Laws that should not leave Liberals so manifestly under-represented as they were. And, for a space, it even seemed that such justifications might never need to be re-examined. In offering to go to America to arrange an Anglo-American plan for an extension of Naval Disarmament, Mac-Donald seemed to improve vastly, in regard both to Disarmament and Anglo-American relations, on the record of Baldwin and Austen Chamberlain;[1] J. H. Thomas's much-publicized trip to Canada in search of trade-openings, which might help the British Unemployed, was also treated, for a time, as a feather in the new Government's cap;[2] and when Snowden went to the Hague and resisted, as unfair to Britain, some of the suggested Young revisions of the Dawes Reparations scheme, he was widely acclaimed in Britain as a more veritable John Bull than his predecessor at the Exchequer, who had been strongly criticized by Snowden for his "unfavourable" war-finance settlements with France and Italy.[3] And despite the fact that Labour was profiting disproportionately from the existing electoral system, the Cabinet finally decided not to drive the Liberals, in default of a soothing phrase, to the desperate resolution of approaching Baldwin for an Electoral Reform pledge embracing Proportional Representation. A paragraph was put into the King's Speech,[4] and comment added by the Prime Minister from the Front Bench,[5] to allow the pre-

[1] Cf. *Hansard*, July 24th, for the Prime Minister's announcement that Britain and America had agreed upon the principle of parity and that work would be suspended on two cruisers, the building of a submarine depot ship as well as two submarine contracts would be cancelled, etc., etc. It hardly seems that the Admiralty could have been pleased.

[2] Cf. John Scanlan, *Decline and Fall of the Labour Party*, pp. 150–79, for some "Red" irony on the subject.

[3] Cf. Viscount Snowden, *An Autobiography*, ii, 778–838, for Snowden's own complacent account with cartoon reproductions of himself as "The Iron Chancellor" and much else.

[4] Cf. *The Times*, July 3rd, for the closing paragraph immediately before the invocation of the "blessing of Almighty God": "At the recent General Election an extended franchise placed in the hands of the whole of My people of adult years the grave responsibility for guarding the well-being of this nation as a constitutional democracy, and My Government propose to institute an examination of the experiences of the election so that the working of the law relating to parliamentary elections may be brought into conformity with the new conditions."

[5] Cf. Viscount Snowden, *An Autobiography*, ii, 772–3, 884–9, for some sardonic treatment of "MacDonald's habit of falling into Scottish metaphysics"

tence to be made that Liberals' electoral grievances were going to be considered. But how characteristically the Ullswater all-party Conference on Electoral Reform was turned, during the ensuing winter, into a trap both for Lloyd George and Baldwin deserves separate treatment in its own place.

Naturally, even at the height of Labour's summer rejoicings over its return to Downing Street and the Government Benches, there was the possibility of the appearance of an ugly skeleton at the feast. The international banking community did not like the various hints in the King's Speech of new legislation for Coal, "inquiries" into Iron, Steel, and Cotton, amendment of Factory Legislation, increases of National Insurance and Pensions expenditure, repeal of the Trade Disputes and Trade Unions Act of 1927, and the rest of the concessions that were being promised to an already impatient following.[1] Two definite commitments made before the Summer Adjournment could be entered into, on July 26th, proved exceptionally critical—the pledge of July 18th that the school leaving age would be raised to an eventual sixteen as from April 1, 1931,[2] and the pledge of July 23rd that there would be a Bill for the pitmen when Parliament returned in the autumn. Obviously the possibility of a "flight from the pound" by a removal of foreign balances from London must already have been in prospect when Bank Rate was raised as high as $6\frac{1}{2}$ per cent on September 26th. By that time, too, it was obvious that the international banking community suspected that Thomas had found little or nothing for helping the British Unemployed in Canada and that, to make matters worse, it suspected also something of the

whenever he wanted to becloud an issue for his own advantage. A few phrases for Lloyd George, followed by others permitting the wiping-out later of any hint of concession, may here be instanced from his first speech in the new Parliament: "There are the rival plans of a second ballot, an alternative vote, and proportional representation, and there is another group. There is a group who consider that, after all, an election does not begin and end by an accurate mathematical representation in this House of the bodies of electors. . . . That is one view, the static view. . . . But the other view is that the real, final purpose of an election is to elect a Government. . . ."

[1] Cf. John Scanlan, *Decline and Fall of the Labour Party*, p. 125, for some of the more vocally impatient miners' M.P.s.

[2] Cf. *Labour and the Nation* whose 1500 words on Education contained the original Labour pledge: "It will take steps, therefore, to ensure that the task of providing the school places required proceeds without delay, will raise the age of compulsory school attendance to fifteen, with a view to its being raised to sixteen as soon as that further reform shall be practicable, will require local Education authorities to develop maintenance allowances on an adequate scale, and will make the necessary financial provision . . . from national funds." In the event, the pledge proved completely abortive.

Stock Market troubles that were to lead Hatry and Lord Kylsant to the dock.[1]

The Prime Minister, however, had, almost from the moment of his return to Downing Street, early in June, concentrated his principal attention on another field, hoping, doubtless, that a successful and prestige-bringing visit to America and Canada would enable him to dominate the Parliamentary proceedings of the winter of 1929–30 better than if he submitted to the grumbling and prodding of the normal autumn Labour Party Conference. As his disabused Parliamentary Private Secretary was later to put it:[2]

it is a question whether his eagerness to visit America or his wish to leave England was the more insistent. He would be leaving censure and criticism. . . . The Labour Party Conference was to be held in October. If he remained in England, he must attend it and, as Labour Prime Minister, . . . give all sorts of promises as to his future plans and proposals. . . . A visit to America was a very pleasant way of escape . . . he got the maximum publicity. . . . A high-sounding joint statement from President Hoover and the British Premier proclaimed a state of moral disarmament. . . .

But in the extract just quoted, the disabused Parliamentary Private Secretary was, perhaps, in the bitterness of the middle 1930s, hardly able to register adequately what Labour's Premier was thought to have accomplished in ending Anglo-American tension on new Naval Construction and in preparing the way for new Five-Power Disarmament talks.[3] Of course, Conservative

---

[1] Cf. Colin Brooks, *How the Stock Market really Works* for a chapter written in April 1930 and called "Hatry and After". Apparently Hatry's financing of his greatest deal yet—in Steel—was rendered more difficult by the return of Labour to Downing Street in June 1929 and the greater hesitation induced in the City. He finally sanctioned the illegalities, which he just failed to cover up in time, and produced the long Stock market troubles with Associated Automatic Machine Corporation ordinaries; Drapery Trust preference; Far Eastern Photomaton shares and debentures, etc., etc., not to mention Wakefield Corporation 4½ per cent Redeemable stock. Lord Kylsant's mishandling of shipping finance, as treated by Colin Brooks, is in *The Royal Mail Case* of 1932.

[2] L. Macneill Weir, *The Tragedy of Ramsay MacDonald*, pp. 224–9.

[3] Cf. *Whitaker's Almanack, 1930*, p. 491, for such entries as these: "Oct. 4, 1929: Mr. MacDonald and his daughter received tumultuous welcome on landing at New York. . . . Oct. 5th. Mr. MacDonald and the President went to the latter's camp on banks of Rapidan River. Oct. 6th. After further conversations a Five-Power Naval Conference was decided upon. Oct. 7th. Mr. MacDonald in a speech to the Senate declared that war between Britain and the United States was unthinkable. Oct. 9th. Mr. MacDonald and Mr. Hoover issued joint statement declaring that competitive building between Britain and the United States was ended. . . ."

opinion was inclined to suspect all MacDonald's moral gestures as presumably involving an over-ruling of the Admiralty's conceptions of Imperial defence in the interests of a personal and party propaganda success in Britain. Yet the Prime Minister's welcome home was sufficiently warm and wide-spread to lend him some extra moral authority when taking charge of a difficult Parliamentary Session destined to drag on to the beginning of August 1930. And though he had actually been on the other side of the Atlantic when the dangerous Wall Street collapse came in the second half of October,[1] the full import of this for Britain was hidden from him and the world. Indeed, there was a distinct *Schadenfreude* about some Socialist comments on Wall Street's plight, and certainly, among its first effects in Britain was a temporary easing of the strain on sterling so that a Parliament, reassembled on October 29th, could be cheered by a reduction of Bank Rate to 6 per cent two days later. All in all, the atmosphere that allowed more Labour gains to be recorded in the Municipal elections of November 1, 1929 hardly needs detailed comment.

The kind of difficult Session for MacDonald that developed between his return early in November and the final prorogation at the beginning of August 1930 can only be allowed the briefest mention here. Suffice it to say that Lloyd George and Herbert Samuel brought his Government some occasional aid against Conservative attacks on what was, from the Tory point of view, over-indulgent or positively reckless Pensions and Unemployment financing.[2] Snowden's Budget, too, earned warm Liberal approval

---

[1] *Ibid.*: "Oct. 21st. Heavy selling on New York Stock Exchange. . . . Oct. 24th. Further selling in Wall Street was arrested by bankers' support. Oct. 28th. More heavy selling occurred in Wall Street. Oct. 29th. Fortunes lost in renewal of sales of stock." The Prime Minister had, meanwhile, visited Canada and sailed for home from Quebec.

[2] Cf. John Scanlan, *Decline and Fall of the Labour Party*, pp. 134–41, for what Lloyd George and Samuel must have known of the struggle Ministers had put up against much extremer demands from the Back-Benches. Clear pledges, it was there claimed, had been given to the Unemployed and there was no reason for not honouring them fully as the pledge to pay £350 millions in annual interest on War Loan was honoured. Money was found for the Armed Services and even for the pensions "of relatives of long dead generals and courtesans" and could and should be found, it was asserted, to honour the figures for Unemployment benefits and allowances that had been demanded from Baldwin's Government. Besides, there was the very general Labour commitment to abolish the "Not Genuinely Seeking Work Clause" under which the Labour Exchanges had been able to demand, before paying benefit, some tangible proofs of work-seeking and which the Back-Benches chose to treat as harsh and stupid though, in point of fact, the Clause was not often put into force as a reason for withholding payments to those observing Exchange routine.

for the most part and, indeed, with its increase of Beer duties, dropping of Safeguarding imposts and preparations for a Land-Tax Valuation, not to mention its somewhat steeper graduation of the now inevitably heightened Income Tax and Death Duties, it was, as the "Reds" complained, rather a Liberal than a Socialist Budget.[1] On the Coal Mines Bill, however, which made some of the Session's leading "crises", the Liberal Leaders were very critical, Mr. Lloyd George, for example, proclaiming that it seemed to contain the worst features of both Capitalism and Individualism without the redeeming features of either. The Government was defeated by a majority of 8 on March 11th when the dangerous notion of authorizing a levy on coal to subsidize coal-exports was in question. Despite the threats of Dissolution that had circulated, Ministers made sufficient concessions, according to Sir Herbert Samuel, to allow him, at the Report Stage and in view of the London Naval Conference, to abandon opposition, and Mr. Lloyd George echoed the sentiment, on April 3rd, when the Third Reading was carried by 277 to 234. Even so, the Lords were able, during the next three months, to insist on four further concessions from a Government whose prestige had already begun to sink under the burden of a fast-deteriorating Unemployment position, not to mention the imperfect success of its Naval Conference[2] and the failure of its Anglo-Egyptian Conference.[3]

It is time to turn to the Unemployment situation which Labour Ministers had claimed, when electioneering in happy ignorance of impending Hatry and Wall Street crashes, to be able to master

---

[1] Cf. *Hansard*, April 14, 1930, for the revelation of an actual deficit of £14,523,000 instead of an estimated surplus of £4,096,000 which Snowden disclosed early and to which he proceeded to add an apparent further deficit of fourteen and a half millions on National Debt financing. These figures, of course, weakened the case both of the "Red" grumblers calling for big increases of expenditure and of the Tories, criticizing the higher taxes.

[2] Cf. *The Times*, April 23rd, for the signature the previous day of a London Naval Treaty which had failed to yield the much hoped for abolition of the submarine or, for special reasons, to receive the unqualified adhesion of France and Italy. Even as between Britain, the United States, and Japan, there were some disappointing sides to the Treaty as readers, say, of the *Daily Mail Year Book, 1931* were to be made aware in no uncertain tones (pp. 72–80).

[3] Cf. *Whitaker's Almanack, 1931*, p. 505: "May 8, 1930. Negotiations with Egyptian delegates in London broke down, Britain being unable to meet demands with regard to the Soudan." This was a special disappointment to Labour which could consider itself entitled to some gratitude from Egyptians, however Nationalist, for having opened the second MacDonald Government by virtually dismissing the "Imperialist" High Commissioner, Lord Lloyd, and offering to negotiate the termination of British military occupation except in the Canal Zone.

satisfactorily and fairly quickly. By December 16, 1929 the figures of the Unemployed, registered at the Labour Exchanges, were already showing, at 1,334,220, a marked deterioration from what they had been when MacDonald had taken over from Baldwin. But, thereafter, they worsened ever more inexorably and catastrophically—1,520,448 at January 27, 1930; 1,583,102 at February 24th; 1,694,016 at March 24th; 1,760,520 at April 28th; 1,855,898 at May 26th; 1,911,749 at June 23rd; and 2,070,088 at July 21st with the figures still rising.[1] And though an Economic Advisory Council was by this time at work which, with its distinguished panel of industrialists and economists to consult, had something of the style of the Economic General Staff suggested in the Liberal Industrial Report; though Economic Missions were about to proceed to the Far East, to Scandinavia, to South America, and to South Africa and the Rhodesias,[2] there seemed little reason to expect that much more could be done than to prevent the position from deteriorating further. In point of fact, even this modest hope was not realized and the Unemployment figures rose, during the winter of 1930–1, to reach the frightening total of 2,662,842 at January 26, 1931.[3]

Characteristically, MacDonald, while keeping control in his own hands, tried, in June 1930, to involve Baldwin and Lloyd George in a sort of joint responsibility with him for the Unemployment situation by summoning them to confer with him. Baldwin, who, in February, had committed himself to use tariffs, if not food-duties, knew sufficient of MacDonald to avoid the Unemployment consultations if holding himself bound to attend the India meetings that, almost simultaneously, became necessary on the completion of the Simon Report by the all-party Statutory Commission. In any case, to have allowed MacDonald to inveigle him into taking sides on the sorry Unemployment polemics going

---

[1] Cf. *Ibid.*, p. 912, for these figures. By August 1930 cotton alone had 257,879 unemployed, 46·5 per cent of its workers; coal had 253,335 unemployed or 23·6 per cent; and the metal trades of the puddling and rolling mills showed an unemployment percentage of 37·2. Possibly the worst-hit town of its size was Blackburn which had 52·7 per cent of its insured workers unemployed.

[2] *Ibid.*, for a section on the Economic Advisory Council (p. 891). Keynes, Stamp, and Henderson are mentioned among the economists while, on p. 892, details of the Economic Missions are set out.

[3] *Ibid., 1932*, p. 918, which shows also during 1931, shipbuilding reaching an unemployment percentage of 55, steel and iron mills 45, cotton 42, docks 40, and coal 31.

on, inside the Labour Party, between Maxtonites and the "Right Wing" and between Mosley and Thomas,[1] would have been fatal to Baldwin's Leadership, which had again been challenged by Lords Beaverbrook and Rothermere as too weak and compliant. Even when Beaverbrook had been bought off, in March, by a partial commitment to a United Empire policy, Lord Rothermere's decision to keep his mighty Press organs very critical of the Baldwin Leadership made plenty of trouble.[2]

Lloyd George was in a different position from Baldwin for several reasons. For one thing, the strains inside the Labour Party were again becoming notorious enough to revive the gossip of 1925-6 of a possible break-up, with the Labour Right driven to seek the Radical alliance.[3] Then, Lloyd George had the National Development Plan of 1928-9 to push. And, finally, the Ullswater all-party conference on Electoral Reform, which had seen its Labour membership blocking, with some obvious approval from the Leadership, every suggestion not calculated to increase still further Labour's already disproportionate membership of the Commons, would have to be improved upon if MacDonald seriously expected Lloyd George's help. But, perhaps, Lord Ullswater's Report, after he had decided at the end of the Conference's fifteenth sitting, that nothing satisfactory was being accomplished, should be treated in a new chapter.

[1] Cf. Viscount Snowden, *An Autobiography*, ii, 845-7, for Maxton's assertions that 250 annual millions more could be got from the Super-Tax payers if Snowden so resolved.

[2] Cf. *Daily Mail Year Book 1931*, pp. 1-3, for a United Empire policy "whose objectives, besides Protection for British manufactures, included (1) A subsidy for the British farming industry. (2) Ruthless economy in public expenditure. (3) No more surrenders in India and Egypt. (4) No diplomatic relations with Moscow until the Bolshevists conform to civilised standards."

[3] Cf. L. Macneill Weir, *The Tragedy of Ramsay MacDonald*, for a very long section (pp. 231-333) on MacDonald's party problems in the 1930-1 period, immediately preceding his break with his following. Weir, his Parliamentary Private Secretary from 1924 to 1931, frankly admits that though he saw some indications, when the mask was dropped, that MacDonald resented any Labour applause for Lloyd George even when the Liberal was siding with the Government against Tory criticism, astonishment overtook him, too, when he realized, after the break of August 1931, that MacDonald really preferred working with Baldwin and the Tories.

CHAPTER XXIV

LABOUR'S SECOND DISASTER

"You have been told by a spokesman of the Labour Party this week that the resources of the country are enormous and that we have money enough to go on spending to our hearts' content. This is appalling ignorance or wilful deception. It is true the resources of the country are great; but the fact is that they cannot continue to be mortgaged for current expenditure. . . . The majority of the Labour Government, after agreeing to most of the economies, shirked the responsibility of placing the proposals before Parliament. . . . So the National Government was formed to deal with the situation. By drastic economies, and by heavy taxation spread fairly over the whole population, the Budget has been balanced. I know the economies we have had to make are disagreeable. It has been no pleasure to impose them. They were necessary to prevent a far more serious reduction in working-class conditions. They are far less drastic than reductions which the Labour Government of Australia has been compelled to make, and far less than the economies made in Germany. After the cuts have been made the unemployed in this country are far more generously provided for than in any other country. In America they are left to private charity or to beg or starve. After the reduction in unemployment pay the benefits are now 17 per cent more in value than the Labour Government in 1924 considered adequate, and at a time when there was a Budget surplus of £30,000,000—not a deficit of £170,000,000. . . . There is no more stern and unbending Free Trader than I am. . . . The Labour Party is not a Free Trade Party. . . . A month ago the Trade Union Council was preparing a tariff policy. When the General Election became imminent they dropped that in order to pose as an anti-tariff party.

"Mr. Henderson is quoted in the *Daily Herald* this morning as having said that if he were faced with a large cut in unemployment pay or a 20 per cent revenue tariff as an emergency expedient he was going to try the value of that expedient. Now he is denouncing tariffs as an expedient to raise prices and lower wages. . . .

"I hope you have read the Election programme of the Labour Party. It is the most fantastic and impracticable programme ever put before the electors. All the derelict industries are to be taken over by the State, and the tax-payer is to shoulder the losses. The banks and financial houses are to be placed under national ownership and control, which means, I suppose, that they are to be run by a joint committee of the Labour Party and the Trade Union Council. Your investments are to be ordered by some board, and your foreign investments are to be mobilised to finance this madcap policy. This is not Socialism. It is Bolshevism run mad. . . ."

Mr. Snowden's broadcast speech of October 17, 1931, regarded as the most decisive of the Election and therefore responsible, as events proved, for preventing a Labour return to power till 1945.

On July 17, 1930 the ex-Speaker, Viscount Ullswater, who had presided over a three-party Conference on Electoral Reform appointed towards the end of the previous year, reported to the Prime Minister that its proceedings had been abandoned. "No good purpose would be served by prolongation", he found for "no agreement had been reached or was likely to be reached. The Conference could only at the best submit a few resolutions carried on Party lines" that could not "fulfil the purpose which was in view when the Conference was appointed". The then Labour Chancellor of the Exchequer, Philip Snowden, was later to admit quite frankly that it was his own party's representatives who had blocked, in what they regarded as their party's interests, any possibility of result from a Conference to which the sorely under-represented Liberals had suggested Proportional Representation or, failing that, the Alternative Vote. Snowden, a theoretical supporter of Proportional Representation, considered all along that the Parliamentary Labour Party's majority was short-sighted in its eager exploitation of its existing over-representation. Indeed, it was when he was at the height of his popularity, after his "achievements" at the Hague,[1] that his influence was available to help the Electoral Reform Conference slowly to take shape, and even after its failure, he was one of the decisive Cabinet influences to secure the Liberals the promise of an Electoral Reform Bill in return for their Lobby support.

Snowden's views are specially worth noting as they were when, writing in 1934, he had no longer the slightest interest in studying the feelings either of the Labour Back-Benchers or of Ramsay MacDonald. It was then that he said of the Ullswater Conference that, from its commencement, the Labour representatives had "deliberately" set out to render it "abortive".[2] And of MacDonald he remarked that his views altered with the balance of party

[1] Cf. *The Nation*, October 5, 1929: "Something more seems to have occurred than an ordinary swing of the pendulum. The new Government has succeeded for the moment in creating the illusion that it is the State; the Conservatives have not only lost office but they have temporarily disappeared from public life. What is the explanation of these phenomena? The startling rise in the Government's stock is, we think, mainly due to the personality, opinions and achievements of that former Ishmael of politics, Mr. Philip Snowden. In the first place he soothed and conciliated the business world. . . . In the second place, he appealed strongly to the Palmerstonian instincts which are latent in so many of his countrymen by his celebrated stand at the Hague. . . ."

[2] Viscount Snowden, *An Autobiography*, ii, 886–7.

advantage. When a General Election gave his opponents more seats proportionately than their votes entitled them to, he held a change to be desirable. But in 1929, when it was Labour that had obtained the disproportionate advantage, he was reported in the *Manchester Guardian* of June 5th as considering Proportional Representation impracticable and without interest for the Labour Party. Labour's majority had, in fact, been gaining most of the advantages, of late, from the three-cornered contests and Snowden's calculation was that it was the unfortunate Liberals, with 58 seats from the 5,300,000 votes of 1929 instead of the proportionate 140, who had been the principal victims. Conservatives, too, who had polled more votes than Labour but yet found themselves, to begin with, a rather powerless Opposition, had their own grievances, the more so when Labour began pushing its own special brands of "Electoral Reform", all calculated to hamstring the other two parties' traditional electioneering. Permitted Election expenditure was to be reduced much lower; the accounts of the Central Party Funds were to be published, and the sums spent on electioneering were, properly divided among the constituencies, to disallow the same amounts of permitted expense to the candidates; the use of motor-cars to bring voters to the poll was to be made illegal save under very restrictive regulation; the University seats were to go and the businessman's second vote (where he enjoyed it in virtue of business premises in another constituency) was to go too; and, finally, the double-membered boroughs that still survived and made some special problems for Labour[1] were to be carved up, in the name of democratic equality, into single-member divisions. It is hardly surprising to learn that

[1] Cf. *Whitaker's Almanack, 1931*, pp. 183, for the electoral statistics in the boroughs that had been allowed to maintain the two-member system traditional for centuries. There was a certain amount of local attachment to it, and this had been honoured, in 1918, in the case of the borough class entitled to two members on the score of population and still anxious to have both members representative of the entire town—Blackburn, Bolton, Brighton, Derby, Norwich, Oldham, Preston, Southampton, Stockport, Sunderland, and Dundee. This, however, in the eyes of strict egalitarians involved a species of plural suffrage, albeit of a more excusable character than the University- or businessman's second vote, and, besides, facilitated the Liberals' task in trying to bargain with Labour, or alternatively with Conservatism, for separate representation. At Preston, for example, there had been a local Liberal and Labour agreement to nominate only one candidate each against two Tories, and both seats had been won. At Norwich, the Conservatives had agreed to nominate only one but the result was different, a Liberal heading the poll but Labour obtaining the second seat. Here are the figures: Shakespeare, Liberal, 33,974; Smith, Labour, 33,690; Jewson, Labour, 31,040; Fairfax, Conservative, 30,793.

old-fashioned Conservatives were soon declaring that Labour would like to make the sowing of envy and malice among one's neighbours the only permissible political activity.[1]

Of course, Labour's position deteriorated fast and continuously throughout the year 1930 as the Unemployment figures rose remorselessly, and soon MacDonald himself was pleased to make the most of the fact that the Liberal Leaders, if not the Tories, had consented to joint Unemployment conference with Government representatives. There were apparently a number of amicable meetings and discussions between a Liberal team composed of Lloyd George, Lord Lothian, and Seebohm Rowntree and a Labour team composed of the Prime Minister, the Chancellor of the Exchequer, and Vernon Hartshorn, the baffled Thomas's successor as Minister in charge of Employment schemes. This new Liberal-Labour co-operation was to have some strange results. For example, Dr. Addison, who had gone over to Labour some years before, after falling out with Lloyd George, was given his former Leader's strenuous assistance when, as Labour's Minister of Agriculture, he pushed to the Statute Book, against determined opposition, the Agricultural Land Utilization Bill of 1931.[2] And there is Snowden's account of another result—a highly confidential meeting in which discussion passed, on September 18, 1930,[3] to party politics proper by way of prospective Agriculture legislation for 1931 and Lloyd George's urgency for faster Road Development, more Housing and a Board of Business Men to advise the Post Office on profitable openings for bigger

[1] Cf. *The Daily Mail Year Book, 1931*, p. 4, for another version of the "snarl" reserved for more moderate and traditional forms of political activity by "the Clydesiders, the Welsh lambs, the Birmingham group, the furious Midlanders". "The Leaven of Unrest had no use for this at all. Moreover, it was the Leaven which had brought Mr. MacDonald and his Ministers to office. Year after year the Leaven had worked—at street-corners, in dreary gas-lit halls, in committe-rooms, in back-kitchens, and in mass-demonstrations. Here was the day and the hour. Their idea of the seats of the mighty was not to sit in them but to stand on them, and to make, out of all office, a super-soapbox from which a thundering blast might be blown against all the evils of our time."

[2] Cf. *Hansard*, November 13, 1930, for Dr. Addison explaining the proposals when moving the Second Reading—proposals with certain basic resemblances to the Liberals' plans for Rural Land. The Third Reading in the Commons on February 10, 1931, agreed to in a Division of 282–226, and the later struggle with the House of Lords majority, represented almost the achievement of Liberal-Labour harmony. And there was much the same feeling about Dr. Addison's Agricultural Marketing Bill (Cf. *Hansard*, February 9th for Dr. Addison's outline), which joined the first on the Statute Book on July 31st, though less amended by the Peers.

[3] Viscount Snowden, *An Autobiography*, ii, 884ff.

Telephone expansion. According to Snowden, it was Lloyd George who raised party issues when affirming that continued co-operation would prove impossible unless Liberals obtained, in return, not office which was undesired, but fairer Parliamentary representation. And he claimed that the Tories had offered to bargain on Proportional Representation as well as to promise the withdrawal of Tory opposition to all Liberal members who helped to turn Labour out. Lloyd George, however, professed his preference for continued co-operation with Labour provided an Electoral Reform Bill was conceded. The House of Lords, he thought, would reject it which meant that the Liberals would keep the Labour Government in office for the two years necessitated by the Parliament Act procedure "to overcome the obstruction" of the Peers. The one real difficulty Lloyd George foresaw to such an arrangement was the Political Levy legislation to which the Cabinet seemed to be committed in reversal of the "Tory Trade Union Act" of 1927. Most Liberal members would, he thought, be unable to support Labour's Political Levy views but provided Electoral Reform arrangements were agreed, Lloyd George had no doubt that the Liberals would endeavour to prevent the Government's defeat.

Lloyd George could hardly have ventured so direct and thorough-going a demand even a few months before, but much else had been going wrong with Labour's hopes besides the remorselessly mounting Unemployment figures. For one thing, the tension inside the Party between Left and Right was once again reaching dangerous proportions, and the autumn Party Conference promised to be a most difficult one for the Cabinet to manage.[1] The Left, with its spearhead in an I.L.P. which both MacDonald and Snowden had abandoned as hopelessly impracticable, was prepared to argue that well nigh every pledge given in *Labour and the Nation* had been broken or evaded. And even if some "management" helped to keep "broken pledges on Education" off the charge-list until 1931, here is the Left's sufficiently lengthy indictment of Government's courses as it was made before the Llandudno Conference of October 6th–10th:[2]

---

[1] Cf. John Scanlan, *Decline and Fall of the Labour Party*, pp. 180–94, for the "Mosley Memorandum" threatening to add to the Cabinet's expected quota of troubles. Mosley had resigned the Chancellorship of the Duchy of Lancaster when Thomas found his anti-Unemployment plans too risky.

[2] Cf. L. Macneill Weir, *The Tragedy of Ramsay MacDonald*, pp. 245–6.

Labour's Second Disaster

This Conference views with alarm the failure of the Government to apply the bold Unemployment policy outlined in *Labour and the Nation*. It believes this failure to be due to the Government's timidity and vacillation in refusing to apply Socialist remedies . . . it has attempted to alleviate the unemployment situation by the expedient of competition with other manufacturing nations for foreign markets, which, as Socialists, we believe to be not only anti-Socialist in principle but also utterly impracticable of attainment. This Conference, believing that a state of national emergency now exists, instructs the Government to use all its powers towards increasing the purchasing power of the workers, reducing workers' hours, initiating a national housing programme, extending credits to Russia and other countries, and, above all, socializing the basic industries and services, using the provision of work or adequate maintenance as its first basic principle, and, if necessary, to make an appeal to the people.

Fortunately for MacDonald, this proved too extreme for the Conference which turned it down by 1,803,000 against 334,000 though, on the "Mosley Memorandum", the "official" view only triumphed by 1,251,000 against 1,046,000 and on a "means test" for child-maintenance allowances, when the School Leaving Age should be raised, only by 1,336,000 against 872,000.[1]

The Liberal-Labour party bargaining on "Electoral Reform" was apparently conducted between a Labour team of Henderson, Snowden, and Lord Arnold and a Liberal team of Ramsay Muir, Herbert Samuel, and Sir Archibald Sinclair.[2] The Liberals accepted the fact that the Parliamentary Labour Party would never concede them Proportional Representation but might allow the Alternative Vote in return for Liberal support against Conservatism on matters calculated "democratically" to reduce Tory representation. As finally debated in Parliament from the beginning of February 1931,[3] "Electoral Reform" involved the ending of the "plural voting" of University graduates for twelve University seats, not one of them represented by Labour; the ending of the "plural voting" on the business premises qualification except in the City of London (and even there bringing disqualification in respect of place of residence voting); the division of the double-membered boroughs into single-member constituencies; the restriction of the use of motor-cars at elections; and, of course, the Alternative Vote, calculated to help Liberal candidates possibly

[1] Cf. *Whitaker's Almanack, 1931*, p. 898.
[2] Cf. Viscount Snowden, *An Autobiography*, ii, 888.
[3] *Hansard*, February 3rd, for the Division, concluding the two days of Second Reading debate, a Division of 295 against 230.

more than those either of Labour or Conservatism. Thus it was much more conceivable that a Conservative voter would indicate a second preference for a Liberal if his first preference for a Tory would not bring victory just as it was conceivable that even an I.L.P. "Red" might indicate that his Alternative Vote should go to a Liberal if his first preference was unattainable.

A so-called "Electoral Reform" Bill, so obviously representing a "ganging-up" of two not very mutually trustful parties against a third, normally stronger than either of them, would not have been easy to carry at the best of times. As has been seen, Lloyd George expected trouble with the House of Lords, and the necessity, under the Parliament Act, of keeping the Labour Government in office while "Electoral Reform" was pushed through the Commons in 1931, 1932, and 1933. In point of fact, there was a considerable section of Liberal opinion, so doubtful of the wisdom of abolishing University seats as part of a rather dubious bargain with a Labour Government in increasing difficulties, that the abstention of some Liberal members seems to be part of the explanation for the defeat, on March 16th, of University Representation Abolition by 246 votes against 242.[1] As an almost united Liberal Party had just made itself responsible for ruining the Government's Trade Disputes and Trade Unions (Amendment) Bill for restoring the pre-General Strike position,[2] the railing of Labour's "Left" can be imagined almost as easily as the growing Conservative conviction that MacDonald's second Labour Government could

---

[1] *Hansard*, March 16, 1931. It is, of course, worth remembering that Liberals enjoyed a greater share of University representation than of representation in the country as a whole. Of the twelve University seats, they held the Welsh University seat, one of the Scottish University seats, and normally one of the seats for the Combined English Universities though, in 1931, Liberal representation here had taken the form of that Independent crusader for "Family Endowment", Miss Eleanor Rathbone.

[2] Cf. *Ibid.*, January 22nd for Jowitt moving the Bill which Norman Birkett, on behalf of the Liberals, had countered both by asserting that it seemed to make a repetition of the General Strike perfectly legal and by holding that the contracting-in for political levy had justified itself. Stafford Cripps, Government's recently-recruited Solicitor-General, asserted, on January 28th, that the Courts, under the Bill he was supporting would have found the General Strike illegal because its primary object was not industrial and may have helped the Second Reading through by 277 against 250. But in the Standing Committee to which the Bill was referred Dr. Burgin moved and carried the official Liberal Amendment to make illegal any strike or lock-out whose effect would be to expose the community, or any substantial part of it, to danger to health or safety by interfering with the supplies or distribution of essential food, water, fuel, light, medical or sanitary services or other necessities of life. This "wrecking amendment", as Labour called it, was carried on February 26th by 37–31 and the angry Government announced the Bill's abandonment on March 3rd.

hardly survive the year 1931. Indeed, after Lloyd George and the Cabinet had resolved to maintain some co-operation in order to save the rest of "Electoral Reform" not to mention the Agricultural Land (Utilization) Bill and Snowden's expected Budget, it gradually became clearer that the House of Lords might have some part to play in the final *dénouement*. The Peers had already struck a serious blow at the Government when venturing to reject an Education Bill which, according to most of them, was not an Education Bill at all but merely a device to keep children a year longer at school in the supposed interests of the Unemployed. And there were certainly strong grounds for arguing that the great majority of children and parents did not want the Bill; that the extra buildings and teaching force necessary required years of planning and effort; and that the total costs, when the maintenance allowances were added to the rest, would render British Public Finance still more suspect in the eyes of an already doubting world. During July, certainly, the Peers, emboldened by the growingly catastrophic Unemployment position and the increasing distaste of the world's financiers for the melancholy procession of Sessional Bills to increase the borrowing limits of the Unemployment Insurance Fund,[1] handled "Electoral Reform" very drastically. On July 9th, for example, the clauses dealing with the business premises qualification, with plural voting, and with the use of motor-cars were deleted in a fashion that, only a few months before, might well have led to a General Election on the good old cries of "The Peers versus the People" and "End or Mend the Lords". But, as it happened, the Government's own death throes were a good deal nearer than those of the Upper House.

When looking behind the scenes, as it is now possible to do, it is

---

[1] The first Bill received the Royal Assent on December 19, 1930 and raised the borrowing limit of £60,000,000 to £70,000,000. By March a second Bill had become necessary, in view of the approaching exhaustion of the seventy millions, and ninety millions became the limit. On June 22nd, the money resolution was passed which prepared the way for the third Bill to take the borrowing limit to £115,000,000. And on each occasion the banking journals of the world thought themselves to have justification for special criticism especially when the Minister in charge, Miss Bondfield, rebutted the case for increasing contributions and decreasing benefits by alleging that heavily burdened industries could not be asked with safety for their share of increased contributions while the unemployed could not have their standard of living further depressed by a decrease of benefits (*Hansard*, June 22nd). And yet Miss Bondfield was the constant target of the "Reds" for declining to look at their schemes of vast increases of Unemployment expenditure.

astonishing to find how little prepared "progressives" were for the actual débâcle of the summer and autumn of 1931. Snowden, for instance, while declining even to consider a revenue tariff,[1] to help him to deal quickly with his deficit problem, loaded his Budget with a vast and contentious scheme of Land Taxation which could not yield a penny until years of difficult and expensive Valuation had been undertaken.[2] And Lloyd George, who had helped to defeat Conservative opposition, was prepared to encourage a joint Liberal-Labour Free Trade campaign to begin during the autumn of 1931,[3] when, as it proved, the "economic blizzard" had intensified to the point of making Free Trade and persistence with the Land Valuation virtually indefensible. There were some Conservatives, indeed, who saw almost poetic justice in the fact that "so-called progress" was hoisted finally with its own petard. On February 11th, when a Conservative Censure motion had been moved on the basis of some alarming official figures placed before the Royal Commission on Unemployment, Snowden, almost in collusion with the Liberals, had accepted instead a Liberal Amendment asking for "a small and independent committee to make recommendations to Mr. Chancellor of the Exchequer for effecting forthwith all practicable and legitimate reductions in the national expenditure consistent with the efficiency of the

[1] Cf. *Hansard*, April 27th, for Snowden's Budget speech, delayed well past the normal date by the Chancellor's illness. The tariff was still described as a means of relieving the better-off at the expense of the poor, and as an indirect attack on, and reduction of real wages. Yet a growing part of his own party, including as he was well aware both MacDonald and Thomas, found the rigidity of Snowden's attitude increasingly difficult to accept and to justify, and there had been hints even from Radical Liberals with a consistent anti-Protectionist past that, in special cases at least, they were prepared to "safeguard" rather than wait indefinitely for the Tariff Convention that certain foreign interests had suggested as soon as the growing likelihood of the abandonment of Free Trade in Britain had become clear unless concessions were made.

[2] Cf. *Ibid.*, May 4th, for Snowden's admission that between ten and twelve million hereditaments would have to be valued by a large force of valuers who would have to be recruited and could hardly begin work before October. The penny tax for every pound of land value would become payable as from 1933 by which time Snowden hoped the valuation would be complete. His rather optimistic figure for the cost of the valuation was £1,500,000, and when the Opposition challenged almost every feature and assumption of the new Land Tax, Cripps went on record, during the Committee stage, begun, under guillotine-arrangements, on June 8th, that extra staff of only 2000 would be needed. It almost seems, from his language of April 27th, that Snowden hoped to make history with the Land Tax for it was described as a landmark on the road of social and economic progress, and as one further stage towards the emancipation of the people from the tyranny and injustice of the private land monopoly.

[3] Cf. Viscount Snowden, *An Autobiography*, ii, 922-3.

services".[1] The May Committee resulted, so called from its Chairman, a distinguished actuary with important war-services to his credit,[2] and the Report of the May Committee, issued on July 31st and finding that one hundred and twenty millions of economies and new taxation would be necessary to balance the national accounts, produced the Government cleavages which broke up the Cabinet. As Lloyd George's ill-luck would have it, he, who had been waiting for nine years for the chance of co-operating in the new Government-making that proved necessary during August, had just been temporarily removed from the scene. He had been operated upon on July 29th, and the doctors ordered four months rest afterwards.[3]

The world's financial community had, naturally, had its anxieties about the British Exchequer and the Bank of England long before the May Report and, indeed, there have been those who have assigned greater importance to André Siegfried's friendly but penetrating indictment, *England's Crisis*,[4] since that work raised the question of whether a kind of national degeneracy might not have set in.[5] Yet the fact that the London money-market had long specialized in "borrowing short" and "lending long" could not but cause growing uneasiness among those who had traditionally used London as their short-term safe-deposit but now heard increasing rumours of dangerous difficulties. Those difficulties lay not merely in the shattering Unemployment figures, the decline in Exports, and the mounting deficits of the

---

[1] Cf. L. Macneill Weir, *The Tragedy of Ramsay MacDonald*, pp. 274–86, for two chapters on the debate and the immediate results. The author, then the Prime Minister's Parliamentary Private Secretary, was convinced that Snowden would have liked to put some Unemployment economies into his Budget but was deterred by what took place at the Parliamentary Labour Party's meeting following the debate.

[2] *Who's Who, 1931*, p. 2154, for Sir George Ernest May listed as "Member of the Council of the Institute of Actuaries; Secretary to the Prudential Assurance Co.; . . . Manager of the American Dollar Securities Committee, 1916–18; D.Q.M.G. Canteens, War Office, 1917–19; Director British Overseas Bank."

[3] *Whitaker's Almanack, 1932*, p. 503.

[4] The short title of the English translation of *La crise britannique au XXe siècle*.

[5] It is only fair to add that Dean Inge had already put the question in a series of works, most critical of democracy, its political leaders, and its trade unions, works, too, which had undoubted effects. The *Outspoken Essays* of 1919; the *Second Series* of 1922; the *England* and *The Lay thoughts of a Dean* of 1926; and *The Assessments and Anticipations* of 1929 had already made Inge "the gloomy Dean" well before the onset of Britain's worst post-war troubles. And, on a somewhat lower level, Sir Ernest Benn had joined in with writing like the *Prosperity and Politics* of 1924; *The Confessions of a Capitalist* of 1925; and *Account Rendered, 1900–1930* of 1930.

Unemployment Fund but in London's inevitable involvement in every major money-crisis. Thus the Austrian bank-crisis of June necessitated, after France had declined the risks, a Bank of England loan to the Vienna Government.[1] Germany, plagued by much worse unemployment and much more perilous politics than Britain, reached the high-point of bank-crisis in July.[2] And that the May Report should suggest, as essential to a balanced Budget, such politically inoperable measures, it seemed, as a saving of sixty-six and a half millions on Unemployment Insurance payments by reducing benefits, increasing contributions, and applying a Means Test to certain categories of recipients, completed the alarm of those who had already begun a "flight from the pound". On August 1st, it had to be announced that the Bank of France and the Federal Reserve Bank of New York had each agreed to place a credit of twenty-five million pounds at the Bank of England's disposal. Yet the "flight from the pound" continued,[3] and before long a further eighty million pounds had to be borrowed, and again in vain. Meanwhile, in an attempt to reassure home and foreign bankers, a Cabinet Economy Committee had been set to work on August 12th, and the Liberal and Conservative Leaders invited for consultation on August 13th. Yet Henderson in the full Cabinet and Bevin in the T.U.C. led a stand against the modified Economy cuts for which the Prime Minister and Chancellor were prepared, and the Government broke up on August 23rd.[4] There were those in the Labour Party who, despite the crisis atmosphere at the Bank and at the Exchequer, both desperate to secure the new Franco-American credit for eighty millions, believed that the outcome would be a summons to Baldwin to take over the difficulties and dangers of forming a new Government.[5]

[1] Cf. *Whitaker's Almanack, 1932*, p. 512, under June 17, 1931.

[2] *Ibid.*, p. 511, under July 13, 1931: "Darmstadter and National Bank closed down. Run on all banks followed. . . ."

[3] It seems obvious that much British money was now joining in the flight, the property of citizens with no confidence at all in the financial acumen of the average Labour M.P., let alone his sense of justice towards anyone unlikely to register a Labour vote.

[4] Cf. Viscount Snowden, *An Autobiography*, ii, 942–3, for Bevin and Citrine voicing the T.U.C.'s objections to any attempt to reduce or limit Unemployment expenditure and their objections, also, to pay-cuts for the Services and the teachers (if not for Judges and Ministers of the Crown). There was apparently, in their view, no need for economies since, according to the sardonic Snowden, everything necessary was obtainable by suspending the Sinking Fund and increasing direct taxation.

[5] *Ibid.*, pp. 951–2, for his frank admission that he left the Cabinet meeting at 10.40 p.m. on the Sunday in the belief that the result of the resignation of the

Such a Government, Labour optimists hoped, after perilously but vainly attempting to enact the May Economy cuts, would be forced to make way for a Henderson Administration, which, if it dissolved at the right moment, might well, with the aid of the Unemployed, the Teachers, the Service men, and the kinsfolk of all those and other affected interests, not to mention the Unions and the T.U.C., give Labour its first independent majority.[1]

Before recounting how political visions of this type were frustrated by events, it is, perhaps, worth remembering that, but for Lloyd George's being laid aside by illness, things might not have been allowed to reach their pass of August 23rd without some attempted counter-action on his part. He had been engaged for years in a Radical effort to establish some Liberal-Labour co-operation, on a fair basis, and would, at this stage, undoubtedly have been readier to move into a Liberal-Labour crisis-Government than into a National Administration containing Baldwin and Neville Chamberlain. But Herbert Samuel was hardly in a strong enough position to take an initiative which might have been open to Lloyd George, and affairs, between August 13th and 23rd, moved to the point where Baldwin, and his massive block of 260 votes to throw for Economy, became an ever-increasing factor in the calculations of MacDonald and Snowden.

The events which followed the Labour Government's break-up on August 23rd, after a Cabinet majority had declined to follow the Prime Minister's view of what the situation demanded, have themselves become the subject of controversy. It has been asked, for example, whether George V had any constitutional right to entrust MacDonald with the formation of a new Government[2]

Labour Cabinet would be that Mr. Baldwin would be asked to form a Government, and with the help of the Liberals would carry measures of economy and additional taxation which would balance the Budget and restore financial stability.

[1] *Ibid.*, p. 958, for Snowden hearing that Mr. Henderson and his colleagues were confident that their action in declining to make a reduction in the Unemployment benefits would assure them a majority. They argued that there were about three million unemployed voters, and these with their families and the Trade Union movement as a whole would vote solidly for the Labour Party.

[2] Cf. Harold Nicolson, *King George V*, p. 466 n., for some apparent sensitiveness at Court on the issue as quickly raised by Professor Laski in some "notorious" writing. It appears from the *Holmes-Laski Correspondence* that the King's Private Secretary tried to convince the Professor that his views were unfounded but Laski's preoccupation with biased uses of the Royal Prerogative remained, and there were several occasions, before 1945, when he was inclined to suspect that Royal powers would be available to complete the sabotaging, by anti-Socialist elements, of future Labour programmes, drafted by Cabinets more

seeing that it was Mr. Henderson who now commanded the confidence of the overwhelming majority of the Labour members in virtue of whose numbers Mr. MacDonald had received his initial mandate. But the Sovereign had the justification of having taken counsel, on Mr. MacDonald's advice, with the Conservative and Liberal Leaders, Baldwin and Samuel,[1] and of having gathered both their willingness to serve under MacDonald and their ability to provide a majority for the Emergency Government and the Emergency Programme which they all thought necessary. The memory of the fatal post-war currency collapses on the Continent, moreover, was sufficiently vivid to forward the quick constitution of a crisis-Cabinet of ten which speedily took up the task of deciding how much further "Economy" would have to be taken than the Labour Cabinet's majority had been willing to go. The fact, too, that Parliament was in recess and some 260 anti-MacDonald Labour M.P.s temporarily off the scene of action was a help to the new Ministers, and so also seemed the eighty millions of Franco-American credit made available to continue the attempt to stay the "flight from the pound".[2]

Virtually the entire Liberal Party from the "advanced Radicals" to the "moderates" of the Liberal Council (and including Lloyd George on his convalescent bed) had approved the course Samuel had so far taken. And, in the abstract, there was a lively enough pleasure that Liberal influences and personalities were to return to the seats of Government earlier than had been expected and, in view of their holding the balance of Parliamentary power, in

zealous than MacDonald's had ever been. Yet the kind of emergency powers that Laski sometimes dreamed of, as proper for Socialist Governments to take against unfriendly forces in the City, the Services, the Carlton Club, and the Court, might have brought a countering British Fascism much nearer to power than it ever came.

[1] Cf. Viscount Samuel, *Memoirs*, pp. 221–2: "Mr. MacDonald's resignation was the necessary consequence of an irreconcilable division in the Cabinet. The King then acted in strict accordance with precedent in following the advice of the outgoing Premier; that was to bring into consultation the spokesmen of the two Parties which together could furnish a majority in the House of Commons able to sustain a new Administration. The invitation to the Prime Minister to return to office, and to form a new Administration on an all-party basis, was the course advised by them . . . neither directly nor indirectly, did any expression reach me of any personal opinion or wish of His Majesty."

[2] *Whitaker's Almanack, 1932*, p. 503: "August 26, 1931: New Ministers received seals of office from the King and held first Cabinet. Joint meeting of Trades Union Congress General Council, executive of Labour Party and Parliamentary Labour Party committee decided to oppose new Government. . . . August 28th: France and United States each placed credit of £40,000,000 at disposal of Treasury."

probably more than their proportionate numbers. Moreover, quite apart from the immediate Economy crisis, there were all manner of subjects from the India Round Table Conference, just regathering,[1] to Schools Reorganization and the Churches[2] on which, it seemed, that a firmly-voiced Radicalism could do better for the "cause of progress" than the maudlin sentimentalism, on behalf of the "masses", so wearisomely and so unnecessarily imported into every practical discussion by the late Government's Back-Benchers and by some of its Front-Benchers too. But what opportunity there was to heal the divisions in a badly-split party proved unavailing, and one day the full story may well be told of how Lloyd George's being laid aside by illness and yet resenting most decisions necessarily taken in his absence, played its part in the final disastrous consummation. In short, Liberals after helping to carry the Economy programme in September 1931, fought the General Election that followed in October, divided into three sundered groups. The group, nicknamed the "Samuelites" and strongly represented in the Government, regarded themselves as the special guardians of the party's Radical traditions and of Free Trade. A second group, which criticized, among other things, the Samuelites' refusal, whatever the need, to budge an inch from the straitest Free Trade orthodoxy, was nicknamed, from their leader, the "Simonites" and, returning from the elections (thanks to some Tory benevolence) at least as strong as the "Samuelites" demanded and obtained virtually equal representation in the "National Government" as reconstituted after the sensational Labour defeats of the 1931 General Election.[3] And the third group was constituted

---

[1] Cf. *The Nation*, January 4, 1930, for the kind of article on India ("Lahore and After") whose strong criticism of Indian extremism had had its effect. Even Gandhi had not been spared—"that veteran saint (whose motives it is doubtless impious to analyse but whose activities it may none the less be a duty to resist)", and his arrival for the Round Table Conference in September 1931 was one of the events of the year in Britain as the Irwin-Gandhi conversations with the Viceroy, which had preceded it, had been in India.

[2] Cf. *Ibid.*, February 15, 1930, for a full-blooded attack on Catholic Churchmen's threats to hold up Hadow Senior School reorganization until their own financial demands for Catholic Senior Schools had been met in full (a threat actually carried out when thirty-five Labour M.P.s, some Catholics and some influenced by Catholic constituency pressure, destroyed their Government's Education Bill in the Scurr Amendment of January 21, 1931). *The Nation's* article, entitled "The Pope Speaks Out", contained so strong an attack on the Papal Encyclical on schools lately published, as almost to recall the "popular" anti-Popery long frowned upon by "progressives".

[3] Cf. *Whitaker's Almanack, 1932*, p. 181, which gave the Samuelites 86 candidates; the Simonites 40, and the Lloyd George group 34. The Samuelite electorate was 1,332,000; the Simonite 870,000; and the Lloyd George 346,000

when Lloyd George, baffled and irritated by his failure to maintain any control of events, decided, in alleged defence of Free Trade, marked out, he claimed, for destruction after the General Election, to throw his personal influence against the National Government's Election chances.[1] It was a fatal invalid's caprice which not only ended his Leadership of the Party[2] but destroyed the results of the immense efforts that had gone into the task of reconstituting a fighting Radicalism under his command. Of course, attempts to revive the Radical tradition have been constant since then from Herbert Samuel's to Joseph Grimond's. But no Leader of Lloyd George's possibilities has ever been available again, and, of course, the new Liberal "splits" of 1931 did not serve to stop, still less to reverse, the slow drift of Liberalism's more energetic and ambitious Radicals towards Labour.

Many plausible justifications have been advanced for the Radicals who drifted into the Labour camp between the 1930s and the 1950s. And whereas the drifters of the 1930s could complain of the erratic personal politics of Lloyd George,[3] the Free Trade stiffness of Herbert Samuel, and the unfortunate Foreign Office tenure of Sir John Simon between 1931 and 1935,[4] such drifters

with a yield of 35 Simonites, 33 Samuelites, and 4 Lloyd George. It was noticed, of course, that Simon was allowed a free run against his Labour opponent, untroubled by Conservative intervention whereas Samuel suffered a dangerous Conservative intervention because of his strong stand against Tariff Reform.

[1] Despite a personal appeal from the Prime Minister, who made a special journey to Churt on October 5th, after being exhorted thereto in a Winston Churchill article in the *Daily Mail* of October 2nd.

[2] Cf. *Whitaker's Almanack, 1933*, p. 575: "Nov. 4, 1931. Sir Herbert Samuel appointed leader of Liberal Parliamentary Party in place of Mr. Lloyd George."

[3] A great deal of what was left in Lloyd George's Political Fund was being spent in 1935 on raising a Council of Action movement which Ministers regarded as hostile to them on nearly every aspect of Home and Foreign policy, and especially in its over-simplification—on Peace Ballot of 1934 lines—of Disarmament and League of Nations issues at a time when dangers from Mussolini, Hitler, and Japan were growing very fast. Labour undoubtedly got some profit from the net results of £400,000 worth of Fund expenditure but then came, almost as a *volte-face*, the visit to Hitler's Germany and a personal discussion, on September 4, 1936, with the Führer. One day, it will be possible to learn whether German discussions of 1940–1 on what to do with a conquered Britain gave some heed to the possibility of making a Pétain-like use of Lloyd George and whether Lloyd George himself, in refusing Cabinet office from Churchill, had not in mind some ultimate reservation of himself for a supreme crisis.

[4] Cf. L. S. Amery, *The Unforgiving Years, 1929–1940*, p. 167, for a brother-Privy Councillor on Simon's mistaken and ultimately ruinous silence at Stresa on Abyssinia. In Amery's view Simon had deliberately decided to avoid complicating the European discussions at Stresa by leaving Abyssinia till it came up at Geneva on the appeal of the Ethiopian Emperor when, as in the Manchurian

of the 1950s as Dingle Foot and Megan Lloyd George were apt to complain that Liberalism has ceased to be a party of movement and of Radical protest. Unfortunately, it is only too true that the Labour Party, and the Trade Union movement on which it is largely based, need forceful Radical criticism almost as much as any institutions in Britain, and, of course, Radical recruits from the professional classes, suspected of having gone over to Labour with Ministerial ambitions in mind, are the last persons from whom criticism of the Unions or of the Party would be tolerated. Yet here is the impression that the Labour electioneering of 1929 is reported by Professor Ramsay Muir to have made:[1]

Nearly all the ardent Radicals at the Summer School had come out of the General Election with a deeper distaste and dislike for the Labour Party. The sources of this feeling are, in the main, three.

(1) The popular propaganda by which they get their votes still rests largely upon the crudest denunciation of "capitalism" . . . a preaching of hatred against all who own capital.

(2) The Labour Party is financed and controlled by the Trade Unions. It is wrong that organized economic interests should wield political power, as they do when a ruling party is directly dependent upon them for its resources. It is just as wrong in the case of the Trade Unions as it was in the case of landlords. Moreover the Trade Unions often exercise a real tyranny over their members which is as dangerous and illiberal as the tyranny which landlords used to exercise (and sometimes still exercise) over their tenants and labourers.

(3) The Labour Party has proved to be a corrupting element in national life, owing to the reckless and unrealizable promises with which its members strive to buy votes.

It is a revelation of the shortcomings of Labour and the Trade Unions to realize that Ramsay Muir almost gave his life in the 1920s and early 1930s not only to a revivification of Radicalism but to the effort to keep it ready and willing to work in double harness with Labour.

Perhaps one more instance should be given of why, for decade after decade, important Radical elements have found it impossible, even for very alluring ends, to consent to slip into the Labour case, a time-gaining inquiry could have been forwarded and, perhaps, an ultimate compromise. Of course, Mussolini took the silence at Stresa (a conference of Britain, France, and Italy, opened on April 11, 1935 and much centred on whether Italy was to be relied on any more to co-operate in resisting the growing Hitlerite pressure in every direction from the Saar in the West to Danzig, Memel, and Austria in the East) as almost a tacit offer not to oppose his African ambitions if he continued co-operation in Europe.

[1] *The Nation*, August 17, 1929

camp, virtually committed to silence on Trade Union abuses and
lax Public Finance in the supposed interests of the working man
and the poor. The name of J. M. Keynes stands very high indeed
among those of the "progressive" thinkers of the 1920s, 1930s,
and 1940s, and during his control of the Radicals' leading weekly,
The Nation, between 1923 and 1931, he worked hard to make it of
use in securing a "progressive" Liberal-Labour alliance, capable
of undertaking a good deal of "advance" in the national affairs. In
the end, he accepted and carried through to success for the Attlee
Government a Loan Mission to Washington for unprecedented
sums which American financiers and politicians were much
readier to discuss with him than they would have been to discuss
them either with a conventional City banker or with one of
Attlee's party hacks. Yet anxious though he always was to work
with Labour if and when he could, anxious to the point of finally
agreeing to the amalgamation of *The Nation* with the *New Statesman* at a time when Lloyd George's relations with Labour were
growing closer,[1] he none the less could not, and would not,
tolerate financial abuses. Here, then, is *The Nation* of December
6, 1930 rebuking Labour for Dole laxity which it refused to have
touched and joining in the growing discussion of the necessity for
a National Government:[2]

The strongest count against the present Government is its failure
to grapple with the abuses of the dole. Miss Bondfield put up a gallant

[1] It may, of course, be surmised that there were other reasons, personal and
financial. Yet *The Nation*'s last number, that of February 21, 1931, said this:
"Our readers are invited to a marriage and a christening, not to a funeral. The
moment is opportune for the union of an independent journal which has given
critical support to the Liberal Party with an independent journal which has
given critical support to the Labour Party. Parliamentary events last week
pointed strongly in the direction of a Liberal-Labour alliance, which, if steadily
developed with common sense and good will on both sides may postpone the
General Election for another two years, and even secure a Conservative defeat
at the end of that period."
[2] The article appeared under the title, "The Call for a National Government". And it is worth remarking that in the very *Nation* number announcing
its merger in the future *New Statesman and Nation* (February 21, 1931), there
was still the following reproof and dire prognostication for the average Labour
Back-Bencher: "The Budget and the Dole seem more likely to split the Labour
Party than to form a barrier between the [Liberal and Labour] Parties. Mr.
Snowden's economy kite produced such a storm among the Back-Benchers, that
various Ministers have hastened to explain it away. It would be comic, if it
were not so dangerous, to observe that a revolt is threatened if the Government
do not reject the advice of the Royal Commission on Unemployment Insurance
before that body has even begun to prepare its Report. Meanwhile, the borrowing powers of the Insurance Fund have been raised from £70 millions to
£90 millions."

fight on the administrative side, and is disarmingly frank in the House of Commons ... but she cannot justify the Act of 1930 or the reluctance to amend it, or the side-tracking of the three-party Committee, or the delay in appointing a Royal Commission, if it is necessary to appoint one. Indeed, her speech in introducing the Resolution to increase the borrowing powers of the Insurance Fund to £70 millions provided enough evidence to insure the conviction of the Government before any impartial tribunal. . . . The most serious part of Miss Bondfield's speech was, however, that in which she described the development of short-time working by arrangement. . . . Later in the debate, Sir Henry Betterton quoted a case of 1,400 coal-trimmers at Cardiff whose earnings average over £4 a week for working a 3½-day week, and each week, on the average, over half of them establish a claim for unemployment benefit. . . . The cumulative effect of a system of this kind is appalling. Like measures of tax-avoidance, the devices for exploiting unemployment insurance take time to spread. Many employers and employees are only just beginning to realize the possibilities. . . . It is not the comparatively few cases in which benefit is illegally obtained that matter; it is the legal abuses that are increasing and perpetuating unemployment which will ruin Britain if they are allowed to work themselves out to their full extent. Here is the national emergency. Here is the real need for a National Government which will have the courage to act firmly and without delay.

In conclusion, it may well be doubted whether the possibility that existed during the whole period between 1925 and 1931 of a new Radicalism being formed by a junction of Labour's Right and Radical Liberalism will ever recur. For one thing, Liberalism's Parliamentary strength has been steadily sinking to the point where it can hardly play the slightest part in attracting Labour's often hard-pressed constitutionalists to thoughts of breaking away completely from Leftists anxious to contrive or force a complete breach with the past. And, of course, even Labour constitutionalists have the habit of affirming that Lloyd George's Radical Leadership of 1927–31 showed a far greater sense of the direction in which Destiny was moving than all the subsequent Leaderships of Herbert Samuel, Archibald Sinclair, Clement Davies, and Joseph Grimond, preoccupied as they all allegedly were with obsolescent issues from Free Trade and Temperance Reform to Assisted House-Ownership and Employee Profit-Sharing. Liberals are naturally irritated by assumptions that the necessary roads of "progress" are only to such destinations as the Municipalization of all Rented Housing, the Nationalization of increasing blocks of Industry, and the steady expansion of "closed shops" and

Comprehensive Schools. There seems little real desire left among the survivors of the old Radicalism to contemplate absorption into a party with policies, plainly threatening the individual with tighter and more doctrinaire controls than those of the oligarchies from which Radicalism had helped to rescue him in the past.

CHAPTER XXV

DECLINE AND FALL OF FREE TRADE

"PROTECTION IN FORCE. The full transformation in the nation's fiscal policy was made by the Import Duties Bill, which was outlined by Mr. Neville Chamberlain in the House of Commons on February 4th. . . . The Chancellor said that the position had improved since the National Government came into existence. . . . But the nation had not really turned the corner. The unemployment figures remained of colossal dimensions. . . . An examination of the trade figures showed that a surplus of £100,000,000 in 1929 had been turned into an adverse balance of £113,000,000 in 1931. . . . The Government desired to correct the balance of payments by diminishing imports and stimulating exports and to fortify the country's finances by raising fresh revenue. They proposed by a system of moderate protection, scientifically adjusted . . . to transfer to British factories and British fields work which was now done elsewhere, and thereby decrease unemployment. The basis of their proposals was a general *ad valorem* duty of 10 per cent . . . there would be a free list, to include wheat in grain, meat, raw cotton and raw wool. . . . An independent advisory committee was to be set up to consider what non-essential articles should be subject to additional duties. . . . So far as the Dominions were concerned, neither the general nor the additional duties would become operative before the Ottawa Conference. . . . The Chancellor said that if foreign countries discriminated against British goods, the Board of Trade would be authorised to impose duties up to 100 per cent upon goods from those countries, but he hoped it would never be necessary. Power to give reciprocal lowering of tariff barriers to foreign countries would also be provided . . . the feature of the debate was the criticism directed to the new policy by the Home Secretary, Sir Herbert Samuel, who with three other Free Trade Ministers had been unable to accept the Government's plan, but at the Prime Minister's request had remained in the Cabinet . . . on February 29th the Bill . . . received the Royal Assent."

The End of the Free Trade era as reported in *Whitaker's Almanack*, 1933, pp. 256–7.

FROM the time of Chamberlain's launching of the Tariff Reform movement in 1903, Radicals became more and more concerned with the danger to Free Trade. This danger, though apparently repulsed triumphantly in the General Elections of 1906, 1909, and 1910, could never be regarded as over whilst the great bulk of the Conservative Party, large bodies of manufacturers and, often enough, considerable sections of workers, in industries particularly affected by foreign competition, continued critical of Free Trade. And it was never easy to explain away the plain man's apparently "common sense" view that free entry to the British market should not be allowed to foreign products, that competed with British-made goods, unless some measure of reciprocity was obtained by Britain. The electoral victories of 1906, 1909, and 1910, indeed, had been won, not because the average voter had been persuaded to accept the eternal validity of "Cobdenism", but because Tariff Reform, as pressed by Chamberlain and his disciples, offered what seemed to many a remedy worse than the disease. Involved Imperial Preference arrangements were suggested under which Canada, for example, in return for offering British exports tariff advantages, would have expected, say, the taxation of American corn and pork entering the British market while its own continued to enter duty-free. It is not surprising that all consumers of food and raw materials could be scared when summoned by the *Daily News*, the *Daily Chronicle*, the *Morning Leader*, the *Star*, and the rest, to contemplate the price-rises that would result from Canada's presumed action on bread and pork and the parallel action to be expected from Australia and New Zealand on Argentine and American chilled meats, from the British West Indies on Cuban sugar, from India on American raw cotton, from Canada on Baltic timbers and wood pulp, from New Zealand on Dutch and Danish dairy-products, and from a variety of lesser colonial interests interested in replacing, with the help of tariff laws, many traditional and satisfactory foreign suppliers of the British market. There was, in fact, a very strong commercial case for the belief that though Canadian and Australian politicians, for instance, might do very well for themselves, their parties, and their Dominions on the kind of Imperial Preference they wanted, Britain might, on balance, prove a heavy economic loser.

It was the difficulties and dislocation of war that first gave the Tariff Reformers their chance. A strong contingent of Conservative Tariff Reformers entered the Government in May 1915, and though the Chancellorship of the Exchequer was put in the hands of McKenna, who had often argued the Free Trade case against them, the exigencies of war and, perhaps, the new company he was in, produced some proposals in his first Budget of September 1915 which bitterly offended the Free Trade doctrinaires of his own party.[1] The McKenna duties have a small place of their own in British fiscal history, and the Free Trade doctrinaires hardly made sufficient allowance for their four-fold effect in raising revenue, discouraging luxury expenditure in war-time, and even conserving foreign exchange and shipping-space. They claimed, indeed, to find British pianos, for example, immediately raised in price owing to the "monopoly" position allowed British piano-manufacturers by the MacKenna tariff and failed to make any allowance for the increased price of everything, especially skilled labour and scarce parts, since August 1914. Yet if the Radical attitude towards industrial "monopolies", established by tariff, was often over-suspicious and mistaken, events proved that there was no mistake about Radicals' forecast that once a tariff was established, a variety of interests would form under its shelter and make the task of removal, even of a temporary tariff, exceedingly difficult.

In June 1916 came the notorious Allied Economic Conference at Paris which, though issuing from the perfectly legitimate purpose, even from the standpoint of the straiter Free Trade Radicals, of studying what might be done through mutual aid in the supply of scarce resources, developed, under the pressure of hard-driven Allies and a war-fanaticized Press,[2] some very dubious aspects. Even Asquith was submitted to a scalding attack from

[1] Cf. *Hansard*, September 21, 1915, for McKenna's Budget speech with its suggested 33⅓ per cent duties upon certain imported luxuries—motor-cars, motor-cycles, cinema films, clocks, watches, musical instruments, plate glass, and hats. The plate-glass and hat duty suggestions were given up, the latter, to some extent, because it would hurt invaded France but the rest were persisted in for the reasons given above. The need to conserve American exchange was already a pressing one.

[2] Cf. *Whitaker's Almanack, 1917*, pp. 803–4, for a section on British and Enemy Trade which shows this normally sober publication catching the infection and treating Mr. Hughes of Australia as an authority. Truth to tell, Mr. Hughes was one of the British Empire's representatives at the Paris Economic Conference, and the *Daily Mail* would dearly have liked to make him more.

the Radicals of *The Nation*[1] when, in reporting to the House the Resolutions of the Conference, he seemed to accept, without protest, some of the notions ascribing Allied economic problems to past German "penetration", "domination", and "attack on our markets". This apparent departure of Asquith "from our old belief that foreign trade is exchange to the new view that it is war" was, doubtless, not very much more than was required by international courtesy and, in any case, the whole matter was being removed, for a space, from the field of action by reference to a Committee. Doubtless, Asquith could hardly have foreseen that legislation on this Committee's Final Report would be in question just when the German menace seemed to be reaching its height in the spring of 1918. By that time, Radical Free Traders were facing a Report which seemed to suggest "Protection" not merely for "Key Industries" and "trades of a special or pivotal kind" supporting munitions or other essential industries but for "any industry of real importance . . . exposed to undue foreign competition, inadequate supplies of raw materials or any other cause", like "dumping" and "sweated goods".[2] A broader road could hardly have been opened for hundreds of industries to claim protective tariffs or alternative subsidies.

Amid the war and peace crises of 1918–20, however, the shape of the commercial future was so problematic as to rule out far-reaching key-industry legislation except in the special case of the Dye Stuffs Industry which, late in 1920, obtained a ten-year ban

[1] *The Nation*, August 5, 1916.
[2] Cf. *Ibid.*, May 11, 1918: "It is at this hazardous moment that the Committee appointed to give substance and meaning to the Paris Economic Resolutions produces its Final Report. Its recommendations do not satisfy fully the extreme demands for protection, and a boycott of the Central Powers. But they go far enough to procure, if they were carried out, a complete reversal of our pre-war commercial policy and a continuance of the war-spirit and war-tactics into the period of peace. The motive of national defence is everywhere thrown out so as to cover a variety of protectionist designs. Key industries are thrust into the foreground. . . . Though no clear definition of a key industry is attempted, the impressive terms tungsten, magnetos, thorium, nitrates are pressed once more into the service. . . . Nowhere is there any intelligible common analysis of dumping, or any reasonable method of . . . ascertaining real wages and real costs of alleged 'sweated goods'. . . . Imperial Preference is to be . . . accorded 'in respect of any Customs Duties now, or hereafter, to be imposed in the United Kingdom'. With regard to Inter-Allied commerce, the Report is ludicrously hesitant while generally agreeing to the Paris proposals for jointly developing and securing essential supplies so as to be independent of 'present enemy countries' . . . . Finally they commit themselves to an indefinite discrimination against 'our present enemies' by the simple imposition of duties upon all goods imported from them."

on foreign imports, save on licence. The unique case for the industry, as explained by the Chancellor of the Exchequer, was that the textile industries had faced ruin on the outbreak of war owing to their overwhelming dependence on German dyes and colours, and that the situation had only been saved by the Government's investing money, promoting manufacturing companies, and giving pledges as to the future which were now to be honoured. The fact that it was Asquithians who had first had to deal with the Dye and Colour difficulties of 1914–16 possibly accounts for the absence of serious opposition to the Dyestuffs Act of 1920. And when, on May 9, 1921, Mr. Stanley Baldwin, as the Coalition's President of the Board of Trade, began moving a series of Safeguarding Resolutions to prepare the way for a five-year Act laying a $33\frac{1}{3}$ per cent duty in protection of Key Industries and such other trades as were suffering from foreign imports sold below the British cost of production, it was the collapsed continental currencies rather than original German sin in malevolent dumping campaigns that figured as the Government's main anxiety. Though, too, the Government undertook to exclude food, drink, and raw materials from the purview of the Act and consented to enlarge the Safeguarding Committee (to examine applications from menaced British trades) from the original three members to five, quite a Free Trade outcry was raised against it both by Asquith's men and by Labour. From the first, the long list of scientific appliances, which figured in the Key Industry section of the Bill, was under attack as involving a blow to scientific development in Britain and the reintroduction of "Taxes on Knowledge".[1] And, in 1922, a major Free Trade demonstration was made when it was discovered that, after Lancashire had succeeded in opening up its old yarn-export trade to Germany, fabric gloves made in Germany from this Lancashire yarn were having a $33\frac{1}{3}$ per cent Safeguarding duty applied to them. The folly of erecting multiple impediments to world-scale movements of trade in the supposed interests of every petty contingent of workers who thought they might be affected—in this case certain sections of British glovers —had already been feelingly dealt with by Asquithians in 1921. And, naturally enough, neither in 1921 or 1922 did Labour really

[1] Cf. *Ibid.*, April 30, 1921, for the Secretary of the Cobden Club; also *The Nation* of August 27, 1921, for an attack on the Coalition Liberal who supported the Bill as an emergency measure evoked by the collapsed continental exchanges, especially Germany's.

consider itself free to argue this side of the Free Trade case adequately.

There has already been some treatment of Bonar Law's General Election of the autumn of 1922 and the formidable majority obtained, a majority due at least partly to the pledge not to introduce Tariff Reform save after a new consultation of the people. Baldwin took over the majority and the pledge in May 1923 as also the plans for an Imperial Economic Conference, sitting alongside the Imperial Conference proper, and bound to consider extensions of Imperial Preference within the limits of the Bonar Law pledge on Tariff Reform as interpreted by the Government. How Baldwin allowed himself to be manœuvred, by Dominion[1] and party pressure, to agree to much more considerable extensions of Imperial Preference than a great deal of the country considered either wise or justifiable has already been recounted. Nor was this all, for he proceeded, on an important party occasion, to make a personal declaration on Tariff Reform which, against his own real intentions, hurried him and a largely unprepared party into the disastrous Election of December 1923. Housewives, fearful of dearer food in the shops, and raw-material users, fearful of having to price British manufactures higher in export-markets that were difficult enough already, turned on and defeated the Baldwin Government.

The minority Labour Government, that succeeded for nine months of 1924, had its place in fiscal history largely decided by the personality and views of its Chancellor of the Exchequer, Philip Snowden. Aided by Asquithian and Radical votes, which were not yet affected by the haunting fears destined to accompany the altogether grimmer Unemployment of 1929–31, Snowden was able to face the combined wrath of British Conservatives and Dominion Premiers who held that Britain was committed in honour to the new Imperial Preferences which had been negotiated at the Imperial Economic Conference of 1923.[2] Even more dangerous politically was Snowden's resolve not to allow the McKenna Duties to function beyond August 1, 1924, since Tories were able, at the autumn elections, to claim, both of him and of

[1] *Supra*, Chapter XVII.

[2] Cf. *Hansard*, June 17 and 18, 1924, for debating in the Commons on Resolutions introduced by Mr. Baldwin though, of course, the result in the Lords, on June 26th was very different. Yet, even in the Commons, the majorities against the Imperial Conference's plans for dried-fruits, tobacco, wines, and sugar were only 6, 13, 17, and 20 respectively.

his Asquithian and Radical abettors, that compared with their "Cobdenite shibboleth" nothing else seemed to matter. Neither the angry and justified Imperial Preference disappointments of loyal Dominions nor the imperilled livelihoods of tens of thousands of British craftsmen in the motor-trades, for instance, seemed really to weigh with Free Trade "fanatics", prepared to antagonize Dominion sentiment and allow Britain's most prosperous, modern, and efficient group of industries to become exposed, at very short notice, to duty-free importation from France and Germany, with their much lower labour-costs, and from the United States, with the tremendous advantages that sprang from its huge home-markets. Naturally, there was a Free Trade counter-case, effectively enough put in Radical journals though not normally earning the old measure of electoral support. Here, for example, is the Radicals' *Nation* on the "doom" that had been forecast for the motor-car trade:[1]

Three or four months ago, in connection with the abolition of the McKenna duties, the country was ringing with the doom of the motor-car industry. Foremost in the terrific propaganda against the abolition of the duties was Mr. W. R. Morris, the governing-director of the great Oxford firm. I forget how many thousand more men his firm were expected to employ if the election last December had gone in favour of Protection and how many thousand fewer . . . if the McKenna duties were abolished. The election did not go in favour of protection and the McKenna duties have been abolished. Is the Morris firm extinguished? On the contrary, I gather from an interview which Mr. Morris has had this week with *The Daily Express* that his company is having a roaring time, that its output during the next twelve months will be more than one thousand cars a week, and that their manufacture will give employment to thousands of skilled men who are at present out of work. This tremendous increase of business is due to the reductions in the cost of the cars. These reductions, Mr. Morris makes it clear, are a direct reply to the menace of foreign competition to which the removal of the McKenna duties subjected the industry. Mr. Morris has met that menace by increasing production, and consequently lowering the production costs, and by standardization which has reduced overhead charges. The result is cheaper cars for the public and increased trade for Mr. Morris. Not a bad result for a policy which was to have brought swift and irretrievable ruin to the motor-car industry.

This type of argument, especially when it was sought to apply its conclusions to some of the really depressed industries, was a

[1] *The Nation,* September 6, 1924.

little too glib as some veteran Radical Free Traders were themselves to admit when the million and a quarter unemployed of the middle twenties became the three millions of the winter of 1931–2. Yet when Ramsay MacDonald dissolved Parliament in October 1924 and attempted to win an "independent" majority, capable, many Conservatives considered, of taking Britain a long way on the Moscow road, Conservatives had, perforce, to make sure of defeating him even if it meant pledging themselves once more against introducing full-scale Tariff Reform without specific authorization from the electors. As Baldwin, on his return to the Prime Ministership, interpreted the mandate received by his vast army of well over 400 supporters in a House of 615, it was to continue further with the Imperial Preference and Safeguarding methods of helping British industry.[1] And the Budget of 1925 did, indeed, reintroduce the McKenna Duties (to yield ten millions in a full year) and a new version of the Imperial Preferences negotiated in 1923[2] as well as bring in a "nakedly protective" duty on hops to safeguard, it was claimed, a deserving but imperilled rural industry and a $33\frac{1}{3}$ per cent Safeguarding impost on imported lace. Two things, too, seemed to stand out, according to disgruntled Radicals, from the long stretches of often tedious debating on the fiscal issues of 1925. Labour apostacy on the Free Trade issue was not merely to be found among some of the Labour Back-Benchers.[3] MacDonald himself was prepared for it if it promised to bring electoral advantage and, certainly, he had sought to have the best of both worlds by criticizing, at one and the same times, both the "excessive" Liberal claims made for Free Trade and Conservative readiness for tariffs without accompanying safeguards for the workers' employment, wages, and conditions.[4]

Some further Safeguarding, in the cases of British cutlery and gloves, was inscribed on the British Statute Book during December 1925. And in his Budget proposals of April 26, 1926, Churchill

[1] Cf. *Hansard*, December 9, 1924 and December 17, 1924, for the inclusion both of Safeguarding and Imperial Preference in the King's Speech and in Baldwin's reply to the Debate on the Address, in which last, indeed, came a species of advance-notice of the setting-up of an Empire Marketing Board.

[2] Cf. *Ibid.*, April 28, 1925, for Churchill's Budget proposals as originally moved.

[3] Cf. *Ibid.*, June 12, 1925, for the several Labour members who supported the Government against a Free Trade motion to postpone the provision for preferential rates on all Empire-grown tobacco, currants, dried-fruit, and wine.

[4] Cf. *Ibid.*, February 16, 1925, for MacDonald, moving an attack on the Safeguarding policy, in terms which were not irreconcilable with the adoption of "Workers' Safeguarding" by Labour.

extended the McKenna Duties to cover commercial vehicles, put a duty on imported wrapping paper, re-enacted Key Industry Safeguarding and promised to put Imperial Preference arrangements on a decennial instead of a year-to-year basis. Of course, the General Strike and the long coal-stoppage of 1926 did nothing to improve the trade or Budget prospects of 1927, and if the often candid Free Trade Radicals of *The Nation* had publicly admitted, at the very beginning of 1926, that Baldwin was showing uncommon conscientiousness in deciding that the hard-pressed Iron and Steel Industries had established a case for Safeguarding which could not, however, be accorded to trades of their importance without some apparent infringement of his presumed pledge against general tariffs,[1] that only made it the more certain that the existing situation could not continue for very much longer. Of course, it is now known that, Exchequer help having become impossible after the sorry history of the Coal Subsidy of 1925–6, some official planning had begun to bring the extraordinarily depressed "heavy industries" some Rating Relief. But, in the meantime, there seemed nothing for it, till a release could be sought, in favourable circumstances, from the pledge against general tariffs, except persistence with Imperial Preference, direct and indirect, and piece-meal Safeguarding when the opportunity offered. Towards the end of 1926, for instance, legislation was passed in aid of British and Empire goods under which foreign-made products had to be stamped with the name of their country of origin, and it became the duty of the retail shopkeeper to label those goods accordingly and even to indicate, in the case of a composite article, what was British-made, Empire-made, or foreign-made. And Safeguarding, in the Budget of 1927, was represented by a five-year duty of 28s. per cwt. on table-ware of

[1] Cf. *The Nation*, January 2, 1926: "The Committee on Civil Research has reported to the Cabinet on the application of the Iron and Steel Industry for Protection under the Safeguarding Regulations. . . . Mr. Baldwin revealed . . . last week that the evidence showed a serious situation. . . . 'The pressure of foreign competition, aided by long hours, low wages, and depreciated currencies, is being severely felt. . . . It became clear, however, . . . that the safeguarding of a basic industry of this magnitude would have repercussions of a far wider character which might be held to conflict with our declaration in regard to a general tariff.' So Iron and Steel are not to be safeguarded for the present; and as for a subsidy, which the Prime Minister once airily adumbrated as a possible way out for those industries, the idea is utterly discredited since Coal has got in first and emptied the till and queered the pitch. . . . We have always regarded Iron and Steel and the Woollen and Worsted Industries as the test cases for Mr. Baldwin's pledge and we respect him for his decision to keep faith."

translucent and vitrified pottery and by the extension of the McKenna Duties to cover foreign tyres.[1] Even before the Budget, too, Ministers had attempted to give British film-production the protection, that would help it from being overwhelmed by Hollywood's glittering flood, in a Film-Quota Bill, which abolished "blind booking", set a time-limit on "block-booking", and required renters, as from 1928, and exhibitors, as from 1929, to engage for a minimum British quota of $7\frac{1}{2}$ per cent, rising by $2\frac{1}{2}$ per cent per annum to 25 per cent. The Government could and did claim the authority of the last Imperial Conference for the view that a situation in which only five per cent of the films shown in the British Empire were British-made, was thoroughly undesirable.[2]

By this time, many Radical Free Traders had come to see the best hope of maintaining Free Trade in the well-founded fears of numerous foreign interests, who still enjoyed, without reciprocity, their best export-opportunities here, that any further raising of their own countries' tariffs against Britain would help British Protectionism to triumph. A remarkable Economic Conference was, in fact, collected at Geneva under the auspices of the League of Nations in May 1927, and its recommendations were all in favour of stopping tariff-increases and making a beginning with tariff decreases instead.[3] Moreover, it was hoped to set up an improved League Economic Organization to push the pious Freer Trade resolutions of 1927 in 1928 and subsequent years. Accordingly, though the Radical Free Traders could not break themselves readily of the habit of sneering at such minor Safeguarding as once more reappeared in the Government's 1928 programme,[4] there came, all at once, some significant admissions

[1] Cf. *Hansard*, April 11, 1927.
[2] Cf. *Ibid.*, March 16th, for Sir Philip Cunliffe-Lister, President of the Board of Trade, moving the Second Reading. And when the Radicals' *Nation* attempted its customary tone of contemptuous superiority towards Protectionism, one correspondent, at least, counter-attacked in regard to "the flood of rubbish from America" and the two millions per annum that would be spent, instead, on British films, even in the Quota Plan's first stages. "And almost the whole of that would go in wages and salaries," concluded the correspondent (*The Nation*, February 26, 1927), who, doubtless had his part in preparing the British film-producer's case for the Board of Trade.
[3] Cf. Butler and Maccoby, *Development of International Law*, pp. 539–40.
[4] Cf. *The Nation*, June 16, 1928: "The latest glorious achievement of the Government is to put up the price of the cheap enamel-ware articles used in the kitchens of the poor. This has been done to help a small industry which only two years ago was for good reason refused a Safeguarding duty by an inquiry. . . . Ask often enough and the compliant authorities will find some means of ful-

which revealed very clearly how near to death Free Trade was already felt to be unless something tangible resulted from the Freer Trade resolutions of the Economic Conference of 1927. Here is the Radicals' *Nation*, attempting to be almost frank in regard to the plight of British Steel, in an article whose title and opening sections must have given most of its readers some awkward jolts until they were somewhat reassured by the conclusion. "HOW DOES FREE TRADE STAND?" was the title, and the article proceeded:[1]

Have recent developments or present tendencies weakened any of the old Free Trade arguments? Some of them, in our opinion, yes . . . the safeguarding of steel would represent a most hazardous policy. None the less, the condition of the industry is so serious, and the part which it plays in our economic life is so important, that we could not for our part assert that the case for Free Trade . . . is as clear and conclusive as it used to be. Whatever the defects of the organization of our steel works, there is not really much margin for a reduction in its costs. Wages are low; profits are mostly negative; selling-prices are well below the general wholesale index-number. It is not easy, therefore, for the industry to regain a really competitive footing. Rather than allow it to suffer a persistent decline, a point would certainly come when it would be preferable to run a big risk with the secondary industries. . . .

We have been arguing, so far, without a reference to the effect which a radical change in our fiscal policy would have on the fiscal policies of other nations. . . . To-day, in the situation created by the World Economic Conference . . . the tariff position is just now exceptionally plastic and impressionable . . . the Continental imagination, influenced largely by the contrast between American prosperity and European poverty, has been impressed by the mutual damage which tariff barriers do, and has been caught by the idea of Europe as an economic unit. . . . The fact that this issue is hanging in the balance should, in our view, be decisive as regards our fiscal policy. Recourse by Great Britain to Protection would suffice to kill the whole Economic Conference idea. To throw our whole weight behind the work of the Conference, unless and until it demonstrably fails, should be a cardinal principle of our statesmanship.

When Snowden's Free Trade zealotry returned to the Exchequer in the summer of 1929, it was, perhaps, inevitable that, despite the

filling the pledge not to introduce Protection while introducing it in wretched fragments under another name. The National Union of Manufacturers, a body of High Protectionists, has been urging Baldwin to speed up Safeguarding; or in words, which they would not themselves employ, to shelter more inefficient industries from the economic consequences of their own inefficiency, at the expense of the home buyer. . . ."

[1] *Ibid.*, August 25, 1928.

persistent warnings of Graham at the Board of Trade,[1] foreign Governments should have felt some relaxation of the pressure from their exporters to offer London, before worse befell, some pledges against any further raising of duties against Britain. And when the great "economic blizzard" began overtaking the world in the winter of 1929–30 and the pressure for still higher "protective" tariffs mounted abroad, the Radicals of *The Nation* contrived, at a serious cost to themselves,[2] to shout a loud warning to Snowden against undertaking the doctrinaire and unreciprocated Free Trade cancellation of the McKenna Duties half-expected in his coming Budget. As *The Nation* put it in an article, which made a sensation:[3]

In our judgement it would be the height of folly, and utterly indefensible, to touch a single one of them [the McKenna Duties]. We think it desirable to state our opinion plainly and emphatically; since it might be most unfortunate if the impression were to get abroad that Free Trade opinion would be solidly behind a course which, under present economic conditions, must do wanton mischief to trade and employment. . . . In the first place, Mr. Snowden, in his coming Budget will be in no position to throw away any part of his existing revenue . . . even if we had not to face a condition of exceptional financial stringency, it would be very difficult on industrial grounds, to justify the choice of the present year for the repeal of the McKenna Duties. We have to reckon this year with the repercussions of the Wall Street slump . . . one repercussion which it is idle to ignore is that many of our industries will have to face keener American competition. In no industry is this factor likely to be more important than in the production of motor-cars. . . . The repeal of the McKenna duties, under those conditions, would undoubtedly entail a large addition to the numbers of the unemployed . . . it is surely to misconceive altogether the place of

[1] Cf. *The Nation*, December 22, 1928, for what Graham knew as well as the Radicals—that if the Free Trade "tradition, with all the historical glamour attaching to it, is once overthrown, it will not be surprising if the Labour Party comes to throw its weight, as it has long done in Australia, on the side of the highest and most extensive tariff system".

[2] Cf. *Ibid.*, January 18, 1930, for the announcement of the resignation of *The Nation*'s editor, H. D. Henderson, after his article of January 4th, was regarded as having sown confusion in the ranks behind Lloyd George.

[3] *Ibid.*, for the retiring editor on "OUR HERESY": "*The Manchester Guardian* describes it as 'a sensational Protectionist article' which has 'created doubt and dismay in the Liberal ranks'. . . . Conservative papers, while congratulating us on our dawning sense of the error of Cobdenite opinions, are no less astonished, and some of them display considerable ingenuity in their search for an adequate explanation." Yet "if it were not for the quasi-theological atmosphere which surrounds the fiscal issue" the fact that a writer, who reasserted his belief that the case for Free Trade in Britain was a very strong one, should yet feel that the time for the repeal of the McKenna Duties had not come, would not have been regarded as strange or sensational.

principle in economic affairs to suppose that you ought to do things in deference to it which are likely to be mischievous in their results. . . . It is not as though it were in the least likely that the repeal of the McKenna duties by Mr. Snowden would serve to fortify Free Trade. On the contrary, it would inevitably stimulate Protectionist agitation. . . .

This leads to our final point. In approaching tariff questions today, it is vital that we should consider the bearing of our actions on the project of the World Economic Conference, the endeavour, by international agreement, to reverse the tendency towards rising tariffs throughout the world. Would the repeal of the McKenna duties help or hinder that endeavour? We are convinced, for our part, that it would hinder it; and we believe that our opinion is shared by those who are closely in touch with the actual work of Geneva.

Helped by writing of this kind, Snowden's Treasury officials did succeed in getting the McKenna Duties maintained even though notice was served in the Budget of 1930 that there would be no renewal of Safeguarding provisions for cutlery, gloves, and incandescent mantles, due to run out at the end of the year. If Snowden's abandonment of Safeguarding in a year, as it proved, of steadily mounting Unemployment won some Radical support,[1] it was of a character to produce more enmity than favour. It was fortunate, indeed, for Snowden that the Empire Free Trade Crusade attempted by Lords Beaverbrook and Rothermere, made more trouble for Baldwin than for anybody else since, in the Protectionist squabbles that resulted,[2] even the opportunity of the Imperial Conference of the autumn of 1930 seemed to go by without much further result than the resolution to reassemble the Imperial Conference's Economic Section at Ottawa in the autumn of 1931. Yet there were all sorts of pointers during a year of mounting and almost world-wide difficulties, accompanied by

---

[1] Cf. *Ibid.*, April 19, 1930: "Mr. Snowden has presented an honest but drastic Budget. . . . That the McKenna duties would have to remain for reasons of revenue we correctly forecast several months ago. On the other hand nobody (except direct beneficiaries and congenital Protectionists) will regret the lapse of the small but irritating safeguarding duties on lace, gloves, cutlery, and gas mantles. . . ."

[2] Cf. *Ibid.*, July 12, 1930, for the differences that had developed in the Tory Party as to how big a dose of Protection could be victoriously suggested at the next Election: "Mr. Baldwin and the Central Office (with better memories of 1923) said, 'Safeguarding and Retaliation but no food taxes.' Lord Beaverbrook said, 'Taxes on foreign foodstuffs are the cornerstone of our policy.' Lord Rothermere (if we understood him correctly) said, 'No Baldwin and no food taxes.' Mr. Churchill and *The Times* said, 'a moderate revenue tariff on imported manufactures'. Then they all agreed for a time on Empire Free Trade, with a referendum on Food Taxes. Then they all fell to quarrelling more violently than before. . . ."

rising tariffs[1] and the abandonment of all real hope of tangible results from the Economic Conference of 1927, to the fact that unconditional Free Trade was being increasingly abandoned as a tenable British policy. That the Manchester Chamber of Commerce should have turned so strongly against "Cobdenism" as was proved by some striking figures, available early in June,[2] and that a "Bankers' Resolution" of July should have asked for a Revenue Tariff on foreign imports, accompanied by free admission for Empire products,[3] is as significant as one rather despairing Radical comment to the effect that if a ten per cent Revenue Tariff had to come, it would be better for Snowden to impose it than a Tory Chancellor with ulterior ends in view.[4]

In point of fact, the next great round in the battle of Protection versus Free Trade was not delayed to Budget Day 1931 but opened in November 1930 when Graham, President of the Board of Trade, announced that the Dyestuffs (Import Regulation) Act of 1920, due to lapse on January 15th, unless legislatively continued, would not be renewed. Radicals supported the Government on the double case which it could argue[5]—the case, first, that a powerful British Dyestuffs Industry, capable of standing on its

---

[1] Cf. *The Nation*, February 7, 1931: "A review of the world's tariff legislation gives plenty of food for reflection. In four countries—the U.S.A., Sweden, Portugal, and Egypt—completely new tariffs came into force; in each case, according to the *Board of Trade Journal* 'the general tendency' of the revision was 'upward'. Tariff changes on a considerable scale occurred also in Canada and Australia; in these cases, too, their 'general tendency' was towards an increase in duties. These developments were symptomatic.... Tariff changes, on balance in the direction of higher duties, occurred in Belgium, France, and Germany; in Spain, Italy, and Greece; in Poland, Finland, and Jugoslavia. India, China, and certain South American States, are tending also to heightened tariff walls.... It only remains for Britain to hurl herself into the mêlée; the effective paralysis of such forces as are tending towards trade recovery will then have been secured...."

[2] Cf. *Ibid.*, June 7, 1930: "About a fortnight ago the Manchester Chamber of Commerce ballotted its 4000 members on national fiscal policy. The questionnaire was couched in a peculiar manner. Members were asked to vote for or against six alternatives, viz. 'In favour of the policy generally known as Free Trade'; 'In favour of a settled policy of imposing protective duties in the manner generally known as Safeguarding'; or for or against a general protective tariff including raw materials and foodstuffs; or excluding raw materials or foodstuffs or both. 2305 valid ballot papers were filled up ... 607 favoured Free Trade; 986 favoured Safeguarding; while the balance were distributed between the other four protectionist alternatives. Undoubtedly Lord Beaverbrook, Lord Rothermere, and Mr. Baldwin ... will hail these figures...."

[3] Cf. *Ibid.*, July 12, 1930.

[4] *Ibid.*

[5] Cf. *Ibid.*, November 29, 1930: "The Government's decision is both sensible and courageous. It has been received, of course, with a howl of execration from the Protectionists."

own feet, had now been built up by consistent sacrifice of the consumer since 1914 and, then, that the dye-and-colour user could
no longer be expected to submit to the long delays and incon-
veniences of petitioning for special permits to import, often from
his pre-1914 German suppliers, the high-quality specialties, not
made in Britain but which had yet given British textiles their one-
time world-appeal. Even Baldwin was driven to fury by what he
considered the shortsighted Free Trade malignancy, capable of
exposing to certain ruin a group of key-industries built up by so
much effort, and despite the Liberal-Labour majority available to
thwart him in the Commons, a way was found to prevent the
undoing of Dyestuffs "Regulation" in the Lords. The Peers
carried an Amendment including the Dyestuffs (Import Regulation) Act in the Expiring Laws Continuance Bill,[1] and as the
continuance of Rent Restriction, for instance, depended on the
Expiring Laws Bill going through, Ministers were counselled,
even by Radicals, to give way. It was hardly the time, certainly,
to venture all on a propaganda battle for Free Trade. Foreign and
Dominion tariffs were moving steadily upwards; a staggering
increase in the British Unemployment figures would almost
certainly have to be announced for the year's end;[2] and, finally,
Russian "dumping" of timber and wheat, produced, it seemed, by
over-driven peasants and "slave camp" labour, and brought in to
the detriment of Dominions, Allies, and friends, seemed to be
clearly established[3] though, of course, the principal cause was
Russia's own terrible plight.[4]

[1] *Ibid.*, December 20, 1930: "The battle of the Dyestuffs Act still rages. . . .
On Monday Lord Hailsham . . . returned to the attack in the House of Lords,
and an amendment continuing the Act for another year was carried by a large
majority. The Government, faced with the alternative of accepting the amendment (subject, it is understood, to a full inquiry into the dyestuffs position) or
of sacrificing, *inter alia*, the Rent Restriction Act, should, we think, give way."

[2] Cf. *Ibid.*, January 10, 1931: "The unemployment figures for December
29th were 2,643,127. This was 234,756 more than a week before. . . . If the
frost continues it looks as though we should get near the three million mark
before the end of February."

[3] *Ibid.*, December 20, 1930: "The latest move in the campaign against 'Soviet
dumping' has taken the form of a letter to the Prime Minister from Sir Hilton
Young, enclosing depositions by three Russian refugees as to the deplorable
conditions under which timber-cutting is carried on, by forced labour, in the
Archangel district. It may be doubted whether the condition of Russian workers
will be improved by an economic boycott of Russian products. . . . The indignation of Tory members . . . would be more convincing if it were less obviously
coloured by hatred of the Soviet Government. . . ."

[4] Cf. *The Economist*, November 1, 1930, for a Russian Supplement which
went fully into the over-ambitious Five Year Plan whose partial breakdown

No one will claim for Snowden's Budget of April 1931, enjoying Radical support though it did owing to its rigid avoidance of tariffs and its preparations to deal with the "land monopoly", that it was particularly far-sighted. In contesting the "outworn fiscal system" on which it was based, Neville Chamberlain prophesied that it was "the last Free Trade Budget", and, in point of fact, Snowden was himself proposing a far severer emergency Budget in September[1] (though one that failed to stop the Suspension of the Gold Standard on September 20th) and handing over the Exchequer to his Tariff Reform critic early in November. They might now be brother-Ministers in a Coalition Government which had just won a shattering Election victory against a Labour Party that, after going on record as preferring tariffs to dealing with the obvious shortcomings of the "Dole" system, had finally affected an electoral somersault and damned tariffs on its electoral banner after all.[2] But the vast majority of the new House of Commons obviously wanted no more Snowden Budgets and would, indeed, have passed right out of control if Neville Chamberlain had not moved to the Exchequer as the Minister primarily responsible for applying the "doctor's mandate", allegedly received by the Government, to rectify the trade position.[3] Part at least of the reason for the country's devalued and unstabilized pound was widely held to have been the increasingly adverse balance of trade, and, perhaps, the most significant thing asked of the new Parliament was "authority to frame plans for ensuring a favourable balance of trade".[4]

It was, indeed, the fact that the pound was both devalued

was to lead not merely to Communist self-exculpation by means of rigged "trials" of "imperialist agents of sabotage" but to the widespread peasant misery and discontent, the military suppression of which was being reported, towards the end of year, from several countries bordering with Russia, notably Estonia and Latvia. Beyond European Russia, there was trouble in Azerbaijan and Georgia.

[1] Cf. *Annual Register*, 1931, English History, p. 77, for some modifications of the original severity after the "Invergordon Mutiny", the sailors, the teachers, the police, and the insurance doctors and chemists being promised ten per cent as the limit of the pay-reductions to be imposed.

[2] Cf. Viscount Snowden, *An Autobiography*, ii, 1063, for part of the virulent broadcast talk delivered on October 17, 1931.

[3] Cf. *The Times*, October 8th, for the Prime Minister's manifesto of the previous day, asking that the Government be left "free to consider every proposal likely to help, such as tariffs, expansion of exports and contraction of imports, commercial treaties and mutual economic arrangements with the Dominions".

[4] *Ibid.*, November 11, 1931.

538

and unstabilized, despite the emergency Budget of September, that had decided Free Traders and Tariff Reformers to stay together as a "National Government" for the General Election.[1] And it was found wise, for all the mutual incompatibilities of the "National Government's" constituent groups to stay together until September 1932 when the pound sterling had been nursed back to surprising strength, though at a lower gold value, on the markets of the world.[2] Meanwhile, the first push towards what proved the definite abrogation of the Free Trade system had been made not by the deeply-divided Cabinet Committee, engaged on exhaustive studies of Balance of Trade statistics, but by one, who in Asquithian days, had counted as a Radical Free Trade leader and who had just been nominated President of the Board of Trade as a supposed check on Neville Chamberlain's pressure for outright Tariff Reform.[3] It was Walter Runciman, indeed, who made history when introducing the new Protectionist programme in the Abnormal Importations (Customs Duties) Bill, put forward, on November 17th, as virtually the first legislative business of the new Parliament. Merchants were undoubtedly importing unexampled quantities of those goods which they considered likely to be hit by tariffs when the Balance of Trade Committee had reported to the Cabinet. Doubtless a new danger to the unanchored pound could have developed, but for Runciman to have asked for powers to impose duties of up to a hundred per cent and to have induced both Snowden and Samuel not to oppose the Bill as a temporary six-months emergency enactment, gives the measure

[1] Cf. *Annual Register*, 1931, English History, p. 80, for the award of some of the credit to MacDonald who had nursed the Liberals by suggesting that, in principle, he largely agreed with them and who, at the same time, was believed to have persuaded the Conservatives not to campaign for tariffs outright but rather for their inclusion in the list of possible remedies that would have to be studied. As Lloyd George, temporarily off the active list though he was, and Ramsay Muir, at the National Liberal Federation, were both strongly opposed to the General Election, certain in the circumstances to produce a large Tariff Reform majority, the care with which Samuel and the Liberal Ministers were handled becomes explicable.

[2] *Ibid.*, p. 79, for the pound's rapid original fall to a gold value of sixteen shillings where it was held relatively stable. As internal prices remained stationary, British exporters were able to offer more tempting prices abroad and trade improved. Yet the desire to reanchor the pound to gold or to something traditionally stable and assured was very widespread in a generation that had seen the great continental currency collapses after 1918.

[3] Cf. Viscount Snowden, *An Autobiography*, ii, 999, for Snowden's part in securing Runciman's nomination. Yet even Runciman had already suggested the cutting-off of luxury imports as a help to the exchange.

of the currency doubts and fears still rampant.[1] And yet Sir John Gilmour's announcement, also uncontested from the Free Trade side of the Cabinet, marked, perhaps, a greater departure from the old orthodoxy. There was to be a Wheat Quota for home-grown milling qualities, and there were to be emergency tariffs of up to one hundred per cent on luxury imports of fruits, vegetables, and flowers.[2]

There had already been, on the part of the Radical stalwarts of the National Liberal Federation, some serious questioning of the course Samuel and the Samuelites had taken in consenting to stay in a "so-called National Government" whose Tory Wing took advantage, it was alleged, of the emergency and of the General Election to force Tariffs forward to inevitable victory.[3] Questioning grew sharper after the severe, if temporary, duties of the Abnormal Importations Act were followed, on February 4, 1932 by the full-scale Tariff plan put forward by Neville Chamberlain even though on the basis that Free Trade Ministers were at liberty to oppose. Those Ministers knew, of course, better than their critics how much the stabilization of the pound at between fifteen and sixteen shillings of its gold value[4] was due to the impression

---

[1] Cf. *Hansard*, November 17, 1931, for Runciman's speech. And of its results, Snowden's *An Autobiography* reported that on the very day the Bill came into force, the Board of Trade's first list was issued under which fifty per cent import duties were imposed on a large number of goods. And further lists quickly followed.

[2] Cf. *Hansard*, November 26th, for Gilmour seeking to make the flour millers' compulsory use of a quota of home-grown wheat less objectionable to the Free Trade conscience by pledging himself against encouraging the extension of wheat cultivation to unsuitable land. But the very phrasing of such assurances, recalling as they did almost the Corn Law Age, was prophetic of the fate awaiting "Free Trade". Nor did the rapid trouble which developed from France, the principal sufferer from the flower, fruit, and vegetable import-restrictions, have much effect in stopping the new course. Gilmour gave thirteen millions as the annual value of the luxury imports he wanted to restrict, and high-tariff France was felt to have little moral case for protest, particularly in view of her poor record of concern for Britain's employment problems of the last decade.

[3] Cf. *Annual Register*, 1931, English History, p. 85, for its account of the activities of Mr. Ramsay Muir as Chairman of the Executive Committee of the National Liberal Federation. His letter of October 9th, sent to Liberal candidates and Associations, attacked the decision to hold an Election as caused by nothing else than Conservatives' desire to "turn a national emergency to party advantage" and another pungent phrase referred to an Election, already foreseen as likely to bring a great majority, hungry for tariffs, to Westminster, as "a wild gamble with the nation's fortunes".

[4] Cf. *Ibid.*, p. 79. It should be added, of course, that Neville Chamberlain's Import Duties Act, that came into force on March 1, 1932, was a relatively moderate measure designed to help the Liberal Ministers, if they so desired, to resist their party stalwarts. Thus the general standard of import duty

made abroad by the existence of an all-party "National Government" pledged to the country's financial salvation. They contrived, indeed, to brave what finally became almost party censure,[1] staying in the Government until after the British delegation returned from the postponed Imperial Economic Conference at Ottawa with inter-Empire tariff agreements more objectionable, in some ways, to the Free Trade conscience than anything yet attempted by the "National Government's" Majority. Despite the party's pressure,[2] however, the ten Ministers who eventually resigned on September 28th, were sufficiently aware of the very limited improvements in the nation's position yet obtained[3] to offer to stay if there could be some modifications in the Ottawa Agreements which were, in fact, far from ideal from the moderate British tariffist's point of view.[4] And even when the ten left the Government, affirming that a bad decision in regard to a revival of world trade, and therefore of British prosperity, was being taken,[5] independent support was still offered to the Government on India, the League of Nations, and Disarmament.

was ten per cent, which looked almost low compared with some of the fifty per cent duties of the Abnormal Importations Act, and there was a long free list, high up on which stood "wheat in grain, maize in grain, meat, live quadruped animals, tea, raw cotton, flax and hemp, wool, hides and skins, newsprint, wood pulp, rubber, metallic ores". There were later additions to the free list also.

[1] Cf. *Annual Register*, 1932, English History, pp. 40–1, for the party strains that developed and the pressure that began for the resignation of the Liberal Ministers.

[2] Cf. *Ibid.*, p. 82, for the pressure of the Liberal newspapers and the denunciation of the Ottawa Agreements, on September 21st, at a meeting of the Liberal National Federation.

[3] Cf. *Whitaker's Almanack*, 1933, p. 642, showing the Unemployment statistics at August 22, 1932 to have been still at the catastrophic height of 2,859,828. Obviously some of the Liberal Ministers were not anxious to resign when a few trades could actually be shown to be in a worsening position, notably shipbuilding and tramp shipping. The amount of idle tonnage in Britain was over 2,000,000 tons, the average level of freight rates was 71·28 compared with 100 in 1913, and the number of new ships launched during 1932, was only 104, of 191,866 gross tons compared with 502,487 tons of shipping launched in 1931 and nearly two millions in 1913.

[4] Cf. *Annual Register*, 1932, English History, p. 85, for the candid admission that the Dominion "concessions" to Britain had, in perhaps the majority of cases, taken the form of raising the general level of duty, payable by countries outside the Empire, rather than that of offering positive reductions to Britain. In short, the "preferences" for Britain were obtained by methods which threatened further obstacles to a revival of world-trade.

[5] It is, perhaps, worth noting as indicating the still anxious situation that, for well over a year after the resignations, the Liberals stayed on the Government side of the House of Commons. Only on November 16, 1933, did the Liberal Parliamentary Party decide to cross the floor to the Opposition side and, even then, with the proviso that nothing factious would be done.

English Radicalism: The End?

It was to end the last chances of the old school of Free Trade Radicalism when the course of 1933 seemed to show the trade improvement of 1932 continuing.[1] It was true, of course, that the most important factor in that improvement was the very departure from gold which the National Government had been vainly formed to avert. Yet the apparent self-assurance and success with which Britain's Empire-minded Tariff Reformers appeared to have arrested the country's decline and commenced the slow climb-back to normality[2] contrasted vividly with the final plunge of the once-envied United States into the fearful financial morass of the winter of 1932–3.[3] And even when President Roosevelt began the successful restoration of American self-confidence, most bankers and financial experts throughout the world preferred Neville Chamberlain's methods in Britain to many aspects of the American "New Deal".[4] Yet the "New Deal" made sufficient popular appeal in Britain for Lloyd George, in the last Radical campaign of his life, to find a place for a "New Deal in Britain" alongside the Peace and Disarmament causes which, in that notorious Peace Ballot season, seemed so much at the heart of the British public as to render campaigning for a "return to Free Trade" singularly uninviting by comparison. By the time Lloyd George had launched his new campaign in January 1935, there was certainly a grave danger that Hitler in Germany, Mussolini in Italy, and the Japanese militarists in Manchukuo would misinterpret the searching of conscience in Britain on the whole subject of Germany's treatment after 1918 as evidence of pacifistic

[1] Cf. *Annual Register*, 1932, Finance and Commerce, p. 66, for the "exceptional success" which was thought to have rewarded the British efforts in a year when the economic crisis in the world as a whole seemed to be intensifying. As a result, too, British prestige was reported to have risen higher than that of any of Britain's financial rivals. Three factors which gave greater confidence to business circles (in addition to the advantages which were supposed to have come from the depreciated pound and the general tariff combined) were listed as the balanced Budget, the successful conversion of the two thousand millions of 5 per cent War Loan to a 3½ per cent basis, and better relations between Labour and its employers.

[2] Cf. *Ibid.*, 1933, Finance and Commerce, p. 70, for the claim that new factories were begun in view of the tariff protection now accorded and that the building industry was correspondingly stimulated; that Bradford woollen mills had worked overtime for several months in 1933; that rayon production was a record; and that iron and steel had done better than for a long time.

[3] *Ibid.*, p. 71, for the almost daily bank failures in the U.S. and the country's reduction to "a state of despair" unparalleled for fifty years or more.

[4] *Ibid.*, p. 72, for the men of experience and "the more responsible economists" who feared the ultimate results of the Rooseveltian experiments whatever their appeal to politicians and the man in the street.

degeneracy and mortal fear of the intensified aerial bombardments now possible. Indeed, the Government knew sufficient of the plans maturing at Berlin,[1] Rome, and Tokyo to begin the Rearmament which, exposing them though it did to Labour attack and Lloyd George's criticism,[2] had at least one curious and not wholly expected result. But how Unemployment began to disappear as a major national problem as a Rearmament, sufficient to cause second thoughts to Hitler, Mussolini, and Tokyo, really began to enter into its stride, is a subject that must be reserved for mention in the next chapter.

[1] Cf. Helmut Klotz, *Berlin Diaries, 1932–33* (British edition, 1934), which, in addition to much evidence of clandestine German rearmament even before Hitler's admission to power, revealed a Hitler plan, submitted to President Hindenburg for a Germano-Russian Military Convention, which would permit Germany to make war on France and Poland and, "thereupon when our business in the west has been thoroughly settled, make an alliance with France and Poland against Russia. . . . The Polish Corridor and Dantzig will come over to Germany, also the Baltic Provinces. Poland will receive the Ukraine and other parts of Russia; France the decisive spheres of interest in South Russia." Parts of this plan were actually undertaken in 1939 and 1941.

[2] Cf. W. W. Hadley, *Munich: Before and After,* pp. 16–17: "In spite of the warnings of the Defence Departments, the arms industries had been allowed to fall into decay. . . . It was the Royal Air Force that caused most concern. In 1918 Britain had more aeroplanes and a larger trained flying personnel than any other country; but now our Air Force was fifth in order of strength. In July 1934, the Government announced that the number of first-line aircraft was to be increased from 844 to 1304 within five years. Strange as it now appears, the Labour Party opposed that new standard as 'unnecessary' and as encouraging 'dangerous and wasteful competition' in preparation for war."

CHAPTER XXVI

FAILURE OF THE LEAGUE OF NATIONS

"Two important events have taken place this week to bring democratic pressure to bear upon the Governments responsible for the draft scheme of a League of Nations. The Committee appointed by the Berne Labour Conference has had an interview with Lord Robert Cecil in Paris. . . . The demands put forward by the Labour International include the immediate inclusion of Russia and Germany in the League. . . . The Committee also demanded the direct election of delegates by Parliaments. Lord Robert Cecil, in reply, saw no reason to believe that election by Parliaments would secure truer representation of the peoples than election by Governments. Clearly . . . there is every reason for democrats to be active.

"The greatest importance, therefore, attaches to Thursday's Conference, which was jointly convened by the Labour Party and the T.U.C. The resolutions submitted . . . include the demands we have specified and make further representations of equal importance—that no armies should be raised by conscription, that the manufacture of armaments should be directly controlled by the League, that a full meeting of delegates should precede any declaration of war, that Labour and women should be adequately represented, that a declaration should be made in favour of freedom of commerce between States, that the League Covenant should form part of the Preliminary Peace Treaty, and that the Permanent Bureau should be directly controlled by the body of delegates and not by the Executive Council. . . . Many democrats will associate themselves. . . ."

> *The Nation*, April 5, 1919, shows how democrats and "idealists" over-forced the League idea from the first.

"Germany had left the League of Nations. I was present at Geneva . . . Hitler asked if I had anything to report. . . . I replied that Germany's position seemed to me a precarious one . . . our resignation from the League was increasing the risks for German rearmament, and awakening premature suspicion . . . he embarked upon a self-justifying monologue. . . . He returned to the question of the League. It was corrupt and rotten, like everything in the democracies. There would be no resistance there. . . . Incidentally, he would now more than ever speak the language of the League. . . . 'And my party comrades will not fail to understand me when they hear me speak of universal peace, disarmament and mutual security pacts.' "

> Hermann Rauschning, *Hitler Speaks*, pp. 109–16 (of October 1933).

"Mr. Lloyd George's Council of Action for Peace and Reconstruction . . . on October 20 . . . published a booklet on 'Peace' in which . . . it proposed that the League should seek to assure to its members not only security against aggression but satisfaction for their just needs. In order that time should be given . . . it suggested that the British Government should propose an armament truce for five years, together with a five-year pact of non-aggression during which no military alliances should be entered into. During this truce the Disarmament Conference should reassemble. . . ."

> The *Annual Register*, 1935, on Lloyd George's last Radical programme.

"Our Socialist friends in England have reproached, and continue to reproach Mr. Chamberlain's Government for its weakness towards the Dictators, its spirit of compromise and its lack of determination and energy. The Opposition complains that the Government is not doing enough to protect nations threatened with attack, and to defend peace. I am, therefore, shocked, and I believe so is the whole of French opinion, at the inexplicable contradiction between the Labour Party's political opposition to the Government and its opposition to conscription."

> M. Léon Blum in *Le Populaire* on April 28, 1939.

BRITISH Radicals' attractions to and repulsions from persons and movements on the foreign scene make a strange record between 1914 and 1939. The questionable Serbian origins and the unsatisfactory Tsarist associations, for instance, of the War of 1914–18 early drove a considerable Radical section, whose best-known names were Trevelyan and Ponsonby, into criticism of their own Government and, finally, into an alliance with, which became an absorption into, the Independent Labour Party, led by MacDonald and Snowden. Under the direction of E. D. Morel, the joint organization, founded by the co-operating anti-war groups of Radicals and Labour men, the Union of Democratic Control, became a body of some importance in moulding "advanced" opinion. And, sometimes, in its years of real importance, say, between 1917 and 1924, there seemed a good chance of its capturing not merely the Trade Union world but even a good deal of the Chapel world for the over-simplified view that the war of 1914–18 was largely the result of "secret diplomacy" and that the abolition of "secret diplomacy" would largely remove the causes of future wars.[1] There did, in fact, come in 1917 revelations of the grasping and secret bargains, on which much of the anti-German alliance was founded, for the U.D.C.'s case to be, in appearance, vastly strengthened[2] and for the U.D.C. Radicals, in complete revolt as they were against Lloyd George's "Fight to a Finish", to resolve to sever their last links with Liberalism, whether Lloyd Georgian or Asquithian. The "idealistic" programmes being written for Henderson and the Labour Party, not to mention President Wilson's "open covenants openly arrived at", made altogether more appeal, and for a few months after Germany's capitulation on the basis of a Peace of the Fourteen Points being accorded to her, the "idealists" seemed justified in hoping for the birth of a new international order as part of the coming peace-making. The importance of a great deal else happening in the world was under-rated or ignored, and finally, in

[1] H. M. Swanwick, *Builders of Peace, Being Ten Years History of the Union of Democratic Control*, tells the story from the U.D.C. point of view.
[2] Cf. F. C. Cocks, *The Secret Treaties*, published in 1918 which, on the basis of Tsarist material published by the Bolsheviks, gave the world a notion, say, of the terms on which the adhesion of Italy and Rumania to the "cause of freedom" had had to be bought. The fact that Asquith was Prime Minister and Grey, Foreign Secretary when such things took place helped other Radicals, like the Buxtons, to sever their last links with their old party.

his anxiety to erect a League of Nations, President Wilson, the very apostle of "open diplomacy", went into the secret horse-trading of the "Big Three" and tied his League Covenant to one of the harshest and most hypocritical Peace Treaties made for over a century. Yet disappointed though they were with President Wilson, the British "progressives" seized on the League Covenant as offering to the world the best chance of a brighter future[1] and even to Germany, if there was the patience, the means of putting right the wrongs of the Peace Treaty.

In 1920, the once-famous League of Nations Union was being organized for the essential purpose of keeping the British Government and people true to the spirit of the League's Covenant and, in fact, it acquired greater authority in Britain than any of its sister-societies acquired in other member-countries of the League. Almost from its birth to the very death-throes of the League after 1937, the League of Nations Union, led by such an unusual Conservative as Lord Robert Cecil and by Gilbert Murray, the Liberal, even when relying for the bulk of its audiences on the "advanced" and the Socialists, was a power in the land. And for fifteen years chapel-goers, and often church-goers too, were innocently taught to look for their temporal salvation to the great annual Geneva Assemblies where so much rhetoric was expended on "humanity's welfare", accompanied by so much manœuvre for unavowed nationalistic ends. Thus, the once-famous Draft Treaty of Mutual Assistance, which was offered, in 1923, to the world as a necessary instrument if Disarmament was to begin,[2] seems, in essence, to have been a web spun by France and her principal co-beneficiaries in the injustices of the Treaty of Versailles,

[1] Cf. A. G. Gardiner, *Life of George Cadbury*, p. 290, for one who was spending largely on missionary work in China and of whom it is reported: "He was profoundly distrustful of Japanese intentions in regard to that country, and looked to the development of the League of Nations as the only means of preserving its integrity and its interest in peace." His widow is reported to have been a generous supporter of the League of Nations Union and to have helped to make its "notorious" Peace Ballot of the 1930s possible.

[2] Cf. *The Nation*, March 8, 1924: "Lord Parmoor has rejected Viscount Cecil's proposal that the Government should appoint a strong independent Committee to consider the Draft Treaty of Mutual Assistance. . . . It is a painful shock to be asked to sanction an arrangement by which that suspicious instrument, a defensive alliance, is to be, not only permitted, but actually encouraged by the League. The question which inevitably suggests itself is whether this method of bringing about a reduction of armaments will not, by setting up competing groups, ultimately lead to a still greater increase of armaments." Lord Robert Cecil, now Viscount Cecil, when helping to draw up the Draft Treaty, considered it worth making great concessions to the French view in order to get Disarmament started.

Poland, Czecho-Slovakia, Rumania, and Jugo-Slavia, to enmesh Britain and the rest of the League into compulsorily coming to their assistance if Germany should ever demand Treaty revision. And if MacDonald's first Government of 1924 finally decided against it, it was only to plump, in the name of humanity, peace, and the need of a speedy Disarmament Conference, for the Arbitration and Sanctions Protocol to which there were also grave objections on somewhat different grounds.[1]

If some of the Radicals of *The Nation* had seen grave reason to fear England's becoming committed to pious-sounding formulas which concealed other Powers' interest in a not very justifiable *status quo*, the stronger objections of the Conservatives can be understood. They considered, indeed, that the Labour Party under MacDonald's Leadership was far too prone to indulge in so-called idealism abroad which, while sacrificing vital British interests and often finally resulting in much more harm than good, was motivated, at least in part, by electioneering considerations at home, and by the snatch for a quick "absolute majority". The Conservatives, in fact, when they returned to power towards the end of 1924, turned their backs both on the Protocol and the Draft Treaty of Mutual Assistance, feeling their way, instead, towards the Locarno Treaties as a more suitable basis for a European *détente*. There was, of course, no enmity to the League in all this for Austen Chamberlain, the Tories' Foreign Secretary, while opposed to the view that the Covenant of the League had changed human nature or the fundamental basis of international politics, was eager to admit that the regular meetings at Geneva of the leading figures of most of the world's Governments was one of the great hopes of the future. But obviously there were going to be fewer dramatic orations at Geneva which could be written up by "progressive" journalists or preached up in "progressive" pulpits as turning-points in world-history.[2] It is curious to see not

[1] *The Nation*, October 11, 1924, under the heading, "A FALSE STEP AT GENEVA": "The idea which the British public has obtained . . . is extraordinarily hazy. It knows vaguely that the principle of the compulsory arbitration of all disputes has been adopted, and it accepts this, without much interest and without any criticism, as a valuable and impeccable achievement. It is, however, vaguely disturbed by rumours that the British Navy has been pledged in some way as the police force of the League. . . . Compulsory arbitration is a grotesquely inappropriate . . . method for settling non-justiciable disputes."

[2] Cf. *Whitaker's Almanack, 1925*, pp. 479–80, for a League of Nations section which gave, unwittingly perhaps, the illusion of continual advance from the "Jan. 10, 1924. Speaking at celebration of anniversary of birthday of the League

merely Labour journalists but experienced Radical veterans like the famous "A.G.G." inclined, at first, to treat the advent of Baldwin's second Cabinet as a calamity for the League. Here is Mr. Gardiner after Austen Chamberlain's first appearance as Britain's principal representative:[1]

Mr. Chamberlain's speech did nothing to relieve the depression that has prevailed in League of Nations circles since the formation of the present Government. With the exception of Mr. Baldwin and Lord Cecil the new Ministry is either frankly hostile or civilly indifferent . . . the names of Lord Birkenhead, Mr. Churchill, Sir L. Worthington-Evans, Sir W. Joynson-Hicks *et hoc genus omne* are sufficient to spread panic in the hearts of those who regard the cause of the League as the capital interest of world politics. I understand it is not even certain that in the absence of Mr. Chamberlain his place at the League would be taken by Lord Cecil. It might even be taken by Mr. Chamberlain's Under Secretary, Mr. Ronald McNeill, who has probably been more openly contemptuous of the League than any man prominently engaged in public life.

For some time, strenuous League supporters, Radical and Labour, continued very suspicious. For example, the advent of the new Baldwin Government almost coincided with the meeting, at Geneva, of two Opium Conferences (the one to follow on the other) which America had decided to attend in the hope, presumably, of doing something for China against three powerful Empires with opium interests—the British Empire of India, Dutch Indonesia, and French Indo-China. Historically, of course, it was British India's opium export which had pressed hardest on China, and the two "Opium Wars", of which British "progressives" were now heartily ashamed though they oversimplified the issues,[2] represented something from which they

Viscount Cecil expressed belief that the League stood stronger than ever" through the "Sept. 6th. Mr. MacDonald and the French Premier submitted joint resolution on disarmament which was passed unanimously" to the final "Oct. 2nd. Assembly concluded after adoption of the . . . Protocol and unanimous passage of resolution in favour of disarmament conference next year."

[1] *The Nation*, December 20, 1924.

[2] Cf. Arthur Waley, *The Opium War through Chinese Eyes*, pp. 25–6, for mention both of the fact that the Chinese authorities were early charged with hypocritical laxity in regard to their non-suppression of Chinese poppy-cultivation and that their particular animus against imported opium stemmed from their belief that it weighed down the Chinese exchange-rate. It should be remembered, too, that after 1906, British India arranged the plan under which its opium exports to China would be reduced year by year in return for China's undertaking to suppress Chinese production. Yet after Indian export had ceased altogether, it was found, in the 1920s, that Chinese production was growing, and, nevertheless, China's representatives were calling for additional restrictions on India in case Indian opium found an illicit way into China.

meant there should be a total departure, leading ultimately to world-wide abolition of opium-smoking and strict world-control of the trade in those opium derivatives, morphia and heroin. Yet, at the first Conference, it was asserted, British India's representative had prevented any discussion of the really radical plan, desired by China and the U.S.A., of India's undertaking a ten per cent reduction of opium export every year,[1] and the Convention, ultimately adopted, had been a mere "attempt to camouflage complete failure". This was, perhaps, exaggerated language for a Convention which did bind signatory Governments to such things as a reduction in the number of opium-smoking divans, propaganda against the opium-smoking habit, and State monopolization of the import, sale, and retail distribution of opium. Yet Britain's anti-opium humanitarians claimed to have special reason for indignation in the fact that Government monopolization, leading, as at Singapore, to a great part of the revenue coming from the opium monopoly, might tend to perpetuate opium-smoking[2] and, besides, they stressed what folly it had been to repel America when, after long suspicion of the League and all its activities, a trial venture to Geneva's alleged good works had been essayed from Washington.

"Progressive" criticism was not much friendlier even after attempts had been made from London to put a better face on its Opium policy. Viscount Cecil himself was not spared in such Radical comments as these:[3]

No one can look with much enthusiasm on the results of the Opium Conference at last drifting to a close at Geneva. The Americans and

---

[1] Cf. *The Nation*, December 27, 1924: "Opposition, on grounds of procedure, was headed by the representative of India, an Englishman appointed by the India Office, in the face of the views of a large body of public opinion in India in favour of reduction as expressed by the Swarajist National Congress." It may be noted that India had always claimed in the past that, if she consented to reduce her export, sacrificing revenue and the interests of some of her population, the result would only be to have her production replaced by illicit export from other territory or illicit production in China itself. Moreover, the Indian Government and the French Government of Indo-China were even more opposed to the suggestion of becoming committed to a rigid plan of progressively reducing the poppy-cultivation area till it would not suffice for much more than the world's medical and scientific needs. They claimed that the traditional opium-eating (as contrasted with opium-smoking) of some parts of their population was strongly established and, in certain climates, not unjustifiable.

[2] *Ibid.*, for the claim that a Government which, like Singapore's, allegedly drew forty-three per cent of its revenues from the opium monopoly, would not be prepared for the "radical reform" being proposed.

[3] *Ibid.*, February 14, 1925.

Chinese have withdrawn altogether. . . . The appointment of Lord Cecil as British Delegate alone saved the Conference from complete breakdown. Under instructions from the Cabinet, Lord Cecil has contended that since British dependencies are impotent to check the smuggling of opium, it is useless for them to attempt to abolish smoking till China and other countries from which the illicit opium comes have got a hold of their own growers and cease to be a source of illegal supply. Within fifteen years from that wholly problematic date, Great Britain, France and Holland will stop all smoking in their colonies . . . a further Convention has been accepted in principle creating the nucleus, at any rate, of machinery for the control of export, import and manufacture of opium derivatives like morphia and heroin. If that can be made a reality, it may compensate in some small measure for the failure of the Conference to do anything at all to limit production or anything effective to reduce smoking.

And all through the years of the second Baldwin Government until the summer of 1929, amid every kind of Radical criticism of the Cabinet's supposed shortcomings at home and abroad, alleged mistakes in regard to the League of Nations or the complicated Disarmament business which it was trying to foster,[1] could cause hotter attack than almost anything else, whether it was the suggested over-tolerance of "white settler" ambitions in Kenya or "Jix's" allegedly exaggerated anti-Sovietism or, finally, Conservatism's more vigorous defence of British interests in Egypt, Palestine, India, or China than the Nonconformist or Socialist conscience quite approved. If, for example, the great *détente* achieved by Chamberlain's Locarno Pacts could not be denied by Labour and won whole-hearted approval everywhere else, the Radical *Nation* was, before long, inclined to lay part of the blame on the Foreign Secretary for the awkward delays and arguments that developed, during 1926, about Germany's admission to the League as a member entitled, from the first, to the Great Power privilege of permanent representation on the League Council. If Chamberlain had been firm from the beginning with Poland, Brazil, and Spain, it was uncharitably contended,[2] instead of trying semi-promises to avoid the trouble they could make by their demand for equality with Germany, considerable perils for the League could have been avoided and Germany's entry contrived

[1] Cf. L. S. Amery, *My Political Life*, iii, 145–6.
[2] Cf. *The Nation*, March 27, 1926: "If he had been more outright instead of conciliatory—especially to Spain's claim—the whole matter of Germany's entry into the League would not have had to be postponed indefinitely and perhaps fatally."

several months sooner than it was. And then came suspicions that Chamberlain, who had certainly found Italy helpful at Locarno and not unco-operative on Britain's troubles in Egypt, Palestine, and elsewhere, was looking over-tolerantly on Mussolini's Fascism and even on its Imperialist ambitions in Abyssinia.[1]

The inveterate tendency of "advanced" Englishmen to blame their own Government if a "forward-looking" negotiation with other Governments broke down was very characteristically displayed in the closing stages of the Baldwin Administration of 1924–9. Thus, after Britain failed to come to terms with Washington, during 1927, on an extension of Naval Limitation,[2] and then succeeded, in the Geneva work of the Preparatory Commission for the Disarmament Conference, in devising a new Anglo-French compromise formula which still displeased America, it was fatally easy for the "Left" to blame Tory stupidity and Admiralty "Die-Hards" for the situation. In point of fact, the revelation ultimately came that behind American ill-will towards successive British naval suggestions, there had been a propaganda campaign, financed by American steel-producers, in aid of the Big Navy groups of Washington who, in any case, could always rely on every vocal help from anti-British elements, some of Irish descent and others, like "Big Bill Thompson" of Chicago, still engaged in making war on George III and British influence generally.[3] Even

[1] Cf. *The Nation*, August 7, 1926: "Sir Austen Chamberlain has been skating on very thin ice in his negotiations with Italy. . . . It is not surprising that the Abyssinians should feel uneasy . . . in December last agreement was reached and Notes were exchanged. The gist of these Notes is that we "recognize an exclusive Italian economic influence in the West of Abyssinia" and undertake to support Italy's project of building a railway between Eritrea and Italian Somaliland, in return for Italian support of our project of building a dam at Lake Tsana for the irrigation of the Soudan. . . . The French appear ultimately to have been squared, but the Abyssinians when they eventually received the text of the Notes in June, addressed a protest to the League of Nations."

[2] Cf. *Minneapolis Tribune*, September 6, 1927, for the kind of quotation from the American Press which could be used with special advantage against the Government and presumably played some part in Viscount Cecil's resignation: "The United States never has had any difficulty in dealing with Liberal Britain; but Tory Britain has been a trouble-maker in Anglo-American relations ever since the time of George III."

[3] Cf. *Chicago Tribune* as quoted in *The Nation* of April 14, 1928, for the saving fact that much of Chicago was delighted when reverses overtook Mayor Thompson and some of his allies in Chicago and the State of Illinois. The quoted paean of victory ran thus: "The Rule in Chicago of Big Bill Thompson, the school-book burning foe of King George . . . is ended. . . . Small has been repudiated. Frank Smith will never again bring disgrace to Illinois . . . Illinois has been purged of her shame. Chicago can again walk proudly among the cities." And after the sensational Washington revelations that came, before long, on the activities of Shearer, the Big Navy publicity man, Baldwin, no

on Far Eastern matters, in which many not normally enamoured
of Tory Foreign Secretaries found Austen Chamberlain's attitude
towards Chiang Kai-Shek's Chinese Nationalism praiseworthy,
there were already those inclined to blame the British Government for failing to obtain an alteration in Japan's gradually stiffen-
ing resolve to separate Manchuria from China proper.

But in 1928, the Manchurian situation was still rather a distant
cloud on the League of Nations horizon, and the "forward-
looking" in Britain were much more inclined to lament what they
considered as the deplorable showing Britain had been allowed to
make at the great League gatherings at Geneva in September
1928. A quotation from a Labour intellectual's report to a Radical
paper seems called for in order to illustrate how near, in "progressive" eyes, a League gathering came to what an Oecumenical
Council must have been in the eyes of the pious Christians of the
Universal Church. Here is P. J. Noel-Baker reporting to *The
Nation* on the Ninth Assembly of the League of Nations:[1]

There were some observers . . . who declared that the Ninth Session
was the most interesting and the most satisfactory which there had ever
been. They admitted that in spite of the seventeen Prime Ministers and
twenty-five Foreign Secretaries who were present, in spite of this really
astounding constellation of political potentates, it was without the
"electric atmosphere" of, say, the Third or Fifth; they admitted that it
had no dramatic achievement to its credit like the Fourth or Sixth; they
admitted that in some of the major League problems of the hour, for
example, in Disarmament, no step forward of even the most meagre
kind was made. But they held that none of these things was of real
importance; that, in the language of *The Times*, the days are over when
the League requires to live on "enthusiasm"; that enthusiasm has been
replaced by something much more important, by a solid and un-
hesitating political acceptance of the League as a vital part of the
Governmental machinery of the world. . . .

But there were three things about the Ninth Assembly that must be
profoundly disquieting to any Englishman who is not satisfied that all
is already for the best in all international worlds. The first was the
composition and the policy of the British delegation . . . its ignominious
performances and its ignoble record; . . . an unreasoning distrust of
every constructive proposal of whatever kind. . . . The second disquieting fact about the Ninth Assembly was its general attitude towards
League finance. This again was due in great measure to an attack led

doubt, considered he had a right to scold those "progressive" elements in
Britain, Radical and Labour, who used the results of Shearer's unscrupulous
activities, as party-weapons against their own Government.

[1] *The Nation*, October 6, 1928.

by the British delegation against the Budget which had been prepared for 1929. . . . Third and last, it was disquieting to observe how a great number of delegations tamely accepted the discreditable episode of the Anglo-French "compromise" on naval armaments, and even agreed to a resolution expressing satisfaction at the "efforts made" by the two Powers concerned.

In the absence of the convalescent Chamberlain and of Viscount Cecil, who had resigned in 1927 because of Disarmament disappointments,[1] the leader of the impugned delegation to Geneva had been Lord Cushendun, Acting Foreign Secretary. A stout Ulster Tory, almost hereditarily suspicious of the glib "progressive" phraseology which was the current coin of the League, he had apparently determined, despite the "progressive" ridicule to be expected, to stand fast on the Foreign Office's claim that there was much to be said for the "Anglo-French compromise" proposal on Disarmament and to stand fast also on its objections to the continuous expansion of the League's Budget, officials, and proposed activities. Britain doubtless paid more than her share of League costs though it was not that but rather the stupidly exigent language that had been used in requiring the financing of a Coal Production Inquiry by the League's Economic Committee that first provoked British Toryism's overt criticism of League Budgeting.[2] Of course, the idealists rushed in to deliver angry scoldings[3] and the Tories, doubtless, suffered heavily in electoral terms but today, it is possible to spare some sympathy for those Tories who, mostly in private, railed at the blindness of those prepared to stake everything on a new world to be fabricated in the

[1] Cf. *Whitaker's Almanack, 1928*, pp. 474–5, under "July 25, 1927. Cabinet Committee conferred throughout day with delegates to Naval Conference on critical situation reached. . . . Aug. 29th. Viscount Cecil resigned Chancellorship of Duchy of Lancaster because of disagreement with Cabinet over disarmament policy. . . . Oct. 19th. Mr. Ronald McNeill [soon Lord Cushendun] appointed Chancellor of the Duchy of Lancaster." Cecil, whose League of Nations and Disarmament partisanship had made him a sore trial to some of his colleagues, had accepted most of the British Admiralty's contentions as justifiable but not to the point of inducing America to break off the negotiations.

[2] Cf. *The Nation*, July 7, 1928: "After Italy had challenged a Committee Report that 'no consideration of economy must be allowed to restrict or delay a marked-out programme', [Sir Austen Chamberlain had said], 'He was not one of those who wished to see the activity of the League or any of its organs unduly extended; at the same time . . . he thought it would be rash to decide . . . that . . . the production of coal should be excluded from the purview of the Economic Committee. . . . It was not, he thought, possible for the Council to say . . . that work must go on regardless of the expense which it involved. . . .'"

[3] *Ibid.*, on "The League, Economy and Humbug", for such abusive language as "The lowest depth of suicidal meanness is reached, however, by those who wish to economize on the work of the League of Nations. . . ."

cynical corridors of Geneva. It was, in essence, the same type of problem that was already earning the British Tory Government the enmity of those demanding, in the name of "progress", Britain's ratification of the Washington Hours Convention and Britain's acceptance of the "Optional Clause". In regard to maximum working hours, the British Government was well aware that some of the Powers, prepared blandly to ratify the Washington Hours Convention, especially if Britain did so, had neither the ability, nor perhaps the will, to set in motion anything like the remorseless enforcement-efficiency of British Mines and Factory Inspection. In fact, ratification might well have meant the acceptance of yet another handicap in competition for world-trade, competition which had already made it unprofitable to employ nearly a million and a half workless Britishers. And as for the "Optional Clause", so much praised at Geneva, there was reason to fear as, indeed, some British Dominions already feared, that it might be used to reopen, all over the world, long-settled questions to the detriment of the British Empire.[1]

When Ramsay MacDonald's second Labour Cabinet took office in the summer of 1929, Government control had passed into the hands of those who owed their position, at least in part, to their professions of the utmost support for the League, for Disarmament, and for every good international cause. Moreover, Lloyd George's Radicals had often been as loud and as insistent in their professions. It was not hard, therefore, in the Government's opening months to impose on the British Admiralty ideas more to Washington's taste than those of 1927 and 1928 had been. But the kind of Five-Power Naval Disarmament Treaty that was so assiduously sought had evaded the British Prime Minister by the

[1] Cf. *Ibid.*, January 28, 1928, for one censure of the Government in a comment on a British Note to the League which had dealt with the "Optional Clause". According to *The Nation*: "Hitherto the British Government have refused to sign the Optional Clause but they have done so in a hesitating and apologetic way, pleading that certain of the Dominions were uneasy lest the Court should claim jurisdiction over disputes relating to immigration policies, and that widely different interpretations were placed by international jurists on Sea Law. Now a very different tone is adopted. . . . This is a very deplorable attitude. . . . It can only mean that we are not prepared to seek justice, however unimpeachable the tribunal, if the other litigant is a state we dislike. . . ." And in regard to the Washington Hours Convention, the same number of *The Nation* had this censure: "The holding up of the Convention by Great Britain is becoming a serious scandal. It has been ratified unconditionally by seven states including Belgium; and France and Italy have ratified it, subject to its adoption by Great Britain and Germany." Germany, naturally, had much the same doubts as Britain and even graver unemployment problems.

summer of 1930 when the strenuous defence by France and Italy of their alleged special interests and needs upset every attempt to produce a Franco-Italian compromise.[1] There were other grave disappointments, too, in the international sphere for those who had claimed that a change of Government at London was all that was necessary for international affairs to move "progressively" forward once more. The Tariff Truce Conference and the resulting Convention, on which so many hopes were placed in London and Geneva, never came near to yielding any worthwhile results.[2] On the international regulation of Miners' Hours, where, it had been hoped, the ground was better prepared than in almost any other sphere, an International Labour Conference at Geneva failed to find the necessary two-thirds majority for the adoption of a Convention.[3] And, finally, the Labour Cabinet itself was driven almost to fury when its growingly difficult mandatory responsibilities in Palestine, as between Jews and hostile Arabs, attracted from the League's Mandates Commission not the sympathy it felt entitled to expect, but something more akin to fault-finding and rebuke. By contrast, Geneva's most acceptable offering, during 1930, to judge from the signatures obtained, was the rather ominous Draft Convention providing for financial assistance for a State which became the victim of aggression.[4]

Despite some of their grievous disappointments with international developments and the growingly catastrophic nature of their unemployment problem, the Labour Ministers, encouraged by well nigh all the "progressive forces" in the country, went on putting a great deal of their hope, for 1931, on the convening of a

---

[1] Cf. *The Nation*, April 5, 1930, for the difficulties that France was making by trying to exact a special "security" pledge in return for Arms Limitation and by refusing to hear of Italy's being assigned a naval strength at all comparable with that of France. Mussolini, on the other hand, refused to accept any inferiority to France.

[2] Cf. *Whitaker's Almanack, 1931*, p. 510, for essential dates: "Feb. 17, 1930. Tariff Truce Conference opened at Geneva. Feb. 20th. Conference appointed committees to consider draft of convention for a tariff truce and to draw up programme of subsequent negotiations for collective agreements designed to facilitate economic relations. . . . Mar. 24th. Tariff Truce Conference concluded with signature by 11 countries of convention to stabilise existing commercial treaties in Europe for a period. . . . Sept. 13th. Mr. Graham announced that British Government intended to ratify Tariff Truce Convention." It is possibly not uncharitable to surmise that most of Britain's ten co-signatories hoped that, by signing, they could help to stave off a Tariff Reform triumph in Britain, and signature, of course, was still very far from ratification.

[3] *Ibid.*, for the date of failure given as June 28th.

[4] *Ibid.*, under October 2, 1930: "Britain and 27 other States signed convention providing for financial assistance to a State which is victim of aggression."

World Disarmament Conference. The Preparatory Commission did, in fact, during November 1930, contrive to put in train the bringing together, into one apparently complete draft, of all the results of the intermittent discussions that had been proceeding since 1925.[1] Unfortunately, theoretically complete as was the draft Disarmament plan presented to the Council of the League of Nations in January 1931, all the figures which alone could give it meaning had been necessarily omitted, being left in the first place to the League Council and, ultimately, to the World Disarmament Conference which that Council was preparing to convene. It was doubtless a misfortune that Labour's Foreign Secretary, Arthur Henderson, accepted the World Conference Chairmanship in May 1931 for, long before that Conference could be assembled in February 1932 there had been so complete a change in Britain that he had lost not merely his office but even his place in Parliament, and naturally Conference prestige hardly gained therefrom. But much worse than that was the increasingly dangerous position developing in Manchuria where, after Sino-Japanese clashes in a Mukden suburb, five Chinese cities were bombed by the Japanese forces and China appealed for protection to the League (September 1931). It was, of course, unfortunate that the world-economic depression was deepening, for there was not the slightest relish anywhere, not even in America, for becoming involved in dangerous quarrels with powerfully-placed Japan from which there might be no issue save fighting. Fortunately, the Japanese Government had not lost control over its forces in Manchuria to the extent that ultimately developed. When the League Council met, therefore, on November 16, 1931 it did not seem impossible that a set of face-saving formulae might be discovered which, however, as in the case of Mussolini's bombardment of Corfu in 1923, would, doubtless, leave the powerful aggressor unpunished if he but consented to allow the League to negotiate for the wronged and

[1] Cf. *Ibid., 1932*, p. 508, for a succinct rendering of what had been going on. "Nov. 6, 1930. M. Litvinoff, Soviet delegate, at opening meeting of Preparatory Commission for World Disarmament Conference, proposed reconsideration of Soviet proposals for more drastic disarmament. Nov. 15th. Commission adopted resolution declaring that each of the high contracting parties agreed to limit expenditure on war material for large armaments, either by specific enumeration, budgetary limitation or a combination of the two. Nov. 21st. Commission approved principle of Budget limitation for naval expenditure. Jan. 20, 1931. Council of League received report of Preparatory Commission. Mr. Henderson urged reduction of armaments and not a mere limitation, and said there was no alliance except that of the Covenant against war, etc., etc."

weaker party. From the point of view of the Foreign Offices of the Powers, the Chinese Nationalists had a far from perfect international record themselves, and Geneva, despite the Covenant and the League of Nations Unions, resounded with the arguments of those who considered that sufficient risks from Japanese resentment were being run already on Chinese Nationalism's behalf, from the first decision, in December 1931, to send out the Lytton Commission of Inquiry to the publication of that Commission's Report in October 1932.[1]

All this time Disarmament business was not standing still though, as in the case of the Japanese "aggression on China", Radical zealots of the League of Nations Union were apt to find little reason for satisfaction in such proceedings as the publication of Disarmament suggestions from the Great Powers, each contrived to weaken potential rivals though always for "reasons of humanity". Thus British suggestions, presented by Sir John Simon in February 1932 after the Disarmament Conference opened, included the abolition of submarines and of gas and chemical warfare, a reduction in the size of warships and of maximum gun-calibres, and a prohibition of land guns over a certain calibre. Italy, for her part, wanted to add capital ships and aircraft carriers to submarines in the list of prohibited weapons of naval warfare, and, doubtless, "national interest" masquerading as world-philanthropy could also be found in Mussolini's readiness to ban, say, tanks and bombing aircraft. Finally, Germany, largely disarmed already under the Treaty of Versailles, demanded to be put on a footing of equality with other Powers and only to be pledged to obey a Disarmament system applied equally to all. Several months of wily manœuvring followed, very different from the seraphic Disarmament pictures painted at meetings or religious services promoted by the League of Nations Union.[2] By July 20th, a Text of a kind, mainly based on the Draft Convention of the Preparatory Commission but still largely without precise figures, was being pressed on a weary Conference, eager to disperse, in the names of Britain, France, Italy, and America.

[1] Cf. *Annual Register*, 1931, p. 283, for the special risks Britain was already taking.
[2] Cf. *The Times* file from February to July 1932 for reports from Geneva. It should be noted that the Conference, after the big opening speeches, virtually divided itself into four Commissions for Land, Sea, Air, and Political Questions, and that some of the most intricate manœuvring took place in these Commissions.

Adjournment came after the Conference, on July 23rd, had accepted the proffered Text by a vote of forty-one Governments though eight Governments had abstained and Russia and Germany had opposed. Germany, too, even under a Government still desperately trying to keep Hitler and his street-fighting Storm Troopers from taking control,[1] repeatedly announced her refusal to return to future Disarmament business until her claim for Armament equality had been conceded.[2] Moreover, significant preparations for German conscription were begun in defiance of the Versailles Treaty,[3] since Hindenburg, Papen, and Schleicher were well aware that Franco-Polish threats of military action would not readily be implemented if their only result would be to bring Hitler to power.[4]

It was probably too late already, in the second half of 1932, to prevent much further deterioration of the international position. Thus, in Japan, a Prime Minister who had sanctioned very risky "forward" moves in Manchuria and in China itself, still fell so far short of the demands of the "ultra-patriotic elements"[5] that he was assassinated by those who failed to see that a Japan, in considerable military and financial difficulties already, was in no

[1] Cf. *Berlin Diaries, 1932–1933*, p. 137, under August 3, 1932: "The reign of terror in the country grows from day to day. A dozen dead has become a normal occurrence. A bad look-out for humanity in general if ever these Brown villains are let loose upon it!"

[2] Cf. *Whitaker's Almanack, 1933*, p. 586, under September 6, 1932: "German Foreign Minister declared Germany would not take part in disarmament conferences until question of equality had been cleared up." This was almost the culmination of a German campaign for equality of status which had included the despatch of the Note of August 31st to France, which Power was, of course, in the name of its "security", the leader of a considerable *bloc* opposed to the German claim. Under September 12th *Whitaker's* noted this result: "France's reply to German Note rejected plea for equality of armaments, but in conciliatory terms."

[3] Cf. *Berlin Diaries, 1932–1933*, p. 180, under October 17, 1932, for one of the several ways in which Versailles restrictions were being evaded by the second half of 1932: "I have been for a day and a half in Brunswick. The training of our officers in the Flying School is proceeding vigorously, and the dropping of 'mail bags' is splendid practice. The course is completed in eight days. Then another thirty-five are taken on. . . . It is to be hoped that nobody spots it." The conscription planning was undertaken under cover of a Presidential decree, setting up a board for "promoting the fitness of Germany's youth", signed by Hindenburg on September 14th.

[4] *Ibid.*, p. 175, under October 5th, however, for the extension of the Franco-Polish military alliance "for another ten years".

[5] Cf. *Annual Register*, 1932, under Japan, for Mr. Inukai's assassination, on May 15th, by a band of young Army and Navy officers after a similar fate had overtaken, earlier in the year, two other important figures who had aroused the ire of the ultra-patriots. On May 15th bomb-throwing at five of the capital's principal buildings was also reported, and the distribution, by officers in uniform, of handbills in Tokyo's streets.

position to claim a domination of the Far East which would inevitably bring Russia, Britain, America, and France into the ranks of her enemies. And though the Emperor himself must have sanctioned the vigorous police-measures against the "so-called patriotic societies" that followed the assassination of May 15, 1932, it became plain, during the winter of 1932–3, that, in the existing megalomania dominating the armed forces, the Japanese were much more likely to defy and abandon the League, which, indeed, they did, than accept the Report of the Lytton Commission, carefully drafted though it was.[1] In Europe, too, Hitler's megalomania was already such that, in December 1932,[2] it was thought fit to save the Disarmament Conference and the non-Nazi Government of Germany by the Five-Power Declaration of December 11, 1932 under which France, Germany, Italy, Great Britain, and the United States recognized, at one and the same time, Germany's claim to equality and France's claim to security. There followed the effort to reconstitute the Disarmament Conference for a second session as early as might be in 1933. Unfortunately, Hitler became Chancellor at the end of January and though he did not think fit, at this stage, to take Germany out of the Disarmament proceedings or the League, the whole record of his movement was of such unbridled and ruthless Nationalist violence, that hopes at Geneva sank very low.[3]

In March, nevertheless, the British Government made its praiseworthy effort to revive Disarmament negotiation by sending its Prime Minister and Foreign Secretary to Geneva with a Draft Convention in which specific numbers were at last suggested for debate, 200,000 troops each, for example, for both France and Germany in Europe and proportionate contingents for every other continental power. International Bombing from the air was to be

[1] *Annual Register*, for the less hostile reception accorded by Japanese opinion to the Lytton Report than had been expected. Yet the Lytton Commission's proposals for Manchuria were ruled out as no longer applicable since Manchurian "independence" was already an accomplished fact.

[2] Cf. *Berlin Diaries, 1932–1933*, p. 210, under December 3, 1932, for an opponent's treatment of a Hitler letter to Hindenburg in which recognition was refused to any Cabinet save Hitler's own.

[3] Cf. *Annual Register*, 1933, English History, p. 15, for the return of Mr. Eden from Geneva early in March with a report that made it plain that the Disarmament Conference was facing ruin, so complete, apparently, was the breakdown of international confidence caused by Hitler's accession to power and the first reports coming out of Nazi Germany. When the Nazis themselves half-expected plans for "preventive" action, especially from France and Poland, the continental situation had obviously deteriorated fast.

forbidden, too,[1] and France and Italy were to ratify the London Naval Treaty of 1931. It was a misfortune that just when some new hope was being felt in Disarmament proceedings at Geneva, during the spring and summer of 1933, the Russian Communists should have seen fit to stage a "sabotage" trial of some British engineers and that President Roosevelt's "New Deal" determination to accept no limitation on American currency manipulation should have wrecked the chances of the World Economic Conference of 1933. By October 1933, Hitler, whose conduct of German affairs had already given rise to the greatest international anxiety, thought it safe to make the British Foreign Secretary's observation at the Disarmament Conference, that Germany had been changing her ground of late, a pretence for abandoning the Conference and the League. And, doubtless, he was informed that though there was abundant proof that there had been a vast acceleration of all the types of armament production forbidden to Germany by the Versailles Treaty,[2] the British Opposition could be trusted to make such hot attacks on Sir John Simon, "Imperialism", and the Versailles Treaty as the real villains of the Disarmament breakdown that Hitler's prime responsibility would be half-forgotten.

It has, of course, always been one of the great risks of British Radical politics that foreign enemies would seek to take advantage of its insatiable urge to crusade against the alleged iniquities of Toryism and of its over-readiness, especially when in Opposition,

[1] It was, doubtless, a mistake for the British negotiators to try and reserve the "police bombing" of "rebels" in remote parts of the British Empire though, in point of fact, warning bombing in Arabian deserts or North-West Frontier mountains had proved useful and relatively bloodless. Yet the international situation was such that the world soon resounded with attacks on British "hypocrisy", and, at home, a Labour Party, led by such an anarchical pacifist as Lansbury, found an anti-Government cry very much to its taste. In the end, the Government undertook not to allow its provisional reservations to block the success of a World Agreement.

[2] Cf. *Berlin Diaries, 1932–1933, passim*, for what even the pre-Hitler Reichswehr had been up to, and the British Government suspicions were subsequently sharpened by the Hitler War Ministry's attempt to purchase twenty-five British aeroplanes at the very time when Nazi attempts to accure the overthrow of the Dollfuss Government in Austria were causing the greatest continental anxiety. Here is an almost incredible Reichswehr boast of July 4, 1932 from the *Berlin Diaries*: "Reckoned in degrees of intensity, we possess a gas, seventeen times as effective as Russia's, twenty-six times as effective as France's, twenty-nine times as effective as England's, thirty-four times as effective as Italy's.... Stolzenberg assures us that the factories will be ready for action by the end of November this year." There were similar boasts on tanks and tank-artillery, which could not be kept wholly concealed from the French Secret Services, though Britain had taken them less seriously till 1933.

to put all possible blame on the London Government for whatever was amiss in the world. So it was in the days of the Jacobins and of Napoleon, so it was again during the days of Salisbury and Balfour, and so it was to be in the crisis years of 1933–9 when such organizations as the League of Nations Union,[1] the Peace Pledge Union,[2] and the National Peace Council,[3] manned in large part by similar elements to those which had made up the essential strength of the old Radicalism, contrived to do Hitler at least as much service as did the British Fascist Movement. And the partisan fanaticism with which the Labour Opposition—often supported by Lloyd George Radicalism—fought the alleged battles of Peace and the League of Nations against the British Cabinet's attempts to rearm itself to meet the growing dangers abroad will one day seem as incredible as the Left Book Club.[4]

One of the most eloquent of those who saw, almost with despair, the increasing urge of "progressive" Britain to set itself on what seemed the certain road to destruction was Baldwin's Colonial Secretary of 1924–9, Leopold Amery. In his very notable auto-biography, Amery ascribed the unsatisfactory character of much post-1931 development to Labour's resentment of its ruinous 1931 defeats, resentment which drove the Socialist rump in Parliament and the "host of embittered candidates outside" to the advocacy, in international as in national affairs, of extreme courses. The Rump's leader, too, George Lansbury, was permitted to declare, as his personal view, that he would "disband the Army, dismantle the Navy, dismiss the Air Force, abolish the whole dreadful equipment of war and say to the world, 'Do your worst'". Just

[1] Cf. L. S. Amery, *My Political Life*, iii, 144: "It brought together all the theoretical idealists who believed in making war to suppress war and the extreme pacifists. . . . Its appeal was both to memories of the wasteful slaughter of trench warfare and to fears, nearer home, of indiscriminate destruction inflicted by bombing attacks. . . . It is difficult, in these more grimly realist days, to begin to understand the atmosphere of delusion which was so steadily and often unscrupulously fostered. . . ." Amery was especially severe on Robert Cecil's part in organizing the notorious Peace Ballot of 1934–5 which, finally by "a series of apparently innocent but, in fact, highly misleading questions, an affirmative answer to which would, in effect, amount to a whole-hearted endorsement" of the extremist view of the function of the League of Nations, produced vast "peace" majorities among the 11,640,066 persons polled.

[2] This organization, whose best-known figure was the remarkable Churchman, "Dick" Sheppard, actually seems to have canvassed, at one stage, the possibility of establishing a screen of its non-combatants between contending armies. 133,000 members were claimed by November 1937.

[3] Which secured for a time the distinguished Chairmanship (1933–6) of the great historical scholar, G. P. Gooch.

[4] Whose main beneficiary, even in Labour's view, was Communism.

as irresponsible, in Amery's eyes, was the Labour Party's resolution at Hastings by which a national war, even in self-defence, would only be supported at the bidding of the League of Nations, a resolution which he coupled with the notorious Oxford Union vote of February 1933 against "fighting for King and Country" as expressing the "same widespread blend of crazy theory and hysterical emotion". The Tory Leaders in the National Governments of 1931-4 were also blameworthy, in Amery's view, for having refrained, until it was almost too late, from a direct challenge to the prevailing platform temper, a temper which allowed Opposition, in the notorious East Fulham by-election of October 25, 1933, successfully to ascribe to Sir John Simon and the National Government the principal responsibility for Hitler's wreck of the Disarmament Conference eleven days before.[1]

The Peace Ballot of the League of Nations Union; Lloyd George's last Radical campaign "for Peace and Reconstruction"; and the readiness of Baldwin to go to the country, in the autumn of 1935, on a policy of League sanctions against Italy on behalf of Abyssinia, represent further landmarks in the history of the often muddled British thinking about the contemporary world. Of course, the credit of the League was largely ruined by its vain attempt of 1935-6 to coerce Italy, by inadequate economic sanctions, into abandoning the ruthless Abyssinian adventure.[2] By 1939, the League had become almost a wraith, and every attempt to use it to stop the terrifying advance of Nazi, Japanese, and Italian aggression appeared increasingly futile. Yet when a new Prime Minister, Neville Chamberlain, began, in May 1937, an alteration of policy, designed to win Italy back into the Franco-British camp, attempting to save Austria, Czecho-Slovakia, and Poland from Nazi subversion, he found himself in continuous

[1] *Annual Register*, 1933, found the municipal elections of November 1933 also markedly affected by the "warmongers" charge against Ministers.

[2] Cf. *Whitaker's Almanack, 1937*, p. 607, for some of the additional degradation the League was suffering in the summer of 1936: "June 30th. Emperor of Abyssinia addressed Assembly and asked for assurance that the aggressor should not triumph. Italian journalists tried to prevent him speaking, and were ejected. July 1st. Mr. Eden told the Assembly that it was British Government's view that the Assembly should not in any way recognise Italy's conquest of Abyssinia. M. Léon Blum said that France stood by the Covenant. July 3rd. A Jew exiled from Germany shot himself in Assembly Hall during debate on sanctions. July 4th. Assembly recommended Council to invite Governments to make proposals to improve the League and advised Co-ordination Committee to end sanctions. Application by Abyssinia for a loan was negatived. President of Danzig Senate, Herr Greiser, asked for removal of League control over Danzig. As he left he 'cocked a snook' at journalists."

difficulties. A strong section of Conservative opinion—let alone the two Oppositions—considered as humiliating and dangerous the Prime Minister's apparent readiness virtually to condone Mussolini's illegalities in Abyssinia and Spain. And ultimately the fact that, in a moment of brutal frankness, on March 7, 1938, he had said, "What country in Europe today, if threatened by a larger Power, can rely on the League for protection? None.", was used against him by Attlee in the post-Munich debates. According to Attlee, Leader of the Opposition, that had constituted almost an invitation to Hitler to invade Austria which he had accepted a few days later, and Sir Archibald Sinclair, too, for the Liberals, contrived, in his speech, to associate himself both "with the flood of relief and thanksgiving which has swept over the world since the Munich Conference" and with Mr. Attlee's view that it was the policy of the Prime Minister which had brought the country to the brink of war.[1]

If the Prime Minister, at Munich, cheered on by the great bulk of the "public", put altogether too much faith in Hitler's assurances, he certainly tried to make amends in the spring of 1939 when issuing the guarantees designed to safeguard Greece, Rumania, and Poland from the fate which had overtaken the Czechs. He rightly held that a modest measure of Compulsory Service was necessary if Britain's pledges were to be taken seriously abroad but if he hoped that Opposition, in view of what it had done years before when deciding to abandon unconditional resistance to rearmament,[2] could be persuaded to accept Conscription also he was mistaken. It was true that rearmament had served powerfully to restimulate some of the hardest-hit industries of the depression,[3] and that the absorption of young men between twenty and twenty-one into the Services could, at length, help to

[1] Cf. W. W. Hadley, *Munich: Before and After*, p. 114.
[2] Cf. *Whitaker's Almanack, 1937*, p. 606–7, under October 6, 1936: "Labour Party Conference by 1,738,000 to 657,000 carried executive's resolution in favour of rearmament." The issue had virtually been decided some time before when Bevin's angry criticism of Lansbury's pacifist activities, in face of the Dictators, had led to Lansbury's resignation at the end of the 1935 Conference. A General Election was then being expected, and in that season of preparations for going to Abyssinia's help, the Conservative programme of air equality with the next strongest power, the organization of industries for speedy conversion to war purposes, and the rebuilding of the British fleet, had some obvious electoral advantages.
[3] Cf. *Northern Echo Industrial Review*, February 6, 1937, p. 20, for such headlines even then in Rearmament's earlier stages as "REARMAMENT BRINGS PROSPERITY BACK TO THE TYNE." "INDUSTRIALISTS BELIEVE THAT THE DARK DAYS ARE OVER."

564

break up the most obstinate pockets of unemployment[1] besides
encouraging Poland against Nazi threats, Rumania against those
of the Nazis' friends, and Greece against Mussolini. Moreover,
the Japanese activities in China, aiming at a degradation of British
prestige, might become more cautious[2] and the Russian negotiators,
considering Anglo-French plans for a joint stand against further
violence by Hitler, less inclined to ask for terms which indirectly
envisaged the reabsorption of the Baltic Republics and a good deal
more.[3] Peace-time Conscription was, nevertheless, resisted by
both Oppositions as contrary to alleged pledges given, in less
serious circumstances, by Baldwin and Chamberlain himself, and
as raising also the possibility of industrial conscription. Despite
the "conscientious objection" and industrial safeguards offered,
over a hundred and fifty years of Radical history made the resistance to Conscription almost inevitable.[4] Yet it may well be that
Chamberlain's last warning to Hitler, after the latter had achieved
the diplomatic triumph of the Russo-German Agreement of
August 24, 1939, would have carried greater weight but for the
apparent divisions in Britain. Chamberlain's words still ring
ominously enough today:[5]

Whatever may prove to be the nature of the German-Soviet agreement, it cannot alter Great Britain's obligation to Poland which His
Majesty's Government have stated in public repeatedly and plainly and
which they are determined to fulfil.

It has been alleged that if His Majesty's Government had made their
position more clear in 1914, the great catastrophe would have been

[1] Cf. *The People's Year Book, 1936*, pp. 122–6, for the admission by a source
not friendly to the Government of the results achieved before rearmament had
really entered into its stride. Steel showed monthly production averages
increased from 583,000 tons in 1933, to 738,000 tons in 1934, and to 802,000
tons in the first nine months of 1935, and the corresponding figures for pig iron
were 345,000 tons, 498,000 tons, and 516,000 tons. But, thought the *Year Book*,
"we are approaching the limit of industrial activity under present conditions . . .
we shall in future have to regard 'the hard core' of unemployment as being very
much higher than it used to be estimated".

[2] Cf. W. W. Hadley, *Munich: Before and After*, pp. 133–4: "The Royal Navy,
after meeting bare needs on the seas nearer home, was not strong enough to
safeguard British interests in the Far East . . . the Japanese knew our weakness
and were impudent in affronts. . . ."

[3] *Ibid.*, pp. 162–3, for the objections in Latvia, Lithuania, and Estonia to the
Russian claims, and the suspicions of the "Red Army" in Poland and Rumania.

[4] Cf. *Hansard*, April 26th, for Chamberlain's introduction of the Conscription
plan as a temporary and emergency measure.

[5] Cf. W. W. Hadley, *Munich: Before and After*, pp. 170–1, for the text of
Chamberlain's letter, as delivered by Sir Nevile Henderson, the British
Ambassador, to Hitler himself at Berchtesgaden.

avoided. Whether or not there is any force in the allegation, His Majesty's Government are resolved that on this occasion there shall be no such tragic misunderstanding.

If the case should arise, they are resolved, and prepared, to employ without delay all the forces at their command, and it is impossible to foresee the end of hostilities once engaged. It would be a dangerous illusion to think that, if war once starts it will come to an early end, even if a success on any one of the several fronts on which it will be engaged should have been secured.

The man with the bowler-hat and umbrella, whose gullibility was the laughing-stock of the Nazis, was obviously not to be gulled again whether by Hitler alone or by Hitler and Stalin in combination. Germany and Russia, in fact, both paid a tremendous price for the almost unparalleled cynicism of their *entente* to recreate the age of the Partitions of Poland. Britain paid a tremendous price also for leading the resistance, and one small portion of that price was the loss of part of her political inheritance. For British Radicalism could never, after 1945, aspire to play even the role that Lloyd George[1] had contrived for it after his fall in 1922. There was the new Radicalism, indeed, of the Labour Party which had inherited some very characteristic attitudes from the old. But the Labour Party was committed, by its basic dependence on the Trade Unions, to economic and social positions that some of the best and most Radical talent in the country has, soon or late, found insupportable.

One great historian, who never surrendered the title of Gladstonian Liberal even when co-operating on Peace and League platforms with Labour's Leaders, put the matter this way:[2] "I rejoice that more persons have wider opportunities and better prospects than ever before. Yet the common man who has pushed his way—with a good deal of assistance from the privileged classes—to the centre of the stage has a great deal to learn. He is as selfish, short-sighted and quarrelsome as those who used to be called his betters no better and no worse. Exhortation is resented or ignored, and, like the rest of us, he is only taught by experience. . . . Acton used to say that the tyranny of a majority is even worse than that of a minority because it is more difficult to remove. Worthwhile democracy means very much more than 'counting heads instead of breaking them'."

[1] He had died, at a great age, shortly before the end of the war.
[2] G. P. Gooch, *Under Six Reigns*, pp. 327–8.

CHAPTER XXVII

LIBERTY OVERSEAS

"A fortnight ago at the Albert Hall the audience cheered the Bolshevists. . . . But ill-informed enthusiasm is only a little better than malignant detraction. . . . Gorky at least is above suspicion . . . Gorky founded the *Novaia Zhizn* at the beginning of the revolution. . . . With the first Bolshevik outbreak of July his voice becomes more desperate. He sees in the endeavour to rouse the ignorant people against the revolutionary government deliberate criminality. . . . The November days came, and with them an increase in Gorky's fear and also of his conviction that the Bolshevist leaders are deliberately setting themselves to arouse all the beastlike instincts of the ignorant mob. . . . The new Government allows no books to be published. All newspapers, save those which incite their readers to acts of redoubled violence against the bourgeoisie are suppressed. . . . The Red Guards, the railway workers, and the Bolshevist officials alone are fed. . . . Of the starvation, Gorky gives one unforgettable picture. . . . Recently the news has come that Gorky himself has joined the Bolshevists. . . . He has accepted the one post which he could not . . . refuse. . . . He is now in charge of the issue of millions of cheap books to the Russian people. He is preparing the end of the tyranny of the beast. He believes that education is the only way; but whether education alone is sufficient who shall say? Will anyone guarantee that Bolshevism in educated Germany would be less bloody than it has been in Russia? Or in England? . . . Gorky's witness of what Bolshevism actually is must serve us. Those who call for it in England . . . will not escape the charge of having gambled with humanity itself. . . ."

The Nation, November 16, 1918, reproves unqualified pro-Bolshevism.

"We have never blamed the German Government for using military force to suppress the Communist risings . . . the case against Herr Noske is rather that he exaggerated all his military measures, gave the soldiers a free hand. . . . With every allowance, however, the fact remains that the semi-Socialist Government of republican Germany rests on a mercenary armed force, which keeps alive the traditions of the old militarism . . . at its present strength of 400,000 men. . . ."

The Nation, August 30, 1919.

English Radicalism: The End?

"It is becoming the traditional policy of Downing Street to satisfy restless, aggressive, thrusting Powers by gifts of other people's property. Did we not attempt to buy off Russia by granting her a sphere of influence in and virtual possession of North Persia? Was it not seriously contemplated giving the Portuguese African colonies to Germany before the War? And so, as Signor Mussolini is determined to distract attention from internal affairs in Italy by Imperialistic adventures in Africa, it is in accord with the new tradition to offer . . . leave to construct a railway joining . . . Eritrea with . . . Somaliland. . . . The rest will follow according to plan . . . the extinction of the independence of Ethiopia. . . ."

The Nation, May 1, 1926, for J. M. Kenworthy, M.P., on Abyssinia's peril.

"The news from India . . . has been important, and at first sight gravely disquieting. A majority of the Indian National Congress assembled at Lahore have substituted complete independence for Dominion Status as the avowed goal of its policy, declared a boycott of the Legislative Councils, declined participation in the Round-Table Conference. . . . Of two things we feel certain . . . the weapon of violence can at this stage of their history lead the peoples of India nowhere at all except to disaster and destruction. In particular we are convinced that the Irish analogy, which has apparently become a favourite theme with the Indian extremists . . . is a radically false one. It is not only that there is no Indian nation as there has always been an Irish nation—that India contains a thousand Ulsters. . . . It is that among the majority creeds and races themselves there is no uniformity of will to make revolution a success. . . . Meanwhile, a foretaste of the difficulties and problems with which the [Round Table] Conference will be faced has been given."

The Nation, January 4, 1930, on Indian "extremism".

I N a charming autobiography, G. P. Gooch, the greatest
historian among the immense Liberal and Radical bands,
who entered the 1906 Parliament and dominated the national
life for the next eight or nine years, has described some of the
leading political interests of himself and of those who acted with
him. South Africa, Botha, Smuts, and the perhaps exaggerated
hopes placed on virtually unrestricted Boer self-government shall
here be omitted, and attention shall be turned first to the large
India Committee, which he joined as an amateur, in order to
forward the liberalizing work of the half-dozen Anglo-Indian
experts like Sir Henry Cotton who provided the leadership. It
becomes plain from Gooch's account what pressure there was
from the Back-Benchers to forward, for example, the Morley-
Minto constitutional reforms, the first Indianization of the India
Council in London, and the Viceroy's Executive Council in
Calcutta and, above all, the announcement of the eventual abolition
of the Indian opium export to China. The pressure was, indeed,
for much more than Minto in India or even Morley at Westminster felt able to concede especially after boycott and murder
followed Britain's refusal to grant the speedy undoing of the
alleged crime of Bengal's partition.[1]

Egypt, too, promptly came into the picture after the Denshawi
"scandal" of 1906 when the "savage retaliation" inflicted on
villagers who had attacked British officers unwittingly shooting
down pigeons regarded as the villagers' own, raised a major
outcry[2] and revived Egyptian Nationalism under Mustapha
Kemal. Gooch joined an Egyptian group in the Commons who
urged that Egypt could not for ever be kept in leading-strings but
that the time had come for beginning to prepare the Egyptian
people for taking control of their own destinies. Yet unlike the

[1] Cf. G. P. Gooch, *Under Six Reigns*, pp. 127–8, for a warm tribute to
Gokhale, who was specially consulted on the Morley-Minto reforms and who,
in Gooch's eyes, was unlike Gandhi in that he was not merely a great Indian but
a citizen of the world. There is a passage, too, recognizing the seriousness of
Morley's problem in Bengal while objecting to the deportation of suspects
under the Bengal Regulation of 1818.

[2] Cf. *Ibid.*, pp. 129–30, for the fifty villagers tried for murder and assault
(one officer had died), the four hanged, the eight flogged, and the ten others
sentenced to long terms of imprisonment. Humanitarians' repulsion was the
greater from the fact that the hangings and lashings took place before the
eyes of friends and relatives of the accused though, it seems, that if Cromer
had not unfortunately been travelling home on leave, he would have contrived
something very different.

group's extremer members, Gooch was not unwilling to pay tribute to the obstacles which Lord Cromer's twenty-five pro-consular years had cleared from the Egyptian people's path. As he said, on Egyptian as on Indian matters, he belonged to the left centre of his party and he separated himself from extremer views both when he decided to vote for the grant of £50,000 made to Cromer after his resignation and when he disapproved of the more virulent pamphleteering use made of the Denshawi incident.

The Persia Committee, in aid of Persian constitutionalism against the sometimes allied forces of Persian and Russian "despotism" was another Oriental interest of the omnivorous Gooch, and if he was out of Parliament by the end of 1911 when the grossest Tsarist bullying of Persia took place,[1] that tended only to increase his desire as a political editor to help Russian constitutionalism as he had once aided it as a member of the Parliamentary Russia Committee. Yet it was the Balkan Committee, recruited largely outside Parliament by Noel Buxton before 1906 and with some apparently important Macedonian "reforms" to its credit since 1903, which seemed to offer Gooch his best chance of forwarding "progress" after becoming its Parliamentary spokesman in 1906. The constitutional revolution of the Young Turks in the summer of 1908, ending as it did Sultan Abdul Hamid's repellent despot-ism, seemed to give "progress" special chances in the Balkans, and great was the rejoicing of the Balkan Committee,[2] confident that the European Christians of Macedonia and Thrace and the Armenian and other Christians of Asiatic Turkey were reasonably certain of better times. There were, for a time, exchanges of courtesies and visits between the Balkan Committee and the Young Turks' Leaders, and possibly a great deal of good might have resulted but for the aggressive Italian War on the Turks of 1911–12, followed by the onslaught of the Balkan League of 1912–13. By the time the greed of Christian Governments in the Balkans had brought a Second Balkan War in 1913, followed by a

[1] Cf. *Whitaker's Almanack, 1913*, p. 477: "Nov. 12, 1911. Russia presented an ultimatum demanding the withdrawal of Treasury gendarmes from the property of the ex-Shah. . . . Nov. 29th. A fresh ultimatum was delivered by Russia demanding the dismissal of Mr. Morgan Shuster and Mr. Lecoffre."

[2] Cf. G. P. Gooch, *Under Six Reigns*, p. 134, for the deputation that went to Constantinople to congratulate the Young Turks, and the subsequent receptions given in London to some of their leaders, notably Enver Pasha. Gooch admits frankly that the Balkan Committee's hopes were dreadfully belied by events, especially in Armenia, and that Gladstonian survivors of the "bag and baggage" school, like G. W. E. Russell, were better prophets.

greedy victors' peace, much of Gooch's *penchant* for Balkan races and for Balkan Christians had gone.[1] He was working for an Anglo-German *détente* as the surest way of preserving world peace, was finding some encouragement in the Anglo-German collaboration which had taken place to localize the two Balkan Wars and was hopeful both of a newly-founded Anglo-German Friendship Society and of the Associated Councils of Churches in the British and German Empires for fostering friendly relations.

War was fated to come, however, just when the Anglo-German *détente* seemed to be making real progress even in the overseas field, and soon the patriotic rhetoric, found necessary on both sides to keep the war-effort of many millions at its maximum, was making a negotiated peace impossible save as a peace of exhaustion or surrender. Meanwhile, of course, both sides tried to reduce their dangers by taking up the pose of radical liberators of non-national territory, dominated by their opponents, and there were, for example, Turco-German attempts to turn Moslem feeling in Egypt and India against Britain as well as Berlin's aid for those planning a Sinn Fein rebellion in Ireland. Ultimately, of course, Germany, to her ruin, took to such desperate steps as suggesting aid to Mexico to recover territory from the United States (bitterly antagonized already though Americans were by the "indiscriminate" submarine campaign) and helping the Russian Bolsheviks to return and agitate their own country in a fashion that proved more effective than Berlin doubtless bargained for. On the other side, too, more and more irretraceable steps were being taken in the effort to enlist support from Italy, Greece, Rumania, the Arabs, the Czechs and, finally even the Zionist Jews in America. The revelations of the 'Secret Treaties", too, when they came from Russia's Bolshevized Foreign Ministry, in the winter of 1917–18, were epoch-making for, in India and Egypt, for example, they served to free large sections of the native leadership from most of the effects of Allied War propaganda. Certainly, by the winter of 1918–19, despite the final Allied victory, India and Egypt were full of bad trouble for the British administrators on the spot, trouble destined to be aggravated, before long, by deep Moslem resentment of the humiliating plight to which the Allies had reduced the Caliph, Constantinople, and the Turkish Empire.

[1] Cf. *Ibid.*, pp. 160–1.

It must be admitted that if some of the post-war difficulties, that overtook Britain at home and overseas, had been foreseen, the strong Radical section at Westminster that was dispersed by the "Khaki Election" of 1918 might never have been dispersed at all. Its members stayed doubtful to the last whether Lloyd George and his immediate personal following of Macnamaras and Addisons, allied as they were, despite their continued Radical professions, to some of the most distasteful jingoism in the country,[1] were not raising the stakes too high in their bid for a "Knock-Out" Victory. History has, of course, largely justified their doubts, yet the fact that the victorious Coalition Government, which had to liquidate the war, could show two or even three faces—Radical, Conservative, and "National Labour"—as it dealt, according to need, with its world-wide problems, allowed it more success than some of its enemies were counting upon. Thus, the Egyptian Nationalist revolution of March 1919 was not only mastered promptly but conspicuous adaptability was shown, especially by Lord Milner, in finding a way forward to a new basis of Anglo-Egyptian relations under which the 1914 Protectorate was abandoned and Egypt became a Kingdom allied to Britain.[2] In India, too, where there had been repeated signs of coming storms and where the Rowlatt Commission of 1917–18 reported evidence of the association of the Bengal seditionists with German plots, the arrival of a Liberal Secretary of State, E. S. Montagu, to forward that "development of constitutional progress" known as the Montagu-Chelmsford Reforms doubtless prevented the troubles of 1919 from proving even graver than they were.[3]

How the Bombay mill-strikes of January and February 1919 coincided with the mooting of a Rowlatt Emergency Powers Bill against sedition and how, despite the Government concession of

[1] Cf. Julian Symons, *Horatio Bottomley*.

[2] Cf. *Parliamentary Papers, 1921*, xlii, 621, for the Report of the Special Mission to Egypt. The admissions that there were probably far too many British officials in the Egyptian Ministries, that the quality of numbers of them left something to be desired, that the British official community was herding together too much and out of contact with Egyptian social life and even that Egypt's right to send diplomatic missions abroad had only been conceded reluctantly show the remarkable frankness of the Report. It began, indeed, with a candid account of the largely successful Nationalist attempt to organize a boycott of its proceedings.

[3] Cf. *Ibid., 1919*, xxxviii, 489, for the Indian Government's *Annual Statement exhibiting the Moral and Material Progress of India* in which all manner of things, even to the activities and views of "the Left" of the Indian National Congress, are discussed in a fashion that some of the older I.C.S. pensioners in Britain must have found strange and disturbing.

making it a three-year Bill only, the Gandhi "passive resistance" was undertaken which led on to the calamities of Amritsar, cannot be treated in detail here. Suffice it to say that, helped, doubtless, by the thorough defeat and humiliation of an attempted Afghan invasion, the Government considered it possible to allow the King to announce, by the end of 1919, that the Prince of Wales would be sent to India, before long, to inaugurate the new Constitution and open the Chamber of Princes. The censure of General Dyer for his conduct at Amritsar, undertaken by the Hunter Committee in 1920, might have helped the Prince if he had been able to reach India when originally intended but illness interposed, and it was Queen Victoria's last surviving son, the Duke of Connaught, who arrived in India early in 1921 to open the new Councils. A new Viceroy in the person of Lord Reading, another Liberal associate of Lloyd George, had the formidable task of trying to enlist their hearty support while preparing for a delayed State visit from the Prince of Wales, in the winter of 1921–2, which would obviously give all the elements of anti-official agitation, from Gandhi to the underground terrorist groups of Bengal, wonderful opportunities of advertising themselves to the world. Yet Gandhi, upon whom the Indian National Congress had bestowed its full "executive" authority, ultimately overplayed his hand especially when he sickened Hindu Liberals[1] by what they considered his anarchic mob-tactics and the reckless pursuit of the Moslem alliance to the point of adopting the Khilafat agitation and attempting some original condonation of the primitive savagery of the Moplah Moslem rebellion in the South. When Gandhi's arrest was finally ordered in March 1922, even so accredited a British Radical organ as *The Nation* considered it unavoidable,[2] and though it protested against the six years sentence soon inflicted as too severe, it was prepared to write down Gandhi's political leadership thus:[3]

As an Indian mystic he has his place . . . as a public man he has a heavy load of guilt for one of the worst massacres in Eastern history. As for the detail of his politics, it does not survive the analysis of it by Sir Sankaran Nair. I should describe Sir Sankaran Nair as an advanced Indian Nationalist. . . . His *Gandhi and Anarchy* simply blasts Mr.

[1] Sir Sankaran Nair's *Gandhi and Anarchy* of 1922 seems to have had a specially marked effect. Yet Jahawarlal Nehru's *Autobiography* of 1936 contrived to avoid all mention of the Moplahs' outrages on the Hindu population, concentrating instead on Moplah prisoner deaths in a military train.
[2] *The Nation*, March 18, 1921.
[3] *Ibid.*, March 25, 1921.

Gandhi's repute for political leadership. . . . Mr. Gandhi's career is not a step on India's march to freedom; it is a long flight backwards. India chose this engaging charlatan when she had better men for her service.

It must be concluded that 1922 marked in India, as in Egypt, the ebb of a tide of most dangerous mob-pressure against British control though, of course, the tide was certain to rise again, for was not Egypt entitled to ask for further negotiations on the reserved points of February 1922 and India to obtain a re-examination, by 1929, of the new Constitution? Yet some temporary basis of settlement had been discovered and, meanwhile, Palestine, Transjordania, and Mesopotamia were being adapted, with some skill, as model British Mandatory Territories under the League of Nations. What obstacles were being overcome may be gauged from a Parliamentary occasion of July 1921 when cheered on from both "Anti-Waste" to the Right and anti-Imperialism to the Left, Mr. Asquith was thus reported:[1]

On the Colonial Office Vote, Mr. Asquith led a powerful assault on our continued occupation of Mesopotamia. On former occasions he used to advise the retention of Basrah and the coast, but he now makes no reservations and appears to urge withdrawal, not only from Mesopotamia but from Palestine. He laughed at Mr. Churchill's pretence that we are bound in honour by our pledges to the natives. The natives have done their best to drive us out, and now with the Sèvres Treaty unratified, we cannot even urge the sanction of an Allied "mandate". Mr. Asquith pointed out how slippery were the steps on which Mr. Churchill was building—the royal "coupon" bestowed on the Emir Feisul, the loyalty of General Jaafer, the gentleman who won both the Iron Cross and the St. Michael and St. George in one war, the "autonomy" of the Kurds, which our aeroplanes promote by dropping bombs when they locate a tribal assembly . . . on a low reckoning Mesopotamia has cost us since the Armistice £100,000,000 excluding the cost of evacuating the troops. . . .

Patience, skill and profitable oil-production, however, helped Whitehall to steer the Mesopotamia problem into quieter waters for a very long period though Palestine, prospering, too, from a vast inflow of Zionist money, became so difficult a political commitment,[2] owing to Arab-Jewish contentions, that Britain was ultimately driven to suggest partition.

[1] *The Nation*, July 23, 1921.
[2] Cf. *Ibid.*, August 30, 1924: "Broadly speaking, Palestine costs the British taxpayer a million a year for the upkeep of military forces necessary for the maintenance of the present régime in the face of overwhelming opposition. . . . A ninety per cent majority of the population can scarcely be expected to accept

Possibly the most typical colonial campaign in the traditional Radical style was, in the 1920s, concerned with Kenya and the alleged predatory ambitions of the white settlers who, having been allowed and even encouraged to move in for Imperial reasons during the days of Salisbury and Balfour, were now a growing community, aiming, it was said, at a complete domination of the vast native majority. Certainly, Lord Delamere, the Leader of the white colonists,[1] had formidable aspirations and influential friends in high places, prepared, it was feared, to yield to his view that much more power and influence should be allowed to elected representatives of the colonists, anxious to embark on "progress" free of the pettifogging trammels of the Colonial Office. The editorial office of the Radicals' *Nation* seems to have given considerable attention to the Kenya situation between 1923 and 1930,[2] and here is almost a song of triumph on what seemed final victory, a song, which from its Biblical language, almost appears to have been written by a missionary:[3]

THE WORD OF ELIJAH. Some time ago we pointed out that the tragedy of Naboth's vineyard was being re-enacted in Kenya, the parts of Ahab and Jezebel being played by the white settlers, of Naboth by the natives, and of the vineyard by the land of Kenya. Since then, the settlers by their demand for an unofficial majority in the Kenya Legislative Council and by their support of various ingenious schemes for "closer union" of our East African possessions have made a determined effort to obtain control over the Government of Kenya. Such control would, of course, carry with it control of Naboth's vineyard—and of something more, for our modern Ahabs do not stone Naboth, they first take his vineyard and then make him work in it for wages. This charming scheme, so characteristic of modernity, has subsequently had a troubled and involved history. First, the Hilton Young Commission was appointed to report . . . and reported on the whole very unfavourably for the settlers. Then Sir Samuel Wilson was sent to report on the

the position of a minority . . . the Jews . . . must relinquish the idea of Zionist domination or even of a Jewish *imperium in imperio*."

[1] There is an account in two volumes by Elspeth Huxley under the title, *White Man's Country, Lord Delamere and the Making of Kenya*. It was on his fifth big-game hunting expedition to Africa in 1897 that, at the age of twenty-seven, he first traversed the Kenya Highlands of which Nairobi is now the centre. He returned early in 1903 and took a ninety-nine years lease of 100,000 acres, offered by a Commissioner anxious to encourage white immigration and big-scale development. Needless to say, there were some heavy losses of borrowed money in the first stages.

[2] There was Norman Leys's book, *Kenya*, of 1924 to provide a background but *The Nation* seems to have had private sources of information.

[3] *The Nation*, July 5, 1930.

Report . . . and reported on the whole very favourably for the settlers. Meanwhile the Labour Government had succeeded to the Conservatives, and it fell to them to make a decision. After a long interval, the word of Elijah, in the person of Lord Passfield, has at last been spoken in two White Papers, *Memorandum on Native Policy in East Africa* (Cmd. 3573), and *Statement . . . as regards Closer Union in East Africa* (Cmd. 3574).

Brief indications have so far been given of what was the "progressive" attitude towards a number of overseas subjects under constant discussion during the period. But certainly the subject debated most earnestly and continuously by "progressives", and with very good reason, was the rise of dictatorships on the ruins of "democratic systems", dictatorships established by force rather than consent and employing terror and, often enough, torture to hold down unfriendly elements in the population. To the dismay of the "progressive", the echoes of their rejoicing over the beginning of real "democracy" in Russia with the election of a Constituent Assembly had scarcely died away when it became plain that "the dictatorship of the proletariat", in the person of Lenin, had no mind to hand over control or even accept some direction.[1] It was the Constituent Assembly which was swept off the scene in a fashion that lent some justification to the numerous anti-Bolshevik revolts of 1918–19 and even to the Allies doing something for movements that appealed in the name of Allied Russia. The bitter Civil War that followed was marked by dreadful atrocities on both sides, and the murder of the Tsar and his whole family, though responsibility was veiled for the time, is now known to have been personally authorized by Lenin himself. Unfortunately, too many of the "advanced" found it easy and politically profitable to evade fundamental questions by assuming that Tsarist misgovernment had made such things inevitable, by "proving" that, in any case, "alleged" Red atrocities were completely outmatched by White[2] and by, finally, ascribing to "criminal Allied intervention" the main responsibility for what

[1] The election machinery was, of course, in action before the Bolshevik *coup d'état* in Petrograd on November 7th or the surrender of the General Staff at Mohilev on December 3rd. *Whitaker's Almanack, 1919*, p. 398, reports the Senate as having been "forcibly dissolved by extremist soldiers" on December 11th and, on December 13th, the report is of "Members of Russian Constituent Assembly dispersed by Bolshevists."

[2] Those old enough to remember such things may even recollect the Finnish Civil War between the Bolsheviks' allies and the Finnish Nationalists providing an early example of this type of "advanced" position-taking.

has turned out to be a permanent denial of political liberty to all but the Communist Party. It may be that one day due credit will be given to those more moderate "progressives" who felt unable to condone Terrorism of the Left any more than Terrorism of the Right and who, even after 1924, declined to join the animated throngs at Russian diplomatic receptions or to consider possibly advantageous visits to Moscow.[1]

A "Terrorism of the Right", early alleged in Finland and, before long, also in Poland, Hungary, and the Balkans, came ultimately through its capture of Italy and Germany, to spell more direct peril for "progressives" in the West than anything else. Here again, as in the Russian instance, it is possible to read "advanced" accounts which ignore essential elements in the case and especially the truth that it was often a "Red snatch" at power that brought counter-action from their opponents. Rosa Luxemburg and Karl Liebknecht figure in "Red" histories as murdered martyrs,[2] opposing the forces that were eventually to bring Hitler to power. Yet in sober fact they were engaged, in January 1919, in raising rebellion, with Bolshevik aid, against a largely Socialist Government, rebellion, too, intended, among other things, to throw out of gear election arrangements for a completely democratic Parliament to take charge of the country. Here is a British Radical account of their rebellion:[3]

For the moment the Spartacus rebellion seems to be crushed in Berlin. The Government's regular troops . . . arrived in large numbers on Saturday, behaved steadily, and on that day and on Sunday, gradually carried one rebel stronghold after another. The casualties may have been about 600 killed; the Russian Bolshevik Radek is a prisoner, and the Spartacus leaders are fugitives. The immediate object of the rebellion was no doubt to make anarchy which would frustrate the National Assembly elections on Sunday. . . .

The first election results under Proportional Representation and Universal Suffrage are now taking place. . . . The Right is doing badly, and the Independent Socialists worst of all. . . .

[1] Cf. G. P. Gooch, *Under Six Reigns*, p. 204. Instead, Gooch was trying to do something for men like Miliukoff, the first Russian Foreign Minister after the Tsar's fall and Baron Meyendorff, once a Vice-President of the Duma. His conclusion on the Bolsheviks was: "Though somewhat less inefficient the new masters were as despotic and ruthless as the old."

[2] Cf. *January Fifteenth. The Murder of Karl Liebknecht and Rosa Luxemburg, 1919.* No. 1, in Manuals for Proletarian Anniversaries (1924).

[3] *The Nation*, January 18, 1919. It seems the writer was not yet aware of the fact that the two leaders mentioned had been detected and killed. There are, naturally, differing accounts of the manner of their end, Bolsheviks choosing to believe the worst.

577

In Italy, too, the part played by some of the provocative post-war striking, openly aimed at factory-expropriation, in bringing adherents and factory- and landowner-subscriptions to the Fascists, is often ignored so that the story only seems to begin with the otherwise inexplicable lorry-forays against Red centres, already in 1921 rising to anarchic heights.[1] Of course, the Italian governing classes were to pay dearly for the mingled cynicism and cowardice with which they finally allowed the apparatus of State to pass into the hands of the leaders and organizers of the huge bands of street-fighters at whose illegalities they had winked so long.[2] The whole world was, in fact, destined to pay for, before long, there were to be growing apprehensions among the "advanced" as to whether Mussolini's success would not attract power-hungry imitators in every land. In Germany, for example, the ambitions of Adolf Hitler were certainly stimulated, and in that suffering country there had already been such threatening displays from the frustrated Right as the Kapp *putsch* of 1920, the Erzberger murder of 1921, and the Rathenau murder of 1922. The attempted Nazi seizure of Bavaria, when it came in November 1923, enlisted Ludendorff's support. And it was not insignificant that the *Daily Mail* should publish, in 1923, its own version of Italian Fascismo's history and that the Labour Publishing Company should issue a very different account.[3] As September 1923 had seen a Spanish Army *coup* sweep aside the politicians and institute, without any obvious sign of public displeasure, the authoritarian régime of Primo de Rivera, the I.L.P.'s urge to issue Matteotti's *The Fascisti Exposed*, during 1924, becomes more

---

[1] Cf. *The Nation*, May 21, 1921: "The Fasci di Combattimento are a cross between the Comrades of the Great War and the Black and Tans. Their nominal head is Mussolini . . . a sort of Bottomley . . . their patron saint is D'Annunzio. . . . Here is a rough record of Fascist activities for seventeen days. . . . Riots with firearms 60; beatings with sticks 34; killed 39 (of whom 6 Fascists), wounded 270; premises raided 40 (two of these Fascist, the rest "Socialist"); premises burnt 70; arrests 2 Fascists, 214 others; local strikes as protests, 11. . . ."

[2] Cf. *Ibid.*, August 5, 1922, for an estimate of the Fascist bands as then numbering "700,000 young bloods", waging "the most naked form of class war which Western Europe has yet seen".

[3] *The "Red" Dragon and the Black Shirts. Story of the Fascisti Movement* is the title the *Daily Mail* gave to a collected account, in seventy-two pages, of what its readers had already been told by its Special Correspondent, Sir Percival Phillips. The opposite account, in 270 pages, was O. Por's, *Fascism*. It is, perhaps, worth remembering that Catholic publishers were also issuing G. M. Godden's *Mussolini. The birth of the new democracy*, obviously not a catalogue of blame.

explicable. Yet Matteotti's murder in June 1924, a worse and more widely-resented scandal than any he exposed when alive, failed ultimately to weaken the Fascist grip on Italy and may in the long run have served to strengthen it.[1] Certainly, a third Dictatorship appeared when General Pangalos seized control in Greece during the summer of 1925.

All this, as it turned out, was not yet the primary danger to the "advanced" and to their social democracy. Pangalos's dictatorship, after all, was short lived, and Primo, in Spain, never built up and doubtless despised, the Mussolini demagogy, complete with fighting street-rowdies. In fact, despite some ominous undertones even in Britain and France,[2] not to mention Mussolini's increasing grip of Italy, it might be assumed that democratic prospects were on the mend between 1925 and the great "economic blizzard" which began towards the end of 1929. It was when German unemployment began rising again catastrophically in 1930 that Hitler, whose denunciation of Jews, Versailles, and traitors, sold to Moscow or the *Entente*, had become part of the German political scene, scented his first chances of establishing an altogether more formidable dictatorship than Mussolini's. And the street-fighter apparatus which some German capitalists, fearful of Communism and Moscow, helped him to perfect, began to assume, in the S.A. and the S.S., forms destined to leave the Italian models far behind. Already by the summer of 1932, a possible Storm Troopers' transfer from the harrying of Communists and Jews in the streets to operations on the Polish and Czech frontiers was being taken seriously at the German War Department.[3]

By 1932, of course, English theorists of the Left had been

---

[1] Cf. G. P. Gooch, *Under Six Reigns*, p. 211.

[2] Hilaire Belloc, *The Jews*, of 1922 was a notorious example in Britain of how Anti-Semitism might be aroused by alleged "friends of the Jews" giving them some candid advice on Zionism, Sir Herbert Samuel and much else. And then, there was circulation of the *Protocols of the Learned Elders of Zion*, *The Alien Menace* and the like. Indeed, there was The Britons Publishing Company and The Boswell Printing and Publishing Company, whose catalogues reveal what might almost have become a Blackshirt Library. The former and smaller enterprise specialized in Anti-Semitic material, the latter in Anti-Bolshevism and Anti-Socialism.

[3] Cf. *Berlin Diaries, 1932–1933*, under July 26, 1932, for Roehm offering the War Department 180,000 Storm Troopers for holding operations against Poland and Czecho-Slovakia while the Reichswehr operated in the West. The War Department's alleged comment was: "The idea isn't bad. If it is possible we shall carry it through, though I can't abide these Brown Shirt rascals."

speculating for some time on how a British Dictatorship threat might come to be used against them and, in point of fact, several times during the 1920s Winston Churchill had been cast for the part of the British Mussolini. But there were mockers among them who claimed that the British ruling classes would never have to meditate the risks of calling in Fascism if the Labour Movement allowed itself to be run out of power as tamely as had been the case in 1924 and 1931.[1] These mockers of "gradualism" were in favour of assuming in advance that yet another "conspiracy" would be attempted against any third Labour Government, even if possessed of a Majority, and that such a Government was therefore entitled to arm itself with drastic emergency Powers usable against all manner of "capitalist sabotage". It was a most dangerous line of advocacy, almost certain to lead not merely to Fascism but to bloodshed and the complete antagonization of still important Radical forces, yet for a time it became the policy of the Socialist League led by Stafford Cripps.[2]

There had been Radicals who had prophesied that Labour would itself breed British Fascism's would-be leader, and they had been able, as justification, to point to Mussolini's violent Socialist past and to Hitler's description of what he stood for as National Socialism.[3] And, of course, it provided an additional reason for Radicals to refuse absorption into the Labour movement to find its most discontented wing, after 1931, forming Mosley's

[1] Cf. John Strachey, *The Coming Struggle for Power*, pp. 318–21, for warm approval, in 1932, for such views as that "The 1924 Labour Government was destroyed by a Red Letter; the last was ended by a Bankers' Order" and that "A Majority Labour Government" committed to gradualism "would do nothing effective . . . until either fascist power would accomplish a *coup d'état* or a new National Government would be formed on the ruins of the old." Strachey's revulsion had led him first towards Mosley's New Party and then into Communism as is obvious from the concluding pages of the book quoted above.

[2] Cf. Patricia Strauss, *Cripps—Advocate and Rebel*, p. 65, for the League's programme for the next Labour Government: "It included the immediate introduction of an Emergency Powers Act to forestall any sabotage by financial or other interests; abolition of the House of Lords; the immediate nationalisation of banks, land, mines, transport, power, iron and steel, cotton, and control of foreign trade; restriction of compensation; acceptance of 'work or maintenace' in principle; and full civil rights for State employees."

[3] Cf. Peter F. Drucker, *The End of Economic Man, A Study of the New Totalitarianism*, p. 26, for other things being noticed: "The three most promising political philosophers of pre-war Europe—the Frenchman, Georges Sorel, the Italian, Pareto, the German, Robert Michels—all started as good Marxists and came out as violent foes of Marxism and as intellectual and spiritual fathers of Fascism." Drucker went on—in the winter of 1938–9—to the astounding assertion that Hitler and Stalin would not only be able to work together but were actually preparing to do so.

New Party or entering Cripps's Socialist League or, finally, like John Strachey, preaching a break-away into Leninite Communism. As Mosley might well have become a "Man of Destiny" if Hitler's success against Britain had been greater than it was, some remarks on his strange political career between 1918 and 1930 are justifiable. The heir to a baronetcy and considerable wealth, he had, after some service in France, entered the "Coupon Parliament" at the age of twenty-two and married Lord Curzon's daughter in 1920. But, before long, the urge to make a mark had led him on to activities on the Irish Question which his brother-Conservatives found unpardonable, and after four years as Conservative M.P. for Harrow between 1918 and 1922, he had to overcome party resistance to retain his seat in the Bonar Law Parliament as an Independent Conservative. By the time of the first Labour Ministry in 1924, he was lending Labour "Independent" support for some time before he announced his conversion. Thereafter he fought his way back into the House for Smethwick as a Socialist, was admitted to the friendship and confidence of MacDonald and accompanied him on a continental tour in the autumn of 1928. When he entered MacDonald's second Government as Chancellor of the Duchy of Lancaster with a place on Mr. Thomas's Committee for combating Unemployment, there were already those who predicted that he would succeed to the party Leadership. Possibly his ultimate chances were made no worse by the fact that he resigned in May 1930 when, despite growing unemployment, he found virtually all his suggestions, summarized in the once-notorious "Mosley Memorandum", treated as inadmissible.

Mosley's long and pertinacious struggle during many ensuing months to convert the Leadership or force its hand, with Back-Bench aid, had some remarkable features—particularly during the Llandudno Conference of October 1930 and at the extraordinary meeting of the Parliamentary Labour Party held on January 27, 1931.[1] It was, to some extent, because he came so near to dividing the Party dangerously between "Mosleyites" and the rest that the Leadership succeeded in defeating him and never more effectively than when urging, privately, that Mosley was merely a rich young man whose ambition was over-reaching itself. Mosley persisted,

---

[1] Cf. L. Macneill Weir, *The Tragedy of Ramsay MacDonald*, pp. 270-2, for the latter occasion.

until March 1931, with the effort to create an Action Group within the party[1] but, under the frown of official disapproval, its numbers sank from forty to twenty. When the final break came, only six Members in all were available as the foundation of a New Party and the six included Mosley himself and his wife, Lady Cynthia.[2] The election of October 1931, moreover, came in circumstances peculiarly unfavourable to the New Party which polled badly and lost all Parliamentary representation.[3]

Though a great deal is still fundamentally unexplained in the story of the New Party's evolution towards an Anti-Semitic Fascism, it is not impossible to find some guidance by checking the twenty-four constituencies before whom New Party candidates placed themselves. Stepney and Whitechapel were two of those constituencies destined, before long, to supply a steady stream of Blackshirt recruits and to become the nucleus of metropolitan Fascism, and both those areas had, for a couple of generations, heard much complaint of Jewish immigrants,[4] Jewish employers, Jewish business methods, Jewish landlords, and much else. It only needed reports of what the Nazis were doing, especially after Hitler became Chancellor, for Blackshirt contingents to become available not merely in the East End, but in Islington, Hackney, Stoke Newington, and many other quarters of London where there were prosperous Jewish businesses and yet much native unemployment and distress. Of course, the very name Blackshirt, and the uniform, is an indication that it was Mussolini, rather than Hitler, who was being originally imitated. And though some of Mosley's Action associates like Oliver Baldwin[5] and John

[1] Cf. John Scanlan, *Decline and Fall of the Labour Party*, p. 214: "Sir Oswald . . . called meetings in committee rooms in the House, and in spite of an attempt to place the meetings out of bounds, some forty members attended."

[2] *Ibid.*, p. 215: "When Sir Oswald finally decided that something more than group meetings was needed his Party of twenty dwindled to six, including himself and Lady Cynthia. All six resigned, and at once all the energies of the Government were devoted to killing the mutineers. . . ."

[3] *Whitaker's Almanack, 1932*, p. 181, shows twenty-four New Party candidates only raising 36,000 votes between them.

[4] Eventually a Royal Commission on the evils attributed to unrestricted Alien Immigration was appointed and its *Report* of 1903 will be found of interest especially as it led to the Aliens Act of 1905. And, of course, there was some Anti-Semitic literature, circulating in Britain, long before Mosley left the Labour Party. One publishing enterprise, under the style of The Britons Publishing Society, had long been selling *The Protocols of the Learned Elders of Zion* and *4 Protocols of Zion* and had on offer, besides, quite a range of leaflets and such works as *The Riddle of the Jew's Success* at 7s. 6d., *The Truth about the Slump* at 4s., and *The Gravediggers of Russia* at 1s.

[5] Cf. *Who's Who, 1931*, for this son of the Conservative Leader, who had

582

Strachey[1] were shocked into a complete break with him when they first discovered him sanctioning, in his party's rooms and meeting-places, exercises in physical force, there was a possible defence in the plea, that after he had left the Labour Party, Mosley's own meetings were broken up by dangerous mobs, and that in Birmingham and Glasgow police protection had to be secured.[2]

It has, of course, been the fashion of Communists and Fascists to demand complete freedom of speech and assembly for themselves until they are prepared to destroy it and all the other democratic "liberties" by force. And the Radical tradition of tolerance for the extremest views is so strong in Britain[3] that matters have normally reached a dangerous stage before any widespread assent can be obtained for "coercion". And if "Reds" were still, in 1934 and 1935, being allowed to experiment unceasingly with organizing "Unemployed Marches and Demonstrations" that might become something more,[4] the case for exceptional vigilance and severity against the Blackshirts was correspondingly weaker. Yet by 1934 a British Fascist movement of some potential strength was certainly being reared, already capable of attracting support from those who feared "Red" plans and activities and wanted Britain rescued, besides, from the depths, as they considered it, of the ignoble pacifism to which Radicalism and Socialism had brought the country.[5] The most

been M.P. for Dudley since 1929 and Labour candidate since 1924. He forfeited the candidature by joining Mosley but saw reason to ask for readmission to the party before long.

[1] *Ibid.*, for another who had been attracted by the vigour of Mosley's Unemployment policies.

[2] Cf. John Scanlan, *Decline and Fall of the Labour Party*, p. 217.

[3] John Stuart Mill's *Essay on Liberty* with its grave warnings against the "tyranny of prevailing opinion" obviously left a deeper mark than he somewhat pessimistically believed, and to hear I.R.A. propaganda in Hyde Park or to witness "Anti-Bomb" demonstrations against Government Establishments in 1961 merely confirms that opinion. There is an autobiography of 1934, *Hyde Park Orator* by Bonar Thompson, which gives some curious views of the dingy and half-fraudulent world of soap-box agitation.

[4] Cf. Wal Hannington, *Unemployed Struggles, 1919–1936*, pp. 312–20, for one who, in 1935, was still making plenty of trouble for the authorities and the new Unemployment Assistance Board in the name of "The National Unemployed Workers Movement", the main source of whose funds was never plain. By 1936, in view of the alleged danger of the capture of the unemployed by "Fascist demagogy", he was inviting the T.U..C., which had good reason to be suspicious, to come in and give some central direction to the "Mighty demonstrations" alleged to be preparing against the new Unemployment Assistance Regulations of July 10, 1936.

[5] It is, perhaps, worth remembering that, on the other side of politics, a writer like George Orwell was, in *The Road to Wigan Pier* of 1937, to voice hearty dislike of "every fruit-juice drinker, nudist, sandal-wearer, sex-maniac,

formidable patron the Blackshirts acquired, for a time, was the great newspaper magnate, Lord Rothermere, though he finally shrank, under the stimulus of an enormous roar of "progressive" indignation, from the odium of swallowing virulent Anti-Semitism with his Anti-Bolshevism. As Rothermere put it himself:[1]

> I refused to give more than ordinary publicity to Sir Oswald Mosley's Blackshirt movement the moment I discovered it had an anti-Jewish bias. I supported it at first with the idea of promoting a right wing appanage of the Conservative Party, which should form a counterblast to left wing activities. Mosley's correct procedure was to develop a Youth movement inspired by anti-Bolshevist ideals, instead of basing himself on Continental models which, obviously, would not appeal to our British mentality or temperament.

Yet if he withdrew special patronage from Mosley's Blackshirts, Rothermere had an obvious admiration for the services he considered Hitler and Mussolini to have rendered their countries[2] as well as a readiness to lead a great Air-Rearmament Campaign which constituted him one of the hopes in Britain of those who wanted the country to be at once too strong and too friendly for the Dictators to dream of attacking.[3] It was, perhaps, as well

Quaker, 'Nature Cure' quack, pacifist and feminist" who seemed to be attracted "with magnetic force" by the "mere words Socialism and Communism".

[1] Cf. Bernard Falk, *Five Years Dead*, p. 174, for one of his ex-editors who made notes of their conversations. Another editor and friend, Colin Brooks, considered that Rothermere reduced the influence of the *Daily Mail* and the associated papers by "excessive reports, very subjectively prepared, of the activities of the Mosley blackshirts or of the later National League of Airmen, ousting big news from its rightful place" (*The Devil's Decade*, p. 147).

[2] Cf. Bernard Falk, *Five Years Dead*, pp. 173–4: "I am not an anti-Semite. . . . In England there is no Jewish question. . . . But in certain Continental countries you have to reckon with a passionate order of nationalism. . . . I admire Herr Hitler for the way in which he has organised the effort of the German people to regain their former standing in Europe, and I wish we had the same vigour behind our air-defence measures as that imparted by General Goering to Germany's supremacy-in-the-air campaign. But one can admire both gentlemen without being saddled with the reproach of being anti-Semitic."

[3] Cf. Colin Brooks, *The Devil's Decade*, pp. 148–9: "When Hitler during his first year in power had shown his intentions fairly plainly, Rothermere turned himself to rearmament. 'We need 5,000 war planes was his slogan.' The result was a burst of execration from the Left at this war-mongering. . . . Before very long he had changed his exordium. 'We need 10,000 war planes.' It sounded, in the late 1930's a wild mad aspiration! . . . There was, however, another side to his policy which was, perhaps, even more exasperating to those with whom responsibility for maintaining circulation rested. The Rothermereian view was that 'the oligrachs of Berlin', as he called them, meant to strike Britain and strike ruthlessly, and that Britain was totally and tragically unprepared to meet the blow. . . . One of the surest ways of inviting a blow is to insult and belittle and deride your potential antagonist; one of the best ways of avoiding a blow is to

therefore for the general cause of "progress" in Britain that all parties in Parliament decided that they had had enough of provocative Fascist tactics in the East End after some notorious affrays in October 1936 faced a dismayed nation with the prospect of a repetition in Britain of full Nazi-style street hostilities.[1] And Sir John Simon's Public Order Bill, to ban the wearing of uniforms in connection with political objects and the maintenance by private persons of associations of military or quasi-military character, was, if specially welcome to Radicals and Socialists, hardly opposed during its rapid progress through Parliament in November and December 1936.[2] Fascism, however, if deprived of one of its most dangerous and provocative means of display, remained a possible peril to "progressives" till the Fascist Dictators were defeated and destroyed,

Yet for years the destruction that finally overtook the Fascist Dictators seemed most unlikely and the chances to be the other way as the notorious case of the Spanish "progressives" seemed to show between 1936 and 1939. Nay, even Stalin, the "Red" Dictator of Moscow, found it wise to make his bargain of August 1939 with Hitler and to cling to it so tightly, despite repeated warnings, that he and his country were almost overwhelmed by the treachery of 1941. And if the British Left, finally freed from its Fascist perils, was able to aim at power in 1945 and hold it till 1951, the main architect of its salvation could not forget or forgive its large share of responsibility for the chances that had been needlessly presented to Hitler. "Delight in smooth-sounding platitudes, refusal to face unpleasant facts, desire for popularity and electoral success irrespective of the vital interests of the state" were faults, indeed, that Winston Churchill found in all the main contestants for political power in Britain in the decade before 1939. But after that general indictment and blame for Mr. Baldwin's "marked ignorance of Europe and aversion from its problems", Mr. Churchill saw reason to condemn "the strong

keep a civil tongue in your head. . . . At a time when Low and his kind were having the time of their lives insulting by cartoon and written abuse the armed dictators, the Rothermere papers annoyed . . . many of the public . . . by publishing tributes. . . ."

[1] Cf. *Whitaker's Almanack, 1937,* p. 602, under October 4, 1936: "Projected Fascist march in East End of London banned by police at last minute. Serious disorders occurred and baton charges followed by many arrests took place."

[2] *Hansard,* November 16, 1936, for Sir John Simon moving the Second Reading.

and violent pacifism which at that time dominated the Labour-Socialist Party, the utter devotion of the Liberals to sentiment apart from reality" and "the failure and worse than failure of Mr. Lloyd George, the erstwhile great war-time leader, to address himself to the continuity of his work".[1]

[1] Winston S. Churchill, *The Second World War* (Abridged Edn.), pp. 43–4.

CHAPTER XXVIII

LIVING AND OTHER STANDARDS

"Allowing for some considerable drop after the war, Mr. Rowntree holds it reasonable to suppose that prices will be 25 per cent above the pre-war level. This would mean a minimum wage of £2 4s. od. for men and £1 5s. od. for women. This is the challenge which Mr. Rowntree puts up to the nation. He is in favour of Trade Boards fixing the minimum for all trades upon this basis. Can it be done? It seems a great matter that agricultural wages in Southern England have got to a 30s. basis in war-time. Can agricultural and low-skilled town-labour support his higher scale in peace-time? . . . We agree with him that the main source to which we must look for raising the real wages of the workers to a sufficient amount is 'an increase of the productivity of industry, whether due to labour organization and machinery, greater efficiency on the part of the workers or management or any other factor'. We believe this increase can and will be got when it is generally recognized that labour cannot be purchased and ought not to be purchasable upon any lower terms.

"We shall be told by Mr. Mallock and others of his school that the insistence upon such high wages for unskilled labour must entail the payment of much higher wages for skilled labour, the whole amounting to a demand which would absorb, and far more than absorb, the entire body of profit, interest and rent. . . . But the experience of war has now shown . . . that the under-production and under-consumption of wealth in pre-war society was immense . . . we ought to be able to double our pre-war industrial product without any increase in the aggregate of human toil. . . . Mr. Rowntree is right in his insistence that Trade Boards shall be set up for all industries and instructed by Statute to fix at the earliest possible date, for men of ordinary ability, minimum wages which would enable them to marry, live in a decent house, and bring up a family of normal size . . . in a state of physical efficiency while allowing a reasonable margin for contingencies and recreation."

The Radical *Nation* reviews *The Human Needs of Labour* by Seebohm Rowntree, the leading social statistician of its own school, September 28, 1918.

"Liberalism rested on a too favourable estimate of human nature and on a belief in the law of progress. As there is no law of progress, and as civilized society is being destroyed by the evil passions of men, Liberalism is, for the time, quite discredited. It would be also true to say that there is a fundamental contradiction between the two dogmas of Liberalism. These were that unlimited competition is stimulating to the competitors and good for the country, and that every individual is an end not a means. Both are anarchical; but the first logically issues in individual ararchy, the last in communistic anarchy. The economic and the ethical theory of Liberalism cannot be harmonized. The result—cruel competition tempered by an artificial process of counter-selection in favour of the unfittest —was by no means satisfactory. But it was better than what we are now threatened with. That the Labour movement is economically rotten, it is easy to prove. In the words of Professor Hearnshaw, 'the government has ceased to govern in the world of labour, and has been compelled . . . to bribe, to cajole, to beg, to grovel. It has purchased brief truces at the cost of increasing levies of Danegeld.' "

Dean Inge's *Outspoken Essays* (1919) criticize so-called "Progress".

O N the standard of living, as it developed in Britain during the first and second quarters of the twentieth century, there are, of course, floods of tendentious accounts, especially from the Left, but also a considerable volume of less partial and more reliable material from such works as *The New Survey of London Life and Labour*, Professor Bowley's statistical studies and Seebohm Rowntree's close investigations of conditions in York at successive stages.[1] There emerges, despite the use and misuse of alleged economic facts for party ends, the truth that what the citizen obtained from life was, on average, tending to rise both in quantity and quality and that what he expected from life was rising considerably faster. In fact, some of the principal prophecies of Marx in regard to the growing mass-misery and destitution to be expected as the "capitalist system" evolved further were so belied by events that a key economist like Keynes could never acknowledge the slightest respect for Marx or for those who, by elaborate glosses, tried to make the facts harmonize with Marxist doctrine. Nor is it surprising that the standard of living should be rising even outside boom years when it is remembered what invention was doing to aid productivity and how wage-earners' bargaining powers were being aided not merely by their possession of Trade Union organizations and the Parliamentary and local government votes but by Trade Boards,[2]

[1] Cf. Rowntree and Stewart, *The Responsibility of Women Workers for Dependants* of 1921 for the elaborate investigation attempted in the effort to settle the relatively minor problem of what allowance to make, when fixing minimum wages for women, for the possibility of their having dependants. The investigation was made in Newcastle, Middlesbrough, Hull, Sheffield, Leeds, Oldham, Manchester, Derby, Nottingham, and Leicester, 67,333 houses were called at, and 13,627 women workers aged eighteen or more were found in them. Of these women 11,982 or 87.94 per cent supported themselves only, and 1645 or 12.06 per cent wholly or partially supported others. After more gathering of these types of economic fact, the conclusion was reached that 65 per cent of women workers' responsibilities for dependants would be eliminated by the adoption of an adequate scheme of widows' pensions and 12½ per cent by improvements in National Health Insurance payments to chronic invalids. Another possibility canvassed was the granting of State aid to wage earners with more than three dependent children. In fact, the whole effort was altogether more basic than the floods of fluent prose poured out so copiously by, say, Garvin from one side or Cole and Laski from the other.

[2] Cf. *Britain's Industrial Future being the Report of the Liberal Industrial Inquiry*, p. 170, n. 1, for the specially rapid increase of such boards in 1919 and 1920. Boot and Shoe Repairing; Brush and Broom; Coffin Furniture and Cerement Making; Corset; Dress Making and Women's Light Clothing; Fur; Jute; Laundry; Mantle, and Costume; Paper Bag; Rope, Twine and Net; and Tobacco represent trades provided with Trade Board safeguards in 1919 alone. And the 1920 list was made up of Aerated Water; Button Making; Cotton

Whitley Councils,[1] and even the increasing spread of birth-control.

Seebohm Rowntree's studies of working-class life in York, the first at 1899 and the second at 1935, are specially apposite because of his intimate knowledge of the ground and of the people covered by his investigators. And his conclusions carry more weight from the fact that his Radical political sympathies are never obtruded.[2] According to Rowntree the proportion of York's working-class population living in abject poverty had been reduced by more than one-half between 1899 and 1935, and the reduction would have been still greater if 1935 had been as good an employment year as 1899. The standard of living available to working people was about thirty per cent higher—and in regard to housing, the improvement was specially marked. In 1899 scarcely a working-class family in York was possessed of a bath or a garden. In 1935 about twenty-five per cent of York's working-class families had both, by 1939 the percentage had risen to thirty-five, and but for the war's halting important slum-clearance projects, the rise over the next few years might have been even more impressive.[3] Meanwhile, the working-day in factory and workshop had been reduced by one hour or more as between 1899 and 1935,[4] and virtually the only development that caused Rowntree concern was the marked increase in what he, somewhat severely, denominated as "gambling" on the result of football games.

York, of course, had some notably "progressive" employers[5]

Waste Reclamation; Flax and Hemp; General Waste Reclamation; Hair, Bass, and Fibre; Hat, Cap, and Millinery; Linen and Cotton Handkerchiefs; Milk Distribution; Perambulators; Pin, Hook, and Eye; Stamped and Pressed Metals; and Toys.

[1] Cf. *The Nation*, August 23, 1924, for a realistic appreciation of what had been effected and what might yet follow. An authority is quoted to the effect that the Whitley Councils "in some cases represent a slight advance on pre-war conciliation machinery, and in other cases a poor substitute for Trade Boards". But it was accepted that much useful work had been done on such matters as apprenticeship, dismissals, promotion, and safety regulation, and that there was a case on the industry-rules for all these and similar matters for extending the authority of the Whitley Councils.

[2] Rowntree had been a member of the pre-war Land Enquiry Committee working with Lloyd George in 1913 and 1914, and his signature will be found on the *Report of the Liberal Industrial Inquiry* of 1928.

[3] S. B. Rowntree, *Poverty and Progress, A Second Survey of York*, p. 464.

[4] *Ibid.*, p. 468.

[5] There are *Lives* of Joseph and Arnold Rowntree that tell part of the story. Arnold Rowntree was Liberal M.P. for York from 1910 to 1918, and Joseph Rowntree, founder and head of the firm, apart from his York welfare interests, felt it right, like his friend George Cadbury, to enter the newspaper field to make sure that causes which he cared deeply about secured some hearing. His interest

with their own welfare and housing schemes and there was, besides, a City Council of ancient and honourable tradition, anxious to give the town efficient and kindly government and to make full use of all the Housing powers which were offered by successive Administrations especially after 1919. Indeed, from Plymouth to Aberdeen the local pride of important or historic City and Town Councils, imitated in due course by County and District Councils, has come to be one of the principal factors helping to improve the quality of the nation's culture and life.[1] And from the days of Alderman Cobden of Manchester and Mayor Chamberlain of Birmingham, a Radical tradition seemed to be associated with the most "progressive" of the local government authorities, rising to a "notorious" climax in the Progressive Party that held control of the London County Council from its initiation in 1889 until 1907. Though a fair number of Town and City Councils were to see a ruling majority, composed largely of the same elements as the L.C.C. Progressives, keep control for a considerably longer time, they could not, of necessity, attract the same national and even international attention that was devoted to the London County Council. And for nearly a generation the London Progressives' decisive defeat by a combination of "the millionaire Press" and the "Keep the Rates Low" Municipal "Reformers" was to be a subject of lamentation, the more so as the rise of a London Labour Party intent on claiming every possible seat for the "People" seemed likely to make "Municipal Reform's" triumph permanent.[2]

It must be admitted, of course, that municipal politics have always had their shocks for well-intentioned middle-class Radicals. In times of prosperity, even the slums become complacent and difficult to stir towards the ballot-box, and when times grow worse,

in *The Nation,* the *British Weekly* and a variety of local newspapers should one day be fully treated.

[1] Most worthily displayed, of course, in the organization of attractive systems of Public Parks and Recreation Grounds, the building-up of City Lending and Reference Libraries, the foundation of important Museums and Art Galleries and the maintenance of high standards of City Building, City Schools, City Housing Estates and City Health services. Naturally, private benefactors, often distinguished citizens, had played an indispensable part in the earlier stages of some of these activities as in the foundation or endowment of the University Colleges which have become the "Redbrick Universities".

[2] Cf. *The Nation,* March 11, 1922: "Base as was the newspaper attack that destroyed the ideals of new London and brought the profiteering spirit back, it would never have succeeded if the Progressive and Labour forces had held together. But Labour . . . by its demand to socialise everything at once threatens to turn every London butcher and milkman into a 'municipal reformer'."

the cry is normally, not for long-term programmes but for short-cuts which few economists could possibly approve. Thus, in the short post-war boom that gave way in 1921, critical observers were struck at once by the large-scale apathy being displayed towards local politics and by the normal working-class family's absorption in its own order of pleasures to the exclusion of all serious concern for the sufferings of Central and Eastern Europe.[1] And when times became worse and prospects grew of a poll of, perhaps, thirty per cent at the next elections, say, to the L.C.C., pessimist Progressives, who were in process of being shouldered off the municipal scene as less the "people's friends" than the London Labour Party,[2] gave this not very cheerful picture of the inevitability of a further prolongation of "reactionary" control resulting:[3]

There is a pathetic atmosphere about the all-night sittings which occur on the annual estimates of the L.C.C. All the old issues so vital to a well-ordered administration of London have now been appropriated by the London Labour Party. The progress of time has turned the demand for steam boats on the Thames into one for motor boats but otherwise all the issues remain exactly as they were when Lord Jessel and the millionaire Press first started their alliance to frustrate progress in London government. Most of the amendments point to the need for the Council to initiate Parliamentary action. The opposition is still demanding that the Council should become the market authority for London, that it shall have powers to run omnibuses and tubes, to tax land values and empty properties, and to take over the administration of the City Corporation's Bridge House Estate Fund. But in the view of the leaders of the Municipal Reform Party, "the time is still not opportune for the Council to initiate action".

By 1926, of course, some of London's Metropolitan Boroughs had passed under Labour control and there were, besides, a con-

---

[1] Cf. *The Nation*, May 8, 1920, on "the mass of a people which is spending wildly, saving little, not working in the least degree up to its possible standard, and enjoying cinemas or Blackpool. Nine out of ten of the now prosperous British citizens do not give a minute's thought in the day to the cries, ever growing fainter, of a perishing Austria or a disease-stricken Galicia, or pause to read the advertisement of a dying Armenia which some despairing philanthropist is flinging into all the daily newspapers. They eat, they drink, they marry, they give in marriage. They refuse to believe . . . that the present exploitation of the world is but transitory, that by limited production in coal, housebuilding and other commodities we are not postponing the period of unemployment but hastening it. Then the idea of a universally high paid employed class giving little return for its labour but set on enjoyment, will come sharply into conflict with the facts."

[2] Cf. *Whitaker's Almanack, 1927*, pp. 547–8, for 6 elected Progressives as against 32 Labour and 84 Municipal Reformers in the Council elected for three years on March 5, 1925. By the 1928 elections, the Progressives, now standing as Liberals, were reduced to 4 elected Councillors. [3] *The Nation*, May 1, 1926.

siderable scattering of "Red" Boards of Guardians[1] and District Councils not to mention a County Council or two[2] as well as a number of City and Town Councils, headed for a time by Glasgow Corporation. Naturally, Progressives who had been ousted in the "march of progress" by more "advanced" men found much to criticize in the way they had been elbowed aside. And, truth to tell, formal discipline and efficiency, at least, did sometimes seem to suffer perceptibly as the "matier" atmosphere between the authority and its employees pervaded, say, the Street Cleansing Department, the Swimming Baths, the City Transport Services, the Electricity Undertaking and, it might be, even the Municipal Libraries and Schools. Moreover, there was often something in the charge that appointments to all manner of posts under the authority from Town Hall Porters and Electricity Meter-Readers to Road Maintenance Men and School Attendance Officers tended to pass by a species of political or personal favour which vividly recalled the "patronage" disputes of a past that was thought to have gone for ever. Possibly what some Liberals and even Radicals thought more objectionable than anything else was the new authorities' readiness to succumb to every type of Trade Union pressure especially in the direction of making a "closed shop" of all manual employment under them.

At any rate, there were numbers of occasions when "Red" local authorities learned to their dismay that the uncommitted "public" could and would turn against them very vigorously indeed. One remarkable instance occurred in November 1928 in the Metropolitan Borough of Bethnal Green, where, thanks to Percy Harris and Major Nathan,[3] a very combative Radical Liberalism had been built up which won the borough's four seats on the London County Council and every seat on the Borough Council too. And one comment in the Radicals' *Nation* was this:[4]

Bethnal Green is a refutation to the Tory claim to be the only bulwark against Socialist maladministration—which is a very real evil in many parts of London. The Borough Council elections of 1928 have

---

[1] The Poplar and West Ham Boards were particularly notorious, and "Poplarism" became a political issue of marked danger to Labour.

[2] "Labour control" of the Durham County Council, for example, is sometimes reckoned to have begun in 1924.

[3] *Who's Who*, 1931, shows Harris to have been Liberal M.P. for South-West Bethnal Green since 1922 and to have been first elected as an L.C.C. Progressive for the Division in 1907. Major Nathan joined him in Parliament as M.P. for North-East Bethnal Green in 1929. [4] *The Nation*, November 10, 1928.

shown that all the Conservative can do is to hand over yet another Council [that of Finsbury] to Labour; whereas the only Council that has been won from Labour has been won by Liberalism. In other words, a truly progressive policy is the only real safeguard against the extremism of the less scrupulous kind of Socialist politicians, for whom the slums of London have been a political paradise for some years past.

Obviously, a greater regard to outward appearances and to conventional "public opinion" needed to be paid if "Red" local authorities were to establish themselves firmly and, it might be, permanently in the industrial areas. In London, for example, this was done well enough for the tremendous triumph to be achieved of gaining control of the L.C.C. in 1934, a control never since lost though in the greatest danger in 1949. The 1934 jubilations were the greater in that a strong contingent of professional-class candidates had been obtained for Labour[1] of the kind historically associated with the Progressives who, as Liberals, indeed, were completely swept from the electoral scene in a fashion that Labour has, for a quarter of a century and more, been vainly trying to effect elsewhere, and especially at Westminster. And in providing two Labour ex-Ministers, the one, Lord Snell, as Chairman and the other, Herbert Morrison, as Majority Leader, the London Labour Party was arming itself to meet three years of Press criticism from the *Daily Mail*, the *Daily Express*, and the *Daily Telegraph*,[2] and the eventual need, in 1937, to meet their renewed electoral assault, with three years of allegedly "prodigal expenditure" to quote from in a fashion that once ruined the Progressives resoundingly.

In some ways, the first Labour Majority's struggle to maintain its hold on the L.C.C. in the 1937 elections was more vital than what had happened in 1934, particularly as the general municipal wind, just then, did not seem particularly favourable. Yet a bold line was taken and the London Labour Party's manifesto offered a three-year plan for rehousing, slum clearance, improved schools,

---

[1] Cf. *Whitaker's Almanack, 1935*, pp. 675–6, for a Labour list that included Sir Alfred Baker, Major Harry Barnes, F.R.I.B.A., F.S.I., Dr. C. W. Brook, M.A., Dr. J. A. Gillison, Mrs. M. O'Brien Harris, D.Sc., J.P., Dr. Somerville Hastings, M.S., F.R.C.S., Dr. B. Homa, Dr. S. W. Jeger, Dr. S. McClements, Canon Mahoney, Ph.D., Mrs. L'Estrange Malone, M.A., etc., etc.

[2] Bernard Falk, *Five Years Dead*, p. 168, quotes Rothermere's own rueful reflections on "the easy manner in which Herbert Morrison and his cohort of Socialists romped home in the L.C.C. elections, though faced with the most violent opposition on the part of the Press of the Right".

and better opportunities for children, more hospital beds, the completion of London's Green Belt and the extension of London's traffic facilities. And though the execution of the plan would obviously cost many millions, the Municipal Reform opponents of Labour failed to get an "Economy" rally from the Ratepayers' Associations sufficient to withstand the alleged enthusiasm excited in London's poorer and grimier quarters by Labour's offer to spend so freely on their account. At any rate, after what was, by L.C.C. standards, a strenuous contest, the Labour Party improved its majority from 14 to 26, securing 75 seats against Municipal Reform's 49.[1] And this majority it was which, owing to Hitler's War, was fated to remain in undisputed charge till 1945, to establish almost a presumptive claim to reconstruct London in its own image and, of course, to obliterate still more the memory of the Radical days of the Progressives.

Yet there was naturally much in the Radical inheritance that the London Labour Party, like the Leeds, Glasgow, Birmingham, and many other Labour parties could not but take over even while trying to obliterate a rival name. There was something strangely reminiscent of the old Progressive days to find Lord Snell, Labour's new L.C.C. Chairman, waxing enthusiastic over the 780,000 children and adults educated under its auspices, the 100 parks and open spaces it administered and the 100 hospitals, institutions, and residential schools it maintained.[2] And Snell recalled several decades of Radical history when recounting his contacts with Bradlaugh and Holyoake, his employment as an Ethical Society lecturer, and his work for the Secular Education League. Yet in the most characteristic passage of his autobiography, as issued in 1936, a pessimism as to twentieth-century developments is to be found, not easily matched among brother-Socialists, less well-read in John Stuart Mill and more convinced that "the best was yet to come". As Snell put it:[3]

The future is with the young. What will they do with the world? I try to keep loyal to my faith in them, but they sometimes frighten me.

[1] Cf. *Whitaker's Almanack, 1938*, p. 614, for the elections of March 4, 1937. And the complete list of members (pp. 737–8) shows that, once again, the total elimination of elected Liberals and Progressives has been effected. A Liberal, in the person of Sir Percy Harris, contrived to reappear most inconveniently in 1949 when 64 Municipal Reformers faced 64 Labour Members and had to be overcome by the use of Aldermanic votes.

[2] Lord Snell, *Men, Movements and Myself*, p. 263.

[3] *Ibid.*, p. 268.

They seem for the most part to be indifferent both to their heritage and to their responsibilities. They may differ from each other about many things, but they are united in their contempt for experience. They are so certain that youth alone is right. They may believe in liberty and progress, but they have no disciplined passion to defend and promote these virtues. They will neither "fight for king and country", nor adequately organize themselves to prevent war. The only things they take on trust are Fascism and Communism. In everything relating to sex they insist upon discussion being free and continuous; but of well-sustained preparation for public work I see very little. The athlete and the cinema-star are their gods.

Obviously, one of the Radical strains inherited by Snell went right back to the anti-hedonism of the Puritans and of the Dissenting chapels.

The whole problem, indeed, of the survival of religious influences, religious agencies, and religious attitudes profoundly interested the age. Professor Harold Laski, for example, a non-believer, very influential on the Left for nearly thirty years,[1] was continually being astonished by such discoveries as that Asquith, the ex-Prime Minister, had never dreamed of doubting the religion in which he had been reared or that G. P. Gooch, "the most learned man in England today", was "an orthodox Christian".[2] And he knew as well as any man the combined strength and weakness that came to the Labour Party from the strange mingling, within its ranks, of a strong corps of Methodist local preachers, a powerful element of Irish Catholic descent under priestly control, and "emancipated" Agnostics of his own variety whose tendency to militancy against "superstition" had always to be kept under control for fear of inflicting irrevocable damage to the "cause".[3] The struggle inside the Labour Party, during the greater part of the second MacDonald Ministry, on the alleged "blackmail" attempted on behalf of Catholic schools makes, in fact, a revealing portion of the story of the years 1929–31 as does, indeed, the

[1] Herbert A. Deane, *The Political Ideas of Harold J. Laski*, for a careful examination of his main writing which, however, leaves unnoticed the huge volume of party journalism and reviewing that heightened his day-to-day importance.

[2] Cf. *Holmes-Laski Correspondence* under date "28.12.1923".

[3] Cf. *Ibid.*, under "24.9.33" for a long struggle with the British Broadcasting Corporation to get something better than a virtually censored ten-minute talk in connection with the Bradlaugh Centenary. The B.B.C. at first suggested confining its account to Bradlaugh's troubles with the Parliamentary Oath. And even when accepting some extension, it still tried to have him described as a "freethinker" rather than an Atheist and to forbid all mention of his efforts for Birth Control.

counter-attack from educationists and Free Churchmen which, as voiced in the Radicals' *Nation*, took on an anti-papal vigour such as had not been heard for many years in those quarters. Here is an article in opposition to Catholic educational claims under the bold title of "THE POPE SPEAKS OUT":[1]

"Let it be loudly proclaimed and well understood and recognized by all," writes His Holiness, the Pope, in his New Year Encyclical letter on the Christian Education of Youth "that Catholics, no matter what their nationality, in agitating for Catholic schools for their children, are not mixing in party politics, but are engaged in a religious enterprise demanded by conscience." Everywhere, in all manner of forms this well-organized and centrally controlled agitation is to be found. Roman Catholics obtain key positions on the education committees of most local authorities. Little bodies of Roman Catholics, particularly in new housing estates, work on industriously . . . to form new Catholic schools in their localities and get them placed upon the rates. . . . In the last general election, overtired priests carefully copied out official questionnaires and ingenuously handed them over the platform to be answered by innocent political candidates; later, congregations everywhere were informed of the answers given, and millions of Catholic votes were in this way swayed from one party to another.

And so the article continued, giving a possibly exaggerated view not, indeed, of what the Catholic hierarchy would have liked to effect but of what it was, in fact, capable of achieving. The writer pointed out, for example, the liberality already shown to Catholic schools and the fact that Burnham Scale salaries, paid out in the name of members of Catholic teaching Orders, represented some incidental subsidization of the Catholic Church itself. He enlarged also on the danger of further subsidization of "a militant minority" intent on reproducing in Britain "the educational system prevalent in Spain, Poland and Portugal". But he was doubtless most provocative when illustrating how Roman Catholic educational principles were opposed to the "progress" that was being made in schools on such matters as co-education and elementary sex-information. As he put it:[2]

In another part of the Encyclical the Pope does not mince words: "it is necessary," he writes, "that all the teaching and the whole organization of the school and its teachers, syllabus, and text-books in every branch be regulated by the Christian spirit, under the direction and maternal supervision of the Church. . . . False and harmful . . .

[1] *The Nation*, February 15, 1930. The contributor was given as R. G. Randall. [2] *Ibid.*

is the so-called method of co-education . . . founded upon naturalism and the denial of original sin . . . upon a deplorable confusion of ideas that mistakes a levelling promiscuity and equality for the legitimate association of the sexes." The other problem which agitates the Pope is the tendency to give to adolescents accurate knowledge which may help them to face, free from superstition, the kind of sex problems which no growing human being can altogether avoid. . . .

The birth-control problem, of course, was never far away when "progress" and ecclesiasticism came to hot debate of the kind pictured above. And there were certainly times when Radical attempts to commit the Liberal Party to the notion that Maternity and Child Welfare clinics might be permitted, in suitable cases, to give some Birth Control instruction came nearer to success than was the case with either of its rivals. Ultimately an "influential and representative" Birth Control Conference tried, on non-party lines, to raise, in the authorities, the spirit required to face Catholic wrath by passing the resolution that "This Conference calls upon the Minister of Health and public health authorities to recognize the desirability of making available medical information on methods of birth control to married people who need it on medical grounds or who ask for it."[1] Some results doubtless followed but the fact that Radical grumbling continued both in regard to Catholics' school policy and their Health Committee policy seems evidence enough that their attitude constituted the principal brake upon the cause of "progress" in those fields.[2]

It is interesting to find other Radical approaches to the problem of dealing with the "needless" poverty and suffering so often accompanying large working-class families. Seebohm Rowntree's researches convinced him that it was when the labourer's family exceeded three children that it tended to be plunged into a long period of abject poverty which normally lasted until the elder children began earning. It was from this viewpoint that he was

---

[1] Cf. *The Nation*, April 12, 1930.

[2] Cf. *Ibid.*, January 3, 1931, under the headline, "THE CATHOLIC CHALLENGE": "The existence of Roman Catholic Schools, however well equipped they may be, is a constant menace to the efficiency of our educational service. If it were not for the fear of Roman Catholic propaganda, other denominations would be much more inclined to consider the abolition of dual control and that would be a general benefit. School text-books are left unrevised because local authorities are reluctant to stir up conflict with local Roman Catholic opinion. Moreover as the century proceeds, the mediaeval tradition of Catholic communities is becoming an obvious menace to the progress of national life. Health services are held up in deference to their superstitious beliefs. Women and children are taught to put up with poverty and degradation."

prepared, like Beveridge when drafting a Social Security Plan in the 1940s, to consider Eleanor Rathbone's projects for Family Endowment or Children's Allowances as offering one set of safeguards against the physical and moral deterioration that overtook the "Disinherited Family",[1] socially costly as it was. There were, too, E. D. Simon's studies of children's rent-allowances of, perhaps, a shilling a week per child to make it possible to rehouse families from the slums in new Council housing. But, perhaps, the Liberal Yellow Book of 1928 may be cited on the whole subject of how far "progressive", in contrast to Socialist, opinion was prepared to go in aid of the family, impoverished by the need of rearing its child-members. After ridiculing such I.L.P. proposals as a universal minimum wage of £4 a week, calculated, as it was, to swallow the entire national income and more,[2] the Liberal Yellow Book pointed out that there were some difficulties even in fixing a reasonable minimum wage industry by industry. Here is a relevant passage:[3]

When we face squarely the problem of the minimum or living wage . . . we come up against the difficulty of determining how many dependents the minimum wage ought to be expected to provide for. It is usually assumed that the wage should be sufficient for the needs of a "normal family", consisting of man, wife and three children. Only a small fraction of workers, however, have precisely four people dependent upon them, and there are a good many who have more. The minimum wage which would be adequate for the few "normal families" would be more than adequate for smaller families, and less than adequate for larger. When a Labour Government in Australia proposed to establish a national minimum on the assumption that every worker

[1] Eleanor Rathbone, *The Disinherited Family: a Plea for the Endowment of the Family* was issued in 1924. *The Nation*'s review at the time had this to say: "After a forcible discussion of various evil results of the present system . . . Miss Rathbone gives a full and interesting account of the experiments in 'family allowances' which have been made, under the stimulus of nationalist sentiment in France and under the pressure of poverty in Germany, by voluntary associations of employers, and of the hitherto abortive attempts in Australia to embody the principle in legislation. . . . In conclusion she examines the relative merits of family endowment by means of a general State scheme and by means of a pooling of funds in the several industries and occupations, concluding that the theoretical advantages are on the side of the former, while for practical and psychological reasons, the latter would probably be easier to introduce. . . .'"

[2] *Britain's Industrial Future*, p. 189: "The Independent Labour Party has taken up the idea as a means of attaining 'Socialism in our Time'. It proposes that every industry should be required to pay a minimum wage which its popular propaganda fixes at £4 a week, and that every concern failing to do so should be taken over by the State . . . in a very short time each industry would be run at a loss. . . ."

[3] *Ibid.*, pp. 190–1.

had a normal family (it was calculated on the basis of Australian standards and costs at £5 16s. 6d. a week) the Government statistician reported that this would require more than the total national income. Miss Eleanor Rathbone has shown that the same result would follow in England; and Mr. Paul Douglas has shown that even the superior wealth of America would be insufficient.

To get over this difficulty it has been suggested (and the proposal has been successfully tried in several continental countries) that employers after the payment of a basic wage to all employees, should pay a fixed sum weekly for every employee into a pool, which should be divided out among those employees with dependents. . . . We think that it might be tried in selected industries as one way of raising wages when prosperity is increasing.

It is interesting to examine the Liberal Yellow Book's assessment, in 1928, of what had been, perhaps, the most characteristic Radical contribution to the post-war industrial scene—the Whitley Councils proposed for every organized industry in which an equal number from both sides of industry would have met for regular consultation. The hopes cherished may be judged from the kind of topics suggested as proper for the Joint Industrial Councils' consultations which included:[1]

(1) The better utilization of the practical knowledge of the workpeople.

(2) The means of securing to workpeople a greater responsibility for determining the conditions of their work.

(3) The settlement of the general principles governing the conditions of employment.

(4) The establishment of regular methods of negotiation.

(5) Methods of fixing and adjusting earnings and of securing to the workpeople a share in increased prosperity.

(6) Technical education and industrial research.

(7) The provision of facilities for inventions and improvements designed by workpeople.

(8) Improvements of processes, machinery and organization.

(9) Proposed legislation affecting the industry.

Utopian though events proved many of the more extravagant hopes attached to Whitleyism to have been, the movement did make remarkable progress in the short post-war "boom" when wages and prices were rising fast and masters and men were consequently often on the best of terms. Naturally, the onset of sharp depression restored the toughest of bargaining to much of the industrial scene, and by 1928 the Radicals of the Liberal

---

[1] *Britain's Industrial Future*, pp. 171 ff.

Industrial Inquiry were having to deny that Whitleyism had proved a complete failure or that the Industrial Court, above all, had not been very well worth while. Here are their conclusions:[1]

Before the end of 1921, seventy-four Industrial Councils had been set on foot. In some industries, notably printing, pottery, quarrying and the electrical trades, the new system has worked well. . . . But, on the whole, the system has not justified the glowing hopes of its founders. 27 of the original Councils have broken down altogether, and some of the others are in a comatose condition. It would be gravely misleading, however, to say as is sometimes said—that the Whitley scheme has failed. . . . One of the important results of the work of the Whitley Committee was the setting-up, under the Industrial Courts Act 1919, of the Industrial Court . . . normally the Court consists of the President (or one of the Chairmen) sitting with two other members. The Court has dealt with over 1,000 cases and its decisions have almost invariably been accepted by both sides. It must be remembered that recourse to it is purely voluntary, and that it can only continue to function so long as it gives satisfaction. . . . . If for any reason the parties to a dispute prefer it, they may go before a single arbitrator or before a special board of arbitrators. The Minister also has power to set up a Special Court of Inquiry, with or without the assent of the parties, not to give judgement, but to lay before the nation a full and unbiased statement of the whole case.

There was certainly a case for arguing that the Radical record on Industry was a good one, and there was an even better case for maintaining that Radicals' efforts on behalf of the agricultural labourer, the smallholder, and the poorer farmer (even when they were not without political motivation) were even more praiseworthy. Unfortunately, Radical rural programmes tended to

---

[1] *Ibid.*, pp. 174–8. It is, perhaps, worth adding the Liberal Industrial Inquiry's explanation of Whitleyism's "limited degree of success". The causes listed were:

"(1). The experiment was launched at what was probably the most difficult moment . . . just at the end of the war when everybody was cherishing fantastic and unrealizable expectations. Everywhere men were being captivated by the rosy haze of the Socialist mirage . . . and the modest promises of Whitleyism seemed trivial by comparison.

"(2) The new system needed, during the years of its establishment, careful help and guidance . . . especially to help it in overcoming the difficulty of demarcation between industries, and in adjusting the general scheme to the varying needs of different trades. . . . But this help from a 'staff of local officers of the Ministry of Labour' was suddenly cut off when the Geddes Economy Committee applied its axe.

"(3) The Councils were not endowed with any definite powers.

"(4) Finally, they lacked precise financial knowledge about the actual financial facts of the industries. . . . One or two of them tried to remedy this by calling upon firms in the industry to supply facts . . . but . . . there was no power to compel. . . ."

suffer from some grave weaknesses quite apart from a bias against "landlordism" very obvious even to the farm-labourer, whom they were trying to help to half-acre holdings and a chance of becoming a farmer himself, and to the farmer whom they were offering to turn into a quasi-owner in an hereditary line besides bestowing new credit-facilities upon him and help in countering dealers' market-rings through co-operative marketing. *The Land and the Nation*, the carefully-prepared Liberal Green Book of 1925, had some real merits and was very dear to Lloyd George's heart. Yet it contained such provocative quotation as the following:[1]

> The average labourer is just as ignorant re the possibilities of half an acre as is the average farmer re the possibilities of 100 acres. Half an acre of land . . . may mean 10s. a week to a labourer without his having to work hard in the evening. . . . But many labourers are against the idea. Their idea of a plot of land is something to be dug by hand and planted with potatoes. And they get quite enough digging during the day. They must be taught how to use these plots.

On the Trade Unions, and the danger of exaggerating the influence they had had in raising working-class standards of living, Radicals had arguments which, doubtless, deserved greater attention than they were receiving, by 1928, in the operative quarters of the industrial cities. The whole of Trade Union influence had, after all, to be turned, against the argument (used, by Radicals, at least as much with suspicious employers as with Trade Unionists) that the main cause of the four hundred per cent rise in the standard of living over the past century had been the increase of productivity[2] which would, naturally, have to be further increased if a further rise in living standards was desired. And there were sour comments from the Trade Union side on such claims and tables as the following, designed to show what social reform legislation, largely Radical-inspired, had further

---

[1] *Land and the Nation*, p. 382, claiming to quote a labourer on the Half-Acre Plan.

[2] *Britain's Industrial Future*, pp. 183–4: "The mistaken notion which is most prevalent on the side of labour is that labour can only improve its position at the expense of capital, and that all the advances which it has been able to secure have in actual fact been won by means of the belligerent action of the Trade Unions. The notion is quite incorrect. . . . Sir Josiah Stamp has shown that during the 19th century the real wages of the workers were on the average quadrupled. All incomes rose in roughly the same proportion . . . the primary cause of the rise of wages has been an increase of efficiency in the production of wealth. . . ."

contributed, mainly at the expense of the rich, to working-class standards:[1]

During the last 30 years we have developed a steeply-gradauted system of taxation by income-tax, super-tax, and death-duties which have taken from the very rich nearly half of their incomes, and up to 40% of their capital at death. These burdens have been imposed partly to meet war-charges but largely to defray the growing cost of the social services, expenditure on which has risen from £22,600,000 in 1891 to £338,510,000 in 1925 including War Pensions. This expenditure has been out of taxation raised mainly from the rich, and has been spent on social services mainly for the benefit of the working classes. Professor Clay has estimated it at 12½% on the total wages paid, or including employers' contributions under Insurance Acts, 14·7%.

		1891	1925
1.	Expenditure under the Education Acts.	11·5 m.	89·4 m.
2.	Expenditure under Acts relating to the Relief of the Poor.	9·1 m.	40·4 m.
3.	Expenditure under the Housing Acts.	·2 m.	18·4 m.
4.	Expenditure under the Public Health Acts.	·5 m.	9·1 m.
5.	Expenditure under the Lunacy and Mental Deficiency Acts.	·9 m.	4·8 m.
6.	Expenditure under the National Health Insurance Acts.	nil.	32·5 m.
7.	Expenditure under the Unemployment Insurance Acts.	nil.	50·6 m.
8.	Expenditure under the War Pensions Acts.	nil.	66·5 m.
9.	Expenditure under the Old Age Pensions Acts.	nil.	25·8 m.
10.	Other Expenditure.	·4 m.	1·0 m.
	Total	22·6 m.	338·5 m.

What the Trade Union leader vastly preferred to have from the other side was, naturally, the sometimes indiscreet airing of a private dream or ambition as when Lord Leverhulme in 1918 nearly drove brother-employers crazy by issuing *The Six-Hours Day* or Keynes, in the darkening days of October 1930, professed to see at the end of the tunnel the great light of a four- to eight-fold increase in the standard of living during the ensuing century.[2] Here, for example, is one report of how rapidly Lord Leverhulme's six-hour optimism became a formidable weapon in the hands of the "Reddest" trade unionists.[3]

The forty hours' week, or even the six hours' day, has suddenly won its way to the front place in the demands of labour. . . . They do not

---

[1] *Ibid.*, p. 245.
[2] Cf. *The Nation*, October 11th and 18th, under the title, "Economic Possibilities for our Grandchildren".   [3] *Ibid.*, March 8, 1919.

pretend that speeding-up will, or ought to, compensate for the loss of hours. They say that is not their concern. What they are after is liberation from the machine. They want more time and energy to live their own lives. . . . But must material output suffer? Must the nation pay for more leisure by any reduction of the economic product? This challenging question is met by one of our most successful men of business, Lord Leverhulme, with a triumphant negative. The opening part of his interesting volume, *The Six Hours Day* sets forth the case for this great reform.

Of course, there were distinct anticipations in Leverhulme of that "Rationalization of Industry" which became one of the leading economic and social problems of the 1920s and 1930s[1] just as in Keynes's journalism there were some anticipations of Galbraith's *Affluent Society*.[2] Yet obviously there was some justification for those Radical politicians and industrialists who doubted (like virtually all Conservatives)[3] whether it was wise to proclaim so confidently that all was nearly well when Britain, with an economic system riddled with every variety of "restrictive practice", was called upon to undertake a major reconstruction, especially in Housing. On Housing, the Radical authority, E. D. Simon, had this to say in 1924:[4]

We need for the United Kingdom 100,000 houses per annum to meet the needs of the increasing population. Towards this we have built since the war less than 60,000 houses per annum. . . . If in addition we are to build enough houses to prevent overcrowding and to clear away the slums in a reasonable time, we must build something like 200,000 houses a year. Even then it might easily take us twenty years. . . . There are two great difficulties . . . difficulties of overcoming the selfishness of organized groups of human beings to whom a great housing scheme would give special advantages at the cost of the community . . . the "capitalists" who supply the materials, and the workers who supply the labour.

[1] Because the concentration of production in each industry's most modern and efficient plants, the rest being eliminated by the industry's organizing itself to purchase them for scrapping, involved the double danger of fostering monopoly production on the one hand, and, on the other, of putting thousands of workers from the scrapped plants (e.g. Palmer's of Jarrow) on the industrial "scrap heap" themselves, with the possibility of a rescue through "Industrial Transference" very remote, at least for the older men.

[2] J. K. Galbraith, *The Affluent Society*, p. 13, on Keynes's construction "of a new body of conventional wisdom, the obsolescence of some parts of which, in its turn, is now well advanced".

[3] The great success of Dean Inge's *Outspoken Essays* of 1919 and the *Second Series* of 1922 was proof enough that his bitter views on "so-called Progress", Democracy and Trade Unionism were widely shared.

[4] *The Nation*, January 27, 1924.

Living and Other Standards

It may be well to end this chapter with a review of some statistics which throw a light on what had happened, say by 1935, to the eighteenth- and nineteenth-century religious basis on which so much typical Radicalism had been reared. Cinemas, the radio and cheap cycling, motor-cycling and motoring might have reduced service-attendance figures on Sundays as well as the domination of Church or Chapel lectures, socials, concerts, and outings[1] over the recreational life of vast masses of the population. Yet Church and Chapel influences were still very strong as many proved, who had almost ceased attendance themselves, but yet sent their children regularly to Sunday School for indoctrination in a faith they no longer actively supported. Two sets of statistics are available to show how Radical readers of the *Daily News*[2] and the Radical intelligentsia of *The Nation*[3] answered a questionnaire on Religious Belief in the summer of 1926. To the question: "Do you believe in a personal God?" 9,991 readers of the *Daily News* answered "Yes" as against 3,686 who answered "No", and 366 who were doubtful. The figures in the case of *The Nation* were 669 believers, 882 non-believers, and 76 doubtful. In regard to personal immortality, *Daily News* readers showed 10,161 believers, 3,178 non-believers, and 704 doubtful while *The Nation*'s readers divided at 723 believers, 759 non-believers, and 145 doubtful. The question, "Do you believe in any form of Christianity?" showed 10,546 believers, 2,879 non-believers, and 618 doubtful among *Daily News* readers and, among those of *The Nation*, 847 believers, 681 non-believers, and 99 doubtful. To the question, "Are you an active member of any Church?" 8,796 *Daily News* readers said, "Yes", against 4,896 who said "No", and 351 who were doubtful while, for *The Nation*, the corresponding figures were 595, 999 and 33. A last set of figures may be quoted from the answers to the question, "Do you regard the Bible as inspired?" 8,950 *Daily News* readers as against 4,635 and 458 doubtful thought the Bible inspired while the proportion in the case of *The Nation* was 474 for inspiration against 1,102 and 51 doubtful.

[1] *Poverty and Progress, A Second Survey of York* treats authoritatively of the changes in these respects at York between 1899 and 1935.

[2] The *Daily News*, October 11, 1926.

[3] *The Nation*, September 18, 1926. *The Nation*'s figures were based on the 1627 completed questionnaire forms received up to date.

EPILOGUE

IN 1945 and, perhaps, for some years afterwards, there seemed a possibility that Labour's hopes of establishing a permanent hold on the State in the name of the majority of the "people" were capable of realization in the fashion that had already given Labour apparently permanent control of such local authorities as, say, the Durham and Glamorgan County Councils, the Leeds and Sheffield City Councils or, to take two of the most firmly-established if least inviting examples, the Poplar and West Ham Borough Councils. And, truth to tell, there were pessimistic moments when Conservative and Liberal Parliamentarians became doubtful whether the domination, say, of the Labour caucuses of the Durham Shire Hall and the West Ham Town Hall might not represent the shape of things to come at Westminster itself in an age apparently prepared to boast that it belonged to the "common man". Of course, such fears at Westminster proved to be exaggerated partly because Labour's claim to have obtained a mandate to create a Socialist State, according to Transport House specifications, was very wide of the mark. The Majority of 1945 seems to have been due, more than to anything else, to the fear of millions of Service men and their families that demobilization might not be as prompt under Churchill as under Labour and that under Churchill, too, much larger numbers would be drafted off for a dangerous and protracted war against Japan in the Far East. In fact, despite other predisposing causes for Churchill's defeat including his unhappy "Gestapo" broadcast, there can hardly be a doubt but that if the Japanese surrender had taken place before, instead of after, the Election, the results would have been very different.

But whatever the truth as to the reasons for Labour's capture of 11,985,733 votes out of a total of 25,018,393 cast and of 393 seats in a total House of 640, events were to make that Majority and its Nationalization and Trade Union shibboleths increasingly unrepresentative and increasingly provocative of the anger and contempt of some of the best economic and financial opinion of the country. Moreover, the 2,253,197 electors who had still voted Liberal despite the certainty of gross under-representation (not to mention the 759,884 Liberal Nationals) were increasingly unlikely to yield to the occasional wooing attempted by Labour in the character of Radicalism's legitimate heir and successor. And, of course, it did not follow that, if the neighbourhood and population imbalance of a Poplar or West Ham had allowed Labour caucuses, of no exalted worth or reputation, to maintain unbroken control for a generation and more (with Conservative, Liberal, Independent, and Moderate criticism sometimes virtually extinguished for years) that the nation, as a whole, would easily submit to something of the Poplar Town Hall pattern becoming established at Westminster and Whitehall. And, in fact, many events of the six Labour years of 1945–51 were of a character to give uncommitted elements in the nation a thorough distaste for what might be in store unless they asserted themselves. There were such gems of Labour eloquence as "we are the masters now" not to mention the costly diatribe on the "vermin" opposed to the new dispensation; strike troubles rarely seemed, to the casual newspaper-reader, more numerous or less justifiable; and, of course, there was the epoch when one Nationalization Act after another appeared to open up vast new fields of patronage or, to use one very expressive phrase, "Jobs for the Boys" from Lord Citrine's £8500 per annum as Chairman of the Electricity Authority to the humbler openings available to lesser lights of the Trade Union world as Colliery Welfare Officers under the National Coal Board, it might be, or Area Chairmen of Gas Consultative Councils. It could be held, moreover, that a large number of thoroughly undesirable Trade Union practices, which had become illegal under the 1927 Act passed in consequence of the General Strike, would reappear again after that Act's repeal. And there was, besides, the 1948 Act which made "professional politics" easier in the Town or Shire Hall by conceding the right to claim for "loss of earnings" due to Council activities in addition to the incidental expenses already allowed.

Two further steps of a character to cause special concern to the uncommitted were taken when it was determined to abolish University representation as "undemocratic" and to reduce the suspensive veto of the House of Lords, under a new Parliament Bill, to a year's duration only. To Labour's party strategists, indeed, the disappearance of twelve University seats, none held by Labour, greatly increased their chances of establishing the permanent majority they were dreaming of, and, as for the new Parliament Bill, the likelihood of an Opposition's building up, in a mere twelvemonth, a sufficiently popular outcry against a projected piece of legislation to deter Labour's Majority, seemed poor. Yet, of course, many unexpected mishaps had overtaken the Labour planners by the time the electorate was called, in 1950, to pass judgement on their record. Nothing, for example, was less likely to take Liberals into the Labour camp than the combination of financial mistakes and Trade Union pressures that had forced a major devaluation of the pound sterling during 1949, and 2,621,489 grossly under-valued votes were cast for Liberal candidates independent both of Labour and Conservatism. Yet Trade Unionists' belief that they were better off, in relation to other classes, than they would have been under any other Government brought Labour a mass vote of over thirteen millions and allowed the Attlee Cabinet to stay in office even though by a majority shrunken from 186 to 8.

But for the next eighteen months, a new financial crisis and a possibly disastrous new devaluation never seemed to be far away, with sterling under constant pressure and suspicion abroad, partly because of what the uncharitable called an unmasterable wage-inflation and partly because the over-ambitious National Health Service, with its free dentures, spectacles, medicines and much else, was running at a level well beyond all prudent Budgetary calculations. The foreign banking community was scandalized that, in such circumstances, it was being proposed to force through Iron and Steel Nationalization, and its attitude hardly became friendlier when a Cabinet majority decided to sacrifice, in the interests of the Budget of 1951, if not Iron and Steel Nationalization, at least the completely "free" principle of the National Health Service. Even this cost some notable Cabinet resignations, and, all in all, the Government's shrinking prestige was of a character to tempt the Persian Prime Minister, Moussadeq, to press on with Persia's own Nationalization projects for taking over all the installations of "the late Anglo-Iranian Oil Company". Nor did the finally futile half-threats from London apparently avail much, either at Abadan or in the world's banking centres, to stave off the conviction that Britain's inept and not very successful Labour Leadership might soon be facing its greatest financial danger yet. At any rate, Attlee's attempt to persuade the country at the General Election of October 25, 1951 to strengthen his hand and give him a new mandate failed when it yielded him only 295 supporters against Churchill's 321.

Eight years were to follow in which, helped by occasional fortunate changes of world-prices in Britain's favour, by remarkably rapid technical developments in world-industry, and by the greater confidence of the world's financial centres, a succession of British Chancellors of the Exchequer was to prove that prudent finance might still do more for Britain's working families than Labour's doctrinaire Nationalization projects or its habit of trying to buy "wage restraint" from the Unions by the part-confiscation of company profits and by the continuation of all manner of unwise or unnecessary food and other subsidies. Indeed, the remarkable popular and Parliamentary majorities obtained by Conservative Governments at the General Elections of May 26, 1955 and October 8, 1959 have, with the growing Liberal tendency to win more votes from Labour than from Conservatism, at last emboldened some of the party chiefs, headed by the Leader, Gaitskell, himself to suggest a change of emphasis. The platform, in fact, outlined by the Labour Leader to the Blackpool Conference, investigating, on November 28 and 29, 1959, the causes of Labour's third successive General Election defeat, contained so little Marxism and so much Radicalism or even Liberalism that the angriest thunder on the Left resulted, despite his conciliatory gestures, when "throwing out of the window" suggestions for a change of party name, for a Pact with the Liberals and for a severance from the Trade Unions. One irate critic claimed that even the Tories could accept Mr. Gaitskell's general phrases, another found that the lost Election had been fought not on a Socialist policy but on "a rehash of the Liberalism of the thirties", and, all told, an open split was barely, and, perhaps, only temporarily avoided.

At this stage, it might be well to give Mr. Gaitskell's definition of his party's "basic first principles". They were:

1. The Labour Party expressed a broad human movement on behalf of the bottom dog—on behalf of all those who were oppressed or in need or hardship. At home their first concern was for the old, the sick, the widowed, the unemployed, the disabled, and the badly housed; abroad it was reflected in a deep concern for the well being of peoples who were much poorer than themselves.

2. They believed in social justice, in an equitable distribution of wealth and income. They demanded that differences should be related not to the accident of birth or inheritance but to how much effort, skill, and creative energy each contributed to the common good.

3. They believed in a classless society, without snobbery, privilege or restrictive social barriers.

4. They believed in the fundamental equality of races and peoples and in the building of an international order which would enable them to live together in peace. They believed quite simply in the brotherhood of man.

5. British Socialism had always contained an essential element of personal idealism—the belief that the pursuit of material satisfaction without spiritual values was empty and that their relations with one another should be based not on ruthless self-regarding rivalry but on fellowship and co-operation.

6. They believed that the public interest must come before private interest. They were not opposed to individuals seeking to do the best for themselves and their families, but the pursuit of private gain should not take precedence over the public good.

Finally, they believed that these objects must be achieved with and through freedom and democratic self-government.

Of course, any party policy-statement is full of papered-over cracks as well as "moral uplift" but, within the limits of what can be done in a formula necessarily designed to attract the adhesion of many millions of members of different backgrounds and interests, Mr. Gaitskell's is an interesting and revealing production. Even extensions of nationalization were, with some reservations, put into a kind of disarming footnote; the old-style nationalization was obliquely criticized as "the setting-up of huge monopolies by Act of Parliament"; and the special fault found with the existing Party Constitution, as devised by Henderson and Webb "over forty years ago", was that "it laid them open to continual misrepresentation. It implied that they proposed to nationalize everything" instead of having "long ago come to accept a mixed economy for the foreseeable future". Indeed, if the kind of negotiation, called for by some Liberals enheartened by their unexpectedly strong polling displays at the General Election, should ever take place for the construction of a "new progressive party" of Radical-Labour Opposition, few better formulas for the new party's constitution could be devised than Mr. Gaitskell's.

Yet even Mr. Gaitskell's formula evades the fact that his party's present plight is the result, above all, of the complete failure of the confident prophecies that were made in regard to the main Nationalization schemes for Coal, Railways, and Dock labour. Having been largely constructed and financed by the Miners', Railwaymen's, and Dockers' Unions for the very purpose of nationalizing their industries, the Labour Party, after 1945, not merely undertook nationalization but "modernization" also, on a costly scale which it often seems difficult to justify by the likely results. Moreover, so far from Nationalization bringing the angelic content to the "workers" so often and so long the theme of Labour rhetoric, it appears that some of the worst and least excusable of the "lightning unofficial strikes" have been enacted in the nationalized industries and that the "working-class militancy" affected by their organizers is frequently a mere cover for Communist disruption. Yet when, at long last, the T.U.C. (not without electoral considerations in mind) began, in 1959, its painful attempt to open an investigation into what might be wrong with the functioning of Trade Unions, it was the largest Union of all, The Transport and General Workers under Mr. Cousins, whose dockers had been among the most inveterate of "unofficial strikers", which gave the T.U.C. a loud public rebuff, certain to be imitated wherever "militancy" was strong.

The Town and Shire Halls, too, where Labour controls have been longest established, often tend to bring the party little national credit as Mr. Gaitskell himself has partially admitted. Nor is it merely a question of over-regulation of Council House tenancies, as is sometimes pretended, or the over-tight discipline of the Labour caucuses, and the plentiful washing of "dirty party linen in public" which results after there has been an expulsion for a display of independence. There is, for example, a long history of suspicion as to the kind of claim for expenses and "loss of earnings" that some Councillors make, and it has transpired that the most notorious Town Hall "scandal" for some years, a "scandal" not apparently without effect on the 1959 General Election, was caused by the Labour majority of the Nottingham Watch Committee reacting sharply to their Chief Constable's attempt, among other things, to investigate twenty-two Councillors' claims on the Town Treasurer. And it is, naturally, the Labour Council which is most apt to assert the "public interest" when attempting to delay de-requisitioning of private property or to make compulsory purchase orders, in conditions and on terms that finally prove morally or legally indefensible. It is in Labour areas, too, that the Council Housing position sometimes tends to become totally inexcusable especially when Councillors allow themselves to be influenced or coerced by Tenant Protection Leagues and their slogan of "No Means Test" into revising or abandoning carefully-prepared schemes of withdrawing the subsidization of house-rents from families who do not need it in order to make it available for those who do. In Scotland there seem to be some special scandals with categories of highly-privileged Council tenantries (including Councillors) enjoying accommodation at a fraction of the mortgage-repayment costs with which the un-privileged have to load themselves and lustily resisting all suggestions of rectification. And to complete their opponents' indictment of some Labour authorities, there have been the ideologically-motivated forcing of "comprehensive schools" on the children of often reluctant parents and the notorious and some-times illegal refusal of Press privileges to journalists who had been declared "black" during the prolonged printing-strike of the spring of 1959.

Some of Britain's ultimate political prospects depend, of course, even more on what happens in the Trade Unions than on what happens in the Town Halls. There can be no doubt, for example, but that "militancy", for all its restless activity and ambition, has normally proved a grave political handicap to Labour, and more especially the Electrical Trades Union type of "militancy", directly associated with Communism and suspect "Red" manœuvre even in the eyes of the T.U.C. And if what used to be called the "Trade Board industries" (since the Act of 1945 more properly denomi-nated Wages Council industries)—specially picked though they once had been because of the past need for official protection of their wage and labour standards—sometimes seem prepared to buy complete bargaining freedom by surrendering their Councils, it must be surmised that much of the "militancy" in traditionally stronger and better-paid crafts is not very warrantable.

A word may be spared, perhaps, for the Co-operative Party, which has proved a very useful ally to Labour but which has expressed opposition to the doctrinaire extension of the National-ization patterns of 1945–51 if not to "public ownership" expansion capable of making use of the Co-operative Societies and the Municipalities. Another type of "public ownership" expansion, mooted by Mr. Gaitskell himself, is the acquisition by the State of blocks of shares in the principal commercial and industrial companies of the country. And it is doubtless worth remembering that, as far back as 1927, the Radical *Nation* had this very pertinent piece of advice to give to the Liberal Industrial Inquiry:

> There are a hundred forms of management and control in which the public interest can be safeguarded without the spur of private interest being lost. It should be a primary task of the Industrial Inquiry to search, for each case separately, the best of these systems . . . the ideal system will be different in almost every case. In very few cases will it be Whitehall nationalization; in a diminishing number of cases will it be unfettered private control.

It has proved to Conservatives' advantage that they have come to appreciate and employ this type of Radical thinking more readily than a Labour Party, almost religiously committed to National-ization. And even more notable in some respects is the way in which the old Radical animus against Monopoly and Restrictive Agreements amongst Industrialists has been allowed to triumph in the Restrictive Practices Court functioning under the Con-servative Act of 1956. But, of course, that Court has no juris-diction over "restrictive practices" on the other side of industry, deeply though the "public interest" is affected.

SELECT BIBLIOGRAPHY

SPECIAL SOURCES

1. The author's collections of coloured and plain wall-posters issued by Unionists, Liberals, the Labour Representation Committee, the Tariff Reform League, and the Free Trade Union in 1905 and 1906 in preparation for or during the General Election of January 1906.
2. A constituency collection of material issued during the Darlington Election contest of 1905-6 between H. Pike Pease (Liberal Unionist) and Alderman Isaac Mitchell (Labour supported by Liberals).
3. A collection of Election addresses issued in North-Eastern England for the same Parliamentary Election.
4. Collections of "F.C.G." cartoons for the *Westminster Gazette* as issued in annual volumes from 1903.
5. The author's own very varied collection of Socialist and Anti-Socialist pamphleteering to 1914.
6. Collections of Liberal, Conservative, and London Municipal Reform handbills and leaflets.

SOURCES IN THE IMPERIAL WAR MUSEUM

1. Diaries of soldiers in the War of 1914-18, including some in type-script.
2. British, Allied, and Enemy propaganda material and cartoons.
3. Files of illustrated enemy periodicals especially those of the *Leipziger Illustrirte Zeitung und Jugend*.
4. Recruiting, War-Loan, War-Rationing, Take-Cover, and similar War-Poster material.
5. Files of the *Suffragette* to 1915 and of *Britannia* (amalgamating the *Suffragette*) to illustrate the war-effort of the women.
6. Files of Norman Angell's threepenny monthly, *War and Peace* and the Churches' periodical *Goodwill* to illustrate the varied parentage of the League of Nations idea.
7. Material on the search for a negotiated peace, 1916-18.
8. Material on the failure of Versailles and the new war-dangers.
9. File of *The Balkan News*, 1915-18 (printed for the Salonika Expeditionary Force).
10. War Resisters' Section on Conscientious Objectors.

615

SOURCES IN "PROGRESSIVE", "ADVANCED", AND OTHER JOURNALISM AND PERIODICAL-WRITING

1. *The Nation* (1907–31), a famous Radical weekly, has been the main authority for the central "battle of ideas between Progress and Reaction". The greater part of its file was made available by the Bradford Public Libraries through the courtesy of Mr. Bilton, the City Librarian.

2. Other "progressive" and "advanced" material used in supplementation came from the following dailies (prices quoted are those of 1914):

   (*a*) *The Northern Echo.*   Halfpenny morning paper for Radicals of the north-east, published in Darlington.

   (*b*) *Daily News.*   Halfpenny Radical morning paper of national circulation.

   (*c*) *Daily Chronicle.*   Shared the Radical halfpenny morning market with the *Daily News* (which absorbed *The Morning Leader* in 1912).

   (*d*) *The Star.*   The sole Radical evening halfpenny for London and the Home Counties after the end of *The Echo* in 1905.

   (*e*) *Manchester Guardian.*   C. P. Scott's Liberal rival to *The Times*.

   (*f*) *Westminster Gazette.*   Liberal evening professional-class paper, very influential during J. A. Spender's long editorship, 1896–1922. But it never paid, and Lord Cowdray, the millionaire-supporter of Rosebery and Asquith, is supposed to have spent several fortunes keeping it alive. It was absorbed by the *Daily News* after his death in 1927.

3. The following "advanced" or "progressive" weeklies and periodicals were occasionally checked or consulted:

   (*a*) *The Workman's Times.*   A Liberal-Labour weekly of some importance in the last years of Gladstonianism.

   (*b*) *The Labour Leader.*   Keir Hardie's organ which, with increasing success, broke Labour away from Gladstonianism and the Liberal Front Bench.

   (*c*) *Reynolds's Newspaper.*   The "extreme Radical" Sunday organ of pre-1914 days, preferred by the zealots to the less indoctrinated *Lloyd's Sunday News*.

Select Bibliography

(d) *The Contemporary Review.* Opinion-making monthly on the Liberal side, long under the joint-editorship of Dr. Scott Lidgett and G. P. Gooch.

(e) *The Review of Reviews.* Founded by W. T. Stead, it made a special point of reproducing foreign political cartoons.

(f) *The Ploughshare.* Turned from quarterly into monthly (February 1916) by a Quaker anti-war and "Social Reconstruction" group.

4. For reference—*The Times; Annual Register; Whitaker's Almanack; The Labour Year Book, 1916.* Some occasional checking with the *Morning Post* and *Daily Graphic* files was also undertaken.

THE PARLIAMENTARY DEBATES AND THE PARLIAMENTARY PAPERS

1. *The Parliamentary Debates.* Referred to or quoted continuously under the old short title of *Hansard* with the date of the speech or the debate under discussion.

2. *The Parliamentary Papers.* Eventually all Blue Books, White Papers and other material presented to Parliament every Session from Royal Commissions, Select Committees, Joint Select Committees, Departmental Committees, the Diplomatic Correspondence, etc., etc., become the Parliamentary Papers of that Session, referred to by the number of the volume in which they are bound and the volume-page where they begin. The total mass of material is formidable as may be judged, for example, from a 1908 Sessional document referred to below as occurring at Volume 125, p. 477 of the Sessional Parliamentary Papers. But good indexes of the Parliamentary Papers are available under subject-heads, and, besides, on administrative, financial, social, and economic matters there are the valuable volumes of the Fords, known as *A Breviate of Parliamentary Papers, 1917–1939* and *A Breviate of Parliamentary Papers, 1900–1916.* The following is a tiny selection of Papers which have been found useful, interesting, or merely curious.

Session	Volume	Paper
1903	IX, 1.	Report from the Royal Commission on the evils attributed to unrestricted Alien Immigration.
1904	CX, 313.	Despatch to H.M. Ambassador at Paris forwarding Agreements between Great Britain and France.
1905	XXXIX, 1.	Report from the Royal Commission on Food and Raw Material Supplies in Time of War.

Session	Volume	Paper
1906	CIV, I.	J. S. Davy's Report on the Poplar Union.
1907	XIV, 529.	Departmental Committee Report on the Miners' Eight Hour Day.
1908	CXXV, 477.	Convention signed on August 31, 1907 between Great Britain and Russia containing arrangements on the subject of Persia, Afghanistan, and Thibet.
1909	XXXVII, I.	Royal Commission Report on the Poor Law and the Relief of Distress.
1911	XLVII, 691.	Correspondence between the Home Office and Local Authorities on Employment of the Military during the Railway Strike.
1912–13	XLVII, 297.	C. Jones's Report on Complaints against the Police during the Transport Workers' Strike.
1913	VII, 95.	Marconi Select Committee Report.
1914	XVIII, 513.	Vice-Regal Commission Report on the Dublin [Larkin] Disturbances [of 1913].
1914	LIII, I.	Army Correspondence on Recent Events in the Irish Command.
1914–16	XXIV, 805.	Royal Commission Report on the Landing of Arms at Howth on July 26, 1914.
1916	VIII, 327.	Consultative Committee Interim Report on [State] Scholarships for Higher Education.
1916	XI, 176.	Royal Commission Report on the Rebellion in Ireland.
1916	XII, 529.	Advisory Committee Report on [1915] Proposals for the State Purchase of the Licensed Liquor Trade.
1917–18	X, 419.	Dardanelles Commission. First Report.
1918	X, 569.	Conference on Reform of the Second Chamber. Letter from Viscount Bryce to the Prime Minister.
1919	XI, 373.	[Sankey] Coal Industry Commission, Interim Reports.
1919	XXXVIII, 489.	[Annual] Statement exhibiting the Moral and Material Progress of India.
1919	LIII, 527.	Treaty of Peace between the Allied and Associated Powers and Germany.
1919	LIII, 987.	A Collection of Reports on Bolshevism in Russia.
1921	XLII, 479.	[Annual] Reports by H.M. High Commissioner on the Finances, Administration and Condition of Egypt and the Sudan for the Year 1920.

Select Bibliography

Session	Volume	Paper
1921	XLII, 621.	Report of the Special [Milner] Mission to Egypt.
1921	XLII, 81.	Correspondence [1913–1921] respecting the Cultivation of Opium in China.
1922	IX, 1.	[Geddes Axe] Committee. First Interim Report.
1922	XIII, 899.	Remarks of the Admiralty.
1923	XI, 975.	Report from the Royal Commission on Honours.
1924	XIX, 985.	[Wheatley's] Rescission of the Poplar Order.
1926	XIV, 1.	[Samuel] Royal Commission Report on the Coal Industry.
1928	XIX, 33.	Proposals for Reform in Local Government, etc.
1929–30	XI, 1.	[Simon] Statutory Commission Reports.
1930–1	XVI, 1.	[May] Economy Report.
1931–2	XXVII, 67.	[Lytton] Preliminary Report on conditions in Manchuria from the Commission of Inquiry appointed by the Council of the League of Nations.
1934–5	I, 535.	Bill [passed cap. 42] to make further provision for the Government of India.

SOME RADICAL BIOGRAPHY

Abraham, William (1842–1922), in *Dictionary of National Biography*.
Baker, J. Allen, M.P., A Memoir, by P. J. Noel-Baker, etc., 1929.
Benn, John, and the Progressive Movement, by A. G. Gardiner, 1925.
Briant, Frank (1864–1934), Obituary Notice in *Annual Register*, 1934.
Buckmaster, Viscount, An Orator of Justice: A Speech biography of, by James Johnston, 1932.
Burns, John, by G. D. H. Cole, 1943.
Burt, Thomas (1837–1922), *Thomas Burt, Pitman and Privy Councillor*, 1924.
Buxton, Noel (1869–1948), *Politics from a Back Bench* by Dr. Conwell-Evans.
Cadbury, George, Life of, by A. G. Gardiner, 1923.
Clifford, Dr. John, by Sir James Marchant, 1924.
Clodd, Edward (1840–1930), A Memoir by Joseph McCabe, 1932.
Dent, J. M. (1849–1926), *Memoirs*, 1928.
Dickinson, G. Lowes, by E. M. Forster.
Evans, Howard, *Radical Fights of Forty Years*, 1914.
Galsworthy, John, Life and Letters of, by H. V. Marrot, 1935.
Gooch, G. P., *Under Six Reigns*, 1958.
Haldane, Viscount, *An Autobiography*, 1928.

Harris, Sir Percy, *Forty Years in and out of Parliament*, 1947.
Hirst, F. W., *In the Golden Days*, 1948.
Hobhouse, Prof. L. T., *His Life and Work*, by Ginsberg and Hobson, 1931.
Hobson, J. A. (1858–1940), *Confessions of an Economic Heretic*, 1938.
Jones, Dr. Thomas, *A Diary with Letters*, 1955.
Keynes, Lord, The Life of, by R. F. Harrod, 1951.
Lidgett, Dr. Scott, *My Guided Life*, 1936.
Lloyd George, David, *A Study*, by Sir Charles Mallet, 1930.
   Tempestuous Journey, by Frank Owen, 1954.
   Lloyd George, by Earl Lloyd George, 1960.
Massingham, H. W., *H. W. M., A Selection from the Writings of*, 1925.
Masterman, C. F. G., by Lucy Masterman, 1939.
Morel, E. D., His Life and Work, by F. S. Cocks, 1920.
Morley, Viscount, *Recollections*, 1917.
Muir, Prof. Ramsay, An Autobiography and Some Essays, 1943.
Nicoll, Sir W. R. (1851–1923), *Life and Letters of*, by T. H. Darlow, 1925.
O'Connor, T. P., *Memoirs of an Old Parliamentarian*, 1929.
Rathbone, Eleanor, A Biography, by Mary D. Stocks, 1949.
Robertson, J. M. (1856–1933). Obituary Notice in *Annual Register*, 1933.
Rowntree, Arnold, by Elfrida Vipont, 1955.
Rowntree, Joseph, A Quaker Business Man, The Life of, by Anne Vernon, 1958.
Samuel, Viscount, *Memoirs*, 1945.
Scott, C. P., by J. L. Hammond, 1932.
Spender, J. A., *Life, Journalism and Politics*, 1927.
Unwin, T. Fisher (1848–1935), Obituary Notice in *Annual Register*, 1935.
Wedgwood, Lord, *Last of the Radicals*, by C. V. E. Wedgwood, 1951.
Wells, H. G., *Experiment in Autobiography*, 1934.
Wilson, J. H. (1833–1914), *Fighter for Freedom*, by Mosa Anderson, 1958.
Wilson, J. Havelock, *My Stormy Voyage through Life*, 1925.

SOME POLITICAL DIARIES, OFFICIAL BIOGRAPHIES, ETC., ETC.

Addison, Viscount, *Politics from Within*, 1924.
   Four and a Half Years, 1934.
Amery, L. S., *The Unforgiving Years, 1929–1940*, 1955.
Asquith, Earl etc., *Life of*, by Spender and Asquith, 1932.
Asquith, Lady, *Autobiography of Margot*, 1922.
Attlee, Earl, *As It Happened*, 1954.
Baldwin, Earl, *Stanley Baldwin*, by G. M. Young, 1952.
   My Father; The True Story, by A. W. Baldwin.
Beaverbrook, Lord, *Politicians and the War*, 1928–32.

Select Bibliography

Birkenhead, Lord, *The First Phase*, 1933; *The Last Phase*, 1935, by his son.
Carson, Lord, The Life of, by H. M. Hyde, 1953.
Cecil, Viscount, *A Great Experiment; An Autobiography*, 1941.
Chamberlain, Austen, Life and Letters of, by Sir C. Petrie, 1939–40.
Chamberlain, Neville, Life of, by Keith Feiling, 1946.
Churchill, W. S., *The World Crisis*, 1923–9.
  My Early Life, 1930.
  Arms and the Covenant (Speeches), 1938.
D'Abernon, Viscount, *An Ambassador of Peace*, 1929–30.
Dalton, Dr. Hugh, *Call Back Yesterday*.
Fitzroy, Sir Almeric, *Memoirs* (1898–1923).
George V, King, by Harold Nicolson, 1952.
Grey of Fallodon, by G. M. Trevelyan, 1937.
Hannington, Wal, *Unemployed Struggles, 1919–1936*, 1936.
Hardie, J. Keir, *A Biography*, by William Stewart, 1921.
Healy, T. M., *Letters and Leaders of My Day*, 1928.
Henderson, Arthur, by M. A. Hamilton, 1938.
Hewins, W. A. S., *The Apologia of an Imperialist*, 1930.
Laski, Harold, *The Holmes-Laski Letters*, 1953.
Law, A. Bonar, The Unknown Prime Minister: Life and Times of, by Robert Blake.
Lawrence, Col. T. E., The Letters of, ed. Garnett, 1938.
MacDonald, J. R., The Tragedy of, by L. MacNeill Weir, 1938.
Maxton, James, The Beloved Rebel, by John McNair, 1955.
Milner, Viscount, The Forsaken Idea: A Study of, by Edward Crank-shaw, 1938.
Montagu, Edwin S., *An Indian Diary*, ed. Venetia Stanley, 1930.
Northcliffe, Lord, *My Northcliffe Diary*, by Tom Clarke, 1931.
Repington, Lt.-Col., *The First World War*, 1920.
Riddell, Lord, *Lord Riddell's War Diary, 1914–1918*, 1933.
  Intimate Diary of the Peace Conference and After, 1933.
  More Pages from My Diary, 1908–1914, 1934.
Snell, Lord, *Men, Movements and Myself*, 1936.
Snowden, Viscount, *An Autobiography*, 1934.
Webb, Beatrice, The Diaries of, ed. Margaret Cole, 1952.
Wilson, Field-Marshal Sir Henry, His Life and Diaries, 1927.
(L. Lyon), *The Pomp of Power*, 1922.
  The Fruits of Folly, 1929.
Potted Biographies, A Dictionary of Anti-National Biography, 1930.

SOME RADICAL VIEWS OF THE BRITISH SCENE

The Liberal Publication Department's Annual Bound Volume of Pamphlets and Leaflets, 1906, 1907, 1908, 1909, 1910, 1911, 1912, 1913.
The Land, The Report of the Land Enquiry Committee, Vol. 1, *Rural*, Vol. 2, *Urban*, 1914.

Essays in Liberalism, Being the Lectures and Papers which were delivered at the Liberal Summer School at Oxford, 1922.

Coal and Power, Report of Mr. Lloyd George's Committee of Liberal members of Parliament and others representative of the different elements in the industry and of the public life of the country, 1924.

The New Way Series of pamphlets, published by the *Daily News*, treated the coal problem as no 8 under the title of *The Problem of the Coal Mines* by A. D. MacNair, 1924.

The Land and the Nation, Rural Report of the Liberal Land Committee, 1923–5 (584 pp.) 1925.

Towns and the Land, Urban Report of the Liberal Land Committee, 1923–5 (288 pp.) 1925.

Britain's Industrial Future, being the Report of the Liberal Industrial Inquiry, 1928.

We Can Conquer Unemployment, 1929.

How to Tackle Unemployment, 1930.

The Council of Action for Peace and Reconstruction.

Booklet on *Peace*, 1935.

Booklet on *Reconstruction*, 1935.

SOME INDIVIDUAL RADICAL CONTRIBUTIONS

Lord Beveridge, *Unemployment: A Problem of Industry*, 1909.

Insurance for All, 1924.

Changes in Family Life, 1932.

Full Employment in a Free Society, 1944.

Why I am a Liberal, 1945.

G. E. Dodds, *Is Liberalism Dead?*, 1919.

Liberalism in Action, 1922.

The Social Gospel of Liberalism, 1926.

Let's Try Liberalism, 1944.

P. Guedalla, *The Industrial Future*, 1921.

A Council of Industry, 1925.

J. M. Keynes, *Economic Consequences of the Peace*, 1919.

A Revision of the Treaty, 1922.

The End of Laissez Faire, 1926.

D. Lloyd George, *The Truth about the Peace Treaties*, 1938.

Ramsay Muir, *Liberalism and Industry*, 1920.

Politics and Progress, 1923.

H. L. Nathan, ed., *Liberal Points of View*, 1927.

Liberalism and some Problems of To-Day, 1929.

J. M. Robertson, *The Political Economy of Free Trade*, 1928.

History of Free Thought in the Nineteenth Century, 1929.

R. S. Rowntree, *The Human Needs of Labour*, 1918.

The Human Factor in Business, 1921.

Poverty and Progress, 1941.

English Life and Leisure, A Social Study (with G. R. Lavers), 1951.

Poverty and the Welfare State (with G. R. Lavers), 1951.

Select Bibliography

E. D. Simon, *A City Council from Within*, 1926.
How to abolish the Slum.
H. G. Wells, *Travels of a Republican Radical in Search of Hot Water*, 1939.
The Fate of Homo Sapiens, 1939.

SOME CONTEMPORARY DESCRIPTIONS OF BRITAIN AND THE BRITISH

1901　*The Heart of the Empire* (Masterman, Gooch, Trevelyan, etc.).
1903　*People of the Abyss*, by Jack London (American on the London slums of 1902).
1905　*England and the English*, by Dr. Carl Peters (German).
1907　*At the Works*, by Lady Bell (Teesside Ironworkers' Lives).
1909　*The Condition of England*, by C. F. G. Masterman.
Pre-1914　*The Pre-War Mind in Britain*, by Caroline Playne, 1925.
1914–16　*The Home Front*, by E. Sylvia Pankhurst, 1933 (East End Poor).
1914–16　*Society at War*, by Caroline Playne, 1940.
1917–18　*Britain Holds On*, by Caroline Playne, 1940.
1919　*Outspoken Essays*, by Dean Inge.
1922　*England After War*, by C. F. G. Masterman.
1926　*In Darkest London*, by Mrs. Cecil Chesterton.
1928　*Industrial Tyneside*, by H. A. Mess.
1930　*Angel Pavement*, by J. B. Priestley (Novel on the "Depression").
1930　*Account Rendered, 1900–1930*, by Ernest Benn.
1930　*Women of the Underworld*, by Mrs. Cecil Chesterton.
1933　*In Scotland Again*, by H. V. Morton.
1934　*English Journey*, by J. B. Priestley.
1938　*Our Present Discontents*, by Dean Inge.
1930–9　*Devil's Decade*, by Collin Brooks, 1948.
1940　*The Fall of the Idols*, by Dean Inge.
1942　*I Saw Two Englands*, by H. V. Morton.
1945　*The Deathbed of the Nation*, by Ernest Benn.
1949　*The Labour Party in Perspective—and Twelve Years Later*, by C. R. Attlee.
And in H. G. Wells's Fiction as follows:
1911　*The New Machiavelli.*
1916　*Mr. Britling sees it Through.*
1926　*The World of William Clissold.*

BRITAIN AND PEOPLES OF OTHER LANDS: A FEW TITLES

Arabs. *Revolt in the Desert*, by T. E. Lawrence, 1927.
"*T. E. Lawrence*" *in Arabia and After*, by Captain Liddell Hart, 1934.
China. *The Problem of China*, by Bertrand Russell, 1922.
A Journey to China, by Arnold Toynbee, 1931.

Egypt. *Egypt*, by George Young, 1927.
  Egypt since Cromer, by Lord Lloyd, 1933–4.
  Egypt, by Tom Little, 1959.
France. *Tableau des Partis en France*, by André Siegfried, 1930.
Germany. *The Fall of the German Republic*, by R. T. Clark, 1935.
  The Berlin Diaries, 1932–1933, ed. by H. Klotz, 1934.
  Hitler Speaks, by H. Rauschning, 1939.
  Our Settlement with Germany, by H. N. Brailsford, 1944.
Greece. *The Western Question in Greece and Turkey*, by Arnold
  Toynbee, 1922.
  Greek Civilization and Character, by Arnold Toynbee, 1924.
India. *Indian Unrest*, by Sir Valentine Chirol, 1910.
  Gandhi and Anarchy, by Sir Sankaran Nair, 1922.
  India as I Knew It, by Sir M. F. O'Dwyer, 1925.
  India, Past, Present, and Future, by Mrs. Besant, 1926.
  Mother India, by Katherine Mayo, 1927.
  India and Britain, A Moral Challenge, by C. F. Andrews, 1935.
  An Autobiography, by Jawaharlal Nehru, 1936.
Irak. *Loyalties: Mesopotamia, 1914–1917*, by Sir Arnold Wilson, 1930.
  Mesopotamia: A Clash of Loyalties, by Sir Arnold Wilson, 1931.
Ireland. *History of Ireland, 1798–1924*, by Sir James O'Connor, 1925.
Italy. *The Awakening of Italy*, by Luigi Villari, 1924.
  The Fascist Dictatorship in Italy, by G. Salvemini, 1928.
  Italy's War Crimes in Ethiopia, by E. Sylvia Pankhurst, 1946.
Japan. *Manchuria: The Cockpit of Asia*, by Etherton and Tiltman,
  1932.
  Japan: Mistress of the Pacific?, by Etherton and Tiltman, 1933.
The Jews. *The Jews*, by Hilaire Belloc, 1922.
  England in Palestine, by Norman Bentwich, 1932.
  The Jews of Britain, by Sidney Salomon, 1938.
Morocco. *Morocco in Diplomacy*, by E. D. Morel, 1912.
Persia. *Persia*, by Sir Arnold Wilson, 1932.
Poland. *The Dark Side of the Moon*, 1946.
  Eastern Europe between the Wars, Professor Seton-Watson, 1945.
Rumania. *Prelude to the Russian Campaign*, G. Gafencu, 1944.
Russia. *An Economic History of Russia*, by James Mavor, 1914.
  The Bolshevik Revolution, 1917–1923, by E. H. Carr, 1950, etc.
  German-Soviet Relations . . . 1919–1939, by E. H. Carr, 1952.
  Stalin, A Political Biography, by Isaac Deutscher, 1949.
  The Bolshevik Myth, by Alexander Berkman, 1926.
  Seeing Red, by Negley Farson, 1930.
  The Moscow Trial, by A. J. Cummings, 1933.
  Stalin and Hitler, by L. Fischer, 1940.
Spain. *Spanish Testament*, by Arthur Koestler, 1938.
  Spain, by Salvador de Madariaga, 1942.
Turkey. *Turkey*, by Toynbee and Kirkwood, 1926.
Yugoslavia. *The Southern Slav Question*, by R. W. Seton-Watson, 1911.
  German, Slav and Magyar, by R. W. Seton-Watson, 1916.

Select Bibliography

World Affairs. *The Survey of International Affairs* series (Toynbee).
The *Documents on International Affairs* (the annual volume edited,
between 1929 and 1938, by Wheeler-Bennett).

A FEW SPECIMEN TEXTS ON A VARIETY OF RELEVANT TOPICS

ANTI-HOME RULE (pre-1914).
1908. Ed. Lord Ashtown.
*The Unknown Power behind the Irish Nationalist Party; its Present
Work and Criminal History* (2nd edn.).
1908? *Watchman.*
Rome and Germany, the Plot for the Downfall of Britain.
1912. Michael McCarthy.
The Nonconformist Treason or the Sale of the Emerald Isle.

ANTI-GERMAN CREDULITIES (post-1914).
1915. Arthur Machen.
The Angels of Mons. The Bowmen and other Legends of the War.
1917. Arnold White.
The Hidden Hand.
   Lord Ponsonby.
Falsehood in War-Time.
1957. Julian Symons.
Horatio Bottomley.

ANTI-"RED" (post-1917)
1919. I. V. Shklovsky.
Russia under the Bolsheviks. (Russian Liberation Committee.)
1921. N. H. Webster.
World Revolution. The plot against civilization.
1924. F. MacCullagh.
The Bolshevik Persecution of Christianity.
1925. G. Popov.
The Tcheka: the Red Inquisition.
1930. Boswell Printing and Publishing Co.
Potted Biographies: A Dictionary of Anti-National Biography (3rd.
edn.).

ANTI-JEW (post-1918)
1920. S. A. Nilus.
The Protocols of the Learned Elders of Zion (English translation from
the Russian work of Nilus dated 1905).
1921. J. H. Clarke. (The Britons Publishing Society.)
England under the Heel of the Jew.
1922. H. S. Spencer. (The Britons Publishing Society.)
Democracy or Shylockracy?
1928. A. H. Lane.
The Alien Menace.

English Radicalism: The End?

A FEW MISCELLANEOUS TITLES AND SUBJECTS ARRANGED CHRONOLOGICALLY

1907 *The Town Child,* by Reginald A. Bray.
Sweating, by Cadbury and Shann.

1908 *Report of the Proceedings of the International Free Trade Congress.*

1909 *Socialism and the Socialist Movement,* by Werner Sombart (trans.).
Socialism and the National Minimum, by Webb, Hutchins, and the Fabian Society.
The Case against Radicalism. A Fighting Brief for Unionist Candidates.

1910 *Emancipation of English Women,* by W. L. Blease.
The Great Illusion, by Norman Angell.

1911 *The Party System,* by Belloc and Chesterton.

1912 *The Servile State,* by Hilaire Belloc.

1913 *The Influence of the Press,* by R. A. Scott-James.
The World of Labour, by G. D. H. Cole.

1914 *National Guilds. An Inquiry into the Wage System and the Way Out,* by A. R. Orage.
Municipal Glasgow, by D. M. Stevenson.

1915 *War and the Balkans,* by N. and C. Buxton.
Nationality and the War, by A. J. Toynbee.

1916 *International Government,* by L. S. Woolf.

1917 *The Choice before Us,* by G. Lowes Dickinson.
Your Part in Poverty, by George Lansbury.
Problems of the Peace, by W. H. Dawson.

1918 *Six-Hour Day and other Industrial Questions,* by Lord Leverhulme.

1919 *Control of the Drink Trade in Britain . . . 1914–1918,* by Henry Carter.
Peace Making at Paris, by S. Huddleston.
Mr. Punch's History of the Great War.

1920 *Sickness of an Acquisitive Society,* by R. H. Tawney.
International Politics, by C. Delisle Burns.

1921 *Nineteen Sixteen–Nineteen Twenty. The Lloyd George Coalition in War and Peace,* by D. Lloyd George.
Solvency or Downfall? Squandermania and its Story, by Viscount Rothermere.
The Call to Liberalism, by C. S. Jones.
Europe—Whither Bound?, by Stephen Graham.

1922 *Labour Policy—False and True,* by Sir L. L. Macassey.
The Campaign Guide (1047 pp.). National Union of Conservative and Constitutional Associations.
The Labour Speaker's Handbook (176 pp.).
Conscription and Conscience. A History, 1916–1919, by J. W. Graham.

Select Bibliography

1923 *The Liberal Handbook* (114 pp.), by H. Storey.
 Mr. Lloyd George and Liberalism, by J. M. Robertson.
 The Capital Levy Explained, by Hugh Dalton.
1924 *My Life for Labour*, by R. Smillie.
1925 *Germany*, by G. P. Gooch.
 The Serajevo Crime, by M. Edith Durham.
 The Socialist Movement, by Dr. A. Shadwell.
1926 *On England*, by Stanley Baldwin.
 The Rise and Decline of Socialism in Great Britain, by Joseph
 Clayton.
1927 *Ethics and Economics of Family Endowments*, by Eleanor R.
 Rathbone.
 On Stimulus in Economic Life, by Josiah Stamp.
1928 *Coal and its Conflicts*, by J. R. Raynes.
1929 *Lure of Safeguarding*, by Comyns Carr and Evans.
1930 *The Financial Aftermath of War*, by Josiah Stamp.
 Modern History of the English People, 1880–1922, by R. H.
 Gretton.
1931 *England Arise!*, by Lord Elton.
1932 *Decline and Fall of the Labour Party*, by John Scanlan.
 Suicide or Sanity? . . . Case for an International Police Force, by
 David Davies.
 Tragedy of the Pound, by Paul Einzig.
1933 *Means to Prosperity*, by J. M. Keynes.
1934 *The Great Depression*, by Lionel Robbins.
 The Crucifixion of Liberty, by A. Kerensky.
1935 *The Next Five Years*, by Harold Macmillan and others.
1936 *Inside Europe*, by John Gunther.
1937 *National Income and other Statistical Studies*, by Josiah Stamp.
1938 *Reports on the British Press*, P.E.P.
 Unto Caesar, by F. A. Voigt.
1939 *In Search of Peace*. Speeches (1937–8), by Neville Chamberlain.
 The New Propaganda, by Amber Blanco White.
 Britain by Mass Observation, by Madge and Harrisson.
 The Twenty Years' Crisis, 1919–1939, by E. H. Carr.
1940 *A Lasting Peace*, by Maxwell Garnett.
 How to Pay for the War, A Radical Plan, by J. M. Keynes.
1941 *Union now with Britain*, by C. K. Streit.
 Mr. Churchill, a Portrait, by Philip Guedalla.
1942 *An Essay on Marxian Economics*, by Joan Robinson.
1943 *Pillars of Security*, by W. H. Beveridge.
1944 *Public Opinion and the Last Peace*, by R. B. McCallum.
1945 *History of British Tariffs, 1923–1942*, by D. Abel.
1948 *Our Partnership*, by Beatrice Webb.
 Individualism and Economic Order, by F. A. Hayek.
1952 *Ten Great Economists from Marx to Keynes*, by J. A. Schumpeter.
1955 *The Political Ideas of Harold J. Laski*, by H. A. Deane.
1956 *The Liberal Tradition: From Fox to Keynes*, ed. Bullock and Shock.

1957 *The Trouble-Makers*, by A. J. P. Taylor.
1958 *The Affluent Society*, by J. K. Galbraith.
1959 *The Second World War* (Abridged edn. with Epilogue 1945–
        1957), by Winston Churchill.
        The End of Empire, by John Strachey.
        Documents on German Foreign Policy 1918–1945. Series C,
        Vol. III. *The Third Reich: First Phase.*
        Northcliffe, by Pound and Harmsworth.
1960 *Lord Derby, "King of Lancashire"*, by Randolph S. Churchill.
        Lord Lothian (1882–1940), by J. R. M. Butler.
        Dean Inge, by Adam Fox.
        The Observer and J. L. Garvin, by A. M. Collin.
        The Private Papers of Hore-Belisha, by R. J. Minney.

ADDENDA

1914 *Report of the Scottish Land Enquiry Committee.*
        Report of the Welsh Land Enquiry Committee.
        The Peace Year Book, ed. Carl Heath.
1915 *The War Lords*, by A. G. Gardiner.
1923 *Select Analytical List of Books concerning the Great War*, by
        G. W. Prothero.
1929 *Can Lloyd George Do It?* by Keynes and Henderson.
1936 *The Record of the National Government*, by Ramsay Muir.
1943 *Contemporary Italy*, by Count Carlo Sforza (trans. 1946).
1947 *The Steep Places*, by Norman Angell.
1949 *Pax Britannica*, by F. A. Voigt.
1954 *Contemporary Issues* (International "Leftist" Periodical).
1959 *Small-Town Politics, A Study of Political Life in Glossop*, by
        A. H. Birch.
1960 *The Growth of Parties*, by Ivor Jennings.
        The Little Band of Prophets, by Anne Fremantle.
        The Thirties, by Julian Symons.
        Curzon: The End of an Epoch, by L. Mosley.

INDEX

Index

Index

Index

635

Index

Index